WRITING BUSINESS LETTERS

Writing Business Letters

By

J. H. MENNING

Professor of Marketing
University of Alabama

and

C. W. WILKINSON

Professor of English, and Chairman,
Business and Technical Communications Courses
University of Florida

REVISED EDITION

1959

RICHARD D. IRWIN, INC.

HOMEWOOD, ILLINOIS

REVISED EDITION
Second Printing, August, 1959
Third Printing, July, 1960
Fourth Printing, July, 1961

Library of Congress Catalogue Card No. 59–12099

PRINTED IN THE UNITED STATES OF AMERICA

Preface

WE ARE grateful to the many teachers, students, and businessmen who have used the first edition (1955) of this book. Their comments have been most encouraging to us in revising for this second edition.

Because so many of them have said, in effect, "We like the spirit, plan, style, and special teaching and learning aids," those features have been retained.

The main changes are:

1. Extensive revision of the problems: bringing them up to date, increasing the variety, and—when advisable—making them shorter.
2. Addition of a new chapter (XIII) bringing together the treatment of good-will letters.
3. Wider coverage and fuller explanation and illustration in the supplement on good language usage (Appendix A).
4. Bringing together the basic legal aspects of letter writing (Appendix B).
5. Improvement of the explanations and illustrative letters wherever needed.

Some of the illustrations are modifications of good letters written by businessmen. As most businessmen and teachers of business writing know, even comparatively good business letters that go through the mail do not serve well as textbook illustrations. Along with their good points, they usually contain defects attributable to carelessness, pressure of time, or the writers' temporary lapses or lack of training. For illustrations, therefore, we have carefully selected actual business letters and then edited beyond merely changing names of companies, products, and individuals. In many instances we have written our own. Yet we are fully aware that some readers will see ways in which they would change some of the illustrations.

Writing *perfect* letters is next to impossible for all of us. Writing even *good* ones does not just come naturally to most of us. If you are content to write letters as many *are* written, instead of as they *should* be, you will gain little or nothing from studying *Writing Business Letters* (or any other book or course on letter writing). But with a concentrated effort to improve, most of us can learn to write superior letters.

In learning anything as complex as writing superior letters, a writer needs instruction in principle, then illustration, and finally PRACTICE in applying the principles. Accordingly, in the first four chapters we have tried to show you the basic principles that apply to all kinds of business letters. The next nine chapters show you how those basic principles and appropriate special ones apply to various letter types: inquiries and requests; replies, favorable and unfavorable; orders and acknowledgments; sales; employment; claims and adjustments; credits; collections; and special good-will letters. Because you will need to write reports too, we have included a compact discussion of them in the last two chapters.

You will grasp each principle and understand its application to a letter type readily by analyzing the many illustrations.

You can then make the principles stick in your mind (and thus make their application habitual) by putting them to use in working out representative problems from the many given at the ends of chapters.

But please remember that this book is not a dictionary, formula book, or cookbook to be followed blindly. Your aim should be creation and origination rather than slavish imitation of textbook models, which often leads to inappropriate copy.

You'll notice that we have thrown overboard much conventional thinking about textbook writing. For example, we have chosen to address you directly instead of writing impersonally. To us, this you-and-we style is better because (1) this is a book of instruction from us to you, and so the natural way to write it is to talk with you; (2) through reading such style you will absorb better stylistic practices to be applied in your letters.

As another example, we have used contractions where they're natural and where they increase readability.

And for still another example, we have not stressed "correctness" as one of the requirements of letter style. For one reason, we think students using this book should have successfully completed a course in English composition previously, and that to repeat much of it would only kill their interest in letter writing. For those who need some review, a teacher can best give it by marking their papers with specific references to Appendix A, which provides ample material on the most likely shortcomings.

Our main reason, however, is that we think "inconspicuousness" is a more appropriate term than "correctness."

We know that errors in punctuation, spelling, sentence structure, grammar, and word choice are undesirable because they distract the reader, slow him up, cause him to lose respect for the writer, and sometimes confuse him. On the other hand, we know that on many points there is considerable disagreement as to what is "correct," that language scholars and wide-awake teachers of writing have discarded many grammar-book rules, that discreet use of so-called "slang" is sometimes effective, and that clearness, naturalness, appropriateness, and simplicity are more important than "correctness" in getting your message across to your reader. For instance, some people will no doubt criticize us for saying ". . . to pop the question," but we think that is an effective expression.

From the many businessmen we have talked and worked with, from thousands of articles in business magazines, from the many textbooks on the subject, from associating with many other teachers on the job and through long and active membership in the American Business Writing Association (including terms as president), and from college students and business people we have taught, we have learned much about letters and effective ways for teaching people to write better ones. We have brought together and modified what we have learned from a combined fifty years of experience. And we have contributed our own ideas. In studying this one concise book, then, you learn what we think is the best that has been thought and said about letter writing through the years. By following its suggestions, you can improve your business letters.

J. H. Menning
C. W. Wilkinson

April, 1959

Table of Contents

Why Study Letter Writing?

"ANYONE CAN Write Letters!"[1] is the forceful statement tossed off by some people, even people who should know better. To realize the fallacy of such a broad and sweeping statement, they have only to recall the times they have struggled over how to get a concession or how to please an irate customer. Almost anyone *can* write letters (and everyone does)—but are they good ones? Unless the writer has some training in letter writing and gives some thought and planning to his letters, they are not likely to be.

The main reason you should study letter writing depends on two facts:

1. You are almost certain to write many business letters during the rest of your life, regardless of the kind of work you do.
2. By studying the principles and practicing the skills and arts of letter writing, you can learn to write letters that will more frequently bring the desired results.

The letter is the most common form of written communication for managing business affairs, and everybody has business affairs to manage. Whether you fail or succeed in managing many of those affairs will depend on whether you send an ordinary letter or a really good one. Through systematic study and practice you can learn to write good ones.

OTHER THINGS YOU LEARN

You will also learn some principles of practical psychology that will enable you to get along better professionally and socially with other people.

When you improve your ability to write clear, concise, persuasive, and natural English (which *is* the desirable language of business), you will also gain accuracy and naturalness in phrasing anything else you have to write or to speak.

---

[1] See C. R. Anderson's witty, thought-provoking, and informative article of the same title in *Writing for Business* (Richard D. Irwin, Inc.).

1

You will also get a further insight into the ways of the business world. Through your study of different types of letters you will learn about practices in getting people to buy, handling orders, granting and refusing credit, making collections, adjusting claims, and selecting employees.

You will also learn how to save time and money on letter writing. As a good letter writer, you can often write one letter to settle a business transaction that would require two or three from an untrained writer. By using form letters and form paragraphs you can cut down on letter costs when the form message will do the job. When, however, you have situations requiring individual letters, you will recognize them and know better than to waste money on forms. You will also be able to dictate or write the necessary individualized letters more rapidly because you will have gained the self-confidence that comes from knowing how to tackle a job. You will write freely and effectively the letters you *have* to write and the many others you *should* write.

Perhaps most important of all, you will realize that every letter you write is an item in your over-all public relations—and will try to make each win, instead of lose, friends.

Letter Volume and Costs

The most recent Post Office yearly report (for the year ending June 30, 1958) estimated the number of first-class letters going through the mail at 32 *billion*—an average of almost 200 first-class letters for every person in the United States. This average includes children, housewives, day laborers, farmers, and many other groups who write fewer than the average number of letters. Business and professional men write many more than the average. In addition, they send out 16 *billion* third-class mailings a year, practically all of which are business letters. The Chicago Post Office alone counted a fraction over 1 billion pieces of third-class mail during this same reported year.

All these letters cost money, too. A businessman can send processed third-class mailings in large quantities, enjoying the advantages of reduced postage rates, for costs varying from 10 to 50 cents. But for first-class letters, when he figures the dictator's and transcriber's time, the stationery, and the stamps, he will find that the average cost is at least $1. And if he includes the other items of a careful cost analysis—such as overhead and depreciation on equipment—he will probably find that the report by *American Business* (June, 1957, p. 24) was right in putting the cost of a typical business letter at $1.70, though others estimate $1.50. Even if you assume that only half the first-class letters are business letters, you're forced to admit that a $30 billion cost figure is not far off. And if you further assume even a modest estimate of 10 cents for mass third-class mailings, you have to add another $1.5–$2 billion to that impressive figure. Letter writing is big business.

Most important, isn't it likely that you will be one in a business or professional group that writes more than the average number of letters? And that you will be at least partially responsible for effective control of this high-cost, but often necessary, way of doing business?

LETTER ADVANTAGES

When you consider the advantages of doing business by letter, it is easy to see why businessmen write so many letters and spend so much money on them. Despite the cost of a letter, it is often the most economical way to transact business. You can't go far (not even across town, if you figure your time and traveling expense) or talk far by long-distance or say much in a telegram for $1.50. But for that money you can put your message in a letter and send it anywhere in the country, or almost anywhere in the world.

Even if you do talk to the other fellow, you do not have a written record, as you do if you follow the almost universal business practice of making a copy of your letter (with either carbon or film). The fact that a written contract can be made by a letter and its answer is one reason why the letter often replaces personal calls and telephone calls even in one's own city.

Still another advantage is that the letter can be prepared by its writer and read by its receiver at their most convenient times. Thus it can get by receptionists and secretaries many times when a telephone call or a personal call cannot. Moreover, the reader usually gives it his full attention without raising partially considered objections and without interruption. That is a decided psychological advantage.

EMPHASIS IN BUSINESS

When executives began to realize how much letters cost, how important letters and reports are to the smooth operation of their firms, and how few of their employees were capable writers, many of them started training programs and correspondence-control programs. At General Electric, Westinghouse, Southern Pacific, Marshall Field, the New York Life Insurance Company, and the big mail-order houses (Montgomery Ward, Spiegel's, and Sears Roebuck), to mention only a few of the leaders, such programs have demonstrated the economy and efficiency resulting from improved correspondence. Even these firms, however, prefer to hire people who can already write rather than train them on company time.

A frequent question in employment interviews and in inquiry letters to professors concerns the ability of college graduates to do such writing. An applicant who presents evidence that he can write good letters and reports becomes a favored applicant for nearly any job.

EMPHASIS IN SCHOOLS

Many of the executives who are aware of the importance of good letters are graduates of the few schools where instruction in business writing has been given since early in the 1900's. These business leaders are the main reason why today in the majority of respectable colleges and universities literally thousands of students are studying and practicing how to write more effectively for business. Without exception, surveys by such organizations as Delta Sigma Pi, The American Association of Collegiate Schools of Business, and the American Business Writing Association have confirmed the high regard of former students for the work.

Business letter-writing instructors frequently hear student comments such as "I learned more English in letter writing than in any other course I ever had!" or *"Everybody* should be required to take a course in letter writing!" or "This course is good preparation for living in general."

COMMON MISCONCEPTIONS

Yet some people—mostly for lack of information—do not respect even university work in business writing. Courses in letter writing are sometimes thought of as being merely about letter forms. Though that is a part, it is only a small part (less than 5 per cent of the space in this book).

One even hears the idea stated that students of letter writing learn the trite, wordy, and nearly meaningless expressions so common at the beginnings and endings of letters written by some untrained businessmen. Actually, you learn to write naturally, concisely, and clearly, to take care of the business without beating about the bush, and to end letters when you are through—without wasting first and last sentences saying nothing.

Still others think that in the study of letter writing the emphasis is on high-pressure techniques (almost to the unethical point) and tricks and gadgets. Just the opposite is true.

You may hear it said that letter writing is "just a practical study." It certainly is practical, for the ability to write good business letters is useful. But it is also a cultural study because its primary purposes are the development of (1) your ability to maintain pleasant relations with your fellow men and (2) your language effectiveness.

WHY THE HIGH REGARD FOR LETTER WRITING?

One of the reasons why courses in business letter writing have found increasing favor with students—as well as with executives and college administrators—is that it is a blend of the cultural and the practical. When Professor George Burton Hotchkiss of New York University said, "It isn't a language, it is a point of view," he did not intend to underestimate the value of effective use of the language in business writing; he wanted to give proper emphasis to the necessity for psychology and salesmanship.

The business correspondent writes to an individual for a definite, practical purpose. Emphatically, he must write with the same exactness as other good writers. Unlike them, however, he does not seek to entertain his reader (or to please himself with his purple passages and "deathless prose"). He seeks an invitation to come in for an interview for a job or a sales demonstration, to secure the appropriate signatures on a contract, to get prospects to visit a showroom, or to secure the agreement of a customer to a delay or a substitution. *Action* is usually his goal. Letter writing is partially a study of probable or estimated human *reaction* as the basis for securing the desired *action.* Since the quality of persuasion is more important to the letter writer than to most writers, a good knowledge of practical psychology is essential in his work.

The good correspondent must learn to do more than just sell goods and services. In his handling of claim, adjustment, credit, and collection letters, he learns tact, patience, consideration of the other fellow, a necessarily optimistic attitude, and the value of saying things pleasantly and positively instead of negatively. These are the reasons why you can expect to enjoy more successful social and business relations with other people after a thorough, conscientious, and repeated analysis and application of the principles of good letter writing.

Furthermore, the good letter writer must learn to be concise, interesting, and easy to follow if he is to hold his reader. For reasons of courtesy a listener will bear with a long-winded, dull, or unclear conversation. He will even ask for explanations. But the reader of a letter feels no such courtesy toward it. The good letter writer therefore edits his work carefully so that he will phrase ideas as effectively in writing as he can in talking. In conversation one can cushion the effect or shade the meaning of his words with the twinkle of his eye, the inflection of his voice, or the gesture of his hand. As he proceeds, he can adjust and adapt his presentation according to the reaction he observes in his listener. With far less chance of failure, he can get along by "doin' what comes naturally." The letter writer has no such chance to observe the effects of the first part of his presentation and adapt the last part accordingly. He must therefore learn to *foresee* the reader's reaction all the way through. That requires a more thorough knowledge of practical psychology, more preliminary analysis of what his reader is like, more careful planning of his message, and more careful phrasing of his thoughts than in oral communications.

Such editing establishes good habits of expression—habits which are carried over to the spoken message. This is the reason we say that you will learn to talk better if you learn to write better. It is also the reason we say that in learning to write effective letters you will learn to do a better job of writing anything else you have to write.

Art, Science, or Skill?

The use of the language—in clear, concise adaptation to one's readers so that they can absorb the message with the least amount of effort and the greatest amount of pleasant reaction—is an art. Several generations of business writers have shown that the proper language for business in general and for letters in particular is just plain good English. Though it is more concise and more precise, it is neither more nor less formal than the conversational language of people for whom letters are intended.

Good business letters are also the result of a conscious use of principles which have evolved since the turn of the century. It would be exaggeration to claim that business letter writing is a science; but it would be folly to ignore the experiences of prominent business writers who have experimented with letters for over fifty years. As a result of their experiences, they have given us a near-scientific framework of principles as a starting point. Though many of these principles have not been demonstrated with scientific exactness, they have taken a great deal of the speculative out of letter writing. We can therefore approach the writing of business letters with a pretty good knowledge of what good letter-writing principles are and *when, where,* and *how* to apply them.

Writing good business letters, then, is neither exclusively an art nor exclusively a science. Yet it is certainly more than what we frequently call a skill. It involves thinking of a very complex kind: analyzing both a situation and a reader, then using good judgment in applying knowledge of English, business, and psychology.

SUMMARY

In studying letter writing, then, you not only learn how to get the desired results from the many letters you will have to write. You will also get a greater understanding of people and how to influence them, an increased facility in the use of language (both oral and written), a more thorough knowledge of business practices and ethics, and a resultant confidence in yourself.

You may want to make a career of business letters. Correspondence supervisors, letter consultants, and direct-mail specialists have found it highly rewarding. But in *any* business, industry, or profession—as well as in your private life—your ability to write a good letter will be a vital tool and a powerful factor in your eventual success.

I. The First Test of a Good Business Letter: <u>Good Will</u>

Tone
   Acceptable Balance of Personalities
     Undue Humility
     Flattery
     Condescension
     Preachiness
     Bragging
   Courtesy
     Anger
     Accusations
     Unflattering Implications
     Sarcasm
     Curtness
     Stereotyped Language
     Physical Appearance
   Sincerity
     Effusiveness
     Exaggeration
     Undue Familiarity
Service Attitude
   Resale Material
   Sales-Promotional Material
   Special Good-will Letters

JUST ABOUT everybody has to write business letters. Most people consider themselves "pretty fair" letter writers, too. Actually, however, the statement, "Anything done by everybody is seldom done well," is as true of business letter writing as it is of any other activity.

If you do write good business letters, you can answer "Yes" to the following questions:

1. Do your letters reflect basic good will?
2. Do your letters follow good persuasion (sales) principles?

3. Is the style of your letters interesting, clear, and inconspicuous?
4. Is the appearance of your letters pleasant and unobtrusive?

You and any other business letter writer should apply these four tests in that order because

—your letter may establish an initial favorable impression because its appearance is pleasant and unobtrusive, yet fail completely because its language is dull, vague, inaccurate, difficult to follow, unnatural, or full of errors;

—its appearance may be good and it may be written in natural, clear style, yet fail because it does not stress benefits to the reader (that is, it does not follow proved sales techniques);

—even with good looks, appropriate style, and peruasive presentation, your letter can fail if it reflects poor tone and/or fails to reflect a desire to be of service to the reader;

—with all four desirable qualities—good will, persuasion, good style, and good looks—it will accomplish its purpose in most instances.

To explain and illustrate these four essentials of any good letter is the function of the first four chapters of this book. To show how the principles are applied in specific letter types is the main function of the other chapters on letters. (The last two chapters are about reports.)

We do not believe you can write the good letters you are capable of writing without understanding and appreciating the relative significance of each of these four essentials. For that reason we ask you to read extensively before you start writing; hence no letter problems appear until the end of Chapter IV.

Most business people define good will as "the disposition of customers to return to the place where they have been treated well." Look it up in your dictionary, however, and you'll find friendly, positive words like *kindly feeling, benevolence, cheerful consent, heartiness,* and *cordiality.* A business letter helps to produce that positive disposition in the reader by developing his friendly, confident feeling toward the firm and the writer representing it.

No business firm or individual would intentionally drive away present or possible future customers by creating ill will or by seeming indifferent. For lack of conscious effort to build good will, however, many letter writers do drive customers away. Proper *tone* and the *service attitude* are the methods of winning the reader's friendliness and confidence—that is, his good will or disposition to return to you because you have treated him well.

TONE

No doubt you have heard someone complain, "It isn't *what* he said— it's the *way* he said it!" Inflections and modulations of the voice, facial expressions, hand gestures—all affect the tone or over-all impression of a spoken remark almost as much as the words do, sometimes even more. The point applies in writing, too—especially in writing letters, the most personal, me-to-you kind of writing. If you want your letters to build good will, you *will make a conscious effort to control the tone.*

Basic to a desirable tone in letters is a balance of personalities (writer's and reader's) acceptable to both. Without an attitude of mutual respect, you will have difficulty achieving in your letters the other two qualities necessary for good tone—courtesy and sincerity.

Acceptable Balance of Personalities. As a writer of good business letters you will need to subordinate your own wishes, reactions, and opinions; the suggestion, "Make it BIG YOU and little me," can be overdone, however. Anything you say that looks up to or down on the reader will throw the relationship off balance.

Undue humility usually backfires. Such a fawning, servile tone as in the following is unwise because it is obviously insincere sounding; no reader expects a writer to have such a humble opinion of himself:

> I'm sorry to ask a busy man like you to take his valuable time to help me; but without your help I do not know how to proceed. Since you are a world authority on . . . , and I know nothing about it. . . .

In addition to the insincere implications, it also suggests an incompetent person whose request for advice is hardly worth considering.

Flattery is another reason why readers question the sincerity or integrity of some writers, especially when it is obvious flattery in connection with the writer's attempt to get the reader to do something or to keep buying. Passing deserved compliments or giving credit where credit is due is something else; it is expected of anybody except a boor. But the reader, sure that the writer has an axe to grind, discounts such passages as the following:

> Your keen discrimination in the matter of footwear is evidenced in your order of the 9th.

> You and you alone can give us the information we need about Gullett razors.

> Your eminent position in commercial aviation, Mr. Pogue, is the subject of much admiration.

Your meteor-like rise in the field of retailing, Mr. Bowan, ...

When an Atlanta girl marries, she immediately thinks of Rich's, the merchandising cynosure of the South!

Flattery also embarrasses many readers and makes them uncomfortable even in the privacy of reading a letter. Instead of gaining favor, the writer loses face and the reader's faith. (When you want to indicate your awareness of the reader's position or accomplishment, handle the reference subordinately.) The writer who began his letter with

You are receiving this questionnaire because you are an authority in the retailing field.

got off to a bad start because of the obviousness of his flattery. He might well have revised his sentence this way:

As an authority in retailing, how do you think the passage of HR-818 will affect co-ops?

Before this reader has time to feel irritation or embarrassment over the initial phrase (it's so short and touched so lightly that he may experience a faint glow of satisfaction), he is forced into a consideration of an impersonal point. Handling a compliment subtly is frequently a question of inserting a complimentary phrase in a statement that, to all appearances, is intended primarily to accomplish something else. The indirect compliments in the following opening imply that the reader's opinion is worth seeking but have no obvious flattery:

How, in your opinion, will passage of HR-818 affect co-ops?

After successful experience in the field, would you say that there is any single area of preparation more important than others for effective public-relations work?

More frequent than undesirable humility and flattery, however, is a writer's implication of too much respect for himself and too little for his reader. Lack of that respect usually reflects itself in (1) condescension ("talking down" to the other person), (2) preachiness (didacticism is another word for it), and (3) bragging.

Condescension is quick evidence that the writer considers himself superior to his reader and maybe does not even respect him. Almost everybody has a good share of self-respect. Nobody wants to be considered a nobody and looked down on or talked down to.

Yet, in attempting to be big-hearted, a businessman insulted his reader when he wrote, "It is unlikely that the machine is defective, but a firm of our size and standing can afford to take it back and give you a new one." In the same category go the sentences, "I am surprised that you would question the adjustment procedure of a firm like Blank's" or "You are apparently unaware of the long history of satisfactory customer relations at Blank's." The statement "We shall allow you to" has condescending connotations that are not present in "We shall be glad to" or "Certainly you may."

A particular danger lies in writing to children, who certainly are not lacking in respect for their own ways of looking at things. When the secretary of a boys' club requested that a department-store manager contribute some boxing gloves to the club, the manager answered: "When you grow up to have the heavy business responsibilities I have and you're asked for contributions by all kinds of charitable organizations, you'll understand why I cannot make a donation to your club." The boy's vocabulary failed him, but what he tried to express was "That pompous ass!" And to make matters worse, the manager began his next sentence with "You are probably unaware. . . ."

A slightly different form of condescending attitude crops up in application letters in a statement like "You may call me at Sheldrake 4601." The implication is that the writer is permitting the reader a privilege when just the opposite is true. An applicant is in no position to appear so aloof.

Repeated use of such phrases as "We think," "We believe," and "We suggest" often are interpreted as condescension. The writer who reflects such a sense of superiority is almost certain to erect a barrier of incompatibility between himself and his reader. Far from attracting a reader, such egocentric talk causes him to sputter, "Well, who does he think he is?" When that happens, the good will of the reader is affected in varying degrees.

Preachiness (didacticism), which is an extension of condescension, is undesirable because

1. Most people (especially Americans) do not like to be bossed.
2. When you tell your reader what he ought to do, you imply that he does not know what to do, and you thus suggest your own superiority.

The juvenile-sounding marketing lecture (because it is so elementary) which some sales writers put into letters to retailers is one of the most frequent offenders. The following are typical:

> The only way for you to make money is by offering your customers merchandise that has utility, good quality, and an attractive price.

It's time for all dealers to get in their Christmas stock!

A retailer would not remain a retailer very long if he did not realize the truth of such statements and act accordingly. Whether he is an old-timer or a beginner, when he reads such preachy statements as the foregoing, his usual reaction is an emphatic negative one like "Who is he to be telling me how to run my business?" or a vigorous "Let me make my own decisions!"

When a statement is flat and obvious, it is frequently irritating to the reader, even though the intent of the writer is good, as in the following:

Satisfaction of your customers means turnover and profits to you.

You need something new and different to show your customers.

You as a business letter writer will do well to examine carefully the expressions "you want," "you need," "you should," and their variations, seeking to eliminate whenever you can without altering the meaning. The following illustration from an application letter is preachy:

The business cycle is changing from a seller's market to a buyer's market. You are going to need a strong force of good salesmen.

Here is one way it could be improved for the reader's acceptance of the idea without irritation:

Now that business is shifting from a seller's market to a buyer's market, you're no doubt thinking about the strong force of good salesmen with which you'll meet competition.

The sales writer in the following example is vague, flat, and preachy:

Spring will soon be here . . . rain in the morning, cold and clear in the afternoon. To be safe, you should carry both a topcoat and a raincoat with you every day. But that's a bother.

He could have improved his presentation this way (among others):

For these early spring days when it's raining in the morning but clearer and colder in the afternoon, a topcoat which is also a raincoat will give you protection to and from work—

—and without your having to worry each morning over "Which shall I take today?"

One of the worst examples of intellectual and psychological browbeating is this:

Do you want Davison's to keep growing and keep getting better?

Of course you do!

Then you should employ only those individuals who want to move
steadily forward and push Davison's on to greater heights.

Far more likely to win the reader's approval is the following version,
with positive phrasing and a studied attempt not to tell the reader how
he should be running his business:

Good merchandise at the right prices is not the only reason Davison's has
grown as it has in the last five years: the team of Davison men and women
has been equally influential.

Careful phrasing can eliminate most of the irritant due to preachiness.

Bragging is another undesirable extension of the writer's ego. And as
advertising and public relations improve, as well as the general educational level, bragging brings to the minds of more and more readers the
sometimes comical, sometimes pitiful, sometimes disgusting, chest-
pounding would-be caveman. Conscious use of superlative wording
("latest and greatest," "outstandingly superior," "final word," and
others discussed in greater detail on p. 21) is a flagrant and obvious
way to make your reader not believe you. Most thoughtful writers will
eliminate such references mentally before words get on paper. But
even experienced writers annoy readers with undesirable—and almost
always unsupported—references to size of the company, efficiency of
operations, or quality of product. The following are examples:

In a business as large as ours—with literally thousands of retailers selling
our products— . . . .

In a firm as large as Bowen and Bowen, such incidents are bound to happen.

You were unfortunately a victim of routine made necessary by the vastness
of an institution so well operated as the White Sands Hotel.

You will understand, I'm sure, that it takes longer than usual when orders
are handled as exactingly as we do.

All business writers will do well to remind themselves that

—silver notes never come from brass horns

and

—an ounce of fact is worth a ton of ballyhoo.

The desirable adjustment to both reader and writer (through elimination of servility, flattery, preachiness, and bragging) will help to improve the tone of your letters; but it will not assure courtesy, the second
element in desirable letter tone.

Courtesy. A dictionary definition of courtesy is "excellent manners or behavior; politeness." Being courteous is being considerate of the other person's feelings through exercising patience and tact. These come only from conscious and determined effort in many cases, because often one's instantaneous, unthinking reaction is an impatient or tactless expression.

Contrary to an oft-stated phrase, people are not "born courteous." (If you doubt that, spend an hour talking with almost any child.) Courtesy in letters is more easily attained by those who have been reared in a circle whose members cultivated self-respect, generosity, and forgiveness in one another; but anyone who anticipates his reader's probable reactions will soon find himself habitually writing the courteous thing.

Courtesy cannot be attained, however, as long as one gives offense. For that reason, correspondents need to keep in mind the major causes of discourtesy.

Anger displayed is almost certain to cause loss of the reader's friendliness toward you and confidence in you. The average business reader has a good deal of self-respect and confidence in the wisdom of his own decisions. When they are attacked, he too feels a wave of anger and a consequent necessity to defend himself. The result is two people seriously estranged. Such sentences as the following are almost sure to produce that result:

We cannot understand why you are so negligent about paying bills.

What's going on in the office at your place?

We certainly have no intention of letting you get away with that!

This is the last straw. (I've had my fill.)

What are you birds up to?

Why don't you wake up?

Crude slang or profanity, especially if used in connection with a display of heightened feeling, is likely to be interpreted as anger, whether or not it is intended as such. Don't use either. (And don't try to be coy and cute with quotation marks for questionable slang or dashes in words that are obviously profanity.)

Petulance (peevishness or fretfulness) is simply anger in a modified degree. It is comparable to the scoldings which children often must receive from parents (and, unfortunately, from teachers too!). Here is how a woman scolded an interior decorator: "When do you expect to return my furniture? You've had it now for more than two weeks. That ought to be long enough to do a little upholstering job." A calm request that the work be finished as soon as possible because of the need for the furniture would probably bring just as quick action, and certainly it would leave the upholsterer in a better mood to do a good job.

Business readers have usually graduated from sand-pile psychology, too. When they read "We have played fair with you; why don't you play fair with us?" they are likely to regard the writer's whining as unnecessarily and undesirably juvenile.

Both anger and petulance are the results of impatience and the unwillingness to accept the responsibilities of successful human relations.

Accusations, on the other hand, are usually the result of insensitivity to how another person will react to a remark. One cannot cultivate tact (skill in dealing with others without giving offense) without a deep and almost constant concern for the feelings of others. The sensitive, thoughtful person knows that people do not like to be reminded of their carelessness or ignorance; he also knows that they will develop an unfriendliness toward the person who insists upon reminding them of their errors. The customer may not always be right, but if you are going to keep his greatest friendliness (good will), you will remember not to call attention to the error if you can avoid doing so and otherwise do it with the least likely offense (impersonal style or by implication). The writer of the following letter displayed an almost completely insensitive attitude toward his reader:

> Much as we dislike doing so, we shall have to delay your order of May 12.
>
> *You neglected* to specify which shade of sweater you desire.
>
> Kindly check your catalog and *this time* let us know whether you want navy, midnight, or powder blue.
>
> We have enclosed an envelope for your convenience.

The following revised version has much better tone and is thus more likely to retain the good will of the reader. It eliminates the accusation and the unfavorable reminder in the italicized words of the preceding example, the sarcasm the reader would probably read into *kindly,* and the pompous-sounding reference to the enclosure.

> Since we want you to be entirely satisfied with the blue sweater you ordered May 12, will you please let us know which shade you prefer?
>
> You may obtain the cardigan style in navy, midnight, or powder. All are popular this spring.
>
> Just check the appropriate blank on the enclosed reply card. As soon as we receive it, we will mail your sweater.

In this revision the reader infers his own carelessness, but he will feel more friendly toward the writer and his firm for the gentlemanlike way of asking for additional information without accusing.

Unflattering implications are usually the result of tactlessness combined with suspicion or distrust. The collection correspondent who wrote "When we sold you these goods, we thought you were honest," implied an idea of much greater impact than the literal statement, an implication which is distinctly unflattering and thus destructive of good will.

The adjustment correspondent who writes, "We are investigating shipment of the goods *you claim* you did not receive," need not be surprised to receive a sharp reply. When he writes, *"We are surprised* to receive your report," or "We *cannot understand* why you have had trouble with the Kold-Hold when other people like it so well," he is establishing by implication his doubts of the reader's reasonableness, honesty, or intelligence.

And the sales correspondent who begins his message implying that he doubts his reader's alertness can expect few returns to his letter:

> Alert hardware dealers everywhere are stocking No-Flame, the fire-resist-ant liquid which more and more home builders are including in their specifications.
>
> Are you prepared to meet the demands of your home-building customers?

In similar vein, the phrases "Do you realize . . . ?" and "Surely you are . . ." immediately suggest the writer's doubts that the reader measures up on either score.

Such lack of tact is frequently unintentional. Most readers, however, do not question whether it is intentional; the result is ill will for the writer and the firm.

Sarcasm, on the other hand, is generally deliberate. And it is usually dangerous in business correspondence. The smile which accompanies friendly sarcastic banter cannot find its way onto paper; unfriendly sarcasm is sheer malice. It is the direct opposite of the attitude necessary for a tone of good will because it shows a lack of respect for the other fellow and a deliberate attempt to belittle him. The sales manager sending the following message to a group of salesmen falling short of their quotas would build no good will:

> Congratulations on your magnificent showing!
>
> We're only $50,000 short this week.
>
> How *do* you do it?

The Community Chest leader who included the following in his public report could hardly expect future co-operation from the division indicated:

> The ABC employees, with an assigned goal of $800, magnificently responded with $452. Such generosity should not go unmentioned.

Sarcasm should never be used in business correspondence except between people of equal intelligence, of equal station in life, and with highly similar senses of humor. To be on the safe side, do not use it at all. The moment of triumph is short-lived; the loss of the friendship of the reader may be permanent.

Curtness, born of impatience and a false sense of what constitutes desirable business brevity, reflects indifference and is thus considered discourteous. The manufacturer sending the following letter was promptly labeled a boor by the woman who received it:

> We have your request for our booklet and are enclosing same.
>
> Thanking you for your interest, we are,

Better to send no letter than this. Booklets usually do a good job. And experiment after experiment has shown that a good letter accompanying a booklet increases the pulling power. On the other hand, a poor letter like this, reflecting such lack of interest, destroys some of the favorable impression made by the booklet.

That correspondent might very well have helped to convert a casual inquiry into a sale if he had taken the time to show interest in serving the customer with a letter like the following, which is superior because of the service attitude reflected, the positive and specific resale material, and the action ending (all of which are discussed later):

> We're glad to send you Siesta's booklet *Color at Mealtime.*
>
> When you read it, you'll understand why we say that in Siesta you can now have handsome dinnerware that is sturdy enough for everyday use, yet surprisingly inexpensive.
>
> No photography, however, can do justice to the delicacy of some Siesta shades or to the brilliance of the others.
>
> Your friendly local dealer will be glad to show you his selection of Siesta. If you want him to, he'll be glad to order additional colors for your examination.
>
> See him soon and start enjoying Siesta's color at mealtime.
>
> Sincerely yours,
> (*Signature*)
>
> You can find Siesta in Omaha at (name and address of dealer).[1]

[1] This letter can easily be set up as a form letter with only this one line and the inside address and salutation individually typed.

Stereotyped language is another mark of discourtesy because it suggests indifference. And nobody likes to have his business treated in an indifferent, routine way. Writers of letters like the following can expect no more feeling of friendliness from the reader than is reflected in the letter—and that is very little:

> We have your favor of the 19th and in reply beg to state that the interest on your mortgage is now $361.66.

> We trust this is the information you desired, and if there is any other way we can oblige, please do not hesitate to call upon us.

Since stereotyped language is primarily a question of style, it is discussed in greater detail beginning on page 52.

Physical appearance is one other factor affecting the apparent courtesy of letters, in the eyes of most readers. Strikeovers, poor erasures, dim type, poorly matched type and processed material, and penciled signatures are like trying to gain admission to the Stork Club when you're dressed in sweat shirt, dungarees, and sneakers. Since this point is developed in a full section later, no further mention is made here.

In putting his best foot forward through courtesy, however, a correspondent must be careful not to trip himself; the attempt to be courteous can be overdone to the point of apparent insincerity and thus destroy the third element in desirable letter tone.

Sincerity. When a reader feels his first flashes of doubt, with a resultant reaction of "Well, I'll take that with a grain of salt," his confidence in the writer is shaken. More than anything else, that confidence is affected by sincerity.

Sincere cordiality is entirely free of hypocrisy. It is unwillingness to exaggerate or fictionalize upon the true state of a situation. Inappropriate cordiality (usually unbelievable and sometimes distasteful) is commonly the result of effusiveness, exaggeration, and undue familiarity. (Flattery and undue humility, it is true, often sound insincere. But in our opinion they are more intimately linked with the desirable balance of personalities discussed in a preceding section.)

Effusiveness means gushiness. It is excessive politeness which *is* often insincere and always *sounds* insincere. "Overdone" means the same thing. Your letters can sound effusive simply because you've used too many adjectives and adverbs, as in the following examples:

> We are extremely happy to place your name on our list of highly valued charge customers, and we sincerely want you to know that we have hundreds of loyal employees all very eager and anxious to serve.

Your excellent choice of our fine store for the opening of a charge account, we consider a distinct compliment to the superb quality of our merchandise and outstanding service. And we're genuinely happy about it.

I was exceptionally pleased to note your name on this morning's list of much-appreciated new charge customers.

It is indeed a pleasure for the house of LeRoi to serve you, and you may feel sure that we shall do everything possible to keep you happy.

The plain fact is that in a business relationship such highly charged personal reactions as those suggested in the foregoing examples do not exist—and any reader knows that. No writer and no firm is going to "do everything possible to keep you happy." Rarely will a credit man be "extremely happy" or "exceptionally pleased" to add a name to a charge list. Phrases like "do all we can" and simply "happy" or "pleased" are appropriate because they are believable.

Furthermore, the coy quality of the following endings is unrealistic in a business situation—and therefore unbelievable:

We do hope you'll come in soon. We can hardly wait!

Don't forget to come in soon. We'll be looking for you!

Simply note your color choice on the enclosed card, mail it to us—and then sit back with an air of expectancy.

The usual cause of effusiveness is a writer's choosing too strong and too many adjectives and adverbs in an attempt to please the reader by making him feel important. You'll do well to watch especially overused words like *very, indeed, genuinely, extremely, really,* and *truly*—all of which begin to gush in a very short time.

Exaggeration is stronger, and therefore more destructive of sincerity, than effusiveness. The correspondent who wrote, "Work is a pleasure when you use these precision-made tools," appears to be overstating his case to his carpenter-reader. And the writer of the following, if he could overhear, should be prepared for an unrestrained, emphatic "BOSH!" when his dealer-customer opens the letter and reads:

New customers, happy and eager to buy, will surely applaud your recent selection of four dozen Tropical Holiday play suits for women.

Especially made for the humidity of Macon, these garments will lead girls and women for miles around to tell their friends that "Thompson's has them!"

Superlatives and other forms of strong wording are among the most frequent reasons why so many letters sound exaggerated, unbelievable, and therefore insincere. The trite "more than glad" is nearly always an insincere attempt to exaggerate a simple "glad." And "more than happy," if translated literally, could mean only slap-happy. The classic illustration is the misguided "What could be finer than . . . ?" Applied to everything, it fits nothing. Furthermore, any reader can supply at least one quick answer of something which in his opinion is finer than the product or service mentioned. What's more, he usually does.

Exaggerated wording is nearly always challenging. Few things are actually amazing, sensational, revolutionary, ideal, best, finest, or perfect. Simple, accurate, specific statements of quality and value not only avoid the impression of insincerity; they are often more forceful than the general superlatives made nearly meaningless by sixty years of American advertising. If you describe products or services in terms like the following, you are inviting negative responses toward you and your firm:

> You'll find that Loomoleum is truly the ideal low-priced floor covering.

> Are you looking for something that will sell like wildfire and give your customers the greatest possible satisfaction?

> Want Amazing Protection
> That Can *Never* Be Canceled?

> It will take you only a few minutes to read this letter. But it may save you and your family years of untold hardship during the years ahead. Here is really a magnificent opportunity if you consider carefully the suggestion now offered— and act without delay!

> Imagine a health and accident policy that can never be canceled. That is truly unusual. Nor is that all!

> WHAT—a lawn mower that trims around the edge of sidewalks and fences while cutting a 16-inch swath of tall grass? Amazing, of course! But look in next month's *Post* and see for yourself.

> This new mower is revolutionary in build, style, performance, and customer appeal. Here is your golden opportunity!

Whether the reader of such statements feels irritation or disgust is relatively immaterial: what counts is that he does not believe them. His confidence in the writer and the house, and therefore his good will, take a sharp downturn.

Undue familiarity also causes a writer to lose favor with his reader in many instances. Sometimes it crops out merely because the writer is uncouth. The reader may feel sympathy for the poor fellow who does not know how to act with people, but he will not have the disposition to return for more uncouthness.

Undue familiarity more frequently results from (1) calling the reader by name too frequently or writing in too informal language to a stranger and (2) making references to subjects which are entirely too personal for business discussions. For an obvious purpose, the writer pretends a closeness of friendship or an overweening interest which does not exist. It is characteristic of the shyster. Like other forms of pretense, it is resented. In the following letter giving information on home insulation to a college professor, the jocularity doesn't just fall flat; it boomerangs!

> Just set the thermostat and relax. That's all you have to do, Professor Eckberg. Pick up your book and settle down in a cozy chair. The Mrs. won't be continually warning you to get your old sweater, or nagging you to shovel more coal on the fire, or to put another blanket on the cherubs.
>
> Yes, Professor Eckberg, ISOTEMP will guard over your household. Take a gander at the statistical table in the folder, *Modern Insulation for Older Homes*. This Table shows that out of every 8,000,000 cases of respiratory diseases, 6,536,042 occurred in uninsulated homes—over 75% from the very type of home you're now living in!
>
> Didn't you say that you spent over $300 for coal last year, Professor Eckberg? That's a lot of money out of a professor's salary; and as you said, "Even then the place wasn't always warm."
>
> If you will fill in and return the enclosed card, we will send Mr. Don Diller, our Milwaukee representative, to answer any of your questions. Incidentally, Professor Eckberg, Mr. Diller is a graduate of the University of Wisconsin with a degree in heating engineering. He may be the guy who slept through half your classes six years ago; but somewhere he learned how to make your home more comfortable and reduce those high coal bills. Then the Mrs. can buy that fur coat she's been nagging you about for when she goes outside, where it *is* cold!

Such diction as *cherubs, gander,* and *nagging* might be used in breezy conversation with an old friend and perhaps in a letter to the old friend but certainly not in a letter to someone the writer does not know. Using the reader's name three times in such short space gives the impression of fawning. And the assumptions and references to family relations and activities are typical of familiarity that breeds contempt. These spring from insincerity; but they are discourteous in the truest sense and thus destructive of good will.

Service Attitude

In addition to a desirable tone as a means of maintaining good will, good letter writers show their readers that the company's interest extends beyond making a profit. A business organization obviously must make profits if it is to exist; both reader and writer accept that premise. To deny it is trying to fly under false colors. The answer is neither to deny nor to affirm: just don't talk about it! Instead, let your letters remind present and potential customers of your thoughtfulness and genuine desire to be of service, through

1. Resale material on the goods and/or the house,
2. Sales-promotional material on other goods (in some letters),
3. Special-occasion letters.

Resale Material. Often a writer needs to assure a reader of the wisdom of his choice of goods or of the house he has chosen to do business with and thus stress satisfaction. In *keeping the goods sold,* resale material fosters repeat orders and forestalls complaints. It is an effective device in meeting competition.

As the phrase is most frequently applied by correspondents to goods and services, "resale" means talk about something in which the reader has already shown an interest, either by inquiry or by actual order. Most buyers would feel better about the product upon reading the following resale idea woven into an acknowledgment letter:

> The Henshaw electric boudoir clocks (8 @ $12) that you ordered March 1 are our fastest-selling models in this price range. Because they are accurate as well as beautiful, they make excellent gifts.

The woman receiving the following would most likely feel much more secure in her choice of a suit—and thus happier with the suit as well as the company that sold it to her:

> Your new suit is one of the Fashion-True line by Andreena. With its simple slenderizing skirt and tuxedo jacket (both Coleman 100% wool), it will give you equal pleasure and comfort at church, at a football game, or at an informal luncheon.

Such material is most effective when it is relatively short and when it is specific. Tell a reader buying a white shirt, for instance, that

> It will launder rapidly and easily because the collars and cuffs are permanently starched.

OR

> It will retain its comfortable shape because it's preshrunk and guaranteed to shrink no more than 1%.

OR

> The buttons will stay on because they are double-lock-stitched.

OR

> Made from long-staple California cotton, your Pallcraft shirt will give you the wear you expect from a shirt of this quality.

But don't try to tell your reader *all* these points in a resale passage. And for your own greatest effectiveness as a writer, don't try just to get by with a lame "Pallcraft shirts are a good buy."

Used most frequently in acknowledgments, resale material on the goods may also appear in certain credit, collection, and adjustment letters.

Resale material on the house consists of pointing out services sometimes called "the little extras" which the firm renders its customers. Especially in the beginning of a business relationship you want to tell your reader about services you render—sales assistance, advertising aids, and the like to dealers. Retail stores often talk of air conditioning, lounges, lunchrooms, and personal shoppers, to mention only a few.

The following excerpt from a letter to a dealer is typical:

> Along with your shipment of Lane candies are some display cards and window stickers which you'll find valuable aids in bringing these delicious candies to the attention of your customers. Our advertising department will regularly furnish you with seasonal displays, and will be glad to help you on any special display problem in connection with the sale of Lane's.

And this—from a retail store to a new charge customer—is also a good sample of resale on the house:

> You are welcome to use Rosen's air-conditioned lounging and rest rooms on the mezzanine, the fountain luncheonette on the first floor, or the spacious parking lot right behind the store. It is absolutely free to customers shopping at Rosen's, no matter if your purchase amounts to only a spool of thread.

Also from a retail department store to a new customer:

> When you cannot come to the store, call or write Lola Lane, our personal shopper, who will gladly do your shopping for you. Most of the time she can have your merchandise on the delivery truck or in the mail the same day she receives your order.

Resale material on the house need not—indeed, should not—be confined solely to letters to new customers. Any time that a new service is added, an old one improved, or a line expanded is an appropriate occasion to tell customers about the firm's continued attempt to give satisfaction.

Resale passages are the writer's attempts to confirm or increase the faith of the reader in goods, services, or the firm he is already interested in. Sales-promotional material on new and different goods or services seeks to promote interest in something else the firm can supply.

Sales-promotional Material. For a number of reasons, sales material about related products is desirable in some acknowledgment, credit, collection, and even adjustment letters. The most obvious business reason is that, regardless of what you try to market, you must constantly seek to sell more of it to more customers all the time. In letters, however, the most significant reason is the concrete demonstration that the firm desires to be of further service. A third function of sales-promotional material is that it can end a letter naturally and easily, with emphasis on further service. The following example illustrates the point:

> Your carpenters' tools, as itemized on the enclosed invoice, were shipped this morning by parcel post; they should reach you by October 15. Thank you for your check, which covers all charges.

> *Resale* The Crossman level, with aluminum frame, is stronger and weighs less than wooden ones; and it will not rust or warp. The true-tempered steel used in the Flex-Line tape is permanently oiled; so you can be sure it will easily and rapidly unwind and rewind every time you use it.

> *Sales* When you receive the fall and winter catalogue we're sending separately, turn to page 126 and read the description of the Bradford 6½-inch electric hand saw. This is the lowest price at which it has ever been offered. To enjoy the savings in time and energy this time-saving piece of equipment offers, use the handy order blank at the back of the catalogue.

You'll need to observe a few precautions in the use of sales material. Above all, it should reflect the desire to be of service rather than the desire to sell more goods. It is low-pressure sales effort, comparable to the way a salesman, after selling a woman a pair of shoes, will casually pick up a matching or complementary purse and say, "Perhaps you'd like to examine this purse, which goes with your shoes so well." Only after the customer displays an interest in the suggested item does the salesman begin a real sales talk. If he makes another sale, that's good. But if he doesn't, it's still good: most customers are pleased because of the demonstrated interest in their welfare or happiness.

If, however, the insatiable sales appetite of "I want to sell you more" is established through selfish, greedy terminology, you neither promote sales nor please the customer. When emphasis is on *what we want* rather than *what you get,* the effect is unfavorable, maybe even repellent, as in the following:

More than 8,000 of these Multimowers have been sold through our factory!

And now that a large demand has been built up for our product, we want to sell it through dealers.

When emphasis is on *order* instead of *service,* Greedy Gus overtones are almost inevitable:

We also sell attractive summer purses, silk and nylon hosiery, and costume jewelry to complete your excellent line of goods. We are sending you our catalogue. And we hope to fill many more orders for you.

In terms of customer good will, this correspondent would have made a better impression had he rephrased the foregoing passage somewhat like this:

The summer purses and costume jewelry shown on pages 29 to 32 of the accompanying catalogue have also sold well for many of our other customers. We'll be glad to handle your order for these items on the same terms as this one. Use the handy order blank and reply envelope in the back of the catalogue.

Appropriateness is also a factor. When a woman buys a suit, a natural item to call to her attention is a blouse; a man buying a suit can be told about shirts, ties, hats, or shoes. But to tell a purchaser of heavy-duty truck tires about the good buy you now have in refrigerators or the buyer of a washing machine about your special on tires would be questionable most of the time because such suggestions appear to be dictated by the greedy desire to further sales rather than an eagerness to render service. Almost always sales material should be on items related to those under consideration.

Before using sales material, consider also the kind of letter you are writing and what it is supposed to do. A letter requiring further action on the reader's part needs final emphasis on that action, not on sales material. In acknowledgment letters, for example, you can use sales-material endings to good purpose when you are sending the goods as requested, but not when additional action by the customer is necessary. Also, while you might use sales material in an early collection letter to a good customer, it is decidedly inappropriate as soon as your letter reflects concern over the account. And in adjustments you may safely use sales material to end a letter making full reparation, because you can be fairly sure the customer is going to be pleased with the results; but its use in a compromise or a refusal is usually questionable.

Both resale and sales material help to sell more merchandise, but they are even more effective as good-will builders because they imply positively and emphatically the general statement, "We are eager to serve you."

Special Good-will Letters.   Also to demonstrate continuing interest in the customer and the desire to serve, special good-will letters subtly use resale material on the goods and the house, and sales material. They have often been called the "letters you don't have to write—but should." Since the customer does not expect them, since they usually bring something pleasant, and since your reader knows you do not have to write them, they are doubly welcome and thus greater builders of good will than some other types. Because they are of great variety in function and occasion and because you can write them with greater understanding and skill after studying other kinds of letters, they are treated in greater detail in Chapter XIII.

[*All the problems for the first four chapters are at the end of Chapter IV because we think you should cover all four basic tests of a good business letter before trying to write any kind of letter. We urge you to read the first four chapters quickly but thoroughly so that you can put all the basic principles to use even in your first letter.*]

II. The Second Test of a Good Business Letter: Persuasion

BECAUSE IN most business letters you are trying to produce an action or a reaction which may lead presently to an action, many correspondents maintain that every letter is a sales letter. In the broad sense that you are usually trying to persuade someone that your suggestion is a good one and/or that yours is a good firm to deal with, that's right.

If you are going to be successful in that mission, you'll want to make conscious use of five principles of persuasion which have proved helpful in getting the desired positive response: (1) planned presentation in the light of your objective, (2) you-viewpoint interpretation, (3) adaptation—even personalization when possible, (4) positive statement, and (5) success consciousness.

PLANNED PRESENTATION

You can make your job of beginning fairly simple and also gain favor with your reader if you will classify your letter according to one of three probable reactions of your reader:

A. Does it contain information which will please the reader? Does it take action that the reader has requested? Does it request action which the reader is prepared to take?

28

B. Does it contain bad news?

C. Or does it request action which the reader is probably not already willing to take?

According to subject matter, you can list hundreds of different kinds of business letters; but for predetermining its beginning and the subsequent development of points, all you need to decide upon is whether your letter is an A-type (good news or neutral information), B-type (disappointing information), or C-type (persuasion leading to action).

Good News or Neutral Letters. Most A-type letters say or imply "Yes," as in favorable replies to requests, acknowledgments in which you can ship goods as ordered, adjustments fully complying with the customer's request, and credit grants. Since you are doing what the reader wants you to do, the first sentence should contain the big idea of the letter; that is what the reader most wants to know. Then you follow up with necessary details in an order of relative importance or natural sequence. Frequently letters of this kind end with a short punch line recalling the benefits of the good news in the beginning, as suggested by Figure 1.

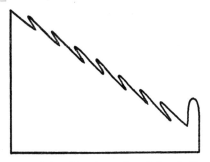

FIGURE 1. "Good news" and "routine" letters.

Letters which merely seek or merely transmit business information follow the same basic order: inquiries and replies about personnel applicants and explanations or identifications of something about the company, its personnel, even its products. All these are situations in which your reader is neutral (neither displeased nor pleased), and so the letters are taken for granted. They should be characterized by the same directness and dispatch in their handling as in the following "Yes" letter:

Your new Admiral desk clock was mailed by insured parcel post this morning and should be at your door no later than January 23.

The same kind of heavy padding carefully protecting your new Admiral in the large corrugated box will be used for all future shipments of fragile articles so that they will arrive in the same perfect condition in which they leave the store.

And now will you take a moment to assist us in recovering from the Post Office by signing the enclosed notification forms and returning them to us with the original clock?

The recipient of the new Admiral on January 26 will no doubt be pleased with its beauty and practicality. It is an appropriate birthday surprise.

Disappointing Letters.   B-type letters, those that say "No" or "Yes, but . . ." (that is, modified refusals), have no such quality of directness. If you have to tell a reader that you can't give him the booklet he wants, that you can't fill his order as he has specified, that you can't extend credit to him, or that you cannot make the adjustment as he has requested, you have a situation which is potentially good-will-killing— especially if you blurt out the disappointing information immediately.

We assume throughout this book that you are a fair-minded person who does not act highhandedly or arbitrarily and that you therefore have good reasons when you refuse anything. We know, too, that in most cases you can show that some of your reasons are beneficial to the other person—as when a mother refuses her child something for the child's good as well as (sometimes even *rather than*) her own. The following psychology of refusing, therefore, depends on your having good reasons, as does any satisfactory refusal.

You know that when you refuse anybody anything to which he thinks he's entitled, he becomes frustrated unless he receives justifying reasons (not just excuses or no explanation at all). You know further that if you begin with the refusal, you will at least disappoint your reader and you may anger him. You also know that an angry person is not a logical one. So, even if you do give good reasons *after* the refusal, they fall on an illogical mind, where they do not take effect. But if you start pleasantly and give justifying reasons *before* a refusal, your reader is much more likely to accept your refusal without irritation because you lead him to see the justice of it. Thus your logical reasons fall on a logical mind; and the reasons which caused you to feel justified in refusing convince your reader that you *are* justified. That psychology directs you to a rather specific plan for all refusals.

To soften the effect, you try to catch the reader's favorable interest in the opening remarks with something from the situation on which both reader and writer can agree. This is commonly called a "buffer." Writers use it for two reasons: (1) to suggest that the writer is a reasonable person who can see two sides of the question and (2) to set the stage for a review of the facts in the case.

After you establish compatibility, you analyze the circumstances sympathetically and understandingly, giving the reasons why you can't do what he wants you to do. Not until you have tactfully prepared the way with these justifying reasons do you want to phrase the disappointing news. You further attempt to soften the blow by embedding this information, by giving it minimum space, and by positive statement.

Nor do you want to end your letter on a note of disappointment; to close, select some point of favorable interest to your reader which demonstrates your desire to retain him as a friend and customer. Graphically, your procedure looks like the line in Figure 2. The following positive refusal illustrates the strategy:

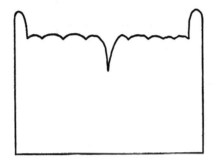

FIGURE 2.   "Bad news" letters.

Your comments, Professor McGinnis, on the effectiveness of the "More Business" series are helpful to those of us at Read's who worked on these practical guides for users of direct mail.

When we first planned the booklets for our customers, we had in mind a check list for a business using direct mail extensively rather than a thoroughgoing treatment suitable for a textbook. Accordingly, our quota for noncommercial users was set at a low figure—partly because we did not anticipate many requests and partly because of present-day paper restrictions.

Since the series has proved so popular with our customers and since fine paper like Read's is increasingly hard to get, we have for over a month been distributing copies only to commercial users, though we are glad to make available what we can to training institutions.

Perhaps you may be able to use the extra copy—sent to you this morning by parcel post—as a circulating library for your correspondence students. Two or three days' use should be ample for most of them, and they're perfectly welcome to copy anything they care to.

Will you give us the benefit of your suggestions for making the series more extensive after you have had an opportunity to test its teachability more thoroughly?

Selling Letters.   The third basic letter siuation,_the C type, if graphed, shows two areas of interest, as in Figure 3. You start off with something that you can be reasonably sure your reader wants or is interested in, thus catching his attentive interest from the start. Develop your letter in concrete pictures of what will benefit him. If you can start off with his agreeing with you and maintain this agreement as you try to convince him of the worth of your proposition, you can wind up with his agreeing that he wants to do what you want him to do.

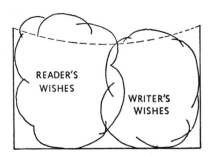

FIGURE 3.   "Selling" letters.

Starting a letter of this kind need not be difficult if you will make your most honest and concrete attempt to figure out what it is the reader wants (or needs) that you can give him. When you have developed the benefits he will derive from complying with your suggestion and have supplied enough evidence for him to believe that your claims are true, then you are in a psychological position to ask him to do what you want him to do.

Prospecting (cold-turkey) sales and application letters, persuasive requests, and some collections follow this pattern, as in the following persuasive request for a confidential manual:

How often have you received—from well-educated people—letters that are not worth your attention?

You as a Public Relations Director and employer are of course interested in this problem. And I as a teacher of business correspondence am too. Here at Harwood we're turning out a thousand students each year who are better trained in writing effective letters than the usual college graduate. But we'd like to do more. We'd like to be sure that we're giving them what business wants.

It's quite likely, you know, that some of these students may some day be writing letters for your company. Wouldn't they be better prepared if we instructors could stress the ideas that you have given special emphasis to in your recent correspondence manual? Both the students and business firms would benefit from your letting us have a copy for our teaching files.

Of course we'd handle the material with whatever confidence you specify. And I assure you we'd be most grateful for this practical teaching aid.

But the ones especially benefiting from your sending a copy would be the students and business firms like Southern Atlantic.

Will you send us a copy today?

The planned steps in all selling are here. Whether you want to call them four steps (Attention, Interest, Conviction, Action, or Promise, Picture, Prove, Push) or three steps (Attentive Interest, Conviction or Evidence, and Action) or more doesn't matter. But it does matter that you get attentive interest quickly by promising a reader benefit, give evidence backing up that promised benefit, and confidently ask the reader to do what you have already decided you want him to do.

Keep in mind what one highly successful direct-mail specialist told his understudies: "Remember, the Three Wise Men came bearing gifts —not seeking them."

That's a good thing to remember in writing "Yes" letters, highly desirable for writing successful "No" letters, and absolutely essential in writing selling letters.

You-Viewpoint

The you-viewpoint or you-attitude does not hinge on actual gift giving, of course. What the direct-mail specialist was referring to is a state of mind: always ferreting out and emphasizing the benefits to the reader resulting from your suggestion or decision and subordinating or eliminating your own.

Of course, it isn't pure unselfishness. All businesses must be motivated by the profit motive. When you try to sell something, obviously you are trying to make some money; but you don't need to put that idea into words. When you attempt to collect, obviously you want—maybe even need—the money; you don't need to put that idea into words. When you apply for a job, obviously you either want or need work to earn some money; you don't need to put that idea into words. Both reader and writer *assume* all these ideas. Putting them into words merely sounds selfish, wastes words, and helps your cause not one bit.

Nor is the you-attitude a question merely of politeness, courtesy, or good manners. The hard business reason for you-viewpoint presentation is that when you show you are aware of and are doing something about your reader's needs or problems, he will react more favorably to your suggestion. In other words, he will do what you want him to if—and only if—you show him that he gets something worth the cost and trouble.

Nothing else is so important to your reader as himself (and when he's writing to you so that you're the reader, he'll take the same stand if he's smart). So by central theme and wording you show that you are thinking of him and his welfare as you write.

The you-viewpoint requires imagination, certainly. The old story of the village half-wit's answer to how he found the mule ("Why, I just thought, If I was a mule, where would I go?") is apt. The ability to visualize the reader's desires, circumstances, and probable reactions and write in those terms is the answer. When you write to secretaries, you *are* a secretary; when you write to doctors, you *are* a doctor; when you write to merchants, you *are* a merchant. It requires that you be able to play many roles. Without that basic outlook and attitude, you-viewpoint presentation may be superficial.

Phrasing helps, it is true. You are more likely to write in terms of the reader if you use more *you*'s and *your*'s than the first-person pronouns *I, me, mine, we, us, our.* But if you apply that test, the sentence, "We want your check" has more you-viewpoint than "We want our check," when obviously neither has any. "Please send your check" is neutral. The reader-dominated sentence might well read, "To keep your account in the preferred-customer class, send your check for $142.63 today," or "Get your account in shape for the heavy Christmas buying coming up by sending your check for $142.63 today." Whether you say "sending *us* your check" or not is immaterial, except that it wastes a word; the *us* is clearly understood. But what is much more significant, the reader-benefit reason—the you-viewpoint—is there.

The following examples may help to clarify the point for you:

WE-VIEWPOINT:	YOU-VIEWPOINT:
We are shipping your order of June 2 this afternoon.	You should receive the Jurgin crosscut saw you ordered June 2 no later than Saturday, June 7.
We have spent 27 years making the Jurgin the finest of its kind.	Back of your Jurgin blade is 27 years of successful testing and remodeling. Because it is taper-ground alloy steel, it is less likely to bind on you than other models.

Making your reader the subject or object of your sentences will help you keep you-viewpoint interpretation. The only way to get it in the first place, however, is to subordinate your own reactions to those you estimate are your reader's probable reactions and then to write in a manner which clearly shows that your reader's interests dominate. An example of well-intentioned writing that is fundamentally writer-dominated is the conventional thank-you beginning: "Thank you for your order of June 2 for one Jurgin crosscut saw blade" and "We are grateful for . . . ." Even worse is the selfish "We are glad to have your order for . . . ." All three variations have this strike against them: they emphasize the personal reaction of the writer rather than something the reader is interested in knowing.

If you can (or will) make shipment, an opening like the following has more you-viewpoint than any of the three foregoing:

> Your Jurgin crosscut saw blade should arrive by prepaid railway express no later than Saturday, June 7.

This is something your reader wants to know! If you can't make shipment, then a resale comment is a better example of you-viewpoint than the selfish statement of pleasure upon the receipt of another order or the disappointing statement that the reader is not now getting what he wants. If shipment will be delayed only a few days, this is a possibility for retaining positiveness and you-viewpoint:

> The Jurgin crosscut saw blade you ordered will give you long and faithful service.

When the reader has done you a favor, some form of "thank you" may be one of the best beginnings you could use. In place of the conventional "Dear Mr. Miller," the salutation—

> Thank you, Mr. Miller!

—has a directness and enthusiasm which are heart-warming. The first paragraph may then concentrate on a more significant point:

> Those articles about palletization which you suggested contain some of the best information I've been able to uncover.

But doesn't the statement of the significance you attach to your reader's contribution adequately establish your appreciation?

We do not mean to imply that an expression of gratitude is out of place. No one ever offended a reader with a genuine, appropriate "thank you." But we do want to stress to you that you can accomplish the same function with some statement which will place more emphasis on your reader—where it should be!

The preceding remarks concerning planned presentation and you-viewpoint apply whether you're writing a special or a form letter—a sales, credit, collection, application, or simple reply. The closer you can come to making your reader nod his head in agreement and think "That's what I want to hear," the greater your possibilities for favorable reception of your letter.

ADAPTATION

When you can make him also think "That sure fits me," you have an additional advantage. Successful adaptation makes your reader feel that your letter has been written with him specifically in mind.

Even in a mailing to a large number of people, you will have identifiable common characteristics (of geography, age, educational level, vocation, or income status, for example) that will enable you to adapt the talking points, language, and style of your letter and to make references to commonplace circumstances and events.

Adapting Talking Points.   In adapting talking points (or theme) you simply seek out and emphasize those reasons that you believe will be most influential in causing your reader to act or react as you want him to. Specifically, you would try to sell a typewriter to a secretary on the basis of ease of operation, to an office manager on ease of maintenance and durability, but to a purchasing agent on the basis of long-range cost. The lawnmower you would sell to a homeowner because of its ease of handling and maintenance you would sell to a hardware dealer because of its salability and his profit margin. A car is more likely to appeal to a man on the basis of economy and dependability of operation; to a woman the appeals of appearance and comfort are stronger. When a man buys a shirt, he is more interested in appearance and fit; his wife is more interested in launderability and long wear.

Accordingly, you adapt your talking points to your reader(s) for increased persuasiveness. This is a fairly simple procedure when you are writing a single letter and is entirely possible in a mass mailing if you study the characteristics common to all people on your mailing list.

Adapting Language and Style.   You adapt language and style, in general, in the light of your reader's age, educational level, and vocation (which influence his social and economic position). As your reader's years, professional and social prestige, and financial status increase, you are safer in using longer sentences, uncommon words, and more formal language. Sometimes you will want to use the specialized terms of vocational classes, such as doctors, lawyers, and insurance men, for instance. Though some of these terms are more technical than you would use in writing to a general audience, to the specialized reader they convey the impression that you, the writer, understand his problems. The application of this suggestion means that when you write to doctors, references to patients, laboratories, diagnoses, and the like help; to an insurance man, prospects, premiums, and expirations are likely referents.

But for all kinds of readers, you won't go wrong if you write in the simple, informal, conversational business style discussed in Chapter III.

Referring to Common Experiences. Better adaptation than language and style, however, are references to common experiences in the reader's life. A reference to vocation, to a geographical factor, to some home and family status—in fact, to any activity or reaction which you can be reasonably sure your reader has experienced—rings the bell of recognition and makes the reader feel that very definitely you are writing to and about him.

In a letter to college students, for instance, the following reference would almost universally bring positive (and in most cases humorous) recognition:

When your teacher talks on . . . and on . . . and on . . . (even when it's two minutes past the bell!).

To parents:

When your child yawns, turns over, and FINALLY goes to sleep.

To doctors:

. . . for the elimination of dust, smoke, and antiseptic odors from your reception room.

To school superintendents:

. . . to reduce the necessary and healthy noise of active adolescents when they're changing classes.

To almost any businessman:

. . . when your files simply won't reveal an important carbon.

To anyone who is or has been a secretary:

An hour's transcription to get in the night's mail—and at 5 minutes to 5!

Any of the preceding phrases could go into a form letter or an individual letter. The more specifically you can phrase these references to make them pinpoint to your one reader, the more effective your adaptation will be.

Personalizing. To further the impression that the letter has been prepared for the reader alone and to heighten the feeling of friendliness, correspondents sometimes use the reader's name, not only in the inside address and the salutation but also in the letter copy. About the middle of the letter, much as one uses a friend's name in talking with him, or near the end of the letter in the same way you frequently use a person's name in ending a conversation, such references as the following help to give the impression that the letter is for one person rather than a group:

> You'll also appreciate the lightness of the Multimower, Mr. Bowen.
>
> Your Atlanta Luminall representative, Mr. Paul Owen, will be glad to call on you and answer any other questions you may have, Mr. Bowen.
>
> Just check a convenient time on the enclosed card and drop it in the mail today.

In individually typed letters the placement of the name presents no problem; in form letters, space is usually left at the end of a line (as in the preceding examples) so that typing in the reader's name is easy, regardless of length. Unless you can match type and print perfectly, however, you may do more harm than good. In any case, use of the reader's name is a more or less mechanical process; it is probably the least effective means of adapting.

You can also increase the feeling of friendliness by the wording of your salutation and complimentary close. *Dear Sir* and *Very truly yours,* though appropriate many times, are somewhat formal and do not reflect the warmth of *Dear Mr. Bowen* and *Sincerely yours* or some other less formal phrasing. The main forms and their order of formality are discussed in detail on page 82.

Of far greater significance are adaptation of talking points and lifelike references to the reader's activities. The following letter answers the lady's questions in salesmanlike presentation and enhances the persuasiveness of the message with special references that could apply to no one but the reader:

> DEAR MRS. JACKSON:
>
> The Stair-Traveller you saw in the June *Home and Yard* will certainly make daily living easier for you and your faithful old servant.
>
> You can make as many trips upstairs and downstairs as you care to *every day* and still follow your doctor's advice.
>
> Simply sit down on the bench (it's about the same size as a dressing-table stool), hold the arm support with one hand, and press the button with the other. Gently and smoothly, your Stair-Traveller takes you upstairs at a rate just a little faster than ordinary walking.
>
> Should the electricity fail in Greenbriar while you're using your Stair-Traveller, automatic brakes bring it to a gentle stop and hold it in place until the current comes on again. Then you just press the button to start it again.

Folded back against the wall when not in use, the Stair-Traveller's simple, straight lines of mahogany will blend in well with your antiques. Your Stair-Traveller will be right at home on your front straight stairway, Mrs. Jackson; it will be more convenient for you there; and, as it is designed only for straight stairways, the installation is simple and economical. Notice the folded Stair-Traveller on page 3 of the booklet I'm sending you with this letter; it looks somewhat like a console table, doesn't it?

To explain to you how simply and economically your Stair-Traveller can be installed, Mr. J. B. Nickle, our Memphis representative, will be glad to call at a time convenient for you. Will you use the enclosed postcard, which is already addressed and partially filled out, to let him know when that will be?

Such specialized references do increase letter costs when they mean writing a personal letter rather than using a form. But many times a personal letter must be used if the letter is to get the job done. Even in form paragraphs and entire form letters, however, some means of adaptation to the reader's situation can be made.

You can find out a great deal about your reader through his letters to you, your credit records (including credit reports), salesmen's reports, and the like. Even a bought or rented mailing list contains the names of people with some common characteristics of vocation, location, age, sex, finances, and buying and living habits. You won't make your letter do all it could do if you don't use your knowledge of these common characteristics to adapt your letter according to talking points and endow it with the marginal pulling power of known references to familiar events, activities, places, or persons.

A word of caution should be sounded here, however: Don't try to be specific beyond the point of likelihood. For example, you may have a mailing list of parents, but you don't know how many children these people have or what the sex is. A reference to "your child" is safe (even if the reader has more than one); a reference to "your children" is not— and certainly not to "your boy" or "your girl." It should be obvious that one could not safely use such tags as "Junior" and "Sister" and certainly not individual names like "Bobby" and "Janie." Only when you *know* that your reader does have a Bobby and a Janie can you afford to be so specific in adaptation.

POSITIVE STATEMENT

Your letters have greater prospects for success if you focus on positive ideas because people—most of them, at any rate—respond more favorably to a positive prospect than to a negative one.

Saying the cheerful, positive thing that people do want to hear rather than the unpleasant or unhappy, negative thing that they do not want to hear is really just an extension of you-viewpoint presentation and tact. It requires, first of all, staying optimistic yourself so that you can see the rosier side of any picture. It comes from constantly superimposing a positive picture on a negative one, thus completely eliminating, or at least subordinating, the negative idea. Translated into letter-writing procedures, it is the result of stressing what something is rather than what it is not, emphasizing what the firm or product can and will do rather than what it cannot, leading with action rather than apology or explanation, and avoiding words that convey basically unpleasant ideas.

Test after test of both advertising copy and letter copy has demonstrated the wisdom of positive statement. That is why nearly forty years ago successful copy writers warned against the denied negative (and today's writers still issue the same warning). That is why the effective writer will write the following positive statements rather than their negative counterparts:

NEGATIVE	POSITIVE
Penquot sheets are not the skimpy, loosely woven sheets ordinarily in this price class.	Penquot sheets are woven 186 threads to the square inch for durability and, even after 3-inch hems, measure a generous 72×108 inches.
We are sorry that we cannot furnish the club chairs by August 16.	After checking with the production department, we can definitely assure you your club chairs by August 29.
We cannot ship in lots of less than 12.	To keep down packaging costs and to help customers save on shipping costs, we ship in lots of 12 or more.
I have no experience other than clerking in my father's grocery store.	Clerking in my father's grocery store for three summers taught me the value of serving people courteously and promptly.
If we can help, please do not hesitate to get in touch with us.	Please call upon us when we can help.

A special form of negativism is the challenging question which invites a negative answer. Although it is devoid of negative wording, the question, "Wouldn't you rather drink Old Judge?" is more likely to bring forth the reply, "No, I'd rather drink Colonel Dalton" or maybe "Make mine Dipsi-Cola!" than it is to get a "Yes" answer. "Who wouldn't want a Kreisler Regal?" will bring something like a bristling

"Not me, brother, I want a Cabriolet!" from most readers, who will resent the presumptuousness of such a question. "What could be finer than an XYZ dishwasher?" will elicit, among other answers, "A full-time maid!" Such questions, along with the apparently harmless "Why not try a Blank product?" get your reader out of step with you and, because they invite a negative response, are thus a deterrent to the success of your suggestion.

Keeping your messages positive also means deliberately excluding negative words. You can't be "sorry" about something without recalling the initial unhappy experience. You can't write "unfortunately" without restating some gloomy aspect of a situation. Nor can you write in terms of "delay," "broken," "damages," "unable to," "cannot," "inconvenience," "difficulty," "disappointment," and others of negative character without stressing some element of the situation which makes your reader react against you rather than with you.

For all these reasons the effective writer will write "ABC Dog Biscuit will help keep your dog healthy" instead of "ABC Dog Biscuit will help keep your dog from getting sick." It's just a question of accentuating the positive.

SUCCESS CONSCIOUSNESS

Success consciousness is the confident assumption that your reader will do what you ask him to do or accept the decision your letter announces. To reflect that attitude in your letters, guard against any phrasing which suggests that the reader may not share your enthusiasm and may not take the action you want him to.

Success consciousness is based on your own conviction that your explanation is adequate, your suggestion legitimate and valuable to your reader, your decision the result of adequate evidence and logical, businesslike reasoning. Thus assured yourself, you are not likely to write something which suggests or even implies that you are not sure of your ground. The sales correspondent who writes

> If *you'd like* to take advantage of this time-saving piece of equipment, put your check and completed order blank in the enclosed envelope and drop it in the mail today.

would be better off if he did not remind the reader of his option to reject the proposal. Simply omitting the phrase "If you'd like" establishes a tone of greater confidence. The one word *if* is the most frequent destroyer of success consciousness.

Likewise, when tempted to write

> *Why not* try a sample order?

the correspondent should remember that the suggestion is stronger with the elimination of "why not." It has not only the disadvantage of suggesting that the writer is not sure of his own case but also the distinct disadvantage of inviting the reader to think of several reasons why he should not do what the letter suggests. When he puts his mind to it, he can probably come up with several reasons.

Hope and its synonym *trust* are second only to *if* as destroyers of success consciousness. In a letter granting an adjustment, the sentence

> We hope you'll approve of our decision.

has greater success consciousness (and thus more reader response) when revised to read thus:

> With this extension of your subscription to *Vacation* you can continue to read each month about the world's most interesting places.

By assumption (implication)—by definitely omitting the doubtful-sounding expression—the writer seems to say, "Of course, you and I realize that this is what you want."

In refusals the following sentence sometimes appears in an otherwise well-written letter:

> We trust you will understand our position.

Usually, however, it appears in a poorly written letter. And it is most frequently the result of inadequate explanation. The writer seems to despair of giving an adequate explanation and to hope that the reader will figure out one for himself. If you find yourself writing or wanting to write such a sentence, go back and see whether your explanation is ample. If it is, omit such a sentence; if it is not, revise your explanation so that it is convincing—and substitute some positive, confident statement for the weak-kneed expression.

Even in simple replies the problem arises with such a sentence as

> We hope this is the information you wanted.

The implications of doubt can be removed quickly and easily with

> We're glad to send you this information.

This principle of success consciousness applies in all types of letters, but it is most significant in selling letters.

A word of caution against high-pressure presumptuousness should be injected here, however. It is one thing to omit a reference to a reader's alternative; it is quite another thing to imply that the reader has no alternative! The application-letter writer who so boldly and confidently asks

When may I come in to see you?

gives the impression that he thinks his reader has no alternative but to see him. With such presumptuousness, he may irritate his reader. Rephrased like the following, his request for an interview would strike most readers favorably:

Will you write me a convenient time when I may come in and tell you more about why I believe I am the aggressive salesman you're looking for?

Sales writers, too, may well consider the advantages of substituting the service-attitude type of action ending for the bromidic, high-pressure, unrestrained endings like "Don't delay!" and "Act today!"

Remember that most readers respect and are more likely to be influenced by the man who is confident, but are likely to be irritated by the man who appears to be pushing and ordering them around.

[*All the problems for the first four chapters are at the end of Chapter IV because we think you should cover all four basic tests of a good business letter before trying to write any kind of letter. We urge you to read the first four chapters quickly but thoroughly so that you can put all the basic principles to use even in your first letter.*]

III. The Third Test of a Good Business Letter: <u>Style</u>

~~~~~~

How to Write Interesting Letters
   Depend Mainly on Content
   Put the Emphasis Where It Belongs
   Write Concisely but Completely
      Ideas Which Don't Deserve to Be Put into Words
      Deadwood Phrases
   Write Vividly: Avoid Indefiniteness
      People in Action
      Active Rather than Passive Voice
      Concrete Rather than Abstract Language
      Specific Rather than General Words
      Enough Details to Make the Picture Clear
   Write Naturally to Avoid Triteness and Pomposity
   Vary Sentence Pattern, Type, and Length to Avoid Monotony
How to Make Your Letters Clear
   Make Them Easy to Read
      Words Your Reader Understands
      Reasonably Short and Direct Sentences
      Adjustment of Paragraph Pattern and Length
      Frequent Personal References
      Itemizations and Tabulations
   Plan Letters for Unity, Coherence, Progress, and Proper Emphasis
   Use Accurate Wording, Punctuation, Grammar, and Sentence Structure
How to Keep Your Style Inconspicuous
   Choose the Right Level of Usage for the Situation
      Informal English
      Formal English
      The Illiterate Level of Usage
   Follow the Conventions
      Spelling
      Poor Word Choice
      Unconventional Punctuation
      Grammar and Sentence Structure

FOR THE third test of a good letter, ask yourself: IS IT WRITTEN IN AN INTERESTING, CLEAR, AND INCONSPICUOUS STYLE?

If your letter is so uninteresting that it isn't read, you've obviously wasted your time.

If your letter is interesting enough to be read but is not clear, you've probably annoyed your reader because you've confused him. If he doesn't drop the matter, he has to write again to find out just what you mean.

And if your style is conspicuous because of something unexpected, inappropriate, or incorrect, it distracts the reader from *what* you've said (by calling attention to how you've said it) and causes him to doubt that your facts and reasoning are any more reliable than your writing. Both weaken the impact of your message, which is the important thing in letters.

Though poets, story writers, and essayists may sometimes write for the beauty of their style, a letter writer's language is only a means of communicating facts and ideas—without distorting or otherwise damaging them in transit.

To be effective, then, your letter style should be interesting enough to be read, clear when read, and inconspicuous.

HOW TO WRITE INTERESTING LETTERS

Depend Mainly on Content. In writing most letters, you should depend on the message, not the style, to arouse and hold your reader's interest. Usually you have an inquiry or some other indication that your reader is interested in your general subject. A first-class letter addressed to him will therefore nearly always get a reading. Tricks of style are unnecessary and even distracting to him. If the bare facts have insufficient appeal to gain the attention of your reader, you can make them both interesting and persuasive if you show him how they affect his life.

If you have no inquiry or other indication that the reader is already interested, you may be right occasionally to forget about keeping your style inconspicuous and to work for temporary attention by means of gadgets, tricks of style, and other artificial means at the beginning of your letter. Even then, however, you will have accomplished nothing unless your stunt leads into the message naturally and yields the stage to it promptly.

But just as many a good story or joke is ruined in the telling, a perfectly good message can become dull if poorly presented. Wordiness, indefiniteness, triteness and pomp, monotony, and difficult reading are the most common offenders. By replacing these with their opposites, you will have a style that will speed up your message rather than slow it down or lose it completely—and that's all that style should contribute to making your letters interesting.

Put the Emphasis Where It Belongs. Since the content of your letter is obviously the greatest means of gaining interest, the big ideas of your message deserve the major emphasis.

Though you may use minor mechanical means of emphasis (underscoring, capitalizing, itemizing, using two colors), your four primary means of emphasizing an idea are (1) position, (2) space, (3) phrasing, and (4) sentence structure.

The most significant ideas you depend on to hold your reader's interest need to be placed in the emphatic beginning and ending positions of the letter, of your paragraphs—even of your sentences.

In addition, you write more about those points which you think need stressing. If you write ten lines about the efficiency of a dishwasher and only two lines about the convenience of it, you have emphasized efficiency more than convenience.

As a third major means of emphasis, you select concrete, specific words and phrases to etch the welcome or important idea in your reader's mind. When the idea is unwelcome or insignificant, you choose general words that merely identify, not stress.

Because an independent clause carries more emphasis than a dependent one, you can also stress or subordinate ideas through your choice of sentence structure. You may have noticed, for example, that the minor mechanical means of stressing ideas were merely named in a dependent clause. The four primary means, however, were each given a separate paragraph of discussion and thereby emphasized by means of space.

In the letters in Chapter II perhaps you noticed that ideas in which the reader is assumed to be interested are almost always used to begin and end letters. They usually begin and end paragraphs. They generally take up most of the space of the letter. They are phrased specifically. And they enjoy the benefits of independent construction instead of dependent. Conversely, unwelcome or unimportant ideas are generally embedded in a middle paragraph, covered just enough to establish their true meaning, and stripped of the emphasis of concrete, specific words.

The letter samples throughout this book make use of these principles for appropriate emphasis and its opposite, subordination.

For fuller discussion and illustration, see C. W. Wilkinson's article, "Controlling Emphasis in Letter Writing," in *Writing for Business* (Richard D. Irwin, Inc., Homewood, Illinois).

Write Concisely but Completely.   Every word that you can spare without reducing the effectiveness of your writing is wasteful if it remains. If you use too many words for the ideas you express, you stretch interest to the breaking point. But if you leave out necessary information and vivid details in trying to achieve brevity, you frequently fail to develop enough interesting ideas to hold or persuade your reader. You therefore face the dilemma of length.

A first step in the solution to that dilemma is a clear distinction between brevity and conciseness. Brevity is mere shortness—which is often overstressed. A common mistake in letter writing is that of sacrificing completeness because of a mistaken notion about the importance of brevity. Writing a letter lacking necessary information (and therefore lacking interest and persuasion) is poor economy. Either the letter is pure waste because it produces no result, or both you and your reader have to write additional letters to fill in the missing links of information. Even those people who say "A business letter should be brief!" do not mean that they are so illogical as to want to make decisions without all the pertinent information.

What these brevity-overconscious people want—what you want—is conciseness—making every word contribute to your purpose. A 50-word letter is brief; but if you can write the message in 25 words, the 50-word letter is not concise. A 400-word letter is not short; but if all the words contribute to the purpose, it is concise. So if you need three pages to cover all your points adequately and make your letter do what you want it to do, you should use that much space. Conciseness, then, comes not from omitting necessary information or details that contribute to clearness, persuasiveness, or interest but from writing all you should say in as few words as possible.

Experience may teach you to compose first drafts of letters that are both complete and concise; but, while you are gaining that experience, you need to

1. Avoid expressing ideas that don't deserve to be put into words and
2. Revise first drafts to eliminate deadwood.

Besides obviously irrelevant material, *ideas which don't deserve to be put into words* are

a) Things the reader already knows which you do not wish to emphasize and
b) Ideas which can be implied with sufficient emphasis.

Because it is often insulting as well as wasteful and dull, avoid using an emphatic independent clause for things the reader already knows.

For example, a heating engineer's letter to an office manager about the discomforts of workers began as follows:

> Three days ago you asked us to investigate the problem of discomfort among your office workers. [Assumes that the reader has a short memory.] We have made our study. [Obviously, or he couldn't be reporting.] Too low humidity is apparently the main cause of your trouble. Your building is steam heated. [Doesn't the reader know?] Therefore your solution is to . . . .

The following revision says or implies everything in that paragraph, avoids the insults, saves most of the words, and is more interesting:

> Too low humidity is apparently the main cause of your workers' discomfort. Since your building is steam heated, your solution is to . . . .
>
> [To show the reasoning behind your suggestion, you do need to mention the fact that the building is heated by steam; but the subordinating *since* implies "Of course you and I know this, but it has to go in for the record and for completeness of logic." When you *have* to establish something or when the reader probably knows but you can't risk his not knowing or remembering, inform him subordinately.]

As a general principle, in answering a recent letter from an individual, don't waste words to say "I have your letter of . . ." or to tell what it said. Obviously, you got the letter or you wouldn't be answering it; and he will remember what it said—at least when you start talking about the same subject. Instead of

> You asked us to let you know when the new model of the Clarion radio came on the market. It is obtainable now.

you can say the same thing with

> The new model of the Clarion is now available.

The fact that you got his letter and the idea of "You asked us to let you know" are clearly implied.

Of course, if the inquiry is not recent or if somebody other than the original inquirer may read the answer (as often happens in big companies), you may need to make specific reference (by topic and date) to the letter you are answering. But even then you can often use a subject line to save words and allow the emphatic first sentence to say something important. Rather than

> On February 20 you inquired about our experience with Mr. James H. Johnson. We are glad to tell you about his work for us.
>
> Johnson was a steady, conscientious worker during the eighteen months he kept books for us.

you might better write

> Mr. James H. Johnson, about whom you inquired February 20, was a steady, conscientious bookkeeper here for eighteen months.

Under no circumstances do you need to waste words as in the following paragraph:

> Permit me to take this opportunity to thank you for your letter which I have just received. In reply I wish to state that we shall be very glad to exchange the electric water heater in question for a similar one in a larger size in accordance with your request.

Through implication you can reduce that wordy beginning to

> We shall be glad to exchange your water heater for a similar one in a larger size.

In most refusals you can save words and your reader's feelings by eliminating the negative statement of what you won't do and concentrating on what you will do. You thus *imply* the negative idea, for economy as well as interest. For illustrations, see "Positive Statement" (p. 39).

If the first draft contains any of the foregoing wasteful expressions, revision should eliminate them and *deadwood phrases* (those which take the long way around or contribute nothing to the ideas expressed).

Consider the following suggestive but far-from-complete list of offenders, in which the deadwood is blocked out or the concise statement follows in parentheses:

long ~~period of~~ time
at ~~a distance of~~ 100 ft.
is ~~at this time~~
at ~~a price of~~ $50
~~important~~ essentials
enclosed ~~herewith~~
remember ~~the fact~~ that
held a meeting (met)
would like to (want to)
during ~~the course of~~ the
~~engaged in~~ making a survey
~~the color of~~ the X is blue
until ~~such time as~~ you can
in regard to (about or regarding)
in the development of (developing)
in this day and age (today or now)
main problem is ~~a matter of~~ cost
in ~~the state of~~ Texas

neat ~~in appearance~~
at ~~the hour of~~ 4:00
eight ~~in number~~
circular ~~in shape~~
throughout the ~~entire~~ week
~~at a~~ later ~~date~~
during ~~the year of~~ 1955
costs ~~the sum of~~ $10
came ~~at a time~~ when
at all times (always)
in the event that (if)
put in an appearance (came)
during the time that (while)
these facts ~~serve to~~ give an idea
made stronger ~~with a view to~~
if ~~it is~~ possible, let me have
~~according to~~ Mr. Johnson (says)
arrived at the conclusion (concluded)

your ~~order for a~~ cultivator was shipped
~~in the opinion of~~ Mr. Johnson (thinks)
that is the situation ~~at this time~~ (now)
the X plow is quite different ~~in character~~
made the announcement that (announced)
for the purpose of providing (to provide)
all the people who are interested in (interested people)
at an early date (soon, if you have to be indefinite)
decide at a meeting ~~which will be held~~ Monday
eliminate needless words ~~that may be present~~
~~there is~~ only one point ~~that~~ is clear, ~~and that is~~
the price was higher than I expected ~~it to be~~
the workers ~~are in a position to~~ (can) accept or reject
the soldering process proved ~~to be of an~~ unsatisfactory ~~nature~~
the general consensus of opinion among most businessmen is that
    (most businessmen think that)
~~the trouble with~~ the light was ~~that it was~~ too dim

Sometimes you can save several words by changing a whole clause to one word. For example:

buying new machines which are expensive—buying expensive new machines;
using processes that are outmoded—using outmoded processes;
saving work that does not need to be done—saving unnecessary work.

Write Vividly: Avoid Indefiniteness.   Even good content concisely stated can be uninteresting if your reader gets only an inactive or fuzzy mental picture. The sharper you can make that picture, the better it will be. You will write vividly if you apply these five techniques:

1. Write about people in action. Make people the subject or object of many sentences.
2. Use active rather than passive voice.
3. Use concrete rather than abstract language.
4. Use specific rather than general words.
5. Give enough details to make the picture clear.

The most interesting thing in the world is *people in action.* Things happen because people make them happen. The most interesting, the most natural, and the clearest way to write about those happenings is to talk about those people who are the principal actors. That is why we suggest that you make people the subject or object of your sentences.

And, since the reader of a letter is most interested in himself, his interest will be influenced by how you put him into the picture as the main actor. "You can save 30 minutes at dinner time with a Pronto pressure cooker" is more vivid than "A Pronto pressure cooker saves

30 minutes at dinner time." (For psychological reasons, if a point is unpleasant, however, make your actor a third person or your message impersonal.)

Consistent use of people as subjects will help you to write in *active rather than passive voice.* The passive "30 minutes at dinner time can be saved" lacks the vividness of the original illustration because it omits the all-important *who.* Besides, passive constructions are usually longer, weaker, and fuzzier than active ones. Excessive use of "to be" verbs (*be, is, am, are, was, were, been, being*) usually produces flat writing, partly because it leads to a passive style. If the basic verb in more than half your sentences derives from "to be," your style will seem flat instead of vivid. "There are" and "It was" beginnings (expletives) delay the real idea of the sentence and frequently force a writer to use unemphatic passive voice. The sentence "There are one million people in Cincinnati" is not so vivid as "One million people live in Cincinnati." "It was felt that . . ." gains vividness when the writer rephrases with "We felt. . . ."

You can eliminate most passives and expletives if you will conscientiously try to use action verbs. People live, run, eat, buy—in short, act. They do not just exist, as indicated by *is, was, were, have been.* The price of a stock *creeps up, rises, jumps, zooms*—or *plummets.* For vividness (and for economy) good writers make their verbs do a big share of the work. Far be it from us to encourage you to needless and frivolous word coinage; but *dip, curve, skyrocket, phone, wire,* and many other original nouns are now commonly accepted verbs because people recognized the vividness of their use as verbs. The more action you can pack into your verbs, the more specific and concrete you can make your writing.

When you *use concrete rather than abstract language,* you give your reader sharper mental pictures. When you write *superiority, efficiency,* and *durability* in telling about a product, your words are abstract; they give your reader only hazy ideas. To make the picture sharp and lively, give the evidence back of the abstraction rather than name the abstraction itself. If you think your product is of highest quality, you must have reasons for thinking so. To establish the idea of superiority in cloth, for instance: thread count? number of washings before fraying? tensile strength? resistance to shrinkage and fading? Note that answers to these questions also show durability.

In job applications you need to put across the ideas of your sociability, initiative, dependability, which you can concretize by citing activities and organizational memberships, ideas and plans you have originated, attendance records, and completed projects. Thus you give evidence of these qualities and let your reader draw the abstract conclusions.

You further eliminate haziness and dullness when you use *specific rather than general words.* An investment, for instance, may be a stock certificate, a bond, a piece of real estate. To illustrate further, stock may be common or preferred. The closer you can come to making your reader visualize the special type of thing named rather than just its general class, the more specific and hence the more vivid your writing is.

Take the verb *walk* as another example. Does a person amble, trudge, skip, or one of the fifty or more other possible ways of walking? When you are inclined to write *contact,* do you mean write, go see, telephone, telegraph? You will present a sharper picture if you name the specific action.

Comparisons help you to explain the unknown or variable in terms of the known. *Slowly* becomes sharper if you say "about as fast as you normally walk." "A saving of 2% when paid within 10 days" becomes more vivid if you add "$2.80, or two free boxes of Lane's choice chocolates, on your present invoice of $140."

You *can* be specific and concrete in the kind of information you give your reader; but unless you *give enough details to make the picture clear,* you will fail to attain vividness. Specifications for a house may indicate that the house is to be painted. But unless they tell the kind of paint, how many coats, and what colors, the painter does not have a clear picture of what he is to do until he comes back and asks. You need to flesh out the skeletons to bring them to life, even if it means some loss of brevity.

Write Naturally to Avoid Triteness and Pomposity. All kinds of trite expressions and jargon—usually the result of hazy thinking, or no thinking, by the writer—are inclined to dull interest and put the reader to sleep instead of stimulating his mind to action. They are even called "bromides" ("Flat, commonplace statements," Webster says) because of the use of bromides as sedatives and sleep-inducing medicines.

A businessman meeting another on the street would not say, "I beg to report receipt of your favor of the 29th ult." And if he is a good letter writer he would not write it either. He would more likely say or write, "Those tonnage figures for April were just what I needed," or "Your suggestions about the committee memberships helped a lot in my decision. Thanks." The first is slow, vague, roundabout, and stilted; the others are clear, direct, and natural.

Bromidic style goes back to the times when businessmen first began to have social status enough to write to kings, princes, and others at court. Feeling inferior, they developed slavish, stilted, and elaborately polite style to flatter the nobility. They "begged to advise" the nobleman that his "kind favor of recent date" was "at hand" and "wished to state" that "this matter" would "receive our prompt attention" and "begged to remain your humble, obedient servant." Today businessmen need not be so meek. Unfortunately, too many sheepishly follow somebody else, learn all they know about letter writing from the letters they receive, and thus continue an outmoded, inappropriate, and unnatural style. Like parrots, they use expressions unthinkingly.

Pompous writing (puffed-up, roundabout, and big-wordy) is as dull and confusing as the use of bromides. Why many businessmen write, "We will ascertain the facts and advise accordingly" when in conversation they would say quite naturally, "We'll find out and let you know," is a mystery. A Washington blackout order during wartime originally read: "Obscure fenestration with opaque coverings or terminate the illumination." A high official who wanted the message read and understood revised it to read: "Pull down the shades or turn out the lights."

A young lawyer was certainly pompous when he wrote as follows about a husband being sued for divorce:

> The defendant is renowned as a person of intemperate habits. He is known to partake heavily of intoxicating beverages. Further, he cultivates the company of others of the distaff side, and wholly, regularly, and consistently refuses, demurs, and abstains from earnest endeavor to gain remuneration.

The judge summed up that "Mrs. Rigoni's husband drinks, chases other women, and refuses to work."

Stuffed-shirt writers frequently use a phrase or a whole clause when a well-chosen verb would express the idea better. For example: "Smith raises the objection that . . ." instead of "Smith objects that (or objects to). . . ." One writer stretched a simple "Thank you" to "I wish to assure you that it has been a great pleasure to have been the recipient of your gracious generosity."

The good letter writer avoids both bromides and pompous wording to make his letters natural. The advice to "write as you talk" can be taken too literally, however. You would have an extremely hard job trying to write just as you talk; and, even if you could, the informal style appropriate to letters is more precise and concise than good conversation. What the advisers really mean is that you should not stiffen up, use big words and trite expressions, or get involved in complicated and formal sentences when you write letters. Rather, let the words flow out naturally and informally in phrases and sentences with the general tone and rhythm of the language actually used by men rather than stuffed shirts.

Write like this—	*Not like this—*
many people	a substantial segment of the population
know well	fully cognizant of
object	interpose an objection
wait	hold in abeyance
carry out the policy	effectuate (or implement) the policy
as you requested	pursuant to your request
before, after	prior to, subsequent to
get the facts	ascertain (secure) the data
ask him	interrogate him
find it hard to	encounter difficulty in
big difference	marked discrepancy
begin (or start)	initiate (or institute)
complete (or finish)	consummate
in the first place	in the initial instance
Haste makes waste	Precipitation entails negation of economy

Vary Sentence Pattern, Type, and Length to Avoid Monotony. Unvaried sentence pattern, type, length, or rhythm causes many a reader's mind to wander. Though the necessary variety should come naturally from writing well, revision can sometimes enliven your style by removing a dull sameness.

The normal English sentence pattern is subject-verb-complement. Most of your sentences should follow that sequence; but if all of them do, they produce monotony. Particularly noticeable are series of sentences all beginning the same way. The following list suggests possible variations of sentence beginnings:

With a subject: A simple way of keying returns is the use of different return envelopes with the several different letters being tested.

With a clause: Because human beings are unpredictable, the sales process cannot be riveted to a formula.

With a phrase: For this reason, no large mailing should be made until tests have proved which letter is best.

With a verb: Should you find that all pull about the same, you have the usual direct-mail dilemma!

With correlative conjunctions: Not only the war situation but also the results of progressive education methods in secondary schools for the last fifteen years will continue to lower the caliber of work in American colleges.

With an adverb: Ordinarily, students like courses in business letter writing.

With a verbal: Allowing plenty of time, the student started his report early in the semester.

With an infinitive: To be a successful business letter writer, a student must be able to lose himself in contemplation of his reader's problem.

With adjectives: Congenial and co-operative, he worked many nights until midnight when we faced a deadline.

Proper emphasis of ideas is the main reason for varying sentence type, but the variation also avoids monotony and retains interest. An important idea calls for statement in one independent clause (a simple sentence). Sometimes, however, you have two equally important and closely related ideas; so you should put two independent clauses together in a compound sentence. If you have two related ideas of different importance, a complex sentence of one independent clause and one dependent shows the real relationship. Choosing sentence patterns in terms of needed emphasis will nearly always result in enough variety to prevent monotony.

Sameness of sentence length (and to some extent, paragraph length) can be just as monotonous as unvarying sentence pattern and type. Together they produce an interest-killing rhythm characteristic of a childish style. Children's books put both listener and reader to sleep—but business letters are not intended to.

Though readability specialists have done a lot of good by inducing some people to keep their sentences down to reasonable length, they have done some harm by leading others who have misunderstood them to write too mechanically in trying to average about 12–16 words a sentence. That is an *average,* remember. Nothing could be more monotonous than a series of 14-word sentences—or of 6-word sentences or of 26-word sentences. Lack of variety in sentence length can be just as monotonous as lack of variety in sentence pattern or type.

How to Make Your Letters Clear

The strongest rebuke a reader can give a writer is "I don't understand; what do you mean?"

Obviously, your message must be clear to your reader, or the interest which induced him to read it accounts for nothing. Conciseness helps clarity, as well as interest, by relieving your reader of the necessity for separating the important from the unessential; and vividness helps by giving a sharp, clear picture. But other more important aids to clearness are •

1. Making your letters easy to read
2. Planning for unity, coherence, progress, and proper emphasis
3. Using accurate wording, punctuation, grammar, and sentence structure.

Make Them Easy to Read.   Readability is a factor affecting interest, but it is more intimately related to clarity. You have the responsibility as a writer to present ideas so that they are understood with the least possible effort. As the difficulty of understanding an idea increases, people are more inclined to skip it. Any time your reader has to back up and reread or has to slow down to understand you thoroughly, you are risking the chance that he will go on and misunderstand, or make the effort and get the point but become disgusted with you, or lose interest and toss your letter aside.

Using only those *words which your reader will understand* immediately and sharply is a first step in making letters easy to read. You will usually be wise to choose the more commonly known of two words; an uneducated person will understand you, and an educated reader will appreciate your making his reading job easy. Though some short words are not well known and some long ones are common knowledge, your letters will be easier to read if you use one-syllable words most of the time. If you have more than 50 per cent more syllables than words, your writing requires more reader effort than it should. And the greater number of polysyllabic profundities you use, the greater the likelihood that you'll strike your reader as a pompous ass.

Keeping your sentences reasonably short and direct will also help to make your letters easy to read and hence clear. An average of 16–20 words is a healthy one for readability. But you need not avoid sentences of 4 or 5 words—or 40, if necessary for presenting an idea exactly. If the average length is not too much above 20, more important than the word count are smooth sequence of thought and directness. A good test to help avoid involved, indirect sentences is to look at the punctuation. It cannot make a basically bad sentence into a good one. If you have to punctuate a sentence heavily, you will be wise to rephrase it more directly. Sometimes the best solution is to break it up into two or three.

Paragraph pattern and length influence readability, too. The usual pattern of letter paragraphs is a topic sentence followed by supporting or developing details. But if you write one sentence which says all you need to on that topic, start another paragraph rather than pad one with needless stuff or cover two topics in it because some composition books ban single-sentence paragraphs.

Frequently a single-sentence paragraph is highly desirable to give an idea the emphasis you want!

Especially in letters, long paragraphs are uninviting and hard to read. First and last paragraphs of more than four lines and others of more than eight should be reconsidered for breaking up.

Frequent personal references (names of people and pronouns referring to them) also make your letters more interesting and readable. Since you and your reader are the two persons most directly involved in the actions, desires, and benefits you write about in letters, most of your pronouns will be "you" (or "you" understood) and "I" (or "we").

Itemizations and tabulations may help to make your whole letter or a paragraph clear and easy to read. For instance, if your topic sentence says that there are three big advantages in using XYZ wafers, the three will stand out more clearly if you number them and list them on separate lines.

Plan Letters for Unity, Coherence, Progress, and Proper Emphasis. You have already studied planning for psychological effect as a principle of persuasion (p. 28); but planning also affects clarity. If you are answering a letter, underscore points in it to be covered. In any case, think your answer through before you start to write; you can't plan anything more than a simple letter by just thinking as you write. Clear letters are usually the product of a three-step process which stresses organization and coherence:

1. Preliminary planning for unity, progress, and proper emphasis
2. Continuous fast writing or dictating for the natural coherence that comes from following a chain of thought straight through
3. Revision for tone (see pp. 10 ff.), conciseness (pp. 47 ff.), coherence, and correctness (pp. 58 ff. and 64 ff.)

The preliminary-planning step requires specific answers to four questions:

1. What effect do I want the letter to produce? Decide specifically what you want to happen as a result of your letter, and make this central purpose clear to your reader. Without keeping the central purpose in mind, you cannot achieve one of the main objectives of organizing—unity. That is, good organization should result in a oneness by showing how every part is related to the general theme or idea.
2. Who is the reader? Until you make a clear estimate of what your reader is like, you cannot hope to apply the principles of adaptation (p. 36).

3. What facts and ideas must I present to produce the desired effect on this kind of reader? You should list not only points of positive interest but probable reader objections to be overcome.

4. What is the best order of presenting the items listed in answer to Question 3? You are already prepared to answer generally as Type A, B, or C (from your study of "Planned Presentation," pp. 28–33). But that is only a general plan for the whole letter. There is much more to organization than that.

You can organize well only by answering all four of the questions in preliminary planning. Good organization is the marshaling of statements and supporting details, the orderly procession of paragraphs, the disposition of parts so that each finds its proper place.

Fundamentally, organization is the process of grouping things according to likenesses and then putting the groups into an appropriate sequence. For example, if you explain in your letter or report how something is made, you should treat that part fully before going on to explain how it operates. Either of these topics may be just one paragraph, or it may be several. But you do want to group together all the details about how it is made before proceeding. Thus you achieve unity of that topic.

Having grouped according to likenesses, you have several choices of sequence for either a whole letter or a paragraph. Your choice for your whole letter will be in terms of letter Type A, B, or C (pp. 28–33). Common paragraph sequences are general-to-specific, cause-to-effect, order-of-importance, nearest-to-farthest (space relations), and order-of-happening (time relations). All of these may be reversed.

In the second step of writing well-organized letters—continuous fast writing—you merely follow your preliminary plan and *keep going.* Write the entire letter without stopping.

In the third step—revising—you may need to reorganize a bit by shifting words, sentences, or whole paragraphs into better position. But usually the main work on organization through revision will be a few changes in wording for better coherence. You may find that some transitional words are unnecessary because of the natural, logical sequence of the sentence and paragraph; or you may need to strengthen coherence by inserting more transitional words like *and, but, for,* and the variants of each (for which see **Coh 3** in Appendix A). Although you do not leave out any necessary bridges between parts, the fewer you can use and make the sequence of thought clear, the better. Try especially to avoid overformal transitions like *the latter, the above-mentioned,* and *namely.*

Use Accurate Wording, Punctuation, Grammar, and Sentence Structure. Proper usage of words, punctuation, and grammar is established by convention, not rules. The important thing is that you use them in writing with the exact significance the reader attaches to them. Words, for example, are mere labels which we apply to actions and things. In Great Britain such simple words as *ton* and *gallon* do not mean the same as they do in the United States.

Moreover, words and sentences sometimes change meanings according to what precedes and succeeds them. For instance, a would-be secretary brought laughs when the last two sentences of her ad for a job read: "No bad habits. Willing to learn." Similarly, the last two sentences in an ad of a big dog for sale read: "Will eat anything. Loves children."

The difficulties of accurate expression are increased by the fact that words pick up related meanings and personal significances from everyday use (connotations, in addition to their denotations or dictionary meanings). Consider the differences between *cheap* and *inexpensive* or between *house* and *home*. And note that *hope, trust,* and *if* all suggest doubt. "You claim" or "you say" even suggests doubt of the reader's truthfulness. The accurate user of words will be alert to connotations and implications—if not to avoid confusion, at least to produce effectiveness.

Exceptional cases of failure to follow the conventions have led to readers' getting a completely wrong idea. But rarely does such failure *leave* a reader confused; usually he can figure out approximately what the meaning is. Of course, if you say *profit* for what is generally spoken of as the "selling price," you will mislead your reader.

Much more frequently, unconventional usage of words confuses a reader temporarily, causes him to back up and reread, or leaves him uncertain of the writer's intention. The words you use should give him not only the general idea but the precise idea quickly. If you say *soon* or *later,* your reader doesn't know just when you mean. If you say checks, notes, stocks, etc., nobody can tell whether you mean to include bonds. (Etc. should be used only if its meaning is perfectly clear, as in "I am particularly interested in the odd-numbered questions, 1, 3, 5, etc." But it then becomes unnecessary, as it usually does when it is clear.) If you are inclined to write *actuarially,* most readers will get the meaning more quickly if you write *statistically.* The advantage of an extensive vocabulary is that you can choose the precise word to give the exact idea. But if you don't use judgment with a big vocabulary, you sometimes use words that leave the reader in the dark or slow him up.

Punctuation marks, like words, mean only what a reader takes them to mean. They can be helpful to him by breaking your sentences into thought groups if you follow the conventions and use them as they are generally used. But if you use a system of your own which your reader does not understand, you mislead him just as if you used words in unfamiliar senses.

For instance, if you put up a sign on a parking lot to mean

No Parking: Reserved for Our Customers,

you will certainly mislead people if you write it

No Parking Reserved for Our Customers.

Fortunately, the system of English punctuation is pretty well established (by convention, not by rules), and most readers know at least the main parts of the conventions. Unfortunately, many people who know how to *read* punctuation marks correctly do not know the conventions well enough to use them precisely *in writing*. If you have any doubts about the following main troublesome areas of punctuation, see the symbol **P** in Appendix A for explanation and illustration:

—Semicolon between independent clauses except with strong conjunction;
—Comma after all dependent clauses at the beginnings of sentences and with nonessential ones elsewhere;
—Comma to separate co-ordinate adjectives;
—Pair of commas around a parenthetical expression unless you want to de-emphasize by parentheses, emphasize by dashes, or avoid confusion with other commas by using parentheses or dashes;
—Hyphen between words used as a single modifier of a following noun or pronoun.

So-called "errors" in grammar and sentence structure probably mislead readers even less frequently than unconventional uses of words and punctuation; but they, too, slow up reading and produce indefiniteness. Of course, the statement "Strawberries should not be planted where tomatoes have been grown for several years" will mislead some reader if you mean "Wait several years before planting strawberries where tomatoes have been grown." And the dangling participle in "Smelling of liquor, the officer arrested the reckless driver" might cause a policeman to be asked why he was drinking on duty. But those are exceptional cases of bad sentence structure. Faulty pronoun references can confuse, too; but usually they don't. Most readers will understand perfectly, despite shifts in number like "The Acme Company is located in Chicago. They manufacture. . . ." Wrong verb forms like "He come to my house at 10 P.M." or the wrong choice between *lie* and *lay* are usually definite, quick, and clear. Even this ungrammatical question asked at a state-line road-block is perfectly clear: "You-all ain't a-totin' no cotton-seeds, is ya?"

Indeed, poor grammar and sentence structure are so infrequently causes of confusion that they hardly need be discussed in connection with clarity. The other factors already discussed are more important influences on clarity; and grammar and sentence structure are more important as factors of the third requirement of good letter style—that it be inconspicuous.

How to Keep Your Style Inconspicuous

An obvious striving for "style" is a sign of immaturity. When a reader starts your letter, he is looking for what you say, not to see how you say it. He will notice your style only if you do something unexpected with it. In reading a well-ordered sentence, he will receive no jolt. But if he consciously responds to an expression as an artificiality, he is distracted and you lose his attention to your message. Simplicity and naturalness are good guides on the right road.

If you make your style too flowery, formal, or stiff for the situation or if you make it too flippant and familiar, it will distract the reader from your message and cause him to question your sense of appropriateness. If you violate any of the conventions of word choice, spelling, punctuation, sentence structure, or grammar, the unconventional practice will both distract him and cause him to doubt your general knowledge and ability. For instance, if you cause the reader to say, "Why, he can't even spell," the *even* strongly implies "So, of course, he can't be depended on to know anything else either."

The two main ways a writer does something unexpected with style and thus draws undue attention to it, then, are

1. Choosing the wrong level of usage for the situation
2. Violating any of the more common conventions of word choice, spelling, punctuation, grammar, and sentence structure.

Both weaken the impact of your message—the important thing.

Choose the Right Level of Usage for the Situation. Language appropriateness, like proper dress, is a highly variable thing. What is effective in one situation may not be suitable in another. Formal dress is no better for a day in the office or a weiner roast than a business suit or sports clothing is for a formal party, or beach togs for anywhere except on the beach.

The first step in choosing the right level of usage is to analyze the situation in the light of the five communication factors (sometimes called the "communication formula") :

1. A writer (or speaker) who has
2. A particular message to communicate through
3. A medium (letter, report, advertisement) to
4. A definite readership (or audience) for
5. A definite purpose.

If any of the factors of communication change, the situation shifts so that a formerly good sentence may become bad, or vice versa. Still, many thoughtless writers almost ignore the last two factors. Only in view of all of them can you classify the situation and choose the appropriate level of usage.

Having classified the communication situation, you can take the second step in choosing the appropriate level of usage by considering the nature of the different levels. Whole books have been written naming and describing them. More concise treatments also appear in some modern college composition books (like Perrin's *Writer's Guide and Index to English*). Some linguists distinguish as many as seven levels, but a more usual classification names three: formal, informal, and illiterate (sometimes called "vulgate").

Informal English is much the most useful level for letters and for most other kinds of speaking and writing today. In it, the writer's interest is more on content than on style. The emphasis is more on being functional than on being elegant. Its general tone is that of the natural speech of educated people in their usual business and social affairs. In its written form it is more concise and more precise than normal conversation; but its vocabulary, phrasing, sentence structure, grammar, and hence its natural rhythm and tone are essentially the same as in good conversation among educated people. That—rather than a literal interpretation of the words—is the meaning of the often-heard advice that you should write as you talk.

But informal English is a broad category, ranging all the way from a style which verges on formal English to that which verges on the illiterate. When informal English approaches the formal, it does not allow slang, shop talk, contractions, or omission of relative pronouns and other connecting words. It may use generally understood allusions, figures of speech a little more complex than similes, and words and sentences that are somewhat long. Some writers insist on the highly questionable requirement of impersonal style (no pronouns referring to writer or reader) for reports and research papers at this dignified-informal level of usage.

Near the deep end of the informal level of usage is what we call "familiar-informal." Its whole attention should be on content, to the disregard of style. It's O.K. if you're writing to a guy you know pretty well or if you have a lot in common with him. It is used where there is no need to establish your dignity or your knowledge of the language. Even Churchill and Roosevelt sometimes joshed each other quite a bit in their messages. As in this paragraph, it uses contractions, a light touch, and rather simple sentence structure and words, including some slang and shop talk. Its value is its freshness, vividness, emphasis, and naturalness. The danger point, which this paragraph flirts with, is that it will be abused in an attempt to be clever and thus will call attention to itself.

Formal English is characterized by precision and elegance of diction, sentence structure, and grammar. Like the man dressed in formal clothes, it often appears stiff and unnatural, more to be admired for its appearance than for any function it may perform. It admits of no contractions, ellipses, or indignities of any kind. Of necessity, it uses many everyday words, but by design it includes many that are not commonly heard. Like the man of high society, it sometimes chooses its associates with more attention to their paternity than to what they are. As a consequence, its words are frequently somewhat rare and long, with histories traceable back to the first word families of Old French or Latin. It is often fraught with abstruse literary and historical allusions. Instead of concerning itself with facilitating the reader's comprehension, it often uses long and involved sentences that are more elegant and rhythmical than functional. Following an unsound belief that they are thereby being more objective, its writers usually strive for an impersonal style. Its worst misguided practitioners—some lawyers, doctors, engineers, and politicians—apparently hoping to achieve dignity (and defending their practices by claiming that they achieve precision)—frequently abuse acceptable formal English by carrying it to the ridiculous extremes of the too technical, the pompous, and the flatulent (now commonly called "gobbledygook" or "bafflegab").

Abused formal English has no reason for being. Even in its best sense, formal English is nearly always unsuitable for business letters. It would be noticed as inappropriate in all but the most formal occasions.

The illiterate level of usage is the third one of them three we dun named. It ain't got no bizness in letters. Ya see, folks who reads letters spects you ta right right. If'n ya writes wrong, he shore sees ya errors and knows ya ain't eddicated so he thinks ya don't know nuthin else neither if ya cain't get yer rightin right.

An easy way to choose the appropriate level of usage for a situation you have analyzed is to ask yourself which type of dress would be most suitable if you were going to see your reader and talk your message to him. If the answer is formal dress, choose formal English or dignified-informal. If the answer is an everyday business suit, use the broad middleground of informal English. If the answer is sporty clothes, use familiar-informal. Only if you are the kind of person who goes to church in dirty work clothes should you feel comfortable while revealing your illiteracy by violating the writing conventions expected of educated people.

Follow the Conventions. We have already seen how following the conventions of wording, punctuation, sentence structure, and grammar affects clarity. But violations of those and other conventions have an even more important bearing on keeping your style inconspicuous. If you go contrary to the conventions, you do something your reader doesn't expect of an educated writer. You therefore distract his attention from your message and lose his respect and his faith in you.

Even the following first paragraph in a letter from a hotel man to an association president is clear. You know what the writer means, despite his poor sentence, but you are distracted and you can't respect him:

> Your recent convention over with and successful, we are wondering if since then you have decided on the next year's meeting city, and you jotting down on the margin of this letter the city and dates selected, this will be indeed appreciated.

From that, don't you get the impression that if he is so sloppy about his language, his hotel might not be a very well-run, clean place to stay?

Spelling is probably the most exactly established convention in the English language. A few words are spelled two ways, but most of them are listed only one way in the dictionary. Because of this definiteness, spelling has acquired much more importance in the minds of most people than it deserves. Though a misspelled word almost never leads to confusion and therefore makes little difference in terms of real communication, most readers (even relatively uneducated ones) will notice your errors and look down on you for them. So, unless you prefer to write in other languages (nearly all of which have more systematic and easier-to-learn spelling), you had better accept your fate and learn English spelling.

Because it is so unsystematic, there is no easy way. Consider yourself fortunate if you have learned to spell by observing the words you read and by listening closely to how words are pronounced. If you have not used those methods, you should start now; but don't assume that pronunciation is always a safe guide. (See **Sp** in Appendix A.)

Poor word choice that is close enough to meet the basic requirement of clarity is usually not so noticeable as misspelling, but it may be distracting and even degrading. Among the thousands of possible bad choices, the pairs listed under Diction in Appendix A give the most trouble. If you are unsure of any of the distinctions, look up the words; any educated reader will notice if you confuse them.

Unconventional punctuation may lead to misunderstanding, but more frequently it distracts and retards the reader. If you have trouble with it, study the material under **P** in Appendix A.

Grammar and sentence structure are so closely related that they should be considered together. They have a definite bearing on clarity (where they have been discussed, p. 60), but they have more significance in terms of making your style inconspicuous. Most of the troubles come from one or more of a writer's

—Having heard uneducated people speak unconventionally, particularly his family and fellow workers (solution: observe the skill of other writers and speakers, study writing, practice)

—Simple carelessness (solution: revision) or

—Trying to use big words and complicated sentence structures before mastering them (solution: remember that they are unnecessary to dignity; write simply, at least until you can use more involved structures precisely and clearly).

In trying to keep your style unnoticed by avoiding violations of the conventions of good English, you would have an easier job if all your readers were modern linguists. One of them (R. C. Pooley, *Teaching English Usage* [New York: D. Appleton–Century Co., 1946], p. 14) says:

Good English is . . . appropriate to the purpose . . . , true to the language . . . , and comfortable to [the writer and reader]. It is the product of custom, neither cramped by rule nor freed from all restraint; it is never fixed, but changes with the organic life of the language.

Language scholars like Pooley know that many of the so-called "rules" of English are

—Latin rules foisted off on English by early writers who knew Latin and thought English should follow the same system, and

—Rules concocted to systematize English by people who ignored the true nature and history of the language.

Here is a realistic interpretation of some points that language scholars make in contradiction to statements of some less well-informed people:

—A split infinitive is undesirable only if it is awkward or unclear.

—*And, but,* and *so* are good sentence beginnings if they deserve the emphasis they get there. The same applies to *however* and other transitional words, but some people object only to *and, but,* and *so.*

—Prepositions are perfectly good at the ends of sentences if you want them to have that much emphasis.

—One-sentence paragraphs are perfectly good. The ban on them is nonsense. Often a one-sentence paragraph, especially the first or last in a letter, is just what it should be.

—Passive voice is usually undesirable because it is weak, wordy, and awkward; but it has been retained in the language because it is useful in some situations (to avoid direct accusations, for example). To ban it completely is high-handed.

—Colloquial expressions and slang are important and useful parts of the language; when the situation calls for the informal level of usage, they can improve language effectiveness.

—Many a word has several possible meanings when used alone; but if the context makes the interpretation readily clear and definite, to ban use of those words or to limit them (*while, since,* for example) to one use is unrealistic and lordly.

—The distinctions between *shall* and *will* are almost completely gone except in formal English; *will* is much more widely used.

Unfortunately, not all your readers will have studied courses on the history of the language and modern English usage or have read books such as Baugh's and Pooley's on those subjects. Many of them will have been misled by linguistically unsound books and teachers. But they will *think* they know what is right and wrong. If you don't do what they think is right, you will distract them and lose their respect.

If you are writing to someone likely to be linguistically misinformed, then we advise you to adhere to the widespread, though unsound, "rules" when you can do so easily. Otherwise, we suggest that you forget the unjustifiable restrictions on the language and give your attention to the more important aspects of good style—interest, clarity, and inconspicuousness through adherence to the universally accepted conventions.

Appendix A covers some common violations of these conventions and gives suggestions for avoiding criticism.

[All the letter problems for the first four chapters are at the end of Chapter IV because we think you should cover all four basic tests of a good business

letter before trying to write any kind of letter. We urge you to read the first four chapters quickly but thoroughly so that you can put all the basic principles to use even in your first letter.

[Since you will remember the principles of good style better if you practice them while concentrating on them alone, however, you may profit by working through at least some of the following exercises.]

EXERCISES

Determine what is not good about the sentences and rewrite them or be prepared to discuss them, as your teacher directs. You may also benefit by finding (in Appendix A) the appropriate symbol(s) for criticism of each sentence and reading the discussion of the symbol(s).

1. (From an ad.) Solid oak posture chairs for secretaries with built-in padding.
2. No lawyer ever learned all the law he practices in the college in which he studied.
3. (From a report on rain-making.) The responsible scientists of the project interpret the long series of experiments to mean that recently proposed artificial weather modification processes are of relatively little economic importance.
4. According to the trade journal *Trusts and Estates,* a greater percentage of common stocks are now included in the investment portfolios of more than 3,000 banks in the United States.
5. To me, this trend toward greater holding of common stocks in banks' portfolios is very surprising and confirms my opinion that the Dow Jones averages, Barron's Business Gauge, and the Security Exchange Commission, which all predict bear market conditions, overstate the extent of our present business recession.
6. There are some milling machine manufacturers that I was unable to contact or that did not answer my letter, however, the figures here cover all the major producers in this area.
7. My own evaluation of Honeywells is the same as that of the authors and should be installed in our plant.
8. It was found that there are 12 main reasons why goods are returned. The most significant of these being entirely or almost entirely customer faults. The 12 reasons are: . . . .
9. When buying from an equipment supplier the prices might be a bit higher than these but would include shipping charges.
10. The size of the plant and the nature of its hazards determine$ the fire brigade set-up necessary.
11. While the clothing field has a large number of returns and is a good place to start, it is not at all representative of the whole retailing world.
12. The channel of distribution being utilized most is the use of a traveling sales force.
13. Mr. Johnson insists on neat, accurate work.

14. Because of its greater tensil, tear, and bursting strength, it assures less shut-downs in the packaging line. *[handwritten: resistance to tear &bursting] [handwritten: fewer]*

15. In order to understand how this method of distribution would achieve its purpose an analysis of it is neccessary.

16. While I worked with the fire crew I was only involved in one run.

17. Unless the Office of Price Administration or an authorized representative thereof shall, by letter mailed to the applicant within 21 days from the date of filing application, disapprove the requested increase in the maximum price, such pricc increase shall be deemed to have been approved, subject to nonretroactive written disapproval or adjustment at any later time by the Office of Price Administration.

18. Common stock can be classified under three main types. These types are: 1) income stocks, 2) cyclical stocks, and 3) growth stocks.

19. The report describes the method of operation of the hydrogen plant and a brief discussion of the Girbotol process.

20. The weights of the machines range from 6,000–6,400 pounds.

21. List the names of individuals who should recieve copies at the left margin.

22. Costs of cleaning materials, Windex and rags were considered negligable and not computed.

23. Seasonal resort investments may often lay idle for as many as eight months out of the year.

24. The concensus of opinion from members of the committee was that poly-ethylene had a high probability of meeting the requirements.

25. This gives the company that choses the paper bag more versatility in their packaging line.

26. Not only is this welder useful in the manufacture of products but also in repairing of equipment where replacement of the damaged parts is expen-sive.

27. By adjusting the screws, the spirit bubble may be centered in it's tube.

28. "Nonconference" groups are those comprised of individuals that are brought together as a result of their association or relationship to the university (i.e., football team).

29. It has been enjoyable making this study for you, as it is a subject I've wanted to learn more about.

30. Arc welding has some advantages over other methods: easier wedge prepa-ration, faster welding speed and it eliminates the use of flux.

31. I am of the opinion that before investing funds in personnel and equipment for such a center, certain pilot projects ought to be undertaken to determine the value of such a project.

32. The report is designed primarily to show the particular need existing in Latin America and recommending a possible solution for it.

33. Included in the shipment are three small one ounce packages and one big 16 ounce package of Alpha bits.

34. Mr. Rich's recommendation for this versatile work was the Brown & Sharpe because he felt it required the least upkeep of the two machines.

35. A complete cost, both initial and operational, estimate will be presented.

36. The varied kinds of work we can perform includes: property surveys, stak-ing out of substations, taking elevations for contours, and steel inventories.

37. The table contains a schedule giving the exact lengths of pipe to be used and also shows the valves and fittings that are needed.
38. The observers were very interested in large projectiles, especially the 4-inch model for aircraft that weighed about 18 pounds.
39. There are three types of meters used. There is the ammeter which measures current, the wattmeter which measures power and the voltmeter which measures the voltage or electrical pressure.
40. After the grain leaves the seperator it falls to a screw conveyor, and then this conveyor carries it to one of eight bins for storage.
41. The purpose of the program was set up for the improvement of reading rate and the improvement of reading comprehension.
42. Direct questions will put one on gaurd, but an impersonal simple question-aire does not arouse defense mechanisms nor create inhibitions.
43. The subcontractors draw the final detailed plans which are called shop drawings for their men in the field.
44. An attempt to explain each individual type would be a long tiring thing both from the standpoint of the reader and myself.
45. After the concrete has hardened the forms are removed from the walls.
46. According to population studies by the Bureau of Social Studies which were published in 1955 the population of Latin America will reach 321 million persons by 1980 if it continues at the present rate of increase.
47. The other type uses the hot escaping exhaust fumes to turn a turbine.
48. Inside the tube is also placed a tiny drop of mercury and a small amount of argon gas.
49. Information on the subject was only available in technical journals.
50. He is an all-purpose individual, doing janitorial work, repairs on equipment and minor repairs on the physical plant.
51. While working in Plant 4, fireproof coveralls and protective glasses are issued as a safety measure.
52. The supermarket manager who can get customers in the habit of shopping in Fowler can plan on a good stable business for many years to come.
53. The business district in that area is El Cajon and it has its own police force in it.
54. This highly satisfactory garbage can is made by the Jordan Company who have been known for years for their outstanding products.
55. The polyethylene derives two advantages here which are:
    a) Heat sealing made possible by its use speeds up the process.
    b) Economy of eliminating excess material.
56. A report is a communication of fact-supported ideas; if you do not communicate the ideas are of little worth.
57. The problems selected for study were choosen through personal interviews with the workers, manager and my own personal experience with the company.
58. The legislators are expected to vote bigger outlays for highways, schools, water, power, and flood-control projects, hospitals, defense, and medical research.
59. Approximately 66 per cent had made their most recent hardware purchase in Tulsa. This is an increase over previous findings of 4 per cent.

60. Thank you for your order and let us know if we can be of service again.

61. Admitting your mistake will take courage, but it is the kind of courage you must have in order eventually to succeed.

62. Minimum and average costs for various items are listed and the individual costs may vary according to taste, budget and needs.

63. Mr. Summerfield did not bother to elucidate his assertion that the mail service was badly disorganized nor his claim that all is well now.

64. At the first registration, all students must pay a $5 deposit to the Bursar which will be returned to the student upon leaving the University.

65. In order to satisfy you completely, will you check your preference on the enclosed card?

66. In conformance with our conversation on March 30, 1959, the *Report of the Uranium Corporation* has been reviewed, to determine wherein the operations of the Corporation may have been presented inadequately; further, suggested changes in format, illustrations, and treatment of text have been developed, for consideration in the preparation of subsequent reports.

67. Simply check your choice on the return card and immediately upon receiving your preference, the typewriter will be on the way to you.

68. You might also show accounts receivable, long-term accounts, and discuss the future outlook.

69. The evaluation of these problems were made by the Department of Market Research.

70. The high pressure air then rushes into the cylinder carrying the oil charge with it.

71. Maybe direct-mail selling could be used as a complimentary device in marketing our product.

IV. The Fourth Test of a Good Business Letter: Appearance

THE APPEARANCE of an individualized letter, as well as the style, is like the appearance of a person: the less it attracts attention to itself, the better. The question of whether your letter has a pleasant and unobtrusive (undistracting) appearance therefore becomes a fourth test of a good letter.

A personalized (individualized) letter sent by first-class mail will nearly always get a reading. Flashy designs and lavish colors in it are like yelling at a person whose attention you already have. Even worse, if your letter is either too messy or too gaudy or if it violates the conventions of letter form, the appearance distracts the reader's attention from the important feature—your message.

Sales letters are sometimes justifiable exceptions. Because they are usually unpersonalized mass mailings, they sometimes struggle to get read at all. In striving to capture attention, their writers may wisely use cartoons, gadgets, and lavish colors IF the unusual appearance is a symbol of the key idea and IF the message quickly takes over the hold on the reader's attention. In general, however, the physical letter should serve only as a vehicle for your message and should not be noticed.

STATIONERY

The first thing that will be noticed if it is inappropriate is your stationery. The most common business stationery—and therefore the least noticed—is 20-pound bond with some rag content in 8½″ × 11″ sheets. Variations acceptable under appropriate circumstances include heavier and lighter paper, different sizes, and various colors and shades.

Paper heavier than 20-pound is more expensive, too stiff for easiest folding, and too thick for clear carbons; and lighter than 16-pound is too flimsy and transparent for letters. (As you know, carbon copies are usually made on lighter paper, both because it is cheaper and because you can make a greater number of clear copies with it.)

The main off-standard sizes are Executive or Monarch letterheads (7½″ × 10½″ or 11″), used mainly by top executives, and half-sheets (8½″ × 5½″), used most frequently in intra-company notes but also often for short replies. A common objection to any odd size is that it does not fit standard files.

Though white is the standard, only the rainbow and your sense of appropriateness to your kind of business set the limits for color variations. Numerous tests have shown that colored papers sometimes produce better results in sales mailings. But existing test results do not prove that any one color will always work best for any kind of letter. If you are sending out large mailings, you may be wise to run your own test on a small sample to see what color works best for that particular situation.

Paper with some rag content is more expensive than all-pulp paper, but it gives the advantages of easier and neater erasures, pleasant feel, durability, and resistance to yellowing.

Whatever the choice of paper for the letter sheets, the same quality should be used for envelopes and second pages.

The acceptable variations in stationery allow you to reflect the personality of your business, just as you select clothes appropriate to your personality. A back-alley repair shop would not use pink-tinted 24-pound bond in the Monarch size. Nor would a bank president select paper that looks and feels cheap. The big points are appropriateness and inconspicuousness. In selecting the paper for your letterheads, then, you will do well to ask whether there is good reason to choose something other than 20-pound bond, 8½″ × 11″. Anything else is more likely to distract the reader's attention from the message of the letter.

Letterhead

Designing letterheads has become a job for specialists who know paper stocks, color, and design; so most paper suppliers provide such specialists, at least as consultants. Any business writer, however, should know something of the main principles and trends.

The main trend for some years has been toward simplicity. Letterheads used to take up a good part of the sheet with slogans, names of officers, and pictures of the firm's plant and products. The good modern letterhead usually takes no more than 2 inches at the top. It uses wording and design to convey the necessary information and an atmosphere symbolic of the business firm it represents. The minimum content is the name and address of the firm. An added trade mark or slogan indicates the nature of the business unless the name makes it clear. Telephone numbers and departmental designations are other common additions. Firms doing much international business frequently give a code address

R I C H A R D   D. I R W I N · I N C.

1818 RIDGE ROAD · HOMEWOOD, ILLINOIS · A SUBURB OF CHICAGO

CHICAGO TELEPHONE: INTEROCEAN 8-9200   *LONG DISTANCE TELEPHONE: HOMEWOOD 92*

PUBLISHERS OF BOOKS IN ECONOMICS AND BUSINESS

for cablegrams. On the theory that age suggests stability, many firms also give their starting dates. Though two or more colors sometimes appear, modern designers are careful to avoid garish combinations, elaborate designs, and usually any color unless it signifies something about the nature of the business. The letterheads for all the letters in this chapter are typical modern forms.

FORMS OF INDENTION AND PUNCTUATION

Letters 1 through 4 have been placed in this chapter as best they could be to tell the story and illustrate the shifts in letter indention and punctuation, along with other points about letter form. They discuss decisions which you will have to make in choosing an acceptable form for your letters. They are integral parts of the explanation; so you should read them thoroughly as well as look at them. The sequence is according to our estimate of present popularity of the different forms (but we realize that some teachers and office managers will not agree). Though it is not chronological, some of the important points to note are:

1. The two big trends are toward simplicity and time-saving.
2. All forms that are consistent are "correct"; but either the outmoded or the ultramodern does tend to characterize the writer. Of course, there is no law against driving a Model T or a horse and buggy or the newest design of sports car; but each does call attention to itself and characterize its user.
3. In studying letter writing you should learn all forms, with their advantages, disadvantages, and dangers; but you should realize that if you go to work for a company, you should use the company's established form unless and until you can persuade responsible personnel of the wisdom of changing.

You should also realize that you can mix forms (with blocked parts and indented paragraphs, for example) and be in perfectly good company. Hanging indention (the first line of the paragraph extending out five or more spaces to the left beyond the other lines) is also an accepted form, though not so common.

PLACEMENT ON THE PAGE

Even with appropriate paper and a well-designed letterhead, you can still spoil the appearance (and thus distract from the message) unless you place the letter on the page properly. Two methods are in common use: the Picture-Frame and the Standard-Line.

Picture-Frame. Typing a letter so that it looks like a picture framed by the white space around it, as in Letter 1, is still the more

MICHIGAN STATE UNIVERSITY

OF AGRICULTURE AND APPLIED SCIENCE • EAST LANSING

COLLEGE OF BUSINESS AND PUBLIC SERVICE • DEPARTMENT OF GENERAL BUSINESS   February 7, 19--

Miss Elizabeth Diller
1328 Waukegan Street
Grand Rapids, Michigan

Dear Miss Diller:

     Both you and your employer are right. Indented form with closed punc-
tuation is "correct"; but so are several others, including the much more
popular semiblock with mixed punctuation I'm using here.

     Since the boss has the right to establish policy, however, you'll have
to type his letters the way he wants them. Of course if he welcomes suggestions, you can tell him that indented form with closed punctuation strikes
most modern readers as behind the times; and you can show him that it costs
him money by slowing you up.

     That form was _the_ style before typewriters came into use. Then one
day a bright secretary decided to quit wasting time indenting and punc-
tuating the lines in headings and inside addresses. That started a continuing trend toward efficiency and simplicity in letter form.

     Since she still indented for paragraphs, the form she used is called
semiblock; and since she continued to use a colon after the saluation and
a comma after the complimentary close, she used what is now called mixed
punctuation. Later dropping of the paragraph indention, and omitting the
useless colon and comma, produced block form with open punctuation.

     Semiblock and block are certainly more widely used today than the
other forms; and the order of frequency in punctuation style is mixed,
open, and closed. But all are correct.

     You may show your employer this letter as the most widely used form
if you want to; but don't lose your job over such a small matter as which
form to use for his letters.

                 Cordially yours,

                 C. W. Wilkinson, Professor

LETTER 1. Picture-frame layout, semiblock with mixed punctuation, elite type.

widely used plan. It takes a little more time than the Standard-Line
method because you have to set the marginal stops according to your
estimate of each letter's length, but it enables you to fit long and short

letters to the page in more conventional fashion. Also, you can save time sometimes by increasing the line length and thus getting on one page material that would require two pages by the Standard-Line plan.

The idea is that a rectangle drawn around the letter (not including the printed letterhead) should look like a picture framed in the marginal white space. You determine the width of side margins according to your letter length and make the top margin the same. The bottom margin will take care of itself automatically. It should be about one and a half times as wide as the other margins.

In gaining experience, a typist soon learns where to set a typewriter's marginal stops for letters of varied lengths. If you are not an experienced typist, however, the following tips and the table of approximate settings may be helpful while you learn to estimate.

Your first step in using the Picture-Frame plan is to determine which size of type you have by measuring on a line of copy or on the typewriter's numbered scale. Though pica and elite type both give you six lines to the inch as you go down the page, pica gives you only 10 characters to the inch across the page, whereas elite gives you 12. That 20 per cent increase in how much you can say in a given space is the reason for the increasing use of elite.

Your second step is to set the paper guide at the left end of the roller or platen. Unless you have studied typing and learned another method, you will make your figuring easier if you

1. Set the typewriter carriage on a round number (40 for pica, 50 for elite)
2. Then set the paper guide so that the center of the page lines up with the type guide.

As your third step, set the marginal stops equal distances from the center number (40 or 50). The elite lines obviously will have to be shorter than the pica lines; but, since they will leave wider margins, including those at the top and bottom, the letter typed in elite will have fewer lines and therefore must have more spaces to the line. The following table gives approximate settings for letters of different lengths on letterhead stationery:

No. of Words in Message	Settings for Pica	Settings for Elite
100 or less	15–65	23–77
125–175	12–68	20–80
200–250	10–70	16–84

If you are using plain paper (without a letterhead), use the settings on the next line above for a given number of words in the table. Settings of 20–60 for pica and 28–72 for elite can be used for short letters on plain paper; and, of course, the last settings in the table will allow more than 250 words if a letterhead does not take up part of your space.

The figures in the table are only approximations to what will fit the page attractively. Several factors pointed out in the two sections on spacing of letter parts affect the number of words that will fall into a given typewriter setting.

Standard-Line. As illustrated by Letter 2, the Standard-Line plan of placing a letter on the page saves time because the typist does not have to reset marginal stops for letters of varied length. Typewriters are set to the company's standard line (usually six inches); thus all letters have the same side margins. The top margin is about the same as the side margins, and the bottom margin about one and a half times as wide. By varying from the standard spacing between letter parts (more or less between the date and inside address, for example, or three spaces instead of two between paragraphs), the typist can adjust letters of differing lengths for proper height.

POSITION AND SPACING OF LETTER PARTS

Standard Parts. The usual business letter has six standard parts. As a general rule, letters are typed in single spacing within parts and double spacing between parts. Exceptions are explained as they come up.

The *heading* or first part of a letter on plain paper must include the sender's address (but usually not his name) and the date. It establishes both top and side margins because it is the first thing on the page, and the end of the line going farthest to the right sets the margin. It may appear on the left, too, in a pure-block form. Such a heading is usually three lines but often more. Thus it affects the number of words that can be fitted into a given typewriter setting.

On printed stationery, the date line can be written as a unit with the letterhead (to complete the heading, as in Letter 1) or as a separate part. As a unit with the letterhead, the typed-in date is placed for best appearance according to the design of the printed part. Usually it retains the balance by appearing directly under the center of a symmetrical letterhead; often it rounds out one that is off balance. Often it is a separate part because of the difference between print and type. As a separate part, it fixes the upper right corner of the letter (as in Letter 4)

UNIVERSITY OF ALABAMA
School of Commerce and Business Administration
UNIVERSITY, ALABAMA

Department of Marketing

February 7, 19--

Miss Elizabeth Diller
1328 Waukegan Street
Grand Rapids, Michigan

Dear Miss Diller:

Though most letters are written according to the Picture-Frame plan, certain outstanding firms for years have saved time with what is called the Standard Line.

Following this system, the secretary never resets the margin stops on her typewriter and begins all letters at the same top position on the page.

If the letter is short, she makes the black material extend over the greater part of the white space by increasing spaces between paragraphs and/or between the standard letter parts.

Thus she saves time consumed in calculating and in resetting margin stops to place extra-short letters on the page.

Some folks might be a little startled the first time they see a Standard-Line letter. But if your letters really have something to say, readers won't pay much attention to an appearance which is a little unorthodox but is certainly justifiable. Some readers won't even be aware of the difference.

Show this one to your employer, too; you may be surprised at his agreeableness.

Cordially yours,

J. H. Menning

J. H. Menning
Professor

LETTER 2.   Standard-line layout, block with mixed punctuation, pica type.

or, in full block, the left corner (as in Letter 2). That is, it leaves the top margin (equal to the side margins) between itself and the letterhead, and its end sets the right margin (or its beginning the left margin). Thus it is the first exception to the general rule of double spacing between letter parts.

The *inside address*—the same as the envelope address—includes the title, name, and address of the person to receive the letter. It establishes the upper left corner of the letter if the date is a unit with the printed letterhead. Otherwise it begins at the left margin, two to six spaces lower than the date line. So it is the second exception to double spacing

---

MICHIGAN STATE UNIVERSITY

OF AGRICULTURE AND APPLIED SCIENCE • EAST LANSING

COLLEGE OF BUSINESS AND PUBLIC SERVICE • DEPARTMENT OF GENERAL BUSINESS

February 7, 19--

Miss Elizabeth Diller
1328 Waukegan Street
Grand Rapids, Michigan

SIMPLIFIED LETTER FORM

Both you and your employer are right, Miss Diller. Indented form with closed punctuation is "correct." But so are semiblock and block forms with open punctuation. Both are more widely used than indented form is.

The further simplified form which I am using here, with all parts beginning at the left margin to save time, is fast gaining favor. This form was first introduced during World War I but did not take hold well until the National Office Management Association (NOMA) sponsored it after World War II. It is based on the ideas that

    --no parts need labels. (The subject line in this letter is clear without a label, isn't it?)

    --if you use the reader's name in the first line or two and write your letters sincerely or cordially, you do not need salutations or complimentary closes.

    --by beginning all parts flush with the left margin and omitting end punctuation, you can turn out more letters at lower cost.

True simplification of letters means more than that, of course; but as far as form is concerned, those are the most important considerations.

Though many outstanding firms have adopted the form, and though it may be almost universal in American business sometime in the future, it may yet distract the attention of readers who aren't used to it.

Perhaps after seeing the advantages of this simplified form, you'll want to change your mind. If your boss asks for your suggestions, or if he welcomes them, you can show him the advantages. He's sure to be impressed by the argument that you can turn out more letters this way.

LETTER 3. Picture-frame layout, simplified form with open punctuation, elite type.

Miss Elizabeth Diller, February 7, 19--, page 2

But since your employer has the right to establish policy, you should set
up his letters the way he wants them. If he wants to pay you to take the
time to type more conservative-appearing letters--which are just as
"correct"--don't give the matter a second thought. Save your patience
and energy for more significant considerations.

C. W. Wilkinson
C. W. Wilkinson, Professor

between letter parts. The typist uses the allowable spacing variations
and the varying number of lines necessary for the inside address to fit
all letters within each 50-word range in the table to the appropriate
typewriter setting. (WARNING: Be careful to spell names right and
to use the proper title; nobody likes to have his name misspelled or to

UNIVERSITY OF ALABAMA
SCHOOL OF COMMERCE AND BUSINESS ADMINISTRATION
UNIVERSITY, ALABAMA

DEPARTMENT OF MARKETING

February 7, 19--.

Miss Elizabeth Diller,
 1328 Waukegan Street,
  Grand Rapids,
   Michigan.

My dear Miss Diller:

Your preference for blocked form with
open punctuation is certainly justified;
it is definitely more popular and is more
economical than the indented form with
closed punctuation which I am using here.

This form is not "incorrect" by any
standard (though it is practically out-
lawed by correspondence supervisors and
office managers). It is the preferred
form of many executives associated with
prominent firms of impeccable standing--
of authoritative position. Such fine men
often got their training in letter writing in the early 1900's.

If your employer is willing to pay for
your extra time in following this form
and chooses to be "old school," that is
his decision.

Sincerely yours,

J. H. Menning

J. H. Menning,
Professor.

LETTER 4.   Picture-frame layout, indented form with closed punctuation, pica type.

be given the wrong title. And *always* put some form of courtesy title
in front of other people's names.)

The *salutation* or friendly greeting, the third standard part, begins at
the left margin a double space below the inside address. As you may observe in Letter 3, some writers omit it. If used, it should be followed
by a colon (:) or no punctuation whatsoever. Since it is the first indication of the formality of the letter, you should give some thought to the

implications in how you address your reader and how you match the tone of your salutation in the complimentary close. The main forms are listed below in ascending order of formality with appropriate complimentary closes:

Dear (given name, nick-name, or such more familiar term as originality can produce and good taste will allow)	Cordially yours or some more familiar phrasing, so long as it remains in good taste
Dear (surname or given name)	Sincerely yours or Cordially yours
Dear (any title plus surname)	Sincerely yours or Yours truly
My dear Mr. (or Mrs.) White	Yours truly or Sincerely yours
My dear Sir (or Madam)	Respectfully yours or Yours truly

"Gentlemen" is the invariable salutation for letters addressed to a company, regardless of formality and regardless of an attention line (even when some of the "gentlemen" are ladies). In line with the trend toward informal friendliness of business letters, most business writers use the person's name in the salutation when they can and match the friendly tone with some form of *sincerely* or *cordially.*

The *body* or message of the letter begins a double space below the salutation. The paragraphs are usually single-spaced with double spacing between, though very short letters may use double spacing within and triple spacing between paragraphs. Since the body is all one part, regardless of the number of paragraphs, the standard double spacing between paragraphs is a third exception to the general rule of spacing. The number of paragraphs therefore affects the fit of a letter to a given typewriter setting. A letter of 250 words in seven paragraphs, for example, will take at least four more lines than the same number of words in three paragraphs. Yet you should not overlook the chance to improve readability by keeping paragraphs short and itemizing points.

The *complimentary close* is typed a double space below the last line of the body. It may begin at the center of the page, or in line with the beginning of a typed heading, or in line with the date line when it is used as a separate part, or at a point to space it evenly between the center and right margin of the letter. The most common forms employ four key words—*cordially, sincerely, truly,* and *respectfully*—each ordinarily used with *yours.* Juggling the order of the key word and *yours* or adding *very*—as Yours truly, Yours very truly, Very truly yours—makes very little difference. The key words are the main consideration. Increasingly, business writers are dropping the *yours* in the forms involving Sincerely and Cordially. And, as you read in Letter 3, many writers favor dropping the complimentary close completely. If you want to drop the salutation and the complimentary close, you'll be in good company; just remember to drop both, not one or the other.

The form of the *signature block* depends on whether the letter is about your private affairs or your company business. In writing about your own business, you space four times and type your name. The typed name is important for legibility—and consideration for the reader. You then pen your signature above it.

But if a company instead of the writer is to be legally responsible for the letter, the company name should appear above the signature. (See Appendix B.) The fact that the letter is on company stationery makes no difference. So if you want to protect yourself against legal involvement, type the company name in solid capitals (that's the way most firms do) a double space below the complimentary close; then make the quadruple space for your signature before your typed name. You also give your title on the next line below the typed name; or, if there is room, put a comma and your title on the same line with your name. Thus you indicate that you are an agent of the company legally authorized to transact business:

```
Very truly yours            Very sincerely yours
ACME PRODUCTS, INC.         LOVEJOY AND LOEB



John Y. Bowen          (Miss) Phyllis Bentley, Treasurer
Comptroller
```

Because the possibility of legal involvement is usually remote, many writers omit the company name from the signature block in order to gain the more personal effect of a letter from an individual instead of from a company. In such instances it is company policy. Though there may be some readers who will feel greater security in dealing with a company instead of an individual and for whom the examples cited above would be preferable, the following form of signature is the preference of many well-known firms and individuals:

Cordially yours   Sincerely yours

H. P. Worthington   (Mrs.) Phyllis B. Hudson,
Assistant Public Relations   Treasurer
    Manager

Women's signatures bring up a special problem. Note that in all the men's signatures illustrated, there is no title preceding the names. (Not even the President of the United States signs anything with either "President" or "Mr." preceding his name.) Without some indication, however, the person who answers a woman's letter does not know whether to address her as Miss or Mrs. Some writers dodge the question by using Ms., but this is far from universal practice. As a matter of consideration for the other fellow, a woman should indicate whether she is to be addressed as Miss or Mrs.—the way Miss Bentley, who became Mrs. Hudson, did in the preceding examples.

Special Parts.   Besides the six standard parts of a business letter, you will often find good use for one or more of the seven widely used special parts.

You can use an *attention line* in a letter addressed to a company if you want a certain individual in the company to read it. If you don't know the person's name, you may refer to him by title. For example, in a sales letter you may ask for the attention of the purchasing agent like this:

Black, Decker, and Smith
1223 South Congress Avenue
Minneapolis, Minnesota

Attention of the Purchasing Agent

Gentlemen:

It's equally good form to write "Attention: Purchasing Agent" or "Attention, Purchasing Agent." Don't be surprised to see "The Purchasing Agent, Please"; it gets the job done perfectly well and without offense. You may center the attention line, if you prefer, and underscore it for increased emphasis. In either position, flush with the left margin or centered, double space above and below. Remember, however, that the salutation remains the same as for any letter to a company—"Gentlemen"—even when you use an individual's name in the attention line:

```
Black, Decker, and Smith
1223 South Congress Avenue
Minneapolis, Minnesota
```

Mr. C. R. Smith, please

Gentlemen:

The *subject line* may save words and help you get off to a fast start by telling your reader quickly what the letter is about or referring him to former correspondence for necessary background which he may have forgot. It usually appears a double space below the salutation; it often appears a double space above the salutation; and, when space is at a premium, it may be placed on the same line as the salutation. To make it stand out, many writers either underscore it or use solid capitals. In centered position or flush with the left margin it is equally acceptable. You can save some time by starting it at the left margin and typing it in solid capitals, as illustrated in Letter 3. The legal forms "Re" and "In Re" are gradually disappearing. The informal "About" is increasing in use. And more and more correspondents omit the word *subject* or its equivalent. The position and wording make clear what the subject line is.

Initials of the dictator and the typist often appear at the left margin a double space below the last line of the signature block. The trend is toward omitting the dictator's initials because of repetition from the signature block; but if they are used, they come first (usually in unspaced capitals) and are separated from the typist's by a colon, a diagonal, a dash, or an asterisk. A good method that saves time is to lock the shift and type all as CRA:MF or just write all in lower case as cra/mf. Some writers place the typed name here and omit it from the signature block, as in the following:

Very truly yours
[quadruple space for signature]
Comptroller

J. H. Jennings : dp

An *enclosure notation,* a single or double space below the identifying initials (or in their place), is a reminder to the person putting up the mail that he must actually make the enclosure. It is especially important in large offices. Sometimes it is reinforced by an asterisk in the left margin at the line in the body referring to the enclosure. The word *Enclosure* may be spelled out or abbreviated *Encl.* or *Enc.,* followed by a number indicating how many enclosures or by a colon and words indicating what the enclosures are.

Carbon-copy designations are useful when persons other than the addressee should be informed of the contents of the letter. The names of people to receive carbons are usually listed after CC (or Cc or cc) at the left margin, a single or double space below either the initials or the enclosure notation if it is used.

Postscripts are rarely used in business today in the original sense of afterthoughts. Rather than arouse his reader's resentment by his poor planning, the modern business writer would have the letter typed over; or, in informal correspondence, he might add a pen-written note when signing. (Incidentally, there is some research evidence that such notes actually increase the pulling power of letters—probably because they give the letter a more personal touch.)

The main use of postscripts now is as punch lines. Since they have the advantage of the emphatic end position, they are often planned from the beginning to emphasize an important point. The well-planned postscript that ties in with the development of the whole letter and stresses an important point is effective.

When you do decide to use a postscript, it should be the last thing on the page, a double space below the last of the preceding parts. The "P.S." is optional; position and wording clearly indicate that it is a postscript.

Second-page headings are helpful for filing and for reassembling multipage letters that become separated (especially true when a letter runs to three or more pages). Since pages after the first should be on plain paper, even when the first page has a printed letterhead, for identification they should carry something like one of the following, typed down from the top the distance of the side margins:

```
Mr. C. R. Jeans            -2-            March 21, 19--
```

or

```
Mr. C. R. Jeans
March 21, 19--
Page 2
```

or (for speed and equal acceptability)

```
Mr. C. R. Jeans, March 21, 19--, page 2
```

The body of the letter continues a quadruple space below this.

Addressing the Envelope; Folding and Inserting the Letter

The envelope should be of the same quality as the letterhead stationery, with the return address printed in the upper left corner in the same design as the printed letterhead. For letters on plain paper, the

return address should be typed in the same place in the style of indention and punctuation used for the letter.

The main address—the same as the inside address, except double-
spaced if it is less than four lines—should be placed in the lower half of
the envelope and balanced between the ends. That is, the beginning
point should be the same distance from the left edge of the envelope as
the ending point from the right edge. Since most addresses are blocked,
it usually boils down to centering the longest line in the address.

If you elect to enjoy the economies of window envelopes, then you
have no problem of addressing the envelope. Just remember to fold so
that the inside address will show through without revealing any other
part of the letter. When you crease the upper part of the letter so that
the window will reveal nothing but the inside address, you usually have
creases that divide the letter into approximately equal thirds. Most
window envelopes used for letters are the No. 10.

When you're not using a window envelope, you fold and insert the
letter according to the size of the envelope you are using. Two sizes
are in common use: the No. 6¾ or commercial size, 3⅝ inches by 6½
inches; the No. 10 or official size, 4⅓ inches by 9½ inches. For the
first, fold the bottom up to within a half to a quarter inch of the top;
fold from right to left about one third the width; then fold from left to
right about one third, so that the last fold just fails to meet the other
edge. For the No. 10 envelope, fold up from the bottom about one
third the distance, then down from the top about one third, so that
the last fold just fails to meet the other edge. In each method you
divide your letter into approximately equal thirds. Then insert the
letter in the envelope with the last fold to the back of the envelope and
the open edge of the letter up. Thus the letter will avoid annoying and
distracting the reader because it will unfold easily, quickly, and naturally in the way he is accustomed to.

Summary

Even such a minor point as folding and inserting a letter is symbolic
of the basic theme in the first four chapters of this book:

1. Using the physical letter merely as a vehicle to carry the message in the
least distracting and the most simple, time-saving way
2. Using language that does not distract from the message but conveys it
as clearly, quickly, easily, and interestingly as possible
3. Persuading the reader by showing him that your proposals are to his individual benefit; and
4. Establishing friendliness and confidence between writer and reader by
showing a sincere desire to serve and an acceptable balance of personal-

ities based on respect and consideration for the reader as well as for yourself.

Fundamentally, the underlying theme in all the sections is consideration for the other fellow.

[The problems in this book are disguised and sometimes slightly modified real situations. Mostly they are from among the more difficult letter-writing situations of business.

We have tried to give you the basic information needed without complicating details. You are expected to fill in details from your own imagination. But you are not to go contrary to the statements or implications in the problems, and your imaginary details must be reasonably likely.

The writing in the problems is intentionally not good, because you would learn nothing from copying our phrasing. So beware of copying sentences and clauses in your letters. Put your ideas in your own words.]

PROBLEMS FOR CHAPTERS I–IV

1. Revise the following letter for improved order of points, you-viewpoint, positiveness, and economy of statement. It is from Wright-Lynch Research, Inc., 50 Rockefeller Plaza, New York 20, to Mr. Joseph Moore, 10 Arcadia Drive, Holland, Michigan.*

   We regret to advise the fact that we have not made the soft wall covering in panels and roll material for sometime—almost 2 years. Duron is available in 10 in. and 20 in. squares, and 10 in. × 20 in. rectangles. Duron increases the overall quality of sound, making it more pleasant and making homes more livable, offices less tiring.

   Duran wall covering has been tested for flame resistance by leading independent laboratories. It has been given the superior rating of "Class A" with respect to U.S. Federal Specification SS-A-118b for Acoustical Materials. It has been rated FHA-Acceptable as a building material in all 48 states. It is easily cleaned with a damp cloth and can even be washed with soap and water. Unlike most acoustical materials, Duron will not crumble or dust, and its colors stay bright. Inert to bacteria and fungus, Duron has wide application in modern hospitals.

   See your dealer today and have him demonstrate Duron's unique acoustical properties, and show you the full range of 24 rich decorator colors including the new, soft pastels. He also has special "tweed" finishes, decorative "accent" tiles and special designs.

   It is one of the easiest of all wall and ceiling coverings to install. It can be applied to almost any existing wall—including concrete and cinder block . . . and over curved surfaces. Duron is just the thing for "problem" walls, for it permanently covers persistent cracks that show through other materials.

---

* For more details on Duron see Problem 8, p. 119.

P.S. Your nearest dealer is Roberts Brothers, 1216 Saginaw Boulevard, Grand Rapids, Michigan.

2. How would you improve this letter from the American Bagless Cleaner, 203 North Wabash Avenue, Chicago 1, Illinois, to F. H. Adams, Apt. B-1, 130 Brantley Ave., New Brunswick, New Jersey?

DEAR SIR:

We are in receipt of your letter of recent date in reference to new brush for your Filter King machine, and suggest that you order the part directly from us.

The price of the brush refill is 65 cents, or the complete floor brush with spring, $1.50. Both brushes are easily installed; therefore, it is not necessary to send the nozzle to us.

As we do not send parts open account, when placing your order kindly enclose remittance to cover and same will receive prompt attention.

Thanking you for your patronage,

Yours very truly,

3. As your instructor directs, criticize or rewrite the following letter from Morris E. Sutliff, president, *World Encyclopedia* to a subscriber:

DEAR SUBSCRIBER:

Our records indicate that we have just received the final payment on your account covering your purchase of the *World Encyclopedia* which you favored us with under the terms of our most attractive combination offer. We hasten to thank you, first for your valued patronage, and secondly, for the excellent manner in which you have handled your payments as they became due, so much so that you have been recorded in our archives as a Preferred Certified Account.

Enclosed you will find a Preferred Certified Account Credit Card. It is for your personal use. Carry it with you and use it as the opportunity presents itself. It will introduce you to other organizations, with whom you may be seeking credit.

You may, of course, refer any such organization directly to us for any supplementary information that may be needed, with the assurance that we will be very happy to tell them of our pleasant experience with you.

We hope that you and yours will enjoy your set of *World Encyclopedia* and the other items that you have obtained in your combination purchase.

We beg to advise you that if, at any time in the future, the facilities of this office can be of service to you, they will always be at your command. Do not hesitate to call upon us for any service we can render you. It will be a privilege to serve you, thereby hoping to indicate in every tangible manner possible our appreciation to you, a preferred patron of our organization.

Very sincerely yours,

4. Rewrite the following letter in order to put the good news first and improve in other ways you consider desirable:

Demopolis Gin and Warehouse Company
Demopolis, Alabama

GENTLEMEN:

We have your postal card dated April 1, requesting prices on Cotton Ties. We are pleased to quote the following prices for your consideration:

Standard 45# Cotton Ties Unpainted (30 Strips and 30 Standard Buckles) $3.95 per bundle.

Prices are subject to change without notice and billings will reflect seller's mill price bases and applicable extras in effect at time of shipment, plus actual transportation charges.

We have Cotton Ties in stock and can promise shipment immediately upon receipt of your order.

It is a pleasure to quote on your requirements and we hope to be favored with your purchase order.

The Southeastern Mfg. Co. of Atlanta is the sender. Sign it as the sales manager.

5. Mr. L. Eskridge, manager of W. C. Gardner Wholesale Grocery Company, Fifth Avenue, Harriman, Tennessee, did not receive an invoice and was concerned about his discount on an order for 5,000 feet of 72″ style M Diamond Mesh Fence from the American Fence and Wire Company, Baltimore. He received the following letter:

In accordance with your conversation today with our Mr. D. R. Hutto, we are mailing under separate cover copy of subject invoice.

You will be pleased to know that the discount will not start until you receive this invoice.

We are sorry you were inconvenienced and thank you for bringing this matter to our attention. This will not happen again.

Rewrite for positiveness, naturalness, and other possible improvements. Price is $2 a foot for the first 100 feet, $1.75 a foot up to 100 feet, $1.60 a foot for the second 1,000 feet, and $1.50 per foot thereafter.

6. What is wrong with this letter from the Langford Roofing Company, Chicago, to the Tanner Hardware Company, Gainesville, Ohio?

Attention: Mr. Edward Bowker

Confirming our phone conversation of April 3, we have entered your order for 20,000# of 9′ and 20,000# of 10′—29 Gauge Tenneseal

Type I Roofing, which is to be shipped by Malone Truck Lines only. We expect to ship this order April 7 or April 8.

It is a pleasure to serve you and when we can be of further service please do not hesitate to call on us.

Our official order acknowledgment will follow shortly and we thank you for your continued business.

Rewrite to make clearer, more natural, and more complete. Particularly observe sentence unity.

7. Set up this letter and rewrite the message for naturalness, conciseness, clarity, and specificness. It's written to the Cherokee Porcelain Enamel Corporation, 4200 Old Kingston Pike, Knoxville, Tennessee, from R. C. Lambert, Assistant Director of Sales, Allied Chemical Company, Cleveland.

> GENTLEMEN:
>
> *Your Order 32158*
>
> In accordance with attached acknowledgment sheets, please be advised the sample no-charge order has been entered for your account.
>
> After you have had an opportunity to conduct experiments with this material, we would appreciate your advice as to its suitability for your end use.
>
> When we may be of further assistance, please do not hesitate to call on us.

The product concerned is a die chemical for permanency of color in the finished porcelain enamel.

8. In the Department of Civilian Defense for your state you have been given the following letter from Steve Gibbs, 4 Frederick Drive, Springfield, to answer:

> At Cub Scout meeting the other day, my friend, Al Hummel said you had a little book on *Atomic War and How to Protect Yourself.*
>
> Please send a copy to me. I've enclosed 10 cents.

A recent study done by the Civilian Defense Department has been written up in a booklet, *Facts about Fallout Protection.* Because of so many requests the supply of the booklet on Atomic War is exhausted, but you'll have more in about ten days and will send him a copy. In sending him this second booklet, minimize the negative effect in his not getting what he has asked for; emphasize efficiency in complying with his request; and favorably present your substitute.

9. Several weeks later than in the preceding problem, you are asked to answer this letter from Mike Goodson. It is laboriously written in pencil.

> Hey—you guys. I wrote you and asked for a copy of your book on Fallout Protection, like my frend Steve Gibbs got. That was over ten days ago. A fine time we'd have protecting ourselves.

In checking the situation, you find that Mike is right. He had requested this book ten days ago, but the address had blurred so that you had sent the booklet to Springdale instead of Springfield. The original copy was returned marked "Unknown." In writing an appropriate reply, check for adaptation, salesmanlike planning, and the elimination of accusations.

10. What is not clear in the following letter to Mrs. C. N. Muirhead, 3005 Red River, Austin, Texas, from City Furniture Store, Dallas?

> We are indeed sorry that we failed to send the hospital casters for your bunk bed with your furniture. We were happy to send it to you.
>
> Thank you for your order and we shall be looking forward to serving you often.

Rewrite the letter for greater clarity and positiveness as well as effective use of resale on the modern black wrought-iron bed, night table, and chair which the store delivered to Mrs. Muirhead. The casters have been sent express charges prepaid, after having been omitted from the first shipment.

11. It's your job as a member of the Promotion Department, *Vacation* magazine, 540 North Michigan Avenue, Chicago 11, Illinois, to revise the following letter, especially to eliminate the unnecessarily tactless accusation. Send the letter to Mr. C. A. Peterson, 41 Bigelow Avenue, Mill Valley, California.

> We have your instructions to change your address from
>
> 41 Aberdeen Road
> Mill Valley, California
>
> to that shown at the top of this letter. You overlooked telling us, however, which of our publications is affected by this change, (*Vision, Business World,* or *House Lovely*). Just answer the questions on the form and return it with this letter, and then we will try to get your magazine to you.
>
> This time be sure to attach an addressing imprint from a recent copy.

12. Comment on the following letter, paying special attention to trite phrases, wordiness, and exaggeration:*

> Once in a blue moon an opportunity presents itself that may mean earning thousands of dollars. That occasion is now on hand and if you are a man of vision and ambition you will recognize your golden opportunity.
>
> You answered our ad in regards to State Distributorship for our sensationally-new cosmetic—Vita-o-zyme Beauty Cream. We shall endevor to give you all the details in this letter so that you are able to fisualize what a State Distributorship can mean to you.
>
> As State Franchise Holder you are also permitted to divide your territory, placing a proper person in your State, again, on a franchise basis. Don't miss this chance of a lifetime.

---

* To re-write this letter see Problem 6, under "Invited Sales" for more details.

As you may know, the cosmetic business is an industry that grows—a tremendous, solid business with sales over billions of dollars. Women spend lots for the pursuit for beauty, youth and charm. The demand for beauty preparations that will stop or limit the ravages of advancing years is enormous and money is no object to gain that intangible something—YOUTH.

We have such a preparation—Vita-o-zyme—the acme of perfection. Remember, please, the cosmetic business will never die out and knows no recession or failure, but sales and steady repeats.

13. Seeking to improve the correctness, positiveness, style, and tone, rewrite the following letter from Ralph Minick, vice president, Enterprise Industries, Inc., 517 James Street, Stanton, Illinois, to R. P. McGregor, assistant manager of sales, Tennessee Coal and Iron Division, Fairfield, Alabama:

Please pardon the delay in answering your letter of October 4th, as we have just completed moving our Stanton plant to a new location.

This move should have been made in early summer although we were delayed in the new plant which has caused a further delay in our expansion program at Swainsboro, Georgia.

We are wondering whether you could, without too much trouble, defer this tonnage until the second quarter as we do not believe the plant will be built and in operation before then.

We dislike to ask you for this further accommodation, although our plans have been delayed that much and it would be greatly appreciated if you could accomodate us.

Many thanks for your kind consideration to our problem.

14. Reuben Tyler, Route #2, Danielsville, Iowa, writes the National Steel Corporation, 525 William Penn Place, Pittsburgh 30, Pennsylvania, the following inquiry:

Would you please tell me the difference between Chrome Steel and Stainless Steel and please tell me the price of these steels?

D. T. Early, manager of sales, answers with the following letter:

We thank you for your letter of September 17, which has been referred to this office for reply. In answer to the first part of your question Chrome Steel, as such, does not reflect any specific type of steel to us, since it could be an Alloy or a Stainless Steel. However, for your information whenever Chromium is specified at over 10% this steel would then be called Stainless.

There are many Stainless Steels produced and each one reflects a different price. Therefore, if you would supply us with more information as to the amount of material needed and also the end use of this material, we would be happy to endeavor to make recommendations for you.

We thank you for your interest in our corporation and if we may be of further aid, please do not hesitate to call on us.

Rewrite Mr. Early's letter for him, omitting unnecessary words, improving tone, and correcting where necessary.

15. Can you see why this letter was graded F? Correct it to raise the grade.

The McGrew—Hill, incoperated

Southeasters sales division

Atlanta, georgia

Feburary 14, 1959

DR. JOHN S. Landers

Proffessor of Marketing

University of Iowas

DEAR SIR: Inquiry about Travis Brannon, your student assist. during his sinior year.

I would appreciate your opinion on Mr. Brannon as a Salesman for McGrew-Hill school books.

How is his attitude toward being away from home for considerable length at a time? Does his personality stand out with an older person?

I discussed the situation thoroughly with Brannon and he seemed quiet intrested. He said he had served in the Army as a Colonel, does he try to make himself superior among his assosiates?

Your reply on Mr. Brannon will be strictly confidential and greatly appreciated.

Sincerely yours

Craig Duncan

Sales Director

16. Rewrite the following letter for easier reading and improved tone. It is signed by the policy supervisor of the Providential Insurance Company, Chicago, and addressed to Mr. Llowel Adams, district manager, Tulsa. An "assured" is the person who is insured or covered under the provisions of the policy.

We are enclosing a set of endorsements with this policy which requires the signature of the named assured. Please have these endorsements signed by the named assured, attach the original to the assured's copy of the policy, retain one copy for your file and return one copy to the Home Office for the Home Office file.

Note that if the named assured has not attained the age of 21 years old, it will be necessary that we also have the signature of the parent or guardian on these same endorsements.

We will expect these endorsements returned within 30 days. If we do not receive the same signed endorsements within this time, it will be necessary to send a notice of cancellation to the assured.

17. Rewrite, correct, improve, and set up in acceptable form the following letter from the Lord Baltimore Press, 1769 Marshall Highway, Baltimore:

> Champlain Co., Incorporated
> 88LLewellyn Av.
> Bloomfield, N.J.
>
> Attn of Mr. C. L. Lewis, Production Mgr
>
> DEAR MR. LEWIS:
>
> Just what are the advantages of your autamatic, in-line cutter and creaser?
>
> Your advertisment in Modern Packaging makes some very interesting claims.
>
> The Lord Baltimore Press is considering your cutter and creaser for their eight color Champlain roto-graveure press. More specific information regarding the advantages of your cutter and creaser would help us to decide the feasability of purchasing one of your machines.
>
> Possible your company has some printed material that would covering following information. If not, would you take a few minutes to answer the following questions.
>
> What is the amount of floor space needed for proper instilation? Would your machine be able to handle the high-rate of production of our press? At this high speed what are the tolerance of register? What are the range of prices for the dies and what is there average life in terms of blanks cut? How long does it take for "make-ready"? Is there any special features or attachments not included in the above questions? And of course, what is the complete installed cost of the unit?
>
> Since our production meeting about this machine is scheduled for next Tuesday, I would hearing from you right away as soon as possible.
>
> Your information shall be appreciated in our decision.
>
> Sign it as the Production Engineer.

18. Rewrite this wordy, confusing, repetitious, contradictory letter:

> A. Harris & Co.
> Main & Akard St.
> Dallas, Tex.
>
> DEAR MISS ROGERS:
>
> I was in your store during the Christmas Holidays and tried to purchase a sweater of either one of two styles that you carried there on the First Floor. The description of the sweaters were as follows:
>
> One was a rough weave, in wool, and had a cut-out neck (low-neck) and I believe it had three-quarter length sleeves, and it seems tha y were of the ragland sleeve—the weave was on the order of the pop-corn weave—
>
> The other was also of a sort of pop-corn weave, wool sweater, and with a straight up neck line, cut straight across at the Throat—top of the

neck,—sort of a turtle neck,—except it did not turn down—I believe it had short sleeves—perhaps with a small cuff on the sleeves or it seems that the sleeve was slightly puffed sleeve (. . . not just the regular straight sleeve). Would you be good enough to let me know if you have either style in size 36 if it has the ragland sleeve, xxxx (or at least in the high necked one). and if you have the cut-out neck sweater will you please neasure one to the size 36 of the high-necked one. I tried on one of them—the one with the ragland sleeve and the size 38 was too large for me, but you were out of sizes 36 when I was there. I wanted one in WHITE light blue, or perhaps a gray. Will you tell me what color you have these and if in size 36 as measured to the high-necked one described (that is my right size). I was so sorry I could not get these when I was there, but as they do not have them here, I would especially like one in *white* of either style—especially the low necked one. If you have size 36 in either, please let me know and if you will hold it for me, I will send you a cashier's check for it— I believe one of the prices was $6.98 (or something like that).

Thank you for your shopping help.

Sincerely yours,

P.S. Let me know color, sleeve style and if size 36 or equivalent preferably light blue or white. (or equivalent)

19. Consider the following letter from the advertising manager of an insurance company to an insurance agency that sells policies of various companies. What about the plan? What about the tone? Rewrite to improve it any way you can.

> This answers your memo of March 26, 19—, asking whether we have any available mats for newspaper advertising on workmen's compensation. No, we do not, Wendell, and for a very good reason. Newspaper advertising is a mass market media. Workmen's compensation insurance is not a mass market product.
>
> Perhaps only one in a thousand reading your ad in the newspaper would be a prospect for workmen's compensation insurance but you would be paying for talking to the other nine hundred ninety-nine people who can't use what you are talking about. For pitching a special type of insurance, you would have to use a media that concentrates on the prospects for that type of insurance, such as a trade publication. You couldn't afford to pay the rates on such a trade publication unless it just covered your selling area. For instance, if your Chamber of Commerce put out a publication that was sent just to your local businessmen and you paid a circulation rate just to reach those people, then it might be feasible.
>
> The best way for you to sell X Company's workmen's compensation insurance, Wendell, would be to take our sales promotion brochure on the XX Plan and start calling on businessmen up and down the street.
>
> Kind regards.

20. The following letter to D. J. Clement, owner of the Campus Supply Store, Knoxville, Tennessee, from the credit manager of the Southern Equipment Company, Memphis, is wordy, vague, and tactless, among other things. Rewrite to improve. You will find your job easier if you'll read the material on credit refusals (check the Index entry for page numbers).

> I have yours of the 10th at hand. In regard to your request for credit beg to state that we would help you if we could. However, it is our policy not to sell on credit to unproven businesses.
>
> You certainly will have to agree with me that there are so many deadbeats in circulation these days that one must be very careful to whom one grants credit.
>
> If you should improve your capital position in the near future we will be very glad to grant you credit in accordance with our policy.
>
> If you still want to buy some of our supplies, we wish you would see fit to pay cash.
>
> Awaiting your reply and hoping to serve you further, I am

21. For the personnel manager, Harbor Glass Corporation, Steuben, Ohio, rewrite the following letter to Mr. Roger Burcham, 2614 Pennsylvania Avenue, Urbana, Illinois. Improve it in any way you can.

> It was very nice of you to spend a few minutes with me last Tuesday when we discussed the opportunities available if you considered associating yourself with our good concern. Amoung the many thing we talked about it was mutually agreed it would be best for all concerned for you to visit our main office and one of our factories to get a better picture of our operation and organization. I also mentioned that I wanted to plan a trip for four or five of you men to visit us in Steuben, Ohio, making the trip over on Friday May 4th and returning to Urbana on Sunday, May 6th. If I recall correctly you were agreeable to make such a trip.
>
> This contemplated trip is now definitely planned and I would like very much for you to go along. I plan to meet you and four other men at the Union Building at 7:00 am Friday morning May 4th for breakfast, immediately after breakfast you can be off for Steuben. All of your expenses will be paid and I am sure you will not only enjoy the trip, but you will definitely see what a wonderful organization we have. One of the other men will be using his car, so even though you may have a car we are not planning for you to use it on this trip.
>
> When you arrive in Steuben you will first report to our main office to meet some of the key personnell, so your attire and the clothes you will need for two evenings of entertainment is entirely to your discretion.
>
> I have enclosed a self-addressed postcard so you can advise me by return mail, definitely, whether or not I can plan on your making this trip and if you will meet with the rest of us for breakfast at 7 am Friday May 4th.

22. The following invitation from the head of the Marketing Department (assume your own institution) to all faculty members in the business and economics division needs improving (for directness and consciseness, among other things). Try your hand at it.

> Each year the faculty of the Department of Marketing presents this institutions's Marketing Award for outstanding contribution to the advancement of marketing to a distinguished business executive. This year the Award will be presented to Mr. Anderson Haskell, the noted publisher of TEMPO magazine.
>
> Mr. Haskell is being given the Award in recognition of the acclaimed TEMPO Study of Consumer Expenditures. This comprehensive basic research program provides unquestionably the best picture of the consumption patterns of American families ever available to the business community. In addition Mr. Haskell is being cited for the TEMPO series of Marketing Round Tables which has brought together top corporate officers and distinguished educators to discuss America's marketing needs and resources. This series has led to a significantly greater appreciation and understandinf of marketing as a national resource of our private enterprise economy.
>
> The Awards Dinner will be held on Wednesday, the 1th, in the Student Center on the Campus, beginning with a reception for Mr. Haskell at 5:30 p.m. in the University Room. Dinner will be served at 6:15. His Awards Address will be at 8:00 p.m. in the Main Auditorium and will be carried on the air.
>
> A number of distinguished business executives from (supply the appropriate city and state names) business community will be present for this occasion. Also, a number of administrative officials and faculty members from other parts of the University will be present. The faculty of the Department joins with me in inviting you to be present for this occasion as an honor to Mr. Haskell. Because of budgetary limitations that all of you will appreciate, we are asking all faculty members, including our own, to pay the cost of the dinner, which is $3.50. If you cannot be present for the reception and the dinner, we would welcome your attendance for Mr. Haskell's address, which will also serve to introduce our new Graduate Symposium in Marketing.
>
> We hope to make this a memorable occasion for Mr. Haskell and other TEMPO executives who will be present. Your presence will help to assure this outcome. I hope that it will be our privilege to have many of you present. We look forward to your acceptance of this invitation and if it will be possible to attend, please call the departmental secretary at your earliest convenience.

23. The following letter from the Tri-States Insurance Company, Jackson, Mississippi, to George Brossier, 421 Gulf States Building, Baton Rouge, Louisiana, comes to you, head claims agent, for signing. Since it is unmailable, rewrite it to improve tone, conciseness, accuracy, and general style.

Re: Our file 7–04–677

We are at a loss to understand the returning of the policyholder's report to us without completing it, concerning the involvment of your driver, Mr. Martin Sparling, with another of our assureds, Mrs. Louise Staples, on the 10th of last month.

We have again checked with the District Agency and they are quite definite that they have received no report of this accident from you at that time.

I again request that you fill out this policyholder's report completely and return same to us immediately, with a note explaining the circumstances of your reporting it to the agent, if you did.

If we do not hear from you within ten days, I shall conclude that you do not wish to cooperate with us in reporting the accident and therefore shall have to recommend to the company that we drop your insurance.

24. In your new job as promotion manager for the Standard American Company, manufacturers of heating and refrigerating (air-conditioning) systems, New York, you have just discovered that the following form is being used to respond to inquiries coming to the firm as a result of national space advertising:

> DEAR MADAM (or SIR): Referring to your inquiry of the 6th in which you ask for a copy of our booklet, 70 Degree Temperature in Arctics or Tropics, wish to advise that the last edition has just been exhausted, and we are unable to advise when other copies will be available. Regretting our inability to help, we remain,

The first thing you did was to issue a directive that the form not be used any more. Then you verified that copies would be available from the printer in two weeks. Now write a letter addressed to Mrs. George Passavant, Bardstown, Kentucky, that will serve as a guide for other such inquiries. You've verified that the dealer nearest her is the Hughes Company, 21 Dalton Avenue, Louisville.

25. Consider this letter from the sales promotion manager of a Michigan insurance company to the Advertising Art Novelty Company of Detroit. You'll probably agree that it is a better-than-average letter for the purpose; but, as one who has studied letter writing, you can probably improve it in some ways. Rewrite to improve it in as many ways as you can.

> Enclosed are orders we have received from our agents to date for 19— Tiger baseball schedules.
>
> Several agents have mentioned to me that they did not order schedules this year because they received their supply late in past years. So that this program will not die out because of lack of agent interest, I sincerely hope you will print and ship the enclosed orders with all possible speed and also any other orders we may send you in the future. I realize it takes time to get the complete televised schedule and that

imprinting and shipping a large number of orders cannot be done in a few hours. However, this is difficult to explain to agents and the trend has been that they simply drop the schedule from their promotional plans. Whatever you can do to speed the orders to the agents will be greatly appreciated.

I want to point out again that the emblem should be corrected on the orders this year. As I explained in an earlier letter, the emblem itself should be vertical, i. e., perpendicular to the bottom of the page.

26. You are president of Andrew Jordan Company, Cincinnati, Ohio, soap manufacturers. To tell your stockholders about the promotion your company has been giving the new deodorant and beauty soap, Pride, you are sending a form letter to them. During the rest of the year you plan to promote Pride with a million-dollar television advertising budget. Jack Farr, whose program has become a household institution throughout the country, went on the air for Pride a month ago under a long-term contract. The board of directors feel that concentrated television programs are better than expensive soap samples distributed to homes. Pride has proved itself worthy of all-out promotion, and the sales power of Farr with American consumers is well known. In addition to having a considerable impact on Pride sales, the company feels that sponsorship of these programs is certain to enhance the prestige of the company and the remainder of the product line. Write this letter designed to win stockholder approval and plug Pride and the company behind it.

27. As assistant sales analyst for Peck and Hill, New York 16, you write letters aimed to get customer reaction to how store personnel handle adjustments. Today's letter goes to Mrs. Eugene March, 198 Windsor Road, Oyster Bay, Long Island, who returned a Darlene 100 per cent orlon sweater, $12.95, size 36 and pure silk Barrie blouse, $15.95, size 38. You want to find out whether she was served promptly and courteously, whether the adjustment was satisfactory, and whether the salesperson helped her select other merchandise, as well as to invite any other comments or suggestions she wishes to make. Refer to the stamped addressed envelope enclosed for her convenience. The objective of the letter is, of course, to build good will by stressing service attitude.

V. Inquiries and Special Requests

Inquiries: Directness, Specificness, Conciseness
Special Requests
  Securing Interest
  Justifying the Request
  Minimizing Obstacles
  Positively Anticipating Acceptance

ANY FIRM that stays in business receives inquiries about products, services, operations, and personnel. When a businessman reads an inquiry concerning the product(s) or service(s) that the firm sells, he is motivated to respond by the possibility of making a sale and a consequent profit—the strongest business motive. Or he may answer an inquiry about routine operations or personnel out of simple friendship, either business or personal. Lastly, he will answer many requests for information about people because it is an established business courtesy to give such information for business purposes (the principle of reciprocity).

The reader's attitude toward such inquiries is receptive. In no case would it be negative; and if it is not one of eagerness to comply, at least it is willingness. Since no problem of motivation exists for you when you write such letters, these inquiries are desirably A-type letters characterized by directness, specificness, and conciseness.

If, however, the request is out of the ordinary—involving the contribution of money or its equivalent, a greater than usual expenditure of time or effort, or the disclosure of confidential information about the firm—the reader's probable immediate and instinctive reaction is negative unless you persuade before you pop the question. The appropriate C-type letter is really a modified sales letter. And so we differentiate between inquiries and special requests. Like all letters, special requests should be specific and concise; but they should not be direct if they are to be effective.

101

INQUIRIES

Since an inquiry seeks information which the reader will probably not object to giving, it follows basically the A-type pattern discussed on page 29. It is sometimes called a "direct request."

If your inquiry is about a product or service and is addressed to the manufacturer, distributor, or other agency responsible for its successful marketing, you need have no concern about whether the letter is welcome. You have no problem of motivating a response; the chance of making a sale motivates. Rather, your problem is that of letting your reader know exactly what you want, so that the willing reader can give you the necessary information with as little expenditure of time and energy as possible.

Resolve this problem by beginning directly and by being specific and concise. Requests for catalogues, price lists, descriptive folders, and other phases of information about products and services should be written with the same directness, specificness, and brevity as the following:

> What choice of colors does a buyer have in the shower curtains you advertised in the November *Ladies' Home Journal?*
>
> At what store(s) are they available in Mobile?

This example, you will note, gets right down to brass tacks with a direct question and the key specific phrase "choice of color" rather than the vague, stereotyped request for "more information." And the pinpointing phrase "in Mobile" further helps the writer of the replying letter to send exactly the information that is needed.

The following letter to a resort hotel is another good example of desirable directness and specificness:

> Please send me descriptive material about your accommodations, recreational facilities, and rates.
>
> My wife, sixteen-year-old daughter, and I are planning a two- or three-weeks' stay in the South this fall and are considering the Edgewater Gulf.

If the letter were sent without the second paragraph, the writer would get the most necessary information in general terms. (He would probably get much more than he needs because the hotel man, not knowing just what to tell, would tell everything and thus waste his own and his reader's time.) With the special information given in the second paragraph, however, the hotel man can write a reply which contains necessary general information and only the special information that would be of interest to this family group.

He would be helped even more had the writer added a specific paragraph indicating special interests, such as:

> My wife and I are primarily interested in the golf facilities; my wife and daughter are also interested in dinner dancing; our daughter insists that she be able to ride horseback every day.

In some inquiries you can help yourself as well as the responder if you make replying easy. Some provision for putting the answer(s) on the inquiring letter accelerates the reply and enables the responding firm to cut down on letter costs. The following inquiry (which is a form letter) about a credit applicant is a typical example (the fact that the subject matter is a person rather than a product or service makes no difference as far as writing style and pattern are concerned):

La Casa Blanca
Albuquerque, New Mexico

The Credit Department, please

GENTLEMEN:

Will you please give us the confidential information requested below?

In applying for credit with us, the applicant gave us your name as a reference.

We shall appreciate this courtesy. Any time we can return the favor, please call on us.

Very truly yours

Credit Manager

Applicant: John Y. Bowen

Length of time sold on credit _____

Credit limit (if any) _____ Credit terms _____

Current amount due _____ Past due _____

Highest credit extended _____ Most recent credit _____

Paying habits _____

Remarks _____

The letter lends itself to form treatment because there are no atypical, off-the-beaten-path questions necessary. (Most business firms have to handle inquiries about credit applicants and job seekers with form letters because of time, money, and personnel limitations.) But, form letter or special letter, the important considerations of directness, specificness, and conciseness remain the same.

When questions are clear cut, enabling the responder to supply specific data in reasonably short form (frequently by just jotting down the answers on the inquiring letter), the desirable plan of the letter is often an explanation of the purpose of the letter, followed by tabulated, numbered questions, as in the following:

SUBJECT: REQUEST FOR FURTHER INFORMATION ABOUT
RECONDITIONED LEKTRASWEEPS

Before deciding whether to drive into Birmingham to inspect the vacuum cleaners you advertised in last Sunday's *News,* I need answers to the following questions:

1. Do the reconditioned Lektrasweeps come equipped with a standard 1-hp motor?
2. What kind and how many attachments do you include at $34.95?
3. Does your written two-year guarantee include replacement or repairs, without charge, of any and all defective parts that might result in the unsatisfactory service of the equipment?
4. If so, will replacement or repairs be made by your representative in my home?
5. Is there a trial period, say for two weeks, at the end of which I could return the cleaner if it proved unsatisfactory, and get a full refund?

I shall be grateful for this information.

Certainly such a letter is easily written and easily read. But if questions require detailed answers for satisfactory information, if out-of-the-ordinary questions are involved, and if they require explanation before the reader can get a clear picture of exactly what the writer wants to know, then they are better set out in expository paragraph form, as in the following letter about a dishwasher:

SUBJECT: INQUIRY ABOUT THE $49.50 DISHWHISK

How complex—and expensive—is installation of the Dishwhisk you advertised on page 68 of the September 23d *Post?*

I'm interested in a dishwasher, and I certainly am attracted by this price. But can your unit be attached without plumbing changes, once the present unit is removed? On my sink now is a unit with hot and cold knobs and a single mixing faucet.

Aerated suds sound economical and efficient, but will low water pressure reduce their cleansing effectiveness? Because low water pressure is the rule rather than the exception in this community, this is an important consideration.

Are new soap and water used for each piece to be washed? The use of an excessive amount of soap and water could easily cancel the initial saving in a short time.

I am interested in your answers to these questions. Also please send the name and address of a local owner of a Dishwhisk and the name of a local dealer.

Note that the inquiry started with a direct question. Such a beginning is the preferable form. The request should come before explanations of why you ask, or interwoven with these explanations, because (1) a question commands more attention than a statement, (2) the reader sees the reason for the explanation, and (3) that arrangement nearly always saves words. Hence the desirability of beginning the following personnel inquiry the way the writer did:

SUBJECT: REQUEST FOR INFORMATION ABOUT JAMES R. SULLIVAN

While Mr. Sullivan worked under you as a part-time instructor in marketing, did he show an aptitude for selling? Was he naturally friendly and able to get along with faculty and students alike?

We are considering him for the job of head salesman in the Georgia, North Carolina, and South Carolina territory. Since he listed you as a former supervisor, we shall welcome your comments in the light of the following explanation.

The job will take much time and energy and will also require that he be away from his family a great deal. Do you think he will do his best work under these conditions? And has he demonstrated physical stamina and willingness suggesting that he can stand up under the strain of much traveling for long periods?

As head salesman he will have to supervise the work of two junior salesmen in this territory. We are interested, therefore, in your evaluation of his leadership ability.

Naturally we are looking for someone who will be permanent, since our men need to know their territories and customers quite well before they can sell enough to suit themselves or us. Do you believe Sullivan will remain in the business world for any length of time, or do you expect him to return to school to continue his graduate work?

We shall appreciate your giving us this and any other confidential information that will help us come to a decision, and shall be glad to help you in the same way when we can.

When you ask your reader to give information about people, as in the immediately preceding letter, both you and he face a special problem. You are asking him to endanger himself with the libel laws. It is your duty to help him protect himself as far as possible. Of course, if he tells the truth, he has the one most important piece of protection; but truth alone is not complete protection in some states. You can help by making his informative letter what the lawyers call a privileged communication. You show him that you have an interest to protect, you promise to keep the information confidential, and (if true) you tell him that the inquiry was authorized. In his response, then, he shows that all

Direct Inquiry Check List

1. Get this letter under way quickly.
    a) A subject line frequently saves your reader's time by establishing:
        (1) The fact that this is an inquiry,
        (2) The nature of the inquiry (the name of the product, service, or person, as the case may be).
    b) Your major question should be emphasized in the first line of the body of the letter.
    c) Make the question(s) specific (not just "some information" but "What colors . . .").
    d) For fast traveling in your opening, imply what you can; if you cannot establish an idea by implication, consider referring to it subordinately.

    Slow, plodding:
    Will you please give us some information about Travis Brannon? He reports that he was once your assistant. We are considering his application for the position of college traveler.

    Fast-moving:
    What would be your reaction if Travis Brannon, your former assistant, walked into your office trying to sell you on McGraw-Hill textbooks?
    e) When you use a subject line, don't depend on it for coherence in the letter or as the antecedent for any pronoun.
2. Cover at least the basic questions to which you want answers.
    a) Analyze the problem and make the minimum number of questions to get the necessary information.
    b) Arrange questions in the most appropriate order: importance, logic, time, or space sequence.
    c) Provide explanations the reader needs.

those conditions exist. Otherwise, inquiries and replies about people are the same as those about other things.

The most important considerations for you to keep in mind about routine (direct) inquiries are to get started in a hurry, to be as specific in your questions as you can, and to explain enough (but only enough) for your reader to answer well and easily. The accompanying check list will help you with most of your inquiry problems, though, of course, it is neither a cover-all nor a cure-all.

Special Requests

Though requests for information about products, services, and people constitute the bulk of inquiries sent by businessmen, sometimes they

Direct Inquiry Check List (Continued)

3. Be careful about the form and wording of the questions.
    a) Ask directly for information; don't hint. "I should like to know if the Lektrasweep has a ½-horsepower motor" is wordy and slow. "Does the . . ." accomplishes the same job better and cheaper.
    b) Word your questions to get the information you want—that is, not a mere "Yes" or "No" when you need explanation for a true picture. Leading questions (phrased to suggest a certain answer) won't get you the information you want, either.
    c) If you want to run a series of questions, tabulate them; solid paragraphs of questions induce mental dizziness.
    d) When you need to interweave questions and explanations, be especially careful to vary sentence form and length to avoid a singsong effect.
4. Express gratitude cordially in first person, future tense: "I shall be grateful (or appreciate)" eliminates the awkwardness and wordiness of "It will be appreciated if . . ." and the presumptuousness of "Thank you in advance."
5. Any time you can refer confidently and positively to the reader's next action in the close, you have a good ending. It can serve as a coherent summary to the entire message, leave your reader clear as to what you want him to do, and serve as a stimulant to his doing it soon.
6. In inquiries about people, establish the privileged aspects.
    a) When you ask a man for information that might get him in trouble, promise confidential treatment of whatever information he may make available to you.
    b) When you have permission to make this inquiry, say so.
    c) Show that you have an interest to protect. That idea is usually established when you state your contemplated relationship with the subject of the letter.

need special favors from people who have no built-in motivation to reply. These special requests are more difficult writing problems than direct requests (or inquiries)—and for a highly understandable reason: most people, when asked to do something even slightly out of the ordinary, can think of two reasons why they should not comply with the request for every one reason why they should.

No one ever has enough money or time to give either of them spontaneously and unquestioningly. No one is willing to reveal business information without first knowing how it will be used and deciding that the purpose is good. To put the question directly in these cases is to get an immediate "No." So the special request has to be a persuasive letter. Like the simple inquiry, the special request is specific and concise, but it is not direct; and, because it usually requires more details in development, it is usually longer.

Favor-seeking letters are C-type letters, as already discussed in Chapter II (p. 32). As explained there, the secret of successful persuasive copy is to (1) offer, suggest, or imply a benefit to the reader—at least talk about something that will be of interest to him as a means of securing his interest; (2) explain the worth of your proposal, to justify it in your reader's eyes; (3) try to overcome objections; and (4) after giving necessary details of circumstances, confidently ask the reader to do what you want him to do.

Securing Interest. If you are going to strike the appropriately persuasive theme, you need to analyze the situation, to select the most pertinent and applicable motive.

Dollars being what they must be in American business thinking, the strongest appeal is one that holds out to the reader the prospects of sales, of saving money, or of promoting good will with an audience wherein sales may ultimately materialize. Such potential-dollar themes hold out to your reader the most concrete form of reader benefit and are responsible for this opening to an advertising manager of a manufacturing company:

> What would it be worth to Rigate to add some 8,000 potential customers to its prospect list?

and this opening to the circulation manager of a magazine:

> Who will be your readers ten years from now?

If you can apply such reader-benefit themes appropriately and remain within the realm of good taste (avoiding the suggestion of bribery), you undoubtedly have the strongest appeal you can make.

In many instances, however, such dollar-minded talk would arouse indignation (especially to professional people who do not advertise) or would not apply. But you need not despair of finding a talking point which will stress the reader's benefit or interest rather than your own. The letter to the correspondence supervisor (back on p. 32) that began—

> How often have you received—from well-educated people—letters that are not worth your attention?

—clearly holds out a benefit to the reader by talking in terms of making Mr. Gaines's job easier. Many times the basis for a busy businessman's filling out a time-consuming questionnaire (or one that asks for information ordinarily restricted to the firm) is his realization that, as a result of the information thus gathered and made available to him, he will be more efficient at his job.

Indirect benefits can also be applied. When you can show your reader how your project (and his contribution) will promote the welfare of a group of which he is a member or in which he has an interest, you can write a strong letter. On this basis you might write a letter inviting a public accountant to speak to a college accounting club or a correspondence supervisor to address a group of teachers of business writing or an alumnus of a professional fraternity to take on a responsible office in the organization. Such appeals are not what is frequently called "altruism" (which Webster defines as "regard for and devotion to the interests of others"), the basis for most charity drives.[1] Though many special-request letters are written with appeals to altruism, in business situations you will write more successful favor-seeking letters if you select and emphasize reader-benefit talking points.

The following letter (asking an advertising manager for free samples) stresses reader benefit throughout—so forcefully as to be almost browbeating, in fact:

How much would it be worth to Rigate to add some 8,000 potential customers to its prospect list?

You can increase the good will toward your company of even more people than this—and at a relatively small cost.

Attracting around 300 contestants and 8,000 on-lookers, "A" Day each spring at the University is a festival of fun—a program of pie-eating contests, sack races, beauty contests, and other collegiate horsing-around.

Prizes for the winners of these contests are contributed by local merchants who realize the sales-building value of such donations. But if we had some prizes which we could give to each participant—winner and loser alike—it would be a good opportunity to introduce under most favorable circumstances someone's product and house.

The loud speakers would blare out, "And in addition, each participant will receive one tube of Picote tooth paste!" 8,000 people would hear this . . . and would laugh . . . and would remember your brand name. And 300 would actually receive your product to use and tell their friends about.

---

[1] Though letters seeking funds for worthy causes are special-request letters and thus within the scope of this analysis, we think it best not to take them up here because they are too highly specialized and because of their frequent civic, religious, and fraternal manifestations. When faced with such problems, you can be sure that the fundamental principles we present here will apply; but for more detailed techniques and "tricks of the trade," check some books like Margaret Fellows and Stella Koenig's *Tested Methods of Raising Money for Churches, Colleges, and Health and Welfare Agencies* (New York: Harper & Bros., 1959).

The special "A" Day edition of the student paper will carry an account of all prizes given, and the program will also list all contributors.

A man of your experience knows the value of such advertising.

Won't you, then, write me (in time for our February planning) that you will send us 300 sample tubes of Picote? You'll be getting some low-cost, effective advertising.

If you will look back at the letter beginnings quoted in this section, you will note that, in addition to highlighting reader benefit (or at least reader interest), these openings are questions. We do not mean to imply that all persuasive requests must begin with a question, but the question beginning commands greater attention than a declarative statement and can be phrased more readily to lead your reader to a contemplation of your suggestion. Too, a question is never as challenging as some statements are, and it can be subtly flattering. In phrasing such questions, however, you will be on safer ground if you eliminate the possibility of either a "Yes" or a "No" answer. To make the reader contemplate the circumstance that will lead up to the request, the following opening makes use of the same strategy:

> What Ford philosophy of management caused the change
>   from "Made in Texas by Texas Labor"
>   to   "Made in Texas by Texans"?

We do not mean to imply that to secure interest in favor-seeking letters you must studiously avoid questions that can be answered with either "Yes" or "No." The following opening addressed to a retailing man of national standing contemplating entering the Texas market is certainly a good one:

> Wouldn't you consider the respect and attention of some 200 key Texas retailers a valuable opportunity to test the true business conditions in that state?

The mental response to such a question is positive. And as long as you can be fairly sure of getting a positive reaction, you are probably on safe ground. The danger lies in getting an irritated answer—whether that answer is a "Yes" or "No" or any of the variants of "So what?" The student who invited the head of a large public accounting firm to speak to a college group and began with

> Do you believe in preparing for the future?

apparently gave little thought to the probable snort or burst of laughter that would result from such a question. He eliminated the irritating aspects (and got closer to the subject of his letter) when he changed his opening to read

> What, in your opinion, are the desirable personal characteristics of the successful public accountant?

True, no reader benefit is implied in this beginning. But it is certainly a subject of practical interest to that reader. Of possibly greater reader-benefit implications is this one:

> What does it cost you when you have to dismiss a well-grounded junior accountant because of his poor personal characteristics?

> The actual cost of additional recruiting and training isn't the only loss, either: the loss of prestige and, possibly, of clients is a greater threat.

Justifying the Request. Having secured your reader's interest with a beginning which holds some promise of benefit or at least talks of something of interest, you usually need to devote the greater part of your letter to explaining what your project is and what good comes of it. Two cautions need to be inserted here, however. The first is that you should not be writing the letter unless you cannot get the necessary information or assistance by your own efforts. The second is: DO NOT BEGIN YOUR LETTER WITH EXPLANATION OR DETAILS OF CIRCUMSTANCES. As in the simple inquiry, you certainly want to be specific. But as they start to read, busy readers (the only kind you send such letters to) aren't even faintly interested in

> The National Association of Advertising Teachers of America, which is made up of some 600 teachers in all sections of the country, is planning its annual convention in New York at the Madison Hotel on July 10, 11, and 12.

Of course, a member of the Association planning to attend the meeting would be. Even a non-member would be, after having been almost or completely persuaded to give a talk to the group. Indeed, he would *have* to be so informed. Details concerning who, what, when, where, why, how (sometimes how much) always need to be clarified—but not until after the big idea of the reader's benefit or contribution has been highlighted. A speaker, for instance, needs to know the nature and size of his audience, the time and place, the facilities available to him, the amount of time allotted to him, and the topic (if you are assigning him one). He may need to know how many other speakers there will be and who precedes and follows him. But such details are not appropriate lead-off points to secure interest. Furthermore, they should be incorporated subordinately as much as possible.

Nobody would read with immediate enthusiasm a beginning like this:

> As a Master's candidate at Harwood University I am preparing a thesis on palletization. Professor H. D. Brunham of our Marketing Department has suggested that I write to you to find out the results of your experience.

Notice in the following copy how the young man seeking this information not only changed his opening to an interest-arousing question but also how he subordinated the necessary but uninteresting details of the original opening:

> Just what are the economies of palletization?
>
> Are they as great as my experience in the service led me to believe?
>
> Has palletization been adopted by an increasing number of business firms since the war?
>
> Regardless of your experience in using pallets, your comments in answering these questions could contribute materially in making a worth-while, authentic, down-to-earth thesis of the one I am preparing as partial requirement for an M.S. degree at Alabama. Too, the finished thesis may well be of practical interest to all users and potential users of pallets.
>
> Perhaps you have some printed material which you can simply enclose in the stamped, addressed envelope I've included. If not, will you take a few minutes to give me in a letter the background of your experience with pallets, the cost of palletizing (with particular emphasis on warehousing), current uses or ideas in palletization, and/or possible sources?
>
> Although I don't have to, I'd like to be able to quote you; but I'll handle the material with whatever degree of confidence and anonymity you specify. And no part of this correspondence will ever be used for any purpose other than research, I assure you.
>
> Since I shall have to assemble material and start writing by June 1, I'd be most grateful if you'd let me hear from you before that date.
>
> If you would like to read the finished thesis for a new idea or two that you might be able to put to work, I'll be glad to lend you my personal copy shortly after August 25.

Frequently you must ask your reader to act by a certain date. When you have to, explain why, as the preceding letter does. Thus you avoid seeming to push a man who is doing you a favor.

Note also that this writer promised discretion in handling the material, attempted to minimize the burdensome aspects, and in the final sentence reminded the reader of possible benefit by way of motivation. (From seven requests the young man received five detailed replies.)

Minimizing Obstacles.   Even though you may have supplied a very good reason which highlights the reader's advantage or interest, in most circumstances there is some fly in the ointment: a negative factor which you have to overcome. It may be a sum of money you are asking for which you feel reasonably certain your reader is going to consider out of line; then you break it down into several payments. It may be that you can offer no fee or a smaller fee than a program speaker is accustomed to receiving; then you cite other (perhaps intangible) rewards. It may be that you're asking for secret information. If so, assure the reader that you will do all you can to protect his interest. Regardless of the case or the circumstance, you can usually find some positive corollary to the drawback.

As added inducement you want to make the job sound as easy as possible and as pleasurable as possible. Phrasing can do a lot here. The following letter is a good example of establishing a negative idea in positive language. The fourth paragraph implies, "See, Mr. Philipson, this really won't be much extra work," and the fifth one implies, "Sorry, there's no pay in this deal."

> Don't you agree, Mr. Philipson, that a business leader who's on the firing line every day can lend real punch to Tau Kappa Rho activities?
>
> Of course, we give TKR's the benefits of brotherhood and a certain amount of social life, but our real reason for being is to get these promising young men realistically oriented to business life while they're still in school.
>
> It's that keen desire of mine to see these future business leaders get superior guidance that makes me ask you to become TKR's Midwest District Supervisor. As you know, the District Supervisor, through letters and visits, helps the local chapters develop and expand business-orienting programs.
>
> Frequently you'd be able to combine business and fraternity trips, I'm sure, for the Midwest District of six states and twenty-two chapters almost corresponds with your sales district. You'd be able to spend many pleasant evenings telling the boys how American does it! And you'd undoubtedly spot a number of promising candidates for openings with your company two, three, and four years from now.
>
> Of course, you'd have an expense account for stationery and traveling. But your real payoff would come from seeing these boys get a head start in their professional lives.
>
> Won't you, therefore, write me that I may nominate you to the General Executive Committee when it meets here in Chicago May 21?

Finally, the mechanical aspects of complying with your request should be reduced to the minimum of detail, time, and money. That is why most questionnaires are fill-in or check-off forms and why a return-addressed reply device requiring no postage ordinarily accompanies such requests.

1. Your opening should be dominated by something of reader interest.
   a) The unmotivated phrasing of your basic request (no buildup, no preparation) is likely to defeat your purpose. Differentiate between the question that arouses interest or suggests a benefit (as in C-type letters) and the question that really gets an answer (as in A-type).
   b) When you can, develop a reader-benefit theme. Altruism is a second-best appeal.
   c) The question with obvious "Yes" or "No" answer is usually not good because it stops rather than starts careful consideration of your proposition. Certainly, eliminate any question that could allow your reader to form a "No" response to your basic request.
   d) Are you promising too much (like total attendance of a group)?
   e) Don't depend on obvious flattery to win the reader's acquiescence.
   f) The use of a subject line is unsound here—as in any C-type letter. It lets the cat out of the bag before you can mention favorable points.
   g) Explanations do not arouse interest; save them for the middle. Until you emphasize the role of the reader—sometimes in terms of what he gives but usually in terms of what he gets—he is not interested in details of what, where, when, or how many.
2. Keep the reader in your passages explaining your proposal.
   a) Do give necessary details to prove that your project deserves his consideration and to enable him to act as you request (such details as size and nature of audience he'll face, conditions under which a task will have to be carried out, for example).
   b) But don't let these details dominate the letter. Give your major positions and space to development of what the reader gets or contributes by complying with your request.
3. Do not phrase the explicit request until most of the reasons (benefits) for the reader's compliance have been established.
   a) Phrase specifically (not "any information you can send" or "anything you can do to help") in a direct request; don't hint.
   b) In language that's free and natural, make the reader's participation sound easy—maybe even fun!
   c) Watch your *shall*'s and *will*'s, which can imply that your reader does not have the right to refuse. *Should* and *would* establish the conditional mood.
4. The potentially negative element is usually present (not enough money, inconvenient time, request for confidential material).
   a) Complete elimination of the negative element is unethical and wasteful (because it usually involves additional correspondence).
   b) Minimize the effect by positive statement—what you *can* do rather than what you cannot—embedded position, and minimum space.
   c) Maintain a tone of positive confidence. Do not apologize for what you can do, regardless of how insignificant it may be; do not suggest that the request is trouble or is trivial.

d) Don't supply excuses for your reader (how busy he is, how many requests he receives). He'll think up enough without your help!

e) If there is a time limitation, establish it specifically, but subordinately, and justify it.

5. After you've covered the significant reasons why he should do what you want him to do and have given adequate details so that he understands exactly what it is you seek, then ask confidently for his action.

a) All good action endings contain four elements: what to do, how to do it, helps and/or suggestions for ease of action, and reason for prompt action.

b) Discard the vague generalities about "early reply," "hear from you soon," and the like. Name the specific action you want him to take: write, phone, wire, come in—whatever is appropriate.

c) Establish your appreciation cordially in first person future—and attach your expression of gratitude to his specific action. Don't "thank in advance"; to do so is lazy and presumptuous.

d) When you include a return envelope (which may be return-addressed but is not logically self-addressed), don't make an issue of it. Refer to it incidentally in a sentence emphasizing something else.

e) Inject a last punch line (preferably a phrase or clause rather than a sentence) which throws emphasis back on your reader: the benefit he receives or the significance of his contribution.

6. Adapt your letter to your reader; when you can, personalize it.

a) Refer casually to a commonplace action or event that you can be fairly sure is characteristic of his job or his community or his geographical area or of his economic status. Even in mass form mailings you can do this.

b) When you use an inside address, use the name also in the salutation.

c) If the letter is of any length, consider calling him by name in the second half of the letter or referring specifically to his home city.

7. The following style suggestions apply any time you have an enclosure; they are not restricted to special requests.

a) Don't divert attention from your letter to the enclosure until you have carried your reader near enough to the end that he'll finish it before turning away; he may not come back.

b) Whether you're enclosing a questionnaire, folder, envelope stuffer, or leaflet, refer to it in subordinate fashion in a sentence emphasizing some other factor of significance.

  Very poor: "Enclosed you will find a folder. . . ."
       "I have enclosed a folder. . . ."
  Passable: "The enclosed folder describes. . . ."
  Better: "Read in the enclosed folder how your dollars help provide medical care for needy children."

8. When you ask for confidential material or evaluative opinion or anything else that might make your reader hesitate, give assurance that you will handle the material in whatever limited way he specifies.

Positively Anticipating Acceptance. After establishing the reader's benefit or contribution, making clear exactly what is wanted and why, and minimizing obstacles, the writer should confidently ask the reader to comply with the request. Hesitant, apologetic expressions belittle the request itself and have the disadvantage of suggesting excuses to the reader as reasons for his refusal. Such expressions as the following hinder rather than help the request:

I realize you are a very busy man, but. . . .

I'm sorry to trouble you for such an apparently insignificant matter; however. . . .

I hesitate to bother you with such a request. . . .

If you consider this a worth-while project. . . .

Eliminate such thinking (maybe by rereading the discussion on "Success Consciousness," p. 41) and forthrightly name the specific action you want the reader to take.

In your favor-seeking letters apply the summary of points on pages 114–15.

PROBLEMS

DIRECT INQUIRIES

1. Mrs. Peter Paul Adams, 1809 West Church Street, Aurora, Illinois, read your ad in the *Chicago Daily News:* "Higgins Reconditioned Bicycle Shop, 589 Grant Street, Chicago. For sale—150 light-weight bicycles, Green, Red, Blue. Sizes 20-inch (recommended for ages 5, 6, 7) $20, 24-inch (for ages 7, 8, 9) $25, 26-inch (over 9) $30. Light weight, seat with coil springs, long handle bars. All rubber tires. Coaster brakes. Red Safety reflector." Billy Jean, her six-year-old daughter, has been following her eleven-year-old sister and two neighborhood children, eight and ten, around the block on her three-wheeler but is plainly unhappy about having to. Mrs. Adams has visited many bicycle shops in search of a two-wheeler with two balancing wheels, because she feels that in a year or two she could take the side wheels off and Billy Jean would have a good bike. But all the shops she visited had two- and four-wheelers for $45–$65, even $75. She had hoped to pick up an inexpensive bike that would do between now and when her eleven-year-old tired of her two-wheeler. Before getting too excited over the $20 price in Higgins' ad, she writes to find out whether there are any reconditioned bikes with the nontip balancing wheels. What if the bicycle breaks down—is there any guarantee? If there are any with side wheels, what sizes are they in? According to the ad a 20-inch would be about right. And color does matter; Billy Jean wants red! Are the all-rubber tires new too? Are the bikes made up of old damaged bikes? If she is willing to pay delivery charges both ways, will Higgins send one for a free trial? Assume that you are Mrs. Adams and write this direct inquiry.

2. As educational director of your church, you write the editor of *Live* magazine, 540 North Michigan Avenue, Chicago, about the recently advertised educational film on comparative religions. To rent one of these costs $8, the advertisement says. You'd like to rent the film and show it not only at a meeting of the Service League but also at the monthly evening dinner meetings of the Men's Club and the Ladies' Club. Do you need a special kind of screen, amplifier, and projector to show this colored film? How long does the film run? What age group or educational level is the film produced for? Most of the people in the League are between the ages of fourteen and eighteen; those in the other groups are twenty-five and up. Is the rental charge per showing, or on a time basis? If on a time basis, how long can you keep the film?

3. You and three other college friends plan to fly to Europe for 8 weeks next summer. By careful planning each has about $2,000 to pay for 8 weeks and transportation. To find out more details, write the World Wide Travel Agency, Madison Avenue, Chicago. Some of the specific questions you want answered are: What does it cost to fly austerity class? How much does it cost to rent a foreign car, and where would be the best place to get such a car? You and your friends plan to stay at low-cost but nice inns, pensions, and hostels in England, France, Italy, and Switzerland.

4. In May the Beta Nu Omicron fraternity, Tuscaloosa, Alabama, had 7 large rugs cleaned and stored by Birmingham Steam and Rug Company, 1406 Second Avenue, because the house was to be torn down to make room for a new Beta Nu home on the same lot. To your surprise, cleaning charges and storage until November 3 amounted to $183.56, according to the statement you (the House Corporation President) got today from Arthur Johnson, assistant manager. Johnson pinned a note to the bill saying that storage charges accumulate at $20 a month and asked whether the fraternity wanted the rugs out by Thanksgiving. Since the new house is in the blueprint stage, with no hope of being finished and ready for rugs until late summer, you write Johnson and ask him what he could sell the rugs for. Also you'd like an approximate price for a new Higglow commercial carpet for the 25′ × 38′ living room (the rest of the floors except the guest room and house mother's living room will be covered by vinyl). The three wool carpets (you think) are in pretty good shape, and you might want to keep them for these reasons. On the other hand, rather than pay $140–$160 more storage, you might prefer to trade them in on living-room carpeting if Johnson will make you an attractive offer. What would it cost to store just the 3 green wool carpets (not all 7), and are they, in Johnson's opinion, worth storing? Write Johnson.

5. You've been pricing new standard and portable typewriters in hopes of buying one for some special work you'll be doing next semester. Portables cost from a low of $61.50 to a high of $209.35 (electric). But, after trying almost every make of portable, you decide that you prefer a heavier, easier-to-operate standard. A good new standard, however, runs over $200,

closer to $250. From your summer job you've saved $130 that you want to use for this purchase. In the *Daily News* of a city several miles away you see the following ad from the Snipe's Typewriter Shop, 198 Dearborn Street, promoting reconditioned models of leading brands:

11-inch carriage, $104.50, 13-inch carriage, $118.50, 15-inch carriage, $132.50. Guaranteed to be in perfect working order. Many fine features for fast, efficient typing (automatic margin control sets both margins, tabulator control stops together or separately, green "color-speed" finger-shaped keys with "luxury" touch). Segment shift. Gray finish.

Before making the trip to the city you send a letter asking for more details about the terms of the guarantee, about the gray finish. (Is this a plastic or all-metal machine?) Does Snipe's have pica-type machines with 15-inch carriage for $132.50? Are there any free-trial provisions? And you'd like to know whether the machine has the keys for the dash (in addition to the hyphen) as well as the plus and equalization signs (or symbols). Just how old are the machines? How extensive is the reconditioning? You think you'd prefer a Remingwood, since that's the kind you learned on.

6. To separate your family room from the dining room in the home you are remodeling you are considering a folding door. In this month's *House Lovely* appears a picture of a wooden folding door in a Minutefold Company advertisement, New Castle Products, New Castle, Indiana. Although the advertisement showed several wood finishes, it did not say what kinds of wood were used or what prices the doors cost. You want a door that will cover an opening of 14 feet. Your ceilings are 9 feet high. Ask Minutefold if the doors come in an appropriate size to fit your opening, if they are soundproof, and if they ever warp. Assume that you live in Vero Beach, Florida. Frequently Vero Beach is damp for days at a time. Since you plan cherry Wellwood paneling, you'd like a blending (or matching) wood. After looking at fabric folding doors in restaurants, schools, and in homes, you think that the wooden door might look less commercial. To find out the answers to these questions write New Castle Products.

7. Imagine that you are about ready to begin building a home for yourself and your family. It will be, as you plan it, a house of three bedrooms, two baths, living room, dining room, and kitchen. You've worked out most details, but the question of heat is still bothering you. In the evening paper, however, you read the write-up about the radiant glass heating apparatus of the Universal Corporation, Cincinnati, and immediately you think that this may be the answer to your problem. Electric wall panels ($20'' \times 30''$) have individual room thermostats. They heat without burning draperies or furniture that's placed near, yet they have ultraviolet ray benefits and are clean (no dust or lint). They operate in a quiet manner (no clicking or blowing), and they take little space. With no more to go on than this article, you decide to write direct to find out such details as cost, availability, operating costs, safety, reliability, method and cost of installation, and any other plausible question that comes to your mind. Since this is an inquiry which re-

quires no motivation of the reader for a favorable response, you will begin directly with a request for information—with no explanations first. Ask at least four questions.

8. You are about ready to begin building a home for yourself and your family. You've worked out most details, but you still have the problem of wall covering for the 12′ × 12′ family room. You'd like it sound-conditioned. In the last issue of *Saturday Evening Post* you read with great interest the two-page ad on Duron wall covering produced by Wright-Lynch Research, 50 Rockefeller Plaza, New York 20, N.Y.

> Now you can absorb noise, insulate and decorate with just one material. . . . DURON wall covering.
>
> In a search for new and better products for America, the Research Division of Wright-Lynch has developed Duron, a versatile new family of soft, flexible multi-cellular materials that have wide application in home and industry.
>
> As a wall and ceiling covering Duron is unique in that it combines three properties in one decorative material. In homes and offices Duron not only adds a new look of luxury, but also makes possible extra year-round comfort and a new degree of restfulness by quieting the increasing noise of modern life.
>
> Composed of millions of tiny air cells, $\frac{1}{4}''$ thick, Duron is soft to the touch, and soft to the eye, too. Duron's 24 rich decorator colors . . . beautiful new pastels . . . special "tweed" finishes . . . tastefully silk screened "accent" tiles . . . make it possible to match every room's mood or motif. And for extra luxury, Duron can be bonded directly to special fabrics, to widen even further the decorative possibilities.

Soft Wall Luxury
Duron Quiets, Reduces Fatigue

Medical science has established that the tiring noise level of today is a big factor in creating fatigue. You can't escape noise. Duron muffles the sounds of traffic, planes and other external noises, and reduces the noise of washing machines, vacuum cleaners, air conditioners, and other appliances which contribute to fatigue. Duron takes the aggravating noise out of the general sound level of homes and offices—absorbs the annoying high frequencies and reverberations.

All-Season Comfort Control

The air-cell structure in new Duron acts like thousands of little thermostats to keep the temperatures in your home even (as well as tempers). Duron keeps temperatures much more level every season because of what engineers call its low "k" factor. The heat loss is far lower and slower since the tiny air cells insulate these surfaces from heat and cold; wall and ceiling surfaces maintain a more even temperature. In summertime, Duron reverses the process.

Easy to Install

Duron can be applied to almost any existing wall . . . including concrete and cinder block . . . and over curved surfaces. Duron is just the thing for "problem" walls, for it permanently covers persistent cracks that show through other materials. Duron is available in 10 in. and 20 in. squares, and 10 in. × 20 in. rectangles.

After talking with two hardware and two tile dealers and discovering that they knew nothing about Duron, you write the company and ask for the nearest dealer. Also you want to know what it would cost to do a 12′ × 12′ room using the tiles on the walls and ceilings. You have two standard windows, a closet door, and entrance door. Can you wash Duron as you do walls?

9. Hundreds of millions of the world's people live in rude shacks, under palm fronds, in caves or hovels. As an engineer for the Grande Oil Company, El Tigre, Azoategui, Venezuela, South America, your job is to build homes as inexpensively as possible for many native workers. Last week in *Time* magazine you read where the Rockefeller brothers' Ibec Housing Corporation, New York 12, N.Y., will market a simple machine that promises much for the homeless millions. Called the Cinva-Ram Block Press, it makes sturdy brick from a down-to-earth mixture of 90–95 per cent dirt and 5–10 per cent cement or other binding admixtures such as lime. Resembling an old-fashioned hand printing press, the machine can be operated by two men, one of whom pours in the soil-cement mixture while the other pumps the long handle to press the brick into shape at a pressure of about 10,000 pounds per square inch. In two days it can turn out enough brick to build a hut-sized house, is light enough (140 pounds) to be packed by mule to backwoods villages, inexpensive enough to serve even the most depressed areas.

Before ordering one, you want to know the price of the machine and about what price each brick would be. During certain times of the year the rainfall is heavy in Venezuela, and you wonder whether there would be any danger of the houses washing away. What if the machine breaks down—how will you get it serviced?

10. The board of directors of the Self-Service Department Stores, New York, met last week to discuss future expansion. After doing market research on a nearby metropolitan city (the closest one to you, the student), they decided that there was a need for this type of store. The night workers would take advantage of the vending machines to purchase goods. Such stores have done well in Geneva and Lucerne, Switzerland, as well as in Chicago, Detroit, and San Francisco. As president of the company, write to the Chamber of Commerce of the nearby city to ascertain how welcome such a branch would be. Would the leading department stores resent the fact that Self-Service would be open day and night? Assume any ordinary facts about your company as a "good citizen" in communities where you operate—memberships in businessmen's organizations, contributions to local fund drives, employment and pay practices (including fringe benefits). . . .

11. Set the clock up a few years and assume that you are responsible for purchasing either built-in furniture or new furniture for 24 bedrooms in a fraternity house (or co-op or small dormitory). One of the recent houses you visited installed Mengel built-ins consisting of two chests and two mirrors, with a closet on each side of the unit. Besides wanting to know the cost of such a unit, you also want to know whether a desk is ever built in too. In building a new house, is it wise to put these units back to back for sound conditioning? With building costs high, you naturally are price-minded but want to get practical, good-looking furniture that will last a long time. How hard will it be to refinish these built-ins is another problem to consider. According to the architect's plan, the built-ins will run along one ten-foot wall in each room. Write to Mengel, Milwaukee, to get information necessary to arrive at your decision of whether to use these built-ins or buy individual pieces of furniture.

12. Spencer Sims, age twenty-two, saw your ad for a salesman in the want-ad section of the *Cincinnati Times* and came in for an interview with you, personnel director, G & M Auto Supply Company, Cincinnati. Before joining the Army, Sims worked as a mechanic one summer and after school during his senior year at high school for Pope's Garage. And during his two years of Army service, he worked in a parts-supply depot and in a motor pool.

    Mr. Pope sold the business, however, and moved to Denver. Sims had lost track of him but had the address of Captain Halgren (now a Major living in Rancho Cordova, California—2613 Ellenbrook Drive). Sims told you how he hated office work when he was a sergeant in the Army parts-supply division, but his maintenance duties with the motor pool he thoroughly enjoyed. He added, "You're welcome to write Captain Halgren and ask any questions about job performance and personal record." Keeping records bores him, he said, for he isn't interested in details. This raises a question in your mind, for, as a sales supervisor later (if he should work into that job), he would have to keep sales records and submit progress reports as well as personnel reports. He seems energetic and enthusiastic, but he may be just putting on, in order to land this job. As you talked about new plants and products, relating them to sales opportunities, you felt that Sims wasn't following you. Is he bright and pleasant enough to sell now and work into a sales supervisor's job later? Sims referred to being tense and nervous while in service, but he seems calm and relaxed now. Even though he's bored with details, is he careful and accurate in record keeping? Write Halgren.

13. Assume the role of Anthony Bush, southeastern director of sales for Vulcan Restaurant Equipment Company, Birmingham, Alabama. The major part of his job is getting first-rate men who have the personality and background for contact work with restaurant people and the perseverance that will let enthusiasm be foremost despite long hours of travel, absence from family, and day-and-night working hours. Eugene Shumaker, southeastern representative for Garland Stoves, South Bend, Indiana, came in to see you yesterday about handling more stoves and during the course of conversation mentioned that he was quitting Garland. Instead of traveling five states,

he'd like to settle for a couple and be home more with his wife and three children. Your company placed some big orders with Eugene during the past several years, but that isn't the whole story. You want to find out more about his sales record and performance of other job duties from Garland's director of sales, Fred Best. Shumaker casually mentioned being tired of the pressure at Garland—got so he couldn't sleep at night. His immediate boss fussed when sales reports weren't in on time. But are these the true reasons he quit?

At Vulcan, Shumaker wouldn't have to write as many reports or travel as great a distance, but sales quotas would have to be met and increased. Perhaps Best can tell you whether Shumaker is indolent, careless about sales reports, or nervous . . . . Or, phrased the more positive way, is he energetic, careful about details, and calm?

Having sold for six years with Garland, he probably knows how to draw layouts for commercial kitchens and how to talk with restaurant people. When you asked if it would be OK for you to write Garland, he replied, "Go ahead. I told them I was quitting in a month." Write Mr. Best.

14. Courtney Landers is behind in payments owed to your client, the Scruggs Department Store, Philadelphia. Assume that you are the store's lawyer and you are writing The Mary Ann Shop, Old Line Lexington, Pennsylvania, to find out whether Courtney still works there, in what capacity, and at what salary. If he is no longer employed there, try to find out where he is and what he is doing to earn a living.

15. Assume the role of president and owner of Manley Brick Company, St. Louis. One of your salesmen tells you about Bill Bingham, an efficient, hard-working business manager in a small prefabricated-housing plant in nearby Bellville, Illinois. Bill has expressed an interest in making a change after a year and a half with Manley.

As an accounting student at the University of Missouri, Bill made all A's and received practically all the honors awards for men the year he graduated. Socially he seems adjusted too, according to your salesman (active in a social fraternity while in college, active in civic and church work, now married to an attractive schoolteacher). After Bill's two years in the Army he worked as an accountant in a small department store in St. Louis for one year. Suddenly he left that job for the work as accountant and assistant business manager at the prefab plant. Apparently the management was pleased with Bill, for he soon was running the plant and making many of the important decisions.

You told your salesman to tell Bill to send an application letter and you'd be glad to talk with him about a management job with your brick company. Promptly Bill writes you an enthusiastic application letter and encloses a data sheet listing four references. When you interviewed him, he seemed likable, interested in people, and the world about him. You decide to write to Milton Bell, president of Bell Pre-Fabricate, Bellville, to find out more about Bill. He impressed you as a hard worker, though perhaps too tense and too eager. Does Mr. Bell think Bill changes jobs in order to have more challenge? The job at the brick company is not for anyone who wants to keep changing all the time. Selling also enters into this management job. Many of the accountants you know do not like selling, nor do they seem to enjoy working with people. If Bill is like this, he'll probably not be happy at Manley.

SPECIAL REQUESTS

1. Looking ahead, let's assume you are a candidate for Judge of Inferior Court of your county. A native, self-educated in the county schools and at the state university, you've been practicing law for twenty-five years. As special assistant to the United States Attorney-General and attorney for the Department of Labor, you handled Children's Bureau cases. You are a member of the American Legion, V.F.W., Marine Corps League, and First Baptist Church. You've taught Sunday school in the Young People's Department for ten years. With juvenile delinquency increasing each year, there's concern in your community about how the court decides on both domestic relations and juvenile cases. Set up a form letter appealing to women in your area (since women probably are more concerned about strong families and well-behaved children). Remind them of the voting date, the second Tuesday of next month, and ask them to vote for you. The judge will be charged with mending broken families and leading youthful offenders into the paths of acceptable behavior. This job calls for a man with deep understanding of human relations. It calls for a man mature enough to deal with adults, but young enough in spirit to fathom the juvenile mind. Each letter will be signed. You'll enclose a 2″ × 4″ card with your picture.

2. The president of the university has come to you, secretary of the Chamber of Commerce, to see if the town and the gown can do more to create a better understanding between the people of your community and the 150 foreign students who are at the university. As a result of your talk, a host program is suggested. You are to write a letter to faculty and town families inviting them to a meeting in the University Room at the hotel, 3:00 P.M., ten days from now to tell them more about the Host Family Plan. Each family is asked to select one student from overseas and to have that student in his home once a month or even more often and at Thanksgiving and Christmas, to see that he has some home to visit for at least the traditional holiday meals. Because many of the students are lonesome at Thanksgiving and Christmas when the other students are gone, the host plan will provide homes for these students during the holidays. To make replying easier, enclose a return card. Because you are writing 200 form letters, you'll set the mailing up with a faked inside address.

3. The J. M. Till Metal and Supply Company, Inc., producers of industrial supplies, 285 Marietta Street, N.W., Atlanta, Georgia, is opening a new warehouse in Tampa the 16th and 17th of next month. Invitations to the opening have been sent to all customers in the Tampa area. But you would like

to have Winston Shirley, Manager of Sales, BCI Division, U.S. Steel Corporation, Fairfield, Alabama, attend both days (from 3:00 to 9:00 P.M.) because you feel that he could help convince the customers that their best source of supply is the Till Company. Also you would like Mr. Shirley to see this new building located at 2736 East Hanna Street. It is similar to the one built in Jacksonville and the one which is being completed in Miami. It is an attractive building, designed to make operations more rapid and more efficient. The plan for the 16th and 17th is to give customers a tour of the building and to show them your stocks, handling facilities, cutting and shearing equipment. In addition, there will be some display panels and exhibits of all types of ferrous and nonferrous metals, as well as valves, fittings, fasteners, and gears.

In your letter to Mr. Shirley, ask him to reserve these dates on his calendar and to let you know if he can come. You'll offer to pay his expenses, though it's doubtful that he would accept (BCI would approve this as a business-promotion expense).

4. Each year, by sponsoring a lecture series, your Business and Professional Men and Women's group raises money to help the Junior Welfare Association. The Junior Welfare uses the money for the health and dental clinic for underprivileged children of the city.

During the past five years you've been able to get interesting lecturers to come to your community and talk for no fee. By charging $5 for a season ticket to the three lectures, your group has been able to give an average $1,500 annually to the Junior Welfare. For the first lecture early in the fall, Mr. J. M. Anderson, accountant with the nearby branch of Bailey, Nevins, and Peal firm, has agreed to talk on recent changes in taxation. And Professor Fred Eastover, authority on finance, talks a month later on "How to Hedge against Inflation." Sometime in the spring (your schedule planned this far in advance is very flexible) you'd like to have T. M. Filbey, 1109 Beach Street, Laguna Beach, California, conduct a one-night lecture on effective letter-writing procedures to about 500 businessmen and women at the Municipal Building at 8:00 P.M. You know that Filbey, a Northeastern University graduate, has been a successful author and consultant for the last ten years, usually commanding sizable fees partially dictated by the size of his audience. Your Business and Professional group has money to pay only his expenses, however. All the proceeds of the lecture series go to the Welfare Association. You'll run several articles about him in the local newspaper and put display cards promoting the lecture in store windows. You can arrange for an autograph party at the local bookstore promoting his recent publication *Writing Business Letters Can Be Fun* as well as his famous book of three years ago, *What the Boss Expects of You.* You'll be grateful if Mr. Filbey will let you know in time for you to make your plans.

5. As president of your fraternity house corporation, assume that your group has signed a contract to build a new house. With building costs taking about all your house fund, you decide to see whether any of the loyal brothers will give to a furnishings and decorating fund. From national you get a

list of members from your chapter who are in the state. You hope to be living in the house by next homecoming. Use your imagination in telling about the house and fund. A reply envelope might help to bring some cash. (You may assume a church student center if you prefer. The list would be of alums having attended this center.)

6. During the current school year your fraternity published and mailed three issues of a house newspaper to all alums. Before sending out a fourth issue you write a form letter to each alum asking for $2.00 annual subscription to help meet publication costs. For over twenty years, entirely at the expense of the active chapter, the publication has come out four times a year. Maintenance of good alum address files, publication and distribution, and other mailings have been taking a considerable sum from the budget each year. Even though you expect to keep the names of all alums on your general mailing list, you hope that each person will want to show his appreciation of the work that the active chapter is doing. An addressed reply envelope and subscription blank are enclosed, and each subscription will be acknowledged in the forthcoming issue. All alums are invited to write any news for publication in the paper. You can assume the title of financial adviser.

7. Change places with your instructor and assume that, to build up your lecture material, you are writing Mr. J. P. Brown, direct-mail consultant service, New York, and ask for his recently published series, "How to Collect by Letter." The ad describing this letter series in *The Reporter of Direct Mail* says to send $50 for the 25 letters. After checking with your library and discovering that its funds won't cover such a series, you write a persuasive letter asking that the series be sent to your university library at no cost. You can acquaint your 90 students this semester (average about 1,000 for 5 years) with Brown's service. Remember that, as a gift to an educational institution, the donation would be income tax deductible. It could be sent to the library and would thus be available for use by the instructor or students.

8. The job of program chairman falls to your lot for the annual Alumni Day at your university. You'll have the state governor, the president of the university, the new football coach (who has assumed this post just this year), and the wives of these men at the noon banquet the third Saturday in October. Now you are attempting to secure a forceful, effective speaker to give the main address. After long consideration (and three refusals from others you have asked) you select Dwight Fitzgerald, president of Fitzgerald Clothing Manufacturing Company, one of the leading citizens of the state and a friend of the university. You'd like Mr. Fitzgerald to talk for 30 minutes on the future of the college graduate. The football coach will be introduced to the alumni, many of whom will not have seen him before. The audience will hear a welcoming speech by the president, who will then introduce Fitzgerald (you hope). Fitzgerald will be the guest of the Alumni Day Committee. You can't pay a fee, but he will be reimbursed by the Alumni Association for his travel expenses. Write the letter.

9. The Chamber of Commerce in your city is promoting a park around a large fishing lake 5 miles from town. With the 40-hour work week (shorter for some), many of the city's residents have time for swimming, boating, water skiing, fishing, and cooking outdoors. Many of the federated clubs have had for their projects this year money for the park. Although many businesses in the city have contributed money, swings, benches, tables, etc., there's not enough cash on hand to have the kind of park most people want. You and several other leading citizens (members of the Chamber of Commerce) decide to promote a benefit show out at the park grounds for the afternoon and evening of the first Saturday of next month. (Assume a date when weather is likely to be suitable.) What you hope to do is get the famous guitar-playing, hill-billy-singing Levis Pate and his band. Pate, idol of the teen-age crowd (through his records and his personal appearances) and native of your state, is to be through your city about the time you plan your show. Try to sell Levis Pate on coming to the park and giving a two-hour show in the afternoon and repeating it at night, with the only reward being the good that it will do. You can have the show well advertised through the newspaper, television, and radio (all donated). The tickets, soft drinks, and popcorn will also be donated by civic-minded firms and sold at regular amusement-area prices. The gate price of $1.50 for adults, 75¢ for children, will be net for this worthwhile project; no expenses will have to come out of receipts. The large bandstand will accommodate the crowd. You'll be glad to get him the kind of props he needs and to see that he has adequate acoustical equipment.

10. One of your jobs as chairman of Business Careers Day at your university is to secure speakers and panel participants. This is an annual event when business people come to the campus and mix with the students at a luncheon and in panel discussions devoted to vocational aspects. Student interest in these discussions is keen; the questions they fire at the panel participants are pertinent, pointed, and helpful! While the event is not intended primarily to get individuals together, there is, of course, plenty of opportunity for individual talks before and after speeches and panel discussions. New business machines and industry exhibits are also interesting and instructive. The eight panels are to deal with careers in such fields as management, marketing, accounting, banking, sales, transportation, statistics, and secretarial administration. Since the only funds available come from the low membership fee paid by students, you have to ask speakers to pay their own expenses and to volunteer their services. Three men you're particularly interested in for panels are all from the same company: Thomas Lusk in marketing, D. J. Lazer in statistics, and Dalton Simmons in management. Write to Mr. Robert Bowman, Vice-President in Charge of Personnel, Armstrong Manufacturing Company, in the nearby city where many of your graduates go to work, inviting him to send these three men from his company to the panels.

11. For the Personnel Management Conference to be held at your university three months from now (Thursday and Friday), prepare a letter to Mr. Burt M. Watson, president of the American Society for Personnel Administration and vice-president of Industrial Relations, Mark Equipment Company,

Buchanan, Michigan, requesting him to be the lead-off speaker for your two-day conference. Topic: "Building a Personnel Department." About 500 representatives from over the state will attend. After the speakers' talks, thirty minutes are allowed for a question-answer session involving audience participation. Registration fees of $15 (including two luncheons) provide funds for paying speakers' expenses but no fees. Ferret out those reasons why Mr. Watson might be induced to come and incorporate them into a persuasive request that will elicit a "Yes." You are the director. After completing an M.B.A. degree at Harvard he worked for two other equipment companies before going with Mark five years ago. You've never heard him speak, but you've read of him frequently in the A.S.P.A. *Bulletin.*

12. Sit in the chair of Professor H. A. Pilons, the man of many activities, who right now, as director of the Oklahoma Business Conference, has the task of lining up some twenty speakers for the meeting about six months from now in Oklahoma City at the Biltmore Hotel.

One man he'd like very much to speak before the retailers' group is Walter Loving, president of Aber-Crombie, New York (about whom he has read in a recent *Time,* Business and Finance Section). Pilons wants especially to have a headliner to attract these men and women to the current meeting because their attendance at the conference has always been the poorest of the groups attending (they don't want to be away from their businesses over the week end). So he has decided to test his ability to persuade big-time operators to come down at their own expense and without a speaker's fee (which most of the men he'd want to invite are accustomed to receiving) in this one letter to Loving before writing all the other letters he will have to send.

The *Time* article tells of Loving's meteoric rise in retailing to the controlling ownership of Aber-Crombie and a half-dozen other stores like it, and quotes him as planning a chain of smaller stores all over the country. Adding to that with talk he has picked up at conventions, Pilons figures that Loving may likely be interested in looking over the situation in Oklahoma, preparatory to opening stores. Pilons decides that this idea is the entering wedge for the letter which will ask Loving to attend the meeting and to talk to the retailers' group meeting (Pilons figures that he can attract at least 100 to it) on the Friday of the meeting, 2:00–3:00 P.M., about bonus systems, promotional practices, or any other personnel-management problem and how he has met it—and then for another hour to lead a group discussion. It's the sort of thing he could do easily and well.

Since the professor needs to plan far ahead, when you write the letter for him (on university-letterhead stationery), you'll ask Loving if he can't let you know within a month.

13. Assume a student wife's role as bread-stretcher, mother of baby (or babies), typist (free service for your husband)—and president of the Spartan Wives Club at a large college or university where several hundred married couples struggle to keep at least the husband and often the wife in school, most of whom start families. The wives meet once a month for some kind of program and socializing over modest refreshments later; both husbands and

wives attend the two big social events a year the club sponsors (a dance, a banquet). To raise money for these events, you and your committee of officers are planning a Spartan Wives Stork Party to be held about three months from now. At that time you intend to auction off to these mothers and mothers-to-be all baby supplies and equipment that you can secure through donations by manufacturers of such clothing, food, strollers, buggies, etc. As a sample of the kind of letter you would send to these firms (stressing the good advertising and the good will they'd gain), address a request to the F. A. Persons Co., Glendale, California, for one of its Rola-Walkas, the conventional stroller in which mothers walk their babies outdoors and often let them sit in to keep control over them as well as to assist the child to learn to walk. Both fathers and mothers will attend the auction; you are sure that you can count on an attendance of at least 300, likely 400, and possibly 500.

14. Under the signature of the District Literature Chairman, Nebraska Women's Federated Clubs, ask Professor Mamie Meredith, of the University of Nebraska Department of English, to judge this year's literature contest. You have four: short story (no more than 2,500 words), nonfiction (no more than 2,500 words), poetry (no more than 32 lines), and book analysis (of Dorian Pasterlok's prize-winning *Soul of a Russian*). In previous years you have had no more than five entries in any division. Deadline is three months from now for contestants to send in entries; you'll have to ask Professor Meredith to evaluate and return the entries—selecting a winner in each division—within a month's time. You have no money for a recompense.

VI. Replies to Inquiries and Special Requests

ANY COMPANY desiring the good will of the public replies to all reasonable inquiries—and does so promptly. If a delay is necessary, some explanation should go forward to the inquirer indicating the reason and approximately when he can expect a complete answer, as in the following note:

> Your request for information about palletization can best be answered by Mr. J. S. McConnough, our Sales Promotion and Advertising Manager, who will be in California for another ten days.
>
> Shortly after he returns to the office, he will write you.

Here is another sample:

> We shall send you your copy of *Color Counts* about March 15, when we expect the revision from the printers.

This new edition will show the true colors and will picture in detail all the popular patterns of Siesta ware, including the ones introduced just this year.

You will enjoy it when you receive it.

The first situation appears to contain no possibilities of sales but, as in the case of any inquiry, certainly represents a good opportunity to make a friend for the firm. The second situation obviously represents someone with an active interest in the product sold by the firm. Proper handling might well lead to a sale.

Because some incoming letters ask only for assistance, whereas others readily indicate a potential customer, this discussion of replies is divided into (1) replies to inquiries without apparent sales possibilities and (2) replies to inquiries with sales possibilities, followed by (3) an analysis of the advantages and disadvantages of form letters.

REPLIES TO INQUIRIES WITHOUT SALES POSSIBILITIES

When someone asks you for something, you either say "Yes" or "No" —in an A-type letter or a B-type letter. For all practical purposes, an undecided, noncommittal response like "Well, I'll think it over" is a refusal and needs to be handled in the inductive style (reasons before conclusion) of a B-type letter. This discussion, therefore, concerns itself with letters complying with the request and those refusing the request.

COMPLYING WITH THE REQUEST

Letters which say "Yes" have the qualities common to all good letters analyzed in Chapters I and II. Particular points you need to watch are the direct beginning, completeness of coverage, and resale.

Direct Beginning. The fundamental principle in all A-type replies is to say "Yes" immediately and thus gain increased good will, as well as save time and words. When you can do what the reader has asked you to do, begin your letter by a statement indicating (in line with the circumstances)

1. That you have done it (preferably),
2. That you are doing it, or
3. That you will do it.

Your compliance with the reader's request is the point of greatest interest to him—of far greater interest than any expressions of gratitude or gladness. And from the standpoint of economical writing, the direct beginning cuts through and establishes many ideas by implication, thus shortening your letter copy considerably. Often the letter need contain no more than the notification of compliance, as in this example:

> We are glad to send you with this letter the last three annual reports of National Reaper, Inc., and add your name to our mailing list to receive future copies as they are released around March 1 each year.

The direct beginning also establishes a cheerful, ungrudging tone for the letter and eliminates pompousness—at least from the all-important beginning. Observe the difference between the following original and revision:

INDIRECT, WORDY, GRUDGING	DIRECT, COMPACT, CHEERFUL
We have your request for our HOW book.	Here is the HOW book you asked for.
It was prepared primarily for material-handling engineers, and so we were not prepared for the numerous requests we have received from schools. We are sending you one, however, and hope you will find it helpful.	It was prepared after extensive research by our own material-handling engineers with the assistance of outside consultants and plant men who specialize in material-handling methods and procedures. We're sure you'll find it useful in the classroom.
If there is any other way we can be of assistance, please do not hesitate to call on us.	Call on us again when you think we can help.

In response to a request for a copy of a manual on letters, the following is a good example:

> Here is your complimentary copy of *Better Letters,* Professor Duke.
>
> I hope you'll be able to use it in developing the practical note you desire in your classes.
>
> Since the manual was compiled from company correspondence and contains actual names and other confidential material, will you please not quote directly from it? I'm sure you'll be able to use it successfully by substituting other names and figures when you want to paraphrase an example.
>
> Several Harwood graduates are doing excellent jobs with Southern Atlantic. I hope you will have other qualified graduating seniors to recommend to Mr. R. B. Jones when he comes to your campus in February.

And in accepting the chairmanship of a civic drive, the writer of the following letter created extra good will for himself:

> You certainly may count on me to do everything I can to make this year's Small Business Division exceed its quota for the Community Chest.

Send me the names of the division members as soon as you can, please, so that we can get organized. I'd like to have a preliminary meeting as soon as possible.

We'll certainly appreciate any suggestions pointing to more effective performance.

One of the shorter replies to the palletization request read like this:

Although there seems to be a dearth of palletization material in textbooks, here are two you may want to study if you haven't already:

Harry E. Stocker, *Materials Handling,* Prentice-Hall, New York, 1956.

Mathews W. Potts, *Materials Handling Equipment,* Pitman, New York, 1958.

The following magazines have market research departments and can supply reprints of articles if you'll write them explaining just what information you wish:

Modern Material Handling, 131 Claredon Street, Boston 16.
Flow, 1240 Ontario Street, Cleveland 13.
Factory Management & Maintenance, McGraw-Hill, New York.
American Machinist, 520 North Michigan Avenue, Chicago.
Industry & Power, St. Joseph, Michigan.
Western Canner & Packer, 121 Second Street, San Francisco.

In the attached envelope I am sending you a copy of our latest catalogue and the last four issues of our house organ, *Material Handling News.*

We're glad to pass these suggestions on to you and to send this material along; we realize that today's students are tomorrow's material-handling engineers.

Good luck on the thesis. Call on us again if we can help.

You will note that not one of the foregoing letters wasted any words referring to receipt of the inquiry. The direct beginning makes such references unnecessary and saves space better used for worthwhile information.

Completeness of Coverage.   Obviously, you need to take up every question in an inquiring letter; when you fail to do so, extra correspondence results (or your reader marks you up as careless, indifferent, or ignorant). There will be times, of course, when you can't answer—sometimes because you don't know, sometimes because it is information you can't reveal. In either case, simply tell your reader that, but don't ignore his question.

When the questions call for strictly factual answers, when the requesting letter tabulates questions and leaves space for answering on the letter, your job is easy. When the necessary answers are evaluative and expository in form, your job is sometimes not so easy.

The following personnel report is in answer to an inquiry about the subject's selling ability, personality, cultural background, character, and integrity. Note that the negative information the writer felt was necessary to establish is embedded in the letter and interpreted along with a positive characteristic of the applicant:

Subject: Confidential report by request on Travis Brannon as a prospective book salesman

Mr. Brannon graded papers, had conferences with students, and did clerical jobs as a student assistant in my office during the fall semester last year. He is a careful, accurate worker with lots of initiative. And he makes friends readily.

I got to know Travis quite well while he made two *A*'s in my courses, Sales Management and Public Relations. His questions in class and in conferences showed a keen understanding of business problems and a calm, practical approach to their solution. And his term reports in both cases showed solid, serious, yet original, business thinking. Impressed with his scholastic performance, his friendliness and ability to get along with people, and his obvious wide range of interests in many things (literature, drama, music), I asked him to be my assistant.

I particularly liked the quickness with which Travis caught on to assigned jobs and the willingness and accuracy with which he did a job every time it came up after I had explained it to him only once. On many small jobs and some not so small he went ahead and did what needed to be done without being told.

As he demonstrated ability, I let him do more and more. And he accepted the added responsibility and authority with obvious delight! As a result of such unbridled enthusiasm, I occasionally had to change a grade or contradict what he had told a student in conference. When that happened, he was noticeably silent for a few days; then he apparently forgot the incident and became his cheerfully helpful self again.

I must say, Mr. Parks, that I never had to lower a grade Travis gave a student! And he was hardest on his friends. I never had one single reason to suspect that any student had an inside track with him. He was completely trustworthy with examinations, grade records, and the like.

Perhaps the most noticeable things about Travis are his eagerness to do his job, his efficiency in making use of all his time, and his general alertness. These qualities, though they sometimes made him officious in interrupting my conferences with students and colleagues, stood him in good stead with students and faculty alike.

I feel sure that if Travis walked into the office of a college professor on almost any campus, the reaction toward him and your company would be favorable.

Resale.   Perhaps our suggestion to incorporate resale material in a reply to an inquiry without sales possibilities may strike you as unneces-

Favorable Reply Check List

1. Make your opening sentence establish the fact that you are doing what your reader has asked you to do.

   a) When you are saying "Yes," say it immediately! Best bet in a situation involving a person is a specific identification of what the person did for you and for how long. When you are sending something, establish that fact in the opening lines.

   b) The most effective way to establish the fact that you're glad to do something is to begin immediately to do it. Specifically, "I am very glad to tell you . . ." is NOT so good an opening as "Henry Benton, about whom you inquired, did typing in the central office from August, 1957, to June, 1958."

   c) DON'T emphasize the obvious: "This is an answer to . . ."; "Concerning your inquiry . . ."; "We have received your letter."

   d) In this direct situation, a subject line can often get you and your reader off to a quick start. In a report about a person, make it identify the name of the person, establish the fact that he is the reader's applicant, and show by some appropriate label that this letter gives information.

2. Specificness of coverage and concreteness in comment are essential.

   a) Answer every question—direct or implied—of the inquiry.

   b) You want to evaluate for the reader when such evaluation will be helpful. But do more than editorialize with "fine," "splendid," "excellent." Back up your statements with specific citation of results and performance. In a personnel report, for instance:

   (1) No applicant just stays on the payroll; he does some work. Tell your reader the specific job duties that the applicant performed for you. If he swept floors, arranged stock, or helped with window displays, say so.

   (2) Analyze the job for which the applicant is presently applying and talk about those things which the applicant did for you that will be significant on this next job.

   (3) A good personnel report tells something about work habits which indicate personality characteristics (co-operativeness, determination, punctuality, or whatever else applies).

   c) Scant, skimpy treatment implies to some readers that you are unwilling to extend an ordinary business courtesy or that you are very dubious about the applicant, the project, or the reader.

3. Tone is all-important.

   a) In a personnel report

sary—even odd. But look back a moment at the contrasting samples relating to the HOW book on page 131 and note the different impressions created. The revised direct sample words the additional comment on the book in such a way as to make the reader realize that he is getting some-

FAVORABLE REPLY CHECK LIST (CONTINUED)

(1) Remember that you are *reporting,* not promising future performance. Stick to concrete facts about what the person did while under your supervision.

(2) Beware of superlatives. Too glowing an account sounds unbelievable.

b) In telling or giving your reader something, don't do it grudgingly or parade your generosity.

4. You often have negative material to handle.

a) You aren't being honest when you entirely eliminate reporting a person's failure to measure up personally or professionally or when you entirely eliminate the drawbacks of something else you are reporting.

b) To keep from sounding caustic, bitter, or even warped, embed negative information and further subordinate through the amount of space and word choice.

c) When you must place restrictions on the reader's use of information or material you give him, be quick, be definite—and, since this is negative material, place the statement in the middle of the letter.

5. Remember the privileged aspects when you write about a person.

a) Label the letter confidential.

b) Indicate that it has been requested.

c) For coherence, incorporate these phrases in either beginning or ending statements.

6. When you are sending something tangible (printed material, a sample, for instance), add a few words of resale.

a) Make them short.

b) Make them as specific as you can.

7. End graciously and confidently.

a) Your expression of willingness ("glad to" or its equivalent)—which is much more appropriate here than it is in the beginning—nullifies any possible curt impression.

b) Don't suggest inadequacy of treatment: "I hope I've answered your questions . . ." or "If this is not what you want. . . ." If you feel that way by the time you finish, you'd better rewrite the letter.

c) Certain expressions are the unfortunate victims of overuse and misuse. They destroy the conversational quality of your writing. "Please do not hesitate to" is just one example of what correspondents call "bromides." "Feel free to" is another.

thing special. Furthermore, it enhances the cordiality established by the direct beginning and eliminates any impression of curtness and abruptness that might be reflected from a one-sentence letter.

Note how in the following letter the writer not only applies resale on the booklet requested but goes a step further by sending something additional and offering to do more:

> Of course you may have copies of our booklet; four of them are enclosed with this letter. They'll certainly help to show those future business leaders you spoke of something about how a direct-mail agency operates.
>
> What's more, we're sending you a dividend: a copy of the speech Mr. Ray made at the DMAA meeting in Detroit last month. Some folks have said that it makes some pretty arresting statements about the uses and limitations of direct mail. You and your students will get something from this too, we think.
>
> Call on us again; we're always glad to do what we can.

Certainly it is not possible to apply resale in every reply. In reports about people, for instance, it is out of place. But in situations where you send information (especially in the form of booklets, brochures, or leaflets), there's every reason why you should try to enhance the desirability of what you've done and to offer to help out again (unless you specifically do not want to).

The check list on pages 134–35 summarizes the more important points to keep in mind as you write replies complying with a reader's request.

REFUSING THE REQUEST

If you care little or nothing about your reader's continued good feeling toward you, you can quickly and easily write a refusal like this:

> I'm very sorry, but company practice forbids giving out information such as you requested.

Even if you care a lot about your reader's continued good feeling toward you, you *can* write a believable turndown letter that begins with the refusal—for example:

> I'm very glad to explain to you, Mr. Willet, why Rigate spends its advertising dollars on radio time and magazine space rather than on the distribution of samples.

But most correspondence supervisors and correspondence counselors advocate what they call the "reason-first refusal." The brevity of the first example above and the dispatch of the second are not desirable in refusals because most people are disappointed, irritated, or downright angry when told they can't have something or can't do something. And in any of these emotional states they will not give full attention to your explanation even though most people instinctively react with "Why?" when they are denied something.

Back of most refusals is some good reason(s) dictated by sound business judgment. And usually it can be told. That is why we say that most refusals have an educating job to do: they usually have to acquaint the reader with some circumstance of which he is apparently unaware. Hence the emphasis on explanation before refusing, as already suggested in the analysis of the B-type letter in the "Planned Presentation" section (p. 30).

Furthermore, one of the first lessons in good human relations that any sensitive person learns is that when you take something away from someone or deny him something, you give a reason, you give him something else to compensate for the loss when you can, and you try to extend some gesture of friendliness.

Simply stated, the desirable pattern for most refusals is

—a buffer beginning (establishing compatibility; defined and illustrated below)
—a review of facts (reasons)
—the refusal itself, subordinated ⎱ OR a counterproposal which implies the
—an off-the-subject ending ⎰ refusal

Before studying an analysis of this suggested structure, however, read the following refusal of the request for toothpaste samples (p. 109):

> Sales-minded businessmen are keenly aware of the advertising possibilities which usually accompany such an occasion as "A" Day at your University.
>
> If they have found such advertising to be sufficiently productive to warrant the cost, they are quick to take advantage of the opportunity; and we here at Rigate are no exception.
>
> After experimenting with many different forms of advertising, however, we have found that we obtain best results at the least expense by advertising in nationally circulated magazines—*Life* and the *Saturday Evening Post,* for example—and by sponsoring the Picote Theatre, which millions of Americans enjoy every Sunday night.
>
> The results of advertising by distributing sample tubes of Picote did not warrant the relatively high cost of manufacturing, handling, and mailing the samples; so we now concentrate on magazine and radio-TV promotion. As a result, we have been able to make a substantial saving which we have passed on to the users of Picote by lowering the price of the product.
>
> In addition to this price reduction, in January and February Rigate will offer an economy-size tube of Picote for just one additional penny with the purchase of a bottle of Rigatine. The first time you drop by your drugstore in January, take advantage of the savings Rigate passes on to its users.

The Buffer Beginning.   When the reader starts to read your refusal, remember, he is hoping for pleasant news. He has probably done a good job of ferreting out those reasons why he thinks you should do as he has asked. The outright refusal presented immediately, because it appears to ignore his feelings and his reasoning, is likely to arouse a negative reaction and cause him to close his mind to anything else you say.

If you pitch right in with a presentation of your reasons, you appear to be arguing with him—and his dander, or at least his suspicion, rises.

To prevent mental impasses and emotional deadlocks, show your reader that you are a reasonable, calm person by indicating some form of approval of him or his project. This is your buffer. Frequently, you can agree completely with some statement made in his request. At the least, you can say something which will establish compatibility, even if it's nothing more than that you have given his proposal serious thought.

The turndown of the request for the correspondence manual (p. 31) could easily begin with

> You are certainly right about the pressing need that is facing most business firms for more effectively trained business correspondents.

Or it could have started this way:

> Students attending Harwood College are fortunate to have a faculty who try so conscientiously to correlate college training and business practice.

Both beginnings acknowledge the receipt of the request, clearly imply that the request has been considered, establish compatibility, and set the stage for the review of the facts resulting in the refusal later.

Three warnings should be sounded here, however. The first is that if you appear to be granting the request, you are building your reader up to an awful letdown! The resultant reaction undoubtedly arouses more negative feelings than the abrupt, unmotivated refusal. Such beginnings as these would mislead most readers:

> I certainly would like to see each Harwood letter-writing student have access to a copy of the Southern Atlantic manual.

> "A" Day surely would be a good opportunity to acquaint potential customers with Picote toothpaste, Mr. Willet!

The second warning is against beginning so far away from the subject that the reader isn't even sure the letter is a reply to his request. The buffer beginning must clearly identify the general subject. Otherwise, incoherence and rambling are inevitable results. Even such a beginning as the following is irrelevant:

> Your interesting letter describing "A" Day brought back to mind many pleasant memories of my own college days.

The job of getting to the facts would be harder with such a start.

Despite the fact that many writers advocate beginning refusals with

I really wish we could . . . ,

we do not believe it can do as good a job for you as some other opening. It is stereotyped, it sounds insincere to many readers, and it invites the belligerent response of "Then why don't you?" But the greatest disadvantage (and the third warning) is that it establishes the refusal unmistakably in the opening line before showing any reason why.

Reasons Rather than Apologies. If you will apply the positive thinking and positive phrasing that we talked about under "Positive Statement" (p. 39) and "Success Consciousness" (p. 41), you will resist the common impulse to apologize anywhere in a refusal *and especially in the beginning.* Certainly, you won't offend most readers with a genuine expression of regret, but apologies are no substitute for action or explanation. And they inevitably force you to phrase in distinctively negative terminology the very idea that you should be avoiding, the fact that you *will not, cannot, are unable to, do not have,* and similar negative expressions.

You will, of course, run into some situations when there are no reasons (nonexistence of certain information or plain and simple unavailability) and some when the reason is so obvious that it need not be put into words.

But in most cases when you have to refuse, that refusal is based on policy. And back of that policy are good business reasons. Those reasons —not the policy—form the bedrock of your explanation. As much as possible, you will want to search out and emphasize those reasons which reflect benefit to the reader—if not directly, then indirectly through a group with which the reader might be sympathetic. This, we will admit, is one of those things more easily said than done. But the writer of the Picote-sample-refusal letter did a good job of relating reader-benefit to his refusal. So did the man who had to tell a ten-year-old boy that a big mail-order house could not take the time to put commemorative stamps on packages sent to the boy's mother:

A stamp collection can certainly be fun, Tommy!

And commemorative stamps can teach you a lot about geography and people.

To get your mother's packages to her as quickly as she likes to get them, however, we use canceled stamps and postage-meter machines. They enable us to cut down on shipping time here at Glover's and help the men at the Post Office to save time, too. They also help us to reduce our expenses. Those are two good reasons why your mother likes to buy from Glover's and two good reasons why we use only these means for paying postage.

I'll bet you can get all the commemorative stamps you want for your collection if you'll just ask some of your relatives and friends to save them for you. Try it and see.

Did you see the big write-up about stamp collections in *Life* magazine June 24? You'd enjoy reading it and looking at all the pictures, I know.

The following letter from a manufacturer refusing a dealer's request for samples also stresses reader benefits:

Congratulations on the 25 years of service that you have given to your community!

Through continued association with retailers, we know that only those whose businesses are based on sound managerial policies and services succeed over so long a time.

We have tried to help in these successes by cutting costs whenever possible and passing these savings on to retailers in the form of lower prices. This aim led us to eliminate the high (and often unpredictable) manufacturing and shipping costs of special samples. You and hundreds of other druggists have benefited from these cost reductions for the past five years.

If you'll fill in and mail the enclosed card, Mr. Robert Abbott, your Walwhite representative, will be glad to arrange a special Walwhite exhibit for your anniversary sale. This attractive display will attract many customers.

Such reader-benefit interpretation cannot be applied in every case. To attempt to would result in artificial, insincere talk. The following letter refusing a request for permission to reprint some sales letters of a mail-order house would not likely offend even when stripped down to its fundamental message:

You can count on a large, interested readership for the article you are writing about the importance of sales letters in business.

In our company, as you know, we depend upon letters exclusively for sales. Of necessity, then, we have tested extensively to find out the most effective procedures. Our highly paid writers are continually revising, sending expensive test mailings, and comparing returns. The best letters represent a considerable investment.

In the past we have had some of our standard letters used without consent by rival companies; so we now copyright all our sales forms and confine them to company use. Should we release them for publication, we would have to incur the same expense once again, for their effectiveness for us would be materially decreased.

I'm sending you some bulletins and a bibliography which may help you with your article. Will you let me know the issue of the magazine your article appears in?

Even though the reasoning is frankly selfish, it is reasonable; and the writing is friendly and positive.

If you establish good reasons, you have no cause for apologizing.

The Derived, Positive Refusal. Ideally, as your reader reads your explanation he sees that it justifies you in refusing, and by the time he finishes the explanation he has inferred the turndown. He may even have phrased it mentally. Thus prepared, he is far more likely to accept your decision without ill feeling.

But you cannot always afford to depend exclusively on implication to establish the "No" unmistakably. You cannot take chances on your reader's misunderstanding. The refusal must be clearly established, but the statement of it need not be brutally negative; in fact, it need not be negative at all. If you will look back at the sample refusals in this section, you will see that the writers established the idea of what they were not doing by a statement of what they were doing. To establish the idea of "We don't distribute samples," one writer said, "So we now concentrate on magazines and radio-TV promotion." He might have expressed his idea more definitely with "We advertise exclusively through magazines and radio-television." Instead of saying, "We cannot let you have samples of our sales letters," another phrased it, "We copyright all our sales forms and confine them to company use." When you incorporate the limiting words *only, solely, exclusively* (even phrases like *confine to* and *concentrate on*), there's no room for doubt.

Saving some of your reasons until after establishing the definite refusal enables you to embed the disappointing news and thus, you hope, reduce the impact of the refusal. In any event, you certainly want to take leave of your reader on a more pleasant note than the refusal.

The Pleasant, Hopeful Ending. In some cases when you must refuse, you can do little but reassure the reader through a few additional words that you are not utterly callous—or even merely indifferent. Good wishes for the success of the project, the suggestion of other sources, possibly the suggestion of being helpful in other ways, sending something other than what the reader has requested—all these are possibilities for ending your letter with a friendly gesture.

Sometimes you cannot comply with your reader's request but can suggest an alternative action which will be of some help to him if he cares to follow your suggestion. Business writers call this a "counter-proposal" or a "compromise proposal." In many instances it can success-

REFUSAL CHECK LIST

1. Your buffer opening must establish compatibility through its pleasantness.
    a) One of the poorest starts is talk about how pleased or flattered you are. It's vain and selfish.
    b) Shift the emphasis to your reader—even though your talk may be no more than how worthwhile you think his project is.
    c) If you appear to be on the verge of granting the request, your refusal is even more disappointing when it comes.
    d) Nor do you want to intimate the refusal at this point. Especially guard against "I really wish we could. . . ."
    e) Beginning too far away from the subject of the request results in incoherence. From the buffer content the reader should be able to tell immediately and unmistakably that this is an answer to his request.
2. Your transition must continue the same line of thought set out in your buffer opening.
    a) To avoid selfish-sounding turns, keep the emphasis on the reader.
    b) At the start of the turn, *although, however, but, yet,* signal unmistakably that there's to be a turn for the worse. Avoid them as sentence or paragraph beginnings.
    c) Avoid, also, the insincere "Although I should like to. . . ."
    d) You must supply the bridging sentence that shows your reader why you are going into the explanation.
3. Give at least one good reason (it may be more) for the refusal BEFORE implying or stating the refusal. That is the most significant procedure in the reason-first turndown.
    a) Ferret out and give emphasis to those reasons which are for the benefit of someone other than yourself. If possible, associate the reader with these benefits.

fully absorb the statement of the refusal and furnish you with the positive ending you seek. The following letter is an example of this technique:

Prudential's employees and clients will no doubt benefit materially from the reports manual you are planning, Mr. Lee—especially if it is the same calibre as the letters manual your staff prepared recently.

I'm sure many college teachers would be glad to furnish you illustrative material. And I am no exception. In the past fifteen years of working with business and college people trying to improve the quality of their reports, I've collected much HOW NOT TO and HOW TO teaching material.

For most of this I have only my single file copy, which I use in teaching a report-writing course three times a year and which I carefully keep in my office.

Refusal Check List (Continued)

b) Don't attempt to hide behind the skirts of "our policy." Policies as such merit little respect; the reasons behind them do.

c) For believability, you need specificness.

d) Stick to plausibilities; family difficulties, financial troubles, acts of God, and the like are suspect (the reader isn't likely to believe you; besides, they're of questionable taste).

4. The refusal itself should be

a) A logical outcome of the reasons given. Ideally, the reader should deduce the refusal before he sees your statement of it.

b) Stated positively—in terms of what you *can* and *do* do rather than in terms of what you can't or don't.

c) Preceded and also followed by positive justifying reasons.

d) Unmistakable. Be sure there's no room for doubt. Make clear that you can't or won't. Consider the wisdom of *only, exclusively, confine to.*

e) Written without negative words like *impossible, must refuse, very sorry to tell you that we cannot.*

f) Without apologies, which just weaken your case. Concentrate, instead, on what is hopeful in the case.

5. Continue to talk long enough to convince your reader of your real interest in him and his problems, without recalling the refusal.

a) Your ending material must be positive and about something within the sphere of the reader's interest.

b) Watch for bromides and rubber stamps in the end.

c) Be wary of the expression "If there is any other help I can give you, please let me know." It can produce some sarcastic reactions.

Though I have no secretarial assistance, one of the students just finishing the course is an accurate, rapid typist who is familiar with the material. I'm sure she would like to do the necessary copying at her regular rate of seventy-five cents an hour. Since there are no more than fifty or sixty pages involved, I feel reasonably sure that securing the material this way would cost you no more than ten dollars, probably less.

I shall be glad to make the necessary arrangements if you would like me to. I'm sure I can have the material to you within four or five days after hearing from you.

Please note again that this writer does not resort to negative phrasing, nor does he mouth apologies. You, too, should resist the common tendency to resort to such expressions as "I regret, I assure you, my inability to do as you asked," "I'm sorry to have to refuse your request," or— much worse—"I hope you will understand our position," especially at the end. For these weaklings, substitute appropriate positive ideas such as those used in the examples in this section.

For writing good-will-building refusals, keep the check list of points on pages 142–43 in mind.

REPLIES TO INQUIRIES WITH SALES POSSIBILITIES

Failure to answer inquiries and requests of the types we have been discussing will mark you as an uncooperative boor and probably lose you a good many sales in the long run; but failure to answer inquiries with direct sales possibilities is sooner or later business suicide.

When someone sends you an inquiry about your goods or services, he shows clearly that he recognizes an unsatisfied need or desire; he further implies that your product might satisfy it. Whether he asks for manufacturing data, a price list, a catalogue or descriptive folder, or the name of your nearest dealer, he seems to be an *interested,* potential customer —in other words, a prospect. IF he receives satisfactory information and treatment, he'll probably be a real customer.

Your job of giving him what he wants is certainly much easier than making a sale through the usual sales letter that has to start from scratch with a "cold" prospect (as discussed in Chap. VIII), because the inquirer is already interested. He has practically invited you to send him a sales letter.

Although you will be able to write better invited sales letters after studying special sales techniques, we take them up here because they are the most significant kind of reply that any business firm sends. They are more than good-will builders: they are sales clinchers. Accordingly, they draw on the principles discussed under "Persuasion Principles" in Chapter II.

As a writer of a reply to an inquiry with sales possibilities, you have no problem of securing attentive interest; your main problem is to tell enough to overcome reluctance, to tell it convincingly, and to get the reader to take the appropriate steps that lead to a sale. Your attention, then, must be given to getting started favorably, answering all questions, subordinating unfavorable information, handling price positively, and stimulating action.

Getting Started Favorably.   When a prospective customer writes you the equivalent of "Tell me more," he certainly is going to feel that he has had cold water thrown in his face with an indifferent reply like this:

There is an Endurtone company in your locality. Kindly contact them with your problem.

Such unconcern sends many readers to other sources for their needs. This, of course, is an extreme example, but it apparently happens often enough to merit special warning.[1]

The thing the reader most wants to know is the information he has requested—as specifically as you can give it to him. He is far more interested in such information than in any of your expressions of pleasure or gratitude. But in most cases involving a detailed inquiry, you will want to check the order of your reader's questions before framing your reply. Some of his requests for information you can answer with more positiveness than others; one of these is what you should start with, as in the following examples:

> With your Pow-R-Pac you will feel safe even when traveling alone at night on the country roads you spoke of.

> The Rover bicycle that you saw advertised in *U.S. Youth* is made of lightweight, high-grade steel of the same quality used in motor bikes.

> Yes, Mr. Baines, the base and standard of the Richmond Lamp you saw in *Home and Yard* are of solid brass. They will blend in tastefully with almost any style of 18th-century furnishings.

When you can answer "Yes," that is the information you should choose for your opening. Such positiveness stimulates enthusiasm and increases the desire to read further.

Answering All Questions. In some instances you cannot give the information your reader has asked of you. For example, the letter about the Stair-Traveller (p. 38) could not give cost details because installation varies according to the placement of the machine in a particular dwelling. The visit of the representative (clearly referred to) would have to clear up that point. If you cannot supply an answer, do not ignore it. Such action on your part only leads to suspicion, irritation, or disgust on your reader's part. Indicate that you are supplying the information in some other way or that you are in the process of finding out.

Most of the time you can give all the information the reader has requested, even though it runs to considerable length. The following reply to the request for more information about Reconditioned Lektrasweeps (p. 104) is a good letter not only because of good you-viewpoint and

---

[1] See Paul Vincent, "Why Inquiries Don't Turn into Orders," *Printers' Ink*, 224:57, 60, 62, 64, August 6, 1948 (reprinted in *Writing for Business*); also Carroll J. Swan, "Neglect of Inquiries Is One War Baby to Eliminate," *Printers' Ink*, 219:20–31, 60–63, June 6, 1947. Also Carroll J. Swan, "How to Follow Leads That Result from Advertising," *Printers' Ink*, 217:37–39, November 8, 1946.

positiveness but also because it answers every question of the inquiring letter:

> The reconditioned Lektrasweep that you asked about has the following attachments: a 6-inch upholstery brush, a 6-inch lamp-shade brush, a 12-inch prober, and a plastic blower attachment, in addition to the standard 12-inch rug brush.
>
> These you will find adequate for any home cleaning. They are the same equipment assembled the same way as in vacuum cleaners costing $40–80 more. Were we to include a 1-hp motor with the Lektrasweep (which is necessary only when spraying attachments are included), the price would have to be considerably increased. Since many satisfied users of Lektrasweep have voiced their approval of Lektrasweep for cleaning purposes only, we continue to eliminate the spray attachments—which do require at least a 1-hp motor for effective use—and thus are able to give you a good low-cost cleaner operating efficiently on a ½-hp motor.
>
> Next time you're in Birmingham, come in and let us demonstrate a Lektrasweep for you in our showroom at 1423 Second Avenue North. After a thorough test (as much as you like) of its effectiveness in picking up dust, lint, and other particles from rugs, upholstery, and walls, you'll see why we sell the Lektrasweep with confidence that customers will be satisfied with its performance in their own homes. Though we consider all sales final (another of the economies resulting in the low price of your Lektrasweep), you have the Lektrasweep guarantee, which protects you against mechanical failures for a full two-year period.
>
> Should the motor fail or any of the parts fail to function because of defective workmanship, you have only to pack the entire unit and attachments in the handy container you'll receive your Lektrasweep in, attach a tag to the container handle, and turn it over to the express man. At the central repair plant in Cleveland, specially trained service men will put your Lektrasweep in service again and return it to you within a week's time. As long as the machine shows evidence of proper care, as explained in detail on the written guarantee we give you at the time of purchase, we absorb the charges for servicing and new parts, and return your Lektrasweep, charges prepaid. The 291 returns to the central plant out of the 10,091 Lektrasweeps sold have been handled to the customers' satisfactions.
>
> I believe we have the sweeper you'll find convenient for your cleaning— and at the price you'd like to pay. When you try it out, you'll see at once the brown crackle finish which will resist nicks and scratches and which will be easy to keep clean. You'll realize the desirability of the quiet operation of the motor, especially in small living quarters. The 20-foot cord enables you to clean an entire room without having to switch from one wall plug to another.
>
> You'll want to see for yourself, I believe; but if for some reason you'd like your Lektrasweep before you can get over to Birmingham, use the enclosed order blank and reply envelope for sending us your payment and

instructions. You can be enjoying easy Lektrasweeping the day after we hear from you.

This is a particularly difficult letter to write because so many of the questions had to be answered with limitations, reservations, or implied "No."

Subordinating Unfavorable Information.   It would have been very poor salesmanship if the Lektrasweep letter had started with—

> The Lektrasweep is equipped with a ½-hp motor.

or with

> No, the Lektrasweep does not have a 1-hp motor.

Likewise, if the writer of the Stair-Traveller letter had elected to begin with

> The Stair-Traveller you are interested in will not work on a stair with a turn in the middle,

the lady's interest would very likely have decreased immediately and maybe vanished. But by establishing favorable information before stating this negative fact and by stating the negative in its positive form ("as it is designed only for straight stairways"), the writer hoped to overcome the effect of the disappointing news. Explaining the necessary installation in terms of simplicity and economy (the positive corollary) further helped to cushion the effect.

Another case will more firmly implant the desirability for positive handling of unfavorable information in invited sales. The inquiry read as follows:

> Please give me the answers to the following questions about the Roanoke lamp advertised on p. 27 of the December *Home and Yard:*
> 1. Is it 3-way?
> 2. Is the shade parchment or paper?
> 3. Is the shade available in a design as well as the single color you pictured? Since the pair of lamps will be in front of plain drapes, my wife would prefer shades with some design.
> 4. Is the Roanoke weighted to prevent tipping?
> 5. Is the base real brass or an alloy?
> 6. If we should order a pair and find after placing them with our 18th-century living-room furnishings that the lamps are not what we want, may we return them and have our money refunded?

Answers to questions 1, 3, 4, and 6 contained negative information. Here is one way of handling this inquiry to turn it into a sale despite the unfavorable circumstances:

Yes, the base and standard of the Roanoke lamp you saw in *Home and Yard* are of solid brass, which will blend in tastefully with almost any style of 18th-century furnishings.

For durability and ease in cleaning, the 10-inch shade is light-weight metal. Either the forest green or the royal red shade will contrast effectively with your drapes, and the quarter-inch gold bands around the top and bottom give the Roanoke lamp a distinction which most of our customers prefer to a design.

The white lining of the shade and the milk-white bone china reflector enable the single 150-watt bulb to give you good reading light—10 foot-candles within a radius of 8 feet, which is more than the minimum recommended by the American Institute of Lighting.

Then, too, the indirect lighting reflected from the ceiling is pleasant for conversational groups.

To make the Roanoke more stable than other lamps of this size and shape, our designers put six claw feet instead of the usual four on the base and thus eliminated the necessity for weighting. Claw feet, as you know, are characteristic of much 18th-century design.

You and Mrs. Baines will agree that the Roanoke is a handsome, efficient lamp when you place a pair of them in your own living room. Should you decide to return them within ten days of our shipping date, we will refund your money less shipping charges.

Use the enclosed order blank and envelope to tell us your choice of color. Include with the order blank your check or money order for $40 (including shipping charges). Within five days after we hear from you, you will be enjoying your Roanoke lamps, which will give you good lighting at a moderate price and will make appropriately decorative additions to your living room.

The letter wisely begins and ends with positive ideas and, as positively as circumstances permit, establishes the negative answers of "No, the Roanoke is not 3-way; no, it is not weighted; no, the shade is not available in a design; no, we won't refund *all* your money if you return them." It does so through the usual means available to any writer: embedded position and positive statement.

Handling Price.   In most business situations no other talk is as loud as that concerned with dollars and cents. Receiving money is pleasant; parting with money is hard.

When you have a genuine bargain, a real price reduction, that information may be the best lead you can choose for your message, provided that your reader has some already established value associated with your product or service.

Most of the time, however, you are trying to sell at an established price. And most of the time you are writing to someone who wishes the price were less! For those two simple and obvious reasons, writers attempt to minimize the effect of price details. They do so by

—Introducing price after most of the sales points have been presented

—Stating price in terms of a unit ("50¢ a wrench" rather than "$6 a dozen")

—Identifying the daily, monthly, or even yearly cost based on an estimated life of the product ("10¢ a night" for a good mattress sounds much easier to pay for than "$79")

—Suggesting a series of payments rather than the total (an alumnus is more likely to contribute "$10 a month for the next year" than he is to contribute "$120 next year")

—Comparing the present price with the cost of some product or activity that the reader accepts readily. ("For the price of six cigarettes a day your child can have better schools" was the punch line of an ad promoting a school-bond drive. And an Episcopal bishop drove home his point with "This means 17¢ per week from each communicant—not a large sum for the Kingdom of God, when we realize that many of us spend twice that amount *every day* for tobacco." Likewise, a sales writer sells air-conditioned sleep for the price of a daily coke.)

—Associating the price with a reminder of the benefits to be gained

The first and the last of the suggestions you can always apply; the others as indicated by the following varying factors.

In general, the higher the income bracket of your audience, the less desirability for applying the techniques.

The higher the price of your product or service, the greater the desirability for minimizing price in one or more of these ways. The less familiar your audience is with your product or service, the greater the desirability that you justify price. Such devices are incorporated more frequently in consumer letters than in letters to dealers.

Often you will be able to omit direct price talk because a salesman will handle it in a face-to-face interview or because you need more information before determining price; sometimes you can shift the burden of price discussion to an enclosure. But when you are trying to close a sale, you must identify what it is going to cost your reader and help him justify the expenditure.

Inducing Action.   Having convinced your reader that your product or service is worth the price you are asking him to pay, you want him to take action before he changes his mind, before he forgets about the matter, before he spends the money for something else, before any of the things that could happen do happen.

A word of caution here, however: the bromidic, high-pressure, general expressions like "Act today!" "Do it now!" "Don't delay!" are more likely to produce reactions ranging from indifference to disgust than the favorable reaction you seek.

As in all persuasive letters, your good action ending

—Makes clear the specific action you want your reader to take

—Clears up any question about how the action is to be taken

—Makes the action easy (and sound as easy as possible)

—Supplies a stimulus to action, preferably immediate action

When your reader finishes your letter, he should know just exactly what it is you want him to do. He should not be in doubt for even a fraction of a second. In invited sales letters, you usually want him to send in an order or take some step in furthering the order, such as invite the visit of a salesman, make a visit to a demonstration or salesroom, or try out the product. The psychological urge is stronger if you name the explicit action rather than resort to the vague "Let us hear from you soon" or any of its equivalents. There will be times when you will have to name two actions and ask the reader to take one or the other; if you possibly can, avoid doing so, for the simple reason that some folks when faced with a choice resolve their dilemma by doing nothing.

Facilitating devices—order blanks, order cards, and postcards or envelopes already addressed and requiring no postage—remove some of the tediousness of taking action. References to them—preferably directing the reader to use them—reassure your reader that what you are asking him to do is simple, requiring little time or effort.

Moreover, through careful wording, you can further this impression. "Write us your choice" suggests more work than "Check your choice of colors on the enclosed card." "Jot down," "Just check, "Simply initial," are examples of wording that suggests ease and rapidity in doing something. Wording like this will help to reduce some of your reader's reluctance to take action.

The final suggestion for a good action ending—that of supplying a stimulus to action—is a matter of either threatening your reader or promising him something. As one well-known, successful letter consultant puts it, "The hurry-up should give 'em something if they do, and take away something if they don't."[2] Talk of limited supply, price rises after a certain date, introductory offers for a limited time, premiums, and the like is all very well *provided it is true* and *provided it is specific* so that the reader is likely to accept your statement as one accurately de-

---

[2] Howard Dana Shaw, "Put Teeth in Your Hurry-Up," *The Reporter of Direct Mail Advertising,* 12:17–18, February, 1950; reprinted in *Writing for Business.*

picting the conditions. Otherwise, readers of even average intelligence and experience read such statements with some skepticism for two good reasons:

1. They have seen too many instances in which such statements were not true. They have also seen "introductory" offers repeated over and over and over.

2. Especially in the United States—where the laws of supply and demand and the principles of mass production make any good product available to those who are interested in buying it—talk of limited supply raises questions about the desirability of the article in the first place. "If it's so good and so popular, why aren't more of them made?" is a frequent, legitimate rejoinder. And a reader might well wonder why a premium must be thrown in: Is the product overpriced? Is there some drawback for which the premium is sop?

Records of mail-order experiences over the years have shown that such hurry-up devices do increase returns in some instances. Scarcities, for instance, during national-emergency periods certainly make a difference in a person's decision to buy. And the desire to save money before another round of inflation hits makes many a buyer reach for his checkbook. But such devices are not universally applicable and far less so in invited sales letters than in uninvited sales.

In many circumstances you have nothing you can use as a stimulus but the desirability of your product or service. You *always* have that, however. In the final analysis your reader bases his buying decision on what the product contributes to his life; when you ask him to part with his money, remind him again of what he will receive as a result. (This is called a "stimulus" or a "clincher." But since many sales writers refer to the four steps of the action ending as the "clincher," we think it's simpler just to call this restatement of benefit the "stimulus.")

Such a stimulus comes appropriately as the ending idea of your letter. Such placement has decided psychological value, too, for it emphasizes the service attitude—rather than the greed that would be stressed if you ended with dollars and cents talk or the mechanics of ordering.

Desirably, the stimulus is short—often only a phrase, at most a short sentence, restating the theme of the letter. The Stair-Traveller letter, for example, could have ended effectively with

Mr. J. B. Nickle, our Memphis representative, will be glad to call at a time convenient for you. If you'll fill out and mail the enclosed postcard, he will come to your home and explain how simply and economically your Stair-Traveller can *make your daily living more pleasurable.*

Another example of the built-in stimulus is this ending from a letter to a farmer about an automatic milking machine:

INVITED SALES CHECK LIST

1. Get started in a hurry!
   - *a*) The direct, specific, favorable answer to one of your reader's questions is the surest way of maintaining the interest you already have.
   - *b*) At least give a good sales point if no question can be answered affirmatively.
   - *c*) "Thank you for"—while perfectly nice—is slow.
   - *d*) Keep out the selfish sounds of "we're glad to have your letter," "we appreciate your interest," and their variants.
   - *e*) Certainly you do not want to begin with an answer containing negative information.
   - *f*) The attention-stimulating opening of the uninvited sales letter is bewildering and wasteful in this invited letter. You already have attention and interest.

2. Establish an order of points that makes for natural coherence and that gives your reader favorable information at the beginning and end of your letter (if possible, at the beginning and end of paragraphs). Embed touchy points, answers that you can be fairly sure are not what the reader wants to hear.

3. Completeness of coverage demands an answer to every question in your reader's inquiry, whether it is stated or implied. Failure to answer a question or at least to explain why you are not now answering it builds suspicion.

4. Psychological description is good selling.
   - *a*) Put this product to work in the life of the reader right from the start, and let reader-use sentences predominate throughout the letter. For example, this has good you-viewpoint:

       As you ride slowly up and down stairs in your Stair-Traveller, you can be absolutely certain that you are safe as well as comfortable. When the current fails in Greenville, Specific Motors brakes hold your Stair-Traveller in place until the current comes on.

       Writing dominated by "our product" presentation rapidly begins to pall, then bore; and it fails to make your reader visualize how he is going to benefit. The statement, "Stair-Traveller is equipped with Specific Motors brakes," is true but is not sales-building style.
   - *b*) For best effect, however, get reader possession and/or participation instead of mechanical *you* beginnings. "You will like" and "you will find" do not necessarily inject you-viewpoint. For example, the passage—

       You will discover that the colors in which the lamp is available blend in with any color scheme. You will also like the extra claw feet on the large brass base, which holds the lamp steadily in place

INVITED SALES CHECK LIST (CONTINUED)

—is improved considerably when revised like this:

Either the forest green or the royal red shade will contrast effectively with your drapes. Six claw feet instead of the usual four
hold your Richmond steadily in place; and your wife will prefer the hollow base and standard at cleaning time.

c) You have to watch especially for denied negatives in invited sales
letters. If a product is *not* something, what *is* it?

d) The enclosure (when you have one) itself is not the significant
idea; the use the reader will make of it is what counts! Reread item
7 of your special-request check list (p. 115).

e) Psychological description is persuasive, but you still need specific
statements for conviction.

5. Adaptation is easy here; your reader's letter gives you many cues.

a) Use his name in the salutation or in the first line or two if you do
not use a salutation. Call him by name again in the second half of
the letter.

b) You can easily work in a reference to his town and/or his firm or
organization.

c) Refer easily and naturally to a commonplace action or event that
you can be fairly sure is characteristic of his job or his community
or of his geographical area or of his economic status.

d) Age, social status, economic status, or professional status makes
adjustment of your style desirable.

6. Try to cushion the shock of price when you have to settle the question.

a) Cover your sales points before talking price unless you are writing
bargain copy (usually not applicable in invited sales letters).

b) Consider the value of minimizing the effect through breaking
down price in terms of time or units.

c) Can you make a comparison of what your product will cost him
with what a familiar product or action costs him?

d) Link the benefit with the cost.

e) Price and method of payment should be understood. Many times
these details may be included on an enclosure. And often they must
be clarified after the visit of a sales representative.

7. Confidently ask this reader to take some action. The closer it comes to
nailing down the order, the better.

a) Phrase the action specifically.

b) Make his response easy.

c) Work in a last plug about satisfaction with the product.

d) Guard against the stereotyped and the high pressure.

154 WRITING BUSINESS LETTERS

And for $77.75—less than you pay for ten sacks of feed—Farm Master Milker can go to work for you. Just leave the enclosed card for the mail carrier tomorrow morning, and our Philadelphia representative will soon be up to give you a demonstration of how Farm Master Milker will *increase your dairy profits.*

For other examples, reread the endings of the Roanoke lamp letter and the letter selling the Lektrasweep.

A final reminder: Invited sales are sales letters in the realest sense; you should, therefore, apply all the points discussed in the section on "Persuasion Principles." The check list on pages 152–53 summarizes the most significant points to keep in mind for a good invited sales letter.

Letters like the invited sales you have read in this section do take time and therefore money—more than many firms can wisely spend.

Unless a firm has practically unlimited money and trained personnel, form messages need to be used some of the time for desirable speed and economy in handling inquiries with sales possibilities.

FORM LETTERS

Forms decrease the cost of correspondence by cutting down on time for dictation, transcription, handling, and filing. The closer you can come to completely eliminating one or more of these steps, the more you can save. The big problem is to determine when you can save enough in costs to justify the loss in effectiveness.

Though most readers like the implied extra consideration of the individual letter, few business people will object to a form because it is a form. They will rightly object to a sloppy form or a form message which does not contain the necessary information. And some will object to a form which tries to masquerade as an individual letter but fails because of discrepancies in type, faulty alignment, or inept wording. But the undisguised form can successfully carry its message in many situations like the following:

Here's Your Copy of
"The Buying Guide
to Fine Furniture."

You will be delighted with the wealth of information condensed into this conveniently indexed booklet.

For here, in a comparatively few pages, are guide-posts used by experts with a lifetime of experience in weighing true furniture values. Here are features which help such experts actually judge furniture "upside down" as well as right side up.

And here are features illustrated and described to guide you in your purchases of furniture so that the pieces you select to furnish your home will give you utmost pleasure as the years roll by.

We're glad you've given us this opportunity to send you this information. For we love fine furniture . . . take great pride in making it . . . and enjoy distributing information about it that may be helpful to you in establishing standards of value.

Even though every piece of furniture bearing the Langston seal is hand-crafted to certified standards of quality, nation-wide popularity makes possible budget prices. For a thrilling surprise, see your dealer, whose name is imprinted on the back page of the booklet.

Even the signature of this letter is processed. When an inquiry comes in, the letter and booklet are inserted in an envelope addressed to the inquirer; addressing the envelope is the only time-consuming step. Thus a reply which could easily cost a dollar or more if individually handled runs to no more than a dime. And the firm gains extra good will by a prompt answer.

You can run off completely processed forms (strict forms) by the thousands at very low cost. The only additional expense is for addressing (of course, you have mailing expense and advertising expense in securing the inquiry; but these are the same whether your message is processed or individualized).

Thus *completely* processed messages are the cheapest. And they can be adapted in talking points and references even to a large mailing list. But completely processed letters have limitations. Personalizing is impossible. And if you process the body and then insert individual inside addresses and salutations, you have two additional problems: greatly increased costs and obvious discrepancies between the two types. Unless the firm sells only one product or has a different form for each product, resale talk on the goods can't be included, although it can be on the firm. Dates cannot be included (usually not important). Completely processed messages can, however, indicate the disposition of the inquiry (or order), express gratitude, convey some evidence of service attitude, and look forward to future business relations, as in the following postcard acknowledgment:

We are glad to give your recent order our immediate careful attention and to follow your shipping instructions exactly.

You may be sure we appreciate this opportunity to serve you and shall be happy to do so when you again decide to order Wolf's fine confections for yourself or as a gift.

Fill-ins enable you to be more specific than you can be in a strict form. For example, the strict form above could read like this as a fill-in (the filled-in parts being in parentheses):

(January 15, 19——)

A (2-lb. box of Wolf's famous Texas Chewie Pecan Pralines) was sent to-day, as you requested, by (parcel post).

Your candy was carefully packed and addressed to (Mr. and Mrs. E. F. Blanton, 2443 Hathaway Road, Syracuse, N.Y.). When it arrives within the next few days we know (they) will enjoy the rich, nutty flavor of this fine candy.

Many thanks for your order. When you want more of Wolf's fine candies for yourself or to please a friend with an inexpensive gift distinctly different, we shall be glad to serve you again.

But even though you can do a good job of matching print and type in a fill-in like this, in almost all instances the irregular spacing calls attention to the fact that the message is a form fill-in. The first two insertions in the example above extend the line of type far beyond what any typist would do if this were individually typed. And see what happens when the recipient's name and address are something as short as "Mr. J. P. Ames, Opp, Iowa"! The line then would be much too short. That is one of the reasons why so many of these are filled in with pen and ink, with no attempt to disguise.

With proper planning, equipment, and patience, however, fill-ins can appear to be individual letters. The following is a good example, where the necessary insertions are the name of the city (at the end of a line, please note), the name of the dealer (displayed attractively with additional spacing all around), and the reader's name (again, at the end of the line and with enough space to allow for a "Miss Rives" or a "Miss Getzendannerich"). A full inside address and date line are also used.

DEAR MISS RIVES:

The enclosed literature describes several Phenix models which we believe will be of interest to you. Although the literature illustrates and describes the instruments, you cannot fully appreciate the beauty of the cabinetry or their magnificent tone without seeing and hearing them.

Phenix instruments are designed for discriminating buyers—for those who have genuine appreciation for refined furniture styling and truly fine musical tone—and they are sold only through high-grade music dealers and selected quality department stores.

We urge you to see these instruments and have them demonstrated to you. You will be thrilled by the perfection of tone that has been attained by Phenix.

Our instruments are on display in Austin at
The J. P. Read Music Company
855 Congress Avenue.
This dealer will be delighted to have the privilege of demonstrating Phenix instruments to you without any obligation whatever, Miss Rives.

Plan to go by for a demonstration.

Sincerely yours

For greatest economy, the preceding letter would be printed; then, when an inquiry comes in *that this form would be a satisfactory answer for,* a typist would need only to type in the date, the inside address, the salutation, and the city, dealer's name, and reader's name in the body of the letter—a matter of two or three minutes. Addressing and stamping (or metering) the envelope would take another two or three.

But because type is hard to match and exact alignment is difficult to make, some firms use an automatic typewriter (also called "robot") for multiple correspondence like this. After the contents of the letter have been decided on, the secretary cuts a kind of stencil of the pattern to guide the automatic typewriter. She inserts paper, types the necessary date, inside address, and salutation, then presses a button, and the machine takes over the typing job. When it comes to the necessary individualized parts, the machine stops, and the secretary types in whatever is necessary. The economy over straight manual typing would not be great if only one such machine were used; most companies, however, have a secretary running at least two at one time, and some have one operator running five at one time! When you consider that these machines produce copy at about twice the speed of the fastest typist and that one typist can easily take the place of three, you can easily see what economies are made.[3]

This economy measure can be applied to form paragraphs as well as to whole letters. The procedure is to write an excellent paragraph covering each frequently recurring point in the firm's correspondence and assign it a code number. These paragraphs are then carefully classified. Some of the classifications may be by type of letter in which the paragraphs are used. For instance, most of the collection man's paragraphs would be useless to the man acknowledging orders, and vice versa. Usually there is a list of standard beginnings and endings. Half-a-dozen ending paragraphs and a dozen beginnings will cover most of the situations. Other paragraphs will be about the various products of the company. Each company correspondent and each typist then gets a book of

---

[3] See Edward N. Mayer, Jr., "20 Kinds of Direct Mail Letters—and How to Use Them Profitably," *Printers' Ink,* 227:40–42, 46, 48, 50, 55, 56, 59, May 6, 1949.

the coded paragraphs, which may be typed manually or made into record rolls for use on an electric typewriter.

When the letter writer starts to dictate, he may write a letter simply as 13, 27, 16, 42. That would mean a four-paragraph letter made up of those standard paragraphs in that order. If he finds no ready-made paragraph for what he wants to say in the second paragraph, he dictates 13, special, 16, 42, and follows with the wording for his special second paragraph. If the same point comes up frequently enough, a good paragraph should be prepared for it and put into the correspondent's book.

Because the paragraphs are used over and over, they are carefully prepared and are therefore better than most correspondents would write quickly under the pressure of dictation. Obviously, the same advantage applies to an entire form letter.

And simple arithmetic shows you that even if you spend thirty to fifty hours on one letter, when you send it to a thousand people, dictation time and transcription time are only a fraction of the time that individual letters would require. In a nutshell that is the whole theory back of form letters. They have to be used to cut correspondence costs, to reduce the burdensome human aspects of the ever-increasing correspondence problems of management, and to expedite replies to people who want and expect information as quickly as they can get it.

Certain dangers exist, however. The greatest is the tendency to use a form when it simply does not apply. When a person writes in asking if Pepperdent has chlorophyll in it, he does not want the answer that "Pepperdent will make your smile brighter because of its new secret ingredient urium! Leading stars of stage and screen praise its refreshing cleansing effectiveness"—all of which may be true but has nothing to do with the inquiry. If the form does not supply the necessary information, consider adding it in a postscript position; many good firms do. If you cannot add it to an existing form, write an individual letter.

Another danger is in broadcasting that the message is a form with such references as:

To all our customers:

Whether you live in Maine or California. . . .

In a broadside (circular) such mass impersonality may be necessary. But in a letter the personal touch pays off. And remember that in every test ever made, the form letter that makes no pretense of being anything else (like the furniture letter on pp. 154–55) results in more returns than the imperfectly disguised form, whether the slipup is due to poor mechanics or inept wording.

One objection to forms is that there is a danger of customers' receiving the same letter more than once. If it does the job, what is the objection? Furthermore, an efficient system where all form messages have code numbers will certainly have some means of recording on the customer's records the symbols of all messages which that customer has received.

Still another danger is in the use of form paragraphs. Unless the paragraphs are all prepared by the same person, stylistic differences will be apparent to some readers. Unless the writers of the paragraphs are careful, they make them too polished to sound natural in a letter; and, even though the paragraphs pass on those two counts, if a poor writer has to write one special to go along with four of the good ones from the correspondence manual, his special may stand out like the proverbial sore thumb.

But form messages can and should be used to help you do a correspondence job that would otherwise prove excessively burdensome.

The question of whether to use a form or not depends on the amount of time and money you have, the recurring nature of the problem, the degree of expediency necessitated—but, most of all, on your own good judgment of whether it will do the particular job.

The suggestions made about form letters in this chapter should be applied to any repetitive letter situation, whether it is one involving acknowledgments, sales, credit, collections, or adjustments. Whether a letter is a form or an individualized letter is not the significant consideration; whether a letter does all it can do to cement good will and build sales is what counts. So, except for occasional incidental references pointing out the ease or wisdom of form treatment in a particular situation, the remainder of this book is devoted to individualized, personalized letters because

1. You can learn more about letter principles and their application that way.
2. You will write much better form letters when you have to as a result of such specific study and practice.
3. In most circumstances calling for a letter, a personal letter will do a more effective job for you than a form.

PROBLEMS

Direct Replies

1. As Fred Best (see Problem 13, p. 121), director of sales of Garland Stoves, South Bend, Indiana, write Anthony Bush confidential details about Eugene Shumaker, one of your top salesmen for the last six years. Shumaker's sales

record fluctuated inconsistently from high sales to low ($10,000 sales in November, usually a slow month, to $2,000 sales in August, usually a record month). When he worked near home, he seemed to sell more. Once away from the family nest, it was hard to get him to send in sales reports or to get him to answer your letters. He knew the restaurant business and could draw up effective commercial kitchens easily, since he was familiar with all gadgets and makes of equipment. Follow-ups on his sales show that restaurant owners like him and appreciate his judgment.

His reasons for quitting, you felt, were that he wanted to move his family south, that he was fed up with so much driving and missed his family. With less pressure, as he might likely have in a smaller company, he might be happy. The recent pressure was making him nervous, as was evidenced by his chain smoking and general restlessness. When he first started, he seemed more interested in details, but during the last three years you've had to be increasingly forceful in getting necessary data. Still, his sales record would warrant your keeping him on if he wanted to stay.

2. A young executive trainee in Des Moines, you have frequently attended alumni meetings of your professional business fraternity, Beta Kappa Phi. It's a good group; you enjoy the programs and the contacts. At a recent meeting you met the national president, and the two of you talked enthusiastically about the worthwhile activities of the fraternity for college men as well as businessmen. You knew you made a favorable impression on him, but you're surprised to receive his letter this morning, asking you to become the state supervisor for Iowa. A quick look in your directory shows you that there are only six chapters, no one of them more than 150 miles from you. And, you reason, all the meetings are in the evening—you wouldn't have to miss many working hours; the fraternity pays traveling expenses; it means only about three trips a month (none in the summer). The more you think about it, the more the idea appeals to you. So you decide to write Mr. Ned Sanderson, President, Beta Kappa Phi, 6097 Fisher Building, West Grand Avenue, Detroit, telling him you'll accept the appointment and asking for further necessary instructions and materials.

3. You are the owner of Pre-Fabricate, Bellville, Illinois, and you are answering the confidential inquiry about Bill Bingham (Problem 15, p. 122) as fairly as you know how. Bill is bright, eager, and too tense. Probably will end up on an ulcer diet if he keeps on driving himself. In many ways you hate to lose him to Manley, but he has reached the top job at your plant and you don't want to hold him back. His wife would like to live in a larger city, and probably Bill would too. He enjoys all the cultural things a city has to offer. Selling probably wouldn't be hard for him for he does enjoy people, is impressive looking, and is persistent. At Pre-Fabricate he has no opportunity to sell. From what you can tell, your 134 employees like him. Just yesterday he worked out a budget problem with one of your truck drivers. Bill spent a long time with the driver, but the driver seemed pleased with the arrangement they worked out. In many ways you'll hate to lose him, but you know that he wants larger horizons. As long as there is opportunity for advancement and challenge, you feel that Bill will stick with a job.

4. As educational director of *Live* magazine, answer the questions in Problem 2, p. 117, with this information: The film comes in two parts; each section lasts 45 minutes. The charge is $8 for each showing, not including shipping charges. No special screen is necessary, and any sound amplifier will work. You are enclosing a more detailed description of the kind of projector they should have to show the film. Teen-agers understand the comparative-religion movie, as do college students. Thirteen thousand high-school students in the Chicago area have seen the movie, and all seemed interested. The University of Chicago has shown it to students in religion during the last year, and they thoroughly appreciated it.

5. As a responsible (and responsive) citizen of the community, you certainly want to do your part to create a better understanding between your town and the students from overseas (see Problem 2, p. 123). Although you cannot be at the meeting in the University Room at 3:00 P.M. to hear more about the Host Family Plan, you want to be a part of the plan. You and your wife (or husband) prefer to "adopt" a European male student; you have spent several summers motoring through England, France, Germany, Italy, and Spain. You would like to have the student over this month for a "cook-out" in the back yard. You remember how much pleasure you got out of visiting in typical European homes. Write the director the necessary letter.

6. Before you write this letter turn to page 124 and read Problem 4. Then assume that, even though you have a crowded schedule, you can conduct a one-night lecture on effective letter-writing procedures at the municipal building at 8:00 P.M. on the specified date. Since you can arrive on an early-afternoon plane, you can participate in an autograph party at the local bookstore, 3:30–5:00.

7. Take a quick look at Problem 10, page 120, before you write this letter. As director of the Chamber of Commerce of your city, you write a welcoming letter to Self-Service Department Stores. When you checked with the leading department stores, they each agreed that the all-day–all-night hours would not hurt their business to any great extent. Since the new store would not hire more than about ten employees, there is no problem in getting help. Another department store, Avon's, operates a cash-and-carry store, and it might offer some competition—similar goods, long hours (9:00 A.M. to 9:00 P.M.), in the factory district. Avon's manager, however, says there's opportunity for a self-service type of store in this fast-growing community.

8. A newspaper editor in Miami, Florida, you have been asked by the Jacksonville *Daily News* to help judge an essay contest. Each year the newspaper awards $1,500, $1,000, and $500 college scholarships to the three Jacksonville high-school seniors who win. Winners are boys and girls who write the best essays on a subject that the newspaper selects and who pass achievement and personality tests. The subject this year is "Crisis in American Education." You and three other judges will read about a hundred essays which will be selected from all the essays turned in. From these, you will select

the six best. Two weeks later you will have to go to Jacksonville and inter-view (at a luncheon) the six, to select three. Since you believe this to be a worthwhile project, you are going to accept, even though there is no fee in-volved. Your expenses to Jacksonville will be paid.

9. Answer the lawyer's letter (Problem 14, p. 122). Your records show (and you remember) that Courtney Landers, age thirty-two, worked for you as a bookkeeper and billing clerk for six months. His address was given as 2209 Main Street, Apartment B-1, Landsdale, Pennsylvania. About three weeks ago he argued with the store manager and was discharged. He was given two weeks' pay in lieu of notice. While in your employ he earned $85 a week. You have no other address for him.

10. Even though it is contrary to your usual policy, you decide you'll send the series *How to Collect by Letter* (Problem 7, p. 125) to the professor as a good-will-building gesture. You hope the teacher and his university stu-dents will profit by the series you're sending separately. The reason you are giving him the series is that you have a few extra copies just as you start to print a revised edition. Perhaps the professor would like to do additional reading in your textbook, *Writing Letters,* published by Hath Company, Chicago. Chapter XI goes into detail.

11. You have been asked by the director and owner of Camp Arrowhead, Men-tone, Wisconsin, to teach swimming, supervise craft making, and be cabin director of a dozen twelve-year-olds of your own sex, June 20–August 20 for $200 and all maintenance. The job appeals to you, and so you are going to accept. All acceptances must be in writing. Write the acceptance.

12. While you were a Captain at Lackland Air Force Base (now a Major—see Problem 12, p. 121), you had under your supervision Sergeant Spencer Sims, an extremely indifferent, slow-thinking (90 IQ) man. According to other sergeants in your office, he was pleasant away from the office. His cleri-cal duties in the parts-supply depot he performed perfunctorily, at best. But when he was shifted to maintenance duties in the motor pool, his perform-ance and attitude improved considerably. Clerical work apparently made him nervous. Because Sims liked working with motors (and seemed to know a great deal about them), you feel that work as a mechanic is probably suited for him. Certainly he was no good with details and record keeping.

Today's mail brings a letter from the G & M Auto Supply Company, Cin-cinnati, signed by Henry Black, personnel director, asking you if you think Sims has the personality to sell. Also—is Sims energetic, bright, and pleasant and careful and accurate in record keeping? The job could grow into some-thing big if he demonstrates ability. Mr. Black says that Sims arrived on time for the interview dressed neatly and conservatively. Write as fair a letter as you can about the man you knew as Sergeant Sims.

13. As Dwight Fitzgerald (Problem 8, p. 125) write the program chairman of Alumni Day at your university, agreeing to talk for 30 minutes at the

noon-day banquet on the future of the college graduate. Assume that you want more information about a point or two in the arrangements and that you collected some interesting information recently when you were on a panel of ten discussing "Growing a Good Executive Crop" at your own manufacturers' association meeting.

Refusals

1. To answer the persuasive request of the Business and Professional Men and Women's group (see Problem 4, p. 124), you (T. M. Filbey) consult your crowded calendar and discover that you have to be at the University of California at the time conducting a letter-writing course via television. You know of several people nearby who perhaps could talk to this enthusiastic group—and at a fee considerably less than yours would have to be. You're glad to see that more people are concerned with effective business letter writing.

2. J. P. Brown (Problem 7, p. 125) has many requests like this—too many, in fact, to send the collection series free. The next issue of *The Reporter of Direct Mail* has an article, "How to Collect by Letter," which summarizes principles but contains no illustrations. Perhaps he and his students would be interested in reading more about the series. Chapter XI from his book, *Writing Letters* (Hath Publishing Company, Chicago), also goes into detail about collection series technique. The reason is the same one why businesses selling tangible products cannot give them away and why doctors and lawyers charge for their services. This is Brown's professional service, by which he earns his living.

3. As Dwight Fitzgerald, of the Fitzgerald Clothing Manufacturing Company (Problem 8, p. 125), you have to write the chairman of Alumni Day that you are flying to Europe next week to inspect some clothing industries and you'll be gone two months. You suggest (do not promise) that perhaps the vice-president, James Noonan, also a graduate of the university, might come in your place. Word the possibility so that the chairman will not feel that you are forcing Noonan on him. Besides visiting ten major companies in Scandinavia and Britain, you plan to visit the University of Helsinki in Finland and Oxford in England.

4. For the E. A. Persons Co., Glendale, California, refuse the request of the Spartan Wives Club (see Problem 13, p. 127) for one of your Rola-Walkas for infants. This is a relatively costly item which you cannot afford to give free in response to the many such requests you receive. You have to make your advertising dollars do the most they can through national magazine pages (such requests would have to be treated as advertising expenses; they could not be treated as charitable contributions). Your contributions go exclusively to orphanages and other such facilities for unfortunate and underprivileged children. Address the letter to Mrs. John Powers, President, 46A, Village Gardens, Baton Rouge, Louisiana.

5. For Porter and Lambert, nationally known manufacturers (and advertisers) of soap and allied products, with headquarters in Chicago, write a turndown letter that will serve as a guide for acknowledging the many requests for contributions. These requests come from a few individuals but primarily from orphanages, homes for the aged, city charity groups of various sorts, and national associations like heart, cancer, and infantile paralysis. Just recently the board decided to refuse all such requests because Porter and Lambert is a national organization and in fairness would have to give to all if it gave to any. Instead, the company gives a percentage of net sales to the Kettering Institute for Medical Research. In this way no one group will be favored—all the Porter and Lambert public will benefit. Sign it for the Director of Public Relations. Address this letter to Mr. P. L. Long, Director, M.O.O.S. Home for Children, Troy, Vermont.

6. Sit in for Professor Meredith (Problem 14, p. 128) and write the letter of refusal to the district literature chairman of the Nebraska Women's Federated Clubs. As worthwhile as you consider the project, it comes when most of the professor's term papers and examinations have to be graded. You are also serving this year on the editorial staff of the American Business Writing Association, and as chairman of the Phonics Committee of the American Linguistics Society. You have no alternative to suggest either. Without dampening the lady's enthusiasm, make it clear that you can't judge the contest entries for her.

7. For the administrator of the Veterans Administration, Washington 25, D.C., answer the following letter:

> DEAR SIRS: I am 11 years old and my name is Chester Rankin, and I have a Belgian sheep dog about a year old. Her name is See-becky and my 2 sisters, and 2 brothers and I think it would be nice if we give her to the blind soldiers. Maybe they would call her See-eye-becky. She is very smart. We would like to give her to help someone.
>
>
> Respfy yrs
> CHESTER RANKIN
> Hondo, New Mexico
>

Touched as you are by the boy's generosity, you have to tell him first that the VA tries to train blinded veterans to use what is called The Long Cane. A cane, after all, is only a piece of wood which does not get old and die and for which no sentimental attachment is formed. Second, dogs must be trained from infancy if they are to be completely dependable for a blind veteran who prefers a seeing-eye dog to The Long Cane. But let him know what a generous offer you think his is and how grateful you are.

8. For the mail-order firm of Butler and Ward, Chicago, write a letter explaining why you no longer have a copy of your Garden Book and why you are not in a position to send one. For the first time, this year you issued a special catalogue devoted to nursery stock. You thought that a million copies would be adequate. But they were not. Now that you know how much in demand such a catalogue is, it is too late to have additional ones printed;

they would not reach the prospective buyers to be available for spring buying. In this letter you want to suggest that these readers see one of the available copies at their local store. Selections are good; prices are very reasonable; you guarantee every plant and will replace if it dies within six months after purchase.

9. Your enthusiastic acceptance letter to Mr. Sanderson out of the way (Problem 2, p. 160) and in your pocket for mailing, you went out to lunch and ran into a former college mate who is province director for a similar organization, Delta Sigma Xi. No sooner were the two of you seated than he began to tell you of the trials and tribulations of his fraternal duties. You listened attentively, making mental notes and already beginning to phrase the polite refusal which—back in the office now—you are going to send Mr. Sanderson (just as soon as you tear to bits the original and the carbon of the "Yes" letter you almost sent).

10. Your supervisor, the director of personnel, Southeastern Utilities Corp., Atlanta, has just handed you the following letter for revision. "Improve it in any way you can," he directed. It is a form letter, addressed in this case to Mr. James Youngson, 541 Blair Lane, Knoxville, Illinois.

> Thank you for taking the time and trouble to come in for a second interview with Southeastern. I enjoyed talking with you about your interests and ambitions and about our job and opportunity.

> There has now been opportunity to review the qualifications of the men under consideration for a training assignment with Southeastern. We have selected those men who seemed best qualified for the limited number of positions available. I am sorry to inform you that you are not among those selected.

> The decision in no way reflects on you or your abilities. We have simply tried to select those men who seemed most likely to be happy and successful in our particular company and our particular type of work. The men we selected seemed best suited from the standpoint of background and experience. The final selection was not an easy decision in any case.

> We do appreciate your interest in Southeastern and thank you for taking the time and trouble to come in for a second interview. And we hope that you will quickly find the right job—the job which will provide the maximum of success and satisfaction for you.

11. Graduated and successfully launched in the career of your choice, you are trying to carve a place for yourself in the community; and so you have assumed duties involving responsibility and extra time in connection with civic, religious, and fraternal affiliations. Today's mail brings a persuasively written request that you take on the job heading up the Red Feather Drive raising funds for needy families in your community. You are refusing because of the time it would take from your professional duties (which you simply cannot afford), and because you feel that you do not have adequate

contacts and knowledge of the community and that someone with more maturity, experience, and knowledge could do a better job. Offer to serve in some minor capacity.

12. For the signature of the Postmaster-General, Washington, D.C., prepare a letter that, with few changes, could be mailed in reply to the many requests received for special commemorative stamps, requests which cannot be honored. Before any new stamp is made, there is a set of rules which the Post Office Department observes. One is that whatever goes on a stamp must be of historical interest. And no live subject may be used. Cities with centennials, animal lovers' leagues, sports associations—to all these and more the Postmaster-General must say no. Each new issue that is approved must have a circulation of at least 75,000,000, to be sure the necessary planning and printing expenses are taken care of. Issues of limited subject or geographical interest would in the long run only increase the cost of running the Department and further decrease the chances for extra services. Address this refusal to the Animal Care League of Westchester, Connecticut.

13. In your capacity as personnel director of the Lancaster Iron Works, Lehigh, Pennsylvania, you have received the request of Mr. Robert V. Carstairs, graduate student at the University of Pennsylvania, making a study of scholarship and success in business. He asks you to give the title, age, college grade average, and salary for each executive in your company. Since he does not ask you to reveal identity, this is really no violation of confidential information; but you consider it more than a mere business courtesy. Even to arrange for some competent clerk to go through your files and copy down the material would be time-consuming and disruptive; so you are refusing the request.

Invited Sales

1. As owner of Snipe's Typewriter Shop, 198 Dearborn Street (Problem 5, p. 117) answer the university student. Machines are stripped and all worn parts replaced by new factory parts. There are no worn parts or faulty mechanism. Parts are guaranteed for 90 days, and any necessary servicing during that time is free. The machines average five to ten years in age. All parts are scientifically cleaned and expertly refinished or polished. All enameled parts are repainted with baked-on enamel. Each machine is assembled, adjusted by specialists. The new models have some plastic parts, but your reconditioned ones are all metal and enamel. You can sell him a 15-inch carriage Regal typewriter with elite type, or a 13-inch carriage C. L. Smyth in pica. Since you've cut the price low, to pass savings on to your customers, all sales are final. In your letter to this student try to sell him on the five-year-old 13-inch C. L. Smyth, gray crackle finish, pica type machine, for $118.50 (though the eight-year-old Regal is a good buy). Perhaps he can come to Snipe's and see the machine's overhead paper bail, automatic ribbon reverse, and keyset tabulators. Each machine comes with a complete instruction book and dust cover.

2. The Dictabell Corporation, 487 Lexington Avenue, New York 17, N.Y., has been running advertisements in *Time, Business Week,* and *U.S. News & World Report* plugging its time-master dictating machine, the Dictabell. "Does Paperwork Stand in Your Way?" the ads read; "Nightwork Goes Easier with the Dictabell Time-Master. . . ." "Reasons Why Dictabell's Time-Master Makes Your Job Easier!"

As sales manager, you prepared a four-page folder in advance of the campaign. It illustrates the machine, explains its uses, and lists two dozen outstanding companies using the Dictabell. A short letter accompanies it. This has been adequate up to now to answer most of your inquiries. A letter in today's mail, however, brings home to you the realization that no form letter ever handles all inquiries satisfactorily; it is signed by Mr. Hubert Talyor, president of Whiteside Mills (Waycross, Athens, and Atlanta, Georgia):

> Being a businessman, I'm naturally interested in new ideas and more efficient ways of cutting down costs in office routine. The Time-Master probably would save time and give my secretaries more freedom to type the dictation from the Dictabell plastic recording. But how much does the machine cost, how long a message can you record on the plastic Dictastrip, and how much does each Dictastrip cost? Is there any guarantee? And what about the plastic deteriorating after it has been in the files for several years? Can you reuse the Dictastrips?

Answer Mr. Talyor, 519 South 20th Street, Atlanta 3, Georgia. The machine sells for $350 plus federal and state tax. It is an electronically controlled stenographer, made of durable, light-weight steel. There is a guarantee of 1 year on parts, 90 days on batteries, and 90 days of free labor. Maintenance on the machine is done by factory-trained personnel at a cost of $24 per year, in the city, and $29 per year outside the city. Each Dictastrip sells for 4¢; they may be purchased in convenient packages of 100 for $4. Dictabell has 250 offices and agents in United States cities, and none of the agents has ever reported any problem with the filing of the plastic strips. Even after a year's storage in an office without air conditioning in Cleveland, Ohio, several Dictastrips were tried, and the recordings were as clear as the day they were made.

Reassure him that this endless belt of thin, tough, uniform red plastic saves time. He can dictate anywhere and at any time, and his secretary can transcribe later; he can even mail several Dictastrips in a standard envelope to his secretary if he's on a trip. Dictastrips take less storage space than carbon copies of letters. It's true that each strip can be used just once, but he can dictate for 30 minutes on one strip. Your Atlanta representative will be glad to bring a machine for a two-weeks' free trial. A reply card is enclosed.

3. You are sales representative of the John Yauger Company, 2030 Seventh Avenue, Miami, the distributors of Minutefold doors. An inquiry from Foster Wells (Problem 6, page 118) has been forwarded to you from the home office in New Castle, Indiana. Besides sending Mr. Wells a 27-page

booklet with pictures of your custom fabric and Woodmaster line doors, you are going to answer all questions in a personal letter. The Woodmaster Minutefold, like the custom fabric, doors come in either 8- or 9½-foot heights. Since the ceiling is 9 feet high, the 8-foot door could be hung on a standard track (1¼″ by 1¼″) attached to a partition dropped one foot from the present ceiling. Woodmaster mahogany finish for a 14-foot by 8-foot door costs $163, while oak, birch, or walnut runs $204. Page 17 of the booklet shows the finishes. These hardwood veneers are laminated to the warp-free particle board core with thermosetting, waterproof synthetic resin glue. All surfaces are coated with conversion clear finish—the finest available today. Standard tests show that this tough, mar-resistant finish cannot be removed without sufficient force to damage the wood itself. The inner core of each 6-inch panel is made of particle board to resist warping and provide maximum dimensional stability. Even though Vero Beach has a wet climate during the winter months, you can assure Mr. Wells there's no need to worry about the woodmaster Minutefold warping in the light of the 1,200 you've installed in the last 4 years. Doors are not 100 per cent soundproof. They are sound resistant. Sweep strips at the top and bottom reduce the noise about one fifth. The action you're seeking here is for Mr. Wells to fill out the reply card you enclose naming a time when you can bring samples and talk with him about installing the folding door.

4. As owner of Higgins Reconditioned Bicycle Shop (see Problem 1, p. 116) answer Mrs. Adams' letter. You have six bicycles with balancing wheels. Three are in the 20-inch wheel size, and three are in the 24-inch size. Which would she prefer? You feel that her daughter would outgrow the 20-inch when she was about eight, but the 24-inch size she could use for many years. You do not send any bike on trial. The guarantee against defective materials and workmanship is for 30 days. She'll have to send $20 with her order and $1.50 for shipping. All unnecessary steel and metal trimmings have been eliminated, so that the bike weighs 5–11 pounds less than ordinary bicycles. The steel frame is strong enough, and it is not made from bicycles that were smashed. All tires and all seats are new. And you do have a red bike in the 24-inch size.

5. As sales manager of Mengel Furniture, Grand Rapids, Michigan, answer the inquiry about built-ins (Problem 11, p. 121), sending a two-page folder, price list, and handy order blank with your letter. Standard units (two 5-drawer maple chests with brass pulls, two beveled mirrors, two 24-inch closets) cover a 10-foot wall. With hat and blanket storage above, a unit figures to the total price of $542. Matching desks can be bought separately for $44 each. When these units are placed back to back, a thin wall can be used between, thus cutting building costs and decreasing the noise from room to room. The University of Michigan has had Mengel built-ins in New Hall for 10 years and just this year refinished the chests at a small price—much less cost than refinishing individual pieces. Fanning Hall, Florida State University, put in built-ins 5 years ago and the building committee plans to do three new dormitories with Mengel. By the time two

closets are built with hardware and doors (labor and material averages $50 a door) and two chests plus mirrors are bought, the cost is more than the price of the Mengels. All seasoned hardwoods and durable fixtures are used.

6. Stratford Laboratories, Inc., Box 462, Ann Arbor, Michigan, developed and tested a beauty cream Vita-o-zyme that works from within, on a moist skin, activating neglected and abused tissues. To get state franchise holders, the company ran an advertisement in *Drug Record.* The response was so favorable that the president, George B. Stratford, wants to send out a letter to each person who answered the ad to tell him more about the cream and to see if he will be a state distributor. Stratford wants the letter sent under his name, but he wants you (an employee of Lutz Direct Mail Agency, Detroit) to write the letter.

You can remind your reader that the cosmetic business is an industry without recession. Well over $4,000,000,000 a year are spent on cosmetics. Revlon and Avon each sell over $100,000,000 yearly. The pursuit of beauty, of youth, of charm is universal. Consumer demand for an outstanding beauty preparation that will stop or limit the ravages of advancing years is enormous, and women—especially those thirty-five and over—will spend money for products that will help them look young. Over 3,000 jars were dispensed free, formula after formula tried and discarded, before the company was satisfied with the product. The result of all this testing is smooth, delicately perfumed Vita-o-zyme. Six months ago Stratford distributed 800 jars for testing. Women who used this secret formula achieved a firmer, softer skin and were enthusiastic over this "Revelation in Beauty Culture."

As Stratford builds up the franchise system, national ads will appear in *Charm, Life,* and *Vogue;* and there will be display cartons for stores and beauty parlors. Vita-o-zyme will sell at $7.50 for the 2-ounce and $12.50 for the 4-ounce jar. Each state franchise holder receives a 65 per cent discount, plus an allowance of 50¢ for advertising and delivery on each jar, provided that the quota is met. The distributor also receives all possible help in setting up an office and in training a sales force. Quotas for the first two months will not be hard to meet: 3 gross of the 2-ounce ($3,240.00) and 1 gross of the 4-ounce jars ($1,800.00)—or total sales of $5,040. With 65 per cent discount, the net cost to a state distributor amounts to $3,-276.00, less 40 per cent discount to stores ($1,310.00), which leaves a balance of $1,965.00. With overhead for delivery at 50¢ per jar ($288.00), the grand total would be $1,677.60 for the 576 jars (4 gross). Stratford is a reliable company; references such as Dun and Bradstreet and the First National Bank, Ann Arbor, will back up this statement. Send along an illustrated folder with testimonials. Ask him in the clincher to become a Vita-o-zyme distributor.

Your state franchise costs $10,000, but an income of $10,000–$25,000 is entirely possible for a man with drive. The state franchise holder can sell local franchises, thus recovering part of his investment, but—more significantly—receiving commissions (called "overwrite") on the sales of all the sales representatives in his state.

7. Answer the letter in Problem 7, page 118, for the Universal Corporation in Cincinnati. Mr. James M. Kirby of North Platte, Nebraska, is considering your electric wall panels for his new home; he likes the noiseless feature, and his wife likes the cleanliness angle. He has included a sketch of his home with room measurements and indicated the kind of insulation he will use. He and Mrs. Kirby are concerned, however, about the possibility of burns to their two children, four and six; about the necessity for additional heavy-duty wiring (with its additional expense); about the costs of operation; and the problems of installation and maintenance in an area where no one, as far as they can find out, has ever heard of your Radiant Glass Panel. As far as burns are concerned, your panels are much safer than metals; a person can touch the exposed surface without burning himself, though if he held his hand to the surface long enough he would, of course, suffer injuries. Additional wiring is necessary, too, but the units operate on 110 volts, not 220. From his sketch you calculate that one unit will heat every room adequately, with the exception of the living room, where he will need two. That makes a total of nine units. Since the units operate most efficiently if no more than three are on one circuit, he should plan on three additional circuits beyond what he is already estimating. They may involve as much as $50 additional expense for wiring—but that's a lot cheaper than the metal ducts and grills of a forced-air or hot-water central heating system. Any reliable electrician can install them; they're no more complicated than a light fixture which is flush with the ceiling or wall. Once installed, there's nothing like a light bulb to burn out and replace. Costs of operation are higher than for gas or oil, certainly. But the rate is almost certain to be lower than the minimum 3¢ per kilowatt hour ordinarily charged by private power companies. With all the electrical appliances that modern homes have, heating costs accumulate at 2¢ or 1½¢ and usually at 1¢ per kilowatt hour. Furthermore, radiant heat at 68° is as comfortable as other forms of heating at 72°. Also, with the individual room thermostats, Radiant Glass Panel users do not have to keep some rooms as warm as others. For these reasons, users in the area around Cincinnati have heated five-room homes during the cold season for $150 additional electricity beyond what they had consumed prior to using radiant heating. (In TVA areas, of course, the costs are much lower; owners of 1,500-square-foot houses heat with electricity for as little as $8 a month.) You can assure Mr. Kirby that his nine panels would maintain his house (with its insulation in side walls as well as ceiling) at 68° for a month of zero weather at a cost of no more than $30. Repeated tests in your own experimental laboratory have demonstrated this, and the experience of 20,000 users in all areas have confirmed it. Radiant Glass Panels carry the seal of approval of the Underwriters' Laboratory Association. You guarantee the units against defective workmanship for one year. Since you have no dealer anywhere near Mr. Kirby, you'll sell to him direct for $75 a panel, cash with order, f.o.b. Cincinnati (your usual charge is $85 a panel installed). Stress again the benefits of the ultraviolet rays, easier housekeeping, and the advantages of individual room temperatures when desired.

8. Answer the letter in Problem 8, page 119, for Wright-Lynch Research, Inc., 50 Rockefeller Plaza, New York 20, N.Y. Duron wall covering is easily cleaned with a damp cloth and can even be washed with soap and water.

Unlike most acoustical materials, Duron will not crumble or dust, and its colors stay bright. Inert to bacteria and fungus, it has wide applications in modern hospitals and would be excellent for children's rooms. Three new Veterans Hospitals in San Francisco, St. Louis, and Chicago have just installed Duron.

If he uses the 20″ × 20″ tile, he'd need about 140 tiles, and the cost would be between $160 and $170; the 10 × 20 averages out to about $190, and the 10 × 10 size, $210 (for tiles alone). Since you have no dealer anywhere near, you'll sell to him direct, cash with order. To help him select the color he prefers, a color chart is enclosed. The "accent" or "tweed" tiles are described in detail on page 9 of the enclosure. Reassure him of the acoustical quality. Radio station WKBT, Memphis, recently installed Duron in its studios. Many listeners wrote the station praising the improved quality of the broadcasting. For the Hi-Fi enthusiast, Duron offers an ideal acoustical treatment for the recreation room. Tell him also about the flame-resistant quality. This wall covering has been tested for flame resistance by leading independent laboratories. It has been given the rating of "Class A" with respect to U.S. Federal Specification SS-A-118b for Acoustical Materials. It has also been found highly acceptable when tested in accordance with the American Society for Testing Materials Specifications C209–55T and E84–50T. And it has been rated FHA-Acceptable as a building material in all 50 states. Suggest he order this modern wall covering direct from you.

9. Since the article in *Time* last month, you have had over 2,000 inquiries about the Cinva-Ram-Block Press. Prepare a letter addressed to the engineer from the Grande Oil Company that will serve as a form for answering the other inquiries (Problem 9, p. 120) with these facts: He can buy the machine for $150. It makes rock-hard bricks for less than a penny apiece. With the proper proportions of earth and cement (90–95 per cent dirt and 5–10 per cent cement for Venezuela) there is no danger of the house crumbling or washing away. The only way to service the machines is to send them back to Ibec in New York. Since there are no intricate or delicate parts, there's not much likelihood of need for service. To help clinch the sale, send along a brochure and order blank.

10. Assume that you are travel consultant for World Wide Travel Agency, Madison Avenue, Chicago (Problem 3, p. 117) and answer the college student's inquiry. For just $450 the student can fly round trip to London from New York on austerity class. He will be served sandwiches instead of a full-course dinner and have 3 inches less space between seats than on tourist class. Paris seems to be the best place to buy and sell a foreign car, especially early in the season. Automobile Club de France, 6 Place de la Concorde, or the AAA 9 Rue de la Paix, will supply details on reputable dealers and help arrange to get the kind of car he wants. Car rentals vary from $7.70 per day, including the first 80 miles (2 cents per mile after 80 miles) in England to an average of $4 a day on the Continent. Although gasoline costs 60¢ a gallon, a light European car averages 30 miles to the gallon. World Wide will be glad to help the students plan their trip and for only $2 will gladly send them booklets giving details about places to stay, eating places, and tourist attractions in each country.

VII. Orders and Acknowledg-

ments

∿∿∿∿∿∿∿∿∿∿∿∿∿∿∿∿∿∿∿∿∿∿∿∿∿∿∿∿∿∿∿∿

BUSINESS BY MAIL

BECAUSE business by mail broadens the market of both buyer and seller and thus serves a need of many people, it is big business. By using the mail you can almost literally buy the variety of products in all the markets of the world, or you can make the world your market.

When you think of buying and selling by mail you may think only of such large mail-order houses as Sears, Montgomery Ward, and Spiegel; but business by mail is much more extensive than that. Think of the increasing volume of mail sales in large department stores like Macy's in New York, Hudson's in Detroit, and Marshall Field's in Chicago; consider the tremendous volume of industrial and mercantile business by mail as manufacturers purchase their supplies and sell their finished products; remember the marketing of seasonal and regional produce (fruit, game, syrup, candy) all over the country and all the year round; include farmers' orders for various supplies, machinery, and replacement parts; and then combine all these and you begin to realize just how big business by mail really is.

Yet buying by mail is not all tea and crumpets; it has some disadvantages:

1. The buyer has no chance to see, feel, and try the product before buying.
2. Under the best of circumstances, a purchase by mail takes from two to ten days for delivery, depending on distance and shipping method.
3. With machinery and appliances requiring installation or servicing, the purchaser may be on his own or may have to depend on the service departments of local stores selling competing goods.
4. The customer has to go to the trouble to write an order.

To help the broadened-market idea (and sometimes lower prices) to overcome these disadvantages, sellers by mail

1. Almost always write catalogues with pictures and full descriptions which often give a better idea of the goods than you can get from clerks about merchandise in local stores; offer excellent guarantees; and follow liberal policies on returned goods.
2. Usually try to fill orders as promptly as possible; sometimes pay shipping charges; send by the fastest possible methods if the buyer is really in a hurry.
3. Publish installation, operation, and service manuals, including carefully numbered parts lists; sometimes make standing service arrangements with local mechanics.
4. Provide well-designed order blanks and stamped, addressed envelopes with their catalogues.

Indeed, the only problems connected with writing an order appear when you do not have the blanks and must write a letter.

ORDERS

An order is probably the easiest kind of letter to write. You have no problem of getting attention or interest, and no conviction or persuasion is necessary in this Type-A letter. The reader is in business to sell goods. If you write clearly enough to let him know what you want and make satisfactory plans to pay for it, you'll get an answer. A poor order letter may, however, cause the reader some trouble and bring results a little different from what you really want.

As a considerate and efficient letter writer, you should write orders that will be easy for a clerk to fill and that will bring you just what you want. The basic requirements, as you can see from almost any order blank, are five:

1. Make them orders, not just hints. An order is the acceptance of a definite offer to sell or is your own offer to buy, usually the latter. When an acceptance is mailed, a legal contract is formed. Such hints as "I am in

need of" or "I'd like to have" are neither acceptances nor offers to buy (though they usually will bring the goods). The usual beginning for an order is "Please send me. . . ."

2. Describe the goods completely. Give the stockroom clerk all the details he needs to select just the items you want from his huge stock. With a catalogue or parts list in hand, you will have no trouble. Tell what catalogue you are using, especially if it is any but a single current one. Though the catalogue number alone usually identifies adequately except for color and size, give four or five clean-cut columns of information, preferably in this sequence: (1) quantity desired; (2) catalogue number, if any; (3) name of product and as many details as are appropriate of model, color, size, material, grade or quality, pattern, finish, monogram initials; (4) unit price (sometimes not given as a separate column); (5) total price for the designated quantity of the item.

In the absence of a catalogue, you probably will not know the identifying number and may not know the price or other pieces of information exactly. Your information will likely go into two or three columns: quantity, name and description, and perhaps estimated total price. To supplement the inexact information, then, you may need to explain more fully by telling how the product is to be used, and in some cases by sending exact drawings.

The final test of completeness is whether you tell everything the stockroom clerk needs to know to fill the order without guessing. Inadequate information will cause delay and costly additional correspondence to clear up the missing information or guesswork and perhaps the wrong goods.

3. Write a separate, single-spaced paragraph for each item, with double spacing between paragraphs. Hanging indention (that is, further indention of lines after the first in each paragraph) will enable the clerk to read easily and check items as he packages them.

4. Make clear how you expect to pay. Otherwise your shipment may be sent by the C.O.D. (cash on delivery) method, which costs you more, or it may be delayed until your credit is checked or your money is received. Some firms require a cash-with-order payment of at least 10% even for C.O.D. shipment. If you have not established credit but want goods charged, you should provide credit information with the order (see pp. 372–73).

If you want neither credit nor C.O.D. shipment, several methods of remitting are open to you. Perhaps the personal check is the most common and convenient; and, when canceled, it serves as a receipt. Money orders (postal, express, or telegraph) are less convenient, but they give greater security to the receiver at the cost of a fee to the sender. The telegraph offers speed, but at a high fee. Certified and cashier's checks and bank drafts provide the same security to the receiver, but they are too inconvenient for ordinary use, except for large amounts. For small amounts, coins, currency, and stamps may be used at the sender's risk. In sending coins, put them in coin cards before putting them into the envelope.

Regardless of how you remit, you should refer to the remittance in the letter and tell its form, amount, and intended application.

And don't forget to include any shipping charges or sales taxes that may be due.

5. Specify the *where, when,* and *how* of shipment. Usually your name and return address cover the *where* unless you are ordering gifts to be sent directly to somebody else. Firms selling by mail try to fill orders the day they come in; but if the goods are temporarily out of stock, it is common practice to hold an order a reasonable time. If you can't wait that reasonable time, you'd better say so. The nature of the goods or your established practice may make the desired *how* of shipment adequately clear. If not, specify.

The following typical order letter illustrates the five points.

Please send me the following items listed in your current spring and summer catalogue:

```
1  60 C 6587L  Glass casting rod, Model
               162, extra light action,
               5 ft. 8 in..............$ 8.95

1  60 CP 6302  Pflueger Summit reel,
               Model 1993L.............. 13.75

2  60 C 6846   Cortland "Cam-o-flage"
               nylon casting line,
               10-lb. test, 100-yd.
               lengths @ 2.30...........  4.60
                    Total              $27.30
```
The enclosed check for $28 covers the price, sales tax, and parcel post charges.

As I plan to go fishing a week from next Saturday (June 26), I will want the equipment by that time.

The following letter did a much more difficult job of ordering. Test it against the five requirements set up for a good order letter. Note how the writer made very clear just what he wanted without benefit of a catalogue or parts list to give him the code numbers and prices of the items.

Please send me the following parts for Little Giant Shallow Well Water System P4/12818. Since I have no catalogue, I am describing each part carefully.

1   Valve rubber, 1 1/4 inches in diameter with 5/16 inch hole. It is one of four that work under springs on the valve plate.

1   Crank pin. Apparently this is a steel pin of highly special design. Its threaded end, 7/16 inch in diameter and 11/16 inch long, screws into the eccentric arm on the end of the drive shaft so that the rest of the pin forms the crankshaft. That is, the big end of the connecting rod fits around it. (See drawings on the attached sheet.) The crankshaft part of this pin is an eccentric 1/2 inch in diameter and 11/16 inch long.

1   Connecting rod, as drawn on the attached sheet. Apparently it is brass or bronze. Please note the specifications as to size of hole. For other models, I know that the sizes are a little different.

I estimate that these parts will cost approximately $4. I am enclosing my check for $5 to cover all charges, including tax and parcel post. You can send me your regular refund check if the charges are less or send C.O.D. for the difference if they are more.

I'll appreciate your trying to fill the order promptly. My pump, much needed these days, is about to quit on me.

ACKNOWLEDGMENTS

Poorly written orders cost their buyer-writers much delay in getting the desired goods, and they cost sellers lots of headaches and money (spent on letters required to get the needed information). But poor acknowledgements, for which the sellers are wholly responsible, cost them much more—in loss of good will and customers.

The acknowledgment letter should be an effective means of increasing good will and promoting business. A man who orders from you evidently has a favorable attitude toward your firm and its goods or he wouldn't be ordering. That is a healthful climate for business. Your job in acknowledging his order is to keep it that way by giving him satisfaction.

He expects to get what he ordered, to get it promptly, and to have his business appreciated. If not, he expects a prompt and reasonable explanation. To give him less is to make a customer for somebody else.

Frequently a businessman who handles a large volume of orders, however, comes to look upon them as routine matters and to write his answers accordingly. In so doing, he forgets three things: (1) the individual customer usually sends comparatively few orders, and they are not routine to him at all; (2) a routine acknowledgment of them strikes him as indifference; and (3) indifference, according to a U.S. Department of Commerce survey, is responsible for at least 67 per cent of lost customers.

There may be justifying reasons (rationing, strikes, impossibility of always estimating demand accurately, as well as incomplete orders from the buyer) why a businessman cannot fill some orders promptly, or at all. But there is no reason why he cannot acknowledge those orders promptly, as the following postcard reply from a large department store does.

DEAR CUSTOMER:

Thank you for your letter concerning *a ladder.*

It is receiving our attention, and you will receive a reply to it as soon as possible.

Sincerely yours,

Obviously, a form postcard cannot do all that a letter can, but it can reflect a service attitude and thus help to retain good will. Least of all is there excuse for not showing appreciation for orders. (Italicized words are the fill-in, typed if you can, penned if you're swamped!):

As you requested, the *turntable for Scrabble has been sent to Mrs. M. W. Colby.*

Thank you for calling on us. We hope that you have found our service convenient and that you will write to us often.

There is scarcely any excuse, either, for the seller who does not do more than the minimum that the customer ordinarily expects. A good businessman makes even a small first order an opportunity to cement a lasting business relationship. Ignoring that opportunity by turning the letter writing over to untrained employees who will give acknowledgments only routine treatment is one way to send customers to competitors. To take the opportunity requires only a knowledge of the basic principles of letter writing plus a knowledge of the kinds of things that need to be said in different kinds of acknowledgments.

POSSIBLE CONTENTS

One element is essential in every acknowledgment; and there are five other supplementary ones from which you may select those best suited to the type of acknowledgment you are writing.

1. An explanation of what you are doing about the order (the one essential element).

2. Resale talk (to keep the customer convinced that he made a wise choice in buying the particular goods and in buying from you).

   It is especially important in the acknowledgment to a new customer or to an old one who has not bought the items before. It serves to reassure both about the quality of the stock you carry; and it reassures a new customer of the reliability of the house as well. In general, resale can be introduced best as incidental phrases interwoven into sentences which carry another message. It is made most effective if it causes the reader to visualize himself using and enjoying your products and services. *Warning:* In trying to resell your guarantee and repair service, don't suggest that your customer is probably going to have trouble with your products and need repair service.

3. Evidence of a sincere service attitude.

   Your best evidence is speed, interest, and care in handling the customer's order. In addition, you can give him information about your various services: different departments, credit, store hours, free delivery, mail- and telephone-order service, and the like. If you have some kind of related goods in which he might be interested, you can mention them in a little low-pressure sales-promotion talk. For example, if he has ordered a tennis racquet, he will need tennis balls.

4. Encouragement of future orders.

   The degree of encouragement should be adapted to the situation. If the thought grows out of sales-promotion material on related goods, you should suggest specific action and make that action easy. The common general endings like "We hope to serve you again soon" and "We look forward to your continued patronage" do little good to encourage future ordering.

5. In the case of a new customer, a hearty welcome.

   Just as you would to a newcomer to any group of which you are a member, you will surely extend a welcome to a newcomer to your business.

6. Evidence of appreciation for the order.

   Your customer, whether new or old, will expect you to show some appreciation for his business and the honor he does you in offering you his trade. Such appreciation may be expressed in a sincere but simple statement of thanks. You can usually save words and convey both a welcome and appreciation better by implication, however, through the interest you take and the service attitude you show in handling the order. At least you can show your gratitude without giving the impression of greedy pleasure in having caught another goose to pluck.

You are not likely to want all these six types of content in one acknowledgment, but in most acknowledgments you will find good use for at least two of the supplementary types as well as the one essential. That does not mean that you need to write a paragraph, or even a sentence, on each one. If you try, you are almost certain to come out with a strange letter. Instead, you may have all six in a two-paragraph letter. Usually all or parts of two or three of them should be combined in one paragraph, and sometimes in the same sentence. Often a well-written acknowledgment will seem to concentrate on the first, second, and fourth types of content but will be so worded that it leaves no doubt about a sincere service attitude, the hearty welcome to a new customer, and gratitude for his business. Just which of the six possible contents of an acknowledgment to use and stress cannot be decided, however, except in terms of the classes of acknowledgments.

After you have checked your orders against your stock, you'll find that you can classify your replies as follows, according to what you will do with the various orders:

1. Standard acknowledgments—of orders which you can fill immediately.
2. Incomplete-order acknowledgments.
3. Back-order acknowledgments—of orders which you can't fill right away (until you replenish stock).
4. Declining acknowledgments—of orders which you turn down.
5. Substitute-selling acknowledgments—of orders which you hope to fill with a substitute, because you don't have exactly what was ordered.
6. Combination acknowledgments—of orders involving more than one of the preceding five situations.

STANDARD ACKNOWLEDGMENTS

Of the six classes of acknowledgments, the most numerous and therefore the most important is the standard—acknowledging an order you can fill immediately. It is an easy letter to write.

Clearly, the standard acknowledgment is a good-news letter (Type A). The beginning should be a direct answer to the biggest question in the reader's mind—what you are doing about his order. To perform its legal function, the standard acknowledgment must identify and accept the order. Thus it completes a contract. The identification is by date and one or more of order number, exact relisting, or sometimes merely a general naming of the class of goods. Certainly, when the list is long or the value great, the goods should be listed on an attached invoice and the invoice referred to in the letter.

To perform its business function, the standard acknowledgment must clear up the financial arrangements and tell when, where, and how you are sending the goods. The approximate arrival date is also desirable, not only as a convenience to the customer but as a basis for the psychologically favorable effect of his visualizing himself actually receiving and using the goods. On small orders to customers who have established credit or sent the exact amount with the order, the financial arrangements are frequently omitted because they are already clear.

If you are acknowledging the first order from a new customer, the acknowledgment will certainly include a hearty welcome and will stress resale and the forward look even more than a letter to an old customer. The welcome is sometimes interwoven or implied in what you are doing about the order; but ordinarily it comes later, frequently combined with an expression of appreciation.

Whether new or old, the customer will probably like you better for expressing appreciation, perhaps even interwoven in the first paragraph. In most cases, however, you can demonstrate gratitude more effectively with statements of how you've handled the order, resale talk, and offers to be of service again.

The middle section of the standard acknowledgment is devoted to the financial details not already completed, any resale talk of more than phrase length, and explicit evidence of service attitude.

Encouragement to future ordering in a success-conscious forward look to the future is the almost invariable ending for the standard acknowledgment.

All this discussion of what goes in the letter, how, why, and where, may make you think that such an acknowledgment is not easy to write. Actually, it is. Here's an example of how the parts are all put together for an effective personalized acknowledgment covering all points specifically:

> You should receive your eight cases of Tuff Paper towels in time for Friday afternoon shoppers; they were sent by prepaid express this morning.
>
> The 27¢ voucher attached to this letter is your change after we deducted $9.20 charges and 53¢ express from your $10 check.
>
> Thank you for your order. I believe this is our first shipment of paper products to you. We are glad that we can serve you in this additional way.

You'll find that these Tuff Papers have a fast turnover, Mr. Ford, because housewives like the way they soak up grease, dust off spots, and save cloth towels from many dirty jobs. And you'll like their attractive small packaging that takes up a minimum of display and shelf space. Your mark-up figures out at exactly 29%.

For more information about Tuff Paper dish rags and window washers, colorful shelf paper that your customers will like for their pantries, and other paper products that every household needs, look in the enclosed booklet. Notice that each article carries the usual Tuff Paper margin of profit.

Perhaps you'd like to take advantage of our regular terms of 2/10, n/60 on future orders. If so, we'll be glad to consider your credit application when you fill in and return the enclosed form. And when you order, if you want window and shelf displays to help you sell, just say so. Then watch Tuff Paper kitchen paper products bring Altoona women into your store for frequent repeat sales.

The trouble with this kind of acknowledgment is that it costs a dollar or more. To be specific on all points, to adapt the message to an individual, and to make it persuasive require an average-length, individually dictated letter. And it will cost money. But when the prospect of numerous future orders depends on the letter, the businessman would be foolish to do less. In some situations enough is involved to make him willing to spend even more to produce the most effective letter he can, rather than risk an unfavorable reaction on the part of the customer.

The inability to recognize situations that deserve full treatment and the general inclination to save even a little time and money on correspondence frequently lead to trouble. Pinching pennies by dashing off personalized letters that are just a little too short to be adequate is poor economy. The result is comparable to throwing out *almost* enough rope to reach a drowning man. If you are going to write a personalized letter, make it a good one. Its cost does not increase in proportion to length. A question you should always answer before cheapening your correspondence is whether you lose more in results, including good will, than you save on costs.

But there are many cases in which a form card or letter serves admirably as an acknowledgment, as we talked about and illustrated in the discussion, "Form Letters" (p. 154). The preceding Tuff Paper letter could be handled in a form message like this one (which, incidentally, *could* get by for acknowledging a repeat order):

You should receive the Tuff Paper products you ordered in just a few days; they are already on the way.

CHECK LIST FOR STANDARD ACKNOWLEDGMENTS

1. Of greatest interest to the reader is the complete, accurate shipment.
   a) Send the goods in the first sentence—to emphasize the good news.
   b) Follow the goods through to arrival and reader satisfaction in using them.
   c) Clearly identify the order by one or more of date, number, specific reference to the goods by name—perhaps a complete listing.
   d) If you list, tabulate—in the letter if short; on a referred-to invoice if long.
   e) Clear up any confusion about payment details.
   f) Consider whether method of shipment should be identified.
2. Resale is part of acknowledgments to reassure the reader about his choice.
   a) Make it specific.
   b) Keep it short.
   c) Adapt it to your product and reader (consumer versus dealer, for instance).
3. Resale on the house, especially important to new customers, may be used with others.
   a) For a consumer: personal shopping, delivery schedules, credit possibilities.
   b) For a dealer: salesmen, manuals, displays, and advertising aids and programs.

Thank you for your order. We are glad that we can serve you in this way.

You'll find that Tuff Paper products have a fast turnover; housewives like the way they can be used for many messy household cleaning jobs and then quickly and easily be disposed of.

You will like their attractive packaging that takes up a minimum of shelf and display space. And the sizable markup!

Read the enclosed booklet for more information about Tuff Paper dish rags, window washers, colorful shelf paper, and other paper products that every household needs.

Use the handy order blank and business-reply envelope in the back of the booklet when you want to order the additional Tuff Paper products that your customers will be asking for.

(Signature)

(Postscript position could handle special material.)

How many of the six kinds of acknowledgment-letter content can you find in the following form letter from *Time?* Clearly, resale is given the major emphasis, and perhaps too much of the letter, but aren't touches of all the others present?

Check List for Standard Acknowledgments (Continued)

> *c*) If you talk advertising programs, give the names of publications and radio or TV stations, amount of space or time, and schedules; and emphasize how the advertising promotes sales: "Your customers will be asking for . . . because of the full-page ads running. . . ."
>
> *d*) If you talk credit, invite application rather than promise without checking.
>
> 4. Sales-promotion material can indicate service attitude and build sales volume.
>
> *a*) Keep it appropriate—usually on seasonal goods or something allied to the purchase.
>
> *b*) You-attitude and specificness are necessary to good sales promotion.
>
> *c*) Emphasize your service to the customer, not your selfish desire to sell more: "We also make . . ." or "We'd also like to sell you. . . ."
>
> *d*) Put the emphasis on reader action when referring to any enclosures you use.
>
> 5. Look forward to future orders.
>
> *a*) If sales-promotion material is the basis, suggest specific action and make it easy.
>
> *b*) If resale talk is the basis, continue in terms of reader satisfaction rather than suggest that something will go wrong.
>
> *c*) Guard against bromides and Greedy Gus wording as you close.

It's fine news that you have joined us as a *TIME* subscriber.

I'm sure you'll be glad of your decision—particularly now when the news is so momentous and exciting, and so personally important. As *TIME* gathers, sifts, and organizes all the world's important happenings for you, I believe you'll want to read it for years to come.

If you have not already started to receive your weekly copies, they will be on their way to you very shortly. And I think you may enjoy them even more if I tell you something that makes *TIME* different from any other magazine:

> Most other magazines try to please one reader with this story, another with that one. *TIME* tries to make sure that *everything* that goes into its pages is enjoyable or important to every reader; that *nothing* gets into *TIME* that you will not find of definite significance—or just plain fun.

For 35 years now, *TIME* has been developing—adding new services, exploring new subjects, continually improving its facilities for bringing you each week's news clear, complete, and alive—to meet and surpass its original promise to "keep intelligent people quickly well informed." And over the years *TIME*'s audience has grown too—from 12,000 in 1923 to more than 2,250,000 families today.

I certainly believe you will enjoy reading *TIME,* as they have. And some day if you care to write us, the editors and I would be very grateful for your comments.

The preceding two letters are strict forms. If the situation is one in which specificness would add to the effectiveness of an acknowledgment, a fill-in rather than a strict form should be used. The letter writer will have to weigh the relative advantages and costs. Fill-ins can serve to make the essential information of the acknowledgment more specific, enhance the service attitude, and provide specific resale talk.

The use of forms in acknowledgments to customers whose orders you can fill may be summarized as follows:

1. Nothing else can quite replace the personalized letter for special, important business requiring full details, specific treatment, persuasion, adaptation, and evidence of personal attention.
2. But even very inexpensive forms (strict forms and fill-ins) may do the job adequately on numerous small orders where profits are low, where an obvious form will be excused, where not all kinds of acknowledgment content are required, and where generalities may suffice.
3. The more expensive forms are still much less expensive than personalized letters; and, in the hands of a skillful user, they have most of the advantages of the individually dictated letter, including the important point of *seeming* like one to each reader as he reads his copy.
4. The man writing acknowledgments should study his situation and make the wise choice of (1) whether to use forms and (2), if so, which kind. He can be foolish either way. Economy dictates that he choose the cheapest that will do the job; but probably the poorest economy of all is to send a form when the situation justifies a carefully prepared personal letter.

Fortunately, most standard acknowledgments are not difficult letter-writing problems. Forms can and should do most of the work.

Acknowledgments of Incomplete or Indefinite Orders

You would think that anybody could write an adequate order; but only one day's work in the order department of a big mail-order house would convince you that many people don't.

When you get an order that is incomplete (and therefore vague), you can either try to guess what the customer wants and thereby risk extra costs and customer dissatisfaction, or you can write for the needed information. Usually you write.

Your real problem is to *keep the order,* instead of causing the customer to neglect your request for the information or to write you in disgust to cancel the order. Drawbacks to your success are the inevitable delay, the extra trouble to the customer, his embarrassment at having written a poor order, and (unless you are very careful) his irritation at the way you write to him about it. The big problem, then, is to avoid or overcome these negatives inherent in the situation.

Since it is a *bad-news* letter (Type B, because of the additional trouble and delay), you will use a buffer. Resale, thanks, and (if a new customer) a hearty welcome are all good buffer material and need to come early in the letter. A problem here is to avoid misleading the customer into believing that you are sending what he ordered. Otherwise his disappointment, when he learns the facts, will be greater.

Very early—perhaps by starting to interweave some of it into the very first of the letter—you should stress the resale element. The more specific it is, the more emphatic it is. If you tell him he will like the product, also tell him specifically why you think so. By reassuring the customer that the product he ordered is good, resale will help to overcome the drawbacks. In this case it has a much more important role than in the standard acknowledgment. Though small bits of it may be scattered throughout the letter, at least some of it comes before the reader learns the bad news —to bolster his original desire in his moment of disappointment. It can be very short:

> Fashion-conscious women everywhere are wearing Ban-lon sweaters like the one you ordered.

When you have thus prepared the reader psychologically, you should let him know the bad news by asking for the needed information. Thus you save words, weaken the bad news by putting the reader's main attention on complying with your request, and avoid any good-will-killing accusations. More specifically, your technique at this important crux of the letter is: In one key sentence beginning with a reader-benefit reason for your request, ask for the information. For example:

> So that we may be sure to send you just the sweater that will suit you best, will you please specify your color choice?

Now, if you add a touch of satisfaction-resale to motivate the requested action, provide an easy way to answer (to overcome the extra trouble), and promise speed (to overcome as much as possible of the delay), you'll probably get the information you want . . . without ruffling your reader's feathers:

> Coming in four subtle shades of harvest brown, lettuce green, tile red, and sky blue, Ban-lon sweaters provide you a pleasant color to match any complexion or ensemble.

Check List for Incomplete Orders

1. Opening: If you are sending any goods, say so immediately and give necessary details.
   a) If not, begin with a short buffer which is basically resale.
   b) Quickly, but subordinately, identify the order by date, number, and/or description.
   c) Slow: "We have received . . . ," "Thank you for your. . . ."
   d) Selfish: "We're glad to have. . . ."
   e) Provide some resale on the problem article before the bad news, but don't imply that you are sending the article now.
   f) Make the resale specific, not "We're sure you'll like these shoes." Why?
   g) Use only brief phrases for resale on *goods sent,* or for any new-customer aspects, until you've asked for the missing information.
2. Ask for the information naturally, positively, and specifically.
   a) The natural transition to the request follows from preceding resale talk.
   b) Preface the request with a reader-benefit phrase—something like "So that you'll be sure to get just the X you want, please. . . ."
   c) Make the request fairly early—but not too quickly or abruptly—to avoid puzzling.
   d) Avoid the accusation and wasted words of such phrasing as "You did not include" or "We need some additional information."
   e) Name the customer's options: color choices, different models, for example.

If you'll just use the handy return card, you'll be enjoying the sweater of your choice within two days after we receive it.

Notice that, though they treat an inherently bad-news situation, nowhere in the four paragraphs of this letter is there any negative expression ("delay," "inconvenience," "incomplete," "regret," "sorry"). Most of all, the acknowledgment does not irritate by accusing with such expressions as "you neglected," "you forgot," or "you failed."

Though we have never seen a letter just like the following, others we have seen lead us to believe that some people would actually write:

We have your order for two Ban-lon sweaters, but you forgot to tell the color. We are merchants and not mind readers. If you will please be so kind as to tell us the color you neglected to name in your first letter, we'll try to get them to you.

The following letter illustrates good technique for an acknowledgment when you can fill part of the order but have to get omitted information about another part. If you want to consider it as a simple acknowl-

CHECK LIST FOR INCOMPLETE ORDERS (CONTINUED)

f) Add explanations to help in the choice, resell, and show your interest in satisfying.

g) Keep the *you*-viewpoint: "You may choose from . . . ," not "We have three shades."

3. Close with a drive for the specific action you want.

a) If many words follow the first indication of what you want done, repeat specifically.

b) Make replying easy (maybe a return card to check or a return envelope).

c) Refer to the enclosure subordinately; the requested action deserves the emphasis.

d) Stress your promptness and his—preferably a date of arrival if he acts now.

e) But keep it logical; post office speed is not that of a Coca-Cola machine.

f) Try to work in a last short reference to reader satisfaction from the article.

(If resale on the house and/or sales-promotion material would be appropriate—as the first surely would be in a new-customer situation—use Items 3 and 4 of the **Check List for Standard Acknowledgments** (pp. 182–83) as additional Items 4 and 5 here.)

---

edgment of an incomplete order, however, you can read it without the first paragraph and the phrase "the file and" in the next-to-last paragraph.

Soon after you get this letter you should receive the very protective locking and fire-resistant Shaw-Walker file you ordered October 2. It is to go out on our Meridian delivery tomorrow.

The sturdy but light Model 94 Royal Standard typewriter you specified is our most popular one this year, perhaps because of its wide adaptability. Readily available in two type sizes and six type styles, it is suitable to all kinds of work and to various typists' tastes.

To be sure of getting the size and style you like best, please check your choices on the enclosed card of illustrations and return it.

Though your letter was written in Executive style elite (12 letters to the inch), you may prefer the more legible Professional style pica (10 letters to the inch) if you are buying for your reporters. It is the most widely used in newspaper work.

All prices are the same—except $10 extra for the modish Script style, which you probably will not want—and your check exactly covers the file and the three typewriters you ordered in any other choice.

By returning the card with your choices of type size and style right away, you can have your three new Royals Friday, ready for years of carefree typing. We'll send them out on the next delivery after we hear from you.

For requesting additional information in business-building fashion, apply the suggestions in the accompanying check list for incomplete orders.

Delays and Back-Ordering

Sometimes the problem in an acknowledgment is that you can't send the goods right away. In the absence of a specified time limit, sellers-by-mail usually try to keep the order on the books if they feel that they can fill it within a time that is really a service to the customer—that is, if they feel that the customer would prefer to wait rather than cancel the order. After a buffer, they tell when they expect to fill the order and usually assume (without asking) that to be acceptable. If the date is so far off that doubt arises as to whether it will be acceptable, they may ask instead of assuming. In either case, the wise businessman will acknowledge the order promptly.

Again your main problem is keeping the order. This time, though, the only drawback to overcome is delay. Again your main element is resale —to convince the reader that he wants the product enough to wait. It may include both resale on the house and on the goods. If the order is the customer's first, resale is even more important and more extensive.

The plan and technique are the same as for the acknowledgment of an incomplete order, at least through the first paragraph and some resale talk.

> Your order 5B631 of April 7 for Tropical brand play suits in the new Wancrest Glachine material is another reflection of your astute buying. From all indications they will be *the* prevailing style this season.

The parting of the ways comes where the one asks for information and the other explains the situation. The explanation should picture the goods on their way (and imply receipt of them) in the first part of a sentence which ends with clear indication that that does not mean now (usually by giving the shipping date).

> By making every effort to get your supply to you before spring, when your customers will start calling for these popular playsuits, we are able to promise you a shipment by April 27.

As always in letter writing, it is better to explain in positive terms what you can do, have done, and will do than to tell in negative terms what you can't do, haven't done, or won't do. A good letter writer will avoid such unnecessary negatives as "out of stock," "cannot send," "temporarily depleted," "will be unable to," "do not have," and "can't send until," as the writer of the preceding paragraph did.

Only a poor businessman is caught short without a justifying reason satisfactory to the reader. When he is, he will be better off to admit it frankly than to give some weak or false excuse. A good businessman will have a reason. He should explain it to his customer, to avoid the impression that he is inefficient. Often it is basically strong resale material if properly interpreted. For example:

> The Wancrest people have assured us that, although we're insisting on the top-quality material which has made these play suits so attractive to store buyers, they can catch up to our recent order and have a new shipment to us by the 21st. Thus we can promise yours by the 27th.

More resale may follow the explanation to make the reader want the product badly enough to wait. Because it has such an important job to do, it is probably more important in the back-order acknowledgment than in any other. It should be short, specific, and adapted to carry its full effect. It may include both resale on the house and on the goods. Since so much of both kinds has already appeared in the letter we're developing here, however, more hardly seems appropriate.

The ending of the back-order acknowledgment may be worded either one of two ways:

1. You may ask outright whether it will be satisfactory to fill the order when you have said you can. This plan is preferable if you seriously doubt that the customer will approve.
2. You may phrase it so that this letter will complete the contract unless the reader takes the initiative and writes back a cancellation. That is, you look forward with success consciousness to filling the order when you have said you can. You assume that your plan is acceptable unless and until you learn otherwise. Your assumption will hold more frequently if you never suggest the thing you don't want your reader to do —cancel.

The following letter illustrates the handling of a back-order problem:

> You will be glad to know that the women's play suits you ordered April 7—
>
>   4 Dozen—Style #16J7 Women's Play Suits 1 dozen each in sizes 12, 14, 16, and 18, in full color assortment, @ $19.50 a dozen, terms 2/10, n/30
>
> —are leading the summer sportswear sales of more than four hundred of our customers from Maine to California.
>
> We are increasing production on this model and have booked your play suits for rush shipment April 27 by air express.
>
> The unusual pre-season popularity of this trimly cut play suit owes much to the shimmering Wancrest Glachine fabric of which it is made. When

we used up our stock of this genuine combed cotton and acetate rayon material, rather than use a substitute we shut down production of this model. A large stock of Glachine fabric is already en route here from Wancrest's famous North Carolina mills; thus we are able to promise your shipment by April 27.

For this chance to prove once again Tropical's continuing fashion superiority, we thank you sincerely.

Much of the back-order acknowledgment technique is the same as that used in standard and incomplete-order acknowledgments. The following check list for back-order acknowledgments points out the similarities and additional considerations.

BACK-ORDER CHECK LIST

1. Opening: Same as for the incomplete-order acknowledgment, p. 186.
2. Positively handling the bad news:
   a) Picture the goods moving toward or being used by the customer before indicating that you do not now have them: "So that you'll have these play suits while the selling season is still going strong, we'll air-express them to you at least by the 27th."
   b) Avoid negatives: "out of stock," "cannot send," "can't send until."
   c) Adapt to the one situation rather than a universal like "In order to give you the very best service we can. . . ."
   d) Give a justifying reason for being caught short—preferably resale in effect, like insistence on quality or surprising popularity.
   e) Do make clear when you *can* ship.
   f) To avoid cancellation of the order, resale is more important in this than in other acknowledgments; interweave it wherever you can and definitely end with it.
3, 4, 5. Apply these items from the **Check List for Standard Acknowledgments** (pp. 182–83) if appropriate, as they will be in writing a new customer.
6. Word the back-order action phrase to stress the action you want.
   a) Ask about it only if you seriously doubt that your plan will be satisfactory; normally you should phrase your letter to complete the contract (that is, accept the offer to buy) unless he takes the initiative and cancels.
   b) Emphasize his acceptance rather than refusal; avoid suggesting what you don't want (cancellation), as in "Unless you prefer otherwise . . . ," "Unless you direct us to. . . ."

ACKNOWLEDGMENTS DECLINING ORDERS

There are only three likely reasons why you would decline an order:

1. The customer has asked for credit, and you are not willing to sell to him that way. In that case the problem is a credit problem and is discussed in Chapter XI.

2. You don't have the goods (or a suitable substitute), and you don't expect to get them in time to serve the customer. You then simply thank him, explain the situation, tell him where he can get the goods (if you know), maybe present resale on the house and sales-promotion material on any other goods which seem likely to interest him, and end appropriately.

3. You don't market your products in the way he has proposed. Most of these problems arise because of one of the following two situations: (1) the orderer is an unacceptable dealer; or (2) you sell only through regular merchandising channels, and he does not propose to go through those channels.

Declining because you don't have the goods is well illustrated by the following letter from an orange grower to a former customer:

> Thank you for your recent and additional order for one bushel of navel oranges.
>
> Although this valley is known as the land "where sunshine spends the winter," a heavy snowstorm and freeze during the latter part of January caused extensive damage to our current fruit crop. Some of the fruit looks and tastes good, but we do not trust it to keep more than a week after it has been picked.
>
> Since one of the qualities you have a right to expect in fresh fruit is its ability to keep and since we are unwilling to risk the chance that you might be disappointed, we are returning your check for the one bushel of oranges.
>
> The damage to our trees is only temporary. We are looking forward to another crop of high-quality fruits next year. May we serve you again next season with some of our choice fruits?

Unacceptable Dealer. A dealer may be unacceptable because (1) you sell only through exclusive dealerships and you already have a dealer in his territory or (2) because he does not meet your requirements for a dealership. For example, some manufacturers will sell only to those who propose to follow standard Fair-Trade practices.

The first part of the declining letter would be the same in each case and (except for the omission of resale) the same as the beginning of other bad-news acknowledgments we have discussed. In the first case, your explanation would be how you operate and why you operate that way plus the simple fact of the existing dealership. In the second case, it would be a simple explanation of your requirements, with justifying reasons. The ending for the one would be a purely good-will ending of "keeping him in mind" in case you should later want him as a dealer. The other would end with an offer to reconsider if a change or additional information shows that he does meet the requirements.

Improper Channels. Some buyers think that all manufacturers or producers should sell to anybody who has the money and omit the middle men who add so much to the cost of goods. Those who howl the loudest on that point also howl the loudest when a producer from afar does not make his goods available in the local stores. There are advantages and disadvantages in both methods of merchandising. Which is the more desirable is a question we need not answer. We must grant, however, that a producer has the right to sell his goods the way he wants to. And whatever his plan, he has, no doubt, chosen it for certain reasons. At least some of them should be in terms of how he can best serve his customers.

Assuming that the firm for which you work has taken the customer-service attitude into account when adopting its merchandising plan, you are in a good position to acknowledge the order of a person who does not (through ignorance or intent) choose to follow your plan. Usually he will be a consumer asking for goods from a wholesaler or producer instead of through the regular retail channel. Some of the customer-service reasons you can point out to him for selling only through local retail stores are the advantage of being able to get goods quickly from local stores; of being able to see, feel, and try them; of being able to get adjustments and service easier—indeed, all the disadvantages a seller-by-mail usually has to overcome are now in your favor.

Your bad-news letter begins in the same way as those acknowledging incomplete orders and orders that you cannot fill immediately: with a buffer, including resale to help keep the customer interested in the goods (on which you *do* make a profit, of course). As before, you are careful not to mislead.

After that beginning, you explain how you merchandise your goods (not how you don't, except by implication) and why you operate that way. As far as possible, you explain the why in terms of benefit to the customer (you-viewpoint). He will not be much impressed by the benefits to you. At least a part of the reader-benefit *why* should come before the part of the explanation which conveys the bad news (by implication) that he can't buy that way, that his order is not being filled.

If your explanation is good, he will agree that that's the best way for him. If your resale talk has been good, he will still want the product, though he can't buy it from you. He will still want to know how he can get it. You tell him exactly how and where, and you give him a last touch of resale to make him place his order the way you suggest.

If you have several equally convenient outlets, you name them all to give him a choice and to be fair to all. This letter follows the directions:

> Karsol shower curtains like the ones you saw advertised will give you the wear you want for rental units.

So that you will be able to select personally the exact patterns which you prefer (from eight different designs offered), we have set up a marketing plan of bringing Karsol shower curtains to you through local dealers only. This way you will save handling, shipping, and C.O.D. charges. You will be able to get your curtains at the White House, located at 300 Main Street in Montgomery, thus speeding your purchases and avoiding unnecessary delays ever present when ordering by mail.

We have recently sent a large shipment of Karsol shower curtains to your local retail store; and you will be able to see for yourself that although these water-proof curtains are of exceptional strength and durability, they are soft and pliable.

Stop by the White House next time you are in town and select your favorite pattern of Karsol shower curtains that will satisfy your tenants.

If you are really a good businessman, you notify the retailers, so that they can write or call the interested prospect if he doesn't come in.

Selling a Substitute

Many times you will receive orders which you can't fill exactly because you do not have the special brand, but you have a competing brand or something else that will render the service the customer obviously wanted. You know that in most cases people do not buy a product for the name on it but for the service they expect from it. If you think your brand will serve (and ordinarily you do or you wouldn't be selling it), you remember your service attitude and try to satisfy the orderer's wants. As a point of business ethics, you should not try to sell a substitute unless you sincerely believe that you can truly serve by saving the customer time and trouble in getting what he wants or by giving him service at least comparable to what he can get elsewhere in terms of cost.

Once you decide that you are ethically (not selfishly) justified in selling the substitute; you need to remember several working principles:

1. Don't call it a substitute. Though many substitutes are superior to the things they replace, the word has undesirable connotations that work against you. Burma Shave uses the connotations effectively in a roadside advertisement reading "Substitutes and imitations—give them to your wife's relations. Burma Shave."
2. Don't belittle the competitor's product. Not only is that questionable ethics, but it criticizes the orderer's judgment—after all, he wanted to buy that product.
3. Don't refer to the ordered product specifically by name any more than you have to—perhaps not at all. Certainly, once should be enough. You want him to forget it and think about yours. When you use its name, you remind him of it—in effect, you advertise it. Conversely, stress your product, perhaps repeating the exact name several times.

Except for the fact that the identification and resale are in general terms broad enough to encompass both the product ordered and the substitute, and show their basic similarity, your beginning of the substitute-selling acknowledgment is the same as those other buffers for bad-news acknowledgments. If you phrase the beginning well, you'll have no trouble making a smooth transition to further talk about the substitute.

> Your repeat order of September 10 for sixty regular-duty batteries suggests that you have found your battery business quite profitable. We're glad to hear it, but we think we can show you how you can do even better in the coming season.

You arrange to introduce the substitute and at least one of its sales points *before* revealing that you can't send what was ordered. You need to convey this negative message fairly early, however, to keep the reader from wondering why all the talk about the substitute. Your best technique is the standard one for subordinating negative messages: Tell what you *can* do in a way that clearly implies what you can't.

> In our continuous effort to find the best automobile accessories and equipment at reasonable prices, we have found that the new Acme battery excels others of its price class in power, endurance at full load, and resistance to cracking. Because of those desirable qualities, we decided two months ago to stock the Acme line exclusively. Though Powell of Dayton still has the Motor King, we think your customers will be ahead in service and you'll make more profits with the Acme.

Once you are over that rough spot, clear sailing lies ahead. You continue your sales talk, concentrating on why you carry the substitute and what it will do for your reader, not on why you do not carry what he ordered. You give a complete, specific description of the substitute's good points in terms of consumer or dealer benefits (as the case may be).

A good test of the adequacy of your sales talk is whether it is all *you* would want to know if you were being asked to change your mind about the two products.

> Because of its 115 amp. power and its endurance of 5.9 minutes at full load, your customers will like the fact that the Acme keeps a hard-to-start engine spinning vigorously and increases the chance of starting. They'll also like the tough new plastic case that avoids the cracking and loss of acid sometimes experienced with hard-rubber cases.

Sometimes your price will be higher than that of the product ordered. If so, presumably you think your product is better. Your method of meeting the price competition, then, is to sell the advantages and then point to them as justifying the price. Prices seem less, too, if you put them in terms of small units. You may hear the price of something announced as only 3 cents a day, for example, instead of $11 a year.

> When you explain these advantages the Acme has over its competitors, you justify at least a $2 higher price in the customer's mind—and you produce a prompt purchase. The Acme battery will back you up, too, in the customer's long experience with it. It carries the usual 24-month pro-rata replacement guarantee. And the fact that it wholesales to you at only $1 more, means an extra $1 profit to you on each sale.

Sometimes you will have to admit (tacitly) that your product is inferior but adequate. Your technique, then, is to sell its adequacy and the fact that it is a good buy because of the price. If the customer had ordered a higher-priced battery than you now sell, for example, you could replace the three preceding paragraphs with these:

> In our continuous effort to find the best automobile accessories and equipment at reasonable prices, we have found that the Motor King is a leading seller. Because of its low price, strong customer appeal, and complete range of sizes, we now offer only the Motor King for all cars. The fact that you could fit *any* car would give you a big advantage over competitors selling brands that come in only a few sizes.
>
> The $2 saving you can offer on the Motor King will have a strong appeal to many of your customers who are unwilling to pay higher prices for more than standard specifications for regular-duty batteries: 105 amps., 48 plates, 5.3 minutes' endurance at full load. The Motor King meets those specifications, and it carries the standard 24-month pro-rata replacement guarantee.
>
> And while your customers would be saving, we estimate that you would be making more profits because of increased volume that would almost certainly come from a complete line at favorable prices.

Usually, however, quality and price are about the same, and you simply sell the product on its merits and as a service or convenience because it is available.

When your selling job is done, you are ready to try to get action. You can do either of two things:

1. You can ask the orderer whether you may fill his order with the substitute, or ask him to fill out a new order specifying it; or
2. You can send the goods and give the orderer the option of returning them entirely at your expense—that is, you pay transportation both ways. Thus no question of ethics arises.

The second way will sell more goods if you word the offer carefully to avoid a sound of high-pressuring. You should use it, however, only in an attempt to give the best service you can. You should make this choice if he indicated pressing need, if you are reasonably sure he will accept,

SUBSTITUTE CHECK LIST

1. Your opening:
   a) For acknowledgment, rely mainly on implication: maybe the date of the order and a general reference to the class of goods.
   b) Make the reference broad enough to encompass A (product ordered) and B (substitute).
   c) But don't call either one by specific trade name, model, or number yet.
   d) Let the buffer comment be resale in effect, on the line of goods or on the house, but not specifically on A.
   e) Intimating at this point that you're going to ship anything could mean only A to the reader.
   f) Establish early the kinship—the similar nature—of A and B, with emphasis on points in B's favor.
   g) Show gratitude for the customer's return to you with his business (if it applies).
   h) The routine "Thank you" or the selfish "We're glad to have" is usually not the best way.
2. Your transition:
   a) Introduction of B should follow naturally from what you have said before.
   b) *Before* revealing that you can't send A, introduce B *and* at least one of its strong points.
   c) Calling B a substitute or "just as good" defeats your strategy.
3. Your statement of unavailability:
   a) As always, stress what you *can* do, not what you can't; saying that you can send only B makes adequately clear that you can't send A.

and if the transportation costs are small. If you do send the goods on option, you can greatly affect your chance of having them accepted by the wording of your offer. Note the difference between these two ways:

a) We believe you will find the Acmes satisfactory. Therefore, we are filling your order with them. If you don't like them, just return them to us collect.
b) Because we are so thoroughly convinced that you will like the Acmes, we are filling your order with them, on trial. When you see how they sell and satisfy your customers, we believe you will want to keep the whole shipment and order more.

The second puts the emphasis on his accepting them, where it should be; the first on his returning them. The second way will sell more goods.

Whether your acknowledgment letter selling a substitute asks approval or explains that you are sending the goods on trial, you should merely ask or suggest the action and make it convenient. A last touch of

SUBSTITUTE CHECK LIST (CONTINUED)

b) Identify A by name no more than once—when you clear it out of stock.

c) Present the bad news early enough to avoid puzzling the reader—and increasing his disappointment when he does get the word.

d) Make perfectly clear that you can't send A.

e) Stress why you carry B rather than why you don't stock A; else you'll be criticizing something the reader chose, knocking a competitor, or disparaging a product you once sold.

4. Your sales message on B:
   a) Sell B on its own merits; it's a good product; no apologies needed.
   b) Seek out the sales points and apply them concretely and specifically.
   c) Interpret these points in terms of reader benefits (consumer or dealer).

5. Overcoming price resistance:
   a) Cover sales points before price unless it is the big advantage.
   b) Justify any price increase in terms of advantages.
   c) Price resistance is less if price-increase talk is in terms of units rather than the whole order and if you make everyday, lifelike comparisons.

6. Word your action ending to keep the order *and* good will.
   a) Make responding easy, as always.
   b) Work in a last plug about satisfaction with the product.
   c) High pressure is out of place in this letter, especially in the end.
   d) If you send the substitute, make clear that he can return it and you pay the transportation both ways; legally and ethically you have to.
   e) But encourage keeping, rather than returning, by where you put the emphasis.

resale may be added, but action should not be urged—certainly not commanded. This type of letter has the onus of suspicion on it from the outset. High pressure is out of place anywhere in it, especially in the end. Here's a good substitute letter:

Your request for another Simpson product shows that you have been well satisfied with these high-quality electrical supplies. One of the reasons we've been able to please you is the practice of introducing new and improved products first.

Our latest electric fan featuring the newest improvements is the Matthews. Because of the new style oscillating gear, this new fan delivers 12% more cubic feet of air per minute than any other fan of similar size. A crackle finish looks new longer because it resists scuffs and scratches.

Since the demand is rapidly growing for the improved Matthews, we now stock it exclusively. You may still be able to buy the Seabreeze from

Gardner, Perkins, and Simons in Cleveland. We believe you'll prefer the Matthews, however.

In addition to the standard 10-inch Matthews priced at $10.83 a fan and the large 12-inch at $14.16 a fan, with the Matthews line of fans you can also offer a new model, the Matthews Midget. This is an 8-inch fan priced at only $7.08. The Midget has all the new improvements found on the larger fans. Like all Matthews fans, the Midget also carries a one-year guarantee.

To order, simply fill out the enclosed card and mail it. We will ship your Matthews fans by freight collect. When you see how well the Matthews fan sells, you will fully realize that you made a sound buy.

The check list for selling substitutes (pp. 196–97) summarizes the points you'll want to observe in writing successful letters of the type.

COMBINATIONS

In acknowledging orders, you will often find one for several items, some of which you have and others of which you don't. To answer such an order, you have to combine the principles discussed for different types of acknowledgments. The writer of the following letter to a new customer had to combine several types because he could send one item immediately, he had to delay another shipment, he couldn't provide another item, and he had to substitute for still another:

Your two dozen 6.00 × 16 Firestone tires are already on their way to you. They should arrive by Motor-Van truck Thursday, ready for your weekend customers.

It is always a pleasure to welcome a new customer to our long list of dealers who look to us for automobile supplies. We shall always try to serve your needs as best we can, by keeping up with the market and providing you with the best goods available.

The 6.50 × 16 tires—which you will receive in about two weeks—are a case in point. In another effort to assure our customers of the advertised quality of all products we handle, we returned to the manufacturer the last shipment of 6.50 × 16 Firestone tires because they had been slightly bruised in an accident while the tires were being shipped to us. Since we are assured of a new shipment in two weeks, may we fill this part of your order then?

In trying to keep our operating costs and consequently our prices at a minimum, we have discontinued handling 4.50 × 21 tires because of the small demand for them. Probably your best source for them is the Kimble Supply Company, 401 S. State Street, Chicago, which carries a large stock of obsolete auto parts and supplies.

When our buyer was in the market last year, he found a new automobile paint that seemed superior to other paints he knew. It is a General Motors product in all colors, with the standard General Motors guarantee. Our other customers have been so well satisfied with its quality and price (only $2.85 a qt. and $9.85 a gallon) that we now stock it exclusively. As I feel sure that you too will be satisfied with this new product, I am filling your order with the understanding that you can return the paint at our expense unless it completely satisfies. I think you will like it.

Since I am awaiting the return of the enclosed card with your decision on the paint (sent with your 6.00 × 16 tires) and the 6.50 × 16 tires to be sent in two weeks, I am holding your check to see how much the refund is to be.

For your convenience and information, I am sending a separate parcel of our latest catalogue and a supply of order blanks. We shall be glad to handle your future orders for high-quality automobile supplies.

Note how that letter would have read if the order had been for only the paint. Read only the second, fifth, and seventh paragraphs.

PROBLEMS

Orders

1. As the manager of the Unusual Foods Shoppe, Jacksonville, Florida, send an order addressed to the National Food Enterprise, New York 6: 2 dozen jars Grund's brandied peaches @ $5.50; 3 dozen 6½-oz. cans La Pariee truffles @ 15.50; 1 dozen boxes Maison sugared rose petals, @ $14.00, to be sent air freight, subject to the usual 2/10, n/30 credit terms you have arranged with National.

2. You are the owner-manager of the Beauty Nook, 1943 State Street, Denver, Colorado. Send a rush order to Elizabeth Hardin, Inc., a cosmetics company in Boston, requesting 36 2-oz. bottles Elizabeth Hardin Tapestry Perfume, $2 each; 24 1-oz. bottles of the same, $1.50 each; 48 6-oz. bottles Elizabeth Hardin Tapestry Toilet Water, $1 each; 48 10-oz. bottles Lanolin Skin Lotion, $1.75 each. You are an established credit customer. You want these sent express, charges collect.

3. You are to represent an organization to which you belong (assume a social or professional fraternity, a religious group, or even a civic organization) at its national convention in Chicago next month. Headquarters are at the Palmer House, where you would prefer to stay for the two nights and three days the convention is in session. You prefer a single at the minimum rate. Ask for such a reservation and ask the hotel to confirm it.

4. You are the owner-manager of the Quality Shoppe, 1293 Biscayne Boulevard, Miami, Florida. Send a rush order to Mary Case, Inc., a cosmetics company in North Philadelphia, requesting 2 doz. 1-oz. bottles Mary Case White Lilac Perfume, $3.50 each; 2 doz. 2-oz. bottles of the same, $6 each; 1 doz. 1-oz. bottles Mary Case Chestnut Perfume, $3.50 each; 1 doz. 2-oz. bottles of the

same, $6 each; 3 doz. 6-oz. bottles Mary Case Fragrance Toilet Water, $2.50 each; 3 doz. 10-oz. bottles Mary Case Jasmine Skin Lotion, $1.50 each. You are an established credit customer. You want these sent air express, charges collect.

5. Smythe's White Fruit Cakes, gourmet holiday food, have been sold for over 50 years by mail from Mobile, Alabama. Packed in attractive metal containers, they are shipped anywhere, delivery and satisfaction guaranteed. The 5-pound cake is priced at $8, the 3-pound cake at $5 (including shipping charges). Assume that you decide to order one to be sent as a gift to a relative or friend and write the necessary letter. The firm name is the same as the product name. Since all sales are cash, assume a postal money order for payment.

6. Help Mr. E. J. Pennington, carpenter, Box 609, Henderson, North Carolina, order tools from Allen and Jason Company, 809 Queen Street, Winston-Salem:

1	99	H01936L	Craftsman $\frac{1}{2}$ HP Motor	$44.50
1	99	H25156	Craftsman Table	26.95
1	9	H2516	$\frac{1}{8}$-in. concave Kramedge cutter	1.98
1	9	H2519	1-in. convex Kramedge cutter	1.98
				$75.41
			Shipping charges	2.66
			3% tax	2.26
				$80.33

With a 20 per cent down payment, he plans to pay the rest out on your Easy Payment Plan of $8 a month.

7. Vacationing during the summer and finding yourself with more time on your hands than you had anticipated, you decide to do some studying for your next semester in school in an attempt to raise your college grade average as well as to have more leisure time when you get back to school. From three of your instructors you secured the necessary information for the textbook in each of the three courses (author's full name, complete title, publisher, place of publication, date of publication)—with the instructors' assurance that the books will be used as texts when you enroll in the courses. You do not have prices, however. So in ordering from the campus bookstore of your choice, you identify exactly what you want, specifying preference for new or used copies, estimating prices, and sending a check or money order for approximately half of the total, with the request to ship C.O.D. for the balance plus extras (tax and shipping charges).

8. For Christmas you decide to order gifts direct from Marshall Field, Chicago 10, Illinois. From the Field Christmas *Fashions of the Hour* you select one twin-initial belt, mahogany, size 34, 33 H 4221, $2.98, with initials CW; 2 genuine South American alligator wallets, 83 H 3194, $15 each; 1 Tiny Tears doll, $11\frac{1}{2}$ inches tall, 49 H 3035, $7.46; 1 soft rubber bowling set, 79 H 02491, $5.54, all to be gift-wrapped and mailed to Mrs. Harvey B. Seeley, 1987 Elm Street, Clinton, Tennessee. Enclose a check to cover presents and mailing and handling charges of $2.70.

Standard Acknowledgments

1. As your instructor directs, acknowledge any of the order letters in the preceding section.

2. As a correspondent in the sales office of the Dallas Hardware Company, Dallas, Texas, you acknowledge an order from F. M. Shaler, Rt. 1, Box 198, Gatesville:

1 Bench Saw Table Top, 99 H 0 1718L	$17.50
1 Saw Guard Assembly, 9 H 21046	6.25
1 Miter Gauge, 9 H 2760	8.50
1 Portable Saw Guide, 9 H 1819	2.95
	$35.20
Shipping charges	1.90
	$37.10

His check covers the amount due and shipping charges; you can send the supplies today, and they should be at his home in two or three days. Since he's a new customer so far as your records reveal, remind him of your fast shipping service and invite his application for credit. The order numbers he used were from last year's catalogue; so you are sending him the most recent issue. On page 80 he can read about the Craftsman portable planer attachment, made of strong, lightweight die-cast aluminum body, $7\frac{1}{2}$-inch shoe in front of high-speed 2-knife cutter blade. The planer cuts $2\frac{1}{2}$-inches wide to $\frac{1}{8}$ inch deep and comes complete with easy-to-follow instructions. Priced just $27.95. Wouldn't Mr. Shaler like to order a planer to go with his other Craftsman tools?

3. As the sales manager for American-tex Company, Miami, Florida, you personally acknowledge the initial order from Jay Whitfield Jolly, Lane Tile and Floor Company, Orlando, Florida, for

2 No. 690 Rugs, 9 × 12, nylon and rayon, solid gray @ $49	$ 98
10 No. 88 V691 Rugs, 9 × 12, flecked cotton, black and white @ $36	360
6 No. 21 B257 Cotton Hooked Rugs, 24 × 36 inches @ $6	36

to be shipped by Bagnet Truck line, shipping charges collect, and paid for by Jolly's check which accompanied the order.

American-tex has been promoting Avisco rayon and nylon rugs in *House Beautiful* and *Better Homes and Gardens,* but sales in Florida have been off. Because of all the sand, many families prefer throw rugs or no rugs at all. Nylon with rayon rugs can be adapted to the casual living because they let the sand filter through, resist dirt, lend nicely to washing instead of dry cleaning, and are springy to walk on; 77,760 tufts of Avisco rayon and nylon per square yard, vat-dyed colors for greater resistance to fading; 100 per cent jute back, coated with plasticized latex locks turfs firmly, makes rug seamless. To go along with the carpet you can send a spot-removing kit that contains different chemicals to be used on different stains. For cigarette burns there's some matching nylon thread that can be simply glued into the spots or spot that's burned. Nylon also comes in tweeds as well as solids in Colonial Green, Coffee Brown, and Straw Tan. The dealer markup is a third. This could grow into a good account; make Mr. Jolly want to do more business with you.

4. This morning's mail brings an order from a new customer to you, sales manager for the Stecks Manufacturing Company, Cleveland, Ohio. L. C. Smith, manager, Smith Office Supply Company, Youngstown, Ohio, asks you to send the following office supplies C.O.D.:

```
1 box (24) Scripto ball-point pens...........................@ $12.00
1 gross Number 2, Medium Soft lead pencils..................@    7.50
3 dozen typewriter ribbons, black record, medium inked, for
    Standard Royal.........................................@   18.00
1 gross Midnight carbon paper..............................@   10.50
```

Shipping charges amount to $1.10. The Scripto he buys for 60¢ and sells for $1.19. You are sending a mixed assortment of the popular "Piggyback" refill Scripto with chrome-plated metal caps in black, red, and blue, a dozen each with fine, medium, and heavy points. You decide to tell Mr. Smith about the new Westerbrook twin cartridge pens. When the pen runs dry, his customers simply replace the cartridge. Taking 33 per cent markup, he can sell the pen for only $3.95 or the pen and matching pencil, $5.15. A dozen cartridge refills sell for 98¢. Separately you are sending sales manuals for the use of his salespeople, and a catalogue describing various sales helps, such as window and counter displays, promotional leaflets, advertising mats, and self-mailing folders. John Shumaker, your salesman in his territory, will be in Youngstown next month and will call on Smith. To make ordering easier, you'll send along a credit application for him to fill out.

5. Wayne Feed Company, 1908 Lake Street, Madison, Wisconsin, orders the following garden equipment from your company, Sipes Brothers, national hardware dealers, 907 Wales Street, Chicago, 9:

```
12 dozen garden hose sprayers............................$1.25 each
2 dozen rust-proof brass insecticide sprayers.................. 5.25 each
4 dozen combination seed-spreader carts.................... 8.00 each
    Shipping charges....................................... 7.57
```

As correspondent, acknowledge this order, send the supplies C.O.D., invite credit by sending a credit application blank, and tell Wayne Feed Company about an allied product. You are sending separately 500 envelope stuffers with description of the combination seed-spreader cart. The cart has double rows of openings for spreading any seed or fertilizer. A lever-controlled plate covers agitator and openings when used as a cart, so that it will haul bricks, dirt, leaves, etc. Hopper holds about a bushel. The usual markup on these nationally advertised products is 40 per cent.

6. Yesterday an order came to you from Town and Country Shop, 416 Tenth Street, St. Paul, Minnesota, for an assortment of Italian and Japanese silk scarves to be sent C.O.D.:

1 dozen Italian silk in assorted patterns, 36 in. square. . . . .$2.50 each
2 dozen pure silk chiffon Japanese scarves 17 × 44 in. . . . . 1.00 each

As sales manager for Paul Kruger Company, 879 Fourth Avenue, New York, welcome this new customer. You'll ship the scarves within the next two days (shipping charges of $1.19). Separately you'll send a catalogue describing other women's accessories, and you'll want to tell about your national advertising—half-page ads in *Seventeen* and *Vogue*. This month your ad features Japanese pure-silk clip-on Kerchiefs. For travel, for riding, for informal living, the Kerchief keeps hair in place and can be worn almost anywhere. He can buy a Kerchief wholesale for $1 and retail for $2.

7. Yesterday an order came to you from Lustwig Gift Shop, 178 University Avenue, Norman, Oklahoma, for toys and games to be sent C.O.D.:

1 dozen Spin and Spell educational games @ $1. . . . .$12.00
1 dozen Beat the Clock @ $1.75. . . . . 21.00
3 dozen Hutch pull toys @ $1. . . . . 36.00
$69.00

As sales manager for Just-Rite Toy Company, 823 Patterson Street, Paterson, New Jersey, welcome this new customer. You'll ship the toys Railway Express within the next three days. Separately you'll send a catalogue describing other toys he might want to get for the buying season ahead. "Spellbound," a playing-card word game described on page 26 of the catalogue, is fascinating and instructive and sought by young, modern parents. He can buy it for $1 and sell for $2.

8. Acknowledge the order from Mr. E. J. Pennington, carpenter (Problem 6, p. 200). Since this is his first order and he is buying on the Easy Payment Plan, he'll have to fill out a blank giving credit information before you can make shipment. (See p. 103.) You also might tell him about your grinders, Dunlap Hack Saws, or Craftsman Files described on page 123 of your catalogue. Craftsman Electric Grinders are UL-approved, built to withstand rugged service, enclosed motor with precision ball bearings, nylon insulation, and guaranteed for 1 full year.

9. Assuming that the credit information on Mr. Pennington of the preceding problem is favorable, write the necessary letter informing him that you are making shipment.

Incompletes

1. Linn and Scruggs, Chicago mail-order outlet, has just received the following order for men's clothes from Mrs. Henry R. Meyers, Box 419, Shadesville, Oklahoma:

GENTLEMEN:

Please send to me at once, C.O.D., the following:

2 No. 45 V 5019 Workmaster cotton coveralls in oxford gray @ $4.49
1 No. 56 V 5501 All-rayon gabardine zipper jacket in light green. Medium size. @ $3.98
1 No. 40 V 754 Gabardine slacks 32-inch waist measure @ $8.98

As the sales correspondent, acknowledge this order and ask for the additional information you will need to fill it. You must know the chest measurement (sizes 34, 36, 40, 42, 44, 46) of this tightly woven, hard-finished sanforized cotton work suit, which has 6 pockets, rule pocket, hammer strap, and side openings for access to clothing underneath.

The gabardine slacks come dark brown, slate gray, or denim blue. Sales points: 40 per cent wool, 60 per cent rayon; slacks with snugtex inside waistband so that slacks stay up and shirt stays in. You do not send C.O.D. shipments without a check or money order for 10 per cent of the total charges.

2. You are the Sales Manager for Mansutta Sheet Company, 986 Minge Street, Atlantic City, Alabama, acknowledging the initial order from C. W. Lewis Department Store, East Lansing, Michigan, for:

3 dozen 100% Nylon Tricot Bottom fitted sheets................$ 72.00	
(twin bed size)	
3 dozen 100% Nylon Tricot Top fitted sheets.................... 115.92	
(twin bed size)	
6 dozen Pacific Fine Percale Bottom fitted...................... 142.56	
(double bed size)	
6 dozen Quality Combed Percale Sheets......................... 142.56	
(twin bed size)	
Shipping Charges.. 8.26	
$481.30	

A check for the correct amount was enclosed. But what the Smith buyer forgot to tell you was whether he wanted the Combed Percale Sheets in fitted or flat style. Both styles sell for the same price; both have 190 threads per square inch after sizing. Flat sheets are finished with 4-inch hem at top, 1-inch hem at bottom; strong tape selvages add strength to sides. On the other hand, fitted sheets save time and work with their tape-bound edges that resist strain, are sanforized for permanent fit with maximum shrinkage of 1 per cent. *House Lovely* has been carrying full-page ads the last two months on Quality Percale. Retail prices are about 70 per cent higher.

3. On one of your regular catalogue order blanks John B. Van Fleet, 1109 Maple Street, Garden City, Kansas, orders—

1 9 × 12 37 H MT9439 Axminster Broadloom Carpet (Shipping	
wt. 39 lbs.)..$ 75.00	
2 24 × 36 in. 37 H 4161 Harmony House Vinyl Braid Aquamarine	
@ $3.17 ea. (Shipping wt. 2 lbs., 12 oz.).................... 6.34	
2 36 × 60 in. 37 H 04163 Harmony House Vinyl Braid Aquama-	
rine @ $7.97 ea.. 15.94	
$ 97.28	
Shipping charges via motor freight........................ 8.00	
$105.28	

—from your Kansas City outlet of Lancaster-Lord, sending his personal check for the correct amount. You, the sales correspondent, have to find out what color he wants the 9 × 12 in (dawn gray, smoke gray, shell brown, shell beige). Wouldn't Mr. Van Fleet like to order a 9 × 12 springy sponge rubber cushion ($23.25, shipping weight 40 lbs.) when he tells you his color preference? Rug cushions pay for themselves in longer carpet life, greater comfort underfoot. They won't attract lint, have no fibers to shed or fray, are mothproofed and vermin-free.

4. Write the preceding letter, assuming that Mr. Van Fleet failed to send a check. You do not make C.O.D. shipments without receipt of 10 per cent of the purchase price and all shipping charges in advance.

5. Horace Berry, Professor, University of Illinois, Urbana, orders a 4-speed automatic phonograph to be sent to his daughter, Janet, 1897 Lake Street, Madison, Wisconsin, for her birthday. Although he sent the $5 down and agreed to pay $5 a month, he didn't tell you what type of case he wanted. No. 57 H 082421 priced at $57.50 comes in an attractive wood case with wrap-around speaker grille. No. 57 H 072411 is in simulated leather-covered wood case, $38.95. The more expensive player has $5\frac{1}{4}$-inch speaker instead of 4-inch speaker, and 45-rpm spindle adapter is included with it but not with the cheaper model. Adapter costs $2.50. Both come with sapphire needle; rubber-padded turntable prevents skidding. In your tactful letter make it easy for Professor Berry to reply. You are the sales manager, Shears, Inc., Chicago 51, Illinois.

6. As a sales correspondent for the Tall Girl Shop, Evanston, Illinois, find out what size dress Mrs. Herman Stribling, 809 Hill Street, Des Moines, Iowa, desires. She ordered a $35.50 black silk tailored dress with short sleeves in extra tall length (which fits women 5 feet 10 inches and over) from your ad in *Glamour*, but gave no size. Sizes range from 12 to 20—which would she like? The $8.50 black silk purse she ordered, you are sending. Her personal check with the order is for the correct amount.

7. From C. P. Baernstein, 1109 Swamp Street, Kenner, Louisiana, comes an order for one 20-inch Kenmake portable electric fan for $31.95, as advertised in the *New Orleans Times* by Spiller Electric Company, New Orleans. The 20-inch, 2-speed Kenmake you sell costs only $21.95, but with adjustable easy-roll stand costs $31.95. Does he want the fan with the stand, or does he prefer the 20-inch, 3-speed automatic, manually reversible fan for $31.95? Both fans you advertised measure $22\frac{1}{2} \times 6\frac{1}{2} \times 23$ inches high. The 3-speed machine has a $\frac{1}{12}$-hp motor, while the 2-speed fan operates with a $\frac{1}{16}$-hp motor. Both are UL-approved, have safety grilles that can be removed to clean, and operate on 110–120 volts. Motors guaranteed for 5 years. Ask Mr. Baernstein (a new customer) whether he prefers the 2-speed with stand or the 3-speed without.

8. In the sales department of the Manning Mills, Inc., Charleston, West Virginia, you are to handle an order which comes in the morning mail from the College Men's Shop, Pecos Avenue, Austin, Texas, for 3 dozen No. 809 Cambridge Dacron sweaters at $60 a dozen with the size assortment given. The order does not specify the color assortment (Carmine Red, Royal Blue, Ca-

nary Yellow, British Green). You check back and see that you shipped the College Shop a larger assortment of these—both sizes and colors—with other items just six weeks ago. This order is obviously a supplement; but for efficient service to the customer you decide to ask the color preference before making the shipment.

Back-Orders

1. Mrs. T. M. Ripley, 10 Panetela Drive, Tampa, Florida, orders three 5-pound Smythe's White Fruit Cakes (see Problem 5, p. 200) to be sent direct and paid for by her $24 check. After heavier-than-seasonal demand for these rich cakes that are packed in attractive metal containers, your stock is exhausted. And you have to wait for shipments of Sultana raisins from Turkey and currants from California. According to the invoice you got today, the raisins and currants are on their way and baking should begin this week. Mrs. Ripley should have her cakes in ten days. Write the necessary letter to convince her that Smythe's White Fruit Cakes are appropriate gifts for any season and well worth waiting for.

2. To your desk in the sales division of Walbridge Clothing Company, New York 21, manufacturers of sport clothes, comes a letter from a good credit customer of yours, Linn and Scruggs Company, Cedar Rapids, Iowa, authorizing a shipment of 3 dozen dacron and cotton walking shorts for women #98745, 1 dozen each of sizes 12, 14, and 16 @ $3.50. Because of the unexpected popularity of the shorts, your stock is exhausted. You've ordered new material, and it is due within a week; so Mr. Palmer, the production superintendent, tells you that he'll have the shorts ready to ship within ten days. Write the letter to Mr. Jesse Reid, explaining that the shorts will have to be given a back-order listing. Word it so that the order will remain on the books and that there will be no likelihood that Mr. Reid will refuse to accept this method of handling the order. Include some resale talk on these easy-to-wash, easy-to-iron shorts with two slash pockets and self-belt.

3. All polio vaccine of the Upham Pharmaceuticals Company, Detroit, Michigan, was called in for examination by the U.S. Health Department because of a recent epidemic involving 50,000 people in the Los Angeles area who were vaccinated with a defective serum from a competing drug company. Answer a letter from John Lutes, owner, Rex Drug Store, Richmond, Michigan, requesting shipment of 100 vials of 10-cc., 300,000 units. Explain that there will be some delay before the order can be filled. You have received oral confirmation from the chief that all Upham vaccine is considered safe by the Health Department and will be returned shortly. That certainly shouldn't be more than two weeks from now and may be sooner. Write Mr. Lutes welcoming him as a new customer and handling the back-order element positively, with emphasis on the fact that he will receive his shipment rather than why he can't get it immediately.

4. In the sales department of The Mohawk Company, Chicago 21, Illinois, manufacturers of floor coverings, you need to answer the letter from J. J.

Shellabarger, Shellabarger Home Furnishings, Warsaw, Indiana, authorizing the shipment of four 100-foot length, 9-foot width rolls of Mirro-Glo (one in each of your four available color mixtures). Up to now Mr. Shellabarger has ordered only small quantities of rugs and carpets. Mohawk has been trying to invade the market for inexpensive floor coverings with Mirro-Glo—thick layer of enamel with plastic resins, baked smooth onto sturdy asphalt-saturated felt back. The price (wholesale, 50¢ a running foot; retail, 75¢) doesn't compare with inlaid vinyl or inlaid linoleum. Yet these rugs are superior to the usual type of enamel surface floor coverings and decidedly less expensive. They can be laid by the homeowner and matched regardless of room size (kitchen, bath, nursery, play room) with no waste. Demand has been greater than you expected, however, and good enamels and high-quality resins have been hard to obtain in large quantities. You hope to resume production within two weeks. It takes five days to apply the enamel and about two days to ship the rugs from Chicago to Warsaw. Write the letter to keep this order on the books.

5. A college gift shop, Ye Olde Quality Shoppe, 1987 University Avenue, Bloomington, Indiana, sells many Japanese lanterns to students for parties and to landlords who use them to cover up old naked bulbs in rented apartments. As correspondent for Imports-Exports, New York 8, N.Y., write Mr. William Holden, manager of the college shop, that the 6 dozen red and green lanterns he requested will have to be back-ordered for what you estimate will be a month (because of unsettled conditions in the East). After checking your warehouse thoroughly, you have found one dozen each of red and green (wholesale $5 each, retail $7.50). Would he like you to send those?

6. J. J. Shellabarger, Shellabarger Home Furnishings, Warsaw, Indiana, orders 3 sets of Fincher Colonial-Style, maple finish dining-room furniture (round drop-leaf table, $55; 4 chairs, $80; server, $50; hutch top for server, $20) from Armony Home, Chicago. The Armony people will gladly send the three sets of authentic early American designed furniture with turned legs, shaped bases, and antique metal pulls as soon as they get the sets from Fincher. A letter yesterday from the Fincher Manufacturing Company said that a recent strike was settled and that all Fincher furniture would be shipped in about ten days. Write the appropriate letter to Mr. Shellabarger from the manager of Armony Home.

Declines

1. On your desk in the office of the sales manager of the Purina Mills, St. Louis, Missouri, appears an order for two cases of Kay Dog Chow (one of your popular new grains) to be shipped direct to Paul Kells, grocer, Frankfort, Kentucky. His check for the correct amount at your manufacturer-wholesalers price is pinned to one of your current mimeographed jobbers' lists. Regardless of how he got the list, you cannot sell to him direct or at jobbers' prices. Your exclusive distributor for his district is the Jackson Wholesale Grocery Company, Louisville, Kentucky. Certainly you want Mr. Kells to handle your popular new dog food; so you will return his check and ask him to place his

order with the Jackson Company. In the light of the ultimate advantages to retailers, make a presentation that emphasizes his advantages rather than your own or your jobber's.

2. Your company, the Royal Candy Company, Davenport, Iowa, receives an order for a 50-pound case of Royal Miniature candies in 1-, 2-, and 5-pound special Christmas boxes to be shipped C.O.D. to William P. Kelton, the Wisconsin Club, Madison, Wisconsin. A check for 10 per cent accompanies the order. The order comes to your desk (you are the sales manager) because the order department has been instructed not to sell to clubs, fraternities, and similar organizations. Complaints from retailers in college localities about wholesalers' selling to these groups made it necessary to have a policy of selling to dealers exclusively. Urge Mr. Kelton to place his order through one of the retailers (supply specific names and addresses) in the Madison area who stock the Royal Miniature candies.

3. Neal Patterson, builder of inexpensive housing, orders from your company, Ibec Housing Company, Washington 16, D.C., a new machine that makes bricks from a mixture of 90–95 per cent dirt and 5–10 per cent cement called the Cinva-Ram Block Press. He enclosed a $50 check and asks that you send the machine direct to Neal Patterson Building Company, El Tigre, Azoategui, Venezuela, South America. The Cinva-Ram Block Press has been most successful because it makes rock-hard bricks for less than a penny apiece. Resembling an old-fashioned hand printing press, the machine can be operated by two men, one of whom pours in the soil-cement mixture while the other pumps the long handle to press the brick into shape at a pressure of about 10,000 pounds per square inch. In two days it can turn out enough brick to build a hut-sized house, is light enough (140 lbs.) to be packed by mule to backwoods villages, inexpensive enough to serve even the most depressed areas.

You are the manager and cannot sell direct to Neal Patterson, but he can order the machine, $150 plus shipping charges, direct from Mingle Brick Equipment and Distributors, Miami, Florida.

4. A letter from Harold Odum, Locust Valley, Long Island, N.Y., for six 4-ounce plastic bottles of Tool-Keep, a chemical compound used to protect all tools from ravages of rot and rust, heat and cold, takes special handling. As the director of sales for the American Equipment Company, New York 7, tell Mr. Odum that you sell only through distributors and that the nearest dealer is the Fink Hardware Company, Oyster Bay, Long Island, N.Y. Keep Mr. Odum sold. One bottle of Tool-Keep ($1) contains protective coating for up to 20 tools and makes tools last longer (stops splitting of wooden handles, prevents rust, and waterproofs joints).

5. Mrs. Gary Silver, 89 Pinehill Drive, Durham, North Carolina, writes your company, the Northern Textile Company, New Port, New Jersey, for "4 white nylon contour bed pads as advertised in this month's *Better Homes and Gardens* . . . regular twin-bed size," to be sent parcel post C.O.D. Although your current series of institutional advertisements has brought the company

quite a bit of correspondence in the form of inquiries from prospective dealers, you have had no direct orders from consumers before. Since you don't sell direct to consumers, you quickly check and see that Scarborough's, Raleigh, is the dealer nearest Mrs. Silver who handles your contour bed pads. Keep Mrs. Silver sold on the bed pads, urge her to buy directly from Scarborough's when she is in Raleigh, and point out to her the advantage in buying there.

Substitutes

1. As sales manager for the Hudson Mail Order Store, 110 North Jackson Boulevard, Chicago, Illinois, answer Mrs. J. H. Pennington, 111 South Walnut Street, Pekin, Illinois. She wants a Magna-Vetic steam iron, $12.95, like her friend and neighbor got from Hudson several years ago. You used to carry the Magna-Vetic, a $12, 4-pound steam iron (not a dry iron), but 6 months ago you found a new and improved iron, the Strip-O-Matic. It weighs less than many women's purses, only 3¼ pounds, and has a larger soleplate— more than 30 square inches (covers wider ironing area in fewer strokes). Fabric dial gives perfect heat for whatever fabric you're ironing, which means no more scorching. Although it's $14.95, you can use it as a steam iron or as a dry iron. When you use it as a steam iron, you don't need to sprinkle anything except heavy cottons, linens, and starched fabrics. The steady flow of steam moistens fabrics, saves you the time and work of sprinkling and of ironing premoistened clothes. You get instant steam. Drop by drop water falls onto the hot soleplate and flashes instantly to steam. Steam stops automatically when iron is placed on heel rest. Use tap water in all but extremely hard-water areas. You can press suits, skirts, and sweaters without a damp pressing cloth. Saves money on pressing bills. Write Mrs. Pennington that you can send her Strip-O-Matic within three days after you receive her order. She can send a check with the enclosed order blank; or if she prefers, you can send it C.O.D.

2. Assume that you are Paul DuPres, manager of the Lamp House, 5489 Woodland Hills, Nashville, Tennessee. A note from Mrs. R. Sidney Staley, 19 Skyline Drive, Clanton, Tennessee, an established customer with a good credit rating, reads: "Please wrap as a baby gift a Humpty-Dumpty lamp in blue and send to Master Cary D. Williams, 10 Riverside Drive, Memphis, and charge the $5.98 to my account. I ordered two of these three weeks ago from you, so am sure you still have them in stock." Apparently, Mrs. Staley bought all your stock. You can send the same style lamp with 10-inch shade (white paper over paper parchment) on enameled wood base with Little Boy Blue instead of Humpty Dumpty. This lamp is also 16½ inches high. Or, if she prefers, for the same price she can send a Child Prayer shadowbox night light with a gold-color plastic frame, pottery figurine of a boy in blue pajamas. The shadow box measures 9½ × 7½ × 3 inches deep.

3. In Boston's jobbing house of Fedders-Mathew, you are handling an order from an old customer, the Quigley Electric Shop, Stranton, Massachusetts, for 2 dozen Oceanbreeze oscillating fans, 1 dozen 10-inch, 1 dozen 12-inch, listed in last year's catalogue at $100 and $110 a dozen, respectively. This

year you have switched to the Frederick because it has more insulation, better wearing qualities, and simpler oscillating mechanism. It delivers 12 per cent more cubic feet of air per minute (1,800 cubic feet for the 12-inch) using the same consumption of electric current. The light-gray and charcoal enamel finish with bright metal grille of the Frederick will hold up well over a long time. Other advantages, the Frederick comes in two more popular sizes, the 16-inch, $140, and 8-inch, $85. Try to sell him on the Frederick 3-speed oscillating fans, but you'll have to tell him that the nearest supply house you know of that sells the Oceanbreeze is Beacon-Williams, New York 10.

4. Mr. Brad Wyatt, 1104 Forty-second Avenue, Springfield, Missouri, a long-time charge customer of yours, the Johnson Company, Kansas City, Missouri, requests "another one of those 10-gallon underground garbage cans like I got from you five years ago. When I sold my house the can went with it and now that I have a new house I want one, maybe even two of those $8 cans."

Since the time Mr. Wyatt bought the Magic-Step, you have found a new, improved heavy-steel can that is painted to resist rust and that has an inner galvanized can that is easily removed for disposal. The new underground can, called the Disposall, comes in only two sizes; the 15-gallon (22 inches high, 14½ inches diameter), costs $10.50, and the 20-gallon (23½ inches high, 15½ inches diameter), $14.50. Both cans come equipped with step-on pedal to open the heavy lid. Convince Mr. Wyatt that with the 20-gallon can he probably will need just one. With these sunken cans there's no worry about tipping and spilling. Send an order blank, a reply envelope, and a picture of the improved can.

5. As chief correspondent in the mail-order department of Gold Cross Craft Shoes, Inc., 975 Forty-fifth Street, New York, N.Y., acknowledge Mrs. Whitney Echols' (Greenbriar Road, Huntsville, Ohio) order for Cross-Country natural pigskin shoes, $20.50—plain style tie oxford. The factory which manufactures this popular model notifies you that all have been con-tracted by the Life-Stride National chain. Your stock of the Cross Country is low. And you have none in 7½ AAA. Your most likely substitute, the Stride-Right pigskin buckle model is also soft, water-resistant, handsome, and priced $2 less. It has the same medium heel for comfortable walking. One advantage of buckle models is that they can be worn appropriately for a wider variety of occasions. Write the letter selling Mrs. Echols on the Stride-Right and then ask her permission to send a pair. You will keep her check until you hear from her.

6. Stallworth's Department Store, 189 Lavaca, Austin, Texas, where you work as head of the luggage department, used to carry Hullibarton Aluminum Travel cases but now carries celanese plastics by Whyte. Formed in two halves from celanese laminate, in immaculate ivory or white, the seamless case is easy to keep clean—inside and out. Removable (snap-in) celanese synthetic lin-

ings and fitted-to-the-hand plastic grip complete a design of tradition-free smartness and style.

Mrs. W. G. Money, 39 Windsor Road, Round Rock, Texas, orders a ladies' overnight case at $46.80 in Hullibarton Aluminum. Since you stock only Whyte celanese plastics, sell her on this less expensive ($32.50) case. This celanese plastic with pale-gold finish hardware and trim is available in five sizes for men and women. Celanese can take wear, so is being used for house appliances, radios, and automotive equipment. Whyte's celanese luggage is able to withstand the hard knocks of airline travel and has a definite advantage in weighing about half what aluminum luggage does. The purchase is a charge.

7. You are chief clerk for King Hardware Company, wholesalers of Chattanooga, Tennessee. You have an order from Hoffman Brothers, Gadsden, Alabama, for 1 dozen auto-size Red Comet fire extinguishers. Your records show that about a year ago you shipped Hoffman 2 dozen Red Comets in the larger sizes. Four months ago you took over the Tennessee distribution of the nationally advertised No-Fire extinguisher and have sold out your entire stock of Red Comet in the size ordered. The No-Fire is a more convenient and dependable instrument than the Red Comet. The 1-quart size comes with clamps prepared for installing it on the automobile steering post without drilling holes or inserting screws. This model is $3 a dozen higher in price than the Red Comet, but the No-Fire line sells better. Since the Hoffman Brothers firm has formerly sold the Red Comet line and may still have some on hand, it may still prefer the Red Comet, which it may still be able to get from the Hardin-Manley Hardware Company, Memphis, the nearest distributor that you know of. Try, however, to get permission to substitute the No-Fire.

8. Delores Roddy, 810 Old Mill Road, Youngstown, Ohio, orders a set of Pyrex mixing bowls to be sent to Mr. and Mrs. Carl Chancey, 1109 Hill Street, Akron, Ohio, as a new-home gift. Because of so many customers' complaints about the breaking and chipping of Pyrex bowls, Marshall Miller Department Store, Akron, stocks stainless-steel sets exclusively. The 3-piece set (1-, 1½-, 3-quart bowls) costs $6.00. She can order the jumbo 6-quart bowl for salads, cakes, for $3.75 or the giant 8-quart bowl that is perfect as a punch bowl or for a really big salad for $5.50. You'll be glad to gift-wrap and send the bowls out to the Chancey home as soon as Mrs. Roddy tells you what to do. The 3-piece stainless steel set costs $2 more than the Pyrex.

9. The Batson Electrical Company, St. Louis, has been selling, along with its household electrical appliances, a glass coffee maker known as the Allstate. This has been a good seller; but recently one of Batson's buyers found the Maid of Honor all-aluminum vacuum-type coffee maker in 4-, 8-, or 12-cup size. Batson tested it, found it to be a good selling product, and decided to stock it exclusively. You, the sales manager, felt that the change was a satisfactory one because you believed that the retail jump of $1.50 was not bad

(Allstate retailed at $6, the Maid of Honor at $7.50; wholesale prices of $4.50 and $6). And, since you were enthusiastic, you sent circulars to all regular customers (you thought) describing the Maid of Honor. But this morning you got a letter from Mr. De Forrest Strunk, Strunk Drug Store, Cairo, Illinois, requesting "a dozen of those glass coffee makers, same as I got last time." Apparently you forgot to tell Mr. Strunk about the Maid of Honor in your campaign, and your salesman didn't tell him when he was in Cairo. Write a letter to Mr. Strunk convincing him of the salability and profitability of the Maid of Honor.

10. Rock-wool fibers with reflective aluminum foil covers provide the most effective insulations the Hobart Home Insulation Company, Boston, offers. Since foil itself reflects a great deal of heat, these batts block heat two ways. Rock-wool mass absorbs heat and foil acts as a vapor barrier. These fire-resistant and odorless batts have a nailing flange for easy stapling.

A letter this morning from Roy Sandlin, Box 465, Mountain View, Vermont, asks for $50 worth of Hobart rock-wool batts covered with Kraft paper. Because you believe these aluminum-foil-covered rock-wool batts are the most effective insulation you can offer, you stock them exclusively. They bring more comfort and protection in the winter by keeping heat from escaping through the roof and walls, and they keep a cooler home in summer by reflecting back the sun's hot rays. A package of 10 batts (48 inches long, 15 inches wide, 16-inch stud distance, 3 inches thick) covers 53 square feet, costs $4.89. It's true that these cost $1.68 more than the paper-covered batts, but they will do a much better job of insulation. Write the letter that will make Mr. Sandlin see the advantages—and send an additional $25 check. Assume a testimonial sales folder and a business-reply envelope.

11. Harry Gilmer, Box 908, Longhorn, Texas, orders 3 pairs, size 34, long, gray, dark-blue, and brown Mc Donald twill gabardine slacks ($7.25 a pair) from The Toggery's men's department, Dallas. Because of its resiliency, strength, easier washing, and shape-holding qualities, a dacron-and-cotton combination has replaced all gabardine for men's trousers in your stock.

The Toggery's recent ad in the *Dallas Morning News* clearly said 80 per cent dacron with 20 per cent cotton. All trimmings, thread, pocketing are made from nylon. Gabardine is made from cotton and rayon, materials that always have to be ironed. Mc Donald's twill dacron-and-cotton trousers can be washed at night and worn the next day with no ironing. These trousers are lighter weight than gabardine trousers. You can send Mr. Gilmer 3 pairs in dacron and cotton at $8.50 a pair and charge them to his account.

Combinations

1. You are one of the personal shoppers for Marshall Miller & Company, St. Louis, Missouri, handling the order of Mrs. Peter Adams, 22 Middleton Park, Trenton, Ontario, Canada, a good mail-order customer whose address has been carried on your books for five years as Scott Field, Illinois, where her

husband was a captain in the Air Force. With the necessary change-of-address information, she also included a notation that Major Adams would be stationed in Canada for two years and she'd be calling on you for lots of shopping help. She enclosed two cards, asking that you send two weeks from now to her nephew, Master Johnnie Manning, 6260 Greenmere Drive, Dallas 26, Texas, one red Thermo-Jack Jacket, No. 1435, advertised in this month's *Miller Modes,* @ $6, and one week later to her niece, Mary Susan Manning, same address, two yellow nylon plisse nightgowns, No. 2156, size 8, @ $3. Both are birthday gifts, she says. Since Mrs. Adams fails to give the size of the boy's water-repellent jacket, ask her for the boy's size (and if she doesn't know, ask his age and, if she knows them, his chest measurement and arm length). This has been a popular choice for school youngsters: soft flannel lining; fabric treated to resist spots and stains; seal of approval of *Good Housekeeping.* Probably because the nightgowns wear well, need no ironing, and are easy to wash, you have sold almost all your stock and have none in size 8. And a month from now is the earliest the manufacturer will promise them to you. If Mrs. Adams would like to make another choice, you'll be glad to handle it for her. If she'd prefer, you can mail Mary Susan one of your special children's birthday-gift announcement cards, which will arrive for her birthday, telling her that she will receive a gift about a week later. It includes a blank for indicating the name of the donor. Word the message so that Mrs. Adams will give you the necessary information and agree to the delayed birthday gift.

2. Mr. Larry Ralph Freeland orders the following equipment from the Aids for Invalids Company, New York, for his newly founded Easy-Rest Nursing Home, Springfield, Massachusetts:

6 Hospital beds, No. 8 H Mt1118 . . . . @135.50	$	813.00
12 Tilt-top bed tables, No. 8 H 02542 . . . . @ 7.97		95.64
2 Folding wheel chairs, No. 8 H M1520 . . . . @ 81.97		163.94
2 Convalescent walkers, No. 8 H M1530 . . . . @ 8.57		17.14
Total		$1,089.72
Shipping charges		54.10
		$1,143.82

Mr. Freeland enclosed a check for $500 and asked to be billed for the rest next month. As the sales manager, you find it's easy enough to bill him for the rest due next month, but there are many other problems involved in this order. You no longer stock No. 8 H Mt1118 hospital beds because you found that there was no market for this rather expensive bed. Instead you stock a $71.97 bed with tubular steel ends in attractive walnut finish with strong, comfortable, twisted link springs. The two ball-bearing cranks make it simple to operate—even a child can raise an invalid. The spring adjusts to regular 18-inch or 27-inch bed height. Ask Mr. Freeland's permission to send these equally good, but less expensive, beds. The all-steel tilt-top bed tables you have on order, but it will probably be two weeks before you can ship them to Springfield. The patients at Easy-Rest will find these tables handy to eat on or play cards on. The top can be tilted up to 45 degrees; the table top adjusts from 25 to 40 inches or can be used flat.

The folding wheel chairs come in two styles: No. 8 H M1504 is a tubular frame chair with plywood back and seat in light oak finish, while No. 8 H M1538 has foam-rubber padded seats, tubular-steel frame done in gray enamel finish. Both chairs fold to 10½ inches for easy storage. Both chairs sell for $81.97. You have no chair No. 8 H M1520 as he ordered. You are sending the two tubular steel convalescent walkers, No. 8 H M1530 today. The walkers are easy to use for they just glide along when they are pushed. No adjusting is needed as the patient's stride increases in length. The steel frame is mounted on steel-domed, rubber-cushioned glides.

3. In the preceding problem assume that you have in stock and are shipping immediately the tilt-top tables, the walkers, and the folding wheel chairs, and write the letter accordingly.

4. Instead of the preceding, assume that you are shipping the hospital beds and tilt-top tables and the walkers.

5. Assume that you are sales manager for Savanah Photo Supply Company, Savanah, Ohio. You have before you a letter from Mr. John P. Anthony, who, as the owner of the Anthony Photo Shop, Clayton, Ohio, wants a 2-gross package of double-weight, luster surface enlarging paper, 5 × 7, which sells for $4.00 a gross; 1 dozen Tower No. 8 box cameras that sell for $5 each wholesale or $10.50 retail; 1 dozen 40 × 40 inch Vyna-Flect projection screens ($14 wholesale). You have the enlarging paper, and you are making immediate shipment of that item. But the response to the Tower box camera promotion has been so successful that you do not have any on hand right now; in fact, the wire from the manufacturer today said it would be ten days before the next shipment would arrive in Savanah. And, to complicate matters, you had a falling-out with the Vyna-Flect Company over price and so now stock the Tower screens exclusively. The Tower screens sell for the same price and have the same advantages (glass-beaded surface, flame-resistant, mildew-proof, pliable, so won't crack, heavy-gauge steel case in charcoal gray, automatic action).

In your letter to Mr. Anthony, you want to assure him that the paper is quality merchandise. You will ask for his approval to send the Tower screen; and you will want to talk in such a way about the Tower box cameras that he will be glad to wait the extra ten or twelve days to stock them. His check covered the order exactly.

6. As sales manager for Pake-Stephenson sport equipment manufacturers-wholesalers, St. Louis, you are acknowledging this order from T. M. Clayton, manager, City Sporting Goods, Jefferson City, Missouri:

24 prs. No. 6 H1400 Leather track shoes, 4 each of size 8, 8½, 9,
9½, 10, 10½ @ $3.50 . . . . $ 84.00
12 prs. No. 6 H2387 Higgins rink skates, 3 each 8, 9, 10, 12 @ $8 . .   96.00
12 prs. No 6 H2303 Higgins sidewalk skates (skates adjust from 8
to 11 inches) @ $2.50 . . . .   30.00

Total $210.00

A check for $210 accompanies the order. The calculations of shipping weights and charges are correct. Evidently Mr. Clayton has a copy of your current catalogue; descriptions and prices are correct. So are the catalogue numbers of the track shoes and sidewalk skates. The number for the rink skates is not, however. No. 6 H2387 is for cowhide baseball shoes. The skates come with top-grain elk tanned-leather shoes, fully cloth lined with double-stitched sole, snug-fit heel, built-in arch support in black or white: No. 6 H2354 (men's black), 6 H2356 (men's white); No. 6 H2355 (women's black), 6 H2305 (women's white). All rink skates have waterproof maple wheels with 16 double-row ball bearings, dustcaps, adjustable cones, snag-proof, indented axles. The sidewalk skates you are sending today. The track shoes he requested you are sending in a week. You've had to wait on top-quality leather to make up these shoes. Delivery should take no more than 3 days. The shoes are some of your best sellers: leather uppers, insoles, mid-soles. Leather taps with leather heel piece. Detachable spikes.

In an attempt to gain another good outlet for Pake-Stephenson equipment, you are sending these people a credit application blank and financial-statement forms for them to fill out and return if they care to. The credit department will be glad to review the application. Since this is a dealer, you'll want to establish the profitability of your items (50 per cent markup) and to talk concretely about the dealer aids you furnish: quarter-page monthly ads in *Field and Stream* and *Boy's Life,* counter displays, and envelope stuffers (which you'll furnish at his request).

What else can you talk about as the basis for the next order?

7. An old customer of yours, Mrs. Irving Clark, 16 Fairview Drive, Athens, Georgia, orders from your college dress shop 1 T4561 American Golfer to be sent and charged to her account. As the personal shopper of Poor's Department Store, Atlanta, answer Mrs. Clark's letter. Since it is between seasons, you are sold out of all American Golfers, but your manufacturer assures you that a shipment will be on its way in 5 days. So you expect new American Golfers in stock in 10 days. Mrs. Clark will have to let you know what color she prefers (brick red, toast brown, ivy green) and what size (14, 16, 18, 20). Enclose a card to make replying easy for her.

8. The Sealy-Glisson Realty Company, Johnson City, Texas, an old customer of the Oil City Office Supplies Company, Houston, Texas, orders "an Easy-Rite steel typewriter table, dark-green finish, like we purchased last summer, and a Tower portable steel safe, gray finish. Charge to us. Ship collect by Talbot Motor Freight." Your files show that the Sealy-Glisson Company purchased table No. 8859, at $12.50. With leaves down, top measures 14½ × 18 inches—with leaves up, a roomy 14½ × 35 inches. Height 27 inches. You don't have this size in stock, and no shipment is on the way. You do have the Garrett (same manufacturer), No. 8996, with caster locks (so it won't gradually move as the carriage is returned) at $14. With leaves down, top measures 16 × 19½ inches—with leaves up 16 × 37½. The improvement is worth the money; furthermore, this would be a more economical buy for the Sealy-Glisson customer than a special order with extra

shipping charges would be. The Garrett also has a handy 16-inch center drawer, 4 inches deep. Although you indicate a willingness to make a special order of the Easy-Rite for your old customer, you subordinate this idea; concentrate instead on a low-pressure effort to get him to choose the Garrett.

Also tell the Sealy-Glisson customer that No. 4441 Tower portable steel safe (8 × 12 × 5½ inches) comes with a Yale pin-tumbler key lock ($20.50), while No. 4493 for $23.50 has a Yale combination lock. The more expensive model also has carrying handles on top and sides. Enclose a folder picturing each safe and ask which safe is preferred. You are the sales manager.

9. When Mr. J. T. Bolton, carpenter, Box 609, Bloomington, Illinois, ordered tools from Allen and Jason Company, 908 Queen Street, Memphis—

1 Craftsman Heavy-Duty Motor	$50.50
1 Craftsman Table 99 Ht25156	26.95
1 9 H 2516 ⅛ in. concave cutter	1.98
1 9 H 2519 ⅛ in. convex cutter	1.98
	$81.41

Shipping charges $2.66, plus 3 per cent tax

—he failed to tell you what size motor he wanted.

All motors are guaranteed for one year; shielded ball bearings are lubricated for 5,000 hours. No. 99 HO1936L, ½ hp, weighs 41 pounds and costs $44.50; No. 99 HO1937L, ¾ hp, weighs 65 pounds and costs $55.50; No. 99 HM1938, 1 hp, weighs 83 pounds and costs $84.50. Which motor does Mr. Bolton want? Because of a strike at the aluminum plant, the Craftsman Shaper Table will be delayed about 5 days.

10. You are the sales manager for the Essick Wholesale Company, Baltimore, Maryland. Today you receive an initial order from T. P. Steck, manager, Steck Office Supplies, Georgetown, Maryland, for the following office supplies to be sent right away:

1 gross Eagle lead pencils, No. 2	$ 4.00
12 Boston K-S pencil sharpeners	10.56
1 box (24) Shafer Ball Point pens	36.00
	$50.56

You can send the lead pencils and pencil sharpeners, but you have to delay the box of Shafer pens. Another shipment of the pens is not scheduled for arrival from the factory until next month. The first shipment sold much faster than you had expected. It is necessary for you to back-order this item until that time, and Mr. Steck must be convinced that he wants to wait. Shafer just recently promoted these all-metal pens with the sterling points in *Life, Time,* and *Look.* To make ordering easier, you are sending a credit application blank and financial-statement forms to be filled out and returned. Remind Steck of the 50 per cent markup and of the special you have this month on No. S-1064 Du-O-Ring composition books @ $1.15 a dozen instead of $2.

11. An initial order from Mr. Lester Burger, retailer, 1190 Plain Street, Naples, Florida, comes to you, the sales manager for the Bob Williams Fishing Equipment Company, Coral Gables:

12 Model 600–2 Spin Cast rods . . . .@ $5.50
12 Model 300 Spin reels . . . .@ 8.00
24 J. C. Higgins aluminum tackle boxes 4.89
3 dozen spools Cuttyhunk linen lines (8 lb. wet test; 12 threads) 0.60

Mr. Burger's check covered shipping charges, total cost, and tax. Mr. John T. Kennedy, your salesman, says Burger is hardworking, has a good location, and therefore should be a good customer. He sells to quality clintele. Today you are sending the rods, reels, and tackle boxes; however, because of strikes and general unrest in Ireland, you'll have to back-order the linen lines. You have some domestic nylon lines, but the linen are guaranteed non-kinking, non-swelling, and non-fraying. They are particularly good for salt-water fishing. Tell Mr. Burger about your one-half page monthly ad in *Field and Stream,* also about the window and counter display cards and racks and envelope stuffers you can send at his request. Indicate a willingness to review his credit application and talk in terms of the credit department. Choose an allied product and specifically tell him about it.

12. Mr. Fred Spencer, 987 California Street, Tulsa, Oklahoma, orders from you (retail sales manager of Rickover, Inc., 9876 State Street, Oklahoma City) the following:

1 No. 4–66 Carter "Cleartype" legal-size carbon paper
(box has 100 sheets) . . . .@ $ 4.50
1 No. 9876 Evans typewriter table in gray enamel finish . . .@ 12.50
1 No. 9061 Typewriter cover . . . .@   1.25
$18.25

You have the table and typewriter cover packed and on the way, shipping charges prepaid, but the special carbon is sold out. Nobody else in Oklahoma City stocks this high-grade, light-weight, well-inked brand. You have been promised that a shipment back-ordered for several weeks will be in Oklahoma City in six to eight days. The day after you get it, you can rush a box to Mr. Spencer. To tide him over, however, you sent a 25-sheet package of Carter "Midnight" legal-length carbon N 9–50 (5 cents a sheet or $1 a package) packed with the table and typewriter cover. You bill it for $1, but he may return the whole package or any unused sheets for credit. When you get the Carter "Cleartype," you'll send it ($4.50 plus 25 cents for shipping). His account now stands at $12.50 for the table, $1.25 for the cover, and $1 for the "Midnight" carbon paper and $1.15 shipping charges. His check for $18.25 is not enough. Explain and ask for the difference. He'll like the table: two drop-leaf shelves at the top and one halfway down on the right, a top center drawer, and hard-rubber casters with braking locks.

13. Because of almost constant sickness, Mrs. J. P. Wainwright orders most gifts direct from Stix and Fuller, St. Louis. As the personal shopper, you acknowl-

edge all such orders and see that the merchandise is selected, gift-wrapped, and mailed. This morning Mrs. Wainwright's letter asks that you send a white nylon No. 2706 stand-out slip, $3.95, to her grandchild, Sandra Sims, 1908 Albert Street, Alton, Illinois, in appropriate birthday wrappings, and a short-sleeved, red, all-dacron sport shirt, size 12, No. 3390, $3.50, to her grandson, Samuel Sims, at the same address. She enclosed two birthday cards for you to put in the packages. In the boy's department you discover that the store has sold all of No. 3390 red sport shirts. The store expects more in a week to ten days. If she prefers, you can send her card along with a gift message from the store telling Samuel that a gift is on its way. In the girl's department you find a complete selection of slips; but, since Mrs. Wainwright did not tell you the size for Sandra, you'll have to enclose a card and get that information from her. Slip No. 2706 comes in sizes 2, 4, 6, 6x. With appropriate resale talk, word the message so that Mrs. Wainwright will give you the necessary information and agree to the delayed birthday gift.

VIII. Sales Letters

~~~~~~

PRODUCTS are made to satisfy needs or desires. In these times of mass production, they are usually made for sale to satisfy the needs and desires of other people—rarely for the maker's own use.

Often the ultimate users are not conscious of their needs or desires until somebody else points them out. If such potential users realize their needs, marketing the product is a matter of making it available when and where wanted at an acceptable price and filling the orders. If not, marketing also involves sales promotion—pointing out needs and desires, and how the product will satisfy them—by personal selling, advertising, and mail.

"THE MARKETING MIX"—AND LETTERS

Thus you have what is sometimes called "the marketing mix"—

—a *product* designed and made to render certain services which the manufacturer determined by research or supposed to be wanted by a sufficient number of people,

219

—a group of *prospects* (the people who need or desire those services, who are not getting them, and who can pay for them),

—the *price* at which the product is salable in quantities sufficient to make manufacturing it profitable,

—the *distribution* system (transportation, storage, personnel, and other facilities necessary to make the product available when and where wanted, and to handle the records and finances of the transactions), and

—the *promotional efforts* that induce purchasing by pointing out to likely prospects just how the product will give them services that they probably want, at a price justified by the benefits.

In this chapter we are concerned with *part* of the last ingredient in the marketing mix—sales promotion by mail. Nobody would claim that selling by mail is the whole of selling, or even the biggest part; but neither would anybody—if he knows what actually goes on in American business—deny that it is a big and important part.

Nor are we concerned with all the many forms of sales promotion by mail. Leaflets, stuffers, broadsides, bulletins, brochures, catalogues, reply cards, order forms—all these supplement and support the objective of the sales letter. To attempt to deal with all these forms of mail selling, however, would be far beyond the practical scope of this book or the college course for which it is primarily intended. We are concerned only with the sales letter, the basic form of mailed sales message.

General Sales Strategy.   Whether you sell by mail or in person, your procedures are essentially the same. You seek to gain the reader's attentive interest, convince him that your proposal is worthwhile, and confidently ask him to take action.

In some cases you already have favorable attention, as when you are answering an inquiry about your product. In those cases your job is to marshal your sales points and adapt them to your reader in a message that answers his questions, convinces, and asks for action. You've already learned to do that—especially in your study of invited sales (Chapter VI).

But in prospecting—or "cold-turkey selling," as many professionals label the procedure—you have the preliminary job of arousing interest so that your reader will be eager to see what you have to say.

The surest way to get your reader to read is to stress some benefit to him. This benefit theme must come from what you have to sell. Obviously, then, you must know a good deal about your product, its uses, and the kind(s) of people who might benefit from it. From analysis of your product and prospect comes the selection of the appeal(s) to be stressed. And from a knowledge of marketing methods and people's buying habits comes the decision of what you want your reader to do after he finishes reading your message.

Analyzing the Product. The first and foremost consideration in marketing any product is the answer to "What will it do for people?" You sell only when you satisfy a need or desire.

Though you need to know a great deal about the physical characteristics of the product you are attempting to sell (such as size, shape, color, length, breadth, height, composition, for example), physical description of the product is not effective selling. The psychological description —interpretation of physical features in terms of reader benefits—is the effective part of selling.

Aluminum cooking ware, for example, may be just metal pots and pans to you. But to a cook, aluminum utensils (in psychological description)

—Give lifetime wear.

—Maintain smooth surfaces because they do not nick, chip, crack, or peel.

—Provide even, uniform heat, thus decreasing the chances that food will burn on the top, bottom, and sides, yet be raw in the middle.

—Enable the cook to do waterless cooking or cooking at a reduced temperature and thus preserve food values that would otherwise be cooked away or poured down the drain.

—Make dishwashing easier.

A dictation machine for a business executive enables him to record his ideas, it is true. But it also enables him to

—Release the high-priced dictation time of his secretary for other duties.

—Dictate when (and, with a portable machine, where) he wants to—as time permits and as ideas occur to him.

—Arrange work for his office staff in his absence.

—Have a record which does not get "cold," which anyone can transcribe with greater accuracy than is often possible with an individual's shorthand notes.

—Have a record which he himself can play back without an interpreter.

Insulation is not just pellets or bats of certain sizes and materials. To a true salesman, it keeps houses warmer in winter, cooler in summer. It thus reduces heating costs in cold months and cooling costs in warm months. It also deadens outside noises. Since it is fire-resistant, it reduces chances of fire and also decreases fire damage if and when fire breaks out. In view of all these reasons, insulation adds to the resale value of a house.

Even a child's tricycle (made of steel and chrome, with first-grade rubber tires) does more than provide pleasure for its youthful owner. It teaches him muscular co-ordination, helps to develop his visual perception and judgment, and develops his leg muscles. It also releases his parents from a certain amount of time spent in direct supervision.

You seek through such analysis of your product to identify the promises of benefit you can make to a reader considering use of your product. Through psychological description you establish for a reader a worth which he might not recognize if he saw the product *only* through his own eyes.

Psychological description is interpretation, which should be given primary emphasis. Physical description is specific detail, evidence incorporated subordinately to bear out the promises established in psychological-description phrases and passages.

For convincing your reader that your product is the one he should spend his money for rather than miss the benefits it will give him, you as a salesman must have details concerning how, of what, by whom, and where it is made and how effectively it operates. The circumstances under which it is sold (warranties, guarantees, servicing) are also considerations affecting your analysis and subsequent presentation. This physical description is necessary for conviction, but in the final sales presentation it is subservient to psychological description—the interpretation of the thing to be sold in terms of pleasure, increased efficiency, increased profit, or whatever benefit you can most specifically promise.

You need to find out as much about your product as you possibly can through observation, examination, use, testing, and reading; only then are you in a position to make wise choices concerning who is most likely to buy, how you can appeal to those people most effectively, and what is the most appropriate action for you to ask your reader to take in furthering the sale.

Of course, your analysis and your interpretation will be affected by whether your product is very new and the only one of its kind (the pioneering stage in marketing), whether it and many others like it are fairly well known to your public (the competitive stage), or whether it is very well known to your public and is the only one of its kind or accepted by the public as unquestionably the best (the retentive stage). But in all three stages your basic selling points come from your analysis of how people use your product to satisfy a need.

Finding the Prospects. True prospects are people who need the service your product will give, can pay for it, and are not getting it. Determining who these people are and their approximate number is part of your market analysis.

Of course, some people who appear to be prospects will already be enjoying the benefits of your product or one like it. In that case, they aren't true prospects. But unless you know for certain (through a list of owners, which you may have for your own product but are not likely to have for a competitor's), you need to find out. And the cheapest way to find out is to solicit them.

If you are selling a product that everybody needs, then all you have to verify is your prospects' ability to pay for it. But few products are used by everybody (and when they are, direct mail is not the best way to sell them; direct mail is a specialized class medium rather than a mass medium).

In determing need, you have to start with logical analysis. For instance, you wouldn't try to sell bikinis to Eskimos or Mackinaws to Cubans because you would assume that they don't need them. You wouldn't try to sell a central heating unit to apartment dwellers. You certainly wouldn't waste your time trying to sell a yacht to government clerical workers. Nor would you sell many hearing aids to college students.

You would seek to sell a piece of office equipment to some business owner or manager, aluminum cooking ware to housewives and restaurant owners, insulation to homeowners.

Sex, age (and, a close corollary, physical condition), family and dwelling status, vocation, geographical location, and financial situation are some of your more significant considerations in assuming that someone is a logical prospect for your product. In some cases you will need to go further than a logical analysis and make a marketing survey.

Most sales letters have to be turned out in large numbers to secure the volume necessary for profit. But even when they go out by the thousands, they are sent to a selected mailing list. And no mailing will be any good if the list of names to whom it is sent does not represent enough real prospects. Once you determine the general classes of people who are prospects, your next step is securing specific names and addresses to provide yourself with a mailing list.

What you want is a list of people in similar circumstances; the more similarities, the better. You can make your own list, rent one, or buy one. If you have the time and the money, you may be able to make a better list than you can buy. The phone book or city directory is a list of people in one city, but they usually do not have enough similarities to justify putting all of them on the mailing list for your product. The yellow pages or other kinds of specialized directories give you at least one other important similarity as a basis for selection. Newspaper clippings and trade reports are helpful in getting names for an initial list or adding names to an already existing one. Often the best list is the firm's present customers.[1] Coupon returns in space advertising will build a list for you.

You can get a big list of low purity (that is, including lots of people who are not really prospects) and low accuracy (lots of wrong addresses)[2] very cheaply. The more specifications (similarities) you put on, the higher the price.

A list house will get you almost any list you order if you're willing to pay the price. There are so many suppliers of lists in all parts of the country that the Department of Commerce issues a directory of them.[3]

Whether you buy, rent, or compile your list, however, for sales effectiveness it must be the correct names and addresses of people with common characteristics. Only then can you adapt your talking points and your references in persuasive fashion, as discussed on pages 36–39.

Choosing the Appeal(s).   From the analysis of your product come your possible sales points. But you can't tell all of them in detail in one letter, or you'll have a cluttered, shotgun-pattern letter instead of a piercing, rifle-bullet message. After listing them, deciding who the prospects are, and getting your best mailing list, your next job is to select for emphasis the central selling point—the one big theme around which your letter is built. It is the answer to this question: What one feature of the product is most likely to induce the prospect to buy? Other supporting points are interwoven, relegated to an enclosure, or left for a subsequent mailing.

People buy for many reasons: to make or save money, to preserve health, to save time, to avoid exertion, to protect themselves or their families, to protect or build a reputation, and for many other reasons, which, if you want to, you can find listed in multitude in countless books on psychology, salesmanship, sociology, and marketing. Pride, love, acquisitiveness, self-indulgence, self-preservation, curiosity, and fear play their parts in inducing interest and stimulating the final action.

Man is both rational and emotional. He needs a rational reason to support an emotional desire for something. Arguing the relative importance of the two in selling is comparable to a vigorous debate over which came

[1] See Homer Buckley's "The Sins of Omission and Commission in Direct Mail," *ABWA BULLETIN,* May, 1942.

[2] About 15 per cent of Americans' addresses change yearly, according to professional mailing-list people.

[3] See "Prospects for Sales," *Business Week,* February 14, 1948, pp. 64–68.

first, the chicken or the egg. In writing good sales letters, if you remind your reader of a need which your product will meet and supply evidence to back up your promise; if you stress what you think is the most important reason why the particular group of readers will buy, you won't need to worry about whether you are employing rational or emotional techniques. You'll be using both. And that's as it should be.[4]

Certainly, effective adaptation is necessary. Your choice of theme for your message will be affected by one or more of the significant considerations of the prospect's sex, vocation, location, age, source and amount of income, and social, professional, or educational status. One of the most obvious differences that affect your choice of theme is that between dealers and consumers. Dealers buy for the *profit* they will make on reselling. That depends on the *number* they can sell and the *markup,* less any expense and trouble necessary in backing up guarantees with replacements, repairs, and service calls. Consumers buy for the various services the product will render. But even in dealer letters you wouldn't write the same things to a large metropolitan eastern store that you would to a small rural southern store.

You can't be certain, either, of the wisdom of your choice of theme. Testing two or more different letters on a part of your list in a preliminary mailing (about which we'll say more later) may help you to arrive at a choice; but sometimes even testing does not resolve your dilemma.

For example in selling steel desks and chairs to fraternity houses, two writers came up with two different themes. One played up comfort and subordinated the factor of appearance; the other stressed appearance to the subordination of durability and comfort:

How many hours of each day do you spend at your desk?

Three? Four? Maybe more?

From experience you know how important it is that your desk be roomy and your chair comfortable.

You can be assured of the comfort and convenience you need with Carroll steel desks and chairs. Especially designed as a study unit for college men, they are also sturdy and good looking.

Wouldn't you be proud to show your rushees uniform desks and chairs?

Fine-looking study equipment will create an initial favorable impression. And they will realize, as you do, that following rush week comes work.

In Carroll steel desks and chairs you'll have study equipment that will stay good looking and provide years of comfortable use. The top has been chemically treated to

---

[4] If you want to pursue this point, read Aesop Glim's "By Reason or by Emotion?" *Printers' Ink,* 229:82, October 21, 1949; also William Tyler's "We Need a Wedding of the Two Techniques," *Printers' Ink,* 219:31–32, May 23, 1947.

Since the desk is 31 inches high, you can cross your knees beneath the top. Or if you want to sit with your feet on the desk, propped back in your chair, you can do so without marring the surface or breaking the steel-welded chair.

Whether you choose the steel top at $20.75 or the linoleum top at $15.75, you don't need to worry about nicks and scratches. Either top, 28 inches wide by 42 inches long, gives you ample room for all the books and papers you have in use. Shelves at one end, and a large drawer, keep your other books and supplies at hand.

And you can have Carroll desks and chairs in battle gray, olive green, or mahogany.

After you've had a chance to read over the enclosed leaflet (which explains the attractive quantity discounts available to you), you'll see why Carroll study equipment was recently chosen for dormitories at Michigan, Iowa, and Princeton.

avoid burns and scratches and to eliminate stains from liquids. Welded-steel construction assures you that your Carroll desk and chair will retain their attractive straight lines. And a choice of battle gray, olive green, or mahogany enables you to select a color which will blend in well with your present furnishings.

Either the steel top at $20.75 or the linoleum top at $15.75 will retain its attractive appearance over the years.

The ample work space of the desk —28 inches wide, 42 inches long, 31 inches high, with shelves at one end and a generous drawer—and the swivel chair of body-comfort design mean comfort for study as well as for long bull sessions.

After you've had a chance to read over the enclosed leaflet (which explains the attractive quantity discounts available to you), you'll see why Carroll study equipment was recently chosen for dormitories at Michigan, Iowa, and Princeton.

Both these letters are well-knit presentations of their selected themes. Each establishes the same information about the product. But we suspect that the first version would sell more chairs to house committees, because on most campuses comfortable study conditions are more important than appearance, and for a longer time than rushing conditions. You would have to test to be sure.

A letter addressed to the appropriate purchasing agent for the dormitories referred to would have wisely stressed still a different possible theme: holding down maintenance and replacement costs.

You'll see further illustration of how sales appeals vary from letter to letter in the two series which appear in the final pages of this chapter.

Identifying the Specific Goal. You may know before you begin your prewriting analysis exactly what you want your reader to do. That's fine. Analysis and writing are then simplified for you. But you'll want to be sure that the action you request your reader to take is logical in the light of purchasing conditions, which are governed by the nature of the product, the circumstances of the customer, and authorized, organized marketing channels. Many sales letters cannot and should not drive for the completion of the sale. All they do is ask for a show of interest (and thus help to weed out all but genuine prospects). You may want your reader only to request a booklet; you may want him to come to your show room; you may want him to give you some information about himself; you may want him to authorize the visit of a salesman; in many instances, of course, you can logically ask him to place an order. Regardless of what the appropriate action is, decide on it and identify it specifically before you begin to write.

All possible versions of the letter about fraternity desks and chairs should have some type of action ending, identifying payment and shipping conditions if an order by letter were appropriate or—more likely in this case—inviting the readers to come to a display room or to authorize the visit of a representative.

WRITING THE PROSPECTING SALES LETTER

After thorough study of your product and prospect, selection of theme, and decision on your specific goal, you develop that theme in a C-type letter patterned by some adaptation of the standard sales presentation: Attention, Interest, Conviction, and Action. If you want to substitute *Desire* for *Conviction* in letters appealing largely to emotion, or if you want to add *Desire* as a third step before *Conviction,* go ahead; it won't alter your basic procedure. If you want to call it Picture, Promise, Prove, and Push, you won't go wrong because of your labels. But don't think of a presentation in four or five or even three parts—like a play in three acts. In a good letter, smoothly written for coherence and unity of impression, you can't separate the parts. Though we analyze the writing of a sales letter in terms of getting attentive interest, establishing belief and trust, overcoming price resistance, and confidently asking for action, the final version of it should be a presentation that is smooth because of its coherence and persuasive because of its singleness of purpose.

Getting Attentive Interest.   If you believe in your product and what it can do for your reader, you'll have no big problem starting a sales letter effectively. All you need to do is hold up the promise of the big benefit your product can contribute to the reader. If it's a genuine benefit and your reader is a real prospect (that is, can possibly use your product and can pay for it), he'll read.

Yet, because of the clamor for attention which many advertisers talk about and write about, many advertisements and letters put on a show with the bizarre and the irrelevant in order to make the reader stop and listen. They seem to say to the reader, "We know you won't listen otherwise; so we're standing on our heads to attract your attention. Of course, standing on our heads won't tell you a thing about our product or what it can do for you, but it'll make you sit up and take notice."

To that, all we can say is, "Sure! The freak at the circus commands attention. And if sheer attention is all you want, walk down Madison Avenue or Michigan Avenue in a bikini or in shorts. You'll get attention. But is it appropriate? Is it in good taste? Will it really help to induce the reader to buy?"

Relevancy is important. Without it, your trick or gadget may be a distraction and a detriment rather than an assist to your sales effort. Tricks are legion, and they create talk, even notoriety, about you. But unless they lead naturally, plausibly, and shortly to what your product can do for your reader, they're not worth the effort and expense.

The American public is a highly educated public. It is quick to criticize or, worse yet, to laugh at advertising and its methods. It hasn't bought the Brooklyn Bridge for a couple of generations. It recognizes a gold brick for what it is worth. The farmer's daughter has been to town—even if it's only via TV. Smug patter about the fourteen-year-old mind is beguiling—and dangerous. Even the fourteen-year-old mind recognizes the difference between "show-off-ship" and real salesmanship.

You'll read much and hear much about tricks, stunts, and gadgets. Good-luck pennies, four-leaf clovers, keys that open the door to everything from business success to a happy home life with your dog, rubber bands (which most of the time only stretch the reader's patience), cartoons, faked telegrams in yellow window envelopes, simulated handwritten messages, names of readers written at the top of the page in red, blue, gold ("the symbol of things precious, and your name means much to us!"), boldface numbers ("2,400,001! What's the 1 for? That's *your* copy!"), shorthand copy, Chinese writing, the early bird with the worm in his mouth, checkerboards, mirrors, alarm clocks—all these and many others may distract from your sales message rather than assist in it unless they enable you quickly to cut through to the benefit your product can render.

Such tricks have been overused and misapplied in so many instances that one advertiser recently sent the following letter (which you'll recognize as a trick in itself):

I have never tried to fool you.

I have never sent you an order form that looks like an authentic bank check, with or without signatures and countersignatures!

And I've never sent you a bond-like certificate apparently so valuable that it startles you briefly—before you throw it away.

I have never used a brown envelope to make you think your tax refund has finally arrived.

In fact, I've never even sent you a postage stamp!

We here at Bowen's think you're too intelligent to fall for such nonsense!

We're convinced that Bowen customers are an alert and critical, not a gullible, audience. New gimmicks and catch phrases are not going to influence you. . . .

You may dream up a trick occasionally that isn't old stuff to most of your audience and that naturally, plausibly, and quickly sets the stage for the introduction of the benefit your product can render. If it can meet the tests of relevance, plausibility, and speed, you may want to use it. A fire-sale letter typed in red may have salutary appeal. A check form made out to the reader, immediately followed by the lead, "What would it mean to you to get a REAL check like this EVERY MONTH?" may plausibly preface sales talk about an annuity or health insurance.

The salesman of a car air conditioner appropriately started his letter with "98.6" in red, followed by "Pretty hot on the road, isn't it?" He followed that up with "69.8" in blue, with the quick assurance that "That's the comfortable temperature you can drive in with an Air-Temp in your car."

The sales manager who sent a letter on cellophane with the lead, "Here's a value for you that is as clear-cut as the paper on which it is written," used a good (but very expensive) gadget to command attention.

So we do not mean to imply that all tricks, gadgets, and humorous letters are undesirable. Certainly, there is the occasional opportune time for the whimsical, the gracefully turned phrase, the chuckling at man and his idiosyncrasies, and the outright humorous. But before you use what you think is a bright, clever, or punny approach, recall the story that seasoned advertisers tell of the woman who asked her husband if he had seen a certain clever ad. "What was it about?" her husband asked. "I don't remember," the lady replied, "but it was right next to that homely X, X and Y ad."

If you can phrase an opening which is deft, novel, and catchy, use it— provided that it paves the way quickly and naturally to the introduction of what your product can do for your reader. If you can't, forget about it. The product-benefit-contribution beginning is always applicable and always good. Associate the benefit with your reader, and you have a good opening.

A business-reporting service used the following successful opening in a letter to contractors:

A lot of money spent
on new construction
in your area—

—is going to wind up in somebody's pocket . . . and it might as well be
yours instead of your competitor's!

Another reporting agency got good attention with this opening:

WHAT SORT OF GOVERNMENT
WILL DOMINATE YOUR BUSINESS
IN THE DIFFICULT PERIOD AHEAD?

A laundry got the favorable attention of housewives with

We'll wash your shirts, iron them to please the man of the house, and wrap
them in cellophane—for two thin dimes.

and another varied the same theme with

Would you wash a shirt, iron it to please the most demanding man, and
wrap it in cellophane—for 20¢?

A savings-and-loan association led with

Do your savings work hard enough for you?

And an insurance company seeking to sell education insurance to parents
of small children paved the way with

A small monthly saving now will buy your youngster a gift worth $113,000.
There's no catch to it.

The $113,000—an estate even a man of wealth could be proud to leave his
son or daughter—is the difference between the average lifetime earnings
of a college graduate and one without this special training, according to a
recent national survey made by the Bureau of Labor Statistics.

Selling an automatic typewriter to office managers, the following
opening (below a clipped-on photograph of a girl powdering her nose
while surrounded by three of the machines referred to) pinpoints a real
problem and its solution:

What happens when a girl "powders her nose" in the offices of the Northeastern Mutual Life Insurance Company?

When her typewriter stops, production ceases. And office costs go up.

A variation of theme for the same product went this way:

"I've had five years' experience with the Mutual Life Insurance Company, can type 120 words a minute, am willing to work each day in-
definitely, do not get tired, and demand no salary."

Would you hire this typist? We did. And this letter was typed by her in
two minutes.

Of course it isn't human. It's a machine—The Robo-Typist—which types any letter you want from a record roll at 120 words a minute.

Note that in all these quoted openings the lead is simply a reminder of a need for which the product is shortly introduced as an agent for satisfying that need. They do not command, preach, cajole, beg, or exhort. They do not challenge. They do not scream in superlatives (finest, amazing) with exclamation points. They do not begin with talk of the product itself ("Now you too can have XYZ dog biscuits!") or the company ("53 years of doing business").

Good openings positively, specifically, and vividly, but believably, say or imply, "I promise you help in handling this specific problem." Thus they get attentive interest through psychological description of the product in use benefiting the reader and cause the reader to want more information, especially on how the product can fulfill the promise.

Establishing Belief and Trust. Having made the promise, a letter must quickly supply evidence to back it up. If the opening is successful, it has established tentative favor or agreeableness rather than serious doubt on the reader's part. In effect, the reader has mentally nodded his head in agreement. The next part of your sales letter—which ordinarily consumes the greatest amount of space—tells him how your product does meet his need and gives specific information that will make him believe you. You thus maintain and continue the agreement you establish in the start of the letter.

Explanations and descriptions of the product in use are how you handle this part. Word pictures of how it works and how it is made, performance tests, testimonials of users, statistics of users, facts and figures on sales, guarantees, free-trial offers, offers of demonstrations, and samples are some of your most common devices. Note how the following letter supplies evidence to support its opening claim. (Yes, it's long—as lots of effective sales letters are. If you are concerned about length, read Howard Dana Shaw's "Stop Worrying about Length," *The Reporter of Direct Mail Advertising*, 11:7, 8, 10, December, 1948; reprinted in *Writing for Business*.)

The Carriage Return Lever
On a Manual Typewriter
Is Costing You Money . . .

. . . and it's money you don't have to spend any more.

Human Efficiency, Inc., of New York City, has completed a series of exacting tests and confirms that you can save as much as one man-hour each day for each typist you employ when you install Speedo Carriage Returns on your manual typewriters.

Watch one of your typists. Every time she returns the carriage to the next line, her left hand makes three movements. When the bell signals the end of a line, her hand moves from the keys to the lever, throws the lever, and then returns to the keys. It looks fast and easy, doesn't it? It is—an expert typist can do it in just one second.

Just one second, but one second becomes one minute when your typist types 60 lines. And that one minute multiplies to one hour every time 3600 lines are typed. From your experience as an office manager, you know that 3600 lines aren't very many for an efficient stenographer to type, especially the short lines required for orders and invoices.

Using a Speedo, your typist performs one step—not three—to return the carriage to the next line. When the bell signals the end of the line, she presses a foot pedal; the carriage automatically spaces correctly and returns to the left margin. One-tenth of a second—not one second—has elapsed.

And because the hands do not have to leave the keyboard, accuracy increases when you install Speedos. Human Efficiency tested 150 women typists using Speedos for two weeks in 20 different large plants. They showed a 16% reduction in errors. Naturally, the amount of time spent in erasing errors was also reduced by 16%.

Part of the explanation for the increase in output and decrease of errors is a reduction in fatigue. Throwing a carriage just once doesn't amount to much, but when your typist repeats the same act hundreds of times she uses up as much energy as she would scrubbing the floor of your office. With the Speedo, however, the strain is not only decreased by two-thirds; it is shifted to the leg and foot, which can bear it far better than the arm. Tests of 45 women typists employed by the Kenoya Wholesale Grocery Company of Columbus, Ohio, showed that after two weeks they increased by 9% the amount of copy produced daily.

Clamped to the carriage-return lever, the Speedo is joined to the foot pedal by a thin wire. The adjustment is simple; you can put one on any standard typewriter in less than five minutes.

Turn to pages 1 and 2 of the enclosed folder and read the complete report of the tests. On page 3 you'll find comments of typists who've used the Speedo and the comments of their office managers. Read how the typists all agree that they had no difficulty learning to use the Speedo efficiently.

Page 4 gives you data on prices and shipping. Note that the Speedo with all its advantages—plus an unconditional 90-day guarantee—is yours for only $4.50. And by ordering a dozen for $46 you save 70¢ on each one.

Fill out the enclosed order blank and send it to us in the return envelope provided. We'll immediately ship your Speedos to you by whatever method you direct, either prepaid or C.O.D. Within 10 days at the most you'll be able to see the increased output and accuracy of your typists.

Surely you remember that sincerity is essential to the reader's belief and trust. That you-viewpoint description is vital. That psychological description in terms of the reader's use and benefits is far superior to mere physical description of the product. And that specific words in positive language are also necessary to effective sales techniques. If not, turn back and review the section on "Persuasion Principles" (pp. 28–43) and the analysis of the invited sales letter (pp. 144–54). All we're suggesting is that you apply the same principles.

Overcoming Price Resistance. You've already studied effective ways of handling dollar talk, too (back in the discussion of the invited sales letter, pp. 148–49). The principles are the same in prospecting sales. Were we to repeat them here, we'd just take up space which would merely waste your time if you remember the former discussion.

Asking Confidently and Specifically for Action. Likewise, if we discussed again what we've already told you and illustrated for you repeatedly about action endings (indicate what you want your reader to do and how to do it, make it easy and make it sound easy, and supply a stimulus to prompt action in a quick reference to the contribution the product can make to the life of the reader), we'd be using your time unnecessarily and adding to production costs. Furthermore, the points are itemized specifically in the accompanying summary check list. It helps you to review and your instructor to evaluate your letter.

ADAPTING TO CLASSES

All good sales letters follow the basic procedures advocated in the preceding pages. Only in their talking points and in their interpretation and references do they differ as they go to farmers instead of bankers, to lawyers instead of engineers, to consumers as opposed to dealers. Much fluff is written and said about letters to women, but there's a lot of evidence pointing to the fact that the American woman—and the homemaker in particular—is a sharp customer, as demanding and calculating in reading the pages of catalogues and magazines as a purchasing agent for a firm is. She's no different when she reads a letter. And much guff circulates about the feminine slant and the masculine slant and which sex should write for which. Such talk is misleading. If you are a person of feeling and imagination and are unselfish enough to forget yourself in analyzing another person's (or group of persons') circumstances, you won't have much trouble writing successfully adapted letter copy.

As an illustration of how tone and talking points differ, study the following two letters. The first is to a homeowner, the second to a dealer. In both cases, the product is a lawnmower which eliminates hand clipping.

Prospecting Sales Check List

1. Get started effectively and economically.
   - *a*) Point up a specific reader benefit in the first sentence.
   - *b*) Establish early the distinctive advantages your product has over competitors; it is often your best central selling point.
   - *c*) If you use a gadget, a trick, an anecdote, be sure it leads naturally and quickly to what your product does.
   - *d*) Beginning too far from the *distinctive* thing your product will do is slow and may be distracting. "In your new home, protection from fire is of major importance," may precede talk about asbestos, fire extinguishers, sprinkler systems, or even lightning rods. Just assume such ideas and get started more directly and specifically.
   - *e*) Don't begin with either an obvious statement or a question to which the answer is obvious: "Do you want to make money?" or "Don't you want all the protection you can get in your home?" The question with the obvious answer is worse if you give the answer, too: "Wouldn't you gladly pay 2¢ a day for increased protection from fire?" might be effective with most property owners, but it wouldn't be if you add "Of course you would!" or "You can do just that with XYZ!"
   - *f*) Suggest or remind but don't preach: "You will want," "You will need."
   - *g*) Build up the desirability of the product before introducing it specifically by name. Don't plunge in with something like "XYZ—the answer to homeowners' prayers!" or "What is XYZ? XYZ, Mr. Homeowner, is a new and different. . . ."
   - *h*) Don't claim too much for your product, especially in the opening.
   - *i*) You'll usually do better to stick to positive selling, at least to avoid the pushover aspects of the predicament-to-remedy approach.
   - *j*) Concentrate on your central selling point in the lead; don't split your appeal by attempting to cover too many points.
2. Back up your opening promise with a persuasive description.
   - *a*) Though the you-viewpoint is not automatically injected with frequent use of *you* ("you will find" and "you will note" are often more wordy than persuasive), when you make the reader the subject or object of action verbs, you help to maintain it.
   - *b*) Guard against stark product description. A sentence is usually off to a bad start with "Our goods," "We make," or "XYZ is made of."
   - *c*) Interpret physical features in terms of the reader's benefit in the use of the product each time you bring out a point. By depicting the reader's use and benefit, you help to avoid incoherence.
   - *d*) Specificness in description is necessary for conviction.
   - *e*) Adapt your letter. Even in a form letter, refer to some action or condition that applies to your list as a whole. Avoid a reference which brands your letter as an obvious form ("Mr. Homeowner"

PROSPECTING SALES CHECK LIST (CONTINUED)

or ". . . whether you live in Maine or California"). See pp. 37–39 for references that make your reader feel that you're talking right to him.

   f) The history of the product or firm will bore most readers.

   g) Eliminate challenging superlatives: "What could be finer than . . . ," "amazing," "unbelievable," "sensational," "the finest," "the best."

   h) Guard against the trite and inappropriate "truly" and "really" as well as the indefinite "that" and "which" in expressions like "that important conference" or "that important date."

3. Be sure to cover all important points with proper relative emphasis.

   a) Give enough detail to sell your reader on reading your enclosure when you have one (you usually do) and even more detail when you do not. For many products, a two-page letter will outpull a one-page letter. "If you're gonna sell, you gotta tell."

   b) Select a more appropriate central selling point.

   c) Stress your central theme for a singleness of impression.

   d) Provide more conviction. Consider construction details, specific identification of tests and specific results (performance under actual conditions, before-and-after comparisons), testimonials, number of users, and guarantees.

   e) After covering most of your sales points, introduce your enclosure with a sentence also incorporating a reference to an action of your reader and establishing a genuine sales point. Acceptable but dull: "The inside pages will give you names of XYZ users." Alive and persuasive: "Turn the page and read what some of the 4,000 users of XYZ have said about it."

4. Remember the price; it is an integral part of any sales message.

   a) Unless you sell on a recognized-bargain appeal (you ordinarily don't), minimize price by ways discussed on pp. 148–49.

   b) Try to keep price out of the ending, certainly the last sentence.

   c) If for good reason you do not talk price, reassure the reader that it is not out of line and offer to give price in some other message.

5. Forthrightly ask for appropriate action.

   a) Name the specific action you want your reader to take.

   b) Be success-conscious. Avoid "If you'd like . . . ," "We think you'd like . . . ," and "Why not . . . ?" "Your signature on the enclosed card will bring you . . ." or "Just sign . . ." maintain the right tone.

   c) Avoid high-pressure bromides: "Why wait?" "Don't delay!" "Order today!" "Do it now!"

   d) Refer casually to the order-facilitating device (card, envelope, order blank).

   e) End with a quick reference to what the product will contribute (a condensed reminder of the central selling point).

Lawnmowing Time

Extra Time for
Summer Rest and Fun!

You can cut your lawnmowing time in half with an easy-operating Multi-mower because you can eliminate the hand clipping and trimming.

The Multimower gathers all the grass it cuts, too.

So with just one run over the lawn with your Multimower, your lawn is in shape. And it's just a light workout. You can cut your grass flush against fences, trees, and flower beds. The interlocking rotary cutters enable you to mow tall grass and tough weeds with no more effort than it takes to cut short grass. And you're less tired when you get through because you push only the minimum weight when you use this 8¼-pound mower. It's light enough for almost any member of the household to use, too.

Even though the Multimower is light, you have a precision mower of sturdy construction and strength-tested materials. The drive shaft is mounted on free-rolling, factory-lubricated, sealed ball bearings which keep dirt and water from rusting these parts. And the cutters are self-sharpening. So your Multimower is always ready for you to use.

If the weather keeps you from mowing your lawn on schedule and grass gets a little too high, simply adjust the handle knob to the cutting height you want, and push your Multimower easily across your lawn, cutting a clean, even 16-inch swath.

Many of the 8,000 enthusiastic Multimower owners have been using theirs for over two years. Some of their statements, along with illustrations and the details of our 90-day structural guarantee, you can read on the two inside pages. You'll see too that we pay shipping charges to your door at the economical price of $29.95. The time you save on the first summer's Multi-mowing is probably worth more than that.

Use the handy order mailer to send us your check or money order. Within a week after you mail it, you'll be able to cut, trim, and gather up the grass on your lawn in only one easy, time-saving Multimowing.

The letter to a dealer stresses the same points, to show why he can expect sales to his customers; but it does so more rapidly and concisely, in order to concentrate on sales aids, price spreads, promptness and regularity of supply, and service as parts of the profit-making picture.

Certainly, of necessity, a dealer is habitually more money-conscious than the average consumer. And his reasons for buying are more complex. He may be more rational in his evaluation of a product than a consumer and probably is more critical. But the approach is the same as in any sales letters: It seeks the answer to the ever-present question, "What will it do for me?" To a dealer, the answer is always "profits"; but profits depend on salability (the features of the product that cause people to buy), on serviceability, and on the markup. A dealer is also interested in promptness and regularity of filling his orders, and in your guarantee and service arrangements.

> When you show a customer a Multimower, a lawn mower completely new in design and principle, which cuts and trims a lawn in one operation, you have a quick sale, a satisfied customer, and a $10.45 profit.

> Men like the Multimower because it gives them more time to spend in enjoyable summer recreation. It cuts right up to walls, fences, trees, and flower beds and thus eliminates the need for hand trimming in spots not reached by the ordinary mower. Its easily adjustable cutting-height regulator and self-sharpening cutters that slice down the toughest kinds of grass, dandelions, and weeds will assure them of having a trim, neat lawn in half the time they've formerly spent.

> Both men and women like the Multimower because its light weight—only 8¼ pounds—means easy pushing. The quiet operation of the interlocking cutters has won approval of 8,000 Multimower users. They like it, too, because it is permanently lubricated. With a minimum of care it's always ready for use.

> No doubt many of your customers have been reading about the Multimower in the full-page, four-color monthly ads that started running in the *Saturday Evening Post* in March and will continue through July. A reprint, along with testimonials and conditions of our guarantee, appears on the next page. Note the favorable guarantee and servicing arrangements.

> In these days of high prices, the $29.95 retail cost of the Multimower will be popular with your customers. Our price to you, including shipping charges, is $19.50.

> By filling out and returning the enclosed order blank along with your remittance today, you'll be sure to have Multimowers on hand when your customers begin asking for them.

The significant points to keep in mind are summarized in the accompanying check list on the next two pages.

TESTS AND TESTING

You will probably recall that earlier in this chapter we referred to testing a mailing and to the returns or the pull or the pulling power of a letter. Testing means simply mailing the letter to a portion of the names on your list to see whether you can get the necessary percentage of people to take the action you want.

But, unless your sample is big enough and unless you carefully control conditions so that you test only one factor at once, you won't have any reliable evidence.

Most tests that have been made have been on sales letters (though a little has been done on collections). You can see why a businessman

DEALER SALES CHECK LIST

1. A dealer-letter opening has to move fast.
   a) In action language, picture the act of selling and endow the product with consumer appeal. The opening cited in the preceding example is effective. You can create the same kind of effect with "What are you going to tell your customers when they come in asking for a Multimower, the new kind of lawnmower they've been reading about in the *Saturday Evening Post?*"
   b) Use a distinctive point of appeal and thus eliminate slow, general copy like "Are you looking for something new and different to show your customers?" or even this: "Would you like to sell a modern, efficient lawnmower that has price appeal as well as quality appeal?"
   c) Avoid exaggeration such as "Do you want to stock an item that will sell like wildfire and give your customers the greatest satisfaction?"
   d) Forget elementary merchandising lectures like "Satisfaction of your customers means turnover and profits to you."
   e) Every good sales letter devotes at least the beginning to the reader. A dealer is interested in your product only when you show him how he will benefit. This one completely forgets the Number-1 man in its selfishness: "8,000 Multimowers have been sold directly from our factory, and now that a large demand has been built up for the product, we want to sell the Multimower through dealers."
2. To stress consumer demand and to avoid selfish-sounding product-viewpoint presentation, explain the high points of the product in terms of retail customers' reactions, demands—and approval, that lead to high-volume sales.
   a) Talk in terms of sales by the dealer—not his use of the product.
   b) Adaptation here means talking of sales demonstrations to customers, wrapping up a purchase and handing it across the counter, ringing up a sale, answering customers' questions, and the like.
   c) The best order probably first takes up the salability of the product; without consumer appeal, the product stays on the shelves. The dealer is interested in price spread, of course, but more interested in a good item which is in demand.

would be wise to test a mailing before risking his money sending 10,000 letters, especially if the mailing pieces are expensive.

One reason for testing is simply to find out whether the mailing will be profitable. Suppose your mailing pieces cost 10 cents each (not unusual in a mass mailing) and you make $1 on each sale. Obviously, you have to make sales to 10 per cent of the list to break even. Now suppose you have a 90 per cent accuracy factor (that is, the percentage of correct

Dealer Sales Check List (Continued)

3. Show how the manufacturer helps to push the sale.
   a) Refer to whatever dealer aids you have as local-demand builders. Without effective sales aids (advertising, displays, mats, cuts), the dealer's selling job is harder.
   b) Give working ideas of size (quarter-page, half-page), extent (time it will run), and coverage (specific medium—magazine, newspaper, radio, and/or TV station—and type of audience).
   c) Interpret any advertising as building consumer interest and promoting interested inquiries at the dealer's: "Your customers have been reading about . . ." or "Many of your customers are already familiar with . . ." or "To help sell your customers. . . ."
4. Continue the interpretation of profitable selling in the price talk.
   a) Price is more appropriately handled late because (1) regardless of your markup, there's not much profit unless the goods move; so you want to establish demand first; (2) price is more naturally handled as you ask for an order and talk payment details.
   b) Include a specific mention of price spread: "You buy for $3 and sell for $5." Or you can cite percentages. Many good letters do both.
   c) Terms and manner of payment have to be cleared up.
5. You will almost always have some enclosures to handle.
   a) You wouldn't want to divert attention to the enclosure until your reader is near enough the end that he'll complete the letter before turning away.
   b) Make the reference to further material carry a real sales point, too. (See Item 7 of the special request check list, p. 115).
   c) Don't depend too heavily on your enclosure to do the selling job; establish enough points so that this dealer-reader has a good idea of what he'll read about in the enclosure.
6. Make the action ending brief and businesslike too.
   a) You're probably on safer ground in avoiding commands to this seasoned buyer.
   b) Exaggerated superlatives are out of place here, too.
   c) Of course, you name the specific action you want him to take.
   d) And you make that action easy.
   e) Use a whip-back or stimulus, suggesting prompt handling and profitable selling.

addresses). Each 100 letters have to bring 10 orders from every 90 people to whom they are delivered. Further suppose the purity (how many names on the list are likely prospects instead of deadwoods) is 70 per cent. That means that your 100 letters have to bring 10 orders from every 63 good prospects (70 per cent of 90). That requires about 16 per cent pulling power from your letter ($^{10}\!/_{63}$). Most sales letters don't do that well. But you could change the situation into one that would be more likely to be profitable by increasing any or all of the accuracy, the purity, or the pulling power—or by decreasing costs of the mailing or increasing the margin of profit on the sale.

Faced with the prospect of a required 16 per cent, you'd probably do some revising of plans in order to lower it. And then, to be on the safe side, you'd mail your proposed mailing to a part of your list. On very large mailings the percentage is small—5 per cent or less. Most experienced mail salesmen will use about a 10–20 per cent random sample. If the replies from the sample meet the necessary percentage figures for profitable operations, you'll go ahead. If they don't, you'll revise or drop the whole plan without losing as much money as you would have if you hadn't tested.

Another reason for testing is to find out which of two messages has the greater pull or which of two times (day or week or month the mailing piece arrives) is more profitable. *But you can test only one factor at a time!*

You can test one color against another; but if you vary size, copy, or time, your test doesn't mean a thing. You can test position of coupon *or* order blank versus order card; but if you allow any variation of other factors, your findings are not reliable. You can test one lead against another; but if the rest of the copy, the color and size of the paper, the envelope and stamp, and the time of arrival are not the same, you still have no basis for saying that one lead is better than the other.

Many test results have been published concerning format and timing. If you talked with enough people in the field or read long enough, you'd be reassured—often vehemently!—that every color you've ever seen is the best color for a mailing. You'd find one man swearing by third-class mail and another at it. You'd find out, however, what all experienced people with judgment discover: Because people and circumstances constantly change, so do the results of testing; what is suggested by a test this week may not be true next week and probably will not be next year; the only way to be safe is to test in each new situation and then follow through as fast as you can.

Even so, you usually expect only 5–10 per cent pulling power. But especially effective copy, carefully selected mailing lists, or unusual offers often increase these percentages. And, obviously, the reverse of these conditions decreases the pulling power sharply.

Because some series depend on large volume and succeed on small margins, even such apparently insignificant things as the time of arrival are important. Experience has shown that such letters should not arrive in an office at the beginning or ending of a week or month or at the homes of laborers or farmers in the middle of the week. Around Christmas time and April 15 (income-tax time) are especially bad times of the year. In general, the fall and winter months are better than spring or summer. Of course, seasonal appropriateness of the goods and geographical locations can easily affect this. Even temporary local conditions may.

By keeping careful records on the tests and on the whole mailing, through the years users develop a considerable quantity of experience data that may help guide them in future work.

Before you accept conclusions, however, know the circumstances back of the quoted figures. The results may be worth no more than the paper they're written on; but they may be reliable.

WRITING SALES SERIES

The sales letters we have been discussing are lone efforts to produce or promote sales. Because single sales letters usually cannot do all the work that a series can, probably *just as many* or more sales letters are sent as part of series as are sent singly. Usually they are obviously processed (form) letters, sent out in large numbers by third-class mail. For further economy, they use some simulated address block instead of an inside address and salutation (like some of the examples in this chapter). By careful phrasing, however, a skillful writer will often succeed in making the one reader of each copy forget the form and feel that he is getting something of a personalized message.

Whether a letter is a single sales letter or one in a series makes little difference in the techniques or preliminary planning, but in one type of series the letter's organization is made more complicated. There are three important types of sales series:

1. The wear-out series
2. The campaign series
3. The continuous series

The Wear-Out Series. Probably the most widely used of sales series is the wear-out series. In it each mailing is a complete sales presentation sent to a large group by almost any firm with a relatively inexpensive product to sell (usually $1–$15). The product almost has to be inexpensive, because one letter cannot hope to succeed in persuading most people to buy expensive items by mail from a complete stranger.

After the market analysis, preparation or purchase of a mailing list, and preliminary planning, comes writing the letter. Probably you and several other executives, and perhaps a letter consultant, will spend hours preparing the letter, or several versions of it. These first few copies may cost several hundred dollars in time and consultant's fees.

Then you test your list, and perhaps several versions of the letter (as formerly explained). If one letter seems to have the best pulling power (and that is high enough to make it profitable), you run off hundreds or thousands of copies, as the size of the mailing list requires, and mail them out at a carefully selected time. Now that the big investment has been divided among so many, the cost per letter is not so big (maybe 10–25 cents).

After an interval usually of one to three weeks, you remove the names of purchasers (unless the product has frequent recurring demand) and send another letter (or sometimes the same one) to the remaining names. Sometimes the second or even the third or fourth mailing brings better results than the first, even with the same letter, because of the buildup of impact.

You continue to repeat the mailings as long as the returns pay you a suitable profit on your mailings—that is, until the effectiveness of the list is worn out.

The Campaign Series.   What has been said about the cost of the first copy, the general preliminary planning, the testing, and the usual interval between mailings of the wear-out series also applies to the campaign series. But there the similarity stops.

Contrary to the wear-out series, the campaign series is preplanned not only for the construction of the letters and the intervals between them; you decide, before you start, how many mailings you will send and how long the whole series will run. It is also different in that it is used mostly to sell or to help sell rather expensive items.

That fact (cost of product) really determines its nature. The theory is that people buy some (usually inexpensive) items quickly, without much thought. Those things can be sold by one good complete sales letter, as in the wear-out series. But before buying certain other types of items (usually more expensive, but not absolutely essential), most people ponder for a month or more and talk over the situation with friends, financial advisers, and other members of the family. To send a letter which first introduced such an item and, after only two minutes of reading time, asked for the decision on an order card would be to pour money down the proverbial rat hole. The reader would laugh at you. Instead of the wear-out, you would use the campaign series for such a situation. Your action requests (at least in the first few mailings) are to get a show of interest:

write for more information, come to a showroom, authorize the visit of a salesman. You usually do not talk price in the earlier mailings and sometimes not at all.

Having done your preliminary planning as explained, you are ready to plan the series. You decide approximately how long most people on the mailing list would want to think over your offer before making up their minds. Then you decide how frequently they should be reminded to keep them thinking about your product or service. On that basis you decide how many mailings you want to send for the whole span of time, the whole series.

Some campaigns correspond to the parts of a sales presentation. Each of the letters emphasizes a particular phase but does not omit the action step ever—just in case some readers may be sold without the full treatment.

The essence of planning the series of letters is to make the whole series cover the parts of a complete sales presentation and knit them together. The series may include from two to a dozen mailings, or even more. In any case, the first letter will try hard to get attention and start working at interesting the prospect. Further letters will develop the succeeding steps in the selling procedure until the last makes a strong drive for action.

The last is not the only one, however, to which a reader can easily respond. Mail salesmen know that they will not usually get any action from more than half of their prospects. But they also know that in almost any large group there are some who will be sold on the first contact. Consequently, they usually provide handy return order forms with almost every mailing.

The Continuous Series. The wear-out and campaign series are different in many ways, but they are much more like each other than like the continuous series. Both the wear-out and the campaign series are usually complete sales presentations which try to bring in orders. The continuous series rarely does. Instead of being used by almost any kind of firm, the continuous series is most frequently used by department stores as a good-will or sales-promotion medium rather than a direct-mail selling system. The mailing list for the continuous series is usually the list of the firm's charge customers, instead of one specially prepared in view of a market analysis for the particular item or service being sold. The continuous series usually costs little or no postage because it is sent with the monthly statements; so the usual interval between mailings is longest in the continuous series. Still perhaps the biggest distinction is the rigid planning of the campaign series as compared with the hit-or-miss, haphazard nature of the continuous series. It commonly includes special mailings at Easter and Christmas but also on almost any other special occasion the sales manager chooses. As such, it does not run for any set length of time or for any definite number of mailings; and it may *promote* a great *variety* of products while the campaign and wear-out series are *selling one.*

~~~~~

The following direct-mail campaign directed to accounting firms, tax services, and law firms emphasizes the economy of making dry photocopies instantly with an Adeco Auto-Copier (costing about $350) instead of having papers and carbons manually typed. Though planned for firms in Alabama, Georgia, and Florida, the letters could just as well be sent within one city or over the entire country. A salesman within a city could readily assemble his mailing list from the yellow pages of the phone book. The Atlanta district manager (for the three states) could assemble his list also from the yellow pages of phone books for the cities in his area (available in any large library, such as the Atlanta Public Library). Or he could buy the list. Certainly a nation-wide mailing list would be more inexpensively purchased than assembled.

The mailings are planned for intervals of about three weeks. For economy they use a simulated address block instead of an inside address and salutation, are printed, and go third class. Each mailing includes a reply card which reads something like this:

Adeco

    Auto-Copier

Yes, I would like to know more about how the Adeco Auto-Copier will help me. Please call me and arrange an appointment.

The card provides blanks for indicating name of individual, position, company, and address.

The first mailing includes a 12-page, two-color booklet containing illustrations, savings estimates and comparisons, and information about the company and its organization.

You can save
Up to 80% on
Copying jobs . . .

. . . by letting your typists make black and white photocopies with the Adeco Auto-Copier.

In less than 45 seconds an unskilled operator can turn out a legally acceptable, error-proof copy of an original—one that would take your typist at least ten minutes to copy manually. If your office produces only fifteen copies a day, the Auto-Copier can save you about $3 each working day.

When you need to turn out large numbers of copies, the Auto-Copier makes them for you as fast as 75 an hour, at proportionate savings.

Your Auto-Copier takes a picture without using a camera. So in turning out copies of complicated tax forms, accounting forms, government records, and deeds, it assures you of error-proof, smudge-proof copies. One compact photocopy unit does it all; the Auto-Copier is a fully automatic, continuous copier and processing unit combined. Since prints are processed and dried automatically, they're ready for your instant use.

And you don't need a separate timer or printer, either. In just two simple steps you can turn out prints made from any original up to 11″ by 17″ whether printed on one or two sides.

Just put the Auto-Copier on any convenient desk or table, plug it in, and you're ready to start. You can copy any confidential material right in the privacy of your own office in just a few seconds. Read the description in the enclosed folder of the Auto-Copier's easy, simple operation.

The Auto-Copier will actually enable you to have one unskilled clerk do the copying work of six expert typists. Just sign and return the enclosed card so that your Adeco representative can stop by and show you how to let the Auto-Copier cut the high cost of duplicating records.

(Signature)

Auto-Copier copies of tax forms are fully accepted and approved by the Internal Revenue Department.

The second letter accompanies a 4-page, two-color folder, headlined "Make dry photocopies of tax returns instantly!" In the upper left corner of the letter appears the picture of a girl operating an Auto-Copier. To the right of the illustration is the headline

MAKE

TAX RETURN COPIES

INSTANTLY

with the Adeco Auto-Copier.

Now your typists can
Turn out tax return
Copies in just a few seconds!

Tax copying work which used to take hours you can now do in seconds with the Adeco Auto-Copier. And these copies are fully accepted and approved by the Internal Revenue Department.

You can actually reduce by one-third to one-half the number of statistical typists which you employ. Since the average statistical typist in this area makes about $60 a week, you'll be able to save $20 each week for each one you now employ. Or your typists can use the time saved to get out your other important papers and reports.

You know how difficult it is to type tax copies speedily, align them accurately, and avoid carbon smudges. With the Auto-Copier, you need to type and proofread only the original, then turn out error-proof, clean, legible copies at a rate as high as 75 an hour—copies that your typists never have to align, erase, or proofread.

And on involved legal reports or contracts you'll find your Auto-Copier especially helpful. Whether your paper is opaque or translucent, you are assured of clear copies, and you can reproduce copies on both sides of a single sheet, too.

Eliminate the expensive, time-consuming job of manually copying tax returns in your office. Whether you're working on state or federal tax forms, corporation or individual, you can get the copies out three times as fast with the Auto-Copier. Just sign and return the enclosed card so that your Adeco representative can come by and show you all the ways you can use an Auto-Copier.

(*Signature*)

Turn to page 4 of the enclosed folder and note the three simple steps in making tax-return copies.

Letter No. 3, accompanied by a 1-page folder, drives for a demonstration (with the post card altered in wording accordingly):

When you need copies . . .

. . . of tax forms, accounting records, government forms, or letters, you can be confident that any made on the Auto-Copier will be as clear, unsmudged, and error-proof as the original. No more faulty copies because of poor alignment or carbons that are too light to use. And your copies are turned out from three to ten times as fast as carbons ever can be.

The average typist, even the good typist, is hard pressed to turn out in one hour even six perfect copies of a tax return or many other government forms that the average business has to produce. The Auto-Copier can turn out 75 perfect copies. And no proofreading or corrections are necessary.

Your Auto-Copier takes up no more space than a standard typewriter. Just plug it in, and your typist is ready to copy. Because the Auto-Copier is completely electric, you can do all your copying work automatically from start to finish.

Try the Auto-Copier for a week. We'll be glad to bring one around for you to see how easily it will fit many of your copying needs. Fill in and return the enclosed card so that your Adeco representative can demonstrate in your office its value to you and your company.

(*Signature*)

Notice Auto-Copier's other exclusive advantages described in the enclosure.

The fourth letter shows an attractive young woman turning out copies on the Auto-Copier. She looks directly at the reader and addresses him:

I've typed thousands
Of tax returns.

And I *know* the Adeco Auto-Copier can save you money because it can reduce your tax copying work up to 80%.

For two years I have typed tax forms in the offices of C. C. Putman, C.P.A., 166 Stallings Building, Atlanta.

Turning out an original copy of a complicated tax form is a job in itself, but typing ten or twelve clear, unsmudged carbon copies is next to impossible.

Now just a minute! I'm not a poor typist. I can type 60 words a minute with no errors on a ten-minute test. That is certainly as good as the average typist, and I believe, confidently, a lot better. But I still have trouble aligning carbons, making corrections, and typing sufficiently clear and legible copies.

With the Auto-Copier I simply type the original and run off as many copies as I need. Reports that used to take at least two days to prepare I can now turn out in one day. Each detail of the original is accurately and legibly reproduced—and the only copy I have to proofread is the original!

Our clients like Auto-Copied forms. And they're fully accepted by the government.

In addition to tax form copies, I use the Auto-Copier for letters, bank records, claims, graphs, or invoices. No more costly retyping or hand copying! And no more messy, time-consuming carbons!

My employer and I agree that the Auto-Copier is the answer to our copying needs. Your Adeco representative would like to show you how the Auto-Copier can solve your copying problems, too. Check the enclosed card today so that he can call on you to demonstrate one in your office.

The letter carries the signature of the young woman, the title indicating that she is secretary to Mr. Putman.

The fifth mailing re-establishes the main talking points and stresses much harder the advantages of having the salesman come in and demonstrate:

Can your typists turn out
75 perfect copies an hour?
With the Auto-Copier they can!

The Auto-Copier will enable you to have one unskilled clerk do the copying work of six expert typists.

In addition, you are assured of perfect accuracy—each detail of the original is accurately reproduced without any possibility of error. And there's no need for tedious, time-consuming proofreading and checking, either.

In turning out copies of complicated tax forms, legal reports and records, and accounting data on the Auto-Copier, your typist can run off up to 20 clear, unsmudged copies in no more than five minutes. Since she can't make errors on Auto-Copied material, erasing time and messiness are eliminated.

You can put your Auto-Copier on any convenient desk or table, since it measures 20″ × 11″. You simply plug it in, and you're ready to start using it. No special installation is necessary. Anyone can run it.

Since Auto-Copies are processed and dried automatically, they're ready for your instant use. You need no developing, washing, drying, or printing space because the Auto-Copier does everything in one simple operation.

Your Auto-Copier representative would like to talk with you about your particular copying needs. He'll also show you how other companies are using Auto-Copier to help cut copying costs. Just sign and mail the enclosed card and he will call to arrange a demonstration in your office.

The sixth mailing is a copy of the first letter, with a reminder memo attached.

Mailing No. 7 is the booklet sent with the first letter. Attached to the booklet is a memo in simulated handwriting:

If you didn't get a chance to read the first copy of the booklet I sent you recently, here's another.

It will show you how the Auto-Copier can help you cut the high cost of duplicating records.

Of course the reply card is also enclosed.

The eighth and final mailing is another memo, this time attached to the same folder that accompanied the second letter:

You can make photocopies of tax forms instantly with the Auto-Copier. Notice in the enclosed folder the three easy steps necessary to turn out tax-return copies fully acceptable to the Internal Revenue Department.

To find out how the Auto-Copier can lighten your tax-copying problems, return the enclosed card.

This next campaign, directed to gift shops, seeks to get owners or managers to stock Jense stainless-steel tableware. A list could be purchased easily. With time (lots of it if the mailing were extensive), it could be assembled from classified directories. Since the product is relatively new, the firm offers to sell on consignment. Because of that factor, for safety, the list has to be checked for credit reliability, and the contractual phrasing of the order blank assumes greater significance.

The first mailing early in September is a box containing a sample spoon of Jense and a price list of the line. The envelope attached to the box by a wire contains the following letter and a reply card requesting more information:

100% markup—
And it sells itself!

Take this sample of Jense stainless-steel tableware and compare it with any tableware—either in your shop or in some competitor's.

It compares favorably in style, quality, and workmanship. It gives your customers more value at a lower price. It's durable and easy to keep. So more and more homemakers today are choosing Jense as their best.

When your customers inquire about Jense, invite them to make the same comparisons you have made. Tell them how durable Jense is because it contains 35% nickel, the highest nickel content in stainless-steel tableware. The homemaker of today does not have to be concerned when her maid or children carelesssly handle her Jense, because it will not bend.

Your customers will like the small amount of care Jense requires. It needs no polishing; it won't discolor or tarnish. Soap and water are all that are needed to retain its lustre. Because Jense requires only a minimum of care, it fits right in with today's living that stresses ease and informality.

The low cost of Jense is a good talking point too. Glance over the price list we sent you. Notice that a spoon like the one we sent you costs your customer only $1.40 and that place settings of six in any of the four graceful patterns run to only $8. And remember that on every place setting of Jense tableware you sell, you make a profit of $4.

Jot down your name and address in the blanks on the enclosed reply card and mail it today for more information about Jense—the graceful, inexpensive, durable stainless-steel tableware that your homemaker customers will buy when you put it on display.

The second mailing is a letter, a folder, an order blank, and reply envelope. The 4-page folder illustrates in color a table place setting in each of the four Jense patterns. These are the same photographs as those appearing in current magazine advertising and are identified as such in the letter. Letter copy stresses the adaptability of Jense to conventional or modern surroundings, to informal or formal entertaining. Of course, it asks for an order. It goes immediately to any dealer who responds to the first mailing; others on the list receive it about two weeks after the first mailing.

About a month after the second mailing (the middle of October), the third mailing goes to all names on the list—whether they have bought or not. A 4″ × 6″ memo to the dealer is folded over an 8½″ × 11″ letter, which is a copy of a consumer sales letter about Jense. The memo reads:

Here's one way
We help you
Push your sales
Of Jense.

The enclosed letter is written just for your customers. It stresses the versatility, easy upkeep, low cost, and extensiveness of Jense.

There's space at the bottom of the letter for you or someone else in your store to sign, and room for a personalizing postscript if you want to add one. All you have to do is mail the letter.

Any items you check on the enclosed order blank will be sent to you within 24 hours after we receive it.

And we'll send you whatever number of letters you specify plus the same number of the leaflets referred to in the letter.

When the dealer lifts the memo, he reads this letter, which is already prepared for his local distribution:

Made especially
For today's busy,
Discriminating hostess.

Whether you prefer traditional or modern surroundings, you can set your table with Jense and have a harmonious setting with beauty and charm.

The painstaking craftsmanship and the new techniques of hand polishing and finishing are combined to give you a tableware beautifully balanced for adaptability and harmony. For informal luncheons or buffets, Jense will complement your arrangement and give it freshness and beauty. And the simplicity of Jense's design will add elegance and distinctiveness to your formal table settings.

In preparation for your parties, you do not have to polish your Jense. Since it is tarnish-proof, its lustre lasts for a lifetime. Just wash it with soap and water, and it will always look its loveliest on your table.

You can have a six-piece Jense place setting for only $8—a minimum investment for quality tableware that you will use on any occasion in the years to come.

With Jense you can also have hollowware in the same pattern as your flatware. Notice in the enclosed leaflet the hollowware that matches each of the four distinctive Jense patterns. And remember that all of this permanently polished stainless-steel tableware is equally at home on your table or in the oven.

Come in soon and choose the pattern especially suited to you.

Around the middle of November the fourth letter (order blank and reply envelope included) stresses the idea of Jense for Christmas shoppers. It is worded so that it can be sent to any dealer on the list, whether or not he has already stocked Jense.

Let Christmas gifts of Jense
Increase Christmas sales for you.

When one of your customers enters your store "just looking around" for Christmas, show her a place setting of Jense.

Tell her how durable Jense is because it contains the highest nickel content in stainless-steel tableware. Remember to point out to her how pleased any owner of Jense is, since this tableware needs no polishing, only soap and water, to retain its satin lustre.

Let her see the four lovely, versatile patterns of flatware and the matching patterns in hollowware which will please any of her friends on Christmas morning and in the years to come.

And when you point out to her that Jense goes from the oven right to the table, she'll see how practical it is too.

You can get your Jense in plenty of time for the peak of the Christmas trade by filling out and mailing the enclosed order blank today.

In view of the Christmas buying season and end-of-the-year activities claiming the attention of shop owners and managers through January, the fifth mailing does not go out until shortly after the first of February. It is a letter with folder, order blank, and reply envelope.

The newest trend
In tableware for
American women . . .

. . . who for years have wanted flatware and hollowware in companion pieces!

Today they can make their table arrangements blend harmoniously when they use Jense flatware and the matching hollowware in the same pattern. That is why an increasing number of American hostesses are setting their tables with Jense stainless-steel tableware in

> Fayette—elegant and distinctive
> Phoebe—contemporary simplicity with classic charm
> Flora—for contemporary or traditional surroundings
> Phellips—unadorned modern for today's casual mood

as illustrated in the folder enclosed.

You can offer your customers any of these patterns in more than 200 different pieces. Whether they want a gravy boat, a pickle fork, or a 36″ tray, they can get it in their chosen pattern of Jense. And every article is sold with a printed guarantee issued by Jense.

Any of your customers will delight in using this heat-proof hollowware that they can put right into the oven to keep warm before serving. And like the flatware, it is tarnish-proof—it never requires polishing, only soap and water.

Right now, take time to designate on the enclosed order blank that you'd like to try Jense—on consignment, if you prefer.

Approximately a month later (about the middle of March), the sixth mailing stresses the appropriateness of Jense as a choice for brides—a reminder of the coming spring and summer buying for brides. It is a letter and order blank with reply envelope. Note that it is so worded that it can go to any dealer's name on the original list.

Today's American bride
Is choosing Jense tableware

Because

It is practical, beautifully designed, inexpensive—and made to last a lifetime.

Today's brides who must be homemakers and career girls have to budget their time as well as their money. Jense helps them do both.

They can use their Jense stainless-steel tableware twice a day or oftener with the complete assurance that it needs no polishing—only soap and water to retain its lustre.

A display of each of the four distinctive patterns will be an invitation to all brides to visit your store. Pieces of the hollowware in the matching patterns and a reminder that they go right from the oven to the table convince women that never before has a homemaker been able to do so much with one set of tableware. Whether buffet or formal dinner—family or special occasion—they can use their Jense to make a beautiful, distinctive arrangement that both their young friends and traditional-minded mothers approve.

Any bride today can afford Jense, and she'll use and cherish it the rest of her life. Even though this stainless-steel tableware contains more nickel than any other she could select, she can choose her pattern in a six-piece place setting for eight for $64, as compared to the $250 she would spend for the same thing in sterling. And the bride's friends will be pleased at the economical price range of her choice.

Make this spring the season to promote Jense. Use the enclosed order blank and easy-reply envelope to tell us the quantity you want.

(*Signature*)

You can assure your customers that the patterns they choose will never be out of stock—they can buy any piece in the pattern of their choice to replace or increase their Jense in the years to come.

The seventh and final planned mailing is sent about a month after the sixth mailing (roughly, the middle of April). But it could go almost any time. It is a carbon copy of the letter sent in the fifth mailing—with order blank, price list, and reply envelope. Clipped to the carbon is a memo 4″ × 5″ reading:

100% markup!

And it sells itself.

This carbon of a letter we sent you earlier is a reminder of why American women buy Jense tableware:

> It is the only stainless-steel tableware with matching flatware and hollowware.
>
> It never needs polishing.
>
> It's equally at home on the table or in the oven.
>
> The four distinctive patterns give them a freedom of choice for tableware adaptable to any occasion.

The price list tells you why Jense is a popular choice of every homemaker. Use the order blank and reply envelope to tell us the Jense you'd like to stock.

PROBLEMS

1. Assume that you are the local distributor for Regal typewriters. As part of your efforts to push sales, you are writing a sales letter to parents of high-school and junior-high-school students stressing the appropriateness and desirability of a portable typewriter for their child (or children). Though such a gift would be more timely at Christmas or graduation or birthday time, at no time would it be inappropriate or unwelcome—or a poor investment. You believe that your portable, called the Futura, is the nearest thing to a standard office typewriter that any portable could be. Though it has the advantages of weighing only 17 pounds (the lightest-weight standard is 30 pounds), including the handsome aluminum carrying case (which also can double as a good-looking overnight case for either boy or girl), it retains the full standard keyboard with keys in exactly the same position (spacing) and slope. It retains Regal's Stroke Control device for easy adjustment to each individual's touch. Margins can be set with a flip of the finger with the special Wizard Margin lever. Regal's Space Meter shows how many lines are left at the bottom of the page. The Wizard Column Set key makes for easy tabulations, at any point along the line. Regal's Two-Pack enables the typist to change ribbons without touching the ribbon and smudging fingers.

   Because the aluminium cast-metal base is one-piece, unitized construction, it can take heavy pounding and other hard treatment that teen-agers might give it, travel with them to college and on through working life. The sandstone, blue, green, or pink that the hats come in adds a decorative note especially pleasing to girls. ("Hats" are the movable parts that flip up and allow you to get at the ribbon spools, etc.)

   In terms of better grades, more interest in school work, the development of a business skill that could mean earning power in high school or college and definitely would be useful during one's working years (plus any other plausible reasons you can think of), seek to get the parents to come to your store or to let you bring a portable model to their home for a demonstration. Since this is a local list, you'd just ask them to call you if they want you to come out, just come in if they prefer to try the Regal portable in the store.

The price of $149.50 (plus applicable taxes) can be handled on easy, convenient installments after a down payment of 10 per cent. The 90-day guarantee covers parts and service.

2. As supervisor of sales promotion for Reduce-Acizor Corporation, 908 North La Cienega Boulevard, Los Angeles 46, California, you write a letter to 5,000 YMCA's in cities over 50,000 promoting the Reduce-Acizor, an electrically operated machine which produces peak waves to exercise external muscles. The peak waves trim down bulges (tighten in inches) by creating a pleasant impulse that exercises the muscles. Depending upon the size of unit and number of accessories desired, the machine costs either $207 (6 pads, 3 knobs, exercises 3 sets of muscles at the same time) or $338 (8 pads, 4 knobs, exercises 4 sets of muscles). The Reduce-Acizors are guaranteed to perform for the first two years, with free adjustments during this same period.

One third of the company's customers are men; so you figure that the Y is a good market. Men want to stay fit and trim and live longer, too. The Reduce-Acizor weighs about 9 pounds, resembles a portable radio, and comes with an assortment of body belts, round rubber pads 4 inches in diameter, straps, and wires. To take a treatment a person just puts the body belt or pad where he wants to reduce, straps it down, turns on the machine, and relaxes for 30 minutes while the machine does the work. In 30 minutes a day for a month a man can lose as much as $4\frac{1}{2}$ inches from his waistline.

Many beauty parlors have Reduce-Acizors and charge an average of $20 for 30 treatments. The YMCA might like to operate on this basis and let the machine pay for itself.

It has the seal of safety from Underwriters' Laboratories. In the past two years the company has sold over 900,000 machines in the United States. Since you are writing a form letter, a simulated inside address would be an economical way of starting. The enclosed folder pictures men using the machine, and the enclosed reply card suggests that the receiver fill it out so that you can let your representative in the area come to see him.

3. Your company, White Mist Chemicals, Inc., 31 W. Fifty-eighth Street, New York 19, N.Y., is promoting a new fur and fabric cleaner, Fur Mist, with a $500,000 campaign. Besides full-page ads in *Ladies' Home Journal, Vogue,* and *Retailing,* you plan a mailing to fur dealers all over the United States. Fur Mist is a preparation for cleaning and mothproofing furs and fabrics. Your national advertisements aimed at women who don't bother to store furs or have them cleaned say that the do-it-yourself product is applied easily, protects and cleans furs and fabrics. The copy reads "So safe, so gentle, yet so efficient is Fur Mist that it is guaranteed to keep even the palest pastels of the costliest mutation minks furrier-fresh, glistening like new, season after

season. Fur Mist is non-toxic and non-inflammable. Don't let dirt film dull the beauty of your furs. Spare yourself the expense of cleaning deep pile fabrics by commercial methods, when all they need is spot-cleaning."

Though these dealers can use Fur Mist themselves, their big profit will come from sales of Fur Mist to women owning furs. Any dealer can make an easy profit on these 12-oz. cans that retail for $4.95. The dealer buys for 40 per cent less. Fur Mist is the only spot-cleaner recommended by Princeton for its furlike fabric Olago.

Besides a tear sheet from one of your recent ads, you enclose an order card. You have card displays and envelope stuffers available. You can assume you are writing to Glisson and Glick, Furriers, 198 Main Street, Peoria, Illinois.

4. For those not returning your card (see preceding problem) you send a second mailing one month later. You go into more detail as to how his customers can keep treasured furs at their soft, gleaming, lustrous best throughout the full wearing period. They can actually "float" out embedded soil, grease, or water-based stains (even lipstick and makeup) from either natural fur filament or furlike fiber; remove every trace, completely clean. They just spray, wipe, and brush garments. Make replying easy with your order card. Offer to send a gross on consignment.

5. The Nojax Company, 2300 Oakton Street, Des Plaines, Illinois, has sold about 8,000 of the product for which the company is named. In an effort to cut down on increased costs of materials and higher costs of distribution, the sales division has decided to try direct mail on the list of the Chicagoland Drivers Club in the metropolitan area, and has asked you (a free-lance direct-mail expert) to prepare a one-page mailing to go with a leaflet and order return card. With the sale of its list, the Club will make available its plates for electroprocessing; so full inside addresses and salutations will be used, as well as the facsimile signature of Emil Nello, the president.

A small welded-steel truck (reminiscent of your little red wagon of kid days), Nojax—with its four rubber-tired roller-bearing wheels—simply takes the place of the flat part of the tire. It weighs 17 pounds. When the tire goes flat, the motorist in 3 minutes (less, if he's agile) can align cart and tire, drive slowly up on it, and drive away; the ramp, which falls down to let the car drive up, is locked into place by the weight of the car (weighing no more than 4,000 pounds). Rubber cushions help hold the tire snugly in place and prevent further damage to the deflated tire. Although one enthusiastic motorist (of the 4,000 in Chicago who've purchased Nojaxes) wrote that he drove 50 miles an hour for 30 miles on his Nojax, 35 miles an hour is the top safe speed advocated by the Company.

At $14.95, plus a few cents C.O.D. and shipping charges, Nojax men think it's a good buy. They give it a 90-day guarantee (not money back, just a promise to make good if anything goes wrong). The Good Drivers League of America endorses it, as well as the Chicagoland Drivers Club. Try your deft hand, then, at selling this oversized roller skate to the 10,000 sample you're going to circularize.

6. Observing good layout for emphasis, set up a form letter to regular customers of W. J. Swartz Furniture Company, Louisville, Kentucky, from Arthur Cobb, manager, inviting them to come to the store and select a free gift from the Gift Shop. From now through the 15th of next month, customers will be entitled to a gift equal to 10 per cent of any furniture purchases they make. For example, if they buy $50 worth of furniture (for cash or on any of the three liberal credit plans), they may choose any item up to a value of $5. They may choose from Three Mountaineers pine accessories, imported brassware, dinnerware, crystal, Westmoreland milk glass, pictures, and other decorative accessories. Ask them to bring the letter and present it to the salesman when they make their purchase and he will see that they get the free gift of their choice from the Gift Shop.

7. Your company, Straus-Duparquet, Inc., Erving, Massachusetts, manufactures Servaides, dinner napkins 17 inches square made of triple-ply, fine-quality cellulose. Market research shows that some commercial feeding operators pay more for rented table linens than the cost of these napkins (one case of 2,000 napkins sells for $18). Where operators use their own linens, pilferage losses and replacements due to fraying and cigarette burning amount to a significant cost. Operators who are using paper service are dissatisfied with the small size and poor quality of the napkins; but operators of fine establishments are interested in a luxury type of paper napkin for cocktail lounge or luncheon service. With economy and quality appeals, write a letter to hotel managers in the Southwest. For our sample you can write to Mr. Robert Homan, Manager, El Rancho, Dallas, Texas. See whether you can convince him that this snowy-white napkin is far superior to ordinary paper napkins. It is intended for use instead of linen in the finest inns, hotels, and clubs where patrons expect the best.

With these large paper napkins that won't slide off laps, the hotel avoids all laborious ironing, sorting, counting, bundling, and handling. Also, Servaides have no holes, no frayed edges, no rust spots or stains. Besides calling his attention to the enclosed napkin, suggest that he order by filling out the reply card.

8. Ernest Patterson, president, Meraton Corporation of America, P.O. Box 1044, Boston 3, Massachusetts, signs the letter that you are to write inviting charter members to join the Meraton Division of the Diners' Club. For $5 a year a member can charge at any Meraton Hotel and have these charges consolidated into a single monthly statement. The same single billing will also cover charges at any of the more than 19,000 Diners' Club hotels, motels, restaurants, night clubs, auto-rental agencies, gasoline stations, auto-repair shops, stores, and other services all over the world, including facilities for the charging of air, sea, and rail transportation. Both new and current Diners' Club members will also receive a special Meraton identification card which will fully retain their present status at all Meraton hotels. Being a member of the Meraton Central Credit Club will be a great convenience on all trips. The firms extending their credit are the kind with which any member will

enjoy doing business. To join, the receiver of the letter just fills out an enclosed application blank and sends $5.

9. To promote your Hang-All clothes hanger for automobiles, you have a list of automobile accessory dealers in California, Washington, and Oregon. The nickel-plated steel Hang-All, manufactured by the Domer Distributing Company, 469 Elizabeth Avenue, Newark 8, N.J., holds up to 100 pounds of clothes, fits all cars, is easily attached and removed, and does not obstruct rear-view vision or use of doors or windows. The rack fits flush with the roof of the car and clamps over the window frame without marring. Be sure to tell your auto-supply dealer that the $2.00 ($3.98 retail) Hang-All is a suitable gift for sportsmen, salesmen, and vacationists. Write the letter assuming an illustration of your Hang-All right under your letterhead and right above your letter copy. The same illustration appears this month and next in *Travel* and *Holiday*. Backed by Good Drivers' League of America, the gadget is already installed in over 10,000 cars in the New York area.
   enclose self addressed card

10. As director of sales for the Ibec Housing Company, Washington 16, D.C., you are promoting Cinva-Ram Block Press that makes bricks at a cost of 1 cent apiece from down-to-earth mixture of 90–95 per cent dirt and 5–10 per cent cement (see Problem 9, p. 120). You have a mailing list of building engineers for oil companies in South America, Saudi Arabia, Syria, and Turkey. Assume an enclosure that pictures the Cinva-Ram at work, but write a covering letter that talks ease of operation, no maintenance, low cost. In six months' time these builders can turn out enough bricks for 90 houses with just one machine. Weighing only 140 pounds, the machine is easy to move from village to village. In Bogotá the machine has provided bricks for over 200 homes at a cost of only $500 for each home. After two years the houses show no wear from extreme weather conditions.

11. Write copy for a sales letter going to fathers of thirteen-year-old boys in your community. You are the manager of the H & M Drug Company. Through the courtesy of a friend who runs the leading family shoe store and maintains a list by birth dates of all children who have made purchases at his store, you have assembled your own list—by dates, name of son, name of father, and address. The letters will be individually typed, using both the father's and the son's names. Your secretary will type out the two or three (rarely more than six) letters coming up each day and mail them about ten days before the birth date. In it you want to stress the desirability of having the young man start good, easy shaving habits with the Corelon Speedshaver, a shaving means which will help to keep skin smooth and clear (no nicks and cuts) and—because electroshaving is so much simpler than other ways —promote good grooming (sometimes a matter of despair to parents of teen-agers). The Corelon (which is pictured and described on an envelope stuffer that you'll enclose with every letter) is a rotary-blade shaver that never has to be oiled or the twin blades sharpened. The rotary blades stroke off whiskers whichever way they grow. Simplest cleaning imaginable: simply

push the button and the head flips back for emptying whisker dust. All this whisker dust is collected in the head; does not spray around the room. The young man would not have to use the bathroom for shaving; he could shave in his bedroom. 90-day guarantee. Cost, $24.95, including handsome traveling case. AC/DC. Ask him to come in for an inspection and demonstration. Suggest the appropriateness of the gift also at Christmas time. Since you would likely be on a first-name basis with many of the men on the list but not with others, after using the exact name in the inside address, in the salutation use phrase form of address like: "Dear Parent of a boy who'll soon be a man."

12. To encourage a full house at your theater for the showing of the "Molshoi Ballet" ten days from now, you write to the prominent people in your community and sign the letter as the manager. This first motion-picture presentation of the famous Molshoi Ballet group of Moscow will be shown for one performance only at 8:30 P.M. Tickets for this performance are now on sale and will be sold to the capacity of the theater at the box office prior to performance. Seats will not be reserved. Prices for this limited and exclusive engagement are: adults $1.50, children 60¢. The engagement of the "Molshoi Ballet" will be the first showing of the performance of a leading Soviet artistic institution since the recent discussions began between this country and the Soviet Union aiming toward regular exchange of cultural products. And it will be the first time that American audiences will be offered an opportunity to witness a complete evening of ballet on film as performed by the Molshoi Ballet group, recognized by critics throughout the world as the standard by which all other ballet groups are judged.

The "Molshoi Ballet" full-length film was produced in London last fall when the entire ballet made its first historic visit to Covent Garden in London and danced before the reigning British sovereign. Filmed by a method of multi-cameras designed to capture the full theatrical impact of a live ballet performance, it is in beautiful Eastman color and in wide screen.

Prima ballerina Galina Bulnova dances the classic "Giselle" in the film, which also has six other ballet divertissements typical of the Russian repertory. There are excerpts from the Molshoi Ballet's production of "The Fountain of Bakchisarai," "Swan Lake," "Ivan Susanin," and "Faust," as well as divertissements "Spring Water," with music by Rachmaninoff, and "The Dying Swan," created by Fokine for Anna Pavlova and performed in this film by Mme. Bulnova. The orchestra of the Royal Opera House in London and the Bournemouth Symphony Orchestra, conducted by Yuri Faier and G. Rozhdestvensky, are heard in the film. The letter is going to a list of faculty, professional, and business people whose names you have marked in the phone book.

13. With the theme "Which is more important to your child . . . the size of his home or the size of his mind?" write a sales letter to parents of grade-school children promoting the latest edition of *Encyclopedia of the World*. An enormous printing materially reduces your costs so that, under the un-

usual direct-from-the-publisher plan, you can pass on these savings to the customer. The 24 volumes "televise" information with 23,494 magnificent photographs, maps, drawings. *Encyclopedia of the World* gives accumulated knowledge of the world in clear, easy-to-read language and superb illustrations. *Encyclopedia of the World* is the largest and most complete reference set published in America for children, containing 26,000 pages and over 38,-000,000 words. With the easy Book-a-Month Payment Plan, the set is easy to pay for. Coming in different bindings, the set varies in price (Service, $100, Leather, $150, Deluxe, $200). Assume a one-page descriptive leaflet and reply card. Ask your reader to fill in and mail the card you enclosed so that he will receive, without cost or obligation, a copy of the beautiful new booklet which contains an exciting preview of the latest edition of the *Encyclopedia.*

14. As sales-promotional director for The House of Gifts, New York 12, N.Y., write a letter to interest families in having their family trees drawn and lettered on heavy parchment. These make appropriate family gifts. You have a mailing list of 5,000 families all over the country who have directed inquiries to the American Genealogical Society within the last five years. In your letter describe this black and white 14 × 16-inch drawing of a tree with places on each branch to print the names of family members. For your sample assume that you are writing Mrs. Walter Guin, 569 Crooks Road, Royal Oak, Michigan. Mrs. Guin has to send you the name of grandparents, parents, and children of her family so that you can complete the tree. A tree with 20 or fewer names costs $5, while a tree with 20–50 names costs $7.50. You plan to include a descriptive folder showing what a sample drawing looks like and include an order blank and business-reply envelope for quick handling.

15. A chemist, working under a research grant provided by the American Equipment Company, St. Paul, Minnesota, perfected a formula for protecting tools from rot, rust, heat, and cold. Tool-Keep stops splitting of wooden handles and waterproofs joints. It actually penetrates wooden surfaces, to set up a weather-resistant, glovelike coating. Besides leaving no sticky surfaces and making tools grip easier, Tool-Keep safeguards metals. As a test, 5,000 tools were treated two years ago in St. Paul. During the two years the tools were exposed to rain, snow, sun, and sleet, but they didn't rust, nor did the handles deteriorate in any way. In a short time this product pays for itself. A 1-gallon metal drum, $10.78 wholesale, $18.75 retail, is enough to paint 512 tools. Besides the full-page ads running in *Hardware Age,* you're going to send a one-page letter to all contractors in the Minnesota-Wisconsin-Michigan area. Your mailing will be a four-page folder: the letter on the first page; two-color illustrations, copy, and endorsements on the rest. (For class purposes, just write the letter and assume the rest.) On the fourth and final page will be an order blank. To cut down on the expense of mailing, use a faked inside address of two or three lines imitative of the three-line inside address. Even your signature as sales manager can be processed.

16. Try a mailing promoting Tool-Keep to hardware dealers in the Wisconsin-Michigan-Minnesota area (see the preceding problem). A 4-oz. plastic bottle with applicator top wholesales for 50¢ and retails for $1.00 and is enough to treat 20 tools. A 16-oz. bottle sells for $2.95, but the dealer pays only $1.77. To make ordering easier you've enclosed an order blank along with pictures of the product. You can offer to send card displays and envelope stuffers to help promote Tool-Keep.

17. The Columbus Record Club, Terre Haute, Indiana, has a special $20 retail value for only $3.98, to those who join the Club, and wants to tell collectors in the Chicago area about it by letter. The offer is this: A book of photographs and illustrations of the war between the states and an album of records of more than 30 songs—songs of sadness, loneliness, suffering, and heartache; songs of love remembered and of patriotic pride. All are performed with consummate artistry by Richard Bales and the National Gallery Orchestra, soloists, and choir. Through the lens of the famous Mathew Brady and others the reader views on-the-spot scenes of Bull Run, Appomattox, and Gettysburg. He meets Lincoln, Grant, and Lee, Stonewall Jackson, Jeb Steward . . . down the ranks to a homesick Michigan trooper. The 60 pages of text tell how the great war songs came to be sung, and the reader meets the men who sing them.

To join the club, the reader signs the enclosed agreement reply card; when it is received, Columbus will mail the book and album. On the card one music classification should be checked (classical, listening and dancing, jazz, or musical comedies), indicating what kind of music the signer is most interested in and wants to collect records of. The signer must agree to purchase 5 selections from the more than 100 to be offered during the coming 12 months . . . at regular list price plus small mailing charge. Your letter should suggest the record collector join the Club to take advantage of this special offer and to enable him to get records of his choice easily. An enclosure pictures the linen-bound, gold-stamped book and album.

18. Choose from the pages of a newspaper or magazine any product selling at $5–$20 that could reasonably be sold by direct mail in one letter. Either copy the ad (with name of publication, date, and page reference) or cut it out and attach it neatly to a description of the mailing list you assume for your letter (remember to indicate distinctions of geography, vocation, sex, age, social or educational status if they apply, and any other pertinent factors). Submit these with your letter, properly adapted to the circumstances.

19. One of your direct-mail jobs is to write a campaign for the Florists' Telegraph Delivery Association to promote flowers as a profitable tool for building good will, creating new sales contacts, and strengthening employee and public relations. FTDA's primary function is to serve as a nonprofit national clearinghouse through which retail members can send and receive out-of-town orders through fellow florists. But member shops have come to depend on the Association for a host of other vital services, including advertising, merchandising, promotional assistance, public relations, and

long-range sales planning. On behalf of the 10,500 retailers who control it (and whose floral orders by wire finance its operations) the Detroit-headquartered FTDA spends $1,600,000 a year on advertising. And it supplies members with scores of sales-promotion aids ranging from electric signs to envelope stuffers. As a test use of direct mail, write a letter for the FTDA shops in New Haven, directed to business executives and mailed in mid-October to support Christmas flower giving.

A special letterhead plays up names, addresses, and phone numbers of the participating shops, together with a dominant display of the Association's name and initials. In this, your first letter copy, point up FTDA members as the top-ranking florists in the city and emphasize their efficient, guaranteed service. But place heaviest emphasis on use of flowers for such purposes as office decoration, employee relations, and customer contact—especially at the Christmas season. Don't forget that such business gifts are income-tax deductible. Emphasize this easy way of Christmas shopping.

20. Instead of showing names and addresses of participating shops, the second FTDA mailing (see preceding problem) is processed on the Association's regular headquarters stationery with no identifying tie-in to local members. It goes out about November 1 and asks prospects to mail a special order form back to Detroit specifying the name of any FTDA florist in their trading areas. In return prospects receive 5 roses with the compliments of that shop.

21. As part of your FTDA campaign (see preceding problem), the third mailing is a follow-up from the florist who sent the 5 red roses. Write this for the Blossom Shop of New Haven, Connecticut, to Mr. J. B. Lewis, 2716 Clairmont Drive. This is on the original FTDA letterhead prominently identifying the Blossom Shop and other FTDA shops in the area. It reiterates reasons why flowers are a logical solution to business gift problems. Flowers are distinctive, create a lasting impression, are always in perfect taste (a bid for a larger slice of the millions that business firms spend on liquor, food, delicacies, and other gifts).

22. The fourth of the FTDA campaign mailing stresses ease of ordering, availability of assortments in every price bracket, and reliability of FTDA service. The hard-sell phase of the campaign reaches its climax with a cleanup letter timed for delivery December 15, reminding executive shoppers that even the last minute is time enough to cover late additions to their gift lists with flowers by wire.

23. The fifth mailing of the FTDA campaign (see preceding problem) reminds your executive that he can keep flowers on his sales force all year round . . . to build lasting cordial relations . . . to express appreciation, congratulations, sympathy, or respect . . . to create lasting sales impressions.

24. At Western Electric, Electronics Park, Syracuse, New York, where you are sales manager, you have worked up the following product description for Western Electric 2-Way mobile radio equipment:

What product does: Offers a quick, efficient method of co-ordinating business activities by instant communication with service employees, regardless of where they are located within a community.

Appearance of product: Comes in compact steel case which includes transmitter and receiver. Western Electric's progress line radio equipment chassis blocks are rack-mounted in a compact 14-inch case. The mobile units will fit under dashboard of a car or truck, leaving ample leg room.

Possible users: Police and fire departments, city sanitation departments, utility companies, fuel-oil supply and service companies, and Civil Defense units.

What product costs: Base units $781; mobile units are $596 each. Operation and maintenance runs from 0.80¢ to $1.20 per day. These figures substantiated by the National Service Association, an organization that compiles statistics on cost of operating and maintaining service equipment, whose members are owners and operators of service businesses.

Guarantee: 5-year guarantee on all equipment, except tubes, which carry a one-year guarantee. Electronic equipment has been tested in Western Electric's laboratories and has approval of Federal Communications Commission.

Method of Distribution: District factory representatives.

Besides some half-page ads in *American Service Journal,* you want to try direct mail to see whether you can pave the way for your salesman. From F. W. Dodge Corporation you purchased a mailing list of 1,500 names of service companies (fuel, electric, police chiefs, city sanitation superintendents, fire commissioners, and utility company supervisors). For your sample you may address it to Mr. William H. Hefferman, Hefferman Fuel Supply Company, 1432 River Street, Whithead, Florida.

Write Mr. Hefferman, using the theme of efficiency and economy. He eliminates backtracking with trucks as well as holding up orders because of lack of communication. With the 2-Way Radio he can increase the number of service calls per day. National Service Association, an organization whose members are engaged in the service industries, reports that a truck driver operating on an 8-hour day can increase his calls by 50 per cent. Western Electric 2-Way Radio is engineered to take rough abuse in driving over bumpy terrain. The FM frequency gives a static-free signal in any weather and from any level terrain. Installation and service will be done by personnel who are licensed by Federal Communications Commission. The booklet you enclose with your letter describes how Kirby Ready Mix Company of Cleveland, Ohio, dispatches trucks by radio and saves money on hauling. To help Mr. Hefferman get more information, you've enclosed a reply card.

25. Two weeks later (see preceding problem) a second letter stresses increased profits and compares the conventional way of communicating with the new Western Electric way. Each truck driver can report to work from home by

2-Way Radio, thereby saving time and money. National Service Association puts the average daily time saved at 2 hours per day per man, or enough time to let each man make at least two more calls. The standard service-call fee can be profit because, prior to the use of radio, the same overhead and labor was written off against fewer calls.

The enclosure describes how Charlie Wilkerson Gas Company, Pensacola, Florida, uses three radio-equipped trucks now to do the work of five not so equipped.

26. The third mailing two weeks later (see preceding two problems) emphasizes fingertip control over business activities. Customers with rush orders can expect service or deliveries within minutes—or only as long as it takes the nearest truck to arrive. Enclose a leaflet showing how one firm saved $100 per month per truck with mobile radio. Also point out that the initial investment, $781 for desk-top station and $596 for each mobile unit, can be cut in half if he'll agree to make his equipment available for Civil Defense in case of a national emergency. The government pays half the cost for two or more units in such an agreement. The action you seek is for Mr. Hefferman to name a time when your salesman can see him.

27. The fourth mailing (one month after the third) stresses installation and maintenance service, engineering design, and financial aid from the government on initial cost of equipment. Urge the reader to visit the nearest sales-service outlet (in this case Miami), where he can inspect the Western Electric and talk with the sales personnel.

28. The fifth and final mailing for the Western Electric 2-Way Radio discussed in the four preceding problems (one month later) is the 10-page brochure plus a letter on smaller-sized stationery so that the top is folded over the cover of the brochure. As the signer of the original letter, write a selling request to the fuel executive as in the preceding letters, asking that he keep the brochure handy for study. After he has had a chance to see how successfully other companies have used the Western Electric, you know he'll want to get in touch with the regional representative or write directly to you.

29. To insurance company office managers write a prospecting letter selling the Griden Adaptowriter. The plant and home office are in Los Angeles, but the letterheads will vary according to each sales district in all major metropolitan areas of 400,000 and over. The letters will be signed by each Manager, Systems Engineering Division. Adaptowriters make possible completely automatic letter writing and envelope addressing. When the original letter is typed (manually, of course), the machine produces a punched tape that will be "read" by the machine for as many duplications of the same message as needed. A second tape with nothing but names and addresses can also be cut. The first time the list must be manually produced; thereafter, it can be run as many times as needed and for a different message and date each time if desired. The two tapes—one with the message, the other the list of names and addresses—are threaded on the machine. The

tape in the Adaptowriter Reader causes the machine to type the date and to space to the position for the inside address. At this point a code in the tape switches the operation automatically to a Mechanized Tape Reader which actuates the Adaptowriter to type in the name, address, and salutation. When this information has been typed, a code switches back to the Adaptowriter Reader, and the machine types the remainder of the message. It can be set to stop at the right spots for manual typing of any personalizing or individually dictated material. The same Mechanized Tape Reader can be used for addressing the envelopes, coded to omit the salutation. Although paper and envelope insertion must be done manually, one operator can readily run half-a-dozen machines—each one producing copy and addressing envelopes at the rate of 100 words per minute. The Adaptowriter and cabinet take no more floor space than an ordinary typewriter and typewriter table. The two side rows of file drawers will store 100,000 tapes of letters averaging 200 words. This process, incidentally, eliminates the necessity for carbon copies or microfilming the particular message.

Your only enclosure with this first mailing is a reply card requesting more information. All the reader needs to do is sign it and put it in the outgoing mail. Do not identify exact cost (which is $2,609, for your information). Address the letter to Mr. Paul Clayton, office manager of an insurance company you know of operating in a metropolitan center in your area. Of course, the mailing will be done on an Adaptowriter; you'll be wise to tell your reader so.

30. For those who return the card asking for more information (see the preceding problem) prepare a letter to accompany a 12-page booklet illustrating and describing Griden's Adaptowriter. It also illustrates and describes your other equipment for check writing and Coordinated Data Processing of schedules and customer credit ledger cards and bills.

Stress the savings in typing costs and the attractive appearance (uniform strokes, no erasures) of Adaptowriting. Ask that the reader fill in the enclosed reply card, naming a time for the regional representative to call. Neither the booklet nor the letter takes up specific price. The letter is addressed to a specific individual and calls him by name in the body of the letter at the end of a line.

31. For those who do not return your card (the two preceding problems), send a second mailing one month later. It is personalized, of course. After the inside address and salutation, develop the central theme of a typist who can turn out 350 personalized letters a day. That would assume operation of two machines; even a moderately paid typist could easily run four machines. Tell the reader that one of your representatives will call for an appointment to demonstrate how the Adaptowriter can save him money and still turn out superior letters.

32. For those insurance company office managers who do not give an appointment to your sales representative (see the three preceding problems), prepare a fourth and final mailing, attempting to sell the Griden Adaptowriter. It goes out one month after the third mailing. Summarize the advan-

tages. Send another copy of the 12-page booklet. Ask him to study it at his leisure. Ask him to call when he is ready to have the sales representative come and demonstrate how the Adaptowriter can help him turn out personalized letters at one fifth the cost of letters manually produced.

33. The Dictabell Corporation (Problem 2, p. 167) officials decide to try prospecting sales letters in addition to their magazine advertising. As sales manager, prepare a personalized mailing intended for insurance companies. Address it to the president by name. For your sample you may address it to Mr. Vincent Puryear, President, Standard Life Insurance Company, Indianapolis, Indiana. Assume the enclosure of the 4-page folder and try to pave the way for a salesman to introduce the free-trial plan. With the sales pitch of cutting costs and avoiding last-minute rushes, write the letter. Enclose a card so that Mr. Puryear can get more information, a booklet.

34. Two weeks later (see preceding problem), send a second letter to Mr. Puryear, stressing how much freedom may be had when the Time-Master dictating machine is used. Mention how simple the machine is to operate. He just inserts the Dictabelt into the machine with one hand, presses the mike, and thinks out loud. Suggest the free-trial plan. Card is enclosed.

35. Two weeks later (see preceding two problems) your letter centers around convenience. With a Dictabell, Mr. Puryear can spend more time with his family. The Time-Master is so compact that he can conveniently carry it home on the days that he never seems to finish dictating. He can dictate when out of town and mail the recording to his secretary. Ask him to return the card authorizing the salesman in his area to call.

36. Three weeks go by (see preceding three problems) before you write that there's no need to worry about being misunderstood when you use Dictastrips, since each message is recorded on a virgin surface and is heard with FM clarity by the transcriber. Any corrections he makes while dictating are clearly indicated, so that his secretary can turn out an even flow of correctly done work. Of course, your letter will want to bring in other points, but the theme can center around the clarity of the recording. Same card is enclosed.

37. Your final letter two months later (review the preceding four problems) summarizes the main sales points of simplicity, freedom, and economy. Tell him that your sales representative will phone for an appointment to demonstrate.

38. In addition to 2-page spreads on Duron wall covering in *Saturday Evening Post,* the officials of Wright-Lynch Research (Problems 8 and 8, pp. 119, 170) want to try a prospecting sales letter to new home builders in California. You will not identify price in this original mailing. The action you seek is the return of a reply card requesting more information. This will be a form letter with faked inside address block signed by J. H. Lynch, president. The sales pitch stresses that Duron wall covering absorbs noise, insulates, and decorates. Not only is it flame-resistant and easy to install, but it is also washable and thus hygienic. Most of the addressees on your list are couples.

39. For those returning your card (preceding problem), you have a 20-page brochure picturing the plain, "tweed," and "accent" tiles and quoting from contractors, new homeowners, and the director of Veterans Hospital, Chicago. A price list with an explanation of how to figure room sizes is also included. Write the covering letter emphasizing how Duron controls sound to just the right level. The action you seek is that your reader go to his nearest dealer, who is identified in the brochure. Address the letter to Mrs. J. P. Stockton, 1296 La Cienega Avenue, Los Angeles 46. Assume the dealer is James D. Morgan, Inc., at 3100 Arizona Boulevard. Of course, you would notify Morgan.

40. For those who do not return your card (the two preceding problems) you send a second mailing two weeks later on the letterhead and under the signature of the regional representative. The action you seek is the authorization of the regional sales representative's call. Though it stresses the insulation quality of Duron—the all-season "comfort control"—beauty and wall luxury are the main messages. Duron introduces something of the graciousness of the past into modern living . . . reminiscent of tapestry and velvet wall hangings of medieval times. Duron is soft to the touch, and soft to the eye, too. Duron's 24 rich decorator colors . . . beautiful new pastels . . . special "tweed" finishes . . . tastefully silk-screened "accent" tiles . . . make it possible to match every room's mood or motif. And the colors retain their original hues after repeated washings. Assume a one-page enclosure that shows a room—in color—walled with Duron. Refer to its economy, but do not talk specific price. Sign for the sales manager of James D. Morgan, Inc., at 3100 Arizona Boulevard, Los Angeles 22.

41. Your third sales mailing (see the three preceding problems) in your Duron campaign also goes on the letterhead and under the signature of the regional representative. The main points to stress are the flame resistance (UL Class A rating) and easy cleaning (damp cloth; can be washed with soap and water). But remind the reader also of the advantages of acoustical control (especially for Hi-Fi and TV) and the attractive decorating possibilities.

42. Your fourth and final mailing in your Duron campaign (see the four preceding problems) is a letter accompanying the 20-page brochure. Briefly restate the major sales points. Invite the prospective home builder to read the booklet and to retain it for future consideration for the time when he will want Duron in his home. Ask him to use the enclosed reply card when he's ready to have you call on him.

43. Vary any of the four preceding problems by addressing the letter to any homeowner in your community. In this situation you'd want to stress that Duron is one of the easiest of all wall and ceiling coverings to install. It can be applied to almost any existing wall—including concrete and cinder block . . . and over curved surfaces. Since it permanently covers persistent cracks, it is just the thing for "problem" walls.

IX. Employment Letters

UNLESS you are an extremely fortunate person, sometime in your life you will very likely write letters which help you get work: summer jobs, jobs launching a career when you graduate from some institution of learning, a change of jobs for more money, for a better location, for work that has greater appeal to you—and even jobs for retirement or widowhood days (maybe dictated by necessity or possibly because you need to keep busy).

Rare is the individual who does not have to ask for work at some stage in his life—and rare is the individual who does not change jobs several times in his life.

And even if you never write such a letter, the assurance and confidence from realizing what you could do if you had to are good equipment for successful living. Too, from a practical standpoint, the experience of job analyzing is desirable preparation for interviewing—an inevitable part of the procedure even when job-seeking is exclusively oral.

As in sales, when you seek work, you are simply marketing a product: you and what you can do. You market that product to some prospect: business firms which can use your services. In some cases those firms make their needs known—through advertisements, word-of-mouth, placement agencies, or recruiting personnel ("talent scouts," many big firms call them). In these circumstances, the application is invited. In other cases, firms do not make their needs known; so it's a case of selling your services to someone who has given little or no thought to your proposition—a straight case of prospecting. You'll find, then, that most job-getting letters you ever write will be directly comparable to either the prospecting sales letter (a C-type letter) or the invited sales letter (an A-type letter). Both must convince someone of your ability to do something (either now or after some training); the big difference between the two is in the approach.

If you are content to accept what life (and your family and possibly a few interested friends) doles out to you, you will probably never write anything but an invited application letter—indeed, you will probably never write a letter seeking employment! But we assume that you would not be reading this chapter if you were not trying to improve yourself. For that reason and others listed below, we believe we can help you more by beginning this analysis with the prospecting letter.

The prospecting application is the logical first choice for training you to write applications, because you will write better applications of any type as a result of thorough analysis and writing of that kind. Moreover, in real-life applications the prospecting letter has these advantages over the invited:

—You have a greater choice of companies and locations.

—You have a chance to be considered for jobs that are often not advertised.

—You can sometimes create a job for yourself where none existed before.

—You don't have as much competition as for an advertised job, sometimes no competition.

—Often it is the only way for you to get the exact kind of work you want to do.

—You can pave the way for a better job a few years later after having gained some experience.

It goes without saying that you need to know what kind of work you want to do before you ask someone to let you do it. You may now know exactly what you want to do—that's fine! Business is looking for the person who knows where he's going. Then you can skip the discussion, "Surveying Work Opportunities," which follows later. You may know exactly the company where you will seek employment and be thoroughly familiar with its products, operations, and policies. Then you won't need to spend as much time as some other folks will in research on your firm, as suggested under "Analyzing Companies."

But if you don't know for sure what you are going to do or for whom you want to work, the following few pages will help you in arriving at this important decision.

And even if you think you know, you will profit from reading—and maybe revising your present plans. Life holds many changes, occupationally as well as personally. Many a job plum turns out to be a lemon. One's goals at thirty or forty are often in sharp contrast to those one had at twenty or twenty-five. Sometimes changes come through economic necessity, sometimes because of health reasons, sometimes because of changes in personal situations (one's marital and family status), sometimes because of shifts in demand for a product or service (the prosperous livery-stable owner in 1900 was no longer prosperous by 1910 and was no longer in business by 1920)—for so many reasons, in fact, that it is folly to try to list them all. For you, probably the most significant reason will be your ambition to get ahead: to earn the right to assume more responsibility in work that is challenging and interesting and thus merit respect and prestige in the eyes of other people, with consequent increased financial returns.

The starting point in your thinking and planning, in any case, is yourself.

ANALYZING YOURSELF

If you are going to sell your services to someone, you will do so on the basis of *what you can do*. That is your marketable product, so to speak, and it deserves the same kind of careful analysis as launching any product does. The training you have (or will have had by the time you apply for work), the experience you've had (which is not so important in many instances as college students assume it to be), and your personal attitudes and attributes are your qualifications which enable you to do something for someone.

Of the three, attitudes and attributes may be the most important:

If you don't like a particular kind of work, you probably won't be successful in it.

Of all the surveys of why people lose jobs, none has ever cited less than 80 per cent attributable to personal maladjustments rather than professional deficiency.[1]

No one but you can decide whether you will like a particular kind of job or not. Your like or dislike will be governed by such general considerations as whether you like to lead or to follow, whether you are an extrovert or an introvert, whether you prefer to work with products and things rather than with people, whether you are content to be confined indoors all your working hours or must get out and move around some of the time or all the time, whether you want to work primarily for money or whether prestige—social and professional respect—and greater security can partially compensate for less money. Certain kinds of work call for much traveling, after-work-hours entertaining, frequent contact with strangers, staying "dressed up" and "on call" physically and mentally; other kinds are just the opposite.

For most readers of this book, training is already a matter of record or will be in the very near future. In some college or university you are laying a foundation of courses pointing to job performance in some selected field: accounting, statistics, law, secretarial work, finance, transportation, marketing, engineering, agriculture, or management. While graduation is a certification of meeting certain time and proficiency standards, the individual courses and projects have taught you to do something and have shown you how to reason with judgment so that you can develop on the job. Unless you intend to forfeit much of the value of your training (which for most people who go through college represents an investment of $10,000–$15,000), you will want to find work in the field of your major preparation. That decision is partially or completely made for you.

Experience, likewise, is already partially a matter of record; you've held certain jobs or you haven't. Between now and the time you graduate you may gain some experience during summers or part time during the school term. If you do, that's good; any experience is better than none. Most employers look with greater favor on the person who has already demonstrated some workmanlike habits and exhibited enough drive to earn than they do on the person who has held no jobs. But if you've never earned a dime, don't think your position is bleak or unique. Much of your extracurricular activity is the equivalent of work experience in

---

[1] See Walter Lowen's "Twelve Real Reasons People Lose Jobs," *Advertising Agency*, 42:69, July, 1949. Reprinted in *Writing for Business*.

the eyes of employers—and in some cases it is even more desirable than job experience. Many employers prefer a less experienced person with vision and judgment than some experienced plodder with none. And, as you know, many employers prefer to give their employees their own brand of experience in training programs. Regardless of your status, when in an application you show that you understand the requirements for the job, you have an effective substitute for experience. Furthermore, if you will discard the kind of thinking that brands your training as "theoretical" or "academic," you will begin to realize that it is as down-to-earth as it can be. And that is true whether that training is in cost accounting or is a study of man and his environment.

But since you may still need to come to a vocational decision, because your training may be applied in many different lines of business or industry with equal effectiveness and because you probably don't know as much about your chosen line of work as you could with profit (most folks don't), you'll do well to do some research.

To get an idea—or perhaps a better idea than you now have—you may want to read a description of job requisites and rewards concerning the kind of work you are considering. Publications like *Occupational Briefs,* Nos. 1–200, and other job-outlook pamphlets published by Science Research Associates (57 West Grand Avenue, Chicago 10, Illinois), and the publication *Occupational Outlook Handbook,* put out by the Bureau of Labor Statistics assisted by the Veterans Administration, will help you. If you check in *Readers' Guide, Industrial Arts Index,* or *Public Affairs Information Service* under the subject heading of the vocation you have chosen or are contemplating, you may find leads to more recent publications.

If you are in genuine confusion over your job choice and have not already done so, you may want to consult some guidance agency for tests and counseling. Most institutions of higher learning have facilities for testing intelligence, aptitude, and vocational interest; so do U.S. Employment Service offices and Veterans Administration offices. And in practically any major city you can find a private agency which, for a fee, will help you in this way. Reading and talking with other people can help you, but only you can make the choice.

Having chosen the particular kind of work you want to do, you will be wise to make an organized search for those who can use your services.

SURVEYING WORK OPPORTUNITIES

If you are dead sure that you have chosen the right kind of work and the right organization, that the firm of your choice will hire you, and that both of you will be happy ever after in the arrangement, then this discussion is not for you.

Most job seekers, however, are better off to keep abreast of current developments as signs of potential trends in lines of employment and specific companies.

The publications of Science Research Associates (already referred to) give you business and employment trends that help you decide whether you are going to have much or little competition in a given line of work for jobs (as well as what is expected from you and how far approximately you can expect to go). The annual Market Data and Directory number of *Industrial Marketing* and Standard and Poor's Industry Surveys analyze major industries, with comments on their current position in the economy (the latter also identifies outstanding firms in each field). The *Dictionary of Occupational Titles* (U.S. Employment Service) and the *Occupational Outlook Handbook* help you to keep informed on vocational needs. The special reports on individual fields which *Fortune* and the *Wall Street Journal* run from time to time are helpful also. And study of trade journals devoted to the interests of the field(s) in which you are interested can be highly rewarding in helping you to decide on a given kind of work.

Once that decision is made—and confirmed—you seek names of specific organizations which could use your services. You can find names of companies in *Career, The Annual Guide to Business Opportunities* (published by Career Publications, Incorporated, Cincinnati and New York), Standard and Poor's *Manuals,* and Moody's *Manuals.* Trade directories are useful. If you are concerned with staying in a given location, the city directory—or even the classified section of the phone book—will be helpful. Even if there is no city directory, the local chamber of commerce can help you.

You are by no means confined to manuals and directories, however. If you are on the alert and are willing to spend a little time, you can assemble a good list of prospects from reading business newspapers and magazines. When significant changes occur within a company—for example, a new plant, an addition to an already existing structure, a new product launched, a new research program instituted, a new or different advertising or distribution plan announced—some newspaper or magazine reports that information. Widely known and readily available sources of such information are the *Wall Street Journal* and the business section of an outstanding newspaper in the region of your interest (the New York *Times,* the Chicago *Daily News,* the Detroit *Free Press,* the Dallas *Morning News,* the New Orleans *Times-Picayune,* the Birmingham *News,* the Atlanta *Constitution* are examples). *U.S. News & World Report* and *Business Week* (in their blue and yellow pages) give you outstanding developments; *Printers' Ink* in its "What's News . . . and Why" summarizes what is happening in marketing. From such reading you can assemble a list of companies, the nature of each business, the location, and sometimes the names of key personnel.

Many companies distribute pamphlets dealing with employment opportunities with the company and qualifications for them; all you have to do is write for one. Sears, Roebuck and Company, American Telephone and Telegraph, Container Corporation of America, and General Electric are only four of the hundreds of companies which publish such information and make it available to placement bureaus, libraries, individuals—anyone who asks.

You can easily assemble a substantial list of firms which, either by outright statement or by implication from some event, could be considered prospects for your services. If from your reading you do not get the address or the name of the key individual you think you should write to, you can usually get the address from one of the manuals or directories already referred to. If it is a corporation you're interested in, frequently you can get a copy of its annual report from a business library in your locality. If not, you can get one by writing for it. The report will also often identify key personnel, one of whom may be the man you should direct your letter to.

Certainly, other people can also be a help to you. Teachers in the field of your interest and business people doing the same thing you want to do can make many good suggestions about qualifications, working conditions, opportunities, and business firms. Before taking their time, however, you certainly should do some investigating on your own.

Analyzing Companies

The more you can find out about the organization to which you write an application letter, the better qualified you'll be to talk concretely about how your preparation fits the company's needs. And remember, that's what you have to do in a successful application—show that you can render service which fits the company's need. For that matter, even if you are fortunate enough to have an interview or a series of interviews arranged for you, you'll want to find out all you can about the company: its history, operations, policies, financial structure, position in the industry—even its main competitors.

Probably the best source of such information—and certainly the easiest for you to obtain—is its annual report. Not all companies issue annual reports; however, any company which is listed on the Stock Exchange is required by law to account to the stockholders for its handling of funds at least once a year. And most annual reports contain much more than financial information; their intended readership includes stockholders, employees, customers, sources of supply—almost anyone, in fact. So they summarize the year's over-all activities in terms of products, employment, sales, stockholders, management conditions affecting the industry and the company (including governmental activities), and a wide range of other topics, as well as present the latest balance sheets and income statements. Careful reading of the last five years' annual reports makes you well informed on the company (much more than many of the employees on its payroll).

Standard and Poor's *Manuals* and Moody's *Manuals* summarize the history, operations (including products or services, number of employees, number of plants), and financial structure.

If you can't find the needed information in sources like these, you may be lucky enough to find it in some magazine. *Fortune,* for example, has published many extensive résumés about specific companies. *Time* does regularly. Indexes—*Readers' Guide, Industrial Arts, Public Affairs Information Service*—may show you where you can find such an article.

From whatever source you can find, learn as much as you can about what the company does, how it markets its products or services, the trends at work for and against it, its financial position, its employment record, what kind of employees it needs and what it requires of them—plus anything else you can.

Fitting Your Qualifications to Job Requisites

Simply put, what you are doing when you analyze yourself in terms of a job is running two columns of answers:

What Do They Want?   What Do I Have?

And, simply put, the answers to both those questions lie in three categories: personal attitudes and attributes, training, and experience—but not necessarily in that order of presentation! In fact, as explained in greater detail in the section, "Compiling the Data Sheet," which follows, you will usually put yourself in a more favorable light if you follow an order emphasizing your most favorable qualification in the light of job requirements. That is rarely little personal details like age, weight, and height. But desirable attitudes and personal traits and habits are basic equipment in *any* employee (and for writing a good application). Without them, no amount of training and/or experience will enable you to hold a job, even if you are lucky enough to get it.

The Right Work Attitude.   Someone puts you on a payroll because you give evidence of being able to perform some useful service for him. That means work. The simplest, easiest, and most effective way to think about, talk about, and write about work is in terms of doing something for someone. The only way you'll convince someone that you can do something for him—better than someone else can—is first to realize that you're going to have to be able and willing to produce; that hard work is honorable; that recognition in the form of more pay, more benefits, and flexible hours comes only after demonstrated ability; that you have to be as concerned with *giving* as you are with *getting* (and preferably more so) and that you have to give more than you get, especially at first; that you know you can learn more than you already know, and are willing to in order to grow on the job; and that glibness does not cover incompetence or poor work habits—not for very long, at any rate.

The only way you earn the right to stay on a payroll is to give an honest day's work and to give it ungrudgingly. That means punctuality, reliability, honesty, willingness, cheerfulness, and co-operativeness.

Of course, it means competence, too. But, without a desirable outlook toward work and the conditions under which it must be carried on, competence can be a secondary consideration. Before you can ever demonstrate competence, you have to gain the approval of other people (if you don't, they'll never admit your competence). You can be good; but if you don't get along well with people, your superior abilities won't be recognized. Even if recognized, they won't be rewarded.

You can be very good, but if you indicate that you think you are, you're going to be marked down as vain and pompous. One of the most frequent criticisms of college graduates is that they have overinflated ideas of their worth. Of course, if you don't respect your own abilities, someone else is not likely to either. But the oft-quoted "Silver notes never come from a brass horn" is something to remember for living in general and applications in particular. The best answer to the problem is your recognition that you can do something because you've prepared yourself to do it, that you have the right mental attitude for doing it under normal business conditions, that you believe you can do it, and that you want to.

Confidence in yourself is essential, but so are humility and modesty. You can achieve a successful blend if you imply both in a specific interpretation of how your training and experience equip you to perform job duties.

Specific Adaptation of Personal Qualities.   The work-for-you attitude in an adaptation implying confidence is basic in any application.

Other attitudes or personal qualities need to be evaluated in the light of the particular circumstance. Affability, for instance, is highly desirable for work in which a person deals primarily with people (sales work, for example); it is not so significant in the makeup of an actuarial statistician or a corporation accountant. Accuracy is more to the point for them, as it is for architects and mechanical engineers. Punctuality, while desirable in all things and people, is more necessary for a public accountant than for a personnel worker; for him patience is more to be desired. While a salesman needs to be cheerful, a sales analyst must be endowed with perseverance (though each needs a measure of both). A young woman asking to be a medical secretary would stress accuracy in technique but, equally, poise and naturalness in putting people at ease; were she applying as a technician, accuracy would be the primary consideration, probably to the exclusion of the other two. Certainly in any position involving responsibility, the candidate for the job would want to select details from his experience which would bear out the necessary personal virtues of honesty as well as accuracy.

While all virtues are desirable—and truth, honor, trustworthiness, cheerfulness are expected in most employees—a virtue in one circumstance may be an undesirable characteristic in another. Talkativeness, for example, is desirable for an interviewer seeking consumer reaction; the same talkativeness would be most undesirable in a credit investigator (who also does a considerable amount of interviewing). Both would need to inspire confidence.

In any application analysis, estimate what you think are the two or three most important personal characteristics and plan to incorporate evidence which will imply your possession of them. The others are then likely to be assumed. You can't successfully establish all the desirable ones. Besides, you have to show that your training and experience are adequate in selling yourself to a potential employer.

Enhancing Your Training. With the desirable work-for-you attitude, you'll think in terms of job performance. If your reading has not given you a good idea of some duties you would be expected to perform on a particular job, you'll profitably spend some time talking with someone who has done the work and can tell you. You cannot hope to anticipate everything you might be called upon to do on a given job (nor would you want to talk about everything in your application); but if you anticipate some of the major job requirements and write about your studies in a way that shows you meet these requirements, you'll have enough material for conviction.

Though a specified level of academic attainment is often stipulated (college graduate, completion of at least two years of college, high-school graduate), for most jobs the academic units of credit and the diploma are not what enables you to perform a useful service. What you learned in earning them does. To satisfy the arbitrary requirement when you apply to some firms, you'll need to establish your graduation (or the completion of as much work as you have done). But the primary emphasis in your presentation and therefore in your analysis and evaluation needs to go on those phases of your training which most directly and specifically equip you for the work under consideration. In planning your application (but not in writing it) you'll need to list, as specifically as you can, job duties that you can be reasonably sure you'll be called upon to perform and, in a parallel column, the training that gives evidence of your ability to do them.

An applicant for work in a public accounting firm knows that he is going to be expected to analyze financial data, prepare working papers, assemble financial statements, and present a report with interpretive comments. The direct evidence of his having learned to do these things is his experience in having done those same things in advanced accounting courses and/or work experience. He must communicate intelligibly and easily his findings to his clients, also; and as evidence of his ability to do so, he cites training in report writing (and letter writing) as well as in speech. If he assumes that pleasant relations with clients are a desirable point to stress, he may cite training in psychology and sociology. In helping his clients to evaluate the significance of what the accountant discovers, he may draw on his knowledge of law and statistics.

A secretarial applicant writes about her dictation performance as evidence of her ability to record her employer's ideas; as evidence of her ability to reproduce them rapidly in attractive letters, memos, or reports, she writes in terms of transcription performance. She enhances her value when she talks in terms of relieving this busy employer of much of his routine correspondence as a result of her training in business writing. Since she can be reasonably sure of having to handle callers both face to face and on the telephone, she cites her training in speech and in office procedures.

If you are interested in selling as a career, your specific training in salesmanship (both oral and written), market analysis and research, advertising principles and practice, and report writing need to be stressed (along with any other specifically desirable preparation that you know about).

Likewise, the management major stresses training in principles, industrial management, and personnel selection and placement. And if he is particularly interested in industrial relations, he will focus on training in industrial management, motion and time study, and labor economics, law, and legislation.

In all instances, applicants need to be selective, concentrating on that training which most nearly reflects the most advanced stage of preparation. For example, the successful completion of an auditing course certainly implies training in beginning and intermediate principles of accounting. Likewise, a person who cites evidence of training in market analysis and research will certainly have had training in marketing principles. The careful selection of the most applicable courses precludes the necessity for listing qualifying courses and thus enables you to place desirable emphasis on the most significant.

Making the Most of Experience. Any job you've ever held that required you to perform some task, be responsible for the successful completion of a project, oversee and account for the activities of other people, influence the actions of others, or handle money is an activity that you can cite with pride to a prospective employer. You may not have been paid for it; that doesn't matter a lot. The college man who directs his campus unit of the community chest drive gets a workout in organization, delegation of authority, persuasion, systemization, persistence, punctuality, responsibility, and honesty and accuracy that is good work experience. It is experience which is more valuable than that of the student who mans a cash register at the local supermarket four hours a day— and nothing else. Especially if both men are aiming at managerial work or some kind of contact work, the man who has earned no pay but has had more experience working with people and assuming authority and responsibility is in a more desirable position.

You may not have held the job for any length of time—maybe for only a summer or over the holidays or briefly part time while in school. But didn't you learn something that increased your ability to render service?

You may have held a job that does not appear to be related to the work you hope to do. The checker at the supermarket, for example, because of financial necessity, has punched his way through college because that is the only way he could prepare for a career in marketing. But haven't his vision and stickability been demonstrated? Hasn't he learned and demonstrated accuracy, the ability to work under pressure, the willingness to be cheerful and polite to customers? And if he has kept his eyes open, he has had a good workout in interpreting consumer demand.

Even the person of limited experience can interpret that experience in an adaptation to job requirements, giving the most significant experience the emphasis of position. The most directly related phase of experience is the one most nearly preparing you to do something. For example, if the supermarket checker had also been a fraternity-house treasurer (involving handling and accounting for money), in an application for accounting work he would want to emphasize the treasurer's duties over the checker's job; were he seeking to do selling, the checker's job would be more significant.

If you are fortunate enough to have a wide range of experience, then your problem is simply one of picking and choosing and presenting in an order of descending applicability to the job sought. Chronology (a time sequence) rarely should be your governing choice at graduation or even for a few years after. As an experienced employee changing companies, you may wisely elect to present job experience in a chronological order (or the reverse), emphasizing progress to the present state of preparation; such order-of-time presentation suggests a well-defined goal and success in attaining it. Few college people are in that position, however.

Whatever experience you elect to present, you want to show as directly and specifically as possible that, as a result of this experience, you come equipped to do or at least to learn how quickly. The surest way to present this information about yourself in the most favorable light is to describe job duties that you have done in line with what you have found out you will be expected to do in the job you're asking for. You will strengthen your application if you interpret the experience to show what it taught you about important principles, techniques, and attitudes applicable in the hoped-for job. Evaluating work experience is the same process as evaluating training; it's the matching up as far as possible the answers to What Do I Have? with the requirements under What Do They Want?

You will rarely, if ever, meet all job requirements, and you will always have some points that are stronger than others. Outright lack of a specific point of preparation or below-average standard are negative points to be handled in the same manner that any writer handles them: embedded position and positive language.

Determining a Favorable Order of Presentation. After you have listed the necessary and the desirable equipment of the person who will be hired and your own specific preparation as defined by personal qualities, training, and experience, you will then need to decide on an order of presentation that is most favorable to you.

Most jobs are secured in the first place because of the employee's competence, not his personal charm or good looks. While undesirable personal attributes and attitudes can keep you from getting the job of your choice (sometimes from getting *a* job!) and may result in your losing the job even if you fool someone and are selected, good personality will not ordinarily get you the job unless you first show ability to do the work. Competence stems from good training or worthwhile experience, or a combination of the two.

If your strongest point is thorough training, that is what you want to start with; if it is experience, begin that way. And within each of these categories, arrange your qualifications so that the best comes first (as any good salesman does).

Without telling your reader what they are, as if he didn't know, be sure to give evidence that you meet all important job requirements. And write up your evidence not in the order it occurs to you or even in an order of what you estimate is of greatest significance in the evaluation but in an order that stresses your strong points.

For this comprehensive presentation, a data sheet is the preferred form.

COMPILING THE DATA SHEET

As one authority said, a data sheet gives your life's history in two minutes, indicates your organizing and language ability, and leaves your letter free to sell.

Whether you call it a data sheet, a qualification sheet, a résumé, or a personal profile, to most readers it means the same basic coverage. Some use the term *résumé* to mean only a summary of jobs held and *personal profile* to mean only personal details. It is pointless to quibble over terminology. The thing for you to remember is that the summary is a tabulation of your qualifications, giving pertinent, specific details concerning your training, experience, and personal data and—except in atypical circumstances—supplying the names of references who can verify what you say about yourself.

We know that company employment forms conventionally ask for personal information first. That practice is partially dictated by custom, partially by the desire for a chronological look at the applicant, and partially by the wish of some prospective employers to have a clear-cut picture of the applicant from the start: such information as physical specifications, age, and marital status. Important as this information is, it is not what gets you a job. When you are preparing your own data sheet, you want to sell yourself. Remember that the company isn't trying to sell you, but you are! You will sell yourself more by emphasizing initially your best point of preparation—either training or experience details, followed by the other. In most cases you have a stronger presentation by establishing these significant details before you take up the

necessary personal information. You can use space that would otherwise be wasted and include some personal description at the outset, if
for no other reason than that many people expect it. Certainly the following illustration gets off to a good start and uses space economically
and in attractive layout.

Jayne C. Bowen's
Qualifications for
Secretarial Work
with Standard Oil
Company

209 Harcourt Place
New Iberia, Louisiana
Phone: PL 5-6977

Appropriate

Picture

Age, 20
Height, 5' 3"
Weight, 118
Hair, black; eyes, blue;
  skin, fair
Religion, Methodist
Single
Born in Louisiana
English-French parents

But we think the three data sheets which are shown later do a better job of establishing these personal details as well as additional significant ones. And they desirably emphasize each candidate's strongest selling point.

JOHN DAYTON HALE'S QUALIFICATIONS FOR

ACCOUNTING WORK WITH PHILCO RADIO CORPORATION

(Address: 4030 Sixth Street, Port Arthur, Texas)

Professional College Training

Three uninterrupted years' study summer and winter (1956-1959) in The University of Texas majoring in accounting; BBA degree, August, 1959, with better than a "B" average.
Courses pointing to a thorough understanding of corporation accounting and financial analysis:

-Accounting-

Cost: Job-order and process cost methods.
Federal Income Tax: Reporting taxes for corporations, partnerships, and individuals.
Procedures: Various systems of accounting with emphasis on special items of the balance sheet--Accounts Receivable and Investments.

Auditing: elementary and advanced; public auditing and internal auditing with emphasis on internal control.
Fiduciary: all business units in voluntary or involuntary bankruptcy; also accounting for estates.
Governmental: Accounting for all types of governmental units.

-Related Courses-

Corporation Finance: financial policies; types of corporate securities--when to issue stocks or bonds.
Money and Banking: the theory of money and how the Federal Reserve System is run.

Business Law: contracts, sales, negotiable instruments, corporation, partnerships, and property.
Economics: basic understanding of the various theories.

Written Communications:
report writing and
letter writing.

Work Experience Requiring Accuracy

1958--   Accountant for D. H. Hicks, General Contractor, Austin, Texas; planning and supervision of accounting system, afternoons and evenings while in school.
1957-59: Records clerk, Texas Fire Insurance Commission, Austin, Texas; part-time.
1956-57: Clerk, Police Department, Austin, Texas; part-time in Corporation Court and Identification Bureau.

You may choose to omit references if you are prospecting or if you are answering a "blind" (anonymous) advertisement and fear the effects of an inquiry at the firm where you are working at the time. Or you may not want to ask references to take time to answer inquiries until you

---

JOHN DAYTON HALE'S QUALIFICATIONS FOR ACCOUNTING WORK, PAGE 2

1955-56:   Superintendent, Bureau of Identification, Police Department, Port Arthur, Texas (fingerprint expert, detective, photographer, interrogator).
1952-55:   Clerk, Identification Bureau, Police Department, Port Arthur, Texas.
1950-52:   Airman, U.S. Air Force.

Personality

Birth date and place:
  Born in Texas in 1932 of Scotch and Irish descent.
Family status:
  Married, with a son.
Physical condition:
  5 feet, 10 inches; 165 pounds; no defects. No absence from work or school due to illness in last four years. Glasses for close work.

Organization memberships:
  Beta Alpha Psi (accounting, professional and honorary)
  Kappa Alpha (social)
  Masonic Lodge
  University Baptist Church
Hobbies:
  Fishing (artificial lure)
  Swimming (water safety and swimming instructor)

References (by Permission)

Dr. C. Aubrey Smith
Professor of Accounting
The University of Texas

Mr. Frank Graydon
Professor of Accounting
The University of Texas

Mr. Joyce Campbell
City Manager
Port Arthur, Texas

Chief R. D. Thorp
Police Department
Austin, Texas

Mrs. Corinne Lundgren
Office Manager
Texas Fire Insurance Commission
Austin, Texas

Mr. D. H. Hicks
1313 Speedway
Austin, Texas

know for sure that you are interested in the job. In either case, you would need to indicate the willingness to supply the names of references upon request or after an interview; the evaluation of those who have supervised you in classrooms and on jobs is of real use to the people who consider employing you.

MARIAN CRANE'S QUALIFICATIONS FOR

EFFICIENT PUBLIC RELATIONS WORK

WITH SOUTHEASTERN HIGHWAY TRANSPORT, INC.

Address until June 1, 1959 Box 1773 University, Alabama	Conservative picture in busi- ness dress. Front view.	Address after June 2, 1959 Box 47 Evergreen, Alabama

Thorough College Training

Three and one half years of work in the School of Commerce, University of Alabama, with only five hours of advanced electives left (for completion by correspondence) after June 2, 1959, for a B.S. degree.

"B" average in the following courses related to public-relations work with Southeastern Highway Transport:

Transportation	Business Statistics
Traffic Management	Business Correspondence
Employee Supervision	Business Report Writing
Personnel Management	

The Experience of Working with People

Active participation in these campus organizations:

Beta Beta Alpha--organization for women Business Administration Majors.	Wica--independent women's social organization.
Newman Club--organization for the promotion of religious social activities of Catholic students.	Campus League of Women Voters-- Meetings used for the discussion of current events, trends, interests.

Three and one half years of life in a co-operative house--an organization of sixteen University girls who co-operate to do all the planning, managing, and work of this living unit.

Co-ordinator of this organization during Senior year. Managerial responsibility.	Active member of the Inter-co-op Council, the board representing all co-op houses on the campus. Working on problems of all the houses as a whole and planning a definite expansion program.
Member of the Advisory Committee, with special duties of talking to any member of this co-op who caused any friction within the house.	

In most cases—and always for college students seeking a career—the names of references to whom the potential employer can write are a necessary part of data-sheet information. Logically, they conclude the presentation.

Since the data sheet must carry a weight of detail and condense the

---

MARIAN CRANE'S QUALIFICATIONS--page 2

General office work with Ford Motor Company of Evergreen, Alabama. Typing, Dictation, Bookkeeping. Summers, 1956, 1957, 1958.

Secretary to Representative Stark in the Legislature during the last session. Spring, 1957.

Office assistant at Radio House, University of Alabama. General office work of typing, dictation, mimeographing. Part-time while in school.

Personal Details

Nativity: Born in 1934 in Alabama
Family status: Unmarried.
Physical characteristics: 5 feet, 4 inches; 120 pounds; blond hair; hazel eyes.

Health: Good. Perfect hearing and eyesight.
Religious affiliation: Catholic.
Hobbies: Participation in sports; listening to classical music; designing and sewing wardrobe.

Persons Who Will Testify

Dr. M. W. Whitman
Professor of Transportation
University, Alabama

Dr. John Robert Blocton
Professor of Business Statistics
University, Alabama

Mr. Layden D. Osmus
Director of Radio House
University, Alabama

Mr. D. R. Lanning
Professor of Marketing
University, Alabama

Mr. L. A. Jarosek, Manager
Ford Motor Company
Evergreen, Alabama

material into a small amount of space, it follows good outlining principles and form. You need to capitalize on the space-saving devices of tabulation and noun phrases (rather than sentences and conventional paragraphs). To facilitate rapid reading, you should use headings, differenti-

---

Qualifications of Harry E. Adams

for Representing Bedford, Mace, and Company in the Field

Until June 1, 1959	Conservative picture in a business suit. Front view.	After June 1, 1959
Box 3652 University, Alabama		Rainbow Drive Gadsden, Alabama

College Training and Teaching Experience

Master of Science degree, August, 1959, University of Alabama, with major concentration on economics and labor.

Courses of value in representing a publisher to the college trade (in addition to specialization):

Public Speaking	Business Correspondence	Business Research
Psychology	Business Report Writing	Advertising
Marketing	English Composition	Business Law

One year (1958-59) of teaching Economic Principles, University of Alabama. Responsibility for planning and delivering lectures and for all testing and grading.

Personal Factors

Appearance: 6 feet tall, 170 pounds, brown hair and eyes, dark skin, conservative dress.
Nativity: Born January 24, 1935, Gadsden, Alabama, of Scotch-English parentage.
Military status: honorable discharge from U.S. Navy after 24 months of service.

Memberships: Delta Chi social fraternity. Baptist Church.
Marital status: single (free to travel).
Hobbies: active participation in tennis, golf, swimming. Frequent bridge and dancing. Wide reading of fiction and business publications.

University of Alabama References

Dr. Ralph M. Hill
Professor of Economics
University, Alabama

Dr. R. E. Lampkin
Professor of Management
Chairman, Commerce
   Graduate Division
University, Alabama

Mr. D. H. Brennan
Professor of Marketing
University, Alabama

Dr. Paul W. Paulings
Professor of Economics
University, Alabama

ate in type for the various classes of information, and observe uniform indentions for rows and columns of information. Parallel construction in phrasing requires special care. (If you stick to noun phrases, you'll eliminate your problems in this respect.)

The data sheet is usually written in impersonal style. For that reason, opinions and comments rarely appear on one.

The best form is that one which enables you to make a favorable presentation of your qualifications, attractively displayed and concisely stated. As long as you handle the same kind of information in the same way, your form will be acceptable. Study thoughtfully the three examples beginning on page 282. You'll note the variation in the use of rows and columns of information, in the type and placement of information, in the classification of the information, and in the points the writers stressed. One is as good as the others; they all did the job for the people who used them.

Your data sheet should preferably be typed. When you type each presentation, you can desirably fill in the name of the organization to which it is being presented and make other minor changes for better adaptation. As a practical matter, however, you may have to run off multiple copies. Printed data sheets are preferred over mimeographed ones. Remember, too, that though about half the potential employers say they do not object to mimeographed data sheets, half of them do.[2] These statistics do not imply that any potential employer prefers processed data sheets. Some will tolerate them, but an equally significant number will not. Unfortunately, you have no way of guessing correctly which class the reader of your application will fall into. So if you can spare the time (or the money), send typed ones—and never a carbon.

With careful planning and only minor changes, if any, you will be able to use the same data-sheet information over and over as you mail out applications for the same kind of job. Often a simple substitution of company name in the heading is all you'll need to do. When the kind of work you're applying for changes, however, re-evaluate your qualifications in the light of the changed circumstances. The last two data sheets shown here would have stressed different aspects of training, had the applicants been applying for work in their majors.

After studying the three examples, review the accompanying checklisted items as a basis for preparing your own data sheet.

---

[2] See Charles E. Peck's "Personnel Men's Likes and Dislikes in the Application Letter and Data Sheet," *Writing for Business.*

DATA-SHEET CHECK LIST

A data sheet is designed to sell you to a prospective employer. It can accompany either a prospecting or an invited application letter—and often is used to start off an interview under favorable circumstances. It tells your complete story, thus enabling your letter to be shorter that it could otherwise be and to concentrate on showing how the high spots of your training enable you to do good work for the firm.

1. Give it a heading, and introduce a photograph and address(es) quickly.

   a) Identify your name, the purpose, the type of work desired, and (preferably) the company to which the application is addressed.

   b) Be sure you apply for work, not for a job title.

   c) Make every word count. Phraseology such as "data sheet of" and "position as" are wordy. Besides, they shift the viewpoint of your presentation away from *work.* "Travis Brannon's Preparation for Public Relations Work with Gulf States Paper, Inc." is a good heading. If Brannon has some good experience to emphasize, he might phrase it "training and experience"; he might even write, as some aggressively sales-minded applicants do, ". . . for effective public relations" (or *efficient* or *productive* or *aggressive,* whatever favorable adjective might apply).

   d) Incorporate your address(es) in the minimum of space.

   e) Leave room for a small photograph; most employers want one. [You can use the space to the side(s) for address(es) and phone number(s).]

2. Emphasis, ease of reading, and space saving are the main factors affecting the physical arrangement.

   a) Balance the material across the page in tabulated form. Instead of one tall, thin column, you can often use 2—or 3 if your lines are short. (Leave ample white space around parts.)

   b) If you have to carry over an item to a second line, indent the second line.

   c) Centered heads carry more emphasis and balance the sheet better.

   d) Numbering captions or items is unnecessary.

   e) Capitalize the main words in centered heads. Underlining captions helps to make them stand out (and if you use side captions, underlining helps to keep them from getting lost).

   f) Remember to identify the second page ("Preparation of Travis Brannon, page 2"—either centered or blocked, with 4 spaces after; then the reader sees at a glance that it is merely an identification, not a part of the coverage).

   g) Difference in type and placement affects emphasis and shows that you are aware of organization principles.

3. Lead with that phase of your background which best prepares you for the particular job sought. If specialized (college) training sells

Data-Sheet Check List (Continued)

you best, make it your first major section. If you've had enough re-lated experience, that may be your best lead. Personal details rarely are important enough to warrant putting them at the top (with the possible exception of stevedores and chorus girls, who don't write application letters), even though many company forms put them there.

4. Training details should point up specific preparation.

   a) In your training section highlight those courses which distinc-tively qualify you for this job. A listing of everything you've studied takes away emphasis from the significant ones. (It also suggests your inability to discriminate between what is and what is not pertinent.) If you find yourself wanting to list a dozen or more, consider setting up a second section which you clearly label "supplementary" or "business-building" courses, as differentiated from the ones specifically preparing you for the job.

   b) Give courses titles which describe the real content of the course. (If you get stuck, consult your college catalogue—though those descriptions are usually more formal and general than you'll want yours to be.) Above all, do not list mechanically with numbers or hours of credit; Marketing 6 means nothing to most readers, and 3 semester hours of credit has widely varying value.

   c) In a description, give specific details of what you did in courses (as well as in activities and on jobs)—especially if the title doesn't make clear what you've learned.

   d) But if the course description establishes no more than the title does, omit the description. It's wordy and dull to write "Princi-ples of Accounting—a study of fundamentals."

   e) Grades (about which most employers want to know) and honors may be interpreted as evidence of achievement. You can incor-porate grade information easily—and with appropriate emphasis —in a caption which applies to your specialized field. Give a grade-average indication in some form which any reader will in-terpret accurately: letter or standing in quartiles or even per-centages. Number systems, however, are confusing, because they are applied so differently at various schools; for example, a 1.5 at Alabama is average; at Texas it will earn you a Beta Gamma Sigma key; at Illinois you'd be flunking out of school.

   f) Such expressions as "theoretical" education needlessly deprecate your work (and retard your own confident thinking).

   g) Establish your graduation (or the completion of your training) early in the training section: kind of degree, field of specializa-tion, school at which earned, and when. For college graduates, date of graduation usually establishes availability date.

Data-Sheet Check List (Continued)

    b) Arrange courses in order of relative significance or applicability to the job.

5. Experience: remember that all is good; some is just better than other.

    a) Give complete data about the work experience you list—whether it is in the business world, civic/social organizations, collegiate activities, or military service. Give an exact job title (if you didn't have one, phrase a descriptive one), the firm/organization for which the work was done, the place, and the specific dates (this absorbs length of service)—usually in this sequence. If the title doesn't make clear what you did, explain your duties to show what you learned to do.

    b) If experience is part time, identify it as such. Otherwise, you may arouse suspicion by apparently claiming to have been two places at once or working at two full-time activities.

    c) You do want the chronology of your life's activities to be accounted for. Any employer looks with suspicion on an unexplained, unaccounted-for year or more beyond the high-school level. But until you have amassed a record of work experience showing cumulative progress toward a particular goal (the job being applied for), you'll probably present a stronger picture of yourself by giving details in their relative order of importance to the particular job sought rather than in the order in which they occurred in your life.

6. The personal-details section should present a clear, true picture of the kind of person you are.

    a) It ordinarily includes physical indications (age, height, weight, general coloring, general condition of health) in addition to geographical and racial origins, religious membership (or preference or affiliation), and marital status. They aren't especially significant, but most personnel people expect to see them. Their presence is taken for granted; their absence arouses suspicion. (Though law may prevent employers from asking, no law prohibits you from volunteering information about race and religion.)

    b) Try combining ideas to reduce overlisting in this section. For instance,

        Birth (or Origin): Born in Birmingham, Alabama, June 21, 1942, of Scotch-Irish parents

eliminates the tedious listing of

        Birth place: Birmingham, Alabama
        Birth date: June 21, 1942
        Age: (as if anyone couldn't figure this out!)
        Extraction: Scotch-Irish

Data-Sheet Check List (Continued)

    c) Organizational memberships (in which you might include your religious affiliation) are an indication of the kind of person you are. If you've taken part in a variety of extracurricular activities, consider making them a separate section shaped to show leadership, adaptability, or some other desirable characteristic—And This Advice Is Especially Pertinent if You Have Little Experience. If they are few in number, include them in the personal-details section.

    d) Indicate leisure-time activities (hobbies); they supplement the basic idea of your personality. (Most people are discharged for personality maladjustments, not job inefficiency, you know.)

    e) Keep opinions off the data sheet; let concrete details of activities and memberships establish the assumption. Otherwise, leave these for the letter or even the interview.

7. References ordinarily conclude data-sheet presentation (unless there is some reason for a "blind" situation).

    a) Give the *names, official titles,* and *official mailing addresses* (complete and accurate in each instance) of references for important jobs and fields of study listed: those men or women who've supervised you on jobs, those professors who've taught you the college work emphasized. The omission of either class arouses suspicion in an application from an individual just out of school.

    b) *Always* give them titles of respect: Mr., Professor, Dr., Honorable—whatever is appropriate.

    c) Unless character references are requested, omit them. (In a prospecting application, you'd never need them; in an invited letter, you might.)

    d) The reason for your listing a reference should be obvious from some detail of your training or experience. If not, make clear with some identifying label.

8. Remember these points about style:

    a) Data sheets are usually impersonal presentations. First- and second-person pronouns (*I, me, mine, you, yours, we, us*) are therefore out of place; and verbs without subjects or headless verbs are hard to read.

    b) Noun phrases are the best choice of grammatical pattern.

    c) A data sheet is ordinarily a *tabulation* (because a writer can get more information in less space that way and a reader can read more rapidly, yet receive the information with the emphasis the writer intends). The solid paragraphs of a letter are out of place.

    d) Items in any list should be in parallel form. (See **Para.**)

WRITING THE PROSPECTING APPLICATION

With a well-prepared data sheet you will have done a good job of lining up your qualifications, of realizing what you can (and can't) do, and of deciding on those phases which most nearly equip you for efficient performance. You are then in much better shape to write a covering sales letter (C-type, as you know) than before. At times you may want to send a prospecting letter without a data sheet. That's your decision. We don't think it's the better decision if for no other reason than that most of the personnel men we've ever talked with or listened to or whose articles we've read prefer to receive the data-sheet summary. Even if you elect not to use one, you'll write a better letter for having prepared one. Having prepared it, you're throwing good money away if you don't let it work for you.

You're also being very foolish if you fail to capitalize on your investment of time, effort (and maybe even cash) by slavishly following the points and aping the style of another person's application letter. The good "model" application letter doesn't exist—and never will for folks of average intelligence and above. They realize that the application letter must be an accurate reflection of the writer's personality as well as aptitudes. And so they will write their own.

Securing Favorable Attention. As in sales letters, the infallible way to secure interest in your application letter is to stress your central selling point in writing about doing something for the reader. Your central selling point may be an ability based on training, experience, or personal qualities or a combination of them. The young man who compiled the last of the data sheets you studied on the preceding pages successfully combined all three:

> With my college background of undergraduate and graduate training, my teaching experience, and a temperament which helps me to adapt easily to college people and circumstances, I believe I could do a good job as a field representative for your firm.
>
> And after talking recently about the nature of the work with R. D. Schott, Southern representative for Leath, I know I'd have the added factor in my favor of being very enthusiastic about the work.
>
> While I certainly don't know all the answers to why college teachers choose certain textbooks, I have taught enough while completing a master's degree at Alabama to realize that format and price are only minor factors affecting a teacher's decision when he adopts a book. Possibly the most significant realization from my year of association with the staff here as a graduate student and instructor is that there is no true "academic" personality—that a successful representative has to be prepared to meet and talk smoothly and convincingly with a very wide range of personalities.

Teaching classes in Economic Problems and Policies, discussing my thesis with committees both collectively and individually, and concrete talk with staff members about teaching problems (in staff meetings and in bull sessions) have helped me to think on my feet, to have self-assurance when speaking to groups and to individuals, and to adapt myself to varying situations. I've learned to feel at home with all types of college teachers.

The fact that I have business training from Alabama rather than liberal arts training from Harvard might actually make me a better representative, Mr. Dayton—especially in the South, which is where I've lived most of my life and which I thoroughly understand and like. That doesn't mean I'm a Dixiecrat or that I fancy myself sipping mint juleps while indulgently watching the capers of pickaninnies. I've traveled over most of the United States (and got to Europe and Japan while in the Navy). I realize that the people and the country in other sections are fine too; so I could work happily in any of your districts.

I believe you'd find me quick to learn; the men I've listed as references on the enclosed data sheet will probably tell you that if you'll write them.

After you've had a chance to verify some of the things I've said about myself in this letter and on the data sheet, will you write me frankly about the possibilities of working for you?

Possibly I could talk with one of your regional representatives in this area as a preliminary step. And I can plan to come to New York sometime this summer if you'd like to talk with me further about my successfully representing your firm.

(You may be interested to know that this letter was mailed to 22 publishers and brought 22 replies within a couple of weeks. Half a dozen of the firms wanted to interview the writer right away, another half-dozen within a month afterward. He had 4 job offers.)

To get started rapidly and pertinently, one applicant began her letter to the American Red Cross this way:

I can be the versatile type of Club Director the American Red Cross seeks.

As a result of five years' specialized training in dietetics and institutional management and ten years' practical experience in meeting and serving people as a volunteer worker in Service Clubs from New York to Trinidad, from France through Germany, I know the kind of program which will best meet the needs and interests of service men and their families everywhere.

A young man just graduating from college got favorable attention with this:

Because I have had an unusual five-year educational opportunity combining the fields of engineering and management, I feel sure of my ability to do efficient work in your industrial engineering department and to steadily increase in usefulness if you employed me.

I could conduct a time study with a technical knowledge of the machines concerned or work on the problems of piece wage rates without losing sight of the highly explosive personnel situation involved.

A nineteen-year-old girl with two years of college summarized her outstanding qualifications in the following well-chosen lead:

As a secretary in your export division I could take your dictation at a rapid 120 words per minute and transcribe it accurately in attractive letters and memos at 40 words per minute—whether it is in English or in Spanish.

There's nothing tricky about these openings. They just talk work.

You may be able to capitalize on a trick in some situations—provided that it shows knowledge of job requirements. The young advertising candidate who mailed a walnut to agencies with the lead, "They say advertising is a hard nut to crack," certainly got results from the message he had enclosed in the walnut. The young man who, in seeking radio work, wrote his message in the form of a radio script marked "Approved for Broadcast" and stamped with a facsimile of the usual log certification indicated above-average knowledge of working conditions. The secretary who started her letter with a line of shorthand characters indicated qualifications from the start. The statistical worker who drew at the top of his letter a line graph showing the Federal Reserve Board Index of Industrial Production and in the opening lines of his letter commented on the significance of its recent movements certainly had a head start on other candidates for the job. If you can think of one like these, one which is pertinent, in good taste, and not stereotyped (such as the balance sheet from an accounting candidate), it may help you. But it is by no means a must.

You do need to concentrate on rapidly and naturally establishing your qualifications with the confident assumption that they can be put to work for the reader in some specific job. Having held out such a promise, you need to back it up.

Supplying Evidence of Performance Ability. Your evidence in an application is simply an interpretation of the highlights of your data sheet. For persuasiveness, you phrase it in terms of doing-something-for-you.

The applicant to the Red Cross whose opening you read on the preceding page continued her letter this way:

With the full realization that the Red Cross is operated on a necessarily economical basis, I can use my thorough college training in institutional organization as a sound basis for financial management, cost control, personnel management, employee training, and job specifications, all of which I know are vital in a well-run Red Cross Club.

When it comes to food service I feel equally as much at home in the planning, selection, buying, preparation, and serving of party food for a group of 500 or 1,000 as I do behind the snack bar of a canteen or planning the well-balanced meals for the hard-working Red Cross girls who live in the barracks. During my year's paid experience as the assistant dietician at Ward Memorial Hospital in Nashville, I successfully supervised the preparation and serving of from 3,000 to 20,000 meals a day.

Having been an Army wife and lived in many places under varying circumstances, I have learned to use my own initiative in developing the facilities at hand. I believe in punctuality but am not a clock watcher, and I know from experience that I can direct people without resentment.

I've always enjoyed and participated in the many sports and social activities that are listed on the enclosed data sheet. As a Red Cross Director I could help others to share their pleasures too. I've learned to be adaptable, patient, resourceful, and—through grim necessity as a widow—cheerful!

The industrial-management applicant followed up his opening like this:

The program I followed at Northwestern University required five years of study because I felt that qualification for the field of industrial management should include basic engineering information. The scope of such courses as Business Organization and Cost Accounting were, therefore, enhanced and expanded by related work in Machine Design and Properties of Engineering Materials.

Three years in the Corps of Engineers of the U.S. Army form the main basis of my experience. A large part of this time was spent in the activities of a section officer in a large engineer depot. The knowledge, skills, and experience I gained concerning layout, storage, freight handling, and heavy packaging relate very closely to the problems of factory management in the production of heavy machinery. While working with the problems of shipping bulldozer blades, I was gaining experience that will aid me in understanding the special techniques required in handling cotton-pickers and tractors.

I've learned how to get my ideas across in business-writing courses here at Northwestern as well as through being a reporter for *The Daily Northwestern.* As a member of the student governing board and the senior council I've had good lessons in cooperativeness and patience. And despite a pretty rugged schedule of classes and extracurricular activities, I've kept myself in good physical condition by participating on my fraternity's intramural basketball and football teams.

The enclosed data sheet and inquiries to the men I've listed there will probably give you all the information you want to know about me before seeing me, but I shall be glad to furnish any further particulars you may wish.

And the secretarial applicant to the exporting firm continued (after her opening) in the following vein, drawing exclusively on her schooling:

In secretarial courses during my two years of study at Temple College, I've consistently demonstrated my ability to handle material at these speeds. And as a matter of practice in my course in conversational Spanish I take down what my teacher and my classmates say. I have no difficulty transcribing these notes later in my own room.

I learned a good deal about your markets and your clientele while doing the research for a report I submitted this semester in marketing, "Some Recent Developments in Latin American Markets." In the process, I became familiar with such publications as *The American Importer, Exporting,* and *The Foreign Commerce Yearbook.*

I'm neat and conservative in my appearance. Early in my life my mother impressed upon me the desirability of a low-pitched voice and distinct enunciation; probably for that reason my speech teacher in college has been especially interested in helping me to achieve poise and dignity before a group of people. On the telephone or in person I could greet your clients pleasantly and put them at ease.

I've had little opportunity to travel in my 19 years, but after I start working I hope to use my vacation time for trips to Mexico, Central America, and South America.

Overcoming deficiencies is the function of the letter, not the data sheet. In almost any application situation you'll have one or more. In many cases the wiser course of action is simply not to talk about it! In other cases, if you feel that it is such an important consideration as to merit identification and possibly discussion, then embed it in your letter and endow it with as much positiveness as possible.

The young man wanting to be a publisher's representative had two strikes against him and knew it: the fact that he had gone through a commerce school plus the fact that he was a product of a state university in the South rather than an Ivy League school. Turn back and note how in the fifth paragraph of his letter he met the issue head on and capitalized on it.

The industrial-management applicant had no experience. But did he apologize for it? Not at all! He held out his service experience confidently and showed its relation to the job sought. "Three years in the . . . U.S. Army form the basis of my experience," he wrote—instead of the weak-kneed statement, "The only experience I've had was in the Army" or even worse, "I've had no experience. But I did serve with the Corps of Engineers in the Army." And the nineteen-year-old secretarial applicant followed positive thinking in admitting her lack of experience and her youth.

Probably one of the finest examples we've ever seen of turning an apparent handicap into a virtue is that of a young woman graduate who at first didn't know where to turn when confronted with the necessity for getting a job. After thoughtful analysis of what she had done in college and how it could be used in business, she sent the following letter to a large Chicago mail-order firm. The third paragraph is sheer genius.

> Isn't one of the significant qualifications of a correspondent in your company the ability to interpret a letter situation in terms of the reader?
>
> Because I believe that I could express an understanding of a situation clearly and imaginatively to your customers (a degree in English from the University of Illinois, an *A* in Business Letter Writing, and the editorship of my sorority paper suggest that I can), will you allow me to become a trial employee in your correspondence division?
>
> Learning your particular business policies and forms in writing letters would come quickly, I believe; I am used to following assignments exactly, and I have no previous working experience to unlearn.
>
> I have a good background in writing. I can type 60 words a minute. And the varied extracurricular activities listed on the enclosed data sheet are my best evidence for telling you that I've successfully passed a four-year test of getting along with people.
>
> Will you call me at TRiangle 6–2401 and name a time when I may come in and talk with you?

It worked! And the same kind of positive approach to any handicap you may have—physical or otherwise—is probably your best way to treat it.

Talking the special language of your reader's business also convinces your reader of your performance ability and helps to overcome any deficiency. In all the samples you've been reading in this analysis you probably noticed that each incorporated specific and special references to conditions or products or activities peculiar to the given job. Such references certainly further the impression that you are aware of job requirements and conditions. The would-be publisher's representative referred to books, teachers, college circumstances, and adoptions (the end and aim of that particular job). The industrial-management applicant referred easily and sensibly to two products of the company, tractors and cotton-pickers. The applicant to the Red Cross referred to service clubs, canteens, and the hard-working Red Cross girls who live in the barracks.

From your research you can readily establish such references. If significant enough information, they may be good choices of talking points for your beginning, as in the following four instances:

> With the recent improvements on the foot-control hydraulic-power lift on Farmall tractors and the construction of a new implement plant at Poplar Bluff, Missouri, the International Harvester Company of Memphis will be selling more farm machinery than ever before. As a salesman of Farmall

tractors and equipment, I am sure that I could help to continue your record of improving sales.

~~~~~

The marked increase in General Motors sales for the first two quarters undoubtedly reflects the favorable public reception of the new passenger car models and the new Frigidaire Cold-Wall refrigerators.

These increased sales plus the increased production as announced in your Annual Report also mean more work for your accounting staff. I can take care of a man-sized share of this extra work, I believe—and with a minimum of training.

~~~~~

The regular Saturday Night Reports that your retail dealers submit show consumer trends which I want to help you translate into continued Bendix leadership—as an analyst in your Sales Department.

~~~~~

The completion of the change-over from coal-burning to diesel engines puts Southern Railway in a far better position to "serve the South." I'd like to help serve the constantly growing Southern industry and population in the years ahead as a member of your traffic department.

Each of these candidates continued to talk the lingo peculiar to the job applied for. For example, the salesman applicant referred knowingly to farmers and farming activities and to the selling activities of making calls, demonstrating, closing, and—probably most important in selling farm machinery—servicing. Such in-the-know references are highly persuasive in any application letter because they establish in a desirable way the impression that the writer is well aware of the work conditions and requirements.

You want to show such knowledge, of course. But if you aren't careful to keep your analysis unobtrusive, you're in danger of sounding dull and flat.

The undesirability of emphasizing analysis instead of qualifications will be clearer to you through comparing the following original letter and the revision. The original is almost painful in its flat, obvious statements. It also uses so much space stating requirements of the job that it fails to establish qualities of the applicant. The revision eliminates the flatness and preachiness through implication or incidental reference.

ORIGINAL	REVISED
It takes a secretary who is versatile, accurate, reliable and dependable for a firm like the Brown Insurance Company. I realize the importance of your having such a secretary,	My year's work as a secretary, four years thorough college training in commercial studies, and life-time residence in Tuscumbia will help me to carry on your necessary office

ORIGINAL	REVISED

and I believe I have the necessary qualifications.

Having graduated from the University of Alabama with commercial studies as my major, I am familiar with such machines as the adding machine, mimeograph, and comptometer. Since my graduation, I have been employed as a secretary with the Reynolds Metal Company. This has given me an opportunity to combine my knowledge with experience.

Insurance takes a lot of time and patience. A large amount of bookkeeping is required because every penny has to be accounted for. My one year of accounting at the University will enable me to keep your books neatly and correctly; and, if it is necessary for me to work overtime, I am in good physical health to do so.

Since the Brown Insurance Company has many customers in different parts of the country, a large amount of business letters and transactions are carried on. As your secretary, I could take dictation at 100 words a minute and transcribe your letters accurately and neatly at 45 words a minute.

Even though accuracy and speed are important, personality is an important characteristic too. Because of the many kinds of people who are connected with this type of business, it is important to have a secretary who not only can file, take dictation, and type, but who can be a receptionist as well. Since I have lived in Tuscumbia all my life, I will know most of your clients as individuals and can serve them in a friendly manner.

functions and further the friendly relations between you and your clients.

Whether you're writing a memo to a salesman, a note to a client, or a letter to the home office, my dictation rate of 100 words a minute and transcription at 45 (which I developed while earning my degree at Alabama and demonstrated daily during my year's work as secretary with the Reynolds Metal Company) will enable me to have them on your desk for signing and mailing within a short time.

To help with the varied kinds of record-keeping in a large insurance agency I can bring to your office the knowledge and skills from a year's course in accounting and efficiency in operating the adding machine, mimeograph, and comptometer. Add to those my knowledge of filing systems which I gained in the office-practices course in school and applied during my year of work. You'll understand why I believe you can trust me to compute premiums accurately, send notices on schedule, and devise and turn out special forms when necessary. I anticipate the unexpected, and I meet it calmly; so I am prepared to handle a number of duties and to adjust to the demands of a busy, varied work schedule (including over-time work when it's necessary).

I realize that in an insurance agency everyone from the janitor to the bookkeeper affects the feeling of the public and that all must exercise friendliness and tact in any contact with a client. I would expect to maintain cordial relations with all your customers quite natu-

Original	Revised
I have enclosed a data sheet for your convenience.	rally and easily because most of them are the neighbors and friends I've lived around all my life.
Will you please call me at 4726 and tell me when I can talk to you?	Mr. Bills and the other references I've listed on the enclosed data sheet will be glad to confirm my statements that I can work efficiently and cheerfully for you as a secretary who is able and willing to do more than turn out letters. After you've heard from them, will you please call me at GR 4-4726 and name a time that I may come in and talk with you?

Though the revision is a little longer, it does a good deal more: it establishes qualifications in a good lead; it talks the special language of the reader; it establishes more qualifications. It also has a much better work-for-you interpretation. But the major improvement of the revision over the original is that it eliminates the preachy, flat statements (particularly at the beginnings of paragraphs) that made a smart girl sound unastute.

Asking for Appropriate Action. Whatever action you want your reader to take next, identify it as specifically as possible and ask confidently that he do it. Ordinarily it is to invite you in for an interview. When he gives you time, he is doing you a favor—and your attitude should reflect that fact. As a self-respecting human being who has something to offer, you do not need to beg or grovel; but you do need to show your realization of the fact that the reader is under no obligation to see you, that the time and place of the interview are arranged at his convenience, and that you will be grateful for his seeing you.

The action ending of the sales letter is slightly modified in the application letter, however. You cannot with good grace exert as much pressure. For that reason, most employment counselors and employers do not advocate using any reply device (an employer is happy to spend three cents to send a message to a potentially good employee, and writing and mailing a letter are routine actions for which he is well set up). But your application action ending still suggests a specific action, tries to minimize the burdensome aspects of that action through careful phrasing, establishes gratitude, and supplies a stimulus to action with a reminder of the contribution the applicant can make to the firm.

You've already seen several action endings in this chapter. But to drive home the point, let's look at the action endings of the four letters with which we started this analysis.

The publisher's-representative applicant was in a slightly atypical situation. He couldn't afford to ask directly for an interview in New York because he had neither the money nor the time right then. (As it turned out, he flew to New York at the expense of the firms on two occasions within two weeks after sending the letter; but that was the result of further correspondence—and it's certainly not anything to count on!) So he wrote:

> After you've had a chance to verify some of the things I've said about myself in this letter and on the data sheet, will you write me frankly about the possibilities of working for you?
>
> Possibly I could talk with one of your regional representatives in this area as a preliminary step. And I can plan to come to New York sometime this summer if you think you'll need another man and if you'd like to talk with me further about my successfully representing your firm.

The Red Cross applicant definitely planned a trip to Washington for job-hunting purposes; so she concluded her letter logically and naturally with:

> When I'm in Washington during the first two weeks in August, I shall be grateful for the opportunity to come to your office and discuss further how I may serve in filling your present need for Red Cross Club Directors. Will you name a convenient time in a letter to me at my Birmingham address?

The industrial-management applicant phrased his in this simple fashion:

> Please dial FAirfax 4–6910 and suggest a time when you can conveniently allow me to discuss my qualifications for work in your industrial engineering department.

And the secretarial applicant confidently asked her exporter-reader:

> Won't you please call me at MAdison 5–5946 and tell me when I may come to your office and show you how well my preparation will fit into your firm?

Such letters as suggested in the preceding pages and in the check list which follows won't work miracles. They won't make a poor applicant a good one. They won't ordinarily secure a job; they can only open the door for an interview and further negotiations.[3] But they will help alert, work-minded, prepared candidates to get started successfully in the business careers of their choice and to advance as they gain experience and upgrade themselves. The check list begins on the next page.

---

[3] For helpful tips on interviewing see C. R. Anderson's "Do's and Don't's for Application Interviews," *Writing for Business.*

PROSPECTING APPLICATION CHECK LIST

(The prospecting application usually accompanies a data sheet but may be sent alone to get a show of interest before the writer sends complete details.)

1. Like a sales letter, the prospecting application must generate high interest from the start.

   a) You can *always* summarize your central selling point of training or experience or a combination of both, and phrase it in terms of doing something for your reader. You can also attract favorable attention by citing some evidence of your research on the company or the field. A human-interest story may be useful, but it postpones the real message.

   b) In focusing on the reader's needs, try to avoid the preaching or didactic, flat statement. What you cite may be fact (picked up from a periodical or the company's annual report), but if it is commonplace to your reader, it kills rather than generates interest.

   c) The implication that you are a know-it-all or that your own up-to-date techniques are better than those in his present setup will rankle. Above all, avoid appearing to be telling this reader how to run his business.

   d) Make clear early in the letter that you are seeking work of a specialized nature. Applying for just any job the reader might have weakens your case.

   e) For a realistic approach, talk *work* and *doing;* you may give the impression of having your head in the clouds with talk of "forming an association"—even *position* and *application.*

   f) Even though your idea establishes your preparation and links it with something the reader needs done, you need verve and vigor. Guard especially against the stereotyped "Please consider my application . . . ," "I should like to apply for . . . ," or any of their variants.

   g) All through the letter, but especially in the beginning, shape your presentation so that biography (chronology) does not drown out what you can do *now.*

   h) Preferably in the first paragraph, but no later than in the second, establish your qualifications.

   i) Mere graduation is a poor lead anywhere and especially in the opening.

   j) Eliminate selfish-sounding statements or even overtones of them.

   k) Don't give this reader an opportunity to shut you off. In too many cases to run the risk, you'll encourage a "No" in answer to "Are you looking for?" or "Are you interested in?"

2. Interpretation and tone are important from the start.

   a) You can maintain a consistent tone, neither apologizing for what you don't have nor bragging about what you do, if you back up your claims.

PROSPECTING APPLICATION CHECK LIST (CONTINUED)

   b) Throughout the letter, then, for conviction, back up your assertions of ability with specific points of training or experience.

   c) Generalizing and editorializing are out of place: "invaluable," "more than qualified," even "excellent."

   d) On the other hand, you are needlessly deprecating your good qualifications with statements like "Although I have never worked in the field . . ." and "My only training is. . . ."

   e) The most persuasive interpretation projects this training or experience right to the job to be done for the reader.

   f) Use enough first-person pronouns for conversational naturalness. But avoid a succession of I-me-my beginnings. The monotony of structure and the selfish implications hinder your cause.

   g) Show the research and thought which have gone into this project. Address the letter to the appropriate individual with his accurate title, if at all possible. Within the letter talk about company operations and trends in the industry. Even a deft, tactful reference to a competitor can be a point in your favor. Your treatment needs enough talk about the company to prove your interest in it and your knowledge of the field.

3. Your training and experience are your conviction elements.

   a) Talk about your experience, schooling, or personal characteristics in terms of accomplishing something on a job or in a course. You can show accomplishment by good verb choices. For example, you may *register for, take, attend, study, receive credit for, pass, learn,* or *master* a course; each denotes a degree of achievement.

   b) The emphasis of a lead should go on a phase of work connected with the job you're applying for rather than on a course or courses . . . or even graduation or the degree.

   c) Refer to training as work preparation (in lower-case letters) rather than courses (in capitals and lowers).

   d) You need highlights rather than detailed coverage in the letter.

   e) But even highlights require specific, concrete detail for conviction.

   f) Your data sheet supplies the thorough coverage in most cases. (If you don't send one, you probably should offer to.) Refer to the data sheet incidentally in a sentence establishing some other significant idea *after* stating your case and *just before* asking the reader to take action.

   g) Don't divert attention too soon.

4. Your personality should be reflected.

   a) Refer to the more significant personal characteristics affecting job performance with the assurance that you have them and preferably with the concrete evidence that you do.

   b) Incorporate phrases which reveal your attitude toward work and your understanding of working conditions.

5. Ask for appropriate action in the close.

Prospecting Application Check List (Continued)

a) Name as specifically as possible the exact action you want this reader to take. And make it plausible under the circumstances.

b) For appropriate tone, don't beg and don't command. And avoid the aloof, condescending implications of "You may call me at. . . ." Just *ask*.

c) Eliminate references to *application, interview, position*. Use action references to *work* and the necessary steps in job-getting (for example, observe the difference between the phrase *talk with* and *talk to*).

d) Clearly imply or state that you will be grateful. If he grants your request, he will do you a favor, remember. Remember, too, that "Thank you for . . ." in present tense may sound presumptuous.

e) Isn't it pointless to remind the reader in any way of his option not to see you? "Just write me at one of the addresses on the enclosed data sheet *if* you can conveniently see me June 25 or 26" relieves the reader of even replying! "Will you write me that . . ." establishes quite a different meaning.

f) A little sales whip-back at the end will help strengthen the impression of what you can contribute.

Writing the Invited Application

A firm makes its personnel or employment needs known by running an ad in a periodical (newspaper or magazine), by listing them with an agency (commercial, where they'll charge you a fee, or governmental like the U.S. Employment Service offices and state-government equivalents, or college placement bureaus), or simply by letting the word spread and waiting to see what happens.

As you probably know, most large companies have recruiting personnel who regularly visit campuses scouting for talented young men and women.

In any of these cases, you don't need to generate interest. You have it! Furthermore, the analysis of job requirements is usually given you. An ad as a bare minimum identifies a job category and the principal duties. If you learn of the opening through an agency, someone there will tell you the principal requirements. Even when you hear of the job through a third person, he will usually know and tell you what you'll be expected to do. Matching up your qualifications with the job requirements is easier in the invited situation than in the prospecting, because your source will usually identify requirements in some order indicating their relative importance to the employer.

If you are equally strong on all points of preparation, you have no problem; you simply take up the points in the order listed. But such a happy condition you'll rarely find. Most often your best talking point is not the most significant requirement, and usually you'll be deficient in some way. The solution is to employ the same strategy that you did in writing the invited sales letter: Tie in your strongest point of preparation with something the reader has indicated he wants done; take up those points wherein you are weakest in middle positions of the letter and attempt to correlate them with some positive point.

Your analysis of job requirements and compilation of a data sheet are exactly the same procedures as in a prospecting situation. Adaptation is simply easier. And, once past the opening, supplying evidence and asking for appropriate action are the same. So we shall not require you to spend time reading about something you already know or can easily turn back to and read. Since the beginnings in the prospecting and the invited applications do differ somewhat, we need to consider why and to make some suggestions that will help you write good ones.

Whether you learn of the job through an ad, through an agency, or via a third person, your beginning is pretty much the same. The first requirement is that it talk work and qualifications; the second, that it identify the job; the third, that it refer to the source of the information. The reason for naming this third function is simply that the reference to the ad, or the bureau, or the person who told you about the job is an automatic attention-getter which favorably reinforces the reader's willingness or even eagerness to read your letter. One good sentence can accomplish all three functions and point the trend of the letter.

The opening of the following letter puts emphasis on work, clearly identifies the specific kind of work sought, and desirably subordinates the reference to the source. Note that after the opening the letter reads much the same as a prospecting application (indeed, if you omit the lead in the faked address block and the first two lines, it could be a prospecting letter). Note also the adaptation of talking points—the stress on experience rather than on formal training.

I'm "sold
on insurance"—

—and I believe I can be the aggressive salesman for whom you advertised in Thursday's *Express*.

Five years of experience in dealing with people very similar to your prospects—in addition to technical training in insurance and salesmanship—would aid me in selling your low-premium accident policy.

As a pipeliner in Louisiana in 1953 I made friends with the kind of men to whom I'd be selling your policies. I had a chance to study people, their hopes and fears and desires for protection and security, while doing case work for the Welfare Society in San Antonio the summer of 1954. And while working as a soda skeet both in high school and in college I learned how to work FOR and WITH the public.

The most significant thing I learned was to keep right on smiling even though dog tired at the end of my 6–12 P.M. shift after having been to school most of the day. And I certainly learned the meaning of perseverance when I had to go home after midnight and get on the books for next-day's assignments.

The same perseverance that earned me *B's* in insurance and income protection, liability insurance, and personal salesmanship will help me find leads, follow them up, persuade, and close a sale. I know that an insurance man makes money for himself and his company only when he sticks to a schedule of calls. But I'm equally aware of the value of patience and the necessity for repeat calls.

Because I'm friendly and apparently easy-going, your prospects would like to see me coming. I was elected a Favorite at Schreiner Institute, and at The University of Texas I was tapped for Silver Spurs, a service-honorary organization. Making these many friends has resulted in my knowing people from all sections of the State.

My build and obvious good health inspire confidence. And since I'm 24 and single, I am free to travel anywhere at any time, as well as to work nights.

Dr. Fitzgerald and the other men I've listed on the enclosed information sheet can help you evaluate me professionally and personally if you'll write or call them.

I should be grateful if you would write me naming a convenient time and place when I may talk with you further about my qualifications for being the hard-working salesman that you want.

Frequently your source—especially an ad—gives you an effective entering cue and provides you with useful reference phrases throughout the letter. The ad the young man answered in the following letter can almost be reconstructed from the key phrases.

Because of my college training in accounting and my work experience, I believe I can be the quick-to-learn Junior Accountant for whom you advertised in the May *Journal of Accountancy.*

Having successfully completed down-to-earth studies in tax accounting and auditing while earning my degree in accounting at Alabama, I should be able to catch on to your treatment of these problems quickly.

And while working as assistant ledger clerk for the Grantland Davis firm in Atlanta one semester, I developed a great respect for accuracy as well as an appreciation of the necessity for the conscientious, painstaking labor so essential in public accounting. There, too, I also saw clearly the necessity for absorbing confidential information without divulging it in any manner to others.

My natural aptitude for synthesis and analysis strengthened by special study of the analysis of financial statements and re-enforced with a broad background of economics, law, and statistics should enable me to handle the recurring tasks of compiling comparative statements of earnings and net worth. And training in writing reports will help me to tell the story to my seniors as well as to clients.

Realizing that the public accountant must gain the confidence of his clients through long periods of accurate, trustworthy service, I welcome the offer of a long-range advancement program mentioned in your ad. I'm not afraid of hard work. And I enjoy the good health essential in the long, irregular working hours of rush business seasons.

Will you study the diversified list of courses and the description of my internship listed on the attached data sheet? Note also, please, the wide range of activities I took part in while maintaining an *A* average. Then will you write the references I've listed as a basis for letting me talk with you further about my qualifications for beginning a career of immediate usefulness to you?

I can start to work any time after graduation June 4.

A variation of source doesn't affect your procedure—except that you emphasize a source that would be influential in your getting the job but otherwise subordinate the source. If you learn of the work through an agency or a third person, the procedure is still the same. Here are some openings bearing out our statement:

Since I have the qualifications necessary to successful selling that you listed in your recent letter to the Dean of Students here at the University of Illinois, I believe I could serve you well as a salesman.

When I talked with Mr. Hugh Lomer this morning, he assured me that I am qualified by experience and professional training for the duties of a field auditor with your firm.

During the four years I worked as a branch-house auditor for the L. B. Price Mercantile Company to put myself through school, I became thoroughly familiar with every phase of accounting work necessary for a branch office of a large installment concern and with the reports required by the home office.

I'd certainly like the chance to prove that my training and personal characteristics parallel the description of the desirable management trainee that you gave to Dr. Morley, Head of our Placement Bureau, when you visited the campus last week.

Two warnings need sounding, however; the first is to guard carefully against the stupid question, the one with the obvious answer. It is usually the result of asking a question which is made perfectly clear from the ad or the situation. When a young lady began her application to a legal firm with—

> Are you looking for a college-trained secretary who can do the work in your law office efficiently and accurately and who is eager to learn law work? If so, I think I can meet your exacting requirements for a legal secretary.

—she was earnestly trying to highlight this employer's needs. But the reader had made perfectly clear in his ad the answer to her question! And an efficient candidate only looked silly in the eyes of this reader.

You don't need to worry about setting out requirements; they are already clearly established. Even this opening is questionable because the answer to it is so obvious:

> Wouldn't that junior accountant you advertised for in the *Tribune* be more valuable to your firm if she had a sound understanding of accounting theory and principles and basic training in industrial accounting?

The reader would probably snort, "More? She wouldn't be valuable if she didn't!"

The second warning is against showing signs of selfish glee over having discovered a job opening of your choice. When you read or hear about the job, you may rightly think, "That's just what I want!"—but don't write that or any variation of it. Resist the impulse and start writing in terms of doing something for this reader: what you can give instead of what you hope to get.

Perhaps a third warning should be sounded against assuming that you don't have much of a selling job to do because the reader is on the asking end. Nothing could be further from the truth.

The competition you're up against when a job is advertised is keen even in the heyday of prosperity. And because many others will apply, you'll have to write a superior letter to be chosen as one of the final few for interviewing.

In fact, there may be such a heap of letters on the man's desk that yours may not even get read. For that reason, you may want to do one of several things so that your letter will command attention and thus be selected for reading. Most of these have to do with the physical impression or the mechanics of sending.

A favorite device is sending the letter by special delivery. Few personnel men ever object. If you are in the same town, you can deliver the letter yourself, with the request that it be turned over to the appropriate reader.

If you insert the letter in an envelope large enough to accommodate an $8\frac{1}{2} \times 11$ page without folding and put a piece of cardboard under it to keep it smooth, the contrast between your letter and all the others that have been folded will call attention to yours.

Cutting out the ad and pasting it neatly at the top of the page may single yours out for attention. Beginning your message with a faked address block which quotes from the ad is another device. Hanging indention may help to make a rushed reader reach for your letter instead of another. Even appropriate color may cause the employer to read yours rather than another in the stack.

When the competition is keen, you'll need to take the time and exert the effort to be sure that your letter is one of the earliest arrivals. That may mean getting up early to get the first edition of the newspaper and having your material in such shape that you can have a complete, well-written letter and data sheet in the hands of the employer hours or even days before less alert candidates get theirs there. Even though you may not get the immediate response that you want, your letter (if it is good), becomes better in the eyes of the employer as poorer ones come in through the mail.

But none of these devices will make much difference if your letter is not written from the viewpoint of contributing to the firm through effective, efficient work.

As you already realize, the items we suggested to you in the prospecting application check list (p. 302) apply equally when you write an invited application. Study them again. Additional considerations peculiar to the invited letter are the following (which is numbered 6 because the last number on the prospecting list is 5):

PROSPECTING APPLICATION CHECK LIST (CONTINUED)

6. When writing an application in response to an ad or the suggestion of an agency or friend:

   a) Primary emphasis should go on putting your preparation to work for the reader. But since your reference to the source is an automatic way of securing attention, you should identify it early.

   b) You don't put yourself in a favorable light when you state an obvious inference from the situation itself ("I read your ad" or "In looking through yesterday's *News,* I came across your ad").

   c) Don't ask questions or phrase assumptions which are clear pushovers. "If you are seeking x, y, and z . . . , then I'm your man." "Are you looking for an employee with x, y, and z? I have x, y, and z."

   d) Postpone salary talk until the interview if you can. If the source specifically names a figure, the assumption is clear that the figure is acceptable when you send your application. If the phrase "State salary required" is included in the description, your reply of "your going rate" or "your usual wage scale" is acceptable to any firm you'd want to work for.

CONTINUING THE CAMPAIGN

If within a reasonable time you do not hear from the person or firm you've applied to, send a letter indicating continuing interest. Write thank-you letters to anyone who spends the time giving you an interview. Make your job-acceptance letter sell you further. And write a nice enough job-refusal letter to make that reader realize he has lost a good person.

Follow-Up Letters.   A good salesman doesn't make one call and drop the matter if he doesn't close the sale. Neither does a sales-minded applicant consider the matter closed if he doesn't hear from his application—or even if he receives the usual noncommittal letter telling him that the firm is glad to have his application and is filing it in case any opening occurs. If you are especially interested in working for a particular firm, you need not hesitate to send another letter two, three, or six months after the first one. It should not be another complete application (yours will still be on file); it is just a reminder that you are still interested.

In order to have a reason for sending a follow-up within a week, ten days, or two weeks after the original application, some applicants intentionally omit some pertinent but relatively insignificant piece of information in the original.

> I noticed in re-reading my copy of the application I sent you last week that I did not list Mr. Frank Regan, Manager, Bell's Supermarket, Anniston, Alabama.
>
> Since I have worked under Mr. Regan's direct supervision for three summers, he is a particularly good man to tell you about my work habits and personality. I hope you will write to him.

Such a subterfuge we cannot commend, if for no other reason than that there are so many other approaches you can make. One acceptable one is this:

> I know that in many organizations applications over six months old are thrown away.
>
> Because that much time has elapsed since I sent you mine (dated April 15), this note comes along to assure you that I'm still interested in working for you, in having you keep my record in your active file, and in hearing from you when you need a man with my qualifications.

Only a lackadaisical applicant would end his letter there, however. With just a few more words he could bring information about himself up to date and perhaps stimulate more interest in his application. He could add something like this:

Since graduation I have been doing statistical correlations at the Bureau of Business Research here at the University. I've picked up a few techniques I didn't learn in class, and I've certainly increased my speed on an adding machine and a calculator.

I still want that job as sales analyst with your firm, however.

The foregoing two paragraphs could be a follow-up letter in themselves.

Election to an office or an honorary society, an extensive trip that has opened your eyes to bigger and better possibilities of the job, a research paper that has taught you something significant to the job, and certainly another job offer are all avenues of approach for reselling yourself and indicating continuing interest.

Thank-You Letters. Following an interview, your note of appreciation is not only a business courtesy; it helps to single you out from other applicants and to show your employer that you have a good sense of human relations.

Even when you and the interviewer have agreed that the job is not for you, you can profitably invest about two minutes writing something like this:

I surely appreciate the time you spent with me last Friday discussing employment opportunities at Monitor and Wager.

The suggestions you made will help me find my right place in the business world now.

After I get that experience you endorsed so highly, I may be knocking at your door again.

When you are interested in the job discussed and feel that there's a good chance for you, you're plain foolish not to write a letter expressing appreciation and showing that you learned something from the interview.

Your description of the community-relations program of Livania opened completely new vistas to me, Mr. Lee.

The functions of the public-relations department in your company as you described them made me much more aware of the significance and the appeal of this work.

As soon as I returned to the campus, I read Mr. Fields' book that you suggested and the pamphlets describing U.S. Steel's program.

Many thanks for your suggestions and for the time you took with me.

I hope that you can let me hear from you within the month that you spoke of.

Job-Acceptance Letters. When an employer offers you a job and you decide it's the one for you, tell him so enthusiastically and happily in a direct A-type letter!

I certainly do want to work with Franklin & Franklin—

—and I didn't need a week to think it over, Mr. Bell, though I appreciate your giving me that much time to come to a decision.

I've filled out the forms you gave me and enclosed them with this letter.

Anything else?

Unless you tell me differently, I'll take off two weeks after graduation. But I'll call you on Friday June 11 to get report-to-work instructions for Monday June 14.

Job-Refusing Letters.   Sometime in your life you'll have to tell someone that you don't want what he has to offer. And you may feel that it's routine, that it doesn't mean anything one way or the other to a busy man who interviews many applicants and has many possibilities available to him. Remember, though, that a human being with all his pride and ego is going to read the letter. And make yourself think, "I don't want that job *now*," for you may want to reopen negotiations at some future point. To wind up negotiations pleasantly and leave the way open for you, write a B-type letter with a pleasant buffer of some favorable comment about the company or the work, some plausible and inoffensive reason, the statement of the refusal as positively as you can phrase it (possibly with the statement of where you are going to work), and an ending expressing good feeling and appreciation or both. The following letter is a good example:

Meeting you and talking with you about working for Bowen's was one of the more interesting job contacts I have had.

The opportunity to learn the business from the ground up and to grow with an expanding company is a challenging one, one for which I am grateful.

As I told you, however, I am primarily interested in product research. Since I feel that my abilities will best be utilized in that way, I am going to work for [a company] that has offered me such employment.

I shall certainly continue to watch your company's progress with interest, and I shall look forward to reading or hearing about the results of your prepackaging program.

Letters of Resignation.   Resignation letters, like job-refusing letters, are modified B-type letters. When you have worked for a firm, you have benefited in some way (in addition to the regular pay you have drawn). Regardless of how you may feel at the time you decide to sever connections, remember that there is something complimentary you can say about how things are run, about what you have learned as a result of your experience, or about the people with whom you have been associated.

Regardless of how bad you think things have been, you can always find something good to say. By all means, say it! Then announce your plans to leave, giving consideration to the necessity for ample time in which to find a replacement. In some cases, no more than two weeks is enough advance notification; sometimes it should be longer if it is necessary that you help to train the person who will take your place.

Remember, however, that you want to stay in the good graces of the individuals who have assisted you in your career. You will be wise to give ample notification, to give credit where credit is due. The suggestion to "Be kind, courteous, and considerate to the people you pass on the way up the ladder of success; you will likely meet them on the way back down" is good advice to keep in mind when you leave a job.

In many circumstances your resignation can be handled orally. And in many circumstances it may be better handled that way. But when you need to write a letter, consider adaptations of the following:

I've certainly enjoyed and learned a great deal about the clothing market from my work as sales analyst at Foley's the past eighteen months.

I shall always be grateful to you and the other personnel who have helped me do the job and to prepare for a more challenging one.

You will perhaps recall that when I had my interviews with you before starting to work, I stressed my interest in working toward duties as a sales co-ordinator.

Since such an opportunity has been offered me by Sakowitz, Inc., I am submitting this resignation; it will apparently be some time before such an opening is available for me in this organization. I should like to terminate employment in two weeks. But I can make arrangements to work a little longer if that will help to train the person who takes my place.

My thanks and good wishes.

Often when another job offer comes your way, you'll feel free to discuss the opportunity with your current employer before making a final decision. Such a conference has many advantages for both employee and employer. Often a counteroffer results, to the mutual satisfaction of both; and the job change doesn't take place. If, despite a counteroffer, you still decide to make the change, you can resign in good graces with a letter somewhat like this:

Your recent offer is one that I appreciate very much, and it made me give serious thought to continuing on at Bowen's.

Let me say again how much I have appreciated the co-operation, the friendliness, and helpfulness of everyone with whom I've been associated here.

314 WRITING BUSINESS LETTERS

After considerably more evaluation, however, I believe that I can make a greater contribution and be a more successful business manager by accepting the position offered me by Lowen's.

I hope that I can leave with your approval by [specific date]; I feel sure that all my current projects will be completed by that time.

You'll hear from me from time to time—if for no other reason than that I'll be interested in how the new credit union works out.

But I'll also want to know how things are going for Bowen's and the many friends I've made here.

When appropriate, a possible talking point is the suggestion of a successor to you; often that's a big help. A constructive suggestion, phrased positively, implies your continuing interest in the organization.

Letters of resignation written by college students who resign after having agreed to work for someone but before actually reporting for work are something we take up with reluctance. Many personnel men regard this as a breach of contract. Certainly a practice of sliding out from under such agreements will soon give you a black eye employmentwise.

We would urge you to give serious thought before definitely accepting a job offer. Don't make the mistake of grabbing the first job offered you, only to have something infinitely more to your liking come along later. We'd further urge you never to let yourself get caught in the position of being committed to two employers at the same time. If you have agreed to go to work for a firm and then have a later offer which you want to accept, do not accept it until you are released from the first contract. To the second potential employer, reply in some vein like this:

I certainly would like to accept your offer to come with your firm. As attractive as your proposal is, however, I must delay accepting it until I can secure a release from the Jenkins firm in Blankville. After my interview with you, I accepted this position, which at the time appeared to be the most promising available.

Can you allow me enough time to write the Jenkins Personnel Manager, explaining my reasons and requesting a release? (Incidentally, I can give him the names of two friends who might be suitable replacements.)

This shouldn't take longer than a week to settle. I appreciate your offer, regardless of how things work out.

If necessary, phone the second potential employer, explain frankly, and get his consent to wait. But for your own protection, get his consent before writing a letter like the following:

As you know, I am now planning to report to work as an executive trainee shortly after the first of June.

Before I made this agreement with you, I had talked with a representative of the Larkin organization in Sometown concerning possibilities of my working there as an analyst in the quality-control division, which is the kind of work I have specifically trained for and know I want to do.

I believe I'd be a better-adjusted and qualified employee in the Larkin job. That is the main reason I ask that you release me from my commitment with you. The fact that Sometown is a considerably larger city and that the starting salary is somewhat larger are only secondary considerations.

No doubt you have other people you can call on to take my place, but you may be interested to know that Don M. Jones and Peter Lawson are interested in the Jenkins program. You can get portfolios on both of them through the Placement Bureau here at school.

Since the Larkin people have agreed to postpone a decision until I have heard from you, I should appreciate a quick reply.

You can rest assured that I shall keep my word with you and that if your answer is "No," I shall report to work as promised and do all I can to be an efficient, co-operative, and cheerful employee.

(Only a Simon Legree would say "no" to the foregoing letter.) If the man releases you, you'd then write the appropriate acceptance letter to the second firm; but you should, as a matter of business courtesy, write a short thank-you letter to the first man.

Two Useful Modifications of Applications

The following two letter possibilities for helping you get the job of your choice are not printed here with the implication that they will take the place of the complete sales presentation we have suggested to you. Because they may help you sometime, we simply remind you of them.

The Job-Anticipating Letter. Most personnel men are willing to give advice. And most of them are pleased with a show of interest in their companies and evidence of long-range planning on the part of a student. Several of our students have had successful results from letters like the following, sent in the junior year of college:

A course in business-machine operation under Mrs. Lora Osmus in the Statistics Department at Alabama gave me skill in their operation and showed me the tremendous possibilities of Burrows equipment for business use.

After comparing Burrows and ABL equipment that was on exhibit Commerce Day and talking with the Burrows representative in charge of your display, I am coming to you directly and frankly for some help.

Since I have completed practically all of the courses required for the B.S. in Commerce, I am free to elect practically all courses I shall study next year before June graduation. On the attached sheet I've listed those courses

I've completed and those I'm contemplating. Will you please rank the ones you consider most beneficial for a prospective Burrows representative?

Naturally, I will regard your suggestions as off-the-cuff assistance that implies no commitment. I'm just trying to equip myself as well as I can to meet the competition for the first available job with your company after I graduate.

I shall be most grateful for your comments.

The Telescoped Application Inquiry.   We realize that good applications take time. They're worth the time, however.

But we also know that sometime, somewhere, you're going to need to send some in a hurry and simply cannot write a complete one. You may be able to make profitable use of the services of your College Placement Bureau in a letter, as one young man did. He was too busy writing a thesis and sitting for graduate examinations to prepare a thorough application. He sent the following request and a reply card to six firms:

> With completion of an M.S. degree in accounting at the University of Alabama and two years of retail-merchandise accounting experience, I believe I could make you a good accountant with a minimum of training —and be able to advance more rapidly than the majority of accountants you could hire.
>
> I am not just an accountant: a well-rounded background of finance, transportation, economics, and other related subjects will enable me, in time, to do managerial work as well.
>
> May I have the Placement Bureau here at the University send you a transcript of my college record together with a detailed record of my experience, faculty rating statements, and names and addresses of former employers?
>
> I shall be happy to furnish any additional information you may want and to be available for an interview at your convenience later if you will check and return the enclosed card.

He received replies from all six firms, it's true. But only one resulted in an interview.

This may be a stop-gap measure some time. But this young man's experience simply reconfirms the fact that an applicant must tell a complete story if he expects to get a show of effective interest.

Although letters exchanging information about applicants are a part of the employment routine, applicants themselves do not write them. For that reason, and because you studied them in Chapters V and VI, we see no point in taking them up here. They are A-type letters, characterized by directness and conciseness. You will find several examples of such reference letters in Chapters V and VI.

Likewise, we do not think that you need to study or write the kinds of letters an interviewer or employer writes to an applicant who is accepted for a position (clearly an A-type, good-news letter) or to an applicant who is not accepted (a B-type, disappointing-news letter). With but simple changes of talking points and references, they follow the principles of their types.

PROBLEMS
Prospecting Applications

1. Assume that you are in your last term of school and graduation is just around the corner. Your greatest interest is in finding work which you like, for which you have been preparing for about four years, and in which you could support yourself now and a family later as you win promotions.

   No job of your choice is revealed in the want ads of newspapers and trade magazines. No placement bureau has provided anything to your liking. So you decide to do as any good salesman does: survey the product (yourself), then the market (companies which in the scope of their operations could use a person who can do what you are prepared to do), then advertise (send these companies a data sheet with a covering application letter), and then follow up with another letter if you don't hear from them. Such a procedure sometimes creates a job where none existed before; sometimes it establishes a basis for negotiations for the "big job" two, three, or five years after graduation. And very frequently it puts you on the list for the good job which is not filled through advertising or from the company staff.

   To analyze the high points of your preparation you will need to study the lineup of courses that under your curriculum you expect to complete by the time you graduate. *This means you'll have to study your college catalogue.* It also means that you will have to make a temporary decision about the kind of work you want to do. You may be a general-business major with an equal interest in management and accounting; but you will—for right now— have to make the decision of which you want to do to earn a living. If you haven't the faintest idea of what you'd like to do, follow the suggestions at the first of the chapter.

   Use the courses you have had and make plausible assumptions (don't go daydreaming and woolgathering; stick to probabilities) about the courses you will have completed on graduation.

   Distinguish between those courses which actually qualify you to do the type of work you are seeking and those which give you background education. If you've had experience directly related to the job you want as a career, that's fine; but any work you've done means qualifications (military experience—active duty—is in almost the same category as on-the-job experience). With these training and work sections mapped out, complete a tentative data sheet with personal details and some appropriate references.

   Then study the market, as suggested under "Analyzing Companies." In actual practice you would compile a list of ten, twenty, or even more companies and send them an application. For this assignment, after some preliminary digging around, select one company and plan a letter–data-sheet combination addressed to that company. Adapt it as specifically as possible to the one company. You may be able to find out the name of the specific individual to address it to; you may not. If not, it can always be addressed to the Personnel Department or to the head of the particular department in which you are interested.

You will benefit from this exercise in application-letter writing only if you approach it earnestly and seriously. It should be a job utilizing your college training. It should be a job geared to what you could reasonably assume will be your level of performance at the time of graduation. (Few just-out-of-college folks can expect to be sales managers, chief buyers, senior accountants, copy chiefs, and the like; you'll have to begin at a subordinate level and work up; you'll want to show in your letter that you realize this fact. On the other hand, don't waste your time and your instructor's applying for something that you could readily do if you had never come to college.) ·

Preferably, you would confine your presentation to a one-page letter and a one-page data sheet. But don't be afraid to go to two pages for either. As in sales letters, some highly successful ones run to two and sometimes even three pages.

In actual practice you would send the letter and data sheet together. As a work-control measure in a classroom situation, however, you are allowed to submit the data sheet (which you should in actual practice prepare *before* writing the letter) and a few days later, the letter.

In a job campaign like this, you would do well to get a reply to each of your letters. If half these replies asked you to send more information, you'd be lucky. If a fourth of your replies asked you to come for an interview, you'd be hitting a jackpot. If even one offered you a job without an interview, you could consider your letter phenomenal!

2. Write a job-seeking letter for work next summer. It should not only enable you to earn some money to apply on your college expenses; it should also be work which will be good preparation for the career you plan when you finish your degree and/or leave college. Too, consider the prestige value of the company name on data sheets you will prepare later in your life.

This may well be the company to which you would send an application upon graduation; if that is the case, shape your letter presentation accordingly.

3. Look over your local situation for part-time job possibilities, perhaps on your college campus or in the college community (close enough for you to arrange a schedule of classes that would permit you to work afternoons five days a week). Since you plan to attend school straight through, you could talk in terms of two years of work. Word the application so the reader will understand that between the end of summer school and fall registration you will either have to work full time or go to your home. Prepare a data sheet and letter that summarize and interpret your background up to the time of writing (of course, you would include subjects you are now studying).

4. You've decided that you want to earn some money, see some new places, and have some fun this coming summer. So you're going to address an application for summer employment to an inn at a resort (possibly one of the national parks). You'll have to indicate a willingness to do housekeeping duties (including kitchen and dining-room duties), though if you have enough maturity and the right kind of experience, you may be able to get some kind of clerical or even more specialized assignment. Since college students chosen for such jobs are really hosts (and hostesses) to the guests, stress poise, dignity, cheerfulness, as well as any talents for entertaining.

5. Modify the preceding problem to this extent: You want to be a counselor at a summer camp for children at least five years younger than you. Choose one with which you are familiar, or find out about one from a friend of yours. Address the letter and data sheet to the camp director (by name if you can get it). Note here the importance of understanding and getting along with youngsters, the ability to direct activities, and the emphasis on athletic abilities. Apply to a camp which is not in your home town or your college town; it should be a residence camp, not a day camp.

6. With plausible assumptions and appropriate modifications, write a job-anticipating letter to the company of your choice. Assume that you have one more year of college studies before graduating.

Invited Applications

1. A good starting point in job-getting is the want-ad columns of newspapers and magazines (especially trade magazines). Study the ones of your choice and find an ad that describes a job you would like to have, requiring qualifications you could reasonably assume at the time of your graduation (or some other assumed time as affected by your intentions). It should be a job utilizing your college training. And it should indicate clearly that letter—not telephone—answers are wanted. Clip this ad neatly to your letter; or, if you find the ad of your choice in a library copy, make an exact copy, with exact reference: name of publication, date of the issue, and page on which you found the ad. You may, instead, choose one of the dozen ads listed later in this problem.

Draw on imagination, experience, and whatever information you can find out to bring the situation as close to reality as you can. Read the ad thoughtfully for what it says and search mentally for those qualifications which are only implied. Then evaluate your own training and experience in the light of this specific job. You can readily distinguish between courses that actually qualify you to do the job you're considering and those which are only background. You can certainly classify your work experience in an order of applicability to the given job. Further, analyze significant personal factors. And, finally, decide upon references. In actual practice you would want to send a data sheet. For this problem assignment you may assume a data sheet much like the one used with the prospecting application and refer to it in your letter.

Submit the letter trying to get the one job for which you are best suited, either from an ad you've found or one of the following (assume the city):

a) Capable-creative-resourceful advertising man for medium-sized daily newspaper. Prefer experienced man; copy, selling, layouts, with general advertising and marketing background; might consider promising beginner. Growing town, progressive paper; bright future. Write fully. Box 823 News.

b) Insurance Manager—Nat'l Banker Life Ins. Co. has one opening due to recent expansion. Must be able to hire and train sales personnel. Prefer college graduate with knowledge of insurance and business. Salary override, commission, and renewal bonuses. For immediate employment, apply J. A. Kenyon, Room 203 Wilson Bldg.

c) Production Manager for small midtown publisher and producer of distinguished and unusual illustrated books. Good experience in color work and visual presentation needed. State experience. Prefer man under 30. Strictest confidence guaranteed. Box 828 *Printers' Ink.*

d) Immediate opening—Lady 20–35 experienced in bookkeeping, typing, and meeting public. Correspondence by dictation about two hours daily —accuracy and neatness more important than speed. Regular salary $70 a week. Good background and personality important. Give details. Box E-49, c/o Press.

e) Steno—general office experience—Must be able to start in 30 days, central location, 5½ day week, permanent, over 21, good starting salary. Write giving experience, telephone, and other essential details. Box D-48, c/o News.

f) Credit and Adjustment Manager of national shoe manufacturer needs assistant. Must be able to interpret and carry out manager's policies, handle routine correspondence, supervise clerical help. Good future for right man or woman. College education, business experience, mature judgment required. Salary $5,000 to $5,500 depending on qualifications. P.O. Box 897, Local 10.

g) Office Manager—young man, 23–35. Knowledge of all types office machines; knowledge of accounting desirable. Must have initiative, ambition, adaptability, eagerness to learn. State full details, salary expected in letter. Large firm with sales-service outlets in key cities of U.S., Europe, Canada, Mexico. Local 8.

h) Secretary wanted for law firm. Write Box D-78, c/o News, stating age, training, and experience.

i) National concern desires insurance or credit reporter. No selling or collecting. College education preferred. Be capable earning above $6,000 annually. Write Manager Box 3366 A South Highlands Station (nearest metropolitan center).

j) Sales Trainee. No traveling, college graduate, preferably in business administration. Age 26–31, well acquainted in city. If you have limited opportunity to increase your income in your present position and are interested in training for a sales career with a national firm whose men in State make from $8,000 to $25,000 annually, with adequate starting salary while learning, write full details in confidence to Box A-45, c/o News.

k) Internal Auditor—Immediate opening in internal auditing department, for young college graduate with major in accounting to train as an internal auditor with growing national manufacturer in Illinois. Excellent opportunity for man with executive potential, ambition, attractive personality. Experience helpful, but not essential. If you are interested in working for an established concern with up-to-date employee benefit, write at once giving full details of qualifications and salary requirement. All replies will be kept confidential. Write A-28, News.

l) Distributor wanted for state by Stratford Laboratories, Inc., Box 462, Ann Arbor, Michigan. Capable man or organization to handle exclusive franchise throughout the state of Vita-o-zyme beauty cream. We want a distributor who is interested in making $1,000 a week, not a month. Distributor receives help in setting up office and in training sales force.

m) Accountant—Growing national concern. Traveling. Company car furnished. Good opportunity for man with ambition, personality, hard-work habits. State age, training, experience in confidential letter to Z-79 c/o News.

2. The director of your college placement bureau (use his name) has just told you about the training program of a large corporation. The personnel director indicated in a letter to your placement officer that the company seeks young college graduates between 21 and 25 (this is not ironclad, however) to train for managerial positions throughout the organization. The training program lasts for a year. During that time trainees work in every division under close supervision and attend a series of classes. Assume a specific company and prepare a letter and data sheet. (If you have already written one for the prospecting application, you would use that form with only slight modifications; for this assignment, then, you may just assume the modified form. If you have not already prepared your data sheet, do so for this assignment.) As in any application, indicate your particular field of interest; but reflect a receptive attitude toward the various phases of the training program, showing your realization of its benefits regardless of the specific work you'll eventually perform.

3. Your college adviser is head of the department in which you are pursuing your major studies. This morning he tells you that a firm you hold in high regard is seeking a person with substantially your qualifications for a particular job you want. Fill in with the necessary specific details and write the letter you would send, assuming that your basic data-sheet presentation will accompany it.

4. The same college adviser (the preceding problem) also suggested several other companies as good prospects but stated specifically that he did not know that there are openings in these companies at present. "They hire a lot

of people," he added, "and if there's no opening now, you can be pretty sure there will be before long." Using his name early in your lead, write the letter (assume the data sheet).

5. This morning, quite unexpectedly, you had an interview with the representative of a firm you'd like to work for. After a half-hour of talk which appeared to be mutually satisfactory and during which time you found out a lot about the company, the representative handed you one of the company employment forms for applying, shook your hand, and ushered you out of the room, saying, "Fill this out and return it to me with a letter of application." With the form filled in neatly and completely, draft the earnest but enthusiastic letter of application this man invited. Be careful to talk work rather than employee benefits. Assume specific names for the representative and the company. He said he would write you after receiving your letter.

Follow-Ups

1. Not having heard from the application letter you sent in any of the preceding situations, write a fairly short letter re-emphasizing your desire to work for the firm. You may want to send it as soon as three weeks after the initial letter; you may prefer to wait longer. Clearly refer to the original application by date and type of work discussed. Include any additional data that you think will help sell you. This letter, however, should not be a rehash of what you have already written. It should identify the action you want the reader to take.

2. Assuming that it is almost a year after you sent your original letter, write a follow-up that reassures the firm of your desire to work there. In the meantime a good deal has happened to you (or should have!). Account for the way you have spent this time in such a way as to show that it is preparation for the job you seek.

3. Assume that you have had an interview as a result of your letter and data sheet. You know that the company representative interviewed several other candidates for the job. In a thank-you letter, confirm your interest in employment by the company and add other details to show that you picked up something from the interview. The representative promised to get in touch with you in a week or ten days.

4. As a result of your determined efforts and good showing, you've been offered the job of your choice. The letter so informing you requests you to fill in an employment form and return it and names a starting date that fits in with your plans. Write the acceptance.

5. Offered a job in response to your application, you have decided that you do not want to accept it because it is not in the field of your primary interest. Write the tactful letter that expresses appreciation for the time spent with you and the interest shown in you and that leaves the way open for you to resume negotiations later if you care to. Comment favorably on some aspect of the company.

6. You have just been informed that you were not chosen for the job you have worked so hard to get . . . and still want. Remember, however, that you were considered, that someone spent a good deal of time with you, and that, employmentwise, nothing is ever final. Write the letter showing appreciation for the courtesies extended you, revealing how you have profited from the contact, and showing your determination to reach your intended goal. Above all, the letter should reflect a friendly feeling toward the company and the representative addressed.

7. In response to your application you receive an invitation to come in for an interview at a time and place convenient for you. Write the acceptance confirming the circumstances.

8. Assume that in response to your prospecting application you receive an invitation to come in for an interview at a time which would be convenient if you had the money for traveling to the distant point. Write the letter which reaffirms your interest. Admit your lack of funds and ask if it is possible to see a representative of the firm at a place which is more accessible to you.

X. Claims and Adjustments

CLAIMS offer you the opportunity to get adjustments on unsatisfactory goods and services you have bought. If you are a seller and therefore the receiver of claims, they offer you an opportunity to discover and analyze defects in your goods and services as a basis for improving them. And your adjustment letters are excellent opportunities for you to build or destroy good will. Whether you make the most of your opportunities in either claims or adjustments depends heavily on your attitude.

Any claim and adjustment situation necessarily involves negatives. Somebody is dissatisfied and unhappy. One of the major jobs in writing either claim or adjustment letters is to keep these emotionally based negatives from stealing the show and making the situation worse. What you have learned about good will, resale, and handling of negative material will be especially important in adjustment letters.

CLAIMS

You will probably write pretty good claim letters if you remember these often-forgotten points and learn what to do about them:

1. *Progressive firms like, instead of dislike, claims because they suggest ways to improvement. So if you think you have a just claim, go ahead.*

Many firms even advertise the request: "If you like our products, tell others; if you don't, tell us." Often they encourage claims by "double-your-money-back" guarantees and the like. For example, one manufacturer of lingerie made such an offer in full-page advertisements in national magazines. The conditions were that the products be worn, washed, and returned with an explanation of any dissatisfaction. The company hoped to get some constructive criticism whereby it could improve its products.

All the simple claims in the following analysis were welcomed because they offered the sellers opportunities to correct defects in their goods and services.

2. *When things go wrong, the firm surely did not intend to mistreat the customer. Almost certainly, the reader of the claim letter had nothing to do with the dissatisfaction. So keep your shirt on!*

Very few manufacturers expect every item they manufacture to be perfect. They know that, even after careful checking, some defects may sometimes show up. Nearly always, they expect to replace or repair defective merchandise which is returned. This is a more efficient system than to insist on perfection in manufacturing and consequently higher prices. The consumer who gets defective merchandise and takes the attitude that the seller tried to take advantage of him, then, is usually wrong in his attitude. In most cases, to get satisfaction all he has to do is to make a simple claim such as the following:

When the set of Syracuse dinner dishes I ordered from you on November 1 arrived the day before Thanksgiving, I found that one of the coffee cups was cracked and one of the dinner plates had a defective design.

The excelsior around the cup was thin—evidently too thin to protect the cup from jars in transit.

I am returning the two imperfect pieces by express. Will you please replace them to complete my set?

Even though a product is defective, almost certainly the fellow who reads your claim letter had nothing to do with it. He probably didn't make it, check it, or sell it to you. To be nasty to him is to be quite unfair, unreasonable, and foolish. The worst kind of unfairness is an accusation against the innocent. And instead of putting him in a favorable mood so that he will be inclined to help you get satisfaction, you turn this possible ally against you if you write a nasty letter.

3. *When you know just what is wrong and what is required to set
things right, you should make a definite claim; otherwise, explain and ask for an inspection.*

Sometimes you can be sure that the only fair adjustment is a refund
of your money or a complete replacement of the product. On other
occasions you can see that replacement of a part or proper adjustment
of a machine will correct the trouble. You therefore ask definitely for
what is necessary to make things right, as in the letter on page 325.

Sometimes, however, the product just isn't right, but you don't
know exactly what is wrong. Your claim then should be an explanation of how the product is failing to satisfy you and a request for the
necessary action. You can make your own estimate and request that action (as in the illustration on p. 330), call in third parties to estimate
(as on automobile insurance claims, like that on p. 328), or ask the firm
to investigate and take the indicated action. Here are two examples:

I think you will be interested in my experience with XXX outside white
house paint used on my house this past summer.

A union painter applied three coats according to directions on the can.
About three months later black streaks began to appear where water runs
from the eaves and valleys.

At first I thought that the discoloration was from the green roof paint or
the stain of the cedar shingles, but the same thing appears on the garage,
which has an unpainted tin roof.

Various theories have been advanced concerning the smutty streaks. Some
friends have suggested mildew, but my common sense says no. Some have
suggested dirt, but it will not wash off. A chemist friend says that there is
a lot of sulfur in the atmosphere here and that it may combine with the
lead of the paint to make a sulfur-lead compound that is a smoky color.

So you see that I don't know what the cause is. But if your paint didn't hold
its color, I'm sure that you are interested in knowing why. And I feel sure
that if you find your product at fault, you will want to grant me an adjustment.

Will you please investigate and let me know your decision?

The DEXTER fluorescent desk lamp I purchased at your store October 5
has been satisfactory in every way but one.

When in use, the lamp operates coolly and soundlessly; but as soon as the
lamp is switched off, something inside produces a humming sound. Not
only is the hum annoying, but I fear that it suggests a fire hazard.

I'm returning the lamp to you for repair or replacement, whichever you
find necessary.

Since I've lots of reading to do, will you please rush it back to me?

4. *Sometimes a touch of humor can relieve the pressure in small claims.*

Somewhat like the nasty tone (Point 2), another common error in writing claim letters is the writer's becoming deadly serious about small matters. A claim for replacement of a defective $3 item makes the writer look silly when written as if it were a matter of life and death. If the situation is really serious, of course, you would not want to treat it lightly. But to avoid the too-serious tone in small matters and make the reader an ally instead of a sneering critic, you can often use humor effectively. You may inject only a touch or two in the letter, or the whole thing may be humorous.

Several dangers confront you if you decide to be humorous: (1) A failing attempt to be funny is worse than no attempt. (2) Humor may make you write a longer letter than necessary. (3) Humor at the reader's expense will nearly always be resented. (4) Humor which verges on the vulgar or sacrilegious may offend.

The following successful letter, which was wrapped around the returned fountain pen, avoids at least the last two dangers.

GENTLEMEN: ATTENTION THE DOCTOR OF THE PEN HOSPITAL

This faithful old "lifetime" has served me well through ten years. But now, like an old man, or an old horse, it needs rejuvenation—perhaps monkey glands.

Here's the diagnosis:

1. The threads are stripped, causing the barrel and cap to part company in my pocket. You know what that means!
2. At times gobs of ink come out.
3. Even though I like a point a little finer and more flexible than this one ever was, it seems to be getting blunter and stiffer.

I know what your lifetime guarantee is; so I'm looking forward to receiving a rejuvenated pen ready for ten more years of service.

5. *Claims need to be classified as (a) direct and (b) persuasive, according to circumstances.*

Direct Claims. Usually a firm will grant an adjustment merely on the strength of a customer's explanation of what is wrong and what he considers a fair settlement. In that case, you would make yourself ridiculous by misjudging the situation and writing a too-strong claim. Unless you have good reason to believe otherwise, you should therefore assume that the firm will be co-operative. Your letter should simply explain the specific facts and state your claim. Little or no persuasion is presumed to be necessary; hence you use no appeal beyond brief reference to a guarantee, reputation for fair dealing, and the like.

This kind of direct claim (Type-A letter) may start with the requested action, or it may start with the date and conditions of purchase. Beginning with the history of the case is a little less antagonizing and a little more persuasive. The middle part is a carefully planned, complete, and specific explanation of the facts. A test of the adequacy of the explanation is to ask whether it is all you would want to know if you had to decide on the claim. The ending, then, is a request for action. It should be as specific as the conditions will permit (Point 3 above). Here are two examples:

> I'm sure you will want to know that the Etherwave console model radio I purchased from you on June 5 is not giving the desired performance.
>
> I was well pleased for the first two weeks, but now I am getting some interference and the tuning knob seems to slip. At least turning it does not change the tuning after the machine is warmed up.
>
> Since I know very little about a radio, I asked a friend to look it over. He thinks that the condenser plates are somewhat loose and have shaken out of tram and a small belt in the tuning mechanism has become loose.
>
> I feel that since this radio is only a month old and is also fully guaranteed, you will agree with me that your firm should take care of the necessary adjustments to insure perfect performance again.
>
> Only one local radio shop has the necessary equipment for tramming radio plates, and the charges are $7.50. However, this shop has no belt to fit my radio.
>
> As I see it, there are two possibilities for action. One is that I send the radio to you for repair. The other is that you send the correct belt to my local shop (The XL Radio Shop, 122 East Washington) and pay the cost of installing the belt as well as the $7.50 for tramming the plates.
>
> I shall appreciate your prompt reply, as I am especially interested in good radio reception during the baseball season.

> GENTLEMEN:
> CLAIM FOR DAMAGES DONE TO MY CAR BY YOUR CLIENT
> (Mr. K. C. Hall, Gary, Indiana—License CG 3035)
>
> On June 9 about 15–20 miles west of Decatur, Illinois, on Highway 48, I was driving 55–60 mph and I overtook a car going about 35. When I was almost even with this car, passing it, something bumped my car hard on the left rear fender and door, shoving me hard to the right and damaging my car.
>
> The something that hit my car (a new four-door XXXX, Illinois license 885–009) was a late-model green XXXXXXXX driven by your client, Mr. Hall. I estimated that he was driving at least 70, for he whished on by me before stopping, just as I went on around the car I had overtaken.

Inspection revealed that his car was damaged on the back part of the right front fender and on the right front door, mine on the left rear fender and door.

Certainly the accident was no fault of mine, for I was driving in an entirely normal and legal manner. Good judgment on his part would have told him that I was going to pass the car ahead, since I was overtaking it at an estimated difference of 20 mph in speed. Thus he should have checked his speed and waited. He probably blew his horn, as he said he did; but I could not hear it because a diesel train on a near-by parallel track was blowing very loudly. He probably realized that I did not hear when I continued to pull left to pass, but he was driving too fast to control his car.

Since I consider him completely responsible for the accident and damages, I hereby make claim for repairs to my car, as listed on any one of the three enclosed estimates.

Persuasive Claims. Sometimes you will have good reason to believe that you will have to be rather persuasive in order to get results on your claim. Your reason may be that you know the reader to be rather reluctant to grant claims, that your case is subject to some question and you need to make as good a case as you can within the facts, or (most frequently) that you have already tried the direct claim and have been turned down.

Whatever the cause, you write a Type-C letter when you need to be persuasive, and you can appeal to any desire that might motivate the reader. Some of the main appeals (more or less in ascending order of force and objectionable tone) are to the reader's desire for (1) customer satisfaction, good will, and favorable publicity; (2) a continued reputation for fair dealing; and (3) legal meeting of a guarantee.

Again your letter is divided rather distinctly into three parts, but their contents are somewhat different from those of the direct claim:

1. You begin by stating and getting agreement on the principle which is the basis of your claim. (In logic, it would be called the "major premise.")
2. You explain all the facts in detail, as in any claim. (The term in logic is the "minor premise.") This part may be several paragraphs long. In it you show clearly the reader's responsibility.
3. You apply the facts or minor premise to the principle or major premise so as to draw a conclusion, as the logician would call it. The conclusion will be that the reader should act in a certain way. You request that he act as the logic has clearly shown that he should.

Here are two examples of how the system works. The first was an initial claim. It was successful, in spite of the fact that a glance may suggest that the writer had no justified claim. A closer look, however, will make clear that he did. The situation was quite different from a person's just buying something and finding a few days later that the seller has reduced the price. The key difference is the salesman's assurance to the claimant that he would not save money by waiting. The appeal is, therefore, to the reader's desire for customer confidence.

> If your customers do not trust your salesmen, it doesn't do much good for you to go to a lot of trouble and expense in selecting and training salesmen, does it Mr. Barnes? That's why I'm writing to you.
>
> On July 5 I was in your store looking at an XXXX suit priced at $67.75. I decided to leave and wait for a late-summer sale, as I frequently do. But your salesman assured me that there would be no sale on XXXX suits, that the manufacturer had never allowed its suits to be sold at reduced prices, and would not this year. So, since I wanted the suit, I bought it.
>
> Now I notice that the price has been reduced to $53.95 and that you are selling at that price.
>
> My plan, you see, would have saved me $13.80. Because I was induced to buy through your salesman's assurance that I could not get the suit cheaper by waiting, I believe you will agree that I am entitled to a refund of $13.80.
>
> I am sure that you want me to trust your salesmen. You can renew my faith if you stand behind what they say.

The following illustration of a persuasive claim was written after a claim brought a proposal to compromise. This letter is an answer to that compromise proposal. It got the money, the full amount without compromise, by appealing to fair-minded analysis of the facts (and hence the injustice of compromise in the case).

> GENTLEMEN:
>
> Subject: Claim #070–6289
>
> If a salesman for the XXXX Casualty Company were trying to sell me a policy and I offered to pay him half the premium he requested, do you think he would take it? I don't. That would be a compromise.
>
> Compromises are for cases where there is doubt about responsibility or about the amount of damage done. In my claim, there is no doubt about either.
>
> Analysis of the facts will show that Mr. Hall ran up behind me so fast that he could not control his car and hit the left rear part of the side of my car. Clearly he was responsible.
>
> I got three estimates of the repair job to be sure of having a fair appraisal of the damages. The lowest of the three was $26. So there is no doubt about the damage.

I am therefore returning the RELEASE AND SETTLEMENT form you sent and asking that you send another based on one of the estimates I formerly sent in. That is the only fair settlement.

I know that your job is to keep your loss ratio down as low as possible while being fair about the obligations the Company assumes in insuring clients. The solution is to settle on the basis of one of the estimates submitted.

I look forward to receiving that settlement.

Policy Complaints. The policy complaint may be like a direct claim or a persuasive one.

Whereas claims ask restitution for mistakes, damages, or unsatisfactory products, policy complaints request correction of poor service or unsatisfactory policies and practices. The following are two typical situations:

If there's anything our customers like better than XXXX strawberry ice cream, it's XXXX chocolate or vanilla. That's why many people were disappointed last Sunday when we received an entire delivery of strawberry instead of the chocolate and vanilla we ordered.

If you remember last Sunday, you know it was a pretty hot day—a good day to sell ice cream. We sold 2,000 cups but turned away hundreds of tired, hungry swimmers because they insisted on chocolate or vanilla. I believe I could have sold the remaining 1,000 cups had they been those flavors.

Our customers like XXXX ice cream so well that we'd like to continue selling it. Perhaps a little more care in packing, or a little better system of labeling, will assure you of delivering the right flavors for my future orders, and thus increase both our sales.

May I depend on you?

~~~~·

Am I right in thinking that Racine Motors wants its policy on direct-sale commissions and co-operative selling campaigns to promote long-range good will and increased sales in this territory?

Because I think so but find the present practice is not working out that way, I think you will want to review your policies in view of my experiences.

Recently one of our salesmen called on a prospect in our territory and found him already enjoying the reliability and efficiency of a 20 h.p. Racine Motor, which we normally stock. Further investigation revealed that he had bought the motor directly from you at a price below our selling price. Yet we have received no dealer's commission on this sale. This is one of several occasions brought to my attention in the past year which prompt me to ask you for clarification of our agreement.

Admittedly with the helpful assistance of your missionary salesmen, we have been able to sell a substantial group of the industrial users in this area on the economy and dependability of the Racine Electric Motor. We want to keep and expand this patronage, but it will be difficult if we are working at cross-purposes with you. It will be to our mutual good if we and you quote uniform prices and if we get our dealer's commission on any direct sales. You gain by being relieved of the marketing functions and by having a ready-made market for your motor, and we gain by getting our just profits and keeping the good will of our customers.

We have been contemplating an expansion of our stock to include your 60 h.p. motor, which would play an important part in our sales program. Please give us a definite working policy so we will know where we stand.

ADJUSTMENTS

ADJUSTMENT POLICIES

Invariably a claim represents loss of good will and of confidence in the goods or in the firm. The adjustment writer's key job is to minimize those losses by satisfying customers as far as possible at a reasonable cost to the company.

Some companies try to dodge the basic problem by almost literally adopting the policy that the customer is always right (the *caveat venditor* philosophy). They figure that the few unfair claims cost less in adjustment losses than the liberal policy pays in good will. The system works best in exclusive and expensive shops with a high type of customer; but a recent survey shows that many exclusive ladies' ready-to-wear shops are concerned because as much as 20 per cent of their sales are returned.

Other firms take the opposite view (*caveat emptor*) and make all sales final. Usually they depend on low prices rather than good will to attract a type of customer to which price is the strongest possible appeal.

The great majority take the middle ground between those two extremes: *Treat each claim on its merits and lean a bit toward giving the customer the benefit of the doubt for the sake of unquestioned fairness and the resulting good will.*

That seems to be the most ethical and the most satisfactory policy to most people. Generally a customer will not leave a firm or product after only one disappointment if the firm applies this honest and reasonable policy with finesse. Usually a reasonable person will allow at least a second chance, unless the adjuster loses further good will by his attitude toward the claim or by his bungling techniques in handling it.

Carrying out the recommended policy therefore requires

1. Careful analysis and classification of each claim according to the cause of dissatisfaction and consequently what adjustment is fair.
2. Retaining a reasonable attitude even with testy claimants.
3. Skill in the use of the tools and techniques of adjustment.

ANALYSIS AND CLASSIFICATION OF ADJUSTMENTS

If the evidence in a claim (and from inspection when deemed necessary) shows clearly that the company or the product was at fault, you may replace the article free with a perfect one, repair it free, or take it back and refund the money. The last is the least desirable for both buyer and seller. He bought the article for the service he thought it would render; if you take it back, he has to make other arrangements or do without that service. If you replace or repair it, you give him the service, regain his good will, and make him a satisfied customer who will perhaps buy from you again and pass on the good word about you and your products to other prospects. Indeed, about the only occasion when you would refund the money is when you see that a perfect specimen of the article will not do the job for him. And even then, if you have another (perhaps larger or better quality) which you think will satisfy, you should try to give him the service he wanted and justify any higher price in terms of advantages.

If responsibility for the dissatisfaction is clearly the buyer's, you will ordinarily refuse the claim. In rare cases you may decide that a compromise or even a full adjustment will be the wise thing because of the amount of good will that can be regained at small cost. The weakness in this decision is that it implies your acceptance of responsibility and increases your difficulty in regaining confidence in your goods and services. Whatever your action, your major job is justifying your decision and (usually, because he was at fault) educating the customer. By writing your letter as education to the buyer in the proper use and care of the product (perhaps regular oiling), you may establish the responsibility by implication, avoid irritating the claimant, and prevent future trouble.

If responsibility for the dissatisfaction is uncertain or divided between buyer and product, you will suggest a compromise or make a full adjustment. Again the educational function of the letter is usually important.

Whether you grant the adjustment, refuse it, or propose a compromise, the discussion of replies to inquiries and requests in Chapter VI prepares you rather well to write adjustment letters, which are, in fact, answers to requests (claims). They are essentially the same in organization and psychology. But there are some basic differences. In answering requests, you have no legal or moral obligations to do anything against your will; in answering claims, you have legal and moral obligations to be fair. Before you write any of the three types, therefore, you need to consider the attitude of the adjuster and special adjustment tools and techniques.

ATTITUDE OF THE ADJUSTER

If a firm's adjuster looks on claims as largely the unfair requests of dishonest people or chronic gripers, in time he may reduce the number of claims. People will refrain from making many claims to such a firm —if they don't stop buying there—because they do not like to be considered either dishonest or unreasonable. Most of them aren't, anyway. Out of 5,000,000 on the list of a big mail-order firm, only 2,712, or one twentieth of 1 per cent, tried to take advantage of the firm in five years. So the adjustment man who looks on everybody who makes a claim as somebody trying to take advantage is wrong in fact and wrong in attitude.

Such an attitude not only drives away customers and claims, but it logically prevents the adjuster from making wise use of the claims he does receive. A wise business firm keeps records of claims for statistical analysis, to show weaknesses in its products, methods, services, and personnel. But if the adjuster considers most claims dishonest, he could not logically use them as a basis for making changes.

If, on the other hand, you start with the attitude that a claimant may be misinformed but is honest and reasonable, you will be right much more frequently, and you will do much better. You will use all claims as pointers to improvements in the firm's goods and operations, and your adjustment letters will show appreciation for the help the customer has given. (Even those claims where the buyer is completely at fault point to a need for better instructions to users.) But, more important, you create a much more pleasant situation in which people buy more freely because they know that they can get reasonable adjustments if anything goes wrong.

In addition to this sound attitude, you need a thick skin to be an adjuster. Many claimants will not have learned to keep their shirts on. If you let their gibes and personal-sounding accusations get under your skin, you are likely to get involved in squabbles and lose customers, even when you win arguments. As a wise adjuster, therefore, you will make it a part of your attitude to ignore personal taunts. You defend yourself, your firm, and your products insofar as you can by explanations; otherwise you accept the claims made. Thus you create a climate of good will and good business.

A claim represents customer dissatisfaction, all right; but it does not necessarily involve really strong negatives which you cannot almost completely overcome with your fair-minded attitude and skillful use of the adjuster's tools and techniques.

ADJUSTMENT TOOLS AND TECHNIQUES

Using Resale. Since the adjustment writer's main job is to regain good will and confidence, you will find resale a highly useful tool. Probably nowhere else in letter writing is it more important. Indeed, the main job of an adjustment man is essentially the same as the purpose of resale—to recover or strengthen good will and confidence in the integrity and efficiency of a firm and/or the quality of its goods. Naturally, then, resale is the main tool for doing that job. The explanations on page 23 tell you how to use the tool.

Making Positive Explanations. Effective resale is impossible, however, unless you avoid the following special pitfalls which frequently trap the untrained adjustment letter writer:

1. Inadequate or inept explanation that leaves the reader thinking that slipshod methods of manufacturing or marketing caused the trouble. If it isn't true, you need to be careful to make that clear by showing how careful you are.
2. Dwelling on the reader's dissatisfaction or the likelihood of his being a lost customer. Reminding him is not the way to cause him to forget these thoughts; but resale through explanation and reassurance is.
3. Passing the buck by attributing the difficulty to a new clerk or an act of God. These have been used so much as excuses that they will not be believed, even when true, unless you are specific. Anyway, the new clerk is a member of the firm; so his errors are reflections on the firm.
4. Trying to hide in the bigness of your firm. If the firm is so big that it can't attend to details that necessarily cause frequent slipups, perhaps that's good reason for the customer to go elsewhere. So such talk is the opposite of resale. About the only way you can use the bigness as acceptable explanation is to sell it in terms of reader benefits along with its weaknesses. That is, explain that through large volume you are able to keep the quality relatively high and the price low, and to correct the occasional slipups.
5. Stressing your open-handedness. The reader does not want to be considered a beggar, given things he doesn't deserve. You'd better refuse unless the facts justify the adjustment, or at least leave a possibility that it is justified. Even our terminology, "Granting the adjustment," is questionable for use in the letters themselves; the word *grant* may connote giving something undeserved.

6. Suggesting future trouble. Though it's unsafe to go out on a limb and promise that the trouble will never happen again, you do not want to suggest that it will by telling what to do when it does. Good technique tells what you have done to assure future satisfaction and provides the necessary instruction for the user to assure proper service. You only put undesirable ideas into his head if you say "If you have any more difficulty, let us know," or even "I don't believe you'll have any more difficulty." In fact, a big problem in adjustments is what to do about the inherent negative in them.

Handling Inherent Negatives.   As an adjustment writer, you therefore need to be a master of the techniques for dealing with negatives. They will be one of your stumbling-blocks, for every adjustment situation is full of them. You will do well to remember the letter writer's definition of *negative* as anything unpleasant to the reader. Moreover, you should remember what a letter writer's code of action is with respect to negative material—avoid it when you can and subordinate it when you can't avoid it. Following that code, you will find that you can usually avoid most of the good-will killers like the following, which creep into the letters of untrained adjustment writers:

you claim	policy	damaged	delay
you say	amazed	broken	inconvenience
you state	fault	defective	regret
you (plus any accusing verb)	surprised	unable	sorry

Two of the items deserve special consideration.

1. Such accusations as "You failed to oil . . ." will almost always destroy rather than rebuild good will. Nobody likes to be accused of things which he should not have done, even though he is guilty. When a skillful letter writer has a compliment to pass, he will make it personal for favorable effect; but if he has an accusation to make, he will cast it into an impersonal statement rather than offend needlessly. Indeed, this is one of the rare occasions in which passive voice is preferable to active if the active voice leads to personal accusation.

2. The term *company policy* has been used so much as an excuse by highhanded or timid adjusters with no good reason for not granting an adjustment that most people now take it to mean about the same as "None of your business" or "I'm afraid to tell the real reason." When a man thinks he has a just claim, he feels that he is entitled to an explanation or reason (not an excuse) before a refusal. Unless he gets it, he is not going to be happy.

Of course, an adjuster can avoid all these negative expressions and still write a distasteful letter. The writer of the following one certainly succeeded in doing so:

> I get awful tired of your raising the dickens with us about late shipment and telling us that your buyer threatens to take his business elsewhere. Don't make me laugh! We had the labels a week ago and the shipment has been ready since Monday. . . . Both you and he should realize that . . . and when you continually pick on us it goes against the grain. . . . Don't be so childish in your attitude. . . . It doesn't work that way. . . . Let's be sensible and reasonable.

To take full advantage of the technique of handling negatives in letters, however, you have to consider more than the words and phrases. When you refuse a requested adjustment, you have to say "No"; you can't avoid the negative idea. But you can subordinate it. Since the technique involves the organization of the whole refusal letter, however, further treatment is best in connection with that topic (p. 340).

GRANTING THE ADJUSTMENT

When you decide to grant an adjustment, you have an easy letter to write. Since it is a good-news letter (Type A), you answer the reader's big question in the first sentence as fast as you can. Not only should this sentence tell him that you are granting the adjustment, but it should be worded carefully to avoid any grudging tone and avoid recalling the dissatisfaction any more than necessary. After all, you might almost as well not grant the adjustment, insofar as good will is concerned, if you grant it in a grudging tone. And, of course, reminding him of his trouble by using negative words would hurt rather than help in your biggest job in this letter—to recover or rebuild good will and confidence in the firm's integrity and efficiency and/or the quality of its products.

The fact that you have granted the adjustment gives you a natural basis for some resale talk on the house. You should use it by interpreting the facts as evidence that you stand behind guarantees, treat the customer right, or some such.

Somewhere in the letter, but not necessarily right after the good news and its interpretation, you should express appreciation for the claimant's calling your attention to the situation (because the information helps the firm to keep goods and services up to par). This "thank you" does several important things quickly: (1) It shows the reader that you are fair-minded and do not take a distrusting or bitter attitude toward claims. (2) It is basically resale in showing that you are interested in retaining (if not improving) your standards for goods and services. (3) It makes the customer feel good because his claim seems welcome and seems to get careful consideration. Of course, if any steps have been or are being taken to prevent recurrence of claims such as you are answering, you should explain them (to rebuild confidence) and give him as much credit as the facts allow. It sounds good to almost any reader to hear that "On the basis of helpful suggestions like yours, we have decided. . . ."

The biggest part of your letter will be an explanation of the situation. Insofar as possible, you point it toward rebuilding confidence and good will. It may be that the product was obviously defective or that the firm was at fault in some way. If there is no good reason or explanation that will put them in a better light, you'd better accept the fact and frankly admit the error or defect rather than make excuses. If you explain specifically how your firm tries to see that everything goes well, most readers will accept that as due precaution and will understand that mistakes do occasionally creep in, despite reasonable care. If you have statistics to show how effective your system is in avoiding mistakes and defective goods, they may be effective in rebuilding the customer's confidence and good will. You want to be careful, though, not to present them in a way that seems to tell the reader he must be odd to have trouble when nearly all your other customers don't.

Though you can't honestly or safely promise that "it will never happen again," you can end pleasantly. Having covered the good news, the explanation, the thanks, and any necessary action of the reader, you can end looking forward, not backward. Apologies or other reminders of the past dissatisfaction merely leave a bad taste in the reader's mouth. Give him a chaser. A light touch of resale—or even sales-promotion material, if you have a related article that you think would serve him well—can boost his spirit and provide you with a sincere, success-conscious look forward to future business. The customer so well treated will probably return.

The following letter illustrates most of the points:

> The enclosed credit memorandum for $15.60 is an example of Strong-Arch's continuous effort to satisfy our customers in prices, merchandise, and service. We are glad to make this adjustment, requested in your letter of November 28, on the 2 dozen pairs, assorted sizes, of Cordovan Brogues that we shipped you last week.
>
> How your shoes were billed can be explained by a look at the mechanics of our billing department. Whenever our salesmen take an order, they enter a symbol for the particular style, size, and color of shoe. In preparing the invoice, the billing department automatically enters the latest price, which in this case was $7.50. At the time Mr. Green took your order this price had been in effect only two days. He erroneously entered the old

price of $6.85, which was detected and changed in billing. On future orders any discrepancies between salesmen's orders and current price lists will be referred to one individual for special handling.

We are grateful for your first order. As these shoes become popular with your customers, we know you will want to add some other Strong-Arch models and styles to your stock. All give long wear and comfort to the customer and good profit margins to the dealer.

In addition to the Cordovan Brogue you may want to offer your customers a new style, the Strong-Arch Loafer. It is made of top-grain cowhide, with leather soles and rubber heels, and double-stitched for longer wear. Page 4 of the enclosed leaflet shows you the Loafer as advertised in this month's *Esquire.* When you order these loafers (at only $4.95 a pair) we'll include in the shipment a split sample shoe so you can show your customers the exact structure.

Though the letter below does not actually send the check in the first sentence, as is usually desirable, it does say emphatically that the adjustment has been granted. This letter is in answer to the claim letter on page 330.

You most certainly will be given a refund on the XXX suit which you purchased, for we support our salesmen in whatever they promise a customer.

The salesman who told you that there would be no sale on XXX suits was sincere in his belief that the price would not be reduced. The XXX manufacturers have never before permitted their suits to be sold at reduced prices. We were notified one week before our summer clothing sale this year that they were permitting a reduction for the first time.

We thank you for calling our attention to this situation, and we are glad to enclose our check for $13.80.

When you again need clothing, see our salesmen in the Men's Department. You can rely on what they tell you, with full confidence that we will back them up.

Sometimes you will need the customer's help on a few details such as filling out blanks for recovery of damages from a transportation company and returning defective articles. Be sure to cover such points in the one letter to avoid unnecessary correspondence; be sure, also, to make the reader's action as easy as possible.

Your Old South cream and sugar set is being mailed prepaid today so that it will arrive two or three days before the wedding.

Since the Old South set is in keeping with Southern traditions, it will attract favorable glances and comments as guests look over the gifts.

This set is being carefully wrapped with plenty of newspaper and shipped in a corrugated box of $3/16$-inch thickness. This is thicker than required by shippers, but it will be standard packing for all Old South china from now on. Your report has helped us to improve our service. Thank you.

To save you the trouble of paying for the second shipment, then getting a refund from the Post Office on the first shipment, we are sending a claim form completely filled out except for your signature. Will you please sign it and use the reply envelope for mailing it back to us?

The bride and groom will like the ante-bellum motif of the Old South set and will attach many pleasant memories to it as the years go by.

The accompanying **Check List for Granting Adjustments** is comprehensive enough to cover most situations, but not all the points are likely to apply to any one letter.

REFUSING THE ADJUSTMENT

The letter refusing an adjustment is obviously a bad-news letter (Type B). Your psychology of saying "No" is therefore important. So, unless you thoroughly understand it, read the explanation beginning on page 30.

For your buffer-paragraph beginning, you look for something in the situation which you and the reader agree on and which is pleasant to him. Even though you are going to disagree on the big point and refuse him, you will usually agree with some of the things he has said in his claim. The appreciation for the information could be used in most cases. You can certainly agree that he was right to come to you.

The dangers to avoid in writing the buffer are:

1. Stating or implying refusal before reasons ("We wish we could").
2. Misleading your reader into thinking that you are going to grant the adjustment ("Our policy of making fair adjustments").
3. Talking irrelevantly or too far off the subject.
4. Recalling the disappointment too vividly ("We regret your dissatisfaction").
5. Making it too short to get in step or too long to suit an impatient claimant.
6. Making an awkward transition to the next part because the buffer is not well phrased.

Though you may introduce a sentence that serves as a transition and as resale on the house, you need to get to your explanation or review of facts and reasons fairly early. And you need to give the facts and reasons fully in a clear system of organization.

Again the explanation is the major part of the letter. There are several special techniques important in it if it is to rebuild good will while refusing to do what the reader asked. You already know better than to

Check List for Granting Adjustments

1. Make the beginning fast, informative, pleasant, and reassuring.
   a) Open with the full reparation.
   b) Avoid any grudging tone.
   c) Give a specific statement of what you are doing.
   d) Build up the favorable reaction with a few resale words implying the reader's pleasure in the use of the restored article or in your fairness.
   e) Too much product resale before explanation may bring an "Oh yeah?"
2. Throughout the letter, avoid emphasis on the disappointing aspects by avoiding negative words.
3. Explain fully, honestly, and reassuringly.
   a) Include a good-will-building sentence—either that you're glad to make the adjustment OR that you welcome the report as an aid in maintaining quality and service—as illustrated in the two preceding letters.
   b) Whichever you choose, be sure your facts follow logically from your wording of the adjustment you've made.
   c) Judicially, impartially—and preferably impersonally—establish the reason for the mishap *in the minimum number of words*. Often you can effectively imply the reason in your explanation of corrective measures taken or of the ordinary care taken.
   d) Whether you name or imply the source of error, give concrete evidence of normally correct, safe shipments of high-quality goods or—if applicable—explain changes you are making to prevent recurrence of the difficulty.
   e) Be quick to admit error; don't appear to be buck-passing.
   f) Avoid suggesting frequency of error.
4. Ask for any necessary co-operation from the customer. For example:
   a) Be definite and polite in asking the customer to sign necessary blanks.
   b) Clear up what is to be done with the original article if you're replacing it.
   c) Make his action as little trouble as possible ("When the expressman calls to pick up the original shipment, just have him . . .").
5. Close pleasantly with a forward look.
   a) Don't tear up your good positive efforts with a backward look apologizing or otherwise recalling the disappointing aspects.
   b) Do leave the customer with a pleasant reminder of the pleasurable use of the perfect article now in his hands, if applicable.
   c) You may end the letter with resale talk, but sales-promotional material on an allied article may well suggest your additional thoughtfulness—and just may pick up an extra sale.

hide behind the word *policy* or to give no reason at all. The reader expects one, and a reasonable and clear one. A flat-footed announcement of what the guarantee states is just as bad as unsupported talk about policy. Since you are refusing, clearly you are not charging responsibility for the dissatisfaction to either the firm or the product. You must clear that point up with adequate explanation as a basis for refusing. That, of course, makes the reader guilty; but you don't want to accuse him directly. Preaching to him or belittling him will only make matters worse. Your best technique is to fall back on the impersonal presentation (something "was not done" instead of "you didn't"), rather than accuse. The reader will be able to see who is responsible if you explain well that your goods and your firm aren't.

In fact, if your reasons and explanations are carefully arranged, they will probably make the negative answer clear by implication without the necessity of stating it. Thus you may subordinate the negative refusal. If not this way, at least you subordinate by burying it (that is, putting it in the middle of a paragraph where it doesn't stand out unduly).

After the refusal, which must be clearly there whether by implication or by direct statement, you may do well to add some more reasoning and explanation in support. Be sure there is enough to make your refusal convincing and justified.

Your ending, then, becomes an attempt to get agreement or the reader's acceptance of your refusal as justified. That is, you write with as much success-consciousness as seems reasonable about the future outlook. This does NOT mean that you write and ask for an answer as to whether your action is all right. If it isn't, he'll let you know without your asking. The following letter illustrates most of the points, especially the clear reasoning that makes direct refusal unnecessary:

> We certainly agree with you that your company has always ordered high-quality products to sell to your customers. We, too, try to keep our products up to a high standard.
>
> That is why we appreciate your fairness in giving us a chance to analyze the sample of screws you sent.
>
> Our chemical analysis shows that the screws are brittle because they are high in phosphorous and low in carbon and sulphur steel, whereas our screws are of a very different analysis. Physical analysis shows that the sample screws have been severely cold-worked without stress relief, whereas our screws are never made that way.
>
> To check our laboratory report, which practically proved that we could not have made those screws, I have checked your former orders and found

that the screws we have sent you were always blue steel finish, instead of the cadmium finish of the sample.

We should be glad to supply you again with our hard but tough screws that will give your customers the quality they have come to expect from you. Our descriptive price list is enclosed. May we look forward to your order?

For a more subtle illustration, analyze the following letter to a customer who had taken his suit to another tailor in another city and asked for payment of the tailor's bill long after the usual free-alteration period ended. (The owner-manager knew all of his student customers fairly well.)

You're right!—your Smart Marx gabardine should fit you well. When you buy a suit of that quality from us, we try as hard as you do to see that you are satisfied in every way before we turn it over to you with our blessings.

I well remember how you liked the rich sheen of the tan 100 per cent wool cloth and the casual look of the patch pockets. But for comfort and becoming fit, we decided that the sleeves should be a half-inch longer and the collar taken up an inch—the same directions that are on the sales slip and the alterations slip which I have on my desk right now, and which bear the initials of one of our tailors and my own. When you came back in the next day and tried the coat on, I honestly thought that it clicked all the way around; and, after carefully noting it from every angle, you agreed with me. I thought we had achieved our goal—your satisfaction.

But we owe you something else: the best quality at the lowest price possible. And one of the small economies that helps to keep the price of your suit lower is that it does not include costs of altering suits for men who have become twenty pounds heavier or lighter. In order to protect all Smart Marx buyers, we limit free alterations to two weeks after purchase, thus giving the wearer ample time to become accustomed to the feel of his new suit and take advantage of the free-alterations privilege if he cares to.

After that time we're glad to make necessary alterations at regular tailors' rates to readjust Smart Marx suits to a wearer's changes in weight that sometimes come during the long life of such good suits.

Since you'll probably want to wear your suit well into the coming season, you might enjoy a pair of the Floorshine shoes we've just received. In russet calfskin they're good for all-around wear. May we show you this style when you return to school early next month?

The accompanying (next two pages) check list will review the highlights of refusing adjustments.

COMPROMISING ON THE ADJUSTMENT

When you decide to try to compromise—usually because of divided responsibility, or uncertainty about responsibility or correction for the trouble—you may use either of two plans.

REFUSED-ADJUSTMENT CHECK LIST

1. Make your buffer beginning positive, related, adequate, and progressive.
    a) Reflect a pleasant, co-operative attitude (try to agree on something).
    b) But begin closely enough to the situation to show that this is an acknowledgment and to lead naturally to the next part.
    c) Don't imply that you're granting the request and thus make refusing harder.
    d) Avoid recalling the dissatisfaction any more strongly than necessary.
    e) Watch buffer length: (1) too short and breezy a buffer does not enable you to match up your reader's and your own tone and tempo; but (2) more than two short paragraphs holds off your facts and reasons too long.
    f) Too much resale on the product—especially in the trouble area— gets a sour-grapes reaction if presented before the reasons for refusal show it was not faulty.
2. Make your facts and reasons courteous, thorough, and convincing.
    a) An immediate plunge (usually at the beginning of the second paragraph) into "a thorough examination" or "our policy" is abrupt. A transitional sentence indicating desire to keep up good service is always acceptable.
    b) The cold, apparently inflexible "our guarantee states . . ." is particularly annoying as the lead in the explanation. Eliminate *guarantee* and *policy*.
    c) Don't accuse the reader or preach at him. Phrase your review of circumstances *impersonally*—and let him derive his own guilt.
    d) Definitely establish the explicit facts—the evidence and the reasoning that are the basis for your refusal which is to follow.

In the first you follow the refused-adjustment plan exactly down *to* the refusal. There you make your proposed compromise instead, explicitly. In effect, you are refusing the adjustment requested and are making a counterproposal—a compromise. When you ask acceptance of it, your success in getting a favorable reply will depend not only on how well you have presented facts and reasons to justify the compromise but on your success-consciousness in presenting it and on your phrasing it to encourage rather than discourage acceptance. You'll have a good check list for the type if you substitute the following for Items 3 and 4 in the **Refused-Adjustment Check List.**

3. Make your counterproposal as logical, helpful relief.
    a) Be careful to make a smooth transition from the explanation

REFUSED-ADJUSTMENT CHECK LIST (CONTINUED)

e) Even intimating the refusal before at least some justifying facts and reasons is a violation of your entire psychology and inductive strategy.

f) Whenever possible, interpret the reasoning to show reader benefits.

3. Make the refusal follow logically, in subordinate and impersonal phrasing; but be sure it is clear and justified.

   a) Preferably the reader sees the refusal coming at the same time or shortly before he sees any definite statement or implication of it.

   b) Give little emphasis to the refusal—certainly not the prominence of a paragraph beginning or ending, or independent-clause structure.

   c) Keep it impersonal and positive. Phrased in terms of what you do rather than what you don't, the refusal is implied clearly.

   d) Be sure it is there, however; unclear is as bad as too strong.

   e) Follow the refusal with more justifying reasons, and show whatever possible reader benefits result from your deciding as you do.

   f) Make your explanation convincing; the quick-brushoff treatment is infuriating.

   g) A counterproposal can sometimes adequately imply the refusal.

4. Make your ending pleasant, positive, and success-conscious.

   a) An off-the-subject ending about store services, seasonal goods that might interest the reader, or some topic of general interest is appropriate.

   b) Do not suggest that you aren't sure of your ground by some worn-out expression like "We trust this is satisfactory" or "We're sure you understand our position." Watch *hope* and *trust;* they suggest doubt.

   c) Apologies are unnecessary reminders of trouble; your careful explanation showing that the fault is not yours has already made the best apology.

(which implies refusal of the requested adjustment) to the counterproposal.

b) Offer it ungrudgingly, without parading your generosity; but let the service element rather than price comparisons or sales pressure prevail.

c) Don't belittle it ("about the best we can do") or make it sound like a harsh penalty ("a service charge will *have* to be made").

4. Use a modified action ending.

   a) Ask permission; you wouldn't go ahead without customer agreement.

   b) Tell what he is to do and how to do it; but don't urge acceptance.

   c) Promise quick attention and satisfactory results, to reinforce your service attitude shown earlier.

The following letter in answer to a strong request for removal of the heater, cancellation of remaining payments, and refund of the shipping and installation charges illustrates the points. You will notice that it offers to compromise to the extent of cancelling the remaining payments, but it proposes another action instead.

> You are right in expecting your Warmall Heater to heat a large room such as your entire store, for that was what it was designed to do.
>
> To do so, however, it must be located so that the air currents can carry its heat to all parts of the room. Our engineer reports that the stove was installed in the proper position but that later remodeling of your store has blocked circulation of air with a half partition.
>
> It would be useless to remove your stove, which can be all you want it to be when properly located. That would mean losing what you have paid for shipping and installation, though we would, of course, cancel the remaining payments. Moreover, you must have heat; and the Warmall will do the job.
>
> We have absolute faith in our engineer's judgment, but your satisfaction is more important. So we want to do what is fair to us both.
>
> At your convenience we can move the stove to the position suggested by our engineer; and if it does not heat to your satisfaction, we will not charge you a cent.
>
> Will you suggest the most convenient time for the change that will make your store warm and comfortable? We can do the job so quickly and efficiently that your business can continue as usual.

A second method of compromising—usually called the Full-Reparation Beginning Compromise—sometimes works better. You follow the plan of the letter granting an adjustment at the beginning, through the explanation. The facts, of course, will indicate divided responsibility or uncertain responsibility. Your resale talk will indicate that the repaired product (or a replacement up to par, in case the original was beyond repair) will give the service the customer wanted. Since he presumably still wants that service, you ask him to take his choice—the refunded money or the product. And, of course, you word it to encourage him to choose the product, because that way you have a customer satisfied with your products as well as your fair-minded practices.

Your main purpose is to restore good will and confidence. Your success depends on a start which offers him all he requested and thereby pleases him, your explanation that shows the justice of a compromise, and your fair-mindedness in letting him be the judge and take his choice. The danger—not a very serious one—is that some people might try to keep both the money and the product. And, of course, you have to be willing to accept his choice if he decides on full adjustment. Here are two examples, one to a consumer and one to a dealer.

> The enclosed check is cheerful proof of our "Money back if not entirely satisfied" guarantee on the Corone cigarette lighter you purchased last December.
>
> Because such a guarantee can be given only on a lighter that will entirely satisfy you, we examined yours very carefully in our Service Department. The shop foreman reports that the sparking ridges on the flint wheel were clogged to a smooth surface with flake particles from a soft flint. After he cleaned the wheel and installed a Corone Hard Flint—the type recommended on the instructions enclosed with each new lighter—your Corone worked well.
>
> You probably remember, Mr. Lewis, that one flick brought an instant flame before the hard flint wore out and was replaced in January. Now that your lighter has been returned to that condition, and still has the attractive styling that caught your eye the day you bought it, you'll probably want it back.
>
> We will be glad to absorb the normal sixty cents cleaning charge and return your lighter to you if you wish. Just send the check back in the enclosed envelope, and your lighter will be in your pocket within two days after we hear from you—ready at a flick to show your friend in Jackson that your Corone really does the job.

> Attached to this letter is a credit memorandum for $43.75, which we cheerfully send you for the five Bear Mountain hunting jackets you returned, and as an indication that you'll always be treated fairly at Bowen's.
>
> Under the assumption that these jackets would find a ready sale at a reduced retail price despite slight imperfections (a button mismatched, a crooked seam, or maybe a little nick in the fabric), we offered them "as is" and priced them at $8.75 instead of the regular $12.75. We felt that marking them "as is" indicated special circumstances.
>
> Generally we follow the accepted business custom of making all such sales final for an entire lot. But as you are a customer of long standing and valued patronage [*Better:* But as we evidently did not make the situation perfectly clear], we are leaving the decision up to you; if you feel that you're entitled to the adjustment, it's yours.
>
> Many of your customers, however, would probably be glad to get nationally advertised Bear Mountains at perhaps $21 instead of the standard $25. And even if you sell these five at, say, only $16, your profit will be about the same as if you sold perfect jackets at full price. So if you'd like to reconsider, and want to offer these jackets at a saving, just initial the face of this letter and send it to us with the credit memo. We'll absorb the freight charges.
>
> Even though slightly imperfect, these jackets are still ready to stand a lot of hard wear. They are made to suit the hunter's needs with ample pockets

for shells and with comfortable tailoring. Selling them should be easy, especially at a discount. We'll look for your decision, but we think you can make a good profit on them at the special price.

Application of the following check list for full-reparation beginning compromises to those two letters will show that they are pretty good and will review the principles for you.

CHECK LIST FOR COMPROMISE WITH FULL-REPARATION BEGINNING

1. The beginning giving the customer everything he has asked for is basic —to dissolve his wrath and get him to listen to reason.
   a) Make it immediately, specifically, and completely (thus identifying the situation).
   b) Build up the wholesome effect by a friendly, adapted expression to emphasize your integrity and reliability and prevent a curt tone.
   c) Don't apologize more; 1a *is* an apology of the most concrete form.
   d) Carefully avoid negative reminders (in the identification, for instance).
   e) Beginning with the compromise suggestion would infuriate most readers. Since they think they're entitled to what they asked, you have to show otherwise before compromising.
2. The explanation must show that you are not wholly responsible.
   a) Don't be too slow about getting to at least some of the explanation.
   b) Interpret it with a reader viewpoint and positive statement.
   c) Do not directly accuse; show blame impersonally (perhaps by customer education on the use and care of the article).
   d) Establish the facts, to show the customer that he is at least partly responsible.
3. Show the service attitude and your fair-mindedness in your proposal.
   a) As the foundation of your proposal, stress serving your customer's interests.
   b) Recall the original desire for the service the product can render— the reason he bought—and apply it to the modified conditions.
   c) Continuing the reader-benefit interpretation, state your proposal.
   d) Follow your suggestion with any other plausible sales points.
   e) Don't parade your generosity in the loss you take. Establish it and let it speak for itself.
   f) Suggest—don't command or preach or high-pressure him. Low-pressure sales effort further indicates your generosity and fairness.
4. The modified action ending should give a choice but encourage the one you prefer.
   a) Tell what you want him to do: reject (return) the full reparation and accept your proposal.
   b) As in any action ending, make action easy.
   c) Do not bog down with apologies or references to the full reparation; he can take it if he wants to, but hope he forgets it.
   d) End with a short suggestion of his satisfactory use of the product.

PROBLEMS

Claims and Policy Complaints

1. Before Dugin's Camera Shop went out of business you bought a Polatake camera (you can see your pictures just 60 seconds after taking them) for $129.95. On the salesman's advice you've used only Polatake's new super-sharp film, which he said made it easy for anybody to get terrific shots. For two months you enjoyed snapping pictures one minute and seeing the finished print the next. Yesterday when you tried to take pictures, they came out overdeveloped, even though you used a new roll of film and were careful about the timing of each picture. Since there are thirty more days before the guarantee expires and since Dugin's is out of business, you'll mail the camera back to the home office (Polatake Land Camera Company, 1305 S. West Twelfth Avenue, Portland, Oregon) and send a letter of explanation. Write the letter.

2. From The House of Lamps, 1241 Dunbar Avenue, Evanston, Illinois, you bought a 14-inch gold and white metal lamp shade to go on a brass floor lamp. You asked the shop to mail the shade to your home. When the shade arrived today, it was badly dented; it won't sit straight on the lamp. Since you want another one right away, write The House of Lamps requesting replacement. Explain how even the box was crushed. You'll be glad to mail back the shade.

3. David M. Stout, a businessman who prides himself on his prompt payment of both personal and business bills, is vexed to the point of writing a letter to the Alabama Gas Company, the utilities company which provides current for his home at 120 Aberdeen Road, Birmingham. Even though the service is fine, the practice of sending bills after the due date is irritating— to him. What happens in his case is that on the 15th or 16th of each month he receives a notice that payment for the month's service became due on the 11th or 12th. The postmark is never earlier than the 13th. Instead of the ten days which statutory regulations provide that the gas company must allow him, he has only five or six. Not only is this practice inefficient; it's ridiculous in the light of how much money the company spends promoting good will in newspaper and billboard advertising. Might not the Alabama Gas Company build more good will by better timing of the mailing of the statements to customers? The customers would then have an opportunity to pay when due rather than receiving bills which are not even mailed when due, yet carry notices of deliquency dates (usually no more than five days after receipt of the bill).

   Write a polite, yet forceful, letter for Mr. Stout, seeking to get a revision of this policy.

4. George T. Speigner, salesman for Honey-Bee Cosmetics, 620 Fifth Avenue, New York City, took a first order for 1 gross Queen Foundation cream $2.75 for 2-oz. jar and retailing for $5.00. (You are manager, Ross's Gift Shop,

Oklahoma City.) When the invoice from the home office came today, you were billed for $3.00 a jar instead of the $2.75 you *thought* you and the salesman had agreed on. Write a letter to the Honey-Bee company asking that you be charged $393.80 instead of $429.60 ($35.80 difference). Shipping charges are the same, regardless; so you need make no mention of that.

5. Beazley and Hann, exterminators, 1498 Euclid Boulevard, Miami, guaranteed that, after three treatments for pests, your home in Hollywood, Florida (1930 Lincoln Avenue), would be rid of all roaches, crickets, silverfish, ants, and termites for at least one year. One month ago you left Miami and let the B & H firm decontaminate—to the tune of $150, as agreed on. When the bill came, however, it was for $175. When you called, B & H explained that there was more to be done than they had thought and that they had had to use some special chemicals for the termites. Even though you felt they had upped the price, you paid them and cheerfully forgot Mr. Cockroach. But last Monday morning the cockroaches and ants had taken over the back porch and kitchen. You called but got no satisfactory answer about when B & H would come to spray, or whether they would. After a trip to the supermarket for commercial bug spray and a bombing of all the small little armies, you believe the only way to get satisfaction from B & H is a firm letter of explanation. Make it clear that the guaranteed time is not up (11 more months of bug-free living, supposedly) and also remind them that you paid $25 more than you had contracted.

6. American Van Lines, 1980 Lake Street, Ann Arbor, Michigan, has just moved your household belongings from that city to Austin, Texas. Upon unpacking and arranging your furniture, you notice that a brass pull on a handsome mahogany Fancher chest is damaged and that the works of your cherry Grandfather's clock (one that has been in your family for 80 years) are missing. Report the circumstances to the company and ask for necessary damage forms for making claim. You paid $12 extra for an additional $2,000 of insurance beyond the carrier's liability during shipment.

7. A month having gone by with no word from the recipient of your gift of a Smythe's White Fruit Cake (see Problem 5, p. 200), you phrased a tactful inquiry to her, only to receive a return reply that boiled down to a bewildered "What fruit cake?" Now write to Smythe's, giving the necessary background information and requesting delivery of the cake or a refund of your money. Since you were careful to put the necessary return-address information on the original order envelope, there is small likelihood that your order was lost in the mails. If it was, you'd like to know, so that you can apply for a refund from the post office.

8. After signing up for Around-the-Globe Program (monthly publications of booklets about individual foreign countries, complete with small pictures that must be pasted in the booklets), you wished to stop getting them, now that you have the Scandinavian countries, France, Britain, Spain, Germany, and Italy; so you wrote a letter asking discontinuation of mailings and enclosing a check for $6.90 ($1.15 a month). The booklet on Russia ar-

rived a week later, followed by the booklet on China, two weeks later. With the last mailing there was a bill for $2.30. Write the Around-the-Globe Program, 416 West Thirteenth Street, New York, making clear that you do not want any more booklets, nor do you feel obligated to pay for the last two mailings. Return the bill and the two booklets with the letter.

9. You received an herb catalogue in response to your request. You ordered fennel, sage, balm, oregano, and rosemary, and planted them in a sunny spot in good soil that you worked until the clods were fine (just as the catalogue suggested). Even though you've been careful to remove all weeds from the herb bed, to keep the top soil loose, and to water the plants as needed, all the herbs except the oregano have died. Even though Jackson and Hopkins didn't guarantee that they would grow, you feel that some adjustment is due you, especially in view of the fact that some of the herbs looked withered when they arrived. Jackson and Hopkins had advertised "healthy, hardy, fast-growing herbs." Also, your shipment reached you ten days later than promised, and it was poorly packed. Write the letter requesting replacement of the herbs which died.

10. While in London two summers ago you bought a Russian squirrel cape (male students assume it was for your wife, sister, or mother) from Bambridge's, Ltd., Brompton Road, Knightsbridge, S.W. (a celebrated store of world-wide reputation). When you asked the saleswoman in the fur department about a guarantee, she smiled and said that Bambridge's backed up everything and casually added "just mail it back." On getting the cape out of storage today, however, you find that around the edges the cape looks worn (the fur has almost disappeared). Before mailing it back, you're going to write a persuasive claim asking that the worn skins be replaced. You might tell that on the strength of your recommendation two of your friends bought identical capes when they were in London this summer.

11. Write the claim letter from Selfridge's Department Store, Philadelphia, to Dale of California, referred to in Problem 9, page 355.

12. From S. A. Stevenson Company, Whitman, Massachusetts, you ordered a charcoal-brown wool suit ($55) through one of the traveling representatives, Arnold McMillen. McMillen took your measurements and said that the suit would arrive in approximately two weeks. A month from the ordering date (today) the suit arrives, but the sleeves are a half-inch too long, and the pants are a good inch too long. The fabric and style are the original selection. Return the suit and ask for a refund of your money. Since it is late in the season, you'd prefer to postpone your purchase.

13. Review the preceding problem and assume that you have checked with a local tailor, who will make the necessary alterations for $4. If Stevenson is willing to airmail a check for that amount, you'll keep the suit; if not, you'll return it. You don't want another two weeks' delay shipping it back and forth.

14. You ordered from Gifts, Inc., 1218 Meridian Avenue, New Orleans, two Lightolier picture lamps with fruit still-life pictures on opaque glass for decoration and lighting in your dining room; you included your personal check for $29.90, including shipping charges. Today they arrive—with a definite crack in one. Write a letter informing the vendor that you are returning both (you need a pair, you feel), express collect, and requesting replacement or refund of your purchase price and in either case refund for the extra return shipping charges.

15. Assume that, instead of the crack in one of the Lightoliers of the preceding problem, one simply will not light up. You've taken it to a local electrical shop, where you learned that the trouble is a faulty plug and that the charges for repairing will be $2 (the minimum for any repair job). Write Gifts, Inc., asking whether you should have the necessary repair job done locally or whether you should send the picture lamp in for repairs. Make clear that Gifts, Inc., is to pay any charges, including shipping charges both ways.

16. On Sunday, the local newspaper ran your (the Cozellia Nursery) ad—a quarter-page display listing various nursery and seed-store items, but emphasizing a long list of rosebushes. The copy you submitted said 95 cents and up; but the paper did not run the "and up," though some of the named roses were patented and Fair-Trade-priced at $2.95 and $3.25.

As Sunday was a beautiful day, many people read their morning papers and came to your place Sunday afternoon to buy some of those special roses at 95¢. Not only did you have lots of explaining to do; but, even with such waste of your time on a busy day, you had several irate customers, and you fear that there were lots more who suspected you of trickery to get them to your place. Certainly you lost much good will. Make a policy complaint to the paper. Incidentally, this is the second error in your ads this spring. Assume that your carbon of the ad copy you submitted is enclosed.

Full Reparations

1. Mrs. Harry B. Crawford, 45 Apple Street, Cairo, Illinois, ordered from the Elgin American, Elgin, Illinois, a mother-of-pearl Elgin Carryall with the initials BER on the front. The Carryall is practical, for it has lipstick case, mirror, and cigarette case all in one. The price, as advertised in last month's *Vogue*, $14.95, includes the charge for initials and shipping charges. This morning she writes you (the adjustment manager) that she got her Elgin Carryall (which she paid for by check) with the initials FEB and that she is sending it back; she wants it either fixed right or her money back. When you check her order you see that she is right, and the only explanation you can find is that Elgin has added new help in preparation for the Christmas rush. From now on, you will have one worker be responsible for checking the initials before the Carryalls are mailed. In two days the correct initials BER can be put on the case, and it can be mailed to her by the first of next week. Make the full adjustment and keep Mrs. Crawford pleased with the Carryall.

2. In the Service Division of the Lanning-Owens Electric Company, Chicago, Illinois, you handle the following letter from Mrs. T. N. Thompson, 125 Windsor Drive, Birmingham, Alabama:

> Two years ago in June we received a Lanning-Owens electric broiler as a gift. We used it for two months before we went back to the University. Since then we have had no housekeeping arrangements until my husband and I finished school and we came back here to make our home; so the broiler has been carefully wrapped and stored all this time. When I finally received it from my home in Mobile and started to use it today, it wouldn't even heat up. A local electric shop estimates the cost of parts and labor at $9!—for a broiler that retails at $19.95 and which has had only very limited use. Since I believe you will see the justice of my request that you repair it for us free, I am sending it to you by express.

In the actual circumstance, this request was granted by an indulgent manager of the Service Division. Write the full reparation the gentleman would have wanted to send Mrs. Thompson in the light of the following facts: one of your servicemen reports that the coils are rusted, despite the heavy chromium top in which they are mounted. They've snapped in several spots —a condition more probably due to heavy rust than to jars in shipments. You wonder how it could have rusted so much without having been washed or having been stored for two years in a very damp spot. The instruction booklet and the terms of the guarantee make very clear that the top containing the heating unit should always be wiped, never washed. Your year's guarantee, like most guarantees on appliances of this type, is one which covers defective workmanship or material which reveals itself under normal use conditions within twelve months; likewise, it exempts the company from mechanical failures due to accident, alteration, misuse, or abuse. Time and moves also account for a certain amount of deterioration which cannot be covered by any guarantee (most of the few reports of defective broilers reach you within the first 30 days of use). Assume your letter is attached to the return carton containing the reconditioned broiler.

3. From Bromberg's Gift Shop, Boston, Edward S. Arnold, 261 Highland Avenue, Apt. 1, Wollston 70, Massachusetts, ordered a 35-piece service for 6 of Brookpark melamine dinnerware for his son and daughter-in-law as an anniversary gift. Regularly the set sells for $69.85, but this month Bromberg's is running a special, selling the set for $29.95. The china was sent by parcel post to Mr. Arnold. He writes that the top of the sugar bowl and two cup handles were broken, and so he wants these broken pieces replaced right away in the same pink hyacinth pattern. Luckily for the Arnolds and you, you still have pink hyacinth in stock and so can send him the replacements in time for the anniversary. Ask that he return the broken china to you.

4. Fifteen days ago Mrs. David Sington, 78 Elmwood Drive, Jasper, Arkansas, who has a charge account with you (Green Gables Gift Shop, Little Rock, Arkansas) selected a monogrammed (DES) glass cocktail shaker with

chrome top, $6.50, to be sent to her in time for her to give it to her husband for an anniversary gift. You sent the attractive gift right away. Today she writes that the shaker arrived in pieces and she wants another one. The chrome top is in good condition; only the glass part would need replacing. Since normal delivery would take about three days, you send it special delivery so it will get to her about one day before the anniversary. Enclose a a claim report form and ask her to sign and return it to you so that you can recover from the post office. She need not send the damaged shaker to you.

5. Three weeks ago, a customer, Mrs. Hugh Tiller, 1091 Wood Avenue, Charleston, West Virginia, purchased from Dayton's Department Store, Richmond, a white Lansworth drip-dry fine cotton blouse ($4.98) with red initial (DBT). When she laundered the blouse (and she said she used mild soap, luke-warm water), the initial turned pink and the red streaked all down the front of the garment. Along with her letter comes the stained blouse with faded initials. You (the adjustment manager) will send her another blouse, size 14. In your letter resell her on Lansworth and Dayton's. Tell this good customer also about your special sale of drip-dry cardigan and slip-over orlon sweaters—regularly priced at $7.98, now $5.

6. As sales director for Smythe's White Fruit Cake (see Problem 5, p. 200), try to pacify the unhappy student who reports to you today that you have taken over a month to deliver the gift cake he ordered to be shipped to the hostess in whose home he had been a guest for several days. The facts are that (1) you got caught short after heavier-than-seasonal demand and had to wait for shipments of Sultana raisins from Turkey and currants from California and (2) someone overlooked notifying either the buyer or the recipient of the atypical delay in shipment (which did stretch out longer than you anticipated). You've resumed baking and shipping, filling orders in the order received; the cake in question is en route. Write the necessary letter to relieve his mind and convince him that a Smythe's White Fruit Cake is an appropriate gift for any season and well worth waiting for.

7. Write the letter that you would send to the hostess who is to receive (or possibly already has received) the gift cake in the preceding problem, assuming that the student asked you to do so.

8. At the manager's desk at The House of Lamps, 1241 Dunbar Avenue, Evanston, Illinois, you start the day with the problems of T. M. Quinn, whose special order for one of your gold and white metal shades you filled about ten days ago. When Quinn and his wife were in Evanston visiting, they bought a handsome metal shade (white with gold leaves) from you and asked you to ship it direct to their home, Alton, Illinois. Apparently in shipping, the lamp shade got severely damaged. Mr. Quinn wants another one right away. He'll gladly send this one back to you if it's necessary. Although you'll not need the lamp shade, you will have to ask him to sign a report claim form which you'll enclose, so that you can collect from the insurance company under the blanket policy covering your shipments. To be sure that his new 14-inch shade gets to Alton safely, you'll pack it in one of your new $\frac{1}{8}$-inch

corrugated boxes and will attach the letter which you are going to write. The original box was only $\frac{1}{16}$ inch.

9. As the adjustment manager for Selfridge's Department Store, Philadelphia, handle the request of Mrs. T. P. Sullivan, Box 1261, Old Bethlehem Pike, Pennsylvania. "A week ago I ordered from your catalogue the black and white flecked corduroy slim jims and supposedly matching vest for our 14-year old daughter. If you'll look in the attached box you'll see that they do not match. Teen-agers are most particular. Please send me a matching set in the same size (12 sub-teen). If you don't have any that match, then credit my account ($10.50)."

   Apparently the corduroy was cut a different way of the goods. There's such a slight difference that at first glance anyone would think the two pieces matched. Fortunately, you found another slim jim set (by Dale of California) that matches and you're mailing it today to Mrs. Sullivan. You're also notifying Dale of California (Los Angeles) of the discrepancy and that you are returning the mismatched garments for replacement.

10. The first letter you opened this morning, as adjustment correspondent of the Miller Department Store, Wichita, Kansas, was from Mrs. Harlan Hays, 1980 Ridge Avenue, Dodge City, who complained that the 10-cup General Eastern automatic coffee maker she ordered from you arrived yesterday dented in several places, the handle scratched, and the top crushed. Mrs. Hays is upset because she had planned to use the coffee pot next week end, when she has out-of-town company. She adds that she is sending it right back and if the Miller Department Store can't send another one before Saturday, she wants her account credited for $29.95. Of course, you are sending Mrs. Hays another automatic percolator, which should arrive in time for the week-end guests, but you also want to send a cheerful letter. You'll want to resell her on the coffee maker that has a brew selector which perks coffee to the desired strength automatically every time and then keeps it hot without reperking. Ask her to sign and return the claim form you're enclosing.

11. The Lansing Heating Supply Company, 1827 Richards Drive, Lansing, Michigan, ordered through the Grand Rapids branch of Warren Williams & Company a quantity of disc holders and sent a sample $\frac{3}{4}$-inch disc holder, stem, and bonnet with the order. The order was forwarded to the main office and works of Williams in Camden, New Jersey; but, instead of sending the sample, someone in the Grand Rapids branch identified the material only by part names and dimensions, specifying $\frac{3}{4}$ inch. Though the usual size of the disc holder is 1 inch, the Grand Rapids order clerk noticed that the sample was $\frac{3}{4}$ inch and clearly specified that. In due course (after a direct shipment from Camden to Lansing), you (at Grand Rapids) receive a request from the Lansing firm for permission to return the materials because they do not fit. Write the Lansing people that the company will accept the materials for credit; upon receipt of them at the Camden plant the Camden plant will issue a credit memo for the amount of the in-

voice ($250) less 10 per cent handling charge. You are the sales engineer at the Grand Rapids branch.

12. In response to the letter in the preceding problem, Mr. H. P. Hume, owner and manager of the Lansing firm, fires back the following: "With reference to your charging us a ten per cent handling cost on materials returned on our order 1412, we will in turn bill you ten per cent for inconvenience. When ordering these items, we not only specified ¾" disc holders, we sent along a ¾" disc holder, stem, and bonnet to be used as samples. It wasn't due to our negligence that 1" discs were sent instead of the ¾" that should have been used. We're returning the items to the Grand Rapids Office." With a sigh and a silent wish that Mr. Hume had made this clear in the original letter, you (the Grand Rapids sales engineer) dash off a hand-o-gram to the shipping department to forward the materials back to Camden, and then you write a letter to Hume indicating that the Williams Company will, of course, give him full credit. You are asking the Camden plant to credit him not only for the cost of the materials but also the shipping charges. You have to accept the fact that someone goofed; your office did, possibly, in not forwarding the samples—though the fault obviously lies with the Camden plant, since the Camden invoice also clearly describes the disc as being ¾" (though the 1" size was sent). Try to regain Hume's confidence and retain his future business.

13. In the position of manager, Gifts, Inc. (see Problem 14, p. 352), you have received and inspected the two fruit-picture lamps. The damage to one is obvious; replacement is obviously necessary. Unhappily, however, you have no replacement. The closest match in a pair suitable for a dining room are flower still-lifes in the same size as the original selection but in predominant blues and greens rather than the reds and yellows of the fruit-picture lamps. Write to find out whether the substitute will be satisfactory or whether you send a refund check.

14. As manager, Gifts, Inc. (see Problem 15, p. 352), you would prefer to send your store check for $2 rather than pay shipping charges both ways and do the repairs yourself. Write the necessary letter.

Refused Adjustments

1. Mrs. Otto Von Willhelm, 2508 Prospect, La Crosse, Wisconsin, bought a charcoal-gray orlon sweater (43 N 4309), $5.98, from your store, Mangles, Madison, Wisconsin, two months ago. Today she returns the sweater and demands credit or a new sweater in size 12. She says, "Our boy, age 10, has not worn the sweater in the last month, but the elbow is worn and the left sleeve has a defective place in the seam at the bottom of the cuff. Surely your merchandise holds up better than this."

After examining the sweater closely, you agree with her that the seam in the left sleeve might have been joined more carefully at the bottom of the cuff, but the elbow has been caught on a sharp object, and it is going to tear even more if it is not mended. You have matching yarn and in a short time one of your expert alterations women can mend the sleeve at no cost, but you cannot give her a new sweater or refund her money. You are having the sweater mended and the left seam joined better and are returning it to her in two or three days. Write the necessary letter. You are the adjustment manager.

2. As manager of a small appliance store, Moeller Electric, 967 Water Street, Decatur, Illinois, you have a complaint from G. T. Kent, Route #4, Decatur, that the motor for his wife's Haring blender "won't run and I couldn't get any satisfaction when I came in last week. I'm returning it. Please refund my $29.95 or repair it like new in line with your 5-year guarantee."

You were talking with a salesman, and so couldn't talk with Mr. Kent right when he came in the store. He left before you could get free. He told the salesman that he lost the guarantee and bill to show that he got it from you, but added that he got it last month and that it had a year's guarantee. Because you've had trouble with Haring blenders, you switched to True-Whiz exclusively two months ago, none of which sell for $29.95; so he could not have got the blender from you. But to be sure that he was not confused as to when he bought the appliance, you check for your store symbol that you've been putting on all merchandise since you've had trouble with a local discount house. Your secret store mark is not there either. Write Mr. Kent, telling him why you cannot give him a new blender or repair this one. Separately you are returning the blender to him.

3. Mrs. Wilson Kennedy (6 Ridge Road, Fresno, California), a good customer of Semmel's Shoe Salon, St. Francis Street, San Francisco, writes the following letter: "I bought a pair of D. Spiller black lizzard pumps from your store last week. Since then I have decided that I do not care for them, and so am returning them. Please credit my account with $35, the purchase price."

After reading her letter, you carefully examine the stylish classic lizard shoes and find that the soles show obvious signs of wear and there's a definite cut on the heel of the right pump. You would never sell a shoe with such a defect—nor would she have bought the pair! To protect your patrons, your company has a policy that shoes cannot be worn and then returned. This policy is designed to insure that all goods sold will be new and without flaw. Write a tactful, polite letter to Mrs. Kennedy, explaining that you cannot accept the shoes for credit. Lizard shoes wear well and look well with most street-length outfits for daytime wear wherever she goes.

4. In the adjustment department of the Speery and Hutchinson Department Store, Columbus, Ohio, acknowledge the following letter from Miss Ellen Terry, 1908 Maple Avenue, Maywood, Illinois: "I received as a graduation gift from my aunt the gown I am returning in the accompanying package. I would like to exchange it for a Van Roost cloud white nylon robe, size 14. Please let me know the difference in price, which I will promptly send you."

The gown is obviously soiled: lipstick on the lace in front and powder stains on the back collar. It could not be put back in stock. That is why you don't make exchanges after two weeks following purchase date—and then only when the goods show no signs of use, wearing, etc. The gown will give her lots of wear. It's comfortable, easy to wash and drip-dry, easy to pack for traveling. It is one of your finest tricots. Your first objective is to show Miss Terry the justice behind your refusal; but you'll also want to convince her that the gown is still a fine gift. You'd be glad to send her the Van Roost white nylon robe; you are enclosing an order form and reply envelope. In knee length, it is $12.95; ankle length, $14.95. Both are trimmed in nylon washable lace.

5. Generally, merchandise which has not been used may be exchanged or returned for credit, provided that not more than ten days or two weeks have elapsed since date of sale. Your firm, Fincher and Bluttman, Jacksonville, observes the ten-day rule. Three weeks ago you sent Mrs. Hinton Sawyer, 6 Fairmont Road, Tallahassee, Florida, 6 pairs of sanforized jeans with sewn-in double knees at $2.49 each. Today you get a letter and the returned jeans. She wants 6 pairs ivy league jeans in 10-ounce black denim with adjustable back strap, at $3.50 each. John, age 10, won't wear the practical, durable blue jeans because all his friends in the fifth grade dress fancier. Inspection of the jeans shows that they have been laundered and there's a snag on the back pocket of one pair. For these reasons and also because more than 10 days have elapsed (policy is clearly stated in your catalogue), you return the jeans. Try to convince Mrs. Sawyer that John can wear these blue jeans for play after school and on Saturdays. They are designed for rough play better than the ivy leagues. You'll be glad to send her several pairs of the ivy leagues if she'll just let you know on the enclosed card. Resell her on the jeans. Extra-strong seams are overlapped and interlocked. These jeans are machine-washable with dark clothes. Sign as the adjustment manager.

6. In response to the preceding refused adjustment, Mrs. Sawyer replies by return mail. She says, in effect, of course the jeans were laundered; her son—and none of his friends either—will wear jeans until they've been laundered because they're so stiff. That's one reason the youngsters prefer the ivy leagues. She has always washed jeans as soon as she bought them. These were washed and ironed but never worn. And she thinks you are being unreasonable with a customer who buys as much as she does. Unreasonable you may seem, but your policy still holds. Had she returned the jeans unworn, unlaundered, with all tags attached, and within 10 days, you'd have been glad to make the exchange.

7. As adjustment manager of Moonbeam Corporation, Chicago 50, Illinois, you have a complaint from Mrs. M. W. Nichols, Route #4, Des Moines, Iowa, that the Moonbeam electric percolator she bought won't heat up. Separately she has mailed the coffee maker. Her letter makes it clear that she feels Moonbeam is responsible. "I've had this pot just six months and have used it every day. I've cleaned the various parts at regular intervals, just like your instruction sheet said to do. But today after I filled the basket with coffee

(percolator grind) the pot wouldn't heat. Please send me a new pot or refund my money."

You check the receiving desk and find the coffee maker in the condition she said it was in. But a closer look reveals that there's water in the heating element. Apparently in her enthusiasm over thorough cleaning, the whole vessel got submerged in water. There would be no way for water to get into the heating element otherwise. The instruction folder clearly said that "the percolator is guaranteed for one year against electrical and mechanical defects in material and workmanship, which will be repaired or parts replaced free of charge during this period. The guarantee does not cover damage caused by misuse, negligence, or use on current or voltage other than that stamped on the appliance." "Wash pot separately, keeping element out of water" is printed on the bottom of the vessel and on the instruction sheet.

You cannot refund Mrs. Nichols the money ($29.95) or send a new Moonbeam, but you can replace the heating element at factory cost ($10.75), which is much less than she would have to pay at a local repair shop. Before you can begin work, however, you'll have to have her signature. You're enclosing a card. You'll return C.O.D.; or if she prefers to save C.O.D. charges, she can send you a payment of $11.75 (including return shipping charges). You can have the coffee maker to her within a week after you receive the authorization card.

8. Mrs. Harry D. McCall, 809 Pinehurst, Athens, Georgia, ordered box springs ($42.95) and mattress ($42.95), 54-inch size Beauty-Foam, from Kent House, 675 Ponce de Leon Avenue, Atlanta, two months ago. Today she writes and wants you to take back the 54-inch wide, 75-inch long and send her Kent House 54-inch box springs and mattress that are 80 inches long. Even though you'd be making a larger sale, for these extra-long beds cost $20 more for each spring and each mattress, the state laws forbid you to exchange mattresses, as described in detail on page 833 of your catalogue. Sign the letter as the adjustment manager.

9. About two weeks ago Miss Sally Johnson, Dunbar, Wisconsin, ordered 3 famous-name record albums at $3.58 each from Shears, Department 139, Chicago, Illinois, and included money order sufficient to cover price and postage. Today you receive a letter asking if she can send the records back and get her money. You have to refuse her; all record sales are final. Each record has been auditioned critically. She was the first to play her records. And she has saved by ordering direct from Shears. The script and language of her letter indicate that she is a high-school student. For desirable specificness, make any plausible references to current hits and popular entertainers.

10. In the Service Department of General Eastern Manufacturing Company, Mineola, New York, acknowledge the request of Lt. Paul Terry (Fort Knox, Kentucky) for replacement of a General Eastern dual-control electric blanket under the stipulations of your two-year guarantee. He explained in his letter that the blanket was a wedding present given to his wife and him just two years and two months ago; that, after one winter's use, it had been

washed and stored the next winter (while the Terrys were stationed in a hot climate); that, upon taking it out of storage for use in their present location, they discovered that it will not heat up. True, he admits in his letter, the guarantee period has expired—but the blanket has been used only one winter. He returned the blanket with his letter attached to the carton.

After getting Lt. Terry's letter and examining the blanket, you (the service manager) and one of your service men come to these conclusions: (1) The blanket was not just tumble-washed, as the directions attached to the blanket specified. It has been squeezed (either by hand or wringer) and crushed so that some of the wires are broken. (2) Since the guaranteed time has expired, you are going to refuse the request to replace with a new blanket. The guarantee is for a calendar period, not time-in-use. You are returning the blanket.

11. As adjustment manager of the Flick Company, Minneapolis, Minnesota, makers of electric shavers, you have a claim letter from Glen Martin, 1805 Old Fox Road, Locust Valley, Long Island, and his shaver, asking for the replacement or repairs under your guarantee covering any defect of workmanship or materials for 90 days.

    Examination reveals that the shaver has been dropped or otherwise given a serious jar. Your guarantee specifies normal use; but it does not cover careless handling. A new head and cutter base are needed. You have to have a check for $7.50 before you will put the shaver in first-class condition and renew your guarantee. Or you'll repair the shaver and return it C.O.D. In a resale plug, remind him that his new Flick Powershave comes with the Superaction edge.

12. Review Problem 2, page 253 (about the Lanning-Owens broiler). As a more practical approach to handling this problem, it is your job to refuse Mrs. Thompson's request for free repair. The entire heating unit will have to be rewired, at a cost of $7.25. This represents actual cost. You'll be glad to do it, but not as a free service. You'll need her authorization, of course. You'll return it C.O.D.; or if she prefers to save C.O.D. charges, she can send you a payment of $8.50 (including return shipping charges). You can have it to her within a week.

13. Sit in for Mr. E. P. Hogue, Stabrite Paint Company, Atlanta (Problem 23, p. 551), and write the appropriate letter to Mr. John Darby, manager of the Apex Cab Company, in Jacksonville, Florida. This is a modification of a refused adjustment.

14. Step in for Richard D. Chater, manager of the fur department of Bambridge's (Problem 10, p. 357), and explain that furs are guaranteed only for manufacturing defect(s). Any worn pelts after six months are replaced at the owner's expense. If the cape is mailed back, Bambridge will be glad to replace or trim off the worn fur. Without seeing the cape, however, no price can be quoted. The volume of Russian squirrel at Bambridge probably means a better match of pelts than at furriers in the states.

15. Two months ago, when C. A. Peterson, 35 Meador Drive, Madison, Georgia, was in your city, he bought an all-transistor pocket radio kit, $39.95, manufactured by Eastern. Today his claim says the thing won't work, though he followed the instructions for soldering and otherwise using the kit. The radio he returned, with his letter requesting full refund, clearly shows that in his soldering he used acid-core rather than the resin-core solder the instructions specify. On your guarantee, therefore, you are *not* willing to refund the $39.95; but, for the $5 fee mentioned in the guarantee, you will fix the radio and return it. Does he want you to? You are manager of Bowen's.

Compromises

1. Assume that you are Arthur Johnson, assistant manager, Birmingham Steam and Rug Company (Problem 4, p. 117), and that you failed to answer the letter from the Beta Nu House Corporation president. You got busy with Thanksgiving rush (one of your busiest times). Two weeks ago Moody called you, and you promised that you would answer his letter. In the meantime the father of your partner died, and you failed to do anything about his letter. Today (mid-December) you get a sharp letter from him saying: "Why don't you answer my questions? Not only have the Beta Nus been charged outlandishly for cleaning and storing the rugs—another unnecessary $20 storage charge has accumulated while you take your sweet time to be businesslike. If you can't tell me what you can sell those rugs for or what you'll give on a new rug, then send them to Belton-Adare Warehouse, 1901 Kicker Road, Tuscaloosa. Mr. Belton will store the whole lot (plus the few other things we have in storage) for an additional $1 a month. And when it comes time to buy new carpeting for the fraternity, we'll go where we can find efficient people who answer our letters."

You certainly owe him an explanation, but even more you want to pacify him with a good price so that he'll buy the new carpet from you. First thing to write him is that the chapter will not have to pay this last month's storage bill, since you did not answer his original letter. After looking at the 7 carpets, you estimate that the old gray worn one you could get $25 for, the 3 nylon-cotton rugs $50 each, and the 3 green matching wool rugs $60 each for a total of $355, which would more than pay the storage and cleaning charges and leave a credit of approximately $60 to be applied on the new carpeting.

If the Beta Nus buy a new carpet for the 25′ × 38′ living room, you'll sell them your regularly priced commercial carpet (ideal for fraternity living) at $9 a square yard instead of the regular $11. The new EAS house on the Alabama campus has just bought this fine-quality Higglow carpet. Suggest that he come to Birmingham and see the selection your company has. Also offer to co-operate if he wants you to send the rugs to Tuscaloosa for storage; you'll do that and will be glad to talk with him later about the new carpet. But with "hard sell" on the quality commercial carpet, perhaps you can get him to Birmingham and make a sale that will please both of you.

2. On your desk this morning is the following letter from T. M. Reed, #6 Green Hill Road, Springfield, Missouri, a good customer for the last three

years of your mail-order house, Loomis Brothers, Chicago: "Five weeks ago I ordered an economy pup tent (6 N 07733) shipping charges collect. Will you please send a tracer and get that tent here so that my boys can enjoy it during camping weather? I wrote you two weeks ago, but you never answered. I want that tent or my $15.50 back." Two weeks ago you sent the tracer and found that the tent went to Springfield, Illinois, instead of Springfield, Missouri. After the tent was redirected to Missouri, it was delivered to his address, but apparently no one was at home to accept it and pay the collect shipping charges. In a few days the tent was back in Chicago. Now to convince him that you are a reliable company and to back up your motto "satisfaction—or your money back" send his money back first, explain what happened, and then try to resell him on this water-repellent tent that is ideal for camping (7 feet long, 5 feet wide, 3½ feet high). For $15.50 (a much lower price than he'll pay at a sporting-goods store) this tent has nylon screen front door with tie-down flap, jointed wood center poles for front and rear, guy ropes, stakes, sewn-in floor. Suggest that he mail you the $2.75 shipping charges (to avoid further complication about collecting when the tent is delivered), when he returns your check and his authorization for you to send it right away. You are willing to absorb the shipping charges (both ways) that you have already paid. Your postcard form notification that you sent two weeks ago in response to his letter has not been returned to you; perhaps it, too, was misdirected. Ask him to reconfirm his address.

3. While Drake Gibson, 12, was visiting his grandparents in Chattanooga, Tennessee, he spent time shopping for a beginning set of golf clubs and bag for, according to his father's instructions, around $30. Drake and his grandfather on Drake's next-to-last day in Chattanooga bought from Files Sport Shop, 1198 Main Street, a red water-repellent duck golf bag with black trim (vinyl pouch on pocket, all-leather cuff, padded leather strap with snap, leather-faced handle), $27.95; 5 irons (Nos. 2, 4, 5, 6, 9) and putter $30; 2 woods (1 driver, 1 brassie with black persimmon heads) $26. Drake had saved $60, and grandfather gladly paid the rest. Before boarding the plane for home (Cincinnati), the boy and grandfather played nine holes at the country club. When Drake got to Cincinnati and showed the clubs and bag to his father, his father was furious that the store would sell him a man's set that costs $83.95 instead of the $30 beginner's youth set he thought the boy should have. Despite Drake's saying that he liked playing with the clubs and that he would give his father $10 from his savings account in order to keep them, Mr. Gibson sent them back to Files, demanding the boy's money back (he'll refund the grandfather's money). In his letter he made it clear that he thought a beginning golfer didn't need 5 irons, nor did he need such a fancy bag. Also he felt that the shafts of the woods were too long for a 12-year-old. From a mail-order catalogue he could order a nylon-stitched vinyl fabric, vinyl-covered cuff, trim bag with padded leather strap, 3 irons, putter, and driver for $29.95.

As correspondent in the Adjustment Department, you feel that a compromise is in order. But with Mr. Gibson in his present state of mind, you couldn't sell him anything. So you send the full refund, then concentrate on selling these same Watson clubs and bag back to him at a bargain price of $60. Though you do not write this to Gibson, when the boy played with the set, the clubs acquired some grass stains and a few scratches; Files would have to sell them as used merchandise anyway. In selling these well-made clubs to Mr. Gibson, some of the points you might bring out are that the set will last him all his life; even if the shaft is a bit long now, he can "choke" the cork neoprene grips for one or two seasons. This duck bag with vinyl trim will take the hard wear that a 12-year-old will give it much better than the light canvas bags the beginning sets come in. The driver and brassie with their metal soleplate that is precision-weighted for extra yardage without extra effort make driving easier for a youngster as well as a man. The select persimmon heads have improved lofts that give more angle to the face for more lift and truer shots. Of course, the clubs are highly rated by the United States Golfing Association. Convince him that he should send you a check for $60 so that you can send him the Watson clubs that will last a lifetime. You'll gladly pay the shipping charges also.

4. As manager of the Bush Typewriter Company, 965 Madison Street, Washington, D.C., you receive a letter and portable Regal typewriter from George Adams (who purchased a Regal portable about 60 days ago on a 90-day guarantee), 95 Hindsdale Circle, Frederick, Maryland, saying: "I want my money back that I'm entitled to under your guarantee. Letters g and h and y and t get hung about every time I use the machine. A friend of mine who is mechanically inclined looked at it and said that the machine was defective. But he fixed it so that it worked for about 10 days. Now, however, the keys are hanging again."

Your service man finds that two of the keys (the y and the h) have been bent completely out of shape. If the machine had been defective, you'd have no way of proving it, now that it has been tinkered with. With new keys the machine works perfectly. Contractually, you are not obligated to return the money. But you agree to, as evidence of your reliability; then, having won his confidence, review the facts and try to get him to authorize the shipment of the Regal back to him. You will absorb the cost of the new keys ($3.25; only 2 had to be replaced; the others could be adjusted) and $1.75 shipping charges. With proper care, the Regal will give him good service. You are writing the letter on his former typewriter.

5. You are the credit manager for Laney Furniture Company (manufacturers of aluminum porch furniture), 1906 Grand Avenue, Jefferson City, Ohio. It's the middle of June and the following airmail letter arrives from a new customer, Parker Biddle, owner of Biddle Furniture Company, Carbondale, Illinois: "The summer furniture I ordered early April for delivery May 1 came today—too late for me to sell before clearance sales start after July 4. Surely you realize that folks want summer furniture in early spring and that in June they hold off for price advantages in July and August clearances. About all I can do with this furniture (24 chairs, 6 umbrella tables, 6 vinyl-coated umbrellas, and 6 coffee tables) is to sell them at no-profit prices, store until next spring (which I don't intend to do), or return them

to you, charges collect. Unless you are prepared to make a significant price concession, that is what I'm going to do. I'm returning your invoice and have instructed the freight people to hold the shipment until I hear from you."

Biddle apparently doesn't realize that your company has had a strike and that you've had to hold up orders. You wrote your regular customers about the strike (and therefore delay), but apparently overlooked him. He has every right to refuse shipment. Returning 392 pounds of merchandise—even by freight—would cost Laney about $20. Rather than lose a new customer because of misunderstanding (and pay shipping charges both ways), you grant the price reduction to encourage him to keep the Laney furniture. You'll knock off what the shipping charges would be ($40) but refer to it in terms of a 20 per cent discount on the $205 total wholesale cost if he'll keep the furniture. Airmail a revised invoice with your letter. You might have to use some resale talk to convince him that he should keep the furniture. Chairs have tubular aluminum frame and shaped armrests; Saran webbing seat and back; tilting garden umbrellas spread 6 feet, have 6 ribs; aluminum coffee tables (30-inch diameter) tilt for easy out-of-season storage.

6. The S. A. Stevenson Company, Whitman, Massachusetts, makes men's suits and overcoats and sells them direct to customers through salesmen. Assume that, as the adjustment manager at Stevenson's, you get a letter from B. T. Steiner, 908 Houston Street, Alpine, Texas, saying that the suit he ordered a month ago through your salesman, Arnold McMillen, finally arrived (two weeks after McMillen promised delivery), but the sleeves are a half inch too long and the pants a good inch too long. The tailor in Alpine will charge $2.50 to make such alterations. The alterations really aren't what is worrying Steiner, however—it's the bill. The all-wool charcoal-brown suit was supposed to have cost $55; he paid your representative $20, with the understanding that the suit would be sent C.O.D. for the balance plus shipping charges. But it came C.O.D. for $46.20. Steiner paid it but sent the suit back to you and requested a full refund ($66.20).

Send him a letter with a check refunding in full. But try to resell him the suit. You did use a better-quality wool than the one he ordered (thus the price difference) because you were out of the less expensive wool fabric he selected. As to why the sleeves and the pants were too long, you have no explanation. The measurements correspond exactly with the original order. You will gladly make the necessary alterations. Offer to refund the additional shipping charges ($1.20) and split the $10 additional charge—for a total of $6.20. Remind him in your letter that he's getting a suit that will last for years, that would cost him $15–$20 more in most men's stores, and that will be tailored exactly for him when the minor alterations are completed.

7. With the Tru-Value Manufacturing Company, New Orleans, as adjustment correspondent, you have to acknowledge the following claim from Mr. Rubin Garner, proprietor of Garner's Family Clothing Store, Hattiesboro, Mississippi:

Two weeks ago I ordered 2 gross of women's cotton house dresses at one of your special prices. Counting on these as one of the special attractions, I advertised heavily. The day of the sale, lots of women came in—but no dresses! Today the dresses arrived. I can't use them. How do you want me to return them to you?

The Southern Railroad did carry the shipment of women's cotton house dresses past Hattiesboro. By the time the error was discovered (at Tuscaloosa, Alabama), it was simply too late to get them back to Mr. Garner at the time promised. Clearly it was not your fault. But the railroad won't stand the loss. The only thing you see to do is to offer him a credit memo for the full amount ($864 plus $12 freight charges), then explain what happened, then offer to let him keep the dresses for $2.50 each instead of the $3 originally agreed upon. Enclose a second credit memo for the $144 and try to convince him of the worth of your proposal.

8. Slip into the role of Jon Loder, manager of Garber Galleries, the interior decorating division of Garber's of Houston, Texas. For Mrs. Howard Gibson of Hempstead you made washable cotton slipcovers for a couch, two lounge chairs, and an ottoman (foot stool). The total bill came to $145. When you took samples to her home, she made a fairly quick and definite decision concerning the covering for the couch and ottoman. It was a longer and harder decision on the lounge chairs, however; there were two patterns between which she found it very hard to decide. One was a light green with gold brocade design (which you told her at the time you considered more appropriate with her period furniture); the other was a slightly darker green with self-pattern (and you agreed that this also was a happy choice). After much discussion, during which both of you agreed that either one was a good selection, you understood her to mean the brocade when she said, "Well, I believe I'll take this one." So you tailored the slipcovers to your usual exacting standards, and promptly returned them to her when finished. Today's mail brings a note from her, not sharp in tone but in obvious disappointment at your having covered the two lounge chairs in the fabric that was her second choice, the brocade. She asks that you come pick them up and do them over in the self-pattern. You're surprised because you honestly thought the brocade was her first choice, and because she did not raise her objection at the time of delivery. When you checked with the driver, he reported that the maid had accepted the furniture in Mrs. Gibson's absence. For this good customer, you will do the job over—and you want to reassure her that you will in the first line of your letter. (She is obviously a social and civic leader in this prosperous nearby community and could help to channel a good deal of trade your way.) But the completed covers would be a complete waste ($60) for you. And you think the ones she has are the better choice. After indicating your willingness to make good and trying to convince her that yours was an unintentional, honest mistake (that you were not trying to force your choice on her), try to sell her on keeping the covers now on the chairs. You'll be glad to credit her account for $20 if she does (and just about break even on the job).

9. As manager of the Corona Sales Company, 876 North Washington Street, Chicago, Illinois, you receive a sarcastic letter and Model B Ditto mimeo-

graph machine from Chester E. Felts, 546 Riverside Drive, South Bend, Indiana. Mr. Felts writes: "I want my money back and am entitled to it under your guarantee of satisfaction or your money back. Model B won't feed regularly and when it does send a page through it prints very unevenly. I know that the trouble is not with my stencils because I tried them on other machines and they did fine. It worked all right for ten days. But when I got back from my vacation (during which time my machine wasn't used) it wouldn't work."

Your service man finds that the rubber feed rollers and the main print roller have softened and deteriorated badly, as any rubber will do when it comes in contact with oil. To you it seems obvious that the soaking in oil while Mr. Felts was away had done its damage. With new rollers on the machine, the stencil prints neat mimeograph copies. You even tried the discarded stencil which Mr. Felts had left on the drum. In making the adjustment you must back up your guarantee; but probably Mr. Felts still needs a mimeograph and can't buy one of the same size and style for less than $100 elsewhere. So you try to sell the machine back to him. Return his money ($89.50) in some favorable way; then, having won his confidence, review the facts and try to get him to return the money to you with his authorization for the shipment of the mimeograph to him again. You will pay for the new rollers ($3.75) and $2.50 shipping charges. With proper care, the Model B Ditto will give him good service.

10. To your desk as sales manager for the Western Office Equipment Company of Denver comes the following letter:

> Gentlemen: I'm returning the file cabinets you shipped me in response to my request of two weeks ago. I specified #3 HM 474 four-drawer steel files at $42.50 and you sent #3 HM 646 at $62.50. If there were only one file involved, I'd probably pay the difference; but as you can see from the invoice I'm returning, there are four. Please refund the $8.62 shipping charges that I paid and send me a credit memo for $250. I'm returning the four, shipping charges collect. As far as I'm concerned you can forget the whole thing.

It is signed by J. M. Forrester, Owner, Forrester Abstract Co., Cheyenne, Wyoming. He has ordered various supplies and equipment from you for at least ten years, has always handled his credit purchases satisfactorily, and has requested few adjustments. You're sorry this happened, of course. Several months ago you sent out a correction slip for your current catalogue, indicating that you no longer carry the #3 HM 474. Since you notified everyone to whom you had mailed a catalogue, you assumed that Forrester realized you'd fill his order with #3 HM 646 (as your correction slip indicated). Possibly it didn't reach him; maybe some of the office help threw it away. Whatever the reason, you certainly want to sell him this superior file with its improvements: heavier steel, baked-on enamel colors (instead of sprayed), satin-finish aluminum drawer pulls (instead of chrome-plated), plus automatic stops that prevent drawers from rebounding or being accidentally removed. You are convinced that they are well worth the additional cost. Before you can hope to convince Mr. Forrester, however, you'll need to refund the $8.62 and assure him that you'll send him a credit memo for $250 as soon as you receive the file cabinets. You'll also want to explain why you did not follow his original instructions. But most of all you want to sell him #3 HM 646. You'll be willing to ship the four file cabinets charges prepaid if he'll reconsider.

1, reinstate good favor.
2, try to sell new files

XI. Letters about Credit

WHAT CREDIT IS

IN LATIN *credo* means "I believe." And woven firmly into the meaning of the English word *credit* are the basic ideas of trust, faith, honor, integrity. For the seller the extension of credit means that he has faith in the willingness and ability of the debtor (the one buying the goods) to pay later. For the buyer, credit is the power to command goods and services based on evidence of that willingness and ability to pay later.

Certainly, credit business is big business; estimates of the amount of business done on credit run from a low of 80 to a high of 95 per cent. You can see, then, that people buy and sell a great amount and a great variety of goods and services without paying at the time of purchase.

Such an arrangement is convenient for buyers; and it enables sellers to increase volume. Like any good thing, however, it is subject to abuse if not handled carefully.

Timing is basic, obviously. That is why all credit terms (2/10, n/30, 3/15, n/90, or the common retail arrangement of payment in full by the 10th of the month following purchase) need to be clearly understood and agreed upon by both buyer and seller at the time of purchase. (The terms 2/10, n/30 mean 2 per cent discount allowed if paid in 10 days, net or full amount in 30 days.) The money you send within approximately 30 days to one of the retailers who supplies you may be used by the retailer to pay a wholesaler for goods which he has agreed to pay for within 60 days; the wholesaler uses his collections to pay for goods from a manufacturer (perhaps in an agreed-on 90 days); the manufacturer uses his money to pay his suppliers as he has agreed to. Thus each one benefits, but each has a responsibility to live up to his agreement if the system is to function.

What Credit Rests On

To help accurately to estimate a buyer's willingness and ability to pay, sellers evaluate potential and present credit customers in the light of what is commonly called the three C's of credit: character, capacity, and capital. To that list many credit men add a fourth C, conditions.

Character is honesty. It is one's good word. We may call it integrity or ethical conduct or sense of moral values. In business it is living up to the spirit as well as the letter of the contract. It is good reputation. And, creditwise, it is meeting obligations as one promises to do.

Capacity is the ability to produce or to earn and thus furnish the means for payment. For a business firm it is the present or potential profit from a business operation such as manufacturing or marketing; for an individual it is usually wages, salary, fees, or commissions.

Capital is the money behind the debtor. It may be cash, of course; but it is also other assets in the form of land, buildings, securities, patents, copyrights, to mention the more common forms. It could, as a last resort, furnish the money for payment in the event of reversals.

Conditions, as used by some credit men, has two interpretations. On the one hand, they mean general business trends. On the other hand, they mean special or local conditions or the trends of the debtor's business as shown in his comparative financial statements.

Because all these four C's—especially the first two—are reflections of personal qualities of an individual, credit letters are surcharged with negative possibilities. When you call into question a man's honesty, earning ability, or judgment, you are treading on potentially dangerous ground. And, since the credit department, of necessity, has frequent contact with the customers of the firm, the chances of unintentionally offending increase. Certainly, credit letters can be one of a firm's greatest means of killing off the good will which the sales, advertising, and even adjustment departments work to build up. With tact, patience, and a positive attitude, however, your credit letters can be good-will builders.

One of the fundamental concepts that will help you to write successful letters about credit is this: The credit privilege is *earned;* it is not handed out indiscriminately, given away—or sold. For that reason your letters should not talk about *granting* credit, though we find that phrasing convenient in talking *about* letters.

On one or more of the three C's an individual or firm merits credit. For many people, character is the primary reason they enjoy credit. They earn little, and they have little or no capital; but they pay their bills and thus earn the right to credit. And this is the bedrock of credit extension. Firms or individuals may enjoy high earnings but will not continue to enjoy ordinary credit privileges with a record of not taking care of obligations as promised (though they will be accorded more leniency by most firms than the debtor of low earning power). Most customers in a good capital position usually can also be rated high on both capacity and character. Certainly, this statement is true with respect to business firms (they are usually the discounters). An occasional individual in favorable capital position may have no earning power and may let bills accumulate, but he does not continue in such lackadaisical fashion very long; the axe inevitably falls.

The Credit Man's Job

Anticipating those who may be unable or unwilling to pay is one of the primary functions of the credit manager. He evaluates credit applicants' credit records and estimates their financial stability in the light of general business ups and downs. He does the same for customers already on the books. Periodically, he reviews accounts (and for business firms the financial statements) for danger signals. He must be on his toes to hold down losses from bad debts.

But if he approves only gilt-edged accounts, he will seriously curtail sales. His job is to contribute to the profits of his firm, not just to conserve them.[1] Accordingly, he must be sales-minded. He needs to be well informed about the firm's goods as a means of making his letters build customer confidence and increase sales. But even more significant, he must realize that marginal risks are vital for profitable operations and that he must give a great part of his time to evaluating and encouraging

---

[1] See Karl J. Krause, "The Credit Man's Responsibilities and Relationships," *Credit and Financial Managment,* 49:26–32, January, 1947. Reprinted in *Writing for Business.*

borderline cases. For his firm and his customers, he is part counselor, part salesman, and part detective. To play these many roles, he must keep well informed.

SOURCES OF INFORMATION

An efficient credit man need not want for information about his customers. He has many sources available to him.

The customer himself is a source. Most Americans are fairly well credit-educated and expect to give evidence of credit responsibility. A consumer applying for credit with a retail outlet is usually willing to supply information about his means of livelihood, names of firms with which he has done business on credit, the name of his bank, whether he owns real estate, and his approximate annual income. Most business firms, in seeking credit, furnish financial statements and references, many of them unsolicited (and they keep right on furnishing those statements year after year). If for any reason the customer does not furnish the information, all the information desired, or the right information—or if you want to verify what the customer has stated—you have several reliable ways of finding out.

Other business firms with which the applicant has done credit business expect to furnish details of their experience when asked. Banks supply information about both individuals and businesses. Local and national credit bureaus (such as the National Retail Credit Men's Association and the National Association of Credit Men) maintain files on concerns and individuals with whom their members have done credit business, which information is available to all members. Credit-rating agencies (like Dun & Bradstreet) publish volumes containing credit reports on business firms; if a firm isn't listed and you are a subscriber to their service, they will furnish a special report if you request it. Your salesmen can help to fill in the picture. Even a trade association in some instances can give you pertinent information.

From whatever source you get your information, it should be filed or recorded in some way to be easily accessible for quick review and bringing up to date. Only by keeping well informed can the credit man be in a position to act with desirable dispatch and wisdom.

No doubt you have observed that we have referred frequently in the preceding discussion to consumers or business firms, thus implying a distinction between the two kinds of credit—retail and mercantile. Though some differences in business practice exist, the fundamental credit considerations remain essentially the same. And the letters follow the same basic principles. Hence we make no differentiation in the analysis, only in the specific letter examples. As a writer of letters about credit—whether exchanges between an individual and a retail business firm or between two business firms (a retailer and a wholesaler, for example)—you may write letters requesting credit, exchanging credit information, granting credit, refusing or restricting credit, and special good-will credit letters. Some of these kinds you will write much more frequently than others (credit inquiries and reports and the credit grant, for example); but in the following analysis and illustration we present them in the order of probable occurrence, not the frequency of use.

CREDIT APPLICATIONS

Most consumers who apply for credit locally do so orally in a visit to the credit department of the business, though some do it with a telephone call. Some applicants, however, not wanting to bother with a visit to the store and realizing that certain investigation will have to be made, prefer to write a letter. Certainly that is the more appropriate action when the application is directed to an out-of-town store.

Since requests are welcomed, a direct-style A-type letter immediately phrasing the request and giving the necessary information is appropriate:

Will you please open a charge account in the name of

Mr. or Mrs. J. T. Holloway
76 Idlewild Drive
Dallas, Texas

We have just moved here from Denver, where our address was 27 Crescent Drive.

Stores with which we have had accounts for about five years in Denver are The White House, Foley's, J. P. Price and Co., and The Town and Country Shop.

I am employed as a supervisor at the L. B. Price Distributing Company, where I earn about $6,500 annually; Mrs. Holloway is not employed.

The Merchants National Bank handles our checking account.

Despite having given enough information to serve as a basis for the extension or refusal of the credit, the writer of the foregoing letter need not be surprised to receive an application from the store; most stores have standard forms which they want all charge customers to fill in and sign. Many of these are credit agreements. They are the same kind of form you might sign if you made application in person. In addition to blank spaces for the kind of information given in the foregoing example, they often have blanks for indicating a business address, for indicating whether the applicant owns or rents his home, whether his bank account is a checking account or a savings account, and for listing personal references. Any adaptation of the form illustrated in the sample credit inquiry on page 103 is suitable. Many firms find a card is easier to work with than a letter. The information wanted and the form are so standardized and routine that an applicant may well write no more than a perfunctory

> Will you please send me the necessary form(s) for arranging a charge account with you?

Requests from business firms of national reputation, solidly capitalized and with an unquestioned rating, are also perfunctory. Information about them is readily available in any number of credit sources. The acceptability of their credit is assumed; so the application for it is only by implication. Signed by an authorized agent (usually a purchasing agent), the letter might contain no more than the following:

> Please ship subject to your usual terms 6 dozen Samson 10-inch locking plier wrenches.

If the agent thinks the company name might not be recognized at once, he might add:

> We are listed in Dun & Bradstreet.

If the company is not listed in any source which can be checked readily, he may write in addition to the order sentence above, the following:

> We have done credit business with
>
> > The L. B. Price Company, Dallas 12, Texas.
> > The Vendo Company, Chicago 18, Illinois.
> > T. L. Painter & Co., Kansas City 9, Missouri.
>
> Our most recent certified financial statement is enclosed.

You can treat the application for credit in such direct, brief style when you are reasonably sure that you can meet the firm's credit tests. When you know you are going to have to ask for special concession(s), however, a persuasive letter patterned after the special request, C-type letter may be in order. The presentation establishes interest by stressing potential profitable business, stresses the capacity of the management, establishes a sensible plan for meeting the obligation, and confidently asks for action. It is a modification of AICA in the sales letters. In the following case the young man was asking for 150 days' credit, knowing that 30 days was the usual time allowed by the Long-Shearer Company:

> There's a lot of auto-accessories dollars floating around in booming Lubbock. Yet the chains sell only a standard line.

An alert independent retailer offering a complete line of parts and accessories could certainly count on the reputation of Long-Shearer accessories to give him a rapid turnover and a good chance to get his share of this increasing market.

Hence my optimism about the store I plan to open June 24. Right on Main Street, near several garages and body shops, the 50-foot-front store is out of the high-rent district, yet accessible enough to get me my share of the walking trade. The market survey I made last week indicates that conservatively I can expect 300 people in my store every day. And the managers of all the garages and body shops within four blocks of my store have promised me they'll buy from me.

They got to know me while I worked in my father's Ford service shop during and after high school. We became better friends in the year and a half I spent in the parts department after serving in the Navy and before returning to the University of Texas to complete my B.B.A. degree. I made friends with them—and I learned a lot about the business. I also made friends of most of the young businessmen in town through membership in Rotary and serving a term as President of Jaycees.

Although my father's death stops my chances to go into the Ford agency because there was a survivor-take-all clause in the partnership agreement, I'm willing to put every bit of the $10,000 insurance money he left me into the new store. My wife and I have no illusions of getting rich quick and are fully prepared to plow profits back into our store so that it will get started on the right foot. You can see from the following allocation of the $10,000 that the store will be financially sound.

With $1,000 for store equipment, $1,800 for operating expenses (including six months' rent at $150 per month), and $1,200 plus a small personal fund for six months' personal expenses, $6,000 will be left to buy an initial inventory. To have the sort of stock I'll need to have an edge on my competitors, I should have an initial inventory of $10,000. I would like to finance a $5,000 Long-Shearer accessories stock by paying $3,000 now, $1,000 in 120 days, and the other $1,000 30 days after that. I plan to finance a $5,000 parts stock from the Auto-Life Company in the same manner. With Long-Shearer accessories selling as well as they do, plus living close to my budget with a wife who's able to give me plenty of help, I'm confident that these estimations allow an adequate margin of safety.

An accessories stock turn of 3, and a markup of 50 per cent, will give me a gross profit on accessories of $7,500 in 120 days. Since I've budgeted my own money for operating expenses for six months, there should be almost all of the $7,500 left to pay for the credit stock and reorder another $5,000 accessories stock. Look over the enclosed order and see if you don't agree that the accessories I've ordered will sell quickly.

You'll notice that the enclosed list of references is filled with a diversified group of Lubbock businessmen, ranging from Mr. Logan, President of the Lubbock National Bank, to Ed Duffie, Manager of the Fix-um Garage.

Any one of these men, as well as the Lubbock Retail Credit Bureau, will be glad to write to you about me.

I shall be grateful for your help in starting my new store. With business progressing as it is in Lubbock, and fast-moving Long-Shearer accessories to sell, I feel certain that the new store will be a success.

EXCHANGES OF CREDIT INFORMATION

The most common exchanges of credit information are inquiries sent to the customer, inquiries sent to references, and reports sent to other firms which request information from you.

Requests for Information from Customer. Many applications for credit do not give all the information which you as a credit man feel you must have before coming to a decision. You write, therefore, directly to the customer, asking him to supply you with the information. The major problem in handling such requests is to avoid arousing the customer's suspicion or in some instances even his indignation or anger. To soften the effect of the delay and to quell the possible suspicion, you write a B-type letter which begins with some pleasant buffer material, stresses benefits to him from complying with the request, shows him that he's being treated as all other customers are, makes action easy, and promises quick action. The following letter to a housewife is typical in stressing "All our customers fill out this application . . ."; it is an appropriate covering letter for the form request discussed on page 372:

> It is a pleasure to know that you want to take advantage of the conveniences of an Allen Tilby charge account, Mrs. Lee.
>
> So that we may assist you as quickly and as easily as possible, will you please fill out the routine credit application which is enclosed? All our customers fill out this application as a help to both them and us. The information is strictly for our confidential files.
>
> You can be sure that we will give your application our immediate attention as soon as we receive it. A stamped, addressed envelope is enclosed for your convenience in returning the application.

A letter to a dealer employs the same strategy:

> Corone fishing gear is a good line to handle. Dealers throughout the country report favorable reaction of fishermen. And our advertising in *Field and Stream, Sports Afield,* and *True* continues to create demand for Corone dealers.
>
> We're just as eager as you are to have your Corone sales start; so will you supply the usual financial information that all our dealers furnish us, along with the names of other firms from which you buy on credit? Most of our dealers use the enclosed form, but if you prefer to use your own, please do.

This confidential information will enable us to serve you efficiently—now and in the future.

Occasionally such a request backfires, with a protest from the customer (sometimes quite vigorous!). In such cases all you can do is write again, using a pacifying buffer, then pointing out the value of credit and the necessity for careful selection of credit customers. The letter reiterates the normalcy of the request and closes with a request for action. It is also a modification of the B-type letter, as in this example:

Only through complete frankness can a dealer like you and a supplier like us work together successfully in a credit relationship. We're glad you let us know unmistakably how you feel about sending financial information concerning your business. And we're sure that as an open-minded businessman you'll want to look at your supplier's side of the story.

We have some pretty definite ideas too—ideas which are the results of selling about 2,000 successful dealers like you several million dollars' worth of Corone fishing equipment in the last 20 years . . . about 90 per cent of it on credit.

Because of our credit arrangements, Corone dealers can do a large amount of business on a small investment. In effect, we take the place of your banker, for the goods we send you on credit are the same as cash. And we don't ask for payment for thirty days. Like your banker, we can't make loans without some evidence of ability and willingness to pay later. The only way we can protect all our dealers against price rises due to losses from bad debts is to examine the financial statements of every credit applicant and to secure statements from his references. If you applied for a loan at your bank, you'd expect to show your financial statement to your banker. We are in the same position as he—except that we have no mortgage to protect us, and we are not so well informed as he is about you and your local market.

The confidential information we've asked you for is strictly for business purposes. It helps both of us. Since the peak sales months are close at hand, I'm enclosing another form and an addressed envelope with a special delivery stamp so that you can get this information back to us in time for us to get your fast-selling Corone fishing gear started to you by the first of next week.

Requests for Information from References. Credit inquiries from one business house to another are routine. As already discussed in Chapter V, they are A-type letters, characterized by directness, conciseness, and specificness. And because they ask for the same kind of information over and over again, in most instances they should be forms (like the one shown in Chap. V, p. 103).

When special circumstances arise, however, which the form letter does not cover, you're probably better off to write a special letter. Like any direct request, it should get right down to business:

> *Subject:* Credit Inquiry about Mr. H. F. Green, Grocer, Venita, Oklahoma
>
> Will you please send us a confidential summary of your credit experience with Mr. Green?
>
> Naturally we'd like to have the usual items which reveal his buying and paying habits.
>
> But since we learned from one of the companies here in McAlester that Mr. Green buys a large amount of his supplies from you and that he has given your name as a credit reference very recently, we'd like to have your explanation of why he did not list your firm when he applied for credit with us.
>
> We shall appreciate your help and shall be glad to assist you in the same way when we can.

Credit Reports. Requests such as the preceding obviously have to be answered. In probably the majority of cases, all you'll need to do is look at your customer's record and fill in the blanks provided on the inquiring letter. But when some atypical factor presents itself (or when the inquiring firm does not provide a blank making your reply quick and easy), you'll need to write a special letter.

We do not mean to imply here that all credit reports are letters, for most of them are not; the bulk of credit information distributed in this country from credit-rating and credit-reporting agencies goes out in special report forms. That is a small point, however, for in report form or letter form, the useful credit summary covers essentially the same material:

—Age of account (how long on the books).

—Credit or trading limit (maximum allowed; sometimes labeled "highest credit extended").

—Buying habits (typical or average purchase, annual volume).

—Paying habits *in relation to terms* (identify the terms and show how customer meets them).

—Present status of the account (amount now on the books, what part is overdue, and how long overdue).

In addition to the foregoing information, you may want to incorporate explanations of the effects of local conditions on the size and timing of purchases or on paying habits. And, of course, any unusual question directly put to you—like the one about Mr. Green—requires a direct answer. Since it is usually the reason for the special letter, it often merits the beginning position, like this:

SUBJECT: CREDIT REPORT ON MR. H. F. GREEN, VENITA, OKLAHOMA

Mr. Green, your applicant for credit, has been on our books since August, 1957. Since our relations have always been satisfactory from our point of view, I suspect that he failed to list our name as a reference because he was a little miffed with us about a month ago because we guessed wrong on one of his vague orders.

We've been safe in allowing him credit up to $700 several times. He has a yearly account of about $4,000; his monthly purchases vary from $300 in the summer to $700 in the fall. When crop money in the fall spurs payments, Mr. Green generally takes advantage of our 2/10 EOM discount. With only a few exceptions, he has paid his net bill by the 30th. On the two occasions that we had to press him for collection, he paid up promptly.

Right now is the slack season in the farming regions; so Mr. Green has let ride his May and June accounts totaling $700.30. Of this amount, only the May bill of $382.40 is now overdue. Since, on June 16, he sent in his $366.60 check in payment of his April account, we know that Mr. Green pays his bills as soon as he gets his money. A retired farmer who still owns three farms, he is the sole owner of his modest store.

I am glad to send you, at your request, this confidential letter about Mr. Green.

On the basis of the information you receive from the various credit sources, as a credit official you evaluate the circumstances and come to a decision. Sometimes you have to say "No"; sometimes you can partially comply with the customer's request; but more frequently, fortunately, you have the pleasant duty of saying "Yes."

CREDIT GRANTS

Certainly the extension of credit calls for a good-news A-type message! The customer is pleased at the confirmation of his good standing and at the prospect of being served by a good business firm. And the members of the firm are happy to add another good name to the list of customers.

The one invariable essential function of such a message is that it must confirm the new credit relationship. Though some credit grants are oral, and in the case of firms of national repute and sound capital structure a credit-granting letter is not written because the credit standing of the firm is assumed, in most cases some written message notifies the customer.

Because of the sheer weight of numbers, most credit grants are form messages, especially when no purchase (and shipment) of goods is involved. Many stores do no more than send a printed announcement card like the following:

THE J. P. BOWEN COMPANY

Is pleased to open a charge
account for you and welcomes you to
our family of regular patrons

We hope you will make regular use
of your charge account

Such a notification sent promptly is certainly better than nothing. Yet it falls far short of what a good credit grant can do to strengthen the credit relationship and stimulate sales.

Explanation of Terms. Unless a firm wants to encourage delayed payments, the initial extension of credit should make unmistakably clear how payments are expected, with the confident assumption that the customer will comply with the terms. Even a form card or letter can easily incorporate a simple statement like one of the following:

> On the first of each month you will receive an itemized statement of your purchases made through the 25th day of the preceding month; purchases made after the 25th appear on the following month's bill. Your payment is expected by the 10th.

> Under our system of cycle billing your statement of a month's purchases will be mailed to you on the 17th of each month; settlement is expected within ten days.

(Under cycle billing, bills are prepared and mailed at various intervals throughout the month: names beginning with *A,* on the 1st; with *B* on the 2d; with *M* on the 16–17th; etc. It is a simple matter to match names and dates in form mailings.)

In special letters the clear, specific explanation of the terms not only can prevent misunderstanding and delay but can also serve as a stimulus for prompt pay:

> Under our regular credit terms of 2/10, n/30, you can save $1.36 on this order alone if your check is in the mail by July 10—which will almost pay for another enamel display tray. Your check for the full $68 by July 30, however, will keep you in the preferred-customer class.

Such specificness is not possible, of course, except in an individually written letter or special paragraph. But the credit grant, whenever possible, should be an individual letter; it is worth the extra money in its salutary effect on the customer.

Establishing the Basis for Credit. In credit grants you may, as an effective credit device, take advantage of the simple, obvious psychology of praise or approval. Most people, when reminded of what makes them desirable or attractive, will work to keep that characteristic as good as it is or to improve it. If a customer is placed on the credit list because of a prompt-pay rating, he should be told so; having been told, he is more likely to strive to maintain that rating. The same is true for some reflections of favorable capacity or capital positions. The reference should not be lengthy; in fact, it is preferably absorbed subordinately in the extension of credit or the explanation of terms. It is a significant reminder to the customer that credit is an earned privilege for which care, thought, and effort must be exerted if it is to be maintained. Too, thus established, it may serve as an effective collection appeal to the customer if the account begins to get slow.

So forceful is this device in the opinion of one experienced credit manager we know that his credit-grant letters to credit applicants with prompt-pay records is only one sentence:

> We have received from your references the reports of your fine pay habits and shall be very happy to have a regular monthly charge account with you.

Obviously, this letter should accomplish more than it does. But it is a good example of the significance of the credit basis.

Here are two other examples of how you can establish the basis:

> Your excellent credit record in Joplin establishes you as a preferred charge customer at Allen Tilby's. And we hope that from now on the charge identification plate enclosed will make available to you a wealth of quality merchandise gathered from the four corners of the world.

> Because of your good credit standing, earned by your personal honesty and the sizable amount of property you own, we have placed your name on our list of regular credit customers.

Form letters can—and do—through careful wording, employ the strategy; the one-sentence letter to prompt-pay accounts is a good example. It is entirely possible to phrase the grant and the basis in broad enough fashion to cover a large number of cases.

To stop with the grant, the basis, and the terms would be foolish, however; a good credit man can also help to further sales—through resale material on goods, resale on the house, or sales-promotional material on other allied goods. All should focus on repeat sales.

Stimulating Sales.   In credit grants, sales-building passages should definitely be low-pressure; if the service attitude does not dominate, the greedy overtones can repel the reader. But the writer of the following letter, you will note, is careful to tie in a service-to-you reference to all his sales-building passages and thus make the customer feel welcome rather than pounced upon:

Your excellent credit record in Joplin establishes you as a preferred charge customer at Allen Tilby's.

And we hope that from now on the charge identification plate enclosed will make available to you a wealth of quality merchandise gathered from the four corners of the world.

On the first of each month you will receive an itemized statement of your purchases made through the 25th day of the preceding month; purchases made after the 25th appear on the following month's bill. You'll be prompt in paying your account on time, we know, for our terms—payment in full by the 10th—are the same as the terms of the stores with which you've been trading in Joplin.

You'll find that our merchandise is just as close as your telephone when you haven't time for shopping. Ask for Paula Penn, our Personal Shopper, who will be glad to assist you. We'll have your purchases at your door by 5 o'clock if your order is made no later than noon.

When you come down to Allen Tilby's, you'll find hundreds of sales personnel eager to help you find exactly the things you want. For all-day shopping or just for a delightful downtown luncheon you may enjoy the delightful Oval Room on the eighth floor. The spacious parking lot just across the street is available to you when you shop at Allen Tilby's.

Since you have just moved to a new home, you may be especially interested in the Home Furnishings Sale, which will extend through next week. Whatever you need, won't you come in soon and let us serve you?

The same considerations enable you to write good credit grants to dealers. Two minor differences exist in circumstances (but not as far as writing principles are concerned): One is terms (discounts, datings, and number of days allowed); the other is the identification of the credit limit. Few credit-granting letters to consumers ever identify a limit (though one may be entered on a credit application); most mercantile credit grants include limits as part of the explanation of terms. To prevent—as much as possible—the limit from appearing to be a penalty, with consequent negative reactions by the customer, a good writer phrases it in positive language, as in the following:

The No-Flame you ordered

20 gallons @ $3.00 . . . . $60.00

was shipped to you freight prepaid this morning by the L & M Railroad; it should arrive in Jackson by the week end. The amount of this shipment has been debited to your newly opened account, which we are glad to open on the basis of your strong personal capital.

Under our regular terms of 2/10, n/60, your No-Flame will cost you only $58.80 if you send your check by May 2; the full $60 is due June 21. In any one 60-day period you may purchase as much as $250 worth of No-Flame or other Bronson products.

With the increasing demand for No-Flame you will find it a rapid seller—and a good profit item at the usual markup of $2 a can. With your shipment you will receive attractive window displays which our other dealers have found helpful.

Silentol, a flame-resistant, sound-decreasing plaster, is another item your home-building customers will like. The cost is only a fraction more than for conventional plaster. For a trial shipment, just fill out the enclosed order blank and drop it in the mail; we'll send your Silentol to you—along with display material—within a few days.

Making the Customer Welcome. Much is said and written in credit circles about making the customer feel appreciated. Indeed, the opening welcoming the customer to the "growing number of satisfied customers" or to the "XX&Y family" is standard with so many credit writers that it is stereotyped. The customer is more interested in finding out the answer to his application than he is in such welcomes or in any of the writer's personal (especially if selfish) expressions of happiness at adding another name to his list. If you grant the credit (and ship the goods when the application accompanies an order), establish the basis, explain the terms positively, then follow with resale and sales-promotional material concretely implying the desire to be of service, your reader will not be in doubt over whether you're glad to have his business. By implication, such welcomes and thank-yous are adequately established.

If, despite these suggestions and illustrations, you feel the necessity for either of these expressions, place it at the end of your letter.

The accompanying check list (pp. 384–85) summarizes our suggestions about credit grants.

CREDIT REFUSALS

In the light of unfavorable reports from references or unfavorable financial position as shown in the applicant's statements, your job will sometimes necessitate refusing credit outright or suggesting some modification of the arrangement the customer has requested. In the case of an old customer, it may be a refusal of a credit-limit revision or a suggestion of curtailed buying. All these situations are inherently disappointing; they are a reflection on the ability of the customer; they *may be* interpreted as a reflection on his honesty; and so they are fraught with negative possibilities.

As in any disappointing-news letter, you need to analyze the situation, search out the hopeful elements, line up your reasons, and write a B-type letter.

As in any refusal, you have to have a reason. The applicant may be too slow in meeting obligations, his receivables or payables may be out of line, or he may be undercapitalized. Whatever the reason, you have to establish it; and in this function you have some educational work to do—without offense, if at all possible.

You certainly do not want to close the door irrevocably on any debtor. A poor account at the time of writing may be a good one a year from then (and if your wise counseling has helped in the improvement, you have established yourself favorably in the eyes of the customer and are thus more likely to receive his business). For that reason, most credit refusals follow a presentation that establishes good feeling in a short buffer, establishes the reasons in an analysis of the circumstances, identifies the deficiency, refuses in positive fashion, suggests how the customer can remedy the deficiency, and invites a later application. If possible, the letter may make a counterproposal and point out its advantages, then ask for action on that basis. The usual ending is an attempt to sell for cash.

In the following instance, involving an order for $176 worth of workmen's overalls, the dealer quickly responded with a financial statement and references in response to the request for them. Accounts receivable and payable were both too large; the trade-association reports offered the explanation that strikes in the mines of the dealer's community affected all local trade. Since the references reported that the customer's payments were good enough during normal times, the credit man sought to cultivate potential business while declining the account at present:

> Your large order for Stalwart overalls suggests the prospects of an early strike settlement in your area. We're glad to hear that. When the miners go back to work, sales in and around Canyon City will rise to a normal level.
>
> A steady revival of business will no doubt help your collections so that both your accounts receivable and accounts payable can be reduced. In that way you can probably quickly restore your current ratio to the healthy 2:1 that we require, since we've found over the years that such a ratio places no burden on our customers. Such an improvement will enable us to consider your credit application favorably. Will you please send us subsequent statements?
>
> You'll probably need your Stalwart overalls sooner than that time, however; they're a popular brand because they wear well. Workmen like the reinforced pockets and knees. They'll easily outsell other lines you might carry.
>
> You can stock this popular brand and thus take advantage of present demand by paying cash and taking advantage of the liberal discount that we

CREDIT GRANT CHECK LIST

1. The direct opening:
    a) When there are goods to be shipped, ship them in the first line and in the first main clause.
    b) If you use two main clauses, ship the goods first; the shipment answers a direct question and implies the granting of credit.
    c) Inject a cheerful, welcoming, ungrudging tone in granting credit. Be careful that your opening sound neither condescending nor preachy.
    d) Include a basic identification of the situation: name the goods specifically (don't call it "order"!), state the amount (of goods and dollars, usually, though sometimes the dollar amount is assumed on the invoice).
    e) In general, it's probably better to identify method of shipment.
    f) Choose words that get the goods to the reader; don't stop with just getting them onto a freight car or at the start of your shipping line.
    g) A touch of resale material (a favorable adjective, for example) is desirable, BUT
    h) Do not slow up your fast-moving opening with too much resale/ good will.
    i) Use figures and symbols in order and acknowledgment letters.
    j) Take care of all legal details: item prices, freight charges, total. You may assume an invoice or tabulate here.
2. The credit agreement/relation:
    a) For credit restraint, explain how he has *earned* this credit extension.
    b) Although you might identify terms incidentally in the opening, you'd explain them here.
    c) Attach your interpretation of the terms to this purchase, with calendar dates: "You can take advantage of our discount terms by mailing your check for only $123.48 on or before July 10. The full price of $126 is due July 30. So you see you get the price of a box of candy by just sending that check a little early." Just a rehashed generalization of what 2/10, n/30 means is pretty dull to retailers.
    d) Concretize this discount talk with specific figures and store-cases interpretation (a free unit of purchase, a month's phone bill . . .).
    e) If you attempt prompt-pay education, be sure your tone implies your confidence that the reader *will* comply. "Your check for the full $126 on or before July 30, however, will keep you in the preferred-customer class."
    f) With its negative potentialities, the credit-limit talk needs a *you*-viewpoint introduction and careful handling. That's why you wouldn't want it in the opening paragraph.
    g) Treat the credit limit as a positive help, not a guarded limitation: He can buy up to $100 (or whatever the limit is) in any one credit period. Label it temporary or provisional.

CREDIT GRANT CHECK LIST (CONTINUED)

b) You can get some very undesirable backwash with an explanation of terms that says or implies, "If you don't like these, we'll change them." You'd not want to obligate yourself; so content yourself with a label of *temporary* and indicate your willingness to review the credit arrangement later.

3. Your resale or sales-promotional material in closing the letter:
   a) Include some comment that reassures him of his good choice (unusual manufacturing process, experience of other users, . . .).
   b) Mention store services (to either a consumer or a dealer) and dealer aids (not to a consumer, only to a dealer). Refer to the dealer aids concretely and make them reasonable (display materials, catalogues, sales manuals, envelope stuffers, newspaper cuts and mats. Never all of these; whatever is appropriate). Make it clear that you have sent them or indicate exactly what you want him to do in requesting. Frequently one sees "Just make a note of how many you want when you send us your next order."
   c) Whenever possible, tell him about allied goods or seasonal goods in which he might be interested; this is frequently the best way to end the letter: with a suggestion of ordering.
   d) Regardless of how you close, let it be a forward look toward future orders.
   e) And apply it specifically to this one case. The old universal that fades out with "We have enjoyed serving you and look forward to supplying your future needs" and its variants is wooden and dull; it's just another rubber stamp.

4. You want to make the customer feel appreciated, of course; but your appreciation—even for a new customer—is better worked in incidentally throughout the letter instead of in obvious sentences or paragraphs.

5. Your best transitions (for tight coherence) are provided by logical order of points discussed. This one holds together without too much cement:
   —Shipment and arrival of goods, incidental credit granting.
   —Basis for credit.
   —Specific credit terms, emphasizing reader's advantage in discounting (when appropriate), assuming prompt payments.
   —Credit limit.
   —Resale of goods and new goods.
   —Store services.
   —Forward look to other orders.

6. Watch the TONE throughout the letter
   a) Avoid FBI implications about the credit investigation and condescending, mandatory, or selfish explanation of the terms.
   b) Remember that proportion affects your tone, too. Too much space given to any point automatically affects your tone (especially true in talk of terms and limits).

can give you (on this order, for instance, the discount would amount to $3.52—more than enough to pay interest for six months on a $100 bank loan). You might cut your order in about half and order more frequently. With a $100 bank loan at 6% and a stock-turn of 12—which is a conservative estimate, Mr. Wolens—you'd make an annual saving of $18 after paying your interest charges. I don't need to tell you that that's 12 pairs of dependable Stalwart overalls absolutely free—overalls that you still sell for $2.50 a pair.

To handle the order in this profitable way, attach your check to the memo I've enclosed and mail both of them back to me in the enclosed envelope. We can have your Stalwart overalls to you in about five days.

Usually you can specifically isolate the sore spot in a dealer's situation and by impersonal, positive phrasing save the customer's pride, suggest the remedy, and leave the way open for future negotiations. In consumer letters involving a retail customer, however, nine times out of ten the reason for the refusal is the customer's failure to take care of obligations. That is a highly personal reflection, one which many retail credit men shy away from by feigning incomplete information and inviting the customer to come in and talk the matter over. We do not agree with the philosophy or the procedure involved in a letter like the following, but some authors do:

> We heartily thank you for the implied compliment you paid the Bowen Company when you applied for a charge account.
>
> According to the usual procedure in opening a new account, we sought information which would serve as a basis for extending credit to you. While we have gathered some very fine reports of a personal nature, the business reports which we have been able to accumulate do not allow us to make a definite conclusion right now.
>
> We realize that we have only one side of the story; so if you would care to come to the store and talk with us, we shall be glad to have you call at your convenience. Perhaps we can arrive at a better understanding.
>
> In the meantime may we serve you on a cash basis? We want to serve you to the best of our ability and to continue to merit your good will.

One of the reasons for writing such a letter, according to its sponsors, is that to tell a customer he has had unfavorable reports submitted by his references is a violation of the confidential aspects of credit-information exchanges. To that we can only raise a polite eyebrow. Unless you divulge names and/or enough specific details to reveal identity of a reference, you're doing no such thing. Furthermore, you're doing a customer a service by pointing out what he must do in order to earn (or restore) his credit standing. Such a retail credit refusal as the following is desirably forthright and businesslike (in the usual pattern of buffer, reasons, positive refusal, forward look, counterproposal in the form of a bid for cash business):

> We appreciate your request for a credit account at Aiken's.
>
> For fifty years Aiken's has been bringing its customers quality merchandise at bargain prices. This, as you realize, requires careful merchandising policies on our part. Not the least of these savings—the policy of paying cash for merchandise, thereby receiving discounts and eliminating interest charges, which we are able to pass on to Aiken customers in the form of lower prices—necessitates that we receive prompt payment from our credit customers.
>
> As you were an applicant for a credit account, we followed our usual practice and asked for information from retail credit sources.
>
> We realize that it is often temporarily difficult to meet all obligations promptly and that very likely in a short time you will have qualified for a charge account at Aiken's by taking care of your other obligations.
>
> You will continue to receive the same courteous treatment that made you favor Aiken's in the first place. We certainly want to have you as a customer. With our will-call, budget, or layaway plans at your disposal, you may own anything in Aiken's within a short time by making convenient payments of your choice. Come in soon and let us serve you in this way.

The following letter refusing credit to a young man just out of college and with unsteady, low-income employment talks concretely and sensibly; it's a good credit-education letter. Note how the writer stressed the idea that character was not the basis for refusal.

> When you wrote to us last week asking for credit, as a member of the Illinois Credit Union we automatically asked the Union for your record. You can well be proud of the report which I received. The complimentary reports on your excellent character indicate a promising future.
>
> There is absolutely no black mark against your record. The fact that you have never defaulted or delayed in paying an account means that you will be able to get credit without any trouble when your income increases.
>
> We could extend credit to you on the basis of your personal record alone, for we know that you fully intend to meet any obligations you undertake. But if some unforeseen expense should come up, with your present income you could not pay your account. As a co-operating member of the Credit Union, we would then be compelled to submit your name as a poor credit risk. Such a report would limit your chances of obtaining credit in the future—perhaps at a time when you need it more than now. For your own benefit, you'll be better off to stick to cash purchases now.
>
> Thank you for thinking of us. We shall look forward to the time when you can comfortably and safely contract for credit purchases with us. In the meanwhile, you can make your dollars reach further by buying from Bowen's for cash, for we can buy in quantity, save on shipping costs, and take

CREDIT REFUSAL CHECK LIST

1. Your opening:
   - a) Your best beginning talks about something pleasant: the good market; the timeliness of the order; the reader's experience, insight, or ambition.
   - b) Beware the selfish note of "We are glad to receive" or "It pleases us."
   - c) As part of the continuous effort throughout the letter to keep your reader from considering buying elsewhere when he finds that he can't buy from you on credit, get resale material on the product early in the letter.
   - d) For a consumer, depict pleasure in use; for a dealer, tie in the reader's profit possibilities with this resale talk.
   - e) References to his order (by either date or letter or order number) should be worked in incidentally while you say something of more significance.
   - f) Be careful not to mislead the reader into thinking that you are extending the credit.
2. Your explanation:
   - a) Stick to the theme of a strong, healthy business for the reader; you then have fewer transitional difficulties and less negative effect.
   - b) By all means, do not begin your explanation with writer-interest reasons.
   - c) By careful analysis of the situation, give justifying reasons BEFORE the refusal.
   - d) The real reason for refusing, of course, is some financial maladjustment (a current ratio or an acid-test ratio out of line) or a record of not paying bills. Meet the issue squarely. To base your refusal on other grounds is shirking. His advantages in cash buying, for instance, are NOT reasons for your refusing credit. If character is not the basis for refusal, be sure to make that fact clear; otherwise the reader will almost certainly think you are reflecting on his integrity.
   - e) Avoid the negative, critical, nosey, or patronizing tone by stating your reasons in terms of helpfulness to the reader, with the positive assumption that he can and will correct the situation.
   - f) Be sure you've made perfectly clear that you will not now grant credit (though this may be done through the statement of your counterproposal).

advantage of discounts. We pass these savings on to you in the form of lower prices. When you buy at Bowen's, your income is inflated because you get quality merchandise at low prices.

Letters limiting the credit of an old established customer are no different from refusals to new customers; they just adapt the talking points.

CREDIT REFUSAL CHECK LIST (CONTINUED)

g) Hiding behind "our policy" evades the issue (and appears selfish); you need to give him the justifying reasons for maintaining it.

h) Phrase your reason for the refusal in terms of your experience with other customers. Do not make it a personal relationship between you and him.

i) Always leave the way open for credit extension later.

j) But you can't make definite promises; the decision will have to be made on the basis of how things look later.

3. Your counterproposal:

a) The cash plan or reduced shipment is the thing you want him to turn to as a hopeful relief upon finding that he cannot get credit; bring this idea in shortly after your refusal.

b) But show first why you're going into all this; preface the discussion with some short, helpful-sounding reader-benefit sentence.

c) If you propose cash with a discount, figure the savings on this one particular order, and concretely enliven by talking about specific units of the product.

d) Possibly project the savings over a year's business to make them loom larger.

e) Can you suggest smaller orders? Especially to a dealer, point out the advantages of local financing?

f) Use the conditional mood in your explanation and your proposal.

4. Your ending:

a) Leave no details uncovered in your proposal of how to handle the present order.

b) In regular action-ending style, drive for his acceptance of your proposal.

c) Success-consciousness (assuming his acceptance) precludes the use of "Why not. . . ."

d) You have to get his approval before taking any action other than the one he specified.

e) Your last picture should show the reader's benefits from trading with you.

5. Your tone:

a) Throughout your letter retain an attitude of helpfulness to the reader.

b) Sales-promotional material on other goods is hardly appropriate when he can't even pay for the ones he has ordered.

It is certainly good to see how well you are selling Carlton heaters. The $635 order for September delivery you gave Mr. Ray indicates a bright outlook for fall sales.

We want to work right along with you. In trying to be of service to you always, however, we often make constructive suggestions. Now, for example, the large order you placed in March, together with this current one, leads us to believe that you may be overstocking Carltons. With this shipment your account would stand about $500 beyond the limit we agreed on when you first started to deal with us five years ago. Since we believe that the proposed balance would be too great a burden upon you because it would throw your payables out of line, we suggest two alternative courses of action.

If your ordering such a stock of Carlton heaters indicates that there is an extensive home-building program going on in Fairview, your comments on local conditions and the information requested on the enclosed form may serve as a basis for extending your credit limit to the point where it will take care of your needs.

Or we will extend to July 10 the 5% discount on your $940 March order. By sending us your check for $893, you will not only put your account in shape for the present order; you will also mark up greater profits on the sale of your Carltons.

We're just as anxious as you are, Mr. Skinner, to send you this latest shipment. Please take one of these courses so that we may ship your new stock of Carltons in time for the fall season.

As in any good refusal, none of these apologizes or harks back to the refusal in the end. To do so indicates that you are not confident in your decision. The check-listed items on the two preceding pages incorporate the major suggestions for handling credit refusals or limitations.

Good-Will Credit Letters

Credit good-will letters—and there is a wide variety of them—are treated in Chapter XIII, "Special Good-will Letters."

PROBLEMS

Credit Grants

1. Harold King, your salesman, has sent in an order from Town and Country Shop, 416 Tenth Street, St. Paul, Minnesota, for—

36 No. 78765 polished cotton blouses, pink, 14, 16, 18 @ $3.00	$108.00
36 No. 9867 polished cotton blouses, white, 14, 16, 18 @ $3.00	108.00
	$216.00
Shipping charges	4.50
	$220.50

—along with a request from Mrs. C. B. Coleman, owner-manager, that she be granted open-account terms. She refers you to her Dan & Broadstreet rating, which you, as credit manager for Paul Kruger Manufacturing Company, 879 Fourth Avenue, New York, find is excellent. King also reports quite favorably that Mrs. Coleman has been in business at her present site for 15 years. She carries quality lines such as Donald Dow, Paul Pines, Penny Potter, and Vera Maxwell. The store is well arranged, with a good full inventory. She seems to cater to the middle- and upper-class women's trade. Write the letter that will tell her you are sending the blouses on standard terms of 2/10, n/30. You can send an attractive card display with a picture of the No. 78765 polished cotton blouse as well as mats picturing both blouses she ordered. Would she like these advertising aids? Besides resale talk on the goods ordered, tell her about the pure silk blouses you're manufacturing for the season ahead. She buys for $8 and can easily sell them at $15.

2. After getting a report from the Credit Bureau on Wayne Feed Company, 1908 Lake Street, Madison, Wisconsin, and after talking with Harry Hutt, your salesman (Sipes Brothers, national hardware dealers, 907 Wales Street, Chicago 9), you are going to grant credit on terms 3/10, n/60 with a $500 limit. Wayne Smith, owner, started the feed store 2 years ago. With some savings and some borrowing and repaying of small amounts, he has managed to stay in business. Rosenfield's Feed Company and Spiller and Spiller Feed Store, old established stores, located within two blocks of Wayne, furnish strong competition. Hutt says that Wayne Smith is energetic, hardworking, and progressive. On the other hand, the Credit Bureau reports that he is slow in paying his personal bills. Because the planting and gardening season is near, you grant credit (3 dozen garden hose sprayers, $1.25 each, and 2 dozen seed-spreader carts, $8 each; but you carefully and specifically remind him of due dates and the advantages of cash discounts. Work in the idea that he has earned the credit on the basis of his going firm. Tell him about some of your various services, sales helps, and other merchandise. Because transportation is good between Chicago and Madison, he'll have fast deliveries which will keep him from carrying a big inventory. You are shipping the sprayers and spreader carts today, express charges collect.

3. It is your job as credit sales manager of the Heritage and Hawkins Wholesale Furniture Company, Chicago, to credit a first order from City Furniture, Peoria, Illinois, for 3 No. 89765 solid cherry (36 × 36) coffee tables @ $75.50; 3 No. 86540 Lawson sofas, muslin covered, @ $88.50; and 4 No. 8432 cherry Hitchcock chairs, @ $42.50, totaling $662, plus $26.00 shipping charges. Dan & Broadstreet gives City Furniture a good rating (central location, 30 years old, owned by same family for 25 years). You're glad to extend your standard terms of 2/10, n/60. Write the letter that will build future business. The usual markup is 50 per cent.

4. As credit manager for the Debcraft Wholesalers, Atlanta, Georgia, you are going to grant Mr. Daniel Wade credit. He operates the small Toggery Shop, 445 Prince Avenue, Athens, Georgia. Send him the following men's robes on terms of 2/10, n/30:

    6 navy rayon robes, size 38, @ $15 .... $ 90.00
    6 wine rayon polka dot print robes, size 36, @ $12.50 .... 75.00
    $165.00

They are lightweight, easy to pack; have own matching snap-close case. Besides three roomy pockets, they have shawl collar and self-belt. You wrote letters to the references Mr. Wade listed for you, and you heard from all of them. Two references stated that on several occasions, especially during the summer, Mr. Wade had to be reminded of his overdue account. Another reference said he had always paid on time, and still another said only once in five years had he been reminded. As far as you can determine, his store is not in a busy district of Athens. He just relocated it, and his capital investment in the business doesn't make you feel that it is a thriving business. Until you determine whether or not he is keeping his account up to date, you are limiting his credit to $250. You need to explain your credit terms and to educate him on the value of his taking advantage of the discount. You might want to tell him about your special on tan leather, soft-soled slippers by Aristo. They're usually $7.50, but now are reduced to $6.25 (sizes 6 to 14 in medium and wide widths). Send a catalogue which describes these slippers on page 47 and which describes some of your other products.

5. L. C. Smith, manager, Smith Office Supply Company, Youngstown, Ohio, filled out the credit application blank you sent him (Problem 4, p. 202) from Stecks Manufacturing Company, Cleveland, and ordered 3 dozen typewriter ribbons, black record, medium inked, for Regal, @ $18.00; 1 gross Barter's carbon paper @ $10.50; 12 Westerbrook twin-cartridge pen and matching pencil sets @ $5.15, to be sent by parcel post. Shipping charges amount to $1.18. John Shumaker, your salesman in his territory, reports that he seems to have good turnover, a neat store, good location with ample parking, yet close to three main office buildings. Grant terms of 2/10, n/30 and tell him of the manufacturer's regular ads in the *Saturday Evening Post, Printers' Ink,* and *Office Management.*

6. As correspondent in the sales office of the Dallas Hardware Company, Dallas, Texas, you are going to grant credit to F. M. Shaler, 569 Main Avenue, Gatesville, owner of Dixie-Fix-It shop, on the basis of his credit application that listed two well-known Dallas firms as well as the First National Bank of Gatesville, all of whom confirmed his credit reliability. Shaler ordered one T256R Draftsman miter box and back saw, $45.75; one Bunlap Push Drill with 8 drill points, 9 G 4216, $3.50; set of 4 chisels, 9 G 3647 (¼, ½, ¾, and 1 inch), $8.50. Just two months ago you sent a cash shipment to him (Problem 2, p. 201) as well as a new catalogue. Refer to something else in the catalogue he might be interested in for his Dixie-Fix-It shop.

7. You are credit manager of the Just-Rite Toy Company, 823 Patterson Street, Weehoken, New Jersey. On your desk are the original order and credit application from The Rocking Chair Gift Shop, Iowa City, Iowa, for

36 decks of Spellbound cards @ $1	$36.00
36 Hutch pull toys @ $1	36.00
12 Beat the Clock games @ $1.75	21.00
	$93.00
Shipping charges	6.15
	$99.15

According to your information (a report from the National Bank and the Credit Bureau of Iowa City), Pierce's new store is satisfactory. Explain the details of your terms (2/10, n/30), and send him some merchandising helps. Most dealers take a 50 per cent markup on toys.

8. As credit manager for American-tex Company, Miami, Florida, you are going to grant credit to Mr. Jay Whitfield Jolly, Lane Tile and Floor Company, Orlando, Florida. Send him the following rugs, shipping charges express collect, on terms of 2/10, n/30: 12 No. 37986 braided vinyl rugs, 24 × 36, 4 beige, 4 green, 4 black multicolor, @ $3.50 ($42.00); 6 No. 38654 hand-hooked cotton rugs, 9 × 12, 3 with green border, 3 with brown border, @ $42.50 ($255). Tell Mr. Jolly about the new Durablend carpet, specially tested for American-tex. Blended of verel with nylon for added strength, Durablend retails for $10.95 a square yard, but he pays only $6.50 a square yard. Any seams which may be needed for wall-to-wall installation are almost invisible. High tufts won't pull out in normal use. Heavy back is coated with plasticized latex. If he would like them, you will gladly send Jolly some envelope stuffers to promote the Braided Vinyl rugs he ordered.

9. Jackson Brock, owner, Blue Mill Restaurant, University Avenue, Iowa City, Iowa (Problem 1, p. 429), orders $4,933.70 worth of equipment (to be paid for in 60 days) from Illini Equipment and Supply Company, Chicago, where you work as credit manager. As scheduled, the Illini truck should arrive in Iowa City in two days; the driver and his helper will install the equipment. Write the letter to Brock granting the credit, shipping the goods, and sending a new catalogue. Page 8 features a new deep-fat fryer that Brock might be interested in.

10. As credit sales manager for Vaughn-Wild, furriers, 1908 Second Street, St. Louis, Missouri, write Mrs. Charles Bismarck, 1908 Alton Street, Belleville, Illinois, that you are sending the Autumn Haze mink cape ($748 including tax) on easy-payment plan with no carrying charges (6 payments, $124 for 4 and $126 for 2). Mrs. Bismarck tried on this cape while in your store last week. For $1 you are sending it insured by Greyhound Bus, and it should arrive tomorrow morning. Although Mrs. Bismarck has never had an account with you, she has accounts at Sticks and Fuller, J. P. Martins, and other leading stores. A touch of resale can help your letter do more than just grant credit. You are enclosing contract forms for her to sign and return.

11. Ramon Garcia, owner of Ramon's Shop, Tucson, Arizona, sends in to the Latinos Food Company, San Antonio 11, Texas, a first order amounting to $56.40 (Problem 10, p. 433). Mr. Garcia sends the following information to show his financial condition: Annual sales, $10,000; total assets, $2,500; no liability as bondsman or endorser. His references report him in good standing with all creditors. Send him a new catalogue picturing the tortillas, enchiladas, tacos, tamales, and other Mexican specialties, along with his canned food.

Credit Refusals and Modifications

1. Hilton and Hilton, wholesale dealers in women's clothing, Philadelphia, received an order for miscellaneous women's furnishings (scarves, pins, earrings, gloves) amounting to $600 from The Dress Shop, 175 Germantown Street, Allentown, Pennsylvania. Robert Pearson, your salesman, reports that Arthur Lutz, a former buyer for Wannamaker's, has just recently started in the retail women's clothing business. He has invested all of his savings. Pearson writes that, while Lutz is a bright, promising, and progressive man of excellent reputation, ability, and good standing in the community, his capital is limited. You are to write Lutz and suggest that he cut the size of his order to about half and that he pay cash (receiving the 2 per cent discount). You will be glad to handle all his orders on this basis until the time comes when you can extend credit to him. To help him display the new scarves and pins, earrings, and gloves, you can send handsome advertising cards. And for his sales help, you will be glad to send a sales manual.

2. As credit sales manager of the Van Buren Company, St. Louis, Missouri, you have to acknowledge the order of Mr. Clark W. Weaver, who (according to the financial statements he sent with his application for credit and his first order for work shirts and pants amounting to $534) is the sole owner of the Weaver Dry Goods Company, Dothan, Alabama. You followed up the references he gave, and they spoke well of his personal integrity and indicated that he is a reasonably good payer. Two said he pays within the terms; 3 said he was 15–45 days slow; 1 said "slow but sure." You are reluctant to extend credit to a man in a predominantly agricultural area who, at a time when farm income is high, has allowed his current ratio (quick assets to liabilities) to fall closer to 1:1 than to the desirable 2:1. Furthermore, with the uncertainty of the government's action on farm supports, you think now is a poor time (from Mr. Weaver's viewpoint as well as your own) for him to be taking on new obligations without straightening out his present ones. You suspect maladjusted inventories and lackadaisical collections. As much as you'd like to fill this order, you have to refuse. It's wiser for him to cut his order in half and pay cash (he'll still get the customary 2 per cent discount). Since rush orders can be handled within four days, he can keep adequate stock on hand. Perhaps later on, when he has reduced his current liabilities and strengthened his cash position, your regular credit privileges of 2/10, n/30 can be made available. After you give him the business reasons for refusing, offer a compromise solution as attractively as you can and strive to convince him that Van Buren shirts and pants are the best buy he can make.

3. As credit manager of the Illini Equipment and Supply Company, Chicago, you are not going to extend credit to Ted Miller and John Sparks, owners of the M and S restaurant, Knoxville, Tennessee, on their order for 1 Hobart dishwasher, model AMA, $1,345, and 1 Scotsman ice maker, SF-75, $748. Their statement shows that the restaurant has sold an excessive amount in meal tickets without retaining sufficient cash for operating ex-

penses. Bad checks from students amount to $300. The property statement shows less than the desired 2:1 ratio of quick assets to liabilities, and the income statements reflect disproportionately increasing expenses. Even though Miller and Sparks think they can put the restaurant in good standing through hard work, the only concession you can make is to give them a 5 per cent discount for cash. Suggest they borrow from the bank on a long-term loan and then buy the equipment they need. Work to keep the door open for the time when they'll be in better financial shape.

4. William Brown, employee of a local bakery for two years, earning a salary of $400 a month, requests that he be allowed to buy a $250 dining-room set on the store's Budget Account plan (3 payments). According to the form he filled out, his wife has been earning about $75 a month sewing for people. You learn (through a local credit investigator) that his wife's employment is part-time and uncertain, and sometimes her income varies. Brown is paying $80 a month on a new car and $65 a month on house payments. He has accounts at three local stores, where his payments have been irregular. Also, the bakery where Brown works has been cutting down on operations during the last six months; it recently released 20 employees. Write the letter refusing the request for a Budget Account but try to interest him in your Layaway plan.

5. Ethel Carpenter, 1908 University Avenue, Coshocton, Ohio, applies to the credit section of your department store (Lampkin's, Columbus) for a charge account. She has been a good cash customer in your store. You investigate and find out that she earns about $4,000 a year and has accounts in a dozen other stores. Further examination proves that she buys more than she needs. She has difficulty paying her other accounts, which are always past due. Although married and divorced and mother of two children (10 and 12), she gets no support from her former husband. Write the letter that will keep her good will but refuse her credit.

6. Carl Suttle, traveling salesman for the James Town Seed and Feed Company, 8067 Broad Street, Newark, New Jersey, sent in an order for grass seed and bulbs, amounting to $400, given him by Ray Spiller, manager of Spiller Feed Company, Long Branch, New Jersey, whose rating is "fair," because he is slow in meeting his obligations. Assume that this order has been referred to you, the credit manager of James Town Seed and Feed Company, for attention. You believe the order is too large to be disposed of by your customer promptly and profitably. Write a letter to Mr. Spiller, suggesting that the order be split up into three parts so that he may cancel unfilled portions of it, should the goods not find a ready sale under the present business conditions. You can ship the first installment now.

7. As credit manager of Unusual Foods, Inc., Boston, you are refusing credit to Sam Johnson, proprietor of The Gourmet Shop (opened four months ago), Princeton, New Jersey, because of the general instability of businesses of this type. Although Johnson's references refer to him to be a hardworking, dependable young man, and his business seems to be taking hold,

still it is your experience that a business of this type has to establish itself on a year-round basis before it becomes a worthwhile credit risk. His store is small. The mortality rate for small gourmet shops is high. From your salesman, David Kelton, you learn that Johnson has made occasional cash purchases from your company during the past two months. Naturally, you would like to increase this cash business and, if the account proves stable, cultivate it later on a credit basis. Write Mr. Johnson a definite but tactful refusal of credit extension, but leave the way open for credit business next year. Stress the value of the 2 per cent cash discount.

8. Van Doren Furniture Company, 198 Main Street, Sioux City, Iowa, has been slow in paying. The last bill (Invoice 8476), amounting to $897.43, became due two months ago. You made several attempts to collect it, but in answer to your last three letters your company has received two remittances totaling only $300. Today you receive a check for $397.43 (leaving a balance of $200) and an order for new goods amounting to $350.50. As correspondent for the Holland Manufacturing Company, 987 Sixth Street, Grand Rapids, Michigan, you are directed to refuse the order on a credit basis (for the signature of the credit manager). The present order will have to be C.O.D., and the Van Doren Company will have to deposit 10 per cent. Also, you'll have to remind this customer about the balance of $200.

9. Bruce Koons, 987 Main Street, Memphis, Tennessee, asks for too much credit for his own good and your own company's safety. He's planning to open a small television repair (and sales) shop, and he's sure he can make a go of it, especially if he can get some extended credit right at the first. He has grown up in Memphis, worked there as a clerk in one of the department stores (selling television sets), joined two civic organizations, and studied business at the University of Tennessee. His order to you (Altec Equipment Company, Atlanta, Georgia) is for $750 worth of supplies, for which he proposes to pay $150 down and the rest in six monthly payments. He plans to begin with $3,500 worth of stock—and you assume that he is making the same proposal to other potential suppliers. You have to refuse because your terms are definitely 2/10, n/30. The mortality rate among TV repair shops is high. But since you'd like to have him stock Altec equipment now and in the future, you point out to him the benefits of getting more capital to start with, offer him a 5 per cent discount for cash with order, and try to build long-time good will and immediate cash business. Assume that you are the credit manager at Altec.

10. Litton and Litton, manufacturers of stuffed animals, Pratfield, Georgia, sends in a first order for $987.50 and a request for credit to Whitehall Wholesalers, Florence, Alabama. As credit manager you look up Litton and Litton's rating and discover that the plant just moved from Chicago six months ago, in order to be closer to suppliers and in hopes of operating with cheaper labor. Sales have dropped in the last year (probably due to the lack of production during the move). To get a better understanding of the financial picture, however, you wrote to some of the wholesalers with whom Litton

has been dealing. They report the following: "Won't sell at present, except on cash basis." "Were prompt in payment. Last five years' account stays delinquent, with payment for one order over 45 days, and another 60 days past due." "New management now that Mr. Litton, Sr. is dead. Son doesn't keep up with business. Owes us over $800."

The letter you have to write is a turndown for credit. He has to get payables in line.

11. Wayne and Lewis Company, 1908 Lake Street, Madison, Wisconsin, sends an order amounting to $4,954 to Sipes Brothers, national hardware dealers, 907 Wales Street, Chicago 9. The firm sold this customer for 10 years on its regular terms and has given a high credit of about $3,000. The books show $3,897 now, $800 of which is due. The payments are made slowly. On the one hand, because of the amount still on the creditor's books, it will not be advisable to refuse the order outright; on the other hand, because of the long history of delayed payments, the amount now due, and the large increase in the size of the order, it will not be wise to grant the full credit. Sit in for the credit manager and write Wayne and Lewis, suggesting that the order be cut to $2,477.

12. As credit manager for American-tex Company, Miami, Florida, you are refusing to fill an order for Jay Whitfield Jolly, Lane Tile and Floor Company, Orlando, Florida, for a dozen 9 × 12 flecked cotton rugs amounting to $432. For three years Jolly has been a fair customer of yours. He owes your firm $1,500, 45 days past due. Acknowledge Jolly's order but refuse to fill it. He can pay cash for this order or, better still, clear up the account before buying more.

13. The Miller Department Store, 987 Third Avenue, St. Paul, Minnesota, has been given a $300 credit limit with your company, Sherman-Goldstein Company, New York 3, distributors of imported silk scarves, ties, etc. The store has exceeded that amount twice recently, and you allowed it. On the second occurrence about a month ago, however, you wrote Mr. Howard Miller to keep within the limit. Now he sends you an order for $189.23, which, with outstanding bills, brings the amount owed you to $358.56. None of this is past due. Write him that you are processing the order, but, before sending the goods, you want a check for at least $100. Perhaps the business has outgrown the present limit. If he will send his latest financial statements, you will take up the matter of increasing the limit.

XII. Collection Letters

THE only sure way to prevent collection problems is to sell strictly for cash. Even with the most careful selection of credit customers, the credit manager (who is usually in charge of collections too) will make an occasional mistake and will allow credit sales to somebody who will not pay promptly.

Unfortunately, however, strict cash selling is also an almost sure way to keep sales and profits unnecessarily low. For that reason, the old battle among the salesman who wanted to sell to everybody, the credit man who would approve sales only to gilt-edged credit risks, and the collection man who insisted on prompt pay regardless of consequences has ended in compromise. Today the thinking salesman accepts the fact that there is no profit if you can't collect; so he does not even try to sell unless there is a reasonably good chance of collection, and he helps the credit man find out about the chances. The credit man accepts the fact that every sale he turns down for credit reasons is a lost chance for more profit; so he approves sales to some marginal credit risks. And the collection man remembers that he not only must collect the money but must retain the good will of customers, or he will drive them away as fast as the sales department can bring them in. Indeed, modern credit theory, as explained in the preceding chapter, stresses selling to marginal risks as a means of increasing sales and profits. If a businessman follows that theory, as most do these days, his collection problems will be numerous —but expected.

DEFECTS OF OLD-STYLE COLLECTION LETTERS

In the early days of credit sales, things were different. Only the best risks could get credit. When one of them did not pay promptly, the businessman was surprised, disappointed in his trusted customer, and irked because his bookkeeping routine was broken. The letters he wrote to collect the money revealed all these emotions. Combined with stock letter-writing phrases, these emotions led to letters characterized by curt, exasperated, injured, accusing, or self-righteous tone, jargon, strong-arm methods, and ineffective appeals to sympathy, fear of getting one's nose smashed, and fear of legal suit.

That is the kind of letter *Time* referred to as "breaking into tears in the first paragraph and yelling for the law in the second." Such letters have caused many people to feel like the man who explained, in response to one of them, that he shuffled his bills and drew six for payment each month, but that further impudence would cause the creditor to be left out of the shuffle next time. The unpleasant tone, jargon, and strong-arm technique were known even to the laundress who "begged to advise" a lawyer that he owed her $6 and that if he didn't pay before the next wash she would put too much starch in his collars.

Indeed, such letters are still sent by businessmen who learned all they know about letter writing years ago only by reading and imitating the poor letters of others and who have never bothered since to learn more modern and effective ways. With some exceptions, collection correspondence is still a notorious blind spot in business. Besides the old faults, all too frequently collectors send obvious form letters to collect long-overdue accounts where a form hardly has a chance, or write many short letters when a good one, only a paragraph or two longer than the first, would do the job. They then defend themselves by claiming that they don't have time or money to spend on individualized letters or long letters or by saying (without testing to find out) that debtors won't read long letters. In tests that have been made, the longer letters nearly always pulled better than the shorter ones, and individual-sounding letters always pulled better than obvious forms in collecting accounts that were very long overdue. The apparent reason is that in the longer letters you can present enough evidence and reasoning to be persuasive.

The several-poor-letters plan delays collections and leaves the business to be financed through borrowing instead of through current collections. One of the main values of promptness is therefore lost. The loss, however, is a small consideration in comparison with the main shortcoming of poor collection correspondence—its disposition to drive away customers that the sales department has brought in only at great expense for advertising and sales promotion. Here are two recent examples:

> We are trying to avoid getting impatient over your delay in settling your account amounting to $124.60. This amount is considerably past due, and your failure to answer our letters (all of which we believe have been polite) has been very annoying as well as discourteous. If you cannot pay the account in full, we should be pleased to be favored with your remittance for part of the amount with approximate date for payment of balance.
>
> Trusting that you will give the above your prompt attention, and with kindest regards,
>
> ~~~~~~
>
> You have classified yourself by failure to answer our letter Re: Olympia Clinic Acct., $8.00. It is therefore our intention to seek other means of collection of this account as we do not intend to let you beat it if at all possible to prevent. We beg to advise that fees for medical services are held by court to be a necessity. So remember, the time to settle a debt is before it gets into court.
>
> It will be to your benefit to communicate with this office at once.

You notice that the only reason given for payment in either of those letters is the implied threat to sue (for $8?) in the second. Such letters increase the difficulty of collecting because they make the reader hate to pay someone he so thoroughly dislikes, and they incense him so that he never wants to do business with the writer again. Frequently the results are:

1. A series of costly collection letters, when one good one would do the job.
2. Final collection only by forcing disgusted customers to pay.
3. Permanent loss of many customers.
4. The unfavorable attitudes passed on by these customers to others.

That's a high price for any firm to pay for keeping a poor collection man —higher than necessary to employ a good one.

ATTITUDES AND OBJECTIVES OF MODERN COLLECTION WRITERS

Modern collection theory and methods are designed to prevent those undesirable consequences. The trained collection man takes the attitude that the debtor should pay because he promised to by a certain date and the time has come. So a collector need never apologize about asking for his money; he has every right to ask for money due him.

In asking, however, he realizes that people pay because of benefits to themselves rather than sympathy for the collector, or any other reason. He therefore not only associates the obligation with the goods through resale talk, but, in persuading the debtor, he points out the benefits of paying now rather than letting the account drag on.

Evidently the modern collection man approaches his job with quite a different attitude from that of his early predecessor. He is not surprised by a delinquency. He knows that most people who do not pay promptly are still honest and that they will pay soon. He knows that some are in temporary financial difficulty and need only a little more time. So he avoids the curt tone. He is not hurt or disappointed as if he were being let down by a trusted friend. So he avoids the injured, pouting tone. He is not the bookkeeper irked by a broken routine. So he avoids the tone of exasperation and self-righteousness. He knows that some delinquents are withholding payment because of dissatisfaction with the goods or charges and that the problem is really one of adjustment rather than collection. He knows that some will have to be persuaded to pay. And he knows that a few—but only a few—are basically dishonest and will have to be forced to pay or marked off as losses; but he realizes that threats of physical violence are illegal and threats of suit destroy good will. Still most important of all, the modern collector (unlike his predecessors) recognizes the true nature of his job.

The trained writer of collection letters today expects his letters to do *two* jobs:

1. They must collect the money, promptly if possible; but
2. They must also retain the good will of the customer if at all possible.

By adding the second job, the collector retains the customer, prevents the unfavorable publicity inevitably carried by a disgruntled former customer, and makes his letter more likely to succeed in its first job— that of collecting. In many cases the second job is more important than the first. Certainly it would be bad business to collect $4.50 by means that lose the good will of a customer who has been buying hundreds of dollars' worth of goods a year.

If the collector has to sacrifice anything, he will yield promptness the most willingly. Yet, in so doing, he is taking four kinds of losses or at least the risk of them:

1. Use of the money for the additional time it is outstanding.
2. Costs of further collection efforts.
3. Additional purchases which may be added to the account before it is closed (and thus will increase the loss if the account is uncollectible).
4. Loss of sales. Customers with overdue accounts commonly trade elsewhere rather than face the embarrassment of buying where they owe money.

To his major objectives, the collector will hang on grimly. If he finds later that he has to give up one of them, he will usually give up good will first, unless the amount due is small and the customer a large-volume purchaser. Sometimes he has to give up even his main objective—collection—but he will not do so without a considerable struggle unless the amount is so small that even the trouble of suing would be worth more in time and effort than would be collected.

For effectiveness in both collection and good will, the modern collector co-operates with the sales department because he knows that both sales and collections are essential to the ultimate objectives of the business—profits. As in acknowledgments of orders, he may even inject some sales-promotion material into *early* collection letters to a good risk, when he feels that it might be of interest to the customer. It not only promotes future sales, but it shows the debtor that the firm still trusts him and is willing for him to buy more on credit. Thus it is a subtle appeal to pride which helps to save the reader's face and his good will. If used at the end of the letter, it relieves the sting and solves one of the correspondent's touchiest problems—how to provide a pleasant ending for a letter in which some element is displeasing to the customer.

Even when resale is not the basic collection appeal (as discussed later), the collection man introduces into his letters a few phrases of resale talk to keep the customer convinced that he made a wise decision in buying *those goods* from *that firm* AND to make the obligation to pay concrete by attaching it to the goods. The following letter includes both resale and sales-promotion talk:

> You probably remember your first feeling of pleasure when you saw the dark, gleaming wood and the beautifully proportioned design of the Heppelwaite bedroom suite you bought here a few months ago. The suite was one of the finest we have ever had in our store, and we were well pleased —as we thought you were—when you selected it for your home.
>
> At the time you purchased your furniture, we were glad to arrange convenient credit terms for you so that you could have your furniture while you

were paying for it. Now if you will look over your bills, you will notice that those for October, November, and December have not been marked paid. The sooner you take care of them, the more you can enjoy your furniture because each time you use it or even see it you will subconsciously remember that you are up to date on your payments.

When you come to the store to make your payments, be sure to see the Home-furnishings Department as well as the Time-payment desk. An entire new line of curtains, slip covers, bedspreads, and scatter rugs is there for your inspection. There are all colors and fabrics made up in the latest styles. From the wide selection, you can choose a beautiful new setting for your Heppelwaite suite.

That letter pretty well exemplifies the attitudes and objectives of modern collection writers: Ask for the money without apology because it is due, persuade by showing the reader benefits to himself, use calm understanding and patience, collect but retain good will, and co-operate with the sales department.

CHARACTERISTICS OF THE COLLECTION SERIES

In trying to attain his objectives of collecting and retaining good will, the efficient collector classifies delinquent accounts and prescribes the best treatment for each. The method he employs may be compared to a process of repeated siftings or screenings. The procedure is a series of mailings, each of which eliminates some from the delinquent list and aids in reclassifying and prescribing for those remaining.

To do its two jobs best, the collection series should have the following characteristics:

1. *Promptness.* It is a well-established fact among credit and collection men that the sooner they start trying to collect after an account becomes due, the better the chance. The U.S. Department of Commerce has found that a dollar in current accounts is worth only 90¢ after two months, 67¢ after six months, 45¢ after a year, 23¢ at two years, 15¢ at three years, and 1¢ at five years.

2. *Regularity.* Not only does systematic handling of a collection problem increase office efficiency, but it has a desirable effect on the debtor. He sees quickly that he is not going to slip through the holes of inefficiency in a haphazard collection procedure.

3. *Increasing forcefulness.* Since the collector wants to retain the good will of the customer as well as collect the money, he starts with as weak a letter as he thinks will work. Like the doctor who uses stronger and stronger medicine or resorts to surgery only as the need develops, the collector applies more and more forceful methods. He resorts to the court only after weaker methods have failed.

4. *Adaptation.* Not all credit and collection men classify their customers into the clean-cut categories of good, medium, and poor risks suggested by some books; but all competent ones vary their procedures according to the quality of the risk (as well as according to the general bases of adaptation already discussed). Usually the poorer the risk, the more frequent the mailings and the more forceful the messages. Whereas three months might pass before anything stronger than a few statements is sent to a good risk, much less time might be used to run a poor one through the whole sifting process and bring him to court.

5. *Flexibility.* The collection procedure has to be flexible to take care of unusual circumstances. The collector would look silly to continue sending letters every fifteen days to a man who had answered an early one with the message that an automobile accident had thrown him financially two months behind but that he would pay the bill by a certain date. After all, you can't get blood out of a turnip.

STANDARD COLLECTION PROCEDURES

The exact plan of a collection series varies according to circumstances. Also, various collection theorists and practitioners use different terms to mean essentially the same things. Most well-planned series, however, are based on a screening process somewhat like that shown in the accompanying tabulation:

Stage	Assumption	Nature	Gist
Notification..... Reminder.......	Will pay promptly Will pay; overlooked	Usual statement Statement, perhaps with rubber stamp, penned note, or sticker; or form letter or brief reference in other letter	Amount due, due date, terms Same as above, perhaps with indication that this is not first notice
Inquiry.........	Something unusual; needs special consideration	One letter	Asks for payment or explanation and offers consideration and helpfulness
Appeal..........	Needs to be persuaded	Letters	Selected appropriate and increasingly forceful appeals, well developed
Urgency.........	May be scared into paying	Letter, sometimes from high executive or special collector	Grave tone of something getting out of hand; still a chance to come through clean
Ultimatum......	Must be squeezed	Letter	Pay by set date or we'll report to credit bureau or sue; reviews case to retain good will by showing reasonableness

Of course, there is no more than one mailing at the notification, inquiry, or ultimatum stage. Their nature makes repetition of them illogical. The number and frequency of mailings in the other stages vary from firm to firm, and even within firms according to the class of customer and other circumstances, such as the type of business (retail or mercantile) and type of sale (open account, installment). In general, the better the credit risk, the greater the number of mailings and the longer the intervals. Usually, however, there are two to four reminders, two or three appeals, and one urgency letter at 10- to 30-day intervals (which usually become shorter near the end).

The assumption, nature, and gist clearly call for modified Type-A messages in the first two collection stages (where no persuasion is deemed necessary) and for Type-C letters in the last three. The inquiry stage is middle ground, where one might well use either. Type-B letters would be appropriate in collections only if the debtor had asked for an unapproved concession, such as an unearned discount.

NOTIFICATION (usually a form telling amount, date due, and terms)

On or about the due date, there is no reason to assume anything except prompt payment if the customer knows how much is due, what for, the due date, and the terms. Most people will pay in response to form notices—the first sifting—which give those facts. A personal letter at this stage would insult most people by implying distrust and concern over the account. Instead of a costly letter, then, the notification is almost always a statement (bill) sent on or about the due date. The forms have the advantages of avoiding insults and saving lots of money on the large mailings by reducing the mailing list for the later, more expensive stages.

REMINDER (usually forms giving basic information and adding a push)

If the notice brings no response, the collector gives the customer the benefit of the doubt, assumes that he intends to pay but forgot, and sends him one or more reminders (the number and frequency depending on the circumstances). The collector knows that most of the remaining delinquents will respond at this stage, and his list will be further reduced. He is therefore as much concerned with avoiding offense as with giving the necessary information (amount, what for, due date, and terms).

Reminders are usually forms, in order to save both money and the customer's face, but they may be of several types.

1. Exact copy of the original notice, or copy plus a rubber stamp such as "Second Notice" or "Please Remit."

2. Copy of the first statement with a penned note, such as "Please remit promptly" or "Thank you." (Very effective in collecting but dangerous to good will, in that the personal attention implies concern and distrust.)

3. Copy of the notice with the addition of a colorful gummed sticker carrying a slogan. Effective examples are "Don't delay further; this is long overdue," "Your prompt remittance is requested," "NOW is the time to take care of this," "Prompt payment insures good credit," "Prompt payments are appreciated," "Don't delay—pay today," "Remember you agreed to pay in thirty days," and "Have you overlooked this?"

Less effective wordings, with the apparent reasons for ineffectiveness in parentheses, are:

We trusted you in good faith; we hope we were not mistaken (undesirable implications and tone, stressing *We*)

We are counting on you; don't fail us (selfish view)

If there is any reason for nonpayment, write us frankly (suggests finding something wrong; lacks success-consciousness)

If this checks up clear, clear it up with a check (same criticism as preceding; the word play is questionable)

4. Brief gadget letter (form).

[Picture of Reddy Kilowatt, beside which is]

I'm wondering why—

My note to you last week didn't bring payment of my wages.

Did you by chance forget to send it in? If you have sent my pay within the last day or two, thanks a lot.

Your faithful servant
REDDY KILOWATT

Doe$ thi$ little note from u$ remind you of anything?

I$n't there $omething that you have meant to attend to—$omething that ha$ nearly e$caped your attention?

If you will take ju$t a moment right now—while the inclo$ed po$tage-free envelope i$ before you—we'll $urely appreciate it.

Amt. $9.08 $incerely your$,
                                           Robert W. Widdicombe

We enclose a small piece of string, just long enough to tie around your finger to remind you that you should send your check today for $48.50 in payment of . . . .

The little alarm clock pictured in this letterhead, like any alarm clock, reminds you that it's time to do something you planned to do. This one is a friendly reminder that you intended to send your check today for $28.65. . . .

5. Incidental reminder (italicized in the example) in a personalized letter mainly about something else.

With fall just around the corner and school starting within a month, no doubt you have been planning to order some more fast-selling Queen candies to have plenty on your shelves before the fall rush begins.

By this time you have surely realized the advantage of handling Queen products in your new store. You will want to take advantage of our special back-to-school offer, too. It includes many delicious assorted candies popular with children.

When you mail your payment of $126 due July 30, covering our last shipment under our invoice No. 134, dated June 30, won't you also include your next order, so we can assure you an early delivery of factory-fresh candies? Notice the variety in our complete line, as shown in the latest catalogue, a copy of which I'm enclosing for your convenience in making your selections.

More of the helpful window and counter displays like those sent with your first shipment are available on request. If there is any other way we can help you to sell Queen candies, let us know. We are always glad to be of service.

If we let xxxxx represent collection talk and —— represent resale or sales-promotion talk, the reminder letter may look like either of the following (usually the first, as in the preceding letter):

THIS	or	THIS
_____		xxxxxxxxxxxxxxxxx
_____		_____
xxxxxxxxxxxxxxxxx		_____
_____		_____
_____		_____

Some collection men prefer the second version. They feel that most people behind in their accounts expect a collection letter and spot it as such. Better then, they reason, to send it under no such masquerades as the first. In the following letters, after the direct request for payment the sales material reassures the customer that the firm feels no concern over the status of the account. The first one is a form letter.

Will you please take a moment to fill out your check for $69.50, the amount due for your August purchases?

And then bring it by the shop so that we can show you all the latest fashions assembled from the choice showings in New York, Dallas, and Los Angeles.

Whether you need a basic outfit or only accessories to complete one, we'll look forward to serving you.

~~~~~~

Now that the end-of-the-year rush has let up, won't you please give your personal attention for a few minutes, Mr. Bowers, to your $95 account for Columbia supplies sent you on December 3?

Personal attention is used advisedly here, for you are concerned—more so than are any of your assistants—with the maintenance of your valuable credit reputation among stationery-supply houses. You will want to continue this good record, of course, by taking care of your first purchase from us, sent to you with our invoice BB103. Please sit down now and send us your check for $95 covering these supplies.

The $42 worth of supplies, ordered on January 26 and shipped with our invoice CB345, brought your account total to $137. Doubtless these Valentine and Washington's Birthday sets enlivened your early February sales. With Easter almost here, the new color books and cut-outs shown in the enclosed folder will soon be in demand. May we send you what you need?

Up through the reminder stage in the collection procedure, the assumption is that little or no persuasion is necessary, but just a notice or reminder. Usually the mailings should be inexpensive forms instead of personalized messages. Thus the firm saves money on the large-volume mailings in the first two stages. Most customers pay in those stages, and their names are removed from the list requiring further, more expensive collection efforts. But perhaps more important than the money saved, forms avoid the sting that personalized, full-length collection messages would carry. You may have noticed that even the incidental reminder in the Queen letter was subordinated in dependent-clause structure to avoid too much sting.

6. Individual-sounding letter solely about collection. For greater force in the last reminder, or to poor risks, or about large amounts, the collector may decide to write a letter that talks collection all the way and seems to be individualized. Since most of his delinquents have so much in common, he may still make it a relatively inexpensive fill-in form if he watches the tone and content carefully, typing each copy (perhaps made of form paragraphs) or matching fill-ins neatly.

The following letter for a mercantile concern, for example, is easily adaptable to a large number of customers. With only one fill-in (for the underscored part, conveniently placed at the end of a paragraph) besides the inside address and salutation, it will serve for a large mailing list. It has a touch of pride appeal along with the reminder to reduce the sting of the apparently individualized message.

As a successful businessman, you know what a good credit reputation means.

You have one.

That's why we immediately extended you 30-day credit on your recent order and why we want to be certain that you are completely satisfied with the goods.

We know that the reports of your good credit reputation were correct. And we likewise know that you'll send us payment as soon as this letter recalls the fact that you owe $85 due November 15 for. . . .

Beyond the reminder stage, however, *obvious* form letters can hardly be expected to do the jobs to be done (though they are sometimes used). In the inquiry stage and beyond, the very nature of the collector's working assumptions seems to call for individualized messages.

For the latest stages of the collection procedure, the collection man fortunately has ample information on the credit application form and in the credit records to do a good job of adaptation in an individually dictated letter. And his earlier mailings have so reduced the list of delinquents that he can afford to give some personal attention to each letter late in the collection procedure.

INQUIRY (giving the debtor a chance to pay or explain; offering help)

When the collector has sent enough reminders to convince himself that oversight is not the cause of delay, he has to start working on another assumption. With a new customer or a poor risk, he may assume that persuasion or force is necessary and skip a stage or two in the usual procedure. With an old customer who has paid regularly, however, he will reason that unusual circumstances must be the cause of delay. He still has confidence in the customer, based on past favorable experience. Certainly he still wants to retain good will. And he is always willing to be considerate of a person temporarily in a financial tight spot.

His plan, then, is to write *one* letter in a spirit of friendly understanding and helpfulness, asking for the money *or* an explanation. Because he prefers the money, he stresses it instead of the explanation of what's wrong or how he can help. But he is careful not to offend this formerly good customer apparently in a temporary jam. And he will not suggest that something is wrong with the goods or the billing (for reasons explained later). His only persuasion is in his frankness, his offer of help, and his considerate attitude. Most people react favorably to requests presented in such a spirit. The letters below illustrate the technique for the inquiry stage:

Because distance makes it impossible for me to come to you for a friendly chat, I ask you to accept this letter as the next best thing.

You now owe us $250, due since May 31, for the shipment of assorted electric fans listed on Invoice X-221. Formerly you always paid our invoices promptly. We conclude that there is some special reason for the delay this time. As your business friends, can we do anything to help you over the rough spot?

Of course, we want our money, but we also want to keep your friendship. What is wrong? What can we do to help?

Will you please send your payment today or let me have a full and frank explanation? Perhaps between us we can work out a plan so that you can bring your account up to date without crowding yourself too much and we can continue to supply your immediate needs.

If you will use the handy return envelope I'm enclosing, your reply will come direct to my desk unopened.

Even though we do not send you a series of strong collection letters about the account you owe us, we do expect you to pay it as soon as you can.

In view of the very satisfactory way you have paid your bills for the five years we have been supplying you, I feel sure that something unexpected has happened to you. Can we help you over the hump?

May we ask that you do one of the following three things:

1. If you possibly can, send us a check today for the full amount of $237.60 for the. . . .
2. Send us a partial payment today and propose a schedule which you can follow to cover the rest.
3. If you honestly feel that you can't spare enough to make a significant partial payment, please explain what the trouble is, what I can do to help, and your proposed schedule for taking care of the account.

I shall have to be able to report some response soon or my boss is going to think I'm not doing my job. May I ask your help in doing 1, 2, or 3?

I wish I could sit down and talk with you for a few minutes about the circumstances that leave January and February charges to you on the books.

But because of distance I can only study our past experience with you, and various kinds of credit information. Everything I have points to your having a quite satisfactory credit standing. Your past record of prompt payment therefore leaves me unconcerned about ultimate collection, but it also leaves me wondering what's wrong now.

Please either make immediate payment of the $157.47 balance due or drop me a note today telling just how you intend to handle the account. You'll find me co-operative in accepting any reasonable proposal for your taking care of it—or better, the $157.47.

You may have noticed that those letters avoid two common collection-letter errors that have their first chance to come up in the inquiry stage.

The first is that, in writing inquiry-stage letters, most collectors and even most writers about collections seem to favor asking questions about the customer's possible dissatisfaction with the goods or charges or both. The apparent purpose of the questions is to secure some kind of answer. Any answer is supposedly better than silence, for two of the same reasons that partial payments are often encouraged—they keep the debtor thinking about his obligation, and they renew his acceptance of it.

But aren't such questions psychologically unsound, if not ethically undesirable? If the debtor had found anything wrong with the goods or the billing, would he not himself have suggested an adjustment, especially after being hounded by the collector's former mailings? If he hasn't reported anything wrong, is it not poor policy to suggest that he should? Isn't the collector practically suggesting that if the debtor will claim that something is wrong, he can gracefully postpone payment and perhaps even get an unjustified adjustment? Isn't the collector offering a gun and inviting the debtor to take a few shots? Certainly, he is working in the opposite direction from both resale talk and success consciousness.

The second common error that has its first chance to show up in the inquiry-stage letter is backtracking—that is, going back to the assumption of an earlier stage in the collection procedure. Apparently in an effort to save the delinquent's face, a timid collector sometimes grabs back at "oversight" (the assumption of the reminder stage) after he has started a letter in the inquiry stage. He is only kidding himself and forfeiting the respect of his reader. If he believes that oversight is the reason for the delay, he should not advance to the inquiry stage.

The same kind of nerveless collector sometimes shows the same tendencies in two other places in the collection procedure. After his inquiry-stage offer of special consideration has been ignored, he sometimes incongruously repeats it in letters of the next stage. The debtor then sees the poor fellow quaking in his boots and takes advantage of him, much as a dog, a horse, or a bull will take advantage of a person who obviously fears him.

Not many businessmen—even those who backtrack in other ways—will send an ultimatum and then back down on it. The ultimatum is such a definite action that to do so would be the worst kind of backtracking. Still a few lily-livered collectors do. They merely spoil customers and lose their respect, just as many mothers do with their children by issuing ultimatums and not carrying them out.

The summing-up on all three kinds of backtracking is simply this: Don't do it. Hold on to one working assumption until it seems unsound.

Then throw it overboard, grab the next one, and don't be diving into the water to retrieve the discard. If you've threatened to sue or report the delinquent unless you get your money by a certain day and the money doesn't come, sue or report. Conversely, don't talk about suing or reporting until you are seriously considering it.

APPEALS (basically reader benefits, made increasingly forceful)

If the delinquent does not respond to a friendly inquiry, apparently he is taking the wrong attitude toward his indebtedness. The collector again shifts his working assumption accordingly. His new assumption is that the debtor must be persuaded to pay. He will not backtrack from that.

Basic Considerations. At the appeal stage the collection letter writer does his main work. In doing it, he keeps in mind four important points.

1. For persuasiveness, write individualized messages. The earlier brief notices, reminders, and inquiries will have collected most of the accounts (the easy ones) as inexpensively as possible in terms of time and good will. The remaining few will be harder to collect. Usually they will require individualized (or at least individual-sounding) letters rather than forms, because they have to be persuasive. By using the information in the credit records, the collector can write individualized messages that are specific and therefore persuasive to a degree impossible in a form that has to be general because it has to fit many people.

2. Develop only one or two points. Scattering shots like a shotgun over several undeveloped appeals weakens the message too much to reach the hard-to-collect-from delinquents. Something like a rifle bullet, with all the powder behind one fully developed central theme, will be more forceful. That usually means longer letters because they must be specific and say enough to make the point emphatic; but they pay off in results.

3. Retain good will as far as possible. Because they are individualized, pointed, full-length collection messages, appeal-stage letters will necessarily carry some sting. Like doctors and patients, however, collectors and debtors have to accept the fact that the needle carrying strong medicine for advanced stages of a disease often has a sting. Still the wise collector, like the humane doctor, will minimize the sting as much as possible without weakening the medicine. He knows that many desirable customers sometimes fall behind in payments; so he is still interested in retaining good will. He knows that nasty-toned, strong-arm methods lose customers and collect no more money than more pleasant methods.

As B. C. Gilbert says ("The Modern Trend in Collections," *Credit Currents,* September, 1954, p. 9),

> Never, in the handling of a delinquent account, is harshness justified . . . you can be firm without being harsh. The average man is a pretty good guy at heart. All you need to do is skillfully stimulate the customer's desire to pay you and you'll both be happy.

The job is therefore to write one or more letters (the number, frequency, and forcefulness depending on the class of credit risk) to persuade the debtor to pay without losing him as a customer.

4. Select a reader-benefit appeal. Successful collection, like successful selling or any other kind of persuasion, involves showing the debtor that he will get something he wants or avoid something he doesn't want—in other words, you-attitude.

Appeals to sympathy (variously called the "poor-me" appeal or the appeal to co-operation) do not meet the requirement. They are fundamentally selfish, lacking in the you-attitude. People don't usually pay to help a creditor but to help themselves get something they want or avoid something they don't. The following letter, for example, is not likely to collect from the purchaser of a brown weasel coat bought during a January fur sale:

> You have often heard of a business house needing money to finance its operations, haven't you? How is a concern going to carry on if there is no source of income to meet its constantly growing bills?
>
> That, Mrs. Rose, is our problem today; hence we are asking you again to send us a remittance to cover the balance of your past-due account. Won't you please accommodate us by balancing your account tomorrow?

Though a cleverly and humorously overdrawn picture of the writer's family in need might bring the money, it is more likely to bring a wisecrack answer. For instance, one man built his letter around a picture of his wife and eleven children, with the note below: "This is why I MUST have my money." The answer was the picture of a beautiful blonde with the note "This is why I CAN'T pay."

Psychological analysis shows that when a sympathy appeal does work, usually it does so because the reader feels a twinge of conscience about putting a good fellow like the writer into a predicament. That twinge is something the reader wants to avoid. So we are back where we started: Show the debtor that by paying he will get something he wants or avoid something he doesn't.

Basically people want

a) To have self-respect and the approval of others (they have to live with both themselves and others) and *b*) To avoid loss of what they have and add to those things (money, property, and the credit privilege, for example).

Appeals to all except the desire for the approval of others are usable in collections. A creditor would not dare (for fear of libel suit) tell the shortcomings of debtors to anybody except other creditors or prospective creditors with an interest to protect. And if he told them, their unfavorable actions would affect the debtor more in terms of *b* than in terms of social disapproval. So a collector can be persuasive by showing debtors how they benefit in self-respect or in economic self-interest.

The true collector is therefore really a salesman. Like a salesman, he makes a careful analysis of the customer, selects the appeal most likely to succeed with the particular individual in the specific situation, and sells him on the idea of paying by showing him the benefit he gets. The resale, pride, and fair-play appeals show the reader how to retain a clear conscience and keep up his self-respect.

The Resale Appeal. Touches of resale belong in every collection letter, to keep the debtor satisfied and to show him what he got for his promise to pay; but resale can also be used as the theme of a whole appeal letter. Essentially it goes back and almost repeats the points a good salesman would make in selling the product. By the time the collector-salesman is through reselling, the debtor will see that he got good value. Whether you call it his integrity, his respect for his word when he made the contract, his sense of fair play, or his pride, he will be prompted to pay by his basic desire to act so that he will have a clear conscience and be able to live with himself.

Though any appeal may be made ineffective or good-will-killing by inept phrasing, the danger is not great in the resale appeal. Really effective use of it, however, requires skillful salesmanship. The collector must be imaginative enough to paint a vivid, interesting picture of the product in use; and he must be willing to make it complete, detailed, and long enough to be persuasive. The following letters illustrate the type:

Now that Asbex and Asbar have had time to prove their profit-making ability to you, can you say that we were right? We said that they would be a good selling team for you.

When you followed up your original Asbex order of April 15 with the April 27 order for ten gallons each of Asbex and Asbar, you showed that you thought the fire-retarding twins would move quickly together. With your good reputation for prompt payment as our guide, we were glad to have such a desirable outlet as your store for this pair of fast sellers. Although your payment of $39 for the first shipment, Invoice BT-41198, is now ten days overdue, you can keep your record intact by sending us a check in the next mail. If you make the check for $156, you can also pay for the second shipment, Invoice BT-41390, on its net date.

From all reports on the way business is in Ardmore, you'll be sending us repeat orders before long. We'll be looking forward to serving you, now that you have learned that Asbex and Asbar fill a recurring need of your customers. With readers of *Life, Good Housekeeping,* and the *Saturday Evening Post,* and more and more satisfied users spreading the good news, you can expect ever-increasing turnover with the twins in your stock.

The following letter from a building-and-loan collector who had made the loan originally and knew the family quite well is even more personal in its resale appeal. The reference to passing pleasures in the second paragraph is a subtle way of letting Mr. Barnes know, without preaching to him, that the collector knows where the money went—into expensive parties designed to keep up with the Joneses.

When you and Mrs. Barnes moved into your new home two years ago, I was very proud that I had something to do with it, for if there is anything that contributes to the pleasure of life it is a good place to live—and especially if that place belongs to the occupant. I feel that there is much more than mere sentiment behind those words "There's no place like home."

Indeed, there is so much of comfort, security, and pride in home ownership that anyone should forego passing pleasures that eat up his income, take the savings, and invest in a home—just as you decided to do.

The importance to you of keeping up your payments on your loan can not be overstressed. Perhaps by now you are used to your home and you take it as a matter of course. But take a walk around the lawn. Note the landscaping; note the beautiful architectural lines of the building. Then go inside and think for a minute how comfortable you, Mary, Jim, and Jane are there. Think where you would be without it. And suppose you were going to build today. Instead of the $18,000 you paid, you would now have to pay about $20,000 because of increased prices in general. Really, you cannot afford to stop enjoying those comforts.

So will you please come in and take care of your March, April, and May payments as soon as possible?

Pride Appeal. Often resale talk is interwoven with a subtle appeal to pride; or the appeal to pride may be more or less independent of resale on the goods. In either case the writer uses all his knowledge of practical psychology to know when to encourage pride by sincere compliments, when to needle it, and when to challenge it. If he bumbles, he may get a surprising answer, as did the collector who asked what the neighbors would think if he came into town and repossessed the debtor's new car. The answer was that the neighbors all agreed it would be a low-down, dirty trick. The collector had erred in challenging when he should have been encouraging pride.

One collector was successful by quoting from a highly favorable credit report on the debtor, asking if he recognized the description, and encouraging him to retain the reputation like that by taking the required prompt action. Others have used the technique of giving percentages of customers who pay at different stages in the collection procedure and saying that, of course, the debtor does not want to be in the minority groups at the end of the list. The essence of success with the pride appeal is to encourage the debtor toward actions he can be proud of and to avoid the use of accusations and implications of shame as far as possible. The following examples show the methods. Note that the first (an early letter) ends with sales promotion, and the last (to a university student) incorporates a reference that is almost a left hook.

Your choice of the navy blue suit, the light tan suit with matching shoes, purse, and gloves, for a total of $182.95, shows the care and pride with which you select your clothes.

We feel sure that you want to show that same pride in maintaining your preferred credit rating. Drop your check for $182.95 in the mail today, and your account, due November 10, will be paid in full.

The next time you are in town, come by and look over our completely new line of Mary Margaret furs. Whether you want to make additions to your wardrobe or merely to see the latest fashions, your visit will be welcomed.

When you applied for credit privileges with us, we of course checked your rating.

"Good" and "Fair" some firms reported, and (according to three) "Excellent." You may well be proud of such a rating.

Let us help you keep your pride in your rating by writing "Paid" after the 30-day overdue balance of $33.88 that now shows on our books for. . . .

Twenty-seven other Lansing residents bought Monora television sets the same week you got yours.

That was just a little over three months ago. Yet twenty-three of them have already been in to take care of their payments as agreed. We made a note of their prompt payments on their records. And they walked out of the store pleased with themselves, their sets, and us.

When you stop to think about it, the good credit rating you establish by promptly paying as agreed is more than a matter of personal pride. It adds to the value and desirability of your account with any store in Lansing. It's a personal recommendation, too, for employers often check the credit record of an applicant for a job.

Take the two minutes now to send us your check. Or bring your payment by the store tomorrow.

Fair-Play Appeal. By using slightly different wording, you can turn the basic appeal to self-respect into an appeal to fair play. The wording may recall the debtor's sense of respect for a contract, his feeling of duty to do what he has promised, or his conscience that makes him do the right thing. It develops the feeling that the debtor should carry out his part of the bargain, since the creditor has been fair in carrying out his. Integrity or honesty may be as good a name for the appeal. Some people call it a request for co-operation. Whatever the name, a well-developed, positive presentation (without accusations) showing the reader that he should pay to be fair is an effective appeal. It goes back to the fundamental idea that the debtor promised to pay by a certain time for certain goods or services. Since the benefits have been delivered, the fair thing is that he should pay for them. Almost everybody wants to feel that he is fair in his dealings with others. Here are two examples of the appeal:

On August 20 we filled your order for a . . . on credit because of our faith in you to pay according to terms. It has no doubt given you the service you expected by. . . .

We were glad to extend open account terms to you; and although this has run far beyond the usual 30 days, isn't it true that we've been fairly decent about waiting this long for our money?

I cannot believe that you want us to suffer a loss because of our good faith in filling your order without cash in advance.

So I'm enclosing an addressed envelope that needs no postage, and I'm appealing to you to use it—this moment—to send the $27.60 due us and to make our contract a two-sided one, the way it is supposed to be.

How would you feel next payday if you received no paycheck? I'm sure you would feel that you had been giving good service and that your employer should pay for it.

When we ask you for the $44.95 for the coat you bought November 18, we are only asking for what is due us.

At the time we placed your name on our credit list, I thought we made clear that accounts are due the tenth of the month following purchase. Perhaps more important, I thought you accepted the terms.

In fairness to us and to yourself, won't you please come in today and settle this account according to our agreement?

Appeals to Economic Self-Interest. Even the man who has no sense of obligation to pay for value received (as developed in the resale appeal), or of pride, or of fair play in treating other decent people fairly will likely pay if it is clearly to his own economic self-interest to do so. You may therefore write forceful collection appeals to a debtor's desire to add to what he has by using his valuable credit privilege or his desire to avoid loss of that valuable asset. The second is frequently called the appeal to fear; but the first is more positive, less likely to hurt good will, and therefore more desirable (especially early in the appeal stage).

Slight shifts of emphasis in the wording, as in the illustrations below, may stress the convenience of credit in future buying or the economics of credit:

The increasing size of your three orders for Mada irons and lamps since June 15 indicates that your business must be good.

With your business growing as indicated, you'll be needing a greater variety of stock. That's just good merchandising. It's also good merchandising to pay for your stock within the sixty-day period allowed.

Please send your check for $260, which is now almost four weeks past due. New Mada stocks are coming in now, and you'll want to be in a position to offer your customers the latest in electrical supplies.

As a successful business manager, you know the value of maintaining a well-stocked inventory. You would probably like now to begin your orders for galoshes, rubber boots, stadium boots, and other long-wearing, quick-selling Red Ball products in preparation for the season just ahead when they will be most in demand.

Perhaps your account for 6 pairs of galoshes, 12 pairs of rubber boots, and 6 pairs of tennis shoes, for a total of $93.50, has kept you from ordering those items you need. Today, while the matter is fresh on your mind, mail your check for $93.50 along with an order for the Red Ball products you'll need soon to supply your customers' requests.

By mailing your order today, you can be sure the shipment will reach you by the middle of the month.

The reassurance of a good coat of clear, fire-resistant Asbex on your house and barn is like the reassurance of a prompt-pay credit rating: each is just an extra measure.

You hope you won't have occasion to use it, but it's mighty comforting to know it's there in case you need it.

As a businessman with many years of experience, you realize how much more valuable a good account is when it is stamped "prompt pay." With such a label, other ranchers around Ardmore have found their credit a real help—especially when the cattle market was slow and little money was coming in.

Because such a reputation is built up only by paying on time every time, you'll want to take care of the $59 for the Asbex you bought over two months ago. When you bring the check around to the store, remind me to show you a new type safety wire fence. It should be just the thing for that new colt pen you were telling us about the last time you were in.

Why is a prompt-pay rating like money in the bank?

Both are able to command goods and services immediately when you want them.

On the basis of your ability to pay and your reputation for meeting payments promptly, we extended credit immediately when you asked for it. Now we ask that you send your check for $98.76 to cover your August shipment of jewelry, sold to you on credit just as if you had drawn on your bank account for it.

Then look through the enclosed booklet. Notice the color pictures of things you'd like to have in stock for Toledo's Christmas shoppers. The Heavy-Hollow Silver Plate described on page 3 is a line for moderate budgets. It's durable as well as handsome, since it's triple-plated silver on copper.

Should you care to order on our regular terms, enclose a check covering your balance of $98.76 and order the new stock; use your credit as if it were another check drawn on money in the bank.

Customers are quick to buy Presto-Lite flashlights at $3.45, aren't they?

That price gives you a substantial 50% markup on each one you sell and helps you meet competition for sales of reliable, durable flashlights.

One of the reasons you enjoy this favorable pricing is that we extend credit only to those outlets with good credit ratings and thus keep down collection costs. When our credit customers pay within the agreed-on 30 days, we can take all cash discounts available from our suppliers and pass these savings on to our customers and their customers in the form of lower prices. If they take 90 days, however, the $2 you pay us for a Presto-Lite would probably increase to $2.15 or $2.20 and would wind up costing your customers around $3.75. That affects both of us, doesn't it?

So that all of us may profit from the real economies of prompt payments, please write out your check for $51 covering the 24 Presto-Lite flashlights you received almost 50 days ago and mail it to us in the enclosed envelope.

Though the following letter speaks of fair play, it is not an appeal to fair play as explained before but to the debtor's economic self-interest in enjoying the benefits of the credit privilege:

Are you playing fair—

—playing fair with yourself, I mean?

You want to continue to get merchandise promptly by merely mailing an order to your supplier. Rightfully you can expect the best of service along with good-quality products when you arrange a businesslike transaction. You will agree that you would not be fair to yourself if your actions caused you to lose this privilege.

The Reliable Paint and Varnish Company has continued to honor this privilege because in the past you have always settled your account satisfactorily. At present, however, you owe us $125, now three months over-due, on Invoice 362773 covering a shipment of thirty-five gallons of white Reliable House Paint.

To treat yourself fairly and to preserve your good, businesslike reputation, you will want to get your account balanced promptly. Please use the enclosed envelope to send your check today and put your account in good condition again.

URGENCY

When the regular collector is getting nowhere with appeals like those in the preceding letters, he may continue with stronger letters or he may turn the job over to a higher executive for the final few mailings. Sometimes he writes the letters himself and sends them out over the signature of the treasurer, the president, the company lawyer, the credit bureau, or a collection agency.

The psychology is to give the reader the feeling that things are getting pretty serious when the moguls have to take over. Though urgency-stage letters are not actually the end of the collection procedure, they are designed to seem close. They therefore answer the question of the lady in the *New Yorker* cartoon who flashed an early-stage collection letter at the collection desk and asked how many more she would receive before she had to pay.

Actually, the letter sent over the signature of the higher executive is usually a forceful development of one of the appeals already discussed. It may go a bit further on the economic interests of the debtor and talk about the cost of facing suit (since the debtor would have to pay the bill and court costs), but usually not. Even now the firm is still interested in good will. It knows that there is still a chance of retaining the customer. If he is lost as a credit customer, it desires to have him as a cash customer and to have him speak of the firm as favorably as possible. So the executive more frequently plays the role of the good fellow who gives a man a last chance. But he still does not turn the screws all the way by setting an end date. The following letter was signed by the company treasurer:

When you began your business, a good reputation in Ardmore made it possible for you to get loans, and your hard work and prompt payments —good reputation again—got you credit on your purchases.

This good reputation is more important to you now than ever before, for with the unsettled world conditions causing wide fluctuations in the securities market, credit agencies are becoming more and more strict in their policies—and businessmen are learning to be more careful in abiding by their requirements.

We have not received your check for the $156 for your invoices 69507, covering our shipment of 10 gallons of Asbex on April 10, and 76305, covering the shipment on April 20 of 10 gallons of Asbex and 20 gallons of Asbar. Some arrangement for this settlement is necessary right away. We are willing to accept your 90-day note at 5% for this amount so that you can protect your credit rating without lowering your cash balance.

We would of course prefer to have your check; but, for the benefit of your business, your customers, and your creditors, won't you please settle your account with us today?

ULTIMATUM

If there is no response to the serious mood, the strong appeal, and the big-heartedness of the executive's offer of still another chance to save the debtor's credit rating, the collector will give the screw its last turn. He now assumes that he will have to squeeze the money out of the debtor. He has decided that as long as he gives this debtor any slack, he will move around in it. The collector therefore notifies the debtor that on a definite date, usually 5–10 days later, he will turn the account over to a collection agency or to a lawyer—unless he receives payment before that time.

Though the language of the ultimatum is firm, it should not be harsh. The action itself, however, is inclined to anger the delinquent customer. To minimize his resentment, the collector commonly reviews the whole case at this point to show that he cannot well do otherwise, that he has been fair and considerate all along (but he does not become self-righteous about it), that he dislikes to take the necessary action, but that it is justified. Carefully worded, this letter may collect and still retain good will because of the fair-play appeal in the whole review. Usually it will at least collect, as these two letters did:

When we sent you your first credit shipment of $95 worth of Christmas supplies under Invoice CA-872 on December 4, we took the step that all stationery wholesalers take when granting similar credit requests: we verified your good credit reputation with the National Stationery Manufacturers' Guild, of which we are a member.

The Guild's certification meant that you invariably pay your bills. When we received a second order on January 26, we were happy to serve you again by shipping $42 worth of Valentine cut-outs and art supplies, under Invoice CB-345. Since then we have tried to be both reasonable and considerate in inducing you to pay by our usual collection procedures. Now we shall be compelled by the terms of our membership agreement to submit your name to the Guild as "nonpay" unless we receive your check for $137 by April 15.

You are no doubt aware of the effects of being labeled by the Guild as nonpay. Credit requests to new supply houses will be refused; old sources will be reluctant to continue supplying you on a credit basis. We want to help you maintain your preferred status so that you can continue to stock your shelves through easy credit mail orders.

With the sincerity of a friend, I urge you to weigh carefully the effects of a bad report and the advantages of a favorable one on your hard-earned and well-thought-of credit rating. I urge you to avoid the necessity of our submitting an unfavorable report. And beyond that, of course, would be a suit in which you would not only pay the bill but the court costs.

All the advantages of an unmarred credit standing among suppliers are yours now. Mail us your check for $137 by the 15th and retain those advantages.

Let's talk once more about your 95-day overdue account amounting to $68 for the butcher supplies you bought July 15.

That buying was done a long time ago, Mr. Forrest, and the sale was made on the basis that you would pay within 30 days. By your acceptance of the goods, you made a contract to pay according to the terms.

Although this contract is legal and binding, we usually use the Wholesale Credit Men's Association, rather than the courts, as our final collection agency. You are probably familiar with this Association and know what a stamp of "bad pay" on its record can do to you. Every supply house is a member. It's almost impossible for any firm to get credit on supplies with a bad record in the Association files; and it's difficult for a retailer to operate without credit.

Think it over and see if it's not worth $68 plus the small amount of time necessary to write out a check. Your account should have been reported as an overdue one before now, but I like to give a man a warning and a last chance.

Let us hear from you with a check enclosed for $68, not later than the 28th.

If an ultimatum like the two above does not bring the money by the date set, the only remaining letter to write is a courtesy letter, not a collection letter, telling the customer of the action that has been taken. Then the case is out of the hands of the writer of collection letters and in the hands of a lawyer. In any event, the collection series ends with the ultimatum.

COLLECTING UNEARNED DISCOUNTS

A special problem which does not fit into the regular collection procedure is that of collecting unearned discounts (that is, discounts taken when sending payment of a bill after the end of the discount period). The difficulty is increased by the fact that the amount is usually small—

always small in comparison with the volume of business the collector is risking in trying to collect. Moreover, some of the larger purchasers know their importance to the collector's firm and try to bulldoze him because of it. They know he would think twice before losing their $200 orders to collect an improper $4 discount.

Fortunately, the collector usually has some advantages on his side, too:

1. When the occasion arises, he is almost certainly dealing with experienced businessmen who understand business practices and will understand a businessman's reasoned analysis.
2. The sizable purchaser has almost certainly investigated various sources of supply and has settled on the collector's. He might be as reluctant to change suppliers as the collector would be to lose him as a customer.
3. If the collector cannot get his money in early to use for financing the business, there is no justification for allowing discounts. He will need that money to pay interest on money borrowed for financing while slow collections are coming in. As a businessman, the debtor will understand that the ultimate end to his action of not paying on time will be a revised system in which he has no possibility of discount at all.
4. The fair-play appeal can be broadened to include playing fair with all the collector's other customers. That is, he cannot well allow one to take the unearned discount while requiring others to pay according to terms.

Armed thus, the collector is ready for the taker of unearned discounts. First, he can certainly start by assuming that the deduction was just a little misunderstanding of the terms. If there is any doubt about whether the terms were made clear, he may assume responsibility, make the terms clear, and overlook the improper deduction THE FIRST TIME.

When there is no doubt, the collector can certainly assume (reasonably enough) that the unjustified deduction is a result of a failure to check the dates—an unintentional chiseling—and that the additional money will be forthcoming after a little reminder. One writer used an analogy for the reminder by telling the story of the boy who presented nine apples as his mother's offering for the harvest festival. When the vicar said he would call to thank the mother, the boy asked him please to thank her for ten apples.

If the collector finds that neither misunderstanding of the terms nor failure to check dates is the reason for the improper deduction of unearned discount, he has a real letter-writing job. Though well armed— with justice, legal advantages, and some psychology on their side— some collectors fear to go ahead. The almost inevitable result is chaos in the collection department, or at least in the discount system. Word gets around.

The bold do better. Their appeals are Item 3 above (the economic justification of discounting practices) and Item 4 (the broadened fair-play appeal). Often a good letter combines both, as in some of the following illustrations:

> From your letter of May 25 we can well understand why you feel entitled to the 2% discount from our Invoice X-10 of April 30. If some of our creditors allowed us discounts after the end of the discount period, we too might expect others to do the same.
>
> The discount you get from us when you pay within a definite, specified period is simply our passing on to you the saving our creditors allow us for using the money we collect promptly and paying our bills within ten days after making purchases. It's certainly true that your discount of $4.57 is small; but large or small, we would have allowed it if we had had your payment in time to use in making a similar saving in paying our own bills. If our creditors gave us a longer time, we'd gladly give you a longer time.
>
> Since they don't, I believe you see that the only solutions besides following the terms are stopping all discounts, taking the loss on all our sales, or being unfair to our many other customers by making exceptions and showing favoritism. I don't think you want us to do any of those things, do you, Mr. Griggs?
>
> When you mail us your check for the full invoice amount of $228.57, we know that you will do so with the spirit of good business practice and fairness.
>
> Thank you again for your order. You will find that our merchandise and attractive prices will always assure you of a more-than-average profit.
>
> The fact that we are returning your check for $2,450 does not mean that we don't appreciate your business. Rather, we want you to use your money for ten more days and, from your experience, to answer a question on which we want your opinion.
>
> Before I ask the question, however, I want to stress the fact that we consider your company an ideal outlet for our products in your area. Apparently you also consider our products a good line to sell.
>
> But evidently we are not in such complete agreement on the matter of cash discount as established in our terms of 2/10, n/30. The question is: Is your money worth 36% a year to you? Under our terms we pay you 2% for the use of your money for twenty days (the time between the discount date and the net-due date) or 36% a year. We do this because it is a trade practice, but there is no justification for it unless we have the money during those twenty days. We have no right, of course, to use your money even part of that time without paying for the use of it; so we are returning your check and asking that you pay the net of $2,500 on the due date, ten days hence.

We believe you will welcome this frank presentation so that you can give discounts your fair-minded consideration. May we have your decision?

That letter did both of its jobs of collecting the money and retaining the customer. Certainly it was not written by the distrusting merchant who told a new employee that if somebody wanted to pay a bill and somebody else yelled FIRE, to take the money first and then put out the fire.

The problem of unearned discount becomes particularly difficult after you have allowed one exception, explained the terms carefully, refused to allow a second exception, and received a reply including statements like these:

> . . . I thought that an organization such as yours would be above such hair-splitting tactics . . . and I resent your hiding behind a mere technicality to collect an additional $3.69 . . . oversight. . . . If you wish . . . a new check will be mailed, but . . . it will be your last from us.

Here's how one collection writer handled that hot potato—successfully:

> I appreciate your letter of December 5 because it gives me an opportunity to explain our request that you mail us a check for $184.50 in place of the one for $180.81.
>
> It was prompted primarily by our sincere desire to be entirely fair to you and all our other customers. For years we have allowed a discount of two percent to all who pay their bills within ten days of the invoice date. Such prompt payment enables us to make a similar saving by paying our own bills promptly. Thus we pass on to you and our other customers the savings their prompt payments allow us to make.
>
> But if our customers wait longer than the ten days to pay us, there is no saving for us to pass on. Of course, an allowance of $3.69 is a small matter, but if we allowed it in one case we would have to allow similar discounts to all our customers or be unfair to some. The principle involved is a serious one, since any exception would have to become the rule if we are to be fair to all.
>
> I feel sure that you want us to treat all customers alike, just as you do in your own business. Certainly I do not think you would like it if you found that we were more lenient with somebody else than with you. Our request for the additional $3.69 is necessary if we are to treat all alike.
>
> Thank you again for writing me and giving me this chance to explain. May we have your check—in fairness to all?

HUMOR IN COLLECTIONS

Generally, past-due accounts are not laughing matters, either for the debtor or for the collector. But small amounts early in the collection procedure are not deadly serious matters either. In the early stages, where little or no persuasion is presumed to be necessary or even desirable, the main job of the letter is to gain attention and remind the debtor. Under these circumstances a humorous letter may be just the thing. Its sprightliness will supply the attention and memory value needed. The light mood will take the sting out of the letter and make the collector seem like a friendly human being instead of an ogre.

A widely known and highly successful collection letter, the famous "Elmer" letter by Miles Kimball, pictures both kinds of collection man. The writer, a friendly human, warns the debtor against the ogre, Elmer, treasurer of the company, who sometimes gets out of hand and writes letters that destroy a reader's will to live. The whole thing is a detailed and ridiculous account of the kind of ogre Elmer is and the disastrous effects of his letters, plus a brief warning to pay now before Elmer writes.

Shorter humorous letters are more usual. For example, there is the one which merely asks for the name of the best lawyer in the debtor's town, in case the collector has to sue. The New York *Journal of Commerce* reported a few years ago that one collector was simply mailing small, live turtles to slow payers. *Time* has long used two humorous letters for people who don't pay for their subscriptions. One, on the back of the front picture cover of the current issue of *Time,* begins "I'm sorry—sorry I can't send you any more than the cover of this week's *TIME.*" It then goes into a brief resale appeal. The other begins with the assertion of how much is due, proceeds to poke fun at the usual collection letter, shows how large numbers of small accounts add up, and ends with the pun that "procrastination is the thief of *TIME.*" Still another journal begins a subscription-collection with

"CHECKING, JUST CHECKING,"

said the telephone lineman when the lady jumped out of the bathtub to answer. I'm just checking to find out whether you want to continue to receive. . . .

The rest of the letter is the usual resale appeal with a standard action ending.

Another device is that called the one-sided or half-and-half letter. The writer presents what is essentially an inquiry-stage collection letter as a narrow column on the left half of the page and asks the reader to use the right half to attach his check or explain.

Though such letters (usually inexpensive forms) may be effective in collecting small amounts early in the series, they are too flippant for large amounts or late-stage collections. The exception is that they might be used just before an ultimatum with the hope of jolting the debtor out of his rut. But we must not forget that

1. The credit obligation is a serious responsibility and we can't expect the debtor to take it seriously if we are undignified about it.
2. Written joshing is more likely to offend than oral banter.
3. Gadgeteering and humor in letters of all kinds is likely to be overrated because we are more likely to hear of the occasional successes than of the numerous failures.

LEGAL DANGERS IN COLLECTIONS

In preparing collection letters, especially those of the late stages, the collector needs to be familiar with the privileges and limitations imposed upon him by law. Reporting delinquents to credit associations which are set up within the law (for mutual protection of members' interests) and threats of civil suit to collect money are both legal. Threats of physical violence are not permissible in the mails, and threats to accuse the debtor of a criminal offense or other threats of extortion or blackmail are illegal. (See Appendix B, p. 599, for more detail.)

The other important aspect of law applicable to collections is libel— that is, the writing of injurious comments about somebody and not taking proper precautions against their being read by a third party. The best way to avoid a libel suit is to avoid making libelous comments. But collectors cannot always do that. Any attempt to collect after the due date may be interpreted as implying dishonesty, unreliability, or slow pay. Any of these may damage the credit or reputation of the debtor and be libelous if read by a third party (even the debtor's secretary), unless the sender has taken reasonable precautions to see that nobody except the debtor reads it. Therefore, all collection efforts after the due date should be sent in sealed envelopes; and, if the sender knows that a secretary or anybody else regularly opens the reader's mail, they should also be marked PERSONAL.

Libel may be both a civil and a criminal offense. That is, the damaged party may sue for damages (civil suit), and the state may impose a fine or jail sentence on the guilty. Truth and good faith (absence of malicious intent) together constitute an adequate defense against both kinds of libel suits. Good faith is usually adequate against criminal charges, and truth is adequate against civil charges in most states, but not in all. To protect himself from legal difficulties, therefore, the collector should:

1. Be sure his past-due collection efforts are sealed, so that only the debtor will read them.
2. Never make defamatory statements or accusations maliciously.
3. Be sure to get his facts right.

BEGINNINGS AND ENDINGS

For most writers the beginnings and endings of letters, including collection letters, are the most troublesome spots. Beginnings are more difficult than endings because the background or point of contact is more varied than the desired action, and therefore the beginning cannot be well standardized.

This much, however, can be said: You have to capture the reader's attention and interest and hold it through the letter. Indentification of the account (the amount due, what for, and when due) should be clear in every case, but those facts do not make good beginnings; the reader has already shown his lack of interest in them. Neither is the beginning job well done by references to former attempts to collect. Such references may sound like whining or may suggest that the debtor can again ignore the request with impunity. Since collections are basically sales letters—selling the debtor on the benefits of paying—the collector will do well to reapply the principle of reader-benefit beginnings.

Just as the salesman drives for an order at the end of his sales talk, so does the good collection writer strive to bring in a check or an explanation that will name a payment date. So the standard action ending—telling what to do, making clear how to do it, making action easy, and providing a stimulus to prompt action—is always proper except in the early stages of the series, where it is too forceful. There resale or sales-promotional talk rather than the request for payment usually ends the letter to imply faith, appeal to pride, perhaps promote sales, and remove the sting. Though the collector always writes with success-consciousness because he expects his letter to bring results, in none except the one serving notice that the account has been placed in the hands of an attorney does he fail to leave the way open for more severe action, as in the following forceful requests:

Please sit down NOW—while your resolution is still strong—and send us your check for the balance of $225 due on your Christmas purchases. Your name will then remain in the preferred-customer file.

Won't you come by our office Saturday night and close this account in such a way that we can write a completely satisfactory comment about you on our records?

We're enclosing an addressed envelope that we expect to see back in our office—with a check enclosed for $100—before the 15th.

Wherever feasible the collection writer will find it advisable to make response easy for the debtor. An already addressed and stamped envelope does that and also provides a strong stimulus to prompt action. The DMAA *Bulletin* (May, 1944) reported that 798 collection letters sent without reply envelopes brought remittances from 42.85 per cent and requests for time extensions from 6.78 per cent for a total of 49.63 per cent answering but that a similar mailing of 798 letters which included reply envelopes brought remittances from 45.12 per cent and requests for extensions from 16.80 per cent for a total of 61.92 per cent responding. Even the casual "Don't bother to write a letter; just slip your check into the enclosed envelope . . ." will show the debtor the friendly attitude you have toward him and will frequently produce the check.

Because collection-letter circumstances vary so much, there are few universal truths about them suitable for a check list such as we have provided for some other types of letters. But the accompanying suggestions (next two pages) will be helpful as a partial check list for collection letters.

Collections

1. As Credit Manager of Illini Equipment and Supply Company, Chicago, you extended credit to Mr. Jackson Brock, owner, Blue Mill Restaurant, University Avenue, Iowa City, for the following equipment to be paid for in 60 days (the prices including delivery and installation):

1 Garnett Range; Gas with automatic oven lighting	$ 428.00
1 Hobart Dishwasher Model AMA	1,345.00
1 Autosan Dishwasher RL-20	1,100.00
1 Refrigerator—Model RA-408 Victory Sta-Kold	725.00
1 Scotsman Ice Maker SF-75 WSF 200# size	748.00
1 Blodgett Oven Combination Roast & Bake Section #908	587.70
	$4,933.70

According to credit information, you found that Brock has been in business 10 years, owns the building that the restaurant is in, owns his home, as well as an 80-acre farm. He bought out his brother in the restaurant business two years ago and has been doing a larger volume of business this year than last. To be able to serve more people, however, he decided to make the restaurant cafeteria style and to replace obsolete kitchen equipment. Since 75 days have gone by and you've not heard from Brock in response to your routine notification on the due date, you wrote him a friendly request containing resale on the house and goods, and sales talk on a related item. Mr. Brock answered the letter with a check for $1,000 and a promise of more to come in

Collection Letter Check List

1. Follow a reasonable philosophy and adapted procedure.
   a) Associate the specific goods with the obligation to pay for them and show that you *expect payment because it is due.*
   b) Identify how much is due and how long overdue in every letter.
   c) After the first two stages, these identifications (in *b,* and perhaps the point in *a*) are *not* good beginnings. You need a Type-C beginning, mentioning reader benefits to get attention.
   d) Stick to your sequence of assumptions for the different collection stages; backtracking shows your weakness and loses reader respect.
   e) Try to get the money *and* keep the customer's good will.
2. Fit the tone carefully to the circumstances.
   a) Avoid seeming to tell the reader how to run his business. (Reader-interest reasons for payment and resale material help to avoid preachiness.)
   b) Nasty, curt, injured, pouting, exasperated, or harsh tone serves only to turn the reader against you and make collection harder.
   c) A condescending or scolding holier-than-thou attitude will bring more resentment than money.
   d) To avoid the condescension of uttering credit platitudes, subordinate references to credit principles and regulations by emphasizing their significance in the particular case.
   e) Show confidence that the debtor will pay, by
      (1) avoiding references to past or future correspondence (which sound like whining and suggest ignoring this letter too), and
      (2) stressing positive benefits of payment (not dire results of nonpayment).
   f) Be sure any humor you use makes a point without irritation or distraction from the seriousness of the credit obligation.
   g) Avoid (1) accusations, (2) apologies for requesting payment, and —except in the reminder and inquiry stages—(3) excuses invented for the reader. Let him find his own—including, at all stages, any fault he may think he finds in the goods or billing.

30 days. Thank him for the check and remind him that, since the account is overdue, you expect the balance within the indicated 30 days.

2. After 45 days and no further word from Brock, write him, outlining a definite payment plan requiring payment immediately of $933.70 and 6 per cent notes dated 30, 60, and 90 days ahead.

3. Still you get no answer from Mr. Brock of the preceding two problems. Today, when the account is 75 days overdue, over the signature of Martin Baier, president, write a letter explaining that he must pay or face the consequences of meeting your attorney in court. Although you establish un-

COLLECTION LETTER CHECK LIST (CONTINUED)

b) Increase the force of your request with more credit and collection talk and less resale or (in early letters to good customers) sales-promotion material.

i) To decrease stringency, reverse *h*.

3. For persuasiveness (after the first two collection stages),

   a) You have to stress what the reader gains by doing as you ask, not your desires.

   b) Remember the effectiveness of a central theme—a unified, fully developed point—as opposed to scattered shots scantily treated.

   c) Select an appeal appropriate to the circumstances and reader.

   d) Any kind of antagonizing works against you, makes persuasion harder.

   e) Individualize your message for greater effectiveness. Even though you use a form for economy, selected form paragraphs and fill-ins can make it seem to be for the one reader.

4. Guard against the legal dangers.

   a) Reporting the delinquent to anybody except those employed to help collect or those who request the information because of an interest to protect (like credit associations) is dangerous.

   b) Don't threaten physical violence, blackmail, or extortion.

   c) Be sure of your facts and show no malice.

   d) Be sure (by sealing and marking "Personal" when necessary) that only the debtor will read your efforts to collect overdue accounts.

5. Adapt your drive for action to the stage of the collection procedure.

   a) A full-fledged action paragraph is too forceful and stinging in early stages.

   b) But in the appeal and later stages, anything short of the full action ending—making clear what to do and how to do it, making action easy, and showing a benefit of immediate action—is too weak.

mistakably the increased costs and the effect on his credit reputation of the legal action, positively tell him what he keeps for himself by paying voluntarily. This letter makes a special effort to be friendly but final; it should not dwell on the threat; instead, it is an earnest and sympathetic plea that Brock forestall the bad results which his inaction will inevitably bring about. Give him 10 days more in which to reply.

4. Vaughn-Wild, furriers, 1908 Second Street, St. Louis, Missouri, where you work as collection and credit manager, sold an Autumn Haze mink cape ($748 including tax) to Mrs. Charles Bismarck, 1908 Alton Street, Belleville, Illinois, on an easy-payment plan with no carrying charges (6 payments, $124 for 4 and $126 for 2). She made the first 4 payments of $124 each when they came due. But now it's ten days past the due date for the fifth payment. Write her a friendly early-stage collection letter with touches of resale.

5. Mrs. Bismarck of the preceding problem ignored your letter telling her that the fifth payment is past due. After ten more days you wrote her another pleasant letter reminding her of the value of mink—how long she can wear the flattering cape and what a value she has. You thought it was a good letter, but she still didn't send you any money. Now (ten days later) that the fifth payment is 30 days late and the sixth and final one due, write her a more stringent letter with the theme that she has to pay only $252—that the cape is more than half paid for. Perhaps she'd like to arrange easier terms with you. If she'll just come in or write you, you'll co-operate with her.

6. The next letter you wrote Mrs. Bismarck of the two preceding problems (ten days later), you sent by registered mail. Apparently she had not moved; the letter was signed for. But she still did not write or come in. In this final letter (ten days later) that you are writing today, give her 10 more days. If she has not sent you some explanation—or, even better, some money—you are turning the case over to your lawyer, Baton and Baton of St. Louis. A lawsuit is expensive. She would do much better to send you the $252 she owes for the fifth and sixth payments right away. You have to remind her that she signed a promissory note with a repossession clause.

7. Laney Furniture Company, Norman, Oklahoma, sent your wholesale firm (Hermitage Company, 191 South Madison Avenue, Chicago) a check for $554.95 to cover your recent invoice. This was the net amount of the invoice less 2 per cent discount on terms 2/10, n/30. The check, however, was sent 10 days after the discount period elapsed. You returned the check and asked for one to cover the net amount of the bill. J. T. Laney (owner and manager) wrote you that other wholesalers allowed the discounting of bills a few days late, and he expected the same consideration from you. As credit manager of your firm, write the letter explaining the origin and purpose of discounts as your reason for insisting on payment according to terms by all your customers. Remember, but do not quote from, the literature of the National Association of Credit Men: "Fairness in respecting discount terms is an absolute requisite to sound business practice. In every case of improper deduction the seller has the definite obligation to return the payment offered." In the Association's Ledger Interchange Service, one of the questions which each creditor must answer is whether a debtor makes improper deductions. Ask for a check in full payment of the account.

8. To get the money, yet retain the good will, of Mr. J. T. Blair, manager of The Sun and Surf Speciality Shop, 143 Beach Street, Ft. Lauderdale, Florida, write a middle-stage collection letter that shows him why it is to his advantage to pay. One hundred and twenty days ago you sent him 3 dozen women's bathing suits amounting to $358.20 (terms 2/10, n/30). His order of Maiden-Swim lastex suits included: 12 blue, Style 2458, sizes 14, 16, 18; 12 black, Style 26759, sizes 16, 18, 20; and 12 red, Style 2634, sizes 12, 14, 16. Mr. Blair has been buying from you (the Maiden-Swim Company, Akron, Ohio) irregularly (and paying the same way) for three years. This is the third letter besides a due-date notice you've written about the last shipment. Write the letter over the signature of the credit manager.

9. Mr. J. T. Blair (see preceding problem) doesn't respond to your third letter either. Try your hand at writing a fourth letter thirty days later that asks for the amount due ($358.20) and explains what you'll have to do (turn the account over to the National Manufacturers Collection System) promptly at the end of fifteen days. You can assume that the winter season is about to begin in Florida; therefore, he should have many customers for these popular swim suits.

10. Forty-five days ago you acknowledged an initial order from Ramon's Shop, Tucson, Arizona, and shipped the following canned Mexican food specialties—

24 Tamales @ 40¢	$ 9.60
48 Tacos @ 60¢	28.80
24 Enchiladas @ 50¢	12.00
48 Tortillas @ 12½¢	6.00
	$56.40

—charged under your regular terms of 2/10, n/30 to Mr. Ramon Garcia, owner of the shop. As credit manager of the Latinos Food Company, San Antonio 11, Texas, you sent a notification of the due date. On this 45th day you write a friendly note, reminding him of the due date and containing resale on one of the items, and sales-promotional material on a new item —pulque dulce pralines—12 to a box. They are prettily packaged, deliciously flavored (6 wrapped in light pink paper and 6 in light green). They are packed in a handsome wooden box with Mexican scenic cover— only $2.00, but he can sell for $3.00. Now write this friendly first personalized letter.

11. On the 60th day you wrote another short, friendly note to Mr. Garcia of the preceding problem. "With a holiday season so near, you'll be asked more and more for Latinos specialty food items. In order to help increase your sales during this busy season, we've designed some festive displays. If you'd like some for Ramon's, just write us a note when you send your check for $56.40 for the Latinos Special Mexican Foods sent you 60 days ago." Now, although the account is 60 days old (30 days overdue), you begin persuasive efforts to make Mr. Ramon Garcia pay. This is a heavy buying season, it's true; but the demand for Mexican Foods is pretty steady—and steady payments will enable him to maintain steady orders and sales. "Keep the account in shape" is the theme.

12. That good letter you wrote Mr. Garcia (preceding problem) went unanswered. So did the ones you wrote when the account was 60 days overdue and the long "let's talk it over" letter that you addressed to him when the account was 80 days overdue. Ten more days have elapsed; so you're forced to turn to outside help if the check or satisfactory arrangement isn't forthcoming. The National Credit Bureau may not get your money for you, but the report you'll have to send within 10 days won't help Garcia's credit standing. For his sake and yours, you would prefer that he pay now and not have this report affect his business—as it will, inevitably. If he pays up

within 10 days, he can still get goods on credit, open new accounts, buy what he needs when he needs it. The letter should tell specifically what will happen, with the viewpoint of helping him avoid it.

13. As credit manager for the Debraft Wholesalers, Atlanta, Georgia, you granted credit to Mr. Daniel Wade, manager of the Toggery Shop, 445 Prince Avenue, Athens, Georgia, on terms 2/10, n/30 for $165 worth of men's rayon robes (6 navy robes, size 38, @ $15 and 6 wine polka dot print robes, size 36, @ $12.50). On the 8th day you sent him the usual form calling attention to the discount date; but when you received no reply, you took it for granted that he would pay during the net period. On the 28th day you sent him another form note telling him that the amount was due by the 30th. But again no reply. So, when the account was 45 days old (15 days overdue), you sent another memorandum note. Still no luck. Now write a collection letter to be sent when the account is 30 days overdue. Keep in mind the goods bought, his use of the credit account, and sales promotional talk for the coming season.

14. The letter you wrote to Mr. Daniel Wade of the preceding problem when the account was 30 days overdue went unanswered. Fifteen days later you wrote what you thought was a persuasive letter, still confident in its assumption. The idea behind this letter was: "We know you don't like this delay any more than we do, and we are sure that you will want to send us your check for $165 for the men's rayon robes sent you on account, now 45 days overdue. Your record clearly tells us you realize the value of paying promptly." Now Mr. Wade's account is 60 days overdue. Write him and tell him that he should pay his obligation to keep the reputation he now enjoys.

15. Still no luck in getting a check from Mr. Wade of the two preceding problems. When the account was 75 days past the due date you wrote: "Please check your books this morning and note especially the 75-day overdue bill for 6 navy rayon robes, size 38, @ $15 and 6 wine rayon polka dot print robes, size 36, @ $12.50 ($165) which you owe us. As a good businessman you probably don't hesitate to extend credit to those customers who pay; but you hesitate when they fail to come through. And you, too, realize the importance of keeping your slate clean. Send us a check for $165 and keep your slate clean." Unfortunately, Mr. Wade ignored this letter too. So now, when the account is 90 days overdue, you are to write the final letter. As a member of the National Wholesale Credit Association you must report accounts delinquent for 90 days or longer. You'll not report him for 10 days; but he must send a check by then for his own good. Point out what he gains by paying, so that what he loses by not paying is clearly established.

16. In the last five years George Harris has purchased over $1,500 worth of appliances from your store, L. L. Adams Appliance Center, 514 Broad Street, Toledo, Ohio. Harris has a good credit rating. Five months ago he bought an all-porcelain automatic washing machine at $305.95, paying a substantial amount and saying he'd take care of the small balance later. To this arrange-

ment you were glad to agree. Three months later the manufacturer of the machine reduced the price on this model $50 in an attempt to free the market for washer-dryer combinations. Shortly after, Harris wrote you, the manager of the Appliance Center, pointing out that since the reduction was more than the balance of his account ($40), he thought some adjustment should be granted.

In your reply you pointed out that the price reduction was that of the manufacturer, that the Appliance Center still had to pay the original cost of the washing machine Harris bought. You further explained that the manufacturer made no adjustment to dealers on models already sold, and so there was no price adjustment which would be passed on to customers. Harris did not reply. You have sent him first-of-the-month reminders on two occasions since, but he still hasn't responded. Write him now, requesting payment of his account.

17. When the Sutton Department Store approved credit terms for Mr. Harvey Kellum two years ago, it had a report from the credit bureau which said: "Mr. Kellum is a labor foreman for Logan Long roofing company. Always pays promptly. His weekly income is about $120 net. Good character and doing good business. Credit good to $300." You can't understand why he'd mar a good credit standing like this by allowing a suit ($85) he bought six months ago to go unpaid for. For such a small amount, you don't sue. Nor will you insist that it all be paid at once. He can work out a time-payment plan to suit his circumstances. You've written him five letters. He must pay something by the end of the month. If he is absolutely unable to pay, you want him to come in and explain. If you don't hear from him by the first of next month, you'll have to turn his account over to your collection agency.

18. Assume that you are the owner and manager of Town and Country, an exclusive women's shop catering to town and college trade in your locality. Accounts average $30–$55, though some run much higher. You send a notification of the amount due on the first of the month following purchase; if the account remains unpaid, on the first of the following month you send an unitemized reminder with a cheerful attached printed sticker which expresses appreciation and requests payment. You now need four letters, all forms to be sent at 30-day intervals thereafter. Each will begin "Dear Friend of Town and Country"; below the signature you plan to run three identifications, like this:

> Amount due _____
> For (item or items) _____
> Bought (date) _____

In handwriting you intend to insert the appropriate information in each case. In the first letter (to come after the account is 60 days past due) sell the shop and its unusual merchandise (David Dowel suits, Toni Sharp originals, imported scarves and gloves). In the second, that will arrive when the account is 90 days past due, find out whether something unusual prevents payment, and whether you can help. In the third letter (120 days) talk credit—arrangements, ratings, and procedures. Your last letter (150 days) must definitely inform the reader that the account will be turned over to the local credit bureau for further handling unless the account is paid in 10 days.

19. You are the credit manager of Truck and Tractor Company, Philadelphia, wholesale dealers of farm supplies. Charles L. Morris, owner of Morris Company, 198 Germantown Street, Allentown, Pennsylvania, one of your dealers, owes you $375.50, which is 4 weeks past due. Morris is reliable but sometimes slow in payment when his own collections are slow. In answer to a recent letter from you, he said that he would pay when his farm customers sold their crops. This will be in about a month. Write him and ask him to sign a promissory note. You can explain that you have some exceptionally heavy bills to meet in payment for incoming stock. You can discount his note and use the proceeds for this purpose. Make the explanation and the request tactfully.

20. One of your charge customers, Mr. Whitfield McMillen, 654 West William Street, Peoria, Illinois, bought a portable Admiral TV from the department store, Gephardt's, where you are collection manager. He paid $10 down and signed a budget contract calling for $15 a month for 10 months for the balance. This month you didn't get his check for the $15, and it is now 6 days past due. Write him a letter calling his attention to the rules of installment buying and stressing the importance of keeping a good credit rating.

21. The City Furniture Company, Davenport, Iowa, where you are employed in the credit and collection department, charged for C. W. Hayes, 6110 Glendale Avenue, same city, a $110 Lawson sofa bought 3 months and 5 days ago. Despite the several collection notices and letters you have sent him, he still has not paid his bill. Today his wife came to the store, ordered a set of 3 snack tables, $14.95, and left before the sales clerk had sent the charge slip to your department. Write the appropriate letter in which you diplomatically point out that you cannot add to his already overdue account and that the $110 must be paid before the tables are sent.

22. You sold Luther Callahan, 1908 Jackson Street, your city, whose credit is unquestioned, a subscription to *Live* magazine (78 weeks, $7.87). When sending the original order, he agreed to pay on receipt of the bill. You have sent him two bills and three follow-up letters without result. Write a letter that will collect the $7.87 and still retain his friendship.

23. The Town and Gown Shop where you work as bookkeeper has as one of its well-to-do customers, Mrs. Burton D. Price, 19 Country Club Hills, of your city. Her account amounting to $258 is now 60 days past due. Mrs. Price has ignored two printed notices and one personal letter. Be courteous but firm in this second personal letter.

24. The Roth Johnson Pharmacy, Hibbing, Minnesota, owes your drug company, Spears, St. Paul, $118.87 for assorted drug and medical supplies, now

3 months overdue. Write a middle-stage letter (the third) making it clear that it is to Roth Johnson's benefit to pay—he can clear his account for future buying.

25. The Roth Johnson Pharmacy (preceding problem) still hasn't paid you the $118.87, now 6 months overdue. Write a sixth and final letter making it clear that you are going to report the account to the credit bureau of your trade association in 5 days. What will this mean to the debtor? Make sure that he understands.

26. You are manager of the credit department of the Fulman and Fuller Manufacturing Company, Salt Lake City, Utah. Write a collection letter to Thomas Senna, 1908 Plain Avenue, Eureka, Utah, who bought a 17-inch table TV and cart both for $155.50, 2 months ago. Mr. Senna agreed to pay for the TV and cart when he received his seasonal bonus. He has failed to pay the debt, despite two notifications and a letter. His monthly salary is $300, but his bonus often is as much as $200.

27. You are with Handley and Minor, your city, selling building supplies. With a recent recession, your city has been suffering a building slump. Brooks Foreman, 1980 Woodland Hills, a reliable local building contractor, owes $167.98, now a month past due. Write an appropriate letter.

28. You are the collection manager of the Credit Finance Company, your city. James D. Owen, 758 Gray Street, die worker in a local factory, has borrowed $65 from you to be repaid $5 a week. He has missed two payments, and the third is 4 days overdue. Write him a letter telling him that you are going to get a judgment in court—then you'll serve a notice of garnishment on his employer, who must deduct the amount from Owen's salary and pay it to you. How will this affect his relations with his employer?

29. A dealer (L. T. Haines and Company, 6790 Prairie Street, Cincinnati, Ohio) owes $96.75, now over a month past due with your company, Mirado Pen and Pencil Company, 198 Wacker Drive, Chicago, manufacturers of pens and pencils. Write him a letter based on the idea that your prices have not been advanced, even though there has been a 10 per cent increase in labor costs. Maintaining the old price has been possible only because of careful management and attention to all details.

30. A week after the date of your (Western Furniture Company, Inc., San Francisco) invoice to Mr. Jonathan Baines, owner-manager of The City Furniture Company, Olympia, Washington, for the furniture that you shipped on terms 2/10, n/60—tables and chairs of Far Eastern woods (bamboo, teakwood, sandalwood) and design—total cost plus freight, $561.75—you sent him a suggestion about taking the discount. The customary notification on the due date followed. Now it's 30 days after due date, and you write a friendly letter showing him the advantages of a prompt-pay rating and telling him about your small miniature chest lac-

quered with small designs that are available in red and black for $30. They are attractive placed at the ends of modern sofas or near low chairs. Suggest he order and send his check at the same time.

31. Although you and your salesman, Hugh Barlow, feel that Mr. Baines of the preceding problem can pay, he still doesn't answer your letters. Since he has one of the two leading furniture stores in town and has been in business twenty-five years, you felt that you had to be patient and wait 30 more days before sending him a second letter. So when the account was 60 days overdue, your letter was basically this: "Maybe there is a *good* reason why your account for $561.75 for furniture sent 120 days ago is not paid. If so, won't you tell me by return mail when you can pay. Like any firm that values your account, we value your good will. A delay in prompt payment—as long as it is explained—doesn't injure your credit rating." Mr. Baines didn't answer this letter either; so now that it's 80 days after the due date, you write him a forceful letter pointing out the value of his credit rating that he worked hard to earn—what it does for him—why he needs it. You omit any sales-promotional material on any other goods, but you can have short resale talk on the furniture ordered.

32. You still had no word from Mr. Baines of the two preceding problems when the account was 105 days overdue. So you wrote him a short, friendly note: "Let's talk with the frankness of friends about the $561.75 you owe us for the furniture sent 165 days ago. It took you years to build up your good credit rating, but you can lose it in a few short months by allowing your bills to go unpaid. Won't you write us today arranging payment for your account, or better still—just send us your check for the full amount." Mr. Baines apparently plans to ignore this friendly letter, too. So when the account is 120 days overdue, you must write the last letter and tell him that he *must* pay or face the consequences. His name will be reported to the National Manufacturers Credit Association. By positively telling what he keeps for himself by paying, you make clear what he loses by not paying. He'll have just 10 days to answer.

33. On the 8th day after you (as credit manager of the Atlanta Equipment Supply Co.) sent a shipment of 2 refrigerated open meat display cases ($600) on terms of 2/10, n/30 to Mr. Dewey Sanders, owner of the Sanders Stop 'N Shop, Tallahassee, Florida, you sent him a cordial note about the end of the discount date, mentioning that the discount saving would pay the phone bill. On the 30th day, the collection routine dictated the impersonal notification which you sent to Mr. Sanders. No reply. So on the 45th day, when normally a second formal notice is used, you sent Mr. Sanders a short personal note, with more resale and sales-promotional than collection talk. Still silence. Now that the collection file reminder shows Mr. Sanders marked for special attention on the 60th day ($600 account, 30 days overdue), you are writing another friendly note, talking up as its central theme the value of a prompt-pay rating as particularly adapted to this grocer in a small city far removed from his sources of supply. This is clearly

an early letter; there is no intimation that the account is in jeopardy, least of all with backward- or forward-looking references to other correspondence.

34. On the 75th day after Mr. Sanders of the preceding problem bought meat display cases from you, you wrote (when the account was 45 days overdue) him another letter trying to show him that his slow-paying habits really cost him money in the long run. "If folks pay for a meat cleaver in the normal time of 30 days, we can sell it for $6. But if the time stretches out 60, 90, 120 days, costs of record keeping, collection, and financing increase; and the meat cleaver you now pay only $6 for would cost 20, 30 or 50 cents more. Isn't it, therefore, the smart thing to pay bills on time?" He didn't answer. Now with the $600 account 60 days overdue, you decide to write him a bit firmer letter, stressing the value of a good credit rating—the reputation for *always* paying bills—especially to the individual proprietor with modest capital. Offer some alternative method of settlement as an example of your fair-mindedness and leniency (a system of part payments, maybe part cash and the balance in a note). But don't give all your space to this; remember it's the check for the entire amount that you want, not partial payment—and certainly not just a bunch of excuses.

35. Mr. Sanders of the two preceding problems paid no attention to your letter written when the account was 90 days old (60 days overdue). Fifteen days after that you wrote another letter that went like this: "Let's talk again about the $600 worth of meat display cases we sold you 105 days ago. If you're experiencing a temporary slump in sales, as many good stores are, we can take your 90- or 120-day 6 per cent note and thus help you protect your good credit rating. Better yet, use the enclosed envelope to send the check—today!" It still didn't work. So 15 days later, when the account is 120 days old (90 days overdue), you face the inevitable: Tell him that he *must* pay or face the consequences of having his name turned in to the National Credit Bureau for a delinquency listing and action by the collection staff. He is no novice, it's true; nevertheless, you'll want to devote a major portion of the letter to telling how the Credit Bureau works. This letter makes a special effort to be friendly but final. It is an earnest and sympathetic plea that Mr. Sanders forestall the bad results which his inaction will inevitably bring about. Give him 10 days more in which to reply.

36. A week after the date of your invoice (Langston and Marion, Importers, Baltimore) to Miss Jennie Cavendish, owner and manager of The Quality Gift Shop, Richmond, Virginia, for 24 imported Rummel figurines @ $4 (express charges were collect) you sent a cheerful note about the 2 per cent discount. She ignored that, as well as the customary notice that you sent on schedule at the end of the net period (30 days). Instead of the customary short printed reminder note that would normally go out 30 days after the due date, you decide to alter the collection procedure and send her a personal letter, talking about the value of a prompt-pay rating. Although this theme automatically hints that the customer *should* pay the account, you decrease the stringency of the request for payment with a sales suggestion:

Isn't it about time for another shipment of quality gift items? Has she looked over the leaflet telling about Waldston dinnerware? In case it has become misplaced, here's another. In this letter you are careful not to say or intimate that she can buy no more until this present amount is paid; you very likely would honor another credit request within the next 30 days. She has bought sporadically from you for the past five years—and paid in similar fashion (never later than 60 days, however). Notice, however, the big difference in tone when you write, *"If you pay, we'll send you more . . ."* as contrasted with "When you send your check, include an order for . . ." Write the letter to be sent out 30 days after payment is due.

37. Your polite letter (preceding problem) went unanswered. In 30 more days you sent another letter, the theme of which was "The favorable prices on Langston and Marion fine imports are partly due to the fact that no collection costs are figured in; if everyone took 60 days to pay instead of 30, the cost of all items would have to be increased a few cents." Surely, you reasoned, a spinster owner of a small business would respond to such persuasion. But she didn't. You know Miss Cavendish can pay; you know that she has a thriving shop that can furnish you with sizable business for many years if your goods give satisfaction and your sales and collection divisions please her. You write her a strong letter, 80 days after the due date, pointing out the value of the credit privilege and the necessity of a sure-pay rating. The theme automatically implies that the account is in jeopardy and that Miss Cavendish *should* pay—and soon. You'll want to send the letter on its own merits, with no references to any letter sent earlier or any that will follow if this one doesn't succeed. This letter talks credit and collection straight through; it contains no sales-promotional material on any other goods, though it may contain resale talk on the Rummel figurines. Now write this letter to be sent 80 days after payment is due.

38. Still you have no answer from Miss Cavendish of the two preceding problems. When the account was 105 days overdue, you wrote a letter to her that went like this: "For five years we have been privileged to serve The Quality Shop by providing fine imported gift items. For five years you have met your obligations. We still believe that our original reports as to your credit integrity were correct. But you must make payment of the $96 for the Rummel figurines sent you over three months ago if we are to continue to regard you in that light. If you can't send the check, perhaps we can arrange a 90-day 6 per cent note for part payment." Miss Cavendish still didn't answer. Now it's 15 days later (the account is 120 days overdue), and you face the final letter in which you tell her that she *must* pay or face the consequences of having her name reported to the National Manufacturers Credit Association. This letter makes a special effort to be friendly but final. Give her 10 days in which to reply. Write the letter to be sent out 120 days after payment is due.

39. Marion T. Dick, orthodontist, 189 Bellview Estates, Birmingham, Alabama, comes to Tuscaloosa (60 miles) once a week (Tuesdays) and has as one of

his patients Susan Haring, daughter of the T. M. Harings, 19 Alaca Drive. When Susan first started teeth straightening, her parents paid $100, with the understanding that they owed $20 every month until the bands and braces were taken off (about 1½ years). Dr. Dick has sent several bills to Mr. Haring for services during the preceding three months, but as yet has just had payment for the beginning $100 cost. Mr. Haring is an executive at a large paper mill in Tuscaloosa, and there is apparently no reason why payment should be withheld. Write a letter for Dr. Dick which you think will collect the money.

40. You are with Parker Brothers, Inc., Salem, Massachusetts, producers of games (Monopoly, Clue, Rich Uncle, Pegity, Pit—always the latest and popular ones). The Little Red House (Trenton, New Jersey), a gift store managed by E. J. Pritchett, has been getting games from you for the last two years. Pritchett, who is a fair risk, owes $85.75, now two months past due. Assume that it is November 1. He has not responded to two statements you have sent him. Write a letter built around the theme that it will soon be time to place an order for the holiday season. He should clear his account for heavier buying.

41. For any business with which you are familiar, write a four-letter form collection series the firm could use at 30-day intervals. Assume that a notification and a reminder precede the first letter and that the last letter informs the reader that his account will be placed in the hands of some other agency for collection within a stipulated time. You may assume also that a return-addressed envelope accompanies each letter.

    If you are not familiar enough with any business to write about it, see the following problem.

42. As instructed by your teacher, assume that the letter for any one of the sales problems has been successful, that several of the buyers have not paid, and that the seller wants a series of four collections to bring in the money. Your instructor will ask you to write all four or any one, specifying the stage(s).

XIII. Special Good-Will Letters

FROM THE preceding discussions and illustrations of various kinds of letters, you certainly realize that every letter should retain and even try to increase the reader's favorable attitude toward the writer and his firm while working primarily on something else.

Certain letters, however, have no other immediate purpose than the cementing of friendly relations between the customer and the house. Though they rarely ask the reader to take any action, indirectly these special good-will letters pave the way for future business.

Crass though it may sound, one businessman realistically summarized the function of good-will letters this way: "Especially on the executive levels, hundreds of letters must be written just to keep in touch and to keep business on the personal basis that we have learned pays off."

Because your readers know you do not *have* to write these letters and do not expect them, they are especially effective in overcoming the impression of store indifference.

All too often the only times a customer receives word from a firm are when someone wants him to buy or to pay for something or when he demands attention by making a claim or threatening to close his account. This apparent lack of interest is borne out in practically all reliable surveys of why firms lose customers. About 7 out of 10 lost customers just drift away. Yet 8 out of 10 are reclaimable if given some attention. Only 1 per cent of lost customers have real grievances that need adjusting. And a large part of the 70 per cent who do drift away would undoubtedly not do so if they were reminded that the business firm appreciates their patronage and has a continuing interest in their welfare.

Where people take their trade depends not just on quality, price, and convenience; these are usually comparable in several different outlets. There may be other reasons, but most of us trade where we do because (1) we like the people and (2) we appreciate the extra-service considerations—the personal and friendly aspects.

In theory, good-will letters sell only friendship. Some do no more than that—ostensibly. But we should admit to ourselves in all honesty that "pure" friendship is a commodity not bought and sold. We should also admit that a letter on a firm's letterhead, signed by a representative of the firm, is promotional, regardless of its personal nature. The cultivation of business is inherent in the circumstance itself. No writer need be reluctant to establish the virtues of his firm's services and goods and to place them at the disposal of his reader. But he should be frank from the outset. The main thing to guard against is appearing to be offering only friendship in the first part of the letter and then shifting to an obvious immediate sales pitch.

Most special good-will letters are low-pressure messages with potential or postponed sales possibilities. These are more accurately called business-promotion letters (or just "promotional" or "promotion"). They should be differentiated from both the personal letter that is just a friendly note with no sales axe to grind and from the obvious and avowed sales letter. It is impossible to draw a fine line of distinction between the two, however, or to establish definitions and classifications that conform with the varying ways different people use the terms.

Certainly some of these "unnecessary" business letters are of such highly personal nature that to use an obvious form would be insulting, to include sales talk or resale talk on either firm or merchandise would be ludicrous, and to write very much would likely result in gushiness. Letters of deserved praise and of sympathy certainly fall into this category. Letters expressing appreciation, extending seasonal greetings, issuing invitations, accompanying favors (or services), or offering helpful information do likewise if they are strictly good-will letters; but the majority of these are form letters including sales-building talk and thus are promotional.

Letters of Deserved Praise.   Letters praising people are essentially congratulatory. Though they may not contain the word *congratulations,* the spirit is there. In them you are recognizing a significant event or accomplishment in the life of your reader: a job promotion, election to an office, receiving an honor, winning a contest, graduation, marriage, birth of a child, completion of a new plant or office, a project or a report successfully completed. All these and many more are instances when you can show not only customers but also friends and acquaintances that you are interested in what happens to them. Some of the better ones are just a few lines:

> When I saw that you've been named Plant Manager of Tri-States, I was delighted!
>
> It's a well-earned recognition.
>
> And it couldn't happen to a more deserving fellow!

(Any salutary effects of the foregoing passages would be lost if the writer followed with such an idea as "Now that you're earning more, surely you'd like to consider more insurance" or "buy more clothes.")

> I have just completed your article about credit control in the recent issue of *Credit World*.
>
> Heartiest congratulations on a job well done!

> I can appreciate your deep satisfaction and pride in John's graduation *cum laude* from Haverford last week.
>
> Congratulations to him—and also to his parents.

> Congratulations to you and your wife on the birth of your son. And good wishes to all of you.

> We share your pride and happiness in the completion of the new Henderson plant.
>
> It is a criterion of business, as well as civic, accomplishment.
>
> Good wishes from all of us. (Or "Sincere wishes for your continued success.")

If these strike you as being more like a telegram than a letter, remember that timeliness is important in letters like these, probably of equal importance with what you actually say. The friendly thought behind the message counts most.

A note like the following would certainly engender good feeling (and probably stimulate the salesman to greater productivity):

> Congratulations, Steve Mason, on winning the home movie camera!
>
> I know it took a lot of planning and hard work to exceed your previous records and to nose out every other salesman in the Midwest District.
>
> You have the personality, the drive, and the intelligence to take you places in your career with General Milling.

Incidentally, I'm glad that you have the camera while your children are little. The film record of their growth will become more treasured to you and your wife as the years go by.

Or this:

Your analysis of production difficulties at the Saginaw plant was one of the clearest, most easily read reports I've ever been privileged to study.

We're carrying out some of your recommendations immediately.

Several of us look forward to discussing the report with you when you return to the home office in about two weeks.

In the meantime, thanks for a job well done.

Many people in both their business and their private lives have discovered the gratifying responses of associates, customers, and just personal friends at the receipt of a newspaper or magazine clipping of interest to the reader. A simple greeting (it may be no more than "Good Morning") and a line or two like "This clipping made me think of you" or "I thought you might be interested in this clipping" are enough. A folder is a common form. People who could expect to use such a mailing often would find a printed form a great saving of time; others would probably send a handwritten or typewritten note like

Let me add my commendation to those you've undoubtedly already received as a result of the enclosed clipping.

It's a pleasure to know a man like you.

The obvious substitutions like "to be associated with" or "to serve" or "to have a friend" readily suggest themselves on the appropriate occasions.

Still another variation of a letter deservedly praising someone is one you write to a third person about a second person who, in your opinion, merits recognition or appreciation or both. The man who wrote the following letter to an airline official made at least two friends for himself:

On your Flight 127 from Chicago to San Francisco last Tuesday, I was pleased with every phase of the service. But I was especially pleased with the conduct of Captain A. L. Lutz.

While at the controls he kept us well informed on flight conditions and frequently pointed out places of interest enroute. When he walked through the cabin, he was the soul of hospitality and courtesy to every passenger— particularly to a six-year-old boy who was making his first flight!

As we came in at San Francisco in bright moonlight, Captain Lutz circled the Bay and pointed out sights of interest; it was a thoughtful gesture that all of us appreciated.

The smooth, pleasant ride was made memorable through the "little extras" of Captain Lutz.

My thanks and commendations to the line and to him.

Any time that someone renders good service is an appropriate occasion to relay, via letter, your understanding and appreciation of its significance. Such a gesture not only impresses the reader with the writer's "humanness"; it can and often does earn him preferential treatment on subsequent occasions.

> When I brought my two children to the glove counter of Burger's today to purchase a Christmas gift for their mother, I appreciated very much the patience and courtesy of the sales woman who assisted us.
>
> I did not get her card; nor can I find the sales slip to give you her sales number. She is of medium build and has black hair (my daughter says she was wearing a beige knitted outfit).
>
> We were in the store about one o'clock and the children had not yet had lunch; they were, therefore, fidgety and a little difficult. They asked to see at least a dozen different styles and colors, some of which even I recognized as duplicates. They asked many pointless questions. They argued with one another. But in helping them arrive at a selection, she remained calm and patient. And she was certainly tactful and diplomatic when our eleven-year-old spilled a box of glove powder all over the counter and onto the floor!
>
> No doubt she will remember us. . . . But please tell her that we remember her too—with gratitude.

～～～～～･

> Last Friday your representative, Mr. John Wade, answered our call for help when one of our motors failed at a crucial time.
>
> We appreciated the promptness with which he came, of course. But we appreciated even more the efficiency which he displayed in getting it running again. He was considerate of all around him and thoughtful enough not to leave a mess for us to clean up.
>
> Our thanks to you and to Mr. Wade; we shall remember on other occasions.

Obviously, it is also often appropriate under such circumstances to write directly to the person whose performance you praise, as in the following instance:

> If such an award were given by the U.S. Chamber Workshop, you'd certainly get the "E" for excellence, John.
>
> Your Thursday afternoon clinic met with more enthusiastic reactions than I've observed in a long time.
>
> It is a rewarding experience to work with people like you.

With a second letter to the speaker's dean (taking only two minutes' dictation time), the writer could spread good will all around:

> Everyone at MSU working with us on the U.S. Chamber Workshop contributed and cooperated in exemplary fashion, Dean White.
>
> We are most grateful to all of you.
>
> John Fohr's Thursday afternoon clinic met with such enthusiastic reaction that I feel I should report the group reaction to you. He had men like Ed Sherrer, the Memphis Division Manager, eating out of his hand!
>
> Deservedly so, in my opinion.

Congratulatory letters, including birthday and anniversary greetings, are practically always individualized. Sympathy letters—the most personal of any special good-will letters—must be.

Letters of Sympathy.   Most of us are accustomed to lending a helping hand and extending expressions of encouragement when friends and family suffer some adversity. The same sympathetic attitude should prevail when a business friend experiences misfortune. Admittedly, letters of condolence are some of the most difficult of the special good-will letters to write because of the melancholy circumstances. But they are certainly appreciated by everyone. When a report of a retailer's illness reaches a wholesaler (or a manufacturer), he can certainly gain good will with a short, human, and essentially positive note like the following:

> Sorry, Sam—
>
> —to hear that you're back in the hospital with another heart flare-up.
>
> But with rest and good care you'll be back at the store sooner than you think.
>
> I've always enjoyed you as a friend and valued you as a business associate; so for two reasons I hope that all goes well with you again soon.

> We were distressed to learn of the automobile accident that hospitalized you and Mrs. Sigler recently.
>
> It's good to know, however, that you are now up and about.
>
> We certainly hope that Mrs. Sigler's condition will improve and that there will be no further complications.

As a result of accident, illness, and advancing age, most of us find ourselves having to write letters concerning the death of someone we've known. To the surviving partner of a business, for example, the following letter would be a comfort. It would help to convince him of the writer's friendly interest and concern.

We were genuinely distressed to learn of the death of Mr. Guin, your partner and our good friend for many years.

Though the firm of Guin and Beatty will feel the effects of his absence, it is too well founded and has been too well operated over the years for any serious dislocations to happen.

The great loss is to the community and the Guin family. The good judgment, vision, and integrity that Mr. Guin displayed as a business leader in your city undoubtedly were also reflected in his private life.

In extending these words of sympathy, we should also like to add a few of encouragement and confidence in the future; we feel sure that would have been Mr. Guin's attitude.

Even though the writer of the preceding letter might not have met the widow (and/or the surviving offspring), certainly no offense would be taken if such a message as the following were received:

For many years we enjoyed a business friendship with Mr. Guin.

We respected him as a good businessman who insisted on high standards in serving the public and was always just, fair, and co-operative in his relations with us. We admired the good judgment, vision, and integrity he showed as a business leader in your community.

To you who saw these and other fine qualities in greater detail and frequency than we were privileged to, we offer our sympathy in respect and humility.

May his contributions to your life in former days make the days to come easier to cope with.

It is impossible for such a letter not to have an emotional impact. But the effect can be lessened if writers will refrain from quoting Scripture or poetry. And sepulchral overtones will not be so powerful if death is accepted as the inevitability it is and the word itself used rather than euphemisms like "passed away," "passed to his reward," and "departed." Certainly, such a letter is going to be a greater comfort when it emphasizes the good characteristics and the outstanding contributions of the dead individual rather than the sorrow and anguish of the survivor. Possibly you will find writing such letters a little less difficult and will write more truly comforting messages if you accept the thought that good, worthwhile people continue to exert their influence in the hearts and minds of those who knew them.

Adversity also strikes in other forms—fires, floods, accidents and lawsuits, labor unrest and work stoppage. When it does, the victim(s) will appreciate a message that says, "We're your friends; we understand the significance of this to you; we hope everything will work out successfully." If you really mean the offer and are in a position to extend it, you can add the equivalent of "Call on us if we can help." The following are examples:

> All of us were sorry to hear of the fire that destroyed your warehouse night before last.
>
> It's a tough break.
>
> We're sure, however, that the same determination and ingenuity that helped you to build your business so successfully will also see you through this temporary set-back.

Now if this writer had some unused storage space and wanted to offer it, he might very well close with

> We have a 30 × 40 room that we won't need for another 90 days; if that will help tide you over in any way, give me a ring.

But to propose to rent the space would change the complexion of the letter and destroy any good will built up in the opening passages.

If a supplier were writing the foregoing to an out-of-town customer, he might want to close with

> We want to do all we can to help you over this emergency. For a customer like you we certainly can stretch our credit terms and expedite deliveries if you want us to.

He might even want to add

> We'd like to show in some way our appreciation of the co-operation you've always shown in our relationship.

Even in letters of condolence, a deftly phrased reference to your appreciation can be appropriate.

Letters of Appreciation. You have no doubt observed that most congratulatory messages also involve an element of thanks; likewise, most thank-you letters contain some commendatory passages. It's really just a question of where you want your emphasis to go.

Letters that emphasize appreciation for strictly good-will purposes are not nearly so numerous as those that are also promotional. When you thank a customer for patronage, for prompt payment, for recommending you or your firm to a friend, these are business-promotion letters with obvious tie-ins to service (including quality of merchandise).

Strictly good-will thank-you letters—in response to a favor extended, for work on a project (member of a fund-raising team, for example), or for a contribution—have their origins in civic, educational, and religious surroundings rather than in business.

> Many thanks for the untiring, cheerful way you worked on the recent Red Feather Drive.

Through effort like yours we exceeded our goal.

Possibly the knowledge that you have helped materially to provide clothing, food, and medical care during the coming year for underprivileged children will be slightly more gratifying with this expression of appreciation.

For the 32,000 youth of Athens . . .

Thanks a million!

Your generous gift to the new Y building is another evidence of your concern for the boys and girls of our city and county.

We want you to know how much we appreciate your co-operation in this project. As citizens and parents, we'll all be happy about our share in it for years to come.

thank you   thank you   thank you

To you these tickets mean an evening of top-notch entertainment, but to the children of Jefferson County the price of these tickets will mean many things.

Every cent of profit from the Junior League's presentation of "Jubilee" will be spent in Jefferson County for Jefferson County children to provide

> Medical care for children at the League's Children's Clinic held every Friday.
>
> Dental care for children at the League's Dental Clinic every Thursday.
>
> Milk for under-nourished children who attend these clinics.
>
> A nursing scholarship of $250 to a student in the School of Nursing who needs assistance.

In addition, the League furnishes clerical help to the Crippled Children's Clinic, maintains a Clothes Closet for needy families whose children attend our clinics, and sponsors the annual Christmas Carolling with the co-operation of the Boy Scouts and Girl Scouts.

League members and the children of our county thank you sincerely for your part in making all this possible.

As a matter of fact, you can't call the preceding letters pure good-will letters; for, obviously, the resale phrases are designed to convince the reader of the worth of the projects and thus prepare him for the next time a request comes along.

Letters written by business firms are even more definitely promotional.

Any time is a good time to send an expression of appreciation to good customers for their patronage or for handling accounts satisfactorily. Even the rubber-stamped notation on a current bill, "One of the pleasures of being in business is serving a good customer like you," has a heartening effect. But most stores do more. Upon the first use of the account some stores send a thank-you note like the following:

> We hope that you enjoyed the initial use of your account which was opened recently, and that you were entirely satisfied with the merchandise and service.
>
> If you have any suggestions to offer that will help make the account more convenient, we shall welcome them. We want to do everything possible to merit your continued patronage.
>
> Thank you for the patronage you have given us; we cordially invite you to make further use of your account.

Usually, however, credit managers wait until the customer has used the account for six months or a year, sometimes longer. Because of the rush of business, such letters all too often are sent only around holiday and special-event times. In too many such cases they don't do the effective job they might because too many other people and stores are sending greetings and good-will letters on those special occasions. Arriving unexpectedly and without apparent reason, the following note is a pleasant reminder of the firm's appreciation:

> Believe us
>
> —your continued patronage and friendship are appreciated.
>
> And to hold your friendship and patronage, we certainly intend to continue giving you the sort of service and honest values that you deserve.
>
> Come see us often.

When an account has not been used for some time and then a debit appears on the ledger, many credit men wisely send a thank-you note:

> Thank you for the purchase you made recently.
>
> It's good to hear you say "Charge it" again, for we've really missed you.
>
> To serve you so well you'll want to come in more often is our constant aim.

Letters thanking customers for paying promptly are simply a more specialized version of the ones we've been examining. They are also effective means of discouraging or reducing collection problems. Such a simple note as the following not only pleases the customer; it reinforces his determination to maintain the good habit:

> Your check this morning in prompt payment of last month's purchases made me think, "I wish all our accounts were handled so efficiently."
>
> It's a real pleasure to service an account like yours, and we thank you sincerely for your co-operation.

You can easily tie in the expression of appreciation with a concrete reminder of the benefits the customer gains from taking care of obligations as he has promised, too:

> Thank you for the splendid manner in which you paid out your recent account.
>
> With your record of prompt payments, your credit at Black's is firmly established. You needn't postpone adding fresh, new things to keep your home alive and interesting. It's thrifty and wise to enjoy these things while you save for them on small payments.
>
> Come in often and make full use of the many services this large, complete home store can render you, whether it's just a window shade or a complete houseful of furniture.

Such letters may appropriately be detailed developments of the theme:

> It's sad but true . . . that ninety-five per cent of our customers rarely hear from the Credit Department.
>
> But believe me, people like you who unfailingly take care of your obligations as promised are a continual source of pleasure.
>
> Month after month, year after year, your prompt payments have enhanced the desirability of your account. We know that such a fine record will continue and thus increase the esteem in which we hold you.
>
> We know that with the ups and downs of business, some payments come pretty hard. All the more reason we appreciate your record.
>
> We know, too, that the excellent business judgment and vision behind such a record is the surest signal of continued success. We are grateful for having been allowed to contribute in a small way, and we look forward to continued happy relations.

Certainly, if you keep your eyes and ears open, you'll find many other occasions for saying thank you to your customers and clientele. When a customer recommends you or your firm to another person, you'll certainly benefit in the long run by sending a cheerful, personalized note like the following:

> It was a pleasure to have you bring Mrs. Stallings into the shop recently. We enjoyed meeting her and seeing you again.
>
> Thank you for this expression of confidence in us. We shall do all we can to serve her well and to continue to merit your patronage and recommendation to your friends.

> It was generous of you to suggest to Mr. Lee that he come to us for quality men's wear.

He came in yesterday and seemed pleased with what we were able to show him.

Thank you. We're looking forward to his next visit.

When a firm writes such letters of appreciation to an individual, no reply is expected. And when an individual takes the time to pay a business firm a compliment or to express appreciation for good service, no answer is *required*. But you establish yourself as a courteous, polite person if you do reply. Furthermore, appropriate resale talk helps to strengthen the friendly feeling as well as to pave the way for future business. The following letter emphasizes gratitude for kind words but adroitly stresses service:[1]

The personnel of our Birmingham station quite proudly sent us your letter complimenting Delta personnel for their assistance in transporting Otto to his new home.

It was a real pleasure to receive such an excellent commendation, and we're happy to pass this along to all those who assisted along the way.

In these days of rapidly growing transportation problems, and with the volume of traffic mounting so fast, we sometimes feel that Delta's past record of outstanding personalized service may not be attainable today in spite of our best efforts.

Then, at just the right time, along comes a letter like yours to show that our station personnel are still doing a good job of public relations. It is a genuine pleasure to hear of the excellent way they handled the many details, and we do appreciate your taking time to tell us.

When you receive suggestions for improved service (some of which will be outright complaints requiring adjustment letters), an acknowledgment *is* required, particularly if you have invited the suggestion.

We certainly thank you for pointing out how we can improve our system for providing free parking to shoppers at Wiesel's.

Starting next Monday we shall have all customers pick up their tokens at the cashier's booth on the ground floor. And we shall have the parking lot entrance to the store completely cleared for easier flow of customer traffic.

We welcome your suggestions for better service and are sure that this change will make shopping at Wiesel's a greater pleasure than it was before.

Letters of Seasonal Greeting. A modified form of the thank-you letter is the one of seasonal greeting. By far the most common time is around Christmas and New Year, though some stores send them

---

[1] Reprinted with the permission of the author, Mr. W. D. Huff, Manager of Customer Relations, Delta Air Lines, Inc., Atlanta.

shortly before Easter, Valentine's Day, or Thanksgiving, when they do not have as much competition from other mailings. Since they must be mass mailings in most firms (to keep down costs), they are rarely personalized.

It is pertinent to point out that the Red Feather letter, the Y letter, and the Junior League letter (p. 450) were all obvious printed forms, thus conserving the funds of the organizations for more worthy causes. Business organizations, also, despite their size and resources, must also conserve employee effort and time (as well as funds) by using some modifications of form treatment in many of the thank-you and seasonal-greeting letters they mail. Ideally, these letters would be individualized from inside address through signature; as a practical matter, they often are not. The undisguised form can be successful, however:

> Business firms too pause at this season to count their blessings.
>
> Good friends and customers like you are one of our greatest.
>
> So we want to tell you how much we appreciate your patronage at the same time we send heartiest wishes for
>
> A VERY MERRY CHRISTMAS AND A HAPPY, SUCCESSFUL NEW YEAR!

With the references to "customers" and "patronage," the letter is promotional in effect. Most emphatically you would not want sales material in a letter with such an opening theme. The following holiday-greeting letter, however, is an overt attempt to cultivate business, and perhaps wisely so in the light of how a savings and loan association functions and the kind of service it provides members:

> GREETINGS AT THE NEW YEAR!
>
> Hearts are never as full of peace and happiness as when friends and loved ones gather in the home at this season of good cheer and fellowship.
>
> Through the years your Association has played a part in providing homes for its members through sound home-financing plans that lead to real debt-free home ownership. Won't you please tell your friends about your Association and recommend its services to them? They will appreciate knowing of the easy, convenient terms upon which a loan may be repaid.
>
> Our officers and directors join in thanking you for your help in the past year, and wish you happiness and health in 19— and for years to come.

Most of the time you will be on safer ground if you exclude such promotional passages and concentrate on a simple wish for the customer's well-being, along with an expression of gratitude.

Letters of Welcome and Invitation. One of the most popular forms of a good-will letter is that greeting newcomers to a community and offering to be of assistance, particularly during the orientation period. Almost always it is an invitation to come in and get acquainted; it also emphasizes the services of the inviting firm. One unusual and unexpected example is the following from a public library:

Welcome to Evansville!

We're glad to have you as new members of our progressive city.

Your library card is ready for your use. We hope you'll be down soon to pick it up and to become acquainted with the staff and the services. For your reading pleasure and research over a hundred thousand volumes are available. Staff members will gladly assist you in finding what you seek. All of the leading magazines and newspapers are available in the lounge.

The children's room is also well supplied with both fictional and non-fictional books on a wide variety of topics of interest to youngsters six to fifteen.

If you enjoy musical recordings, you may want to check out some of the thousand-odd albums ranging from the most recent popular music to the classics.

We shall be glad to give you maps of the city, to supply directions—in short, to help you in any way we can to know Evansville better than you now do.

The library is open from 9 A.M. until 10 P.M. every week day. We are glad to answer telephone inquiries during that time.

Please come in soon.

Such a letter—with no sales axe to grind—is the essence of good will in its spirit. It is more likely to be accepted at its face value than the usual letter from a firm with commercial/profit aspirations, such as the following:

As a new resident of our Friendly City, you are cordially invited to visit the Federal Bank. We should like to get to know you. Even though you may have already selected a bank, it would be a pleasure to welcome you to Blankville personally and to explain the many services the Federal offers its customers.

The Federal has given prompt, courteous, and efficient banking services to the people of Blankville for over 75 years, and we would appreciate the opportunity of serving you.

Among the conveniences in Federal's modern banking quarters are the four drive-in tellers that enable you to bank without alighting from your car. And in the parking garage right in our own building you may have 30 minutes of free parking while taking care of your banking business.

You may also bank around the clock at the Federal; a complete mail deposit service and a twenty-four hour depository are located in our parking garage.

> Furthermore, branch banks in Freeport and in Norwood can accommodate you when you do not wish to come downtown.
>
> You have complete banking facilities when you bank with the Federal.
>
> Won't you come in for a friendly visit soon?

Most readers would probably recognize this letter for the wolf-in-sheep's-clothing that it is. It is an obvious attempt to get a new account, and the attempts to establish friendly feeling are thin and transparent. Better to discard the talk of "get to know you" and "friendly visit" and get right down to brass tacks established with an opening like "Since you are a newcomer to Blankville and will need a conveniently located bank with complete facilities, may we tell you what we can offer you at the Federal?"

On the other hand, the invitation to a special event extended in the following letter would probably be read with interest; it builds good will because it expresses a desire to render service; no resale (except that inherent in the action itself) or sales talk distracts:

> Will you be our guest?
>
> Beginning next Thursday, May 31, and every Thursday after that for the rest of the summer, Brentling's will present prominent lecturers and editors reviewing the most talked-about recent books.
>
> All the reviews will be held in the auditorium on the sixth floor (air-conditioned, of course, like the rest of Brentling's) and will begin promptly at 2 P.M.
>
> This Thursday Miss Evelyn Kuppenheimer, popular literary editor of the *Times,* will review Angeline Locke's *Voodoo on the Levee*—a powerful, gripping story of the ante-bellum South.
>
> We hope you will be with us to enjoy this initial literary treat and as many of the others as you possibly can.

Someone connected with credit control can easily maintain a list of newcomers to the community and mail a form letter—which can easily be individualized—like this one (which does not promise credit, please note, but only invites the application):

> Welcoming you to this community gives us a great deal of pleasure. We hope soon to count you as one of our good friends. Our credit department will be glad to handle your credit application at your request.
>
> We invite you to use our lounging and rest rooms on the mezzanine or the fountain luncheonette, where you can get a deliciously prepared, well-balanced luncheon at reasonable prices. Rollins' spacious parking lot, located only 15 feet from the rear entrance to the store, is absolutely free to you when you shop here, no matter if your purchase is only a spool of thread.

On Rollins' remodeled third floor you'll find home furnishings. The advice of our interior decorators is available to you at no obligation. And in the remodeled downstairs you'll find an entirely new and complete food mart and new homeware section.

We are here to serve you. And we hope that you too will soon feel as one of our customers recently was kind enough to say to us, "The longer people live in this community, the more they trade at Rollins'."

When you can verify the credit reliability (usually an easy thing to do), you may elect to set up the account and so inform the reader:

We know that stores, too, make a difference to a person making a home in a new community.

To serve you in as friendly manner as possible is one of our aims. As an earnest assurance of our desire to show you every possible courtesy that will make for a permanent and happy business friendship, we have opened a convenient charge account in your name.

The next time you are in the store, simply say "Charge it" to the person waiting on you.

We hope to see you soon—and often.

The following special invitation letter is frankly a low-pressure sales letter. It does offer a service in making shopping easier, but the primary emphasis is on sales.

For our best customers we're having an Open House the evenings of Wednesday, December 7, through Saturday, December 10. The store will be open until 9 these evenings, and you are invited to come and "just look" to your heart's content.

Refreshments will be served from 6 to 8, and our sales personnel will simply act as hosts. No public announcement will be made of this event.

With an eye to Christmas giving, you may want to examine some of the popular pocket-size transistor radios or portable TV's. Many G-E and R.C.A. models will be available for your inspection. The Whirlpool portable dishwasher is an especially welcome gift for a busy wife and mother. And of course the 19— models in G-E refrigerators, washers and dryers, and other appliances will be on display. Any attendant will gladly demonstrate one of these for you.

This Open House is intended as a departure from business routine—one that will give us a better opportunity to get acquainted with you and give you the opportunity of working out your Christmas gift problems at leisure. Won't you come in one or more of these evenings?

Letters seeking the revival of an account are but modified versions of invitation letters. When an account remains unused for any length of time—say three months or six months, depending on management's choice—it may be a signal that the customer is drifting away because of store indifference, or it may be the result of a real grievance. Letters inviting the customer back to the store, reselling the store's merchandise and services, stressing "How can we serve you better?" and finally asking forthrightly, "May we continue to serve you?" can be mailed individually or in a series. One of the finest we've ever seen is this one:

> Spring fever?
>
> Here's a SURE cure—a Beachstone suit, coat, or dress, spiced with the right accessories.
>
> Easy to choose, easy to buy, too. Simply use your charge account at Wilson's. It's as good as new and just waiting for your "charge it" to be as useful as ever.
>
> So come in soon! See and try on the beautiful new spring apparel, millinery, shoes, and other accessories that we have assembled for your Easter pleasure.

You can easily pattern any such letter after this one, which is built on sales-promotional material and an action ending suggesting a visit to the store. Letters built around special events, such as Christmas, readily supply a theme (though they may lose some effect by competition with many others):

> A welcome warm as Santa's smile awaits you at Bowen's!
>
> We're all decked out with our Christmas bests; so it's an easy job to find the right gift for everyone on your Christmas list.
>
> Practical gifts, starry-eyed gifts . . . and all conveniently in one store . . . Bowen's . . . where you can just say, "Charge it" for ALL your Christmas giving.
>
> With warmest holiday greetings

Accompanying a new credit card, one letter solicited the renewal of the customer's business with:

> Ordinarily we'd send you this enclosure with our monthly statement. Since your account hasn't been used recently, we're sending it along with some "Back to School" suggestions.
>
> You may be thinking of complete outfits for your own child or a "Back to School" gift for a favorite niece, nephew, or friend. You'll find complete selections of dependable quality Bowen merchandise in every department.
>
> Your charge account is just as good as ever—whether you come to the store, phone, or shop by mail.

Some writers studiously avoid asking whether anything is wrong. (See p. 411.) Some stores send a dozen or so mailings before asking. A favorite form is the letter written on only one half of the page (usually the left side) with a caption, "Here's Our Side of the Story." At the top of the right side blank space appears another caption, "Won't You Tell Us Your Side of the Story?" Regardless of the format, most of these letters make a request much like this one:

> One of my duties as Credit Manager of Bowen's is to check up on our service.
>
> Since your account has not been used for quite some time, the only way we can be sure we have pleased you with our merchandise and service is to hear directly from you.
>
> Just use the handy form and the convenient stamped envelope enclosed to tell us whether you want us to keep your charge account open.
>
> We will certainly do our best to please you.
>
> Will you write us . . . now?
>
> We'll surely appreciate it!

Letters Accompanying Favors. Often as a good-will reminder a businessman or firm finds some novelty or favor that he can mail inexpensively along with a note reiterating the desire to be of service, such as the following from a women's shoestore:

> The specially treated purse-size brush accompanying this letter is for your use in keeping your handsome EVERETT suede shoes spotless wherever you wear them.
>
> Accept it with our compliments and the hope that you will be completely happy with your recent selection from EVERETT's collection of footwear for the discriminating woman.

In a somewhat humorous vein one company recently mailed a pocket-size calorie counter to an extensive list of customers and prospects with this short note:

> "Everything's expanding—especially my waistline," grumbled a friend recently.
>
> Just in case you (or someone you know) may need to fight this perennial battle of the bulge, we're sending you this handy calorie counter that you can use at home or at a banquet or at a lunch counter.
>
> Accept it with our compliments—and the hopes that we'll be seeing you soon.

Small gadgets galore are used in this manner. Just as in tricks in sales letters, however, they are better if related to the product or service of the firm. A real-estate agency might appropriately send a pocket- or purse-size map of the city to which a person has just moved, along with the following:

Welcome to Jacksonville.

To help you get places faster and to know your new city better, we're sending you a map showing the principal thoroughfares and location of the principal landmarks and facilities.

Note that the Coleman Agency is located in an accessible area with adequate parking facilities nearby.

We would welcome the opportunity to help you in any way we can.

Letters Offering Helpful Information.   Large companies sponsoring radio and TV programs, as well as research projects and publications, rapidly accumulate names and addresses of people who are interested in being kept informed. As part of the public-relations or goodwill program, many of these companies periodically send letters like the following:

Perhaps you will be interested in a program, "Life under the Sea," scheduled for Sunday, January 22, at 8 P.M. over NBS-TV.

"Life under the Sea" was directed by Emile Ravage, with the assistance of the marine biologist Albert Gaudin. It is the third in a series of such productions sponsored by the Rawlston System.

We hope these programs will help to broaden public understanding of science and to encourage some young people at least to consider scientific careers.

We shall welcome your comments after you have seen the program.

As a teacher of advertising, perhaps you will be able to use the accompanying brochure, "The Evolution of a Woman's Home Journal Ad."

You are welcome to quote liberally in your classes and to reproduce anything in it.

At least, we hope you will enjoy reading it.

The exciting events in Detroit leading up to the introduction of the new models last month made a story too detailed to print completely in TEMPO.

If you read the condensed version in the issue of two weeks ago, you'll agree that the accompanying report-analysis we're sending to selected educators and businessmen is a worthwhile expansion and supplementation. If you didn't . . . well, we think you'll want to now.

Letters Anticipating Resistance.   In the interest of forestalling complaints and minimizing dissatisfaction, many business executives give advance notice when something like an interruption of service, a curtailment of service, or a price increase is scheduled to take place. (The same kind of advance mailing can also pave the way for the call of a solicitor for charitable contributions.) In almost all instances these letters (often only postcards) must be obvious forms. They need to stress service—improved service, if possible; at least, maintaining superior service or quality of goods—as an antidote for the inherently negative material the message has to establish. This message of a power company is typical (dates and times varied according to areas and so were stamped in):

> In order to provide better service for you and our other customers in your area, we have installed new equipment, which we plan to place in service
>
> April 15, 19—
between 1 and 2 P.M.
>
> To safeguard the men who do this work, we shall have to shut off power during this time. Service will be restored as promptly as possible. We appreciate your co-operation in making this improved service possible.

A notification of price increase is really just a modified sales letter. Admittedly, it is never an easy letter to write. But, with specific details supporting the increase, it may be successful in retaining some customers who would otherwise be lost. The following notice went to all customers of a diaper service:

> DEAR CRIB CUSTOMER:
>
> When we first started lending mothers a hand with laundry for infants and babies, diapers cost 90¢ a dozen. After World War II, we had to pay $2.61.
>
> Paper during the same period increased from 6¢ to 17¢ a pound and soap from 8¢ to 22¢.
>
> To continue giving our customers satisfactory service, we had to increase our prices in the late 40's.
>
> In the meantime all these items have continued to increase in price and now are from one-fifth to one-half more than they were then. Wages for our help, taxes, and other costs that we cannot control have also risen appreciably.
>
> And so in order to continue the same twice-a-week pick-up and delivery, and the same high standards of cleanliness and sanitation that we know you as a parent want for your child, we shall have to receive payment for services as listed on the enclosed card. These prices will go into effect at the beginning of the month.
>
> Please note that these increases average approximately 3¢ a day. You still are paying only 35¢ a day for service that makes life much easier for you, conserves your strength, and provides your child clothing that is sterilized to a degree impossible in most homes.
>
> We appreciate the opportunity to serve you and shall continue to do all we can to merit your confidence and your patronage.

It would be possible to classify and illustrate hundreds of situations in which a special good-will letter would be appropriate and would cement a friendship for you and your firm. If you are alert to conditions if you keep informed about what is happening to your clientele, if you honestly like people and enjoy pleasing them, you certainly won't lack for opportunity to write such letters. You'll be surfeited with occasions! In this short treatment, therefore, we have tried to concentrate on the most common instances; it is intended as a springboard for your thinking and practice rather than an extensive catalogue.

Special good-will letters can do a big *extra* job for you; but remember that *all* your letters should build good will through courteous, sincere tone and the service attitude.

PROBLEMS

1. Since your firm, the J. M. Till Metal and Supply Company, Inc., 285 Marietta Street, N.W., Atlanta, Georgia, is opening a new warehouse at 2736 East Hanna Street, Tampa, Florida, you are to write an invitation to all customers in the Tampa area inviting them to a grand opening from 3:00 to 9:00 P.M., the 16th and 17th of next month. Each customer will have a tour of the building and will be shown stocks, handling facilities, cutting and shearing equipment. Also there will be some display panels and exhibits of all types of ferrous and non-ferrous metals, as well as valves, fittings, fasteners, and gears. Mr. Winston Shirley, Manager of Sales, BCI Division, U.S. Steel Corporation, and Edward J. Walsh, Manager of American Steel and Wire, Cleveland, will greet people. These are two of your biggest suppliers.

2. Jones and Armstrong Steel Company, P.O. Box 356, Pittsburgh, Pennsylvania, has just promoted Victor A. Key to Secretary and General Manager, Luther V. Clasen to Plant Manager, and W. H. Tankersley to Purchasing Agent. These men have combined experience of more than forty years in the steel business and are well qualified to fill their respective places. Write a letter telling your customers of this good news.

3. Select one of the three men in the preceding problem and write a note of congratulations. You can assume that you are assistant manager of sales for Tennessee Coal and Iron Division, Fairfield, Alabama, and that you know pretty well the man you're writing. Make any reasonable, likely assumptions about him and your relationship to him.

4. As the general manager for the Milton-Hamilton Hotel, St. Louis, write the letter you would send to convention officials of various groups holding meetings at your hotel. You will not only want to welcome them and assure them of good service but also to inform them of your official convention pin, which will help to identify them as persons in charge and to secure co-operation from all employees in carrying out their wishes. Ask them to present the letter to the assistant manager at the time they register. Assume a specific date

for the convention of the American Association of University Professors and address the letter to Dr. John H. Bowman, 226 Upham Hall, University of Michigan, Ann Arbor (unless your instructor specifies otherwise).

5. One of the many promotional projects of the magazines *Tempo, Living,* and *Success* (all with executive offices in New York) to build and maintain good will is the sending of reprints to a wide variety of names. A letter always accompanies each mailing. In the role of the director of education, write the letter to accompany *Success*'s sixth annual directory of the 500 largest industrial corporations. It is to go to college teachers of business writing, counselors, deans, and directors of placement bureaus in about 2,000 colleges and universities in the United States. The directory appeared as a supplement in last month's issue. Besides names and titles of major officers in each company, it contains useful data concerning financial standing (capital issues, sales, return on investment, for example) and number of employees.

6. As educational director for *Tempo* (see preceding problem) write a letter to accompany a reprint collection of your series "The Changing American Market." It is to go to college teachers of marketing.

7. Assume now the role of sales manager for *Living* (see the two preceding problems) and write a letter to go along with your brochure, "The Story of a *Living* Ad." It describes step by step how an ad promoting Sunburst raisins was developed, from its original suggested form to the finished four-color, full-page appearance in a recent issue. The mailing will go to college teachers of advertising.

8. For your Standard Service dealers (filling stations) prepare copy for a letter accompanying a calorie counter. The counter is a handy pocket-sized rotating disc that enables anyone to keep accurate count of meals away from home as well as at home. The name and address of the local dealer are imprinted on the counter, and the letter carries his identification in the signature. This is just another good-will promotional device. You'll have the counters and letters printed in large quantities and inserted in envelopes. The dealer orders whatever number he needs for his local list (at about half the actual cost) and arranges the addressing himself for local distribution. Though you want to include some resale on Standard Service, your primary emphasis is on the convenience of the calorie counter.

9. Clyde Jackson, salesman for Cole Supply Company, Peoria, Illinois, sends $5 and fills out an application blank of the Meraton Central Credit Club (see Problem 8, p. 256). Over the signature of Ernest Patterson, president, Meraton Corporation of America, P.O. Box 1044, Boston 3, Massachusetts, welcome Jackson as a charter member. Enclose his Meraton Credit Card that's good for 12 months and resell him on the convenience and pleasure in being a member.

10. Assume that you are in the credit department of a department store you are familiar with and prepare a letter to charge customers who've not used their

accounts for three months. Build the letter around sales-promotional material on seasonal goods. The obvious action sought is to get them back to the store. It will be a personalized letter.

11. Prepare a follow-up letter to be sent at the end of six months to those charge customers whose accounts are still unused (see preceding problem).

12. Prepare a third letter for use at the end of eight months, as indicated in the preceding problem.

13. Prepare a fourth letter for sending, one month later, to the people in the preceding problem. Without stressing poor merchandise or service, invite the customer's comments and suggestions.

14. Prepare a letter for inactive accounts for use shortly before one or more of the following special times, as your instructor directs: Valentine's Day, Easter, summer-vacation time, Independence Day, Labor Day, back-to-school time, Thanksgiving, Christmas, winter-vacation time.

15. As the credit sales manager of Tru-Fit, Inc., Racine, Wisconsin, manufacturers of men's underwear, take time out to write a short personal note to the many owners and managers of men's shops, department stores, and other outlets who discount or pay promptly within your 30-day terms, commending them for their efficiency, stressing the desirability of their account, and subtly reselling Tru-Fit men's wear. Let the sample you write to Mr. Horace Crown, Manager, The Men's Shop, 1423 Commonwealth Square, Providence, Rhode Island, serve as the guide for the letters you will write to others.

16. Write the letter that Mr. Crown in the preceding problem might wisely send to his retail customers expressing appreciation for prompt payments (note that there is no discount here; also a much wider range of stock).

17. Assume you are the owner of any business you are familiar with and write a form message that could be sent to any credit customer a year after the account was entered on your books. Assume that the customer has promptly paid all obligations when due. The inside address and salutation would be filled in in each case.

18. At some point in your life you have been impressed with the attention given you by an employee of a firm. Perhaps it was a clerk who went out of the way to find something for you or who took special pains to see that you were fitted well or who made a special effort on a rush order. It might have been a reservations clerk for a railroad, airline, or steamship company. It might have been a hostess or a stewardess on a plane. Write a letter to the business, commending the employee. Recall the specific instance and be specific in telling why and how the employee gave you good service. Use the employee's name or describe the circumstances so exactly that there could be no mistaking who it was. Assume that you are writing the letter two or three days after the happy incident.

19. You are president of your professional fraternity, Beta Alpha Xi. Mr. James C. Marlin, an outstanding man in the profession, has just driven over at his own expense from a nearby city and talked to your group on a professional topic. Write a thank-you to Mr. Marlin that is specific enough to assure him that you and your group appreciate his generosity and realize something beneficial from his efforts.

20. You have just finished heading a campus drive collecting funds for crippled children. Write a note to one of your divisional chairmen that will serve as a guide for all the others you'll send. It should express gratitude and congratulations for the good job done as well as resell the cause.

21. Write a letter of congratulations to someone you know who has been honored, who has accomplished something outstanding, who has been promoted, or something akin to these. Include enough specific comment about the event or deed to show your realization of its significance.

22. As head of a public library in a city of between 50,000 and 100,000 population, write the letter you would send welcoming newcomers to the community and extending your services. The letter should resell the community and the library. Assume the enclosure of a small map of the city which conveniently folds to pocket or purse size. The letter will be personalized with inside address and salutation and mailed as you receive names and addresses from the local credit bureau.

23. As librarian at your school, write a form letter with the salutation "Dear Colleague" to go to all faculty members, inviting them to see the one showing of a special film that you'll have a week from Sunday at 3:00 P.M. in the Reference Room. It is a color film, 80 minutes long, showing many details of the U.S. Library of Congress. The title is simply "The Library of Congress." Reginald McDavid, Congressional Librarian and poet of renown, describes many of the services of the Library. Even grammar-school youngsters might enjoy the interior shots—especially those showing the Constitution, the Declaration of Independence, and other priceless documents.

24. Assume that you are the owner of any business you are familiar with. Write a note expressing appreciation for business given you by your customers. It will be an obvious form letter. Adapt your message seasonally as indicated by the assumed date of your letter.

25. Select some school, civic, or professional group of which you are or have been a member (or would like to be). As president, write a letter to members explaining why the dues are being raised. Explain the increase in terms of additional goals of the organization.

26. You are president of Andrew Jordan Company, Cincinnati, Ohio, soap manufacturers. To tell your stockholders about the promotion your company has been giving the new deodorant and beauty soap, Pride, you are sending a

form letter to them. During the rest of the year you plan to promote Pride with a million-dollar television advertising budget. Jack Farr, whose program has become a household institution throughout the country, went on the air for Pride a month ago under a long-term contract. The board of directors feel that concentrated television programs are better than expensive soap samples distributed to homes. Pride has proved itself worthy of all-out promotion, and the sales power of Farr with American consumers is well known. In addition to having a considerable impact on Pride sales, sponsorship of these programs is certain to enhance the prestige of the company and the remainder of the product line. Write this letter designed to win stockholder approval and plug Pride and the company behind it.

27. As assistant sales analyst for Peck and Hill, New York 16, N.Y., you write letters aimed to get customer reaction to how store personnel handle adjustments. Today's letter goes to Mrs. Eugene March, 198 Windsor Road, Oyster Bay, Long Island, who returned a Darlene 100 per cent orlon sweater, $12.95, size 36, and a pure silk Barrie blouse, $15.95, size 38. You want to find out whether she was served promptly and courteously, whether the adjustment was satisfactory, and whether the salesperson helped her select other merchandise, as well as to invite any other comments or suggestions she wishes to make. You are enclosing a stamped, addressed envelope for her convenience. The objective of the letter is, of course, to build good will by stressing service attitude.

XIV. Reports: Importance, Nature, and Five-Step Process of Preparation

~~~~~~

HISTORY AND PRESENT NEED

IN THE early history of man, reports were not needed. Every man was his own complete business firm or the overseer of a small group of people under his command. As on-the-spot manager of his affairs, a man saw all the facts he needed for making decisions about how to operate his business. For example, when a shipowner captained his one small ship, he saw all the operations and consequently needed no reports. The one central purpose of most reports—*to help the receiver make a decision by providing facts and ideas he does not have*—was taken care of by the shipowner's personal observation of all the information he needed.

Then some men gained power over large groups of others as their employers, masters, or tribal chieftains. When one of these bosses sent an underling out to do some work or to scout an enemy tribe, the boss wanted a report indicating difficulties encountered, or to be encountered, and the underling's suggestions of materials, personnel, necessary time, and plans for overcoming the difficulties. For example, when a successful shipowner built a second ship and put a hired captain on it to develop trade along a different route, the owner needed reports of the second ship's activities if he was to make wise decisions about future operations. Thus the ship's log came into being as one early form of written report. The impossibility of the manager's being in two places made reports necessary. So overcoming the problem of distance is the first specific function that reports may serve in achieving their general purpose of helping the receiver make a decision.

When businesses grew to where the manager could not find time to oversee all operations even under the same roof and some of the processes became so technical that the manager did not have the knowledge to evaluate all of them, reports became more and more widely used for two more reasons: time and technology.

With the increasing complexity of business and government, records became more important too; and, as their fourth possible function, written reports provided permanent records for the files, thus preventing later repetition of work and making it possible (through extra copies) to inform interested secondary readers.

As executives became responsible for more and more varied activities, the wiser ones also began to realize that they could not do all the desirable thinking about new products, new or improved processes, and new marketing methods. They therefore invited employees with initiative to submit their ideas in what are generally called "initiative" or "justification" reports. Thus reports began to serve management in a fifth way as vehicles for creative ideas.

If you bring these trends up to the present world of complex economies and governments—

—Where top management may be thousands of miles from some operations

—Where management cannot possibly find time to oversee all the activities even in one large building

—Where some of the processes are so technical that no man could be competent to decide wisely about all of them

—Where numerous records must be kept and several people informed

—Where competition pushes a company to use all the creative brain power of all employees in developing new ideas

—you see that reports have become an absolutely essential tool of modern management in making decisions.

For that reason, management today expects almost every employee to be able to write reports. Personnel men frequently check on this ability in each job applicant. For the employee who doesn't have the ability, many firms have set up required on-the-job training programs during low-pay apprentice periods. The reports which a trainee is required to submit not only help to determine the division of the company where he will be assigned; they often determine whether he will be retained by the company at the end of the training period. Even after a man is a full-fledged employee, management may continue to study his reports not only for information and ideas in solution to problems but for evidence of the employee's ability to communicate clearly, quickly, and easily. Since a man's reports of his activities are frequently the best indication that management has of how well he is doing his job, employers often use them as an important basis in deciding about promotions and salaries. Thus reports often serve in a sixth way—as a basis for evaluating the employees who write them.

Indeed, modern management cannot well perform as it does without its important tools—including reports.

Imagine a board of directors trying to decide on a proposed new plant without a report showing that reasonably expected profits from increased production will cover estimated costs. Isn't the question of a promotion for a staff member usually settled on the basis of a report of his activities and worth? Would a board approve a suggested new product without a report showing that income from sales would likely be great enough to leave a profit after covering production and distribution costs?

Most reports have to answer one or more of the following three general questions:

1. Will a given new proposal pay? The answer is not always in terms of money but must be in some kind of benefits—usually higher quality or quantity, or less time, money, material, or effort. Maybe safety or good will.
2. Which is the best (or better) way? Often the answer is a choice between the present way and a proposed new one. But it may be between or among products (Smith or Royal typewriters for our offices; Chevrolet, Ford, or Plymouth for our fleet; repair the old or buy a new . . .).
3. Is it feasible? Can you imagine approval of anything like Michigan's Mackinac Straits Bridge without an engineering report on the feasibility of building it, as well as reports on the economic justification and

methods of financing, not to mention the hundreds of reports necessary in the constructing job.

Indeed, can you imagine any board of directors, president, governor, manager, superintendent, or department head in any organization—public or private—approving substantial expenditures, changes in operations, or new regulations without reports (some of which may be oral) of studies showing that beneficial results will justify the action? Those in charge just don't make important moves without some kind of justifying reports. Even a dictator with egotism less than belief in his own omniscience or his having a private line to God will want staff reports, to follow or ignore as he wishes.

NATURE AND CLASSIFICATION OF REPORTS

Just as a building, piece of furniture, or anything else should be designed according to its functions, so should reports. In the foregoing discussion of the functions of reports, you have seen several implications of their nature. Yet the word *report* is such a broad concept that it cannot be well defined in a few sentences. All known attempts at definition are either incomplete, too general to be useful, or not quite true. (For example, if you say that reports interpret facts, you are obviously talking only about analytical reports and omitting the numerous informational reports, which do not interpret the facts they present.) The best way to get a clear idea of the meaning of the word *report* is to consider the usual characteristics of reports, along with the special characteristics of different types.

Usually, but not always, a report—

1. Is a management tool designed to help an executive in making decisions. Thus it is *functional* writing for the *benefit of the reader*. The reader, not the writer, is the important person involved. Since he wants *useful* information which he does not already have, a report is quite different from a term theme turned in to a professor.
2. Is an assigned job. The *justification* (or *initiative*) report may be an exception; but even it may be written in response to a standing invitation to submit ideas (as in a suggestion box). Otherwise, *periodic* reports (at regular intervals, such as weekly, monthly, quarterly) are assigned as part of a new employee's regular duties, and *special* reports are assigned as occasions arise requiring them.

   Usually the assigner will make clear whether he wants an *informational* report just giving the facts or whether he wants an *analytical* report giving the facts plus interpretation into conclusions and/or recommendations. If he doesn't, the report writer should find out from him. Otherwise the writer may be embarrassed to be called in and told to finish his job—to analyze the facts and show conclusions and recommendations. Or perhaps more embarrassing, if the writer has gone too far and seemed to infringe upon the executive's prerogative of deciding what to do, he may be told to keep his opinions and recommendations to himself and leave the decision making to the boss.

3. Goes up the chain of command. A few reports go between people of equal rank, as between two department heads; and some (directives) downward from executives (but most reports that executives write are to still higher authorities—boards of directors, legislatures, or the people who elected them).

4. Is written for one reader or a small, select group of readers. A report writer can therefore adapt his talking points and language well. Usually, there is one immediate reader, who may send the report on up the chain of command to just a few higher executives. The corporation annual report, aiming primarily at stockholders and employees, still aims at an unusually large readership for a report.

5. Gets more than normal attention to organization. Of course, all good writing is organized; but because reports are usually expositions of complex facts and ideas for practical purposes and are for busy readers, report writers work harder at organization than most other writers.

6. Makes more than normal use of the techniques and devices for communicating clearly, quickly, and easily: commonly understood words; short, direct sentences and paragraphs; headings, topic sentences, and brief summaries; itemizations; graphic presentations; and specific, concrete, humanized writing.

7. Is expected to be accurate, reliable, and objective. No executive wants to base decisions on a report writer's errors, assumptions, preconceptions, wishful thinking, or any kind of illogicality. Though no person can be strictly objective—because his selection of facts to include and his evaluation of them are based on his whole background and the kind of person he is—the report writer strives to be as objective as possible.

8. Follows the special form best suited to its particular functions. Thus we speak of such special forms as *letter, memo, credit, justification,* and *complete* reports. If the name *complete* suggests that the other forms are incomplete, it is justified in doing so. The others actually leave out some details relevant to the situation because those details are adequately implied or are already known to the reader.

Preparing a complete analytical report is a five-step process: planning the attack on the problem, collecting the facts, organizing the facts, interpreting the facts (this step omitted in preparing an informational report), and writing up the report in appropriate style. Since any or all of the five steps may be necessary in varying degrees in the preparation of a particular report in any form, we present those five steps before explaining and illustrating different forms.

PLANNING THE ATTACK

Planning the attack is a job to be done at the desk—the head work before the leg work. It involves six procedures, in the following sequence:

1. Get a clear view of what the central problem is. If you can't see the problem you're shooting at, you're not likely to hit it.

   This procedure requires reflective thinking. It may also require a conference with the man who needs the report. As a check, you can try writing a concise and interesting title that clearly indicates the content. If you can also write in one sentence a precise statement of the purpose, clearly indicating what you intend to cover and what you don't, you have the necessary clear view of the problem.

2. Consider conditions that influence the report—the use to be made of it, its importance, and the attitude, degree of interest, and knowledge of the reader(s), for example. In considering use, don't overlook the facts that reports are commonly filed for future reference after they have served their immediate purpose and that therefore they need to be clear to other readers ten years later; and that the immediate superior who asked for the report may have to send it on up the chain of command for approval before anything can happen. So it needs to be intelligible to possible readers other than the immediate one. The reader's knowledge of the subject has considerable influence on how much background and detailed explanation you need to give. His attitude, as well as your reputation as an authority, will influence how persuasive you need to be (whether you use the convincing inductive plan or the faster, more interesting, but possibly less convincing deductive plan). His known biases and special interests may influence what you should stress and whether you must use impersonal style. Your relationship to the primary reader will indicate how formal or informal the style should be. Limitations on time, money, or availability of data may affect how thorough you can be and whether you can use costly plates and charts.

3. Divide the central problem into its elements, the main divisions in an outline of the topic. The idea of dividing to conquer applies in report writing as well as in military strategy. When you are faced with a sizable job, you can't tackle it whole without getting into a tizzy or psychological block—like the dog choked by trying to swallow a whole hunk of meat without biting it into pieces. Of course, not all problems divide alike, any more than all jigsaw puzzles do; but the dividing process is a job of finding the natural divisions of the whole. Some topics to consider in many problems are history, disadvantages of present system, advantages of proposed system, costs and means of financing, personnel required, effects on good will, method of installation, materials required, time involved, safety, increases or decreases in quality, market, competition, convenience, and availability of land. (See pp. 482 ff. and 527 ff. for help on outlining.)

4. Raise specific questions about each element. The questions further divide the problem, lead to subheads in your outline, and point more directly toward collecting data for answers. If cost is one of the elements, for example, you want to ask what the costs are for operating one way and what they would be under a revised system. You would then want to question further about how to find the costs in each instance. And you might do well to break the questions down further into first costs, operating costs, and depreciation; costs for personnel, for upkeep, for power, and the like. Specific questions on good will might include those about customers, stockholders, workers, and the general public.

5. Take stock of what you already know. You may pose a hypothesis, but don't let it close your mind to other possible solutions. Don't assume that you know the answer until all the facts are in. You certainly don't want to start out to prove a preconceived notion. Get a clear concept of the assumptions you are willing to make, and separate those which are to be held without further checking from those which are to be checked. Jot down answers known for the questions raised and the tentative answers to be checked. Clearly indicate gaps in information that are to be filled by data to be collected, and jot down what you think tentatively are the best sources and methods for getting the missing data—experts, books, and articles, and maybe the man for whom you're writing. Or maybe you need to plan a survey—kind and size of sample, kind of survey, and the like.

6. Make a working schedule. Assign time blocks estimated to be necessary for each of the remaining steps in producing the report: collecting remaining data, organizing, interpreting, and writing up the final report. If you plan a survey, remember that the mail requires time and that people don't always respond to questionnaires immediately. For any except the most routine kind of reports, be sure to allow some time for revising early drafts to put the final report in clear, interesting, and inconspicuous style and form. But the first item on the working schedule is the next step in report preparation—collecting the facts.

COLLECTING THE FACTS

For collecting complete and reliable facts, the report writer may use any or all of the four basic methods of securing information: library research, observation, laboratory research, and surveys. The first provides secondary (secondhand) data, and the others provide primary (firsthand or new) facts. In most cases the report writer should use at least two of the methods in a way to get at the essential facts and assure reliability of them.

Library Research.   Study of published books, articles, theses, brochures, and speeches is the most universally useful and is usually the best first step. When you face any problem of consequence, somebody else has probably faced the same or a closely related problem and written up something worth while about it. And when pertinent data are

already written up, getting the facts by reading them in the other fellow's collection is nearly always the easiest and quickest way—easier
and quicker than the laborious process that the original writer went
through to get them. Besides being the quick and easy way to collect
facts, it may also give a bird's-eye view of the whole problem, acquaint
the report writer with terminology and methods he may not have
thought of, refer to other good sources, show formerly overlooked
natural divisions and aspects of the problem, and, in general, help the
writer to revise his tentative plan of attack.

Fortunately libraries are pretty well standardized. They have a great
variety of regular reference books such as

Encyclopedias (*Americana, Columbia,* and the *Britannica,* which is the
    most thorough)
Census reports (U.S. government censuses of agriculture, business, hous-
    ing, manufacturing, population, and other breakdowns)
Yearbooks of various trades and professions (commerce, shipping, agricul-
    ture, engineering, and others)
Almanacs (notably the yearly *World Almanac* with a surprising variety and
    amount of information, both statistical and otherwise)
Atlases (especially those by Rand McNally)
Dictionaries of many different kinds (the big *Webster,* for example, giv-
    ing lots of information besides that about words)
Directories (such as Kelly's for merchants, manufacturers, and shippers;
    Thomas' for American manufacturers, Ayer's for newspapers and maga-
    zines)
Who's who in various fields (including the *Directory of American Scholars,
    American Men of Science,* and *Who's Who in Business,* for example)
Statistical source books (*Statistical Abstract of the United States* and Ayer's
    Directory)

These are just a few main examples of the numerous reference books
that are usually placed conveniently out on tables or in open shelves in a
library. Constance Winchell's *Guide to Reference Books* tells about
them and many more.

The standard key to books in the stacks is the card catalogue arranged
alphabetically by author, subject, and title.

But because libraries available to most writers will not have all the
books published on their subjects; because it takes months for books to
be published, bought by libraries, and catalogued for distribution; and
because not all topics are written up in full-book treatment, the report
writer often finds that his best up-to-date printed sources are periodicals.
Fortunately, most of them are covered in one or more of the numerous
periodical indexes, both general and specific for almost any field. The

accompanying table (next page) describes the main current ones; but if you do not find one for your specific field, ask the reference librarian.

And if the abbreviations or the system of indexing is not immediately clear to you, the preface always explains.

Whatever library key you use, you need to develop resourcefulness. Often when you look under one topic (say "Business Letter Writing" or "Report Writing") you will find little or nothing. Don't give up. You have to match wits with the indexer and try to think of other possible wordings he might have used for the topic. He might have put "Business Letter Writing" under "Business English" or "Commercial Correspondence" and "Report Writing" under "Technical Writing" or something else.

When your resourcefulness brings you to a book or article that seems to be useful, scan it to see what (if any) of it is grist for your mill. If it seems pertinent, check its reliability. Consider both the textual evidence and the reputation of the publisher and of the author for (1) any possible slant or prejudice, (2) the question of whether the author is a recognized authority in the field, and (3) the question of whether the material is up to date. Reading a review in a related journal can help in judging the worth of a book. A sound report writer will not be duped by the usual undue worship of the printed word; he knows that the mere fact that something is in print does not make it true.

If the material meets the tests for reliability, take notes—A SEPARATE CARD OR SHEET OF PAPER FOR EACH BOOK OR ARTICLE—according to your needs. When in doubt, take fuller rather than scantier notes than you think you need; it's easier to omit later than to come back for more.

Some parts you may want to take verbatim, but usually not; direct quotation should be used rarely, and then only to gain the impact of the author's authority or to take advantage of his conciseness, exactness, or aptness of phrasing. If you do quote, be sure to quote exactly and not change the original meaning by lifting a small part from context in which it meant something different. In most cases you can save words and express the idea better for your purposes if you paraphrase. When you paraphrase, however, be sure not to change the original meaning. In some cases you may see that you can save time later by writing your notes as a review of the article or book—that is, from your own point of view, giving the essential content of the article plus your comment on it—because that seems to be the form it will take in the final report. In other cases you will condense, digest, or abstract the article.

Whether you quote, paraphrase, review, or abstract the article or

MAIN CURRENT INDEXES

Title	Coverage	System	Publication Facts (Most Frequent Issue and Cumulation)
Readers' Guide to Periodical Literature	General American magazines	Alphabetically by author and subject	Semimonthly; semiannually
Industrial Arts Index	Business, scientific, engineering, technical, and semitechnical American and Canadian magazines	Alphabetically by subject and author	Monthly; annually
Accountant's Index	International technical books, magazines, and newspaper articles	Alphabetically by topics, authors, and titles	Supplemented irregularly about every three years
Engineering Index	Domestic and foreign literature on engineering	Alphabetically by topics	Annually, plus continuous card-file service
New York Times Index	The news in the paper	Chronologically and alphabetically by subjects, persons, and organizations	Semimonthly; annually
Agricultural Index	International on all printed sources	Alphabetically by subject and title	Monthly except September; quarterly
Education Index	Professional literature	Alphabetically by author and subject	Ten issues yearly; three-year
Public Affairs Information Service (*PAIS*)	Government documents and pamphlets of general, technical, and economic interest	Alphabetically by subject	Weekly except August; annually
International Index to Periodicals	Humanities, social sciences, and sciences; emphasis on history, international relations, political science, and economics	Alphabetically by author and subject	Monthly; three-year periods
For books: *Cumulative Book Index* (a supplement to the *United States Catalogue*)	Any book published in the United States	Alphabetically by author, title, and subject	Monthly; quarterly

book, you need to list in your bibliography all printed sources used directly in the preparation of the report; so you need to take the necessary information while you have the book or magazine in hand. Though bibliography form is not standardized, the usual information is author's name (surname first, for alphabetizing), title of book or article and magazine, publisher and place of publication for books, volume and page numbers for magazines, and the date. For use in citations in the text, you always need to record the specific pages used.

Observation. The second method of collecting data—observation —is used here to include not only its usual meaning but also investigation of the company records. As such, it is the main method used by accountants and by engineers for their inspection and progress reports. Their job of collecting data by observation usually involves no particular problem of getting at the facts. The important part is more likely to be knowing what facts to consider. That requires keeping in mind what the purpose is, so as to notice everything relevant and to relate each pertinent fact to the whole situation. The technique is well exemplified by a skilled policeman's investigation of a murder scene or of an automobile accident scene. Camera, measuring tape, and note pad are standard equipment for outside observation, just as the accountant's special paper, sharp pencil, and calculator are for inside inspection of the records. Still the most important pieces of equipment are sharp eyes to see the situation, judgment to evaluate it, and (most important) imagination to see the relevance of a particular observed fact to the whole problem.

Observation has the advantage of being convincing, just as the testimony of an eyewitness convinces a jury more than circumstantial evidence; but it has the disadvantage of not getting at motives. That is, it may answer *what* but not find out *why.* And unless the observer is careful, he may put too much stress on a few isolated cases or facts.

Laboratory Experimentation. For the most part, laboratory experimentation (which is closely related to observation as a method of collecting facts for reports) is useful in the physical sciences rather than in business and the social sciences and in industrial rather than commercial operations. And, of course, the methods used vary almost infinitely according to the particular experiment to be done. They are best taught by a specialist in the particular physical science, in the laboratory with equipment, rather than through a small section in a textbook mainly about something else. Regardless of his field of science, however, the laboratory researcher is as zealous as the report writer about the reliability of his results. The basic requirements for reliability in laboratory research are three:

1. Accurate equipment. If the laboratory balance is inaccurate or if the tachometer or thermometer misrepresents the facts, the results of an experiment using them will be unreliable.
2. Skilled techniques. If the technician doesn't know how to set his microscope, he won't be able to see an amoeba; and if he can't pipette both accurately and fast, he will be no good at Kahn tests.
3. Sufficient controlled repetition of results. If the laboratory researcher takes two specimens just alike, treats them exactly alike except in one

way (perhaps inoculates one, keeping the other for a control), and gets different results (say one gets a disease and the other does not), he makes a strong start toward convincing us. If he repeats the experiment and exactly the same happens every time (100 per cent), he need not make many repetitions to be thoroughly convincing. For every drop from 100 per cent, however, the scientist has to multiply his tests many times to produce similar faith in them. Testing one variable at a time is basic. If different soil, seed, and temperature are used, different results cannot be attributed to anything.

Experts in certain phases of business can use experimentation that closely parallels laboratory methods if they are careful about their equipment, techniques, and controls. For example, marketing specialists can test the comparative effects of different advertising campaigns and media, sales-promotional devices, prices, and packaging. Their problems of equipment and technique are psychological instead of mechanical and manual, and their controls are difficult to set up to make sure that only one element is changed; but experts can and do manage all three to assure reasonable reliability. (See pp. 237–40 on testing sales campaigns.)

Surveys.   Often in business the quality to be tested is not subject to exact laboratory examination—the sales appeal of a new car, for example. The only place to get an answer to that is from the people. In fact, the survey for fact and opinion vies with library research as a method of collecting data for business and social science reports. It is particularly useful in discovering WHY people do certain things and in FORECASTING what will happen (frequently an important job of reports).

Regardless of which of the three kinds of surveys you use—mail questionnaire, personal interview, or telephone interview—certain basic problems, principles, and techniques are involved.

The first problem is determining what people you will survey. In some cases you may decide that the opinion of a few experts will be worth more than the answers of thousands of the general public. If the whole group involved (called the "universe" by statisticians) is small, you may decide to ask all of them. But in most cases you take a sample.

For sound results you then have to decide on how large a sample is necessary. That will depend on the degree of accuracy required and on the variety of possible answers. For instance, if + or − 10 per cent is close enough, your sample can be much smaller than if you have to be accurate within a range of 1 per cent. And if you have to forecast election returns only in terms of Democratic, Republican, and other votes, your sample can be much smaller than if you have to forecast the purchases of the fifty or more makes and body styles of cars. As an even simpler illustration, it is certainly easier to predict the fall of a coin (only two choices) than of a pair of dice with eleven possibilities.

Even your adequate sample must be stratified (sometimes called "representative"), or your results can go wild. That is, each segment of the universe must be represented in the sample by the same percentage as in the universe. If 50 per cent of your universe are farmers and 70 per cent telephone subscribers, then half your sample must be farmers and 70 per cent telephone subscribers. Adequate size and stratification together make a sound sample.

A sound sample can still produce unsound results, however, unless your techniques of getting answers from it are also sound. If you start out by surveying a minimum sound sample but get answers from only half of it, the sample of actual answers is unsound because it is too small. If you survey more than enough and get a large enough sample of answers but 100 per cent of one stratification group answers and only half of another group answers, your stratification in results is thrown off and made unreliable. You may therefore have to toss out excess returns from some groups to keep returns from all groups in proportion to the original stratification. But, of course, the best method is to get 100 per cent returns from all groups—an ideal rarely accomplished.

How can you induce people to answer survey questions? Sometimes the reader is already so much interested, because his benefit is obvious, that you need not point it out to him. You can therefore begin directly with the request for help, as in the direct inquiry letters discussed on page 102. At other times you have a selling job to do, as in the persuasive requests discussed on pages 106 ff. Whether you are using mail questionnaire, personal interview, or telephone interview makes little difference in the approach. But to misjudge the situation and make a direct inquiry when you need a persuasive request may result in decreased returns.

Fundamentally, your persuasive method is the same as in persuading people to do anything, as in sales and collection letters: show them a benefit to themselves. It may be a gift or reward, direct payment of a fee, or less obvious and less material benefits such as appeals to pride and prestige (but not obvious flattery), appeals to their desire for better service or more efficiency in their kind of work, or the possibility of their getting answers to some questions or solutions to problems that they encounter in their own work. The last two are frequently the best (because they avoid suggesting a bribe or being too mercenary, as the first two might), and they are more immediate and tangible than the others. For instance, a personnel man who has to read lots of poor application letters is likely to answer a textbook writer's or a teacher's questions about what is desired in application letters—because of the possibility that he may as a result get more good applications and thereby make his work easier. A frequent method of inducing answers is the offer of a copy or digest of the survey results.

A big point to remember in making persuasive requests is to show a benefit *before* making the request. Then if you explain who is making the survey and why; make answering as easy, quick, and impersonal as possible; assure respondents that you will honor restrictions they put on use of the information; and ask pointedly just what you want them to do, enough people will usually do it to make your results reliable. Skilled approaches, both oral and written, often bring percentages of answers that surprise the untrained who have tried their hands and failed. (See pp. 106–16 for more detailed explanation of writing persuasive requests.)

The approach you use will be a major factor in determining your success in getting returns, but the questions you ask and how you ask them will affect both the percentage of returns and the worth of the answers. For that reason writers of questionnaires and people planning interviews keep in mind the following main principles used by professionals:

1. Ask as few questions as you can to get the necessary information. Don't ask other people for information you should have dug up for yourself, possibly in the library. And don't ask a question when you can figure the answer from the answers to others. To avoid unnecessary questions—which reduce returns—write down all you can think of, group them, then knock out the duplicates. (There is one kind of permissible duplication: double-check questions which get at the same information from different approaches as a check on the validity of answers.)

2. Ask only what you might reasonably expect to be answered. Requests for percentages and averages are either too much work or over the heads of many people. Questions requiring long memory may frustrate and bring erroneous results. And most people don't even know *why* they do many things.

3. Make your questions as easy to answer as possible (perhaps by providing for places to check); but provide for all likely answers (at least the "no-opinion" answer and perhaps the blank to be filled as the respondent wants to).

4. Make your questions perfectly clear. To do so, you may sometimes have to explain a bit of necessary background, but the question must be clear. If you ask "Why do you use X peanut butter?" you may get "It is cheapest," "A friend recommended it," and "I like its smooth texture and easy spreading" from three respondents. If you really want to know how the customer first learned of X, you should phrase the question that way

to get answers parallel to the second. If you are interested in the qualities that users like (as in the third answer), you should ask that specific question. Questions about *how* cause as many different interpretations as those asking *why,* and require the same kind of careful wording. Also, double-barreled questions (Did you see X and did you like it?) will confuse the reader if he wants to answer one part one way and one the other.

5. Carefully avoid leading questions—questions which suggest a certain answer, such as one to agree with the questioner's obvious view.
6. Insofar as possible, phrase questions to avoid the "prestige" answer—the respondent's answering according to what he feels he ought to think in order to make the best impression.
7. Avoid unnecessary personal prying. When your question is necessary to your basic purpose, make it as inoffensive as possible (for instance, by asking which named *income group* the respondent falls in, if that will serve your purpose, rather than his exact income).
8. Arrange questions in an order to encourage response—not too hard or personal ones at first, related ones together in a natural sequence to stimulate interest and aid memory.
9. Insofar as possible, ask for answers that will be easy to tabulate and evaluate statistically; but when they are important, don't sacrifice shades of meaning or intensity of feeling in the answer for easy handling.

After you have decided on the questions you want answered, your next problem is deciding which type of survey (mail questionnaire, personal interview, or telephone interview) will best serve your purposes. No one is always best. The main bases for your decision are as follows:

1. The kind and amount of information requested. People are more willing to tell you personal information—and more of it—than they are to put personal facts in writing or to do very much writing. The more-or-less anonymity of the interviewer and reluctance to talk long over the telephone with strangers are against the telephone method, but generally people consider talk cheaper and less dangerous than written statements. On the other hand, factual information (especially statistics, percentages, and averages) which may not be known at the moment may be dug up and written, because the respondent can take a little time with a mail questionnaire.
2. Costs. Within one telephone-exchange area, if your group is not large, the telephone is the cheapest method; but if it involves long-distance charges, they become prohibitive unless the group is small. The mail questionnaire has the advantage of wide geographical coverage at no additional cost; and the bigger the group, the greater the advantage, because copies of a good set of questions can be duplicated at little extra cost. The personal interview is almost always the most costly (mainly in interviewer's time) unless the group is small and close together. You need to consider cost per return, however; and since the mail question-

naire usually brings in the lowest percentage, its advantages may not be so great as at first thought unless a good covering letter and set of questions mailed at an opportune time induce a high percentage of answers.

3. Speed in getting results. If you have to have the answers today, you can get some of them by telephone (and by personal interview if your sample is not too large and the people are close together); but you can't get them by mail. Mail answers will flood you in about four days and dribble in for a week or more after that, unless you make clear that you need the information by a certain time (a point which needs careful justifying to avoid the bad manners of rushing a person to do you a favor).

4. Validity of results. In personal and telephone interviews people may give you offhand answers to get rid of you because the time of the call is inconvenient, and they may answer according to what they think is your view. In mail questionnaires they can choose the most convenient time and are more likely to answer thoughtfully or not at all. But those who choose not to answer may be a special group (say the less educated who don't like to write) and may thereby unstratify your carefully stratified sample. On the other hand, certain segments of the population have fewer telephones than others and thereby skew a telephone sample. And certain kinds of doors (maybe apartment dwellers') are hard to get into for personal interviews. But everybody has a mailing address where a mail questionnaire will reach him. Again, on the other hand, the personal interviewer may pick up supplementary information (such as the general look of economic conditions around the home and incidental remarks of the talker) that will provide a check on answers given—an impossibility by telephone and mail. Either the personal or telephone interview can better clear up any confusion about questions and thereby get appropriate answers. But in view of costs and time, the mail questionnaire is less likely to be limited to a too-small group or one that is geographically or economically limited.

5. Qualifications of the staff. Some people who can talk well and thus get information may not be able to write a good questionnaire and covering letter; and, of course, the opposite may be true. Even some good talkers have poor telephone voices that discourage that method. And others have disfigurations that discourage personal interviews.

If you select an adequate and stratified sample, induce the people to answer by showing a benefit, ask good questions, and use the most suitable type of survey, you can use surveys to get a great variety of valuable information for use in reports.

Organizing the Findings

However you collect the necessary facts for your report, you have to organize them for presentation and, if you're writing an analytical report, for your interpretation. You can't well evaluate a bridge hand until you have grouped the cards into the four suits and arranged the cards in order within the suits—mentally if not physically.

Basically, organization is the process of putting related things into groups according common characteristics *and your purpose* (playing poker instead of bridge, for example), and then putting the groups into a desirable sequence. In the process you may find that you have insufficient evidence for some points in your tentative outline and therefore have to get more; that some of your information seems contradictory and has to be reconciled; that some is really irrelevant or too detailed and needs to be discarded; or that you need to revise your tentative outline because the information does not logically classify according to your first plan. You will want to make sure, also, that things the reader needs to compare are close together.

Certainly you need to check your outline before going further. You may now be able to see enough interpretations of your data to make a sentence outline, as you couldn't earlier because sentences require you to *say something about* the topics. If you can, it will be easier to follow, it will force more careful thinking, and it will give your reader the essence of your report (not just the list of topics discussed but the key statements about those topics).

Whether you use full sentences or noun-phrase topics, close adherence to the following principles is necessary for a good outline:

1. Stick to one basis of classification as you break down any topic into its parts. College students can be classified according to credit hours earned as Freshmen, Sophomores, Juniors, Seniors, and graduates. You can't logically classify them as Juniors, Protestants, and Democrats. That shifts bases in helter-skelter fashion from credit hours earned to religion to politics. Thus you have overlapping of topics. And the divisions of an outline should be mutually exclusive.

   The proper basis of classification to use will be determined by your title and purpose. If your title is "Reasons for (or Why) . . . ," the major divisions of your outline can't logically be anything but the list of reasons. If the title is something like "Factors Influencing . . ." or "Ways to . . . ," each major division of the outline will have to be one of those factors or ways. (This does not forbid giving the introduction, conclusions, and recommendations similar major-division status in a table of contents. (See Item 4, p. 527.)

   In outlines of comparison leading to a choice, use the criteria (bases on which the choice depends) rather than the subjects (the things between or among which you must choose) as the major divisions. Your criteria are the things on which your choice will stand or fall, and hence they deserve the emphasis. (See Item 2, p. 527.)

2. Follow one good system to show the relationship of all the parts. The most widely used is symbolized with Roman capitals (I, II, III, etc.) for the major topics (which are logical divisions of your title), sub-divided as capital letters (A, B, C, etc.), subdivided as Arabic numbers (1, 2, 3, etc.), subdivided as lower-case letters (*a, b, c,* etc.).

3. Cover all categories—that is, all the divisions at any level must add up to the whole. All the capital Roman divisions together must add up to everything covered by the title, and all the capital letters under I must total I. In the example cited under Item 1, if you classify students according to political affiliation, you would most certainly have Republicans as well as Democrats, in addition to others. If you classify according to religion, you would certainly have to include non-Protestants along with Protestants.

4. Use no single subdivisions. If you start to divide I by putting a sub-head A, you must logically have at least a B; you can't divide anything without having at least two parts.

5. Organize for approximate balance. That is, try not to let some of your divisions cover huge blocks of your subject and others almost nothing. You probably need to reorganize on a different basis if you have five major divisions (say Roman capitals) and any one of those is more than half of the whole report. Of course, the nature of your subject may force you to imbalance. If you are writing about American politics, for example, the Democratic and Republican parties will each be bigger parts than all the rest, which you might group under "Others" or "Miscellaneous" for approximate balance. Inevitably some parts in the outline will be treated at greater length than others, but approximate balance is desirable.

6. Consider the psychological effects of the number of parts in any classification. Of course, the nature of the topic may dictate how many you have. For instance, according to credit hours earned, the classes in a university are just five—from freshmen to graduates—no more and no less. In breaking down some topics, however, you have some choice in the number. Having too few suggests that there was no need for the breakdown, or that you have not completed it; having too many puts a strain on the reader's mind to remember them. In some cases you may be wise to shift to a slightly different basis of classification that will lead to a more suitable number of divisions; and in other cases you can group some of the less important classes together.

7. Use parallel grammatical structure for parallel things. All the capital Roman divisions are parallel things; all the capital-letter divisions under one of them are parallel, but not necessarily parallel with those under another Roman division. They may all be complete sentences, all nouns or noun phrases (probably the best), or all adjectives.

8. Put the parts of each breakdown into the sequence most appropriate for your purposes. The over-all sequence or plan of a report is usually one of the following four:

   a) Direct (sometimes called "deductive"), giving the big, broad point first and then following with supporting details. This plan arouses more interest than some other plans do because it gets to the important things quickly, saves the busy reader time if he wants only the big idea, and provides a bird's-eye view so that he can read the rest more intelligently. It is therefore desirable if the reader is likely to be sympathetic with the big decision or if the writer is such an authority that his unsupported word would be readily accepted at least tentatively. But it risks the danger that the reader will raise objections at first and continue to fight the writer all the way through.

b) Inductive (sometimes called "scientific"), giving a succession of facts and ideas leading up to the big conclusions and recommendations at the end. The inductive plan is slow and sometimes puzzling until the conclusion tells where all the detailed facts lead to; but it is necessary in some cases for its strong logical conviction, especially when the reader is known to be opposed to the conclusions and recommendations that are coming.

c) Narrative (usually chronological accounts of activities). If there is no good reason against it—but there usually is—the narrative style of report is both the easiest to write and the easiest to read. The main objections are that it doesn't allow you to stress important things (it may have to begin with minor details, and the biggest things may be buried in the middle) and it doesn't allow you to bring together related things that have to be seen together for clear significance.

d) Weighted (that is, according to importance). The weighted plan's basic advantage is that it enables you to control emphasis by putting the most important points in the emphatic positions, first and last.

Whatever the over-all plan of organization, report writers use meaningful headings and subheads, topic sentences or paragraphs, standard transitional words and sentences, and summarizing sentences to indicate organization, to show the coherence of parts in the organization, and to tell the skimming reader the essence of the sections. The summarizing sentences, however, grow naturally out of the interpretation of the facts.

INTERPRETING THE FACTS

If the report is just informational, the writer is ready to write it up when he has organized his facts; but if it is to be analytical, he has then to study the facts and make his interpretation into conclusions and/or recommendations for the boss, as required. Since the reader wants a sound rather than a prejudiced basis for his executive decisions, the report writer's first consideration in making the interpretation is objectivity.

Nowhere else in report writing is objectivity more important—or harder to achieve. Since the writer is a person, his thinking is influenced by his whole background and personality; but he strives to be as objective and logical as possible. He knows the following two basic kinds of unobjective attitudes to avoid if his report is to be unbiased:

1. Preconception. If the writer thinks he knows the outcome and closes his mind to other possibilities before he collects and evaluates the facts, he may be influenced by that preconception to overlook or undervalue some facts and overstress others.
2. Wishful thinking. If he has a strong desire that the investigation turn out a certain way (because of a money interest or any other kind), he finds it hard not to manipulate facts (like the referee who has bet on the game) to make them lead to the desired result.

In addition to these dangerous attitudes to avoid if he is to be un-prejudiced, the report writer keeps in mind (as his second considera-tion) that if his interpretation is to be sound, it must avoid the pitfalls to logical thinking (called "fallacies"). Though some of them—like cir-cular argument and shifting the meaning of terms—are not likely to trap a report writer, the following are dangerous:

1. Using unreliable sources (both books and people), which may be un-reliable because of basic prejudice, because they are uninformed, or be-cause they are out of date. Though these things would have been checked in the process of collecting data, they might be checked again in the interpreting process.
2. Making hasty generalizations—that is, drawing conclusions on the basis of too little evidence (maybe too small a sample, too short a trial, too little experience, or just too few facts).
3. Using false analogies. Though true analogies (comparisons of things that are similar in many ways) are effective devices for explaining, by comparing unknown things to others the reader knows, even at their best they are weak as logical proof. And false analogies (applying prin-ciples valid in one case to another case where they don't belong) are tools of shysters and traps to the careless thinker. Essentially the same error results from a false analogy and from a person's putting a thing in the wrong class (say a persuasive-request situation misclassified as a direct inquiry) and applying the principles of the wrong class to it.
4. Stating faulty cause-and-effect relationships, such as
   a) Assigning something to one cause when it is the result of several.
   b) Attributing something to an incapable cause (for instance, one that came later).
   c) Calling something a cause when it is the effect of another cause.
5. Begging the question—just assuming, rather than giving evidence to support, a point that is necessary to the conclusions drawn.
6. Using emotional persuasion (usually characterized by strong and nu-merous adjectives and adverbs, or any kind of emotionally supercharged language like that of a defense attorney pleading with a jury) to in-fluence the reader, instead of depending on logical conviction through marshaling of fact.

7. Failing to distinguish, and make clear to the reader, what is fact, what is opinion, and what is merely assumption.

The report writer's third consideration in making his interpretation is discovering the really significant things to point out to the reader. If he avoids basic prejudice prompted by preconception or wishful thinking, avoids the pitfalls of various fallacies, and knows what to look for, he should be able to interpret the facts and draw sound conclusions. He can then turn them into practical recommendations that are general or concrete and specific, according to instructions when the report was assigned.

Some bosses want answers to all of what to do, who is to do it, when, and where; others feel that the report writer with so specific a solution to the problem infringes upon their prerogatives of making decisions. But all expect him to show the significance of his facts to the problem. In addition to an organization and presentation of facts that lead to the conclusions, the reader will expect the report writer to point out lesser interpretations along the way.

Causes, symptoms, effects, and cures are always important. So (in terms of graphic statistical data) are high points, low points, averages, trends, and abrupt changes (especially if you can explain their causes). Without going into disturbingly technical statistics, you can probably interest your reader in such measures of central tendencies as the mean (call it average), median (mid-point), and mode (most frequent item). Sometimes you might well use indicators of dispersion, such as standard deviation, range, and the -iles (percentiles, deciles, quartiles).

Certainly, your reader will be interested in comparisons that give significance to otherwise nearly meaningless isolated facts. For instance, the figure $7,123,191 given as profit for the year has little meaning alone. If you say it's 7 per cent above last year's profit, you add a revealing comparison; and if you add that it's the highest ever, you add another. If your volume of production is two million units, that means less than if you add that you're now fourth in the industry as compared with tenth two years earlier.

Breaking down big figures into little ones also helps to make them meaningful. For instance, the capital investment may be put in terms of so much per employee, per share of stock, per stockholder, or per unit of production. The national debt becomes more meaningful if given per citizen; the annual budget makes more sense if presented as a per-day or per-citizen cost; library circulation can best be put in terms of number of books per student.

Whatever the analysis reveals, the report writer needs to state it precisely. He therefore guards carefully against stating assumptions and opinions as facts. And he selects gradations in wording to indicate the degree of solidity of his conclusions. The facts and analyses will sometimes (but rarely) prove a point conclusively. They are more likely to lead to the conclusion that . . . , or indicate, or suggest, or hint, or point to the possibility, or lead one to wonder—and so on down the scale. Usually you can do better than stick your neck out by claiming to prove things you don't or draw your neck in too far with the timorous last three of these expressions. But phrasing the ideas well is a problem for the fifth and last step in report preparation—writing it up.

WRITING APPROPRIATE REPORT STYLE

The final writing-up of the report will not be difficult if the preceding four steps of preparation have been done well. But if your methods of collecting data have been faulty, you're trapped.

Since a report is usually the basis for an executive decision which may be costly if it is wrong, the executive reader rightfully expects the report writer to answer two important questions: What are the facts? How do you know? The second question means that the report writer must explain his sources and methods as a basis for the reader's judgment of the report's soundness. The only exceptions are in the reports of unquestionable authorities (whose word would be taken at full face value) and in cases where the methods and sources are already known or are clearly implied in the presentation of the facts.

In short reports, the sources and methods are best explained in incidental phrases along with the presentation of data, as in the following:

Four suppliers of long standing report him as prompt pay and. . . .

Standard quantitative analysis reveals 17 per cent carbon. . . .

Analysis of the balance sheet reveals. . . .

In the complete analytical report, the introduction explains methods and mentions printed sources (which are explained more specifically in the bibliography and in footnotes and/or other citations in the text).

At least any report writer except the recognized authority precludes what one reader expressed as "the distrust I have of those people who write as if they had a private line to God."

Documentation. Since printed materials are frequently used in collecting data for reports, citing those sources is an important means of assuring the reader about the soundness of the facts. On page 476 you have already seen the kinds of information to be put in a bibliography, but not bibliography and footnote forms. Unfortunately, the forms are not standardized; so unless you are sure that both you and your reader(s) understand other generally acceptable forms used in your field, we recommend the following for your bibliography:

> Wilkinson, C. W., J. H. Menning, and C. R. Anderson, *Writing for Business,* Richard D. Irwin, Inc., Homewood, Illinois, 1955.

(Some writers would add "413 pp." to this entry; many reputable writers would not—any more than they would add the price, though that is a common addition in reviews.)

> Wilkinson, C. W., "The History and Present Need of Reports," *The ABWA Bulletin,* 19:14–15, April, 1955.
> OR
> Menning, J. H., "A Half Century of Progress in Business Writing," *The ABWA Bulletin,* XV (January, 1951), pp. 4–11.

At those points in the report text where you make use of printed sources, you also tell the reader about them by specific references or citations. One way of doing so is footnoting, which is decreasing in use because footnotes heckle readers. A better method for most situations, and now coming into wider and wider use, is to interweave the minimum essentials of a citation subordinately right into the text, like this:

> Wilkinson says ("The History and Present Need of Reports," *The ABWA Bulletin,* 19:14, April, 1955) that reports now commonly serve one or more of the following five functions: overcoming separation of management and workers, saving time, overcoming technological incompetence, providing a file record, and supplementing the executive's own ideas with those of others.

For other illustrations, see pages 46, 231, and 599.

Still footnote citations (indicated by matching raised numbers in the text and before the footnote) may be necessary in some cases to avoid overcomplex sentences of a long citation interwoven in the text. In such cases, the first footnote, plus whatever bibliographical information may be given in the text, is a complete reproduction of the bibliographical entry with two minor changes: the author's name is in the normal order (given name or initials first), and the page reference is the specific page or pages used for that particular part of the report. Later footnotes to the same work can be shortened forms with the specific page number and just enough information for the reader to identify the source.

The practice of using Latin abbreviations (such as *op. cit., ibid.,* and *loc. cit.,* to mention only a few) that have long confused many people is disappearing along with footnotes. Except in scholarly writing for other scholars, the trend is toward using English words and a few standard abbreviations like "p." for page and "pp." for pages. People who communicate effectively know that if they want to be understood, they have to use language their readers understand.

Another citation system coming into wider use, especially in science and industry, involves these steps:

1. Numbering the listings in the bibliography after they are arranged in the usual (alphabetical) way,
2. Using the numbers and the specific page numbers, usually separated by colons and enclosed in parentheses, at the points in the report requiring documentation—usually just before the periods at the ends of sentences, and
3. Using a standard footnote to explain the first citation, somewhat like:

[1] In these parenthetical citations, the number before a colon refers to the item with that number in the bibliography and the number(s) following a colon refer(s) to the page(s) in that item.

Objectivity in Presentation. Clearly, the report reader expects the writer to demonstrate that he has been as objective as is humanly possible in collecting the data, in organizing and interpreting them, and finally in writing them up.

That does not mean, however, that you must follow an old rule and use impersonal style (which is sometimes erroneously called "objective" style). You can be just as objective when saying "I think such and such is true" as when saying "Such and such seems to be true" or even "Such and such is true." The second and third versions mean only that the writer thinks something is true. The only sound objection to the first version is that it wastes two words, not that it is personal style.

Whatever justification there is for recommending impersonal style in reports, as many books do, is that methods and results are usually the important things, and therefore they, rather than the persons who did the research, deserve emphasis as subjects and objects of active verbs.

But since things happen because people make them happen, the most natural and the clearest, easiest, most interesting way to tell about them is to tell who does what. A report about research done by its writer therefore naturally includes *I*'s; and if the writer keeps his reader(s) in mind, it also naturally includes *you*'s. To omit them is unnatural and dull, because you go out of your way to avoid the natural subjects of active verbs—or use too many inactive ones. It leads to lots of awkward, wordy, and weak passive-voice constructions; it gives away the third leg (Frequent Personal References) to Rudolf Flesch's three-legged stool of easy readability so that the stool falls; and it DOES NOT gain objectivity. The Japanese gained no objectivity—did not dodge the wishful thinking any more than they established the wishful sinkings—by reporting in impersonal style that "Eighty-seven American ships have been sunk in the Pacific." What they did gain was weak, awkward, and dull passive voice (p. 589). They might better have gained the interest and readability value of personal references—without increasing the basic prejudice—by reporting to the American troops that "We have sunk 87 of your ships."

Actually, more destructive to objectivity than the use of a personal style is the use of too many or too strong adjectives and adverbs, or any kind of feverish, high-pressure, hot-under-the-collar writing. Such a heightened style—using emotional connotations, fancy figures of speech, and other techniques of oratory—has its place where the author feels deeply and wishes his reader to feel deeply about the subject; but it is out of fashion today, is sometimes distrusted, and is inappropriate in reports anyway because both writer and reader are expected to think hard rather than feel deeply.

Except for the fact that letter style allows more use of emotional persuasion than report style does, the discussion of style in Chapter III applies to reports as well as letters. Report writers certainly use commonly understood words, short sentences so direct that they require little punctuation, short paragraphs so direct that they require few transitional words, and itemizations. But since the report writer often covers so many more topics, and at greater length, he has a bigger job of showing the relationship of parts to one another and each to the whole. In addition, report writers also make more extensive use than letter writers of two other techniques of presenting ideas clearly, quickly, and easily for the reader: headings and subheads and nonverbal means of communication.

Headings and Subheads. Because they are usually longer than letters and because the reader may want to recheck certain parts, reports use headings and subheads, in addition to topic and summarizing sentences, to show the reader the organization, where he has been, and where he is going. For the same reasons and purposes, we have used headings in this book. If you have not thought about them already in those lights, for illustration flick back through some parts of the book with which you are well acquainted and see if they don't serve those purposes.

Skill in using heads and subheads can be a valuable technique in your writing, not only of reports but of anything else that is very long—maybe even long letters.

The only reasonable test of how far to go in putting in subheads is this: Will they help the reader? If so, put them in; if not, leave them out.

Despite the fact that headings and subheads are great helps to readers, no single system of setting them up is in universal use. More important than what system you use is that you use some system consistently and that the reader understand it. Most readers understand and agree on the following principles:

1. A good heading should indicate clearly the content below it, should have reader interest, and should be as brief as possible without sacrificing on either of the other two requirements. Trying to keep titles too short, however, frequently leads to sacrifice of exactness. Usually a short heading is too broad (includes more than the discussion below it covers), or it tells nothing about the topic. Of course, you do not always want the heading to try to tell any more than the topic to be discussed, lest the reader fall for that dangerous thing—a little learning—and read only the head. But in mass communications such as newspapers and magazines, you feel lucky to get most readers to read even the headings; so you tell as much as you can in them. Note the difference, in examples from annual reports, between "Profits" and "Profits up 8% from last year," and between "Position in the industry" and "Position in industry changes from 8th to 4th." In other reports where some readers might only skim, you can help them a lot by making your headings tell the big point about the topic instead of just naming the topic to be discussed.

2. The form and position of the head must make its relative importance clear at a glance. That is, headings for all divisions of equal rank (say the Roman-numbered ones in an outline) must be in the same type form and position on the page, but different from their superiors (of which they are parts) and from their inferiors (their subdivisions). Putting heads of different levels in the same form and position is confusing; it misrepresents the outline.

3. Centered heads are superior to side heads in the same form (compare second- and third-degree heads below); heads in capitals are superior to those in caps and lower case; and heads above the text are superior to those starting on the same line with the text (compare third- and fourth-degree heads below).

4. Heads should not be depended on as antecedents for pronouns or as transitions. The one word *This* referring to an immediately preceding head is the most frequent offender. Transitions between paragraphs and between bigger subdivisions should be perfectly clear if the headings were removed.

5. In capital-and-lower-case heads capitalize the first word and all others except articles (*a, an,* and *the*), conjunctions (for example *and, but, for, because*), and prepositions (such as *to, in, of, on, with*).

Those principles are illustrated and further explained in the five-level breakdown below. If you need a further breakdown for your report, you can type the first heading in spaced C A P I T A L S and move each level of heading up one notch. Note that *above* second- and third-degree heads the spacing is *two* more than the double spacing of the discussion and that *below* them it is *one* more than the text spacing.

FIRST-DEGREE HEADING

The title of your whole report, book, or article is the first-degree heading. Since there is only one title, no subhead should be written in the same form. As illustrated here, the title is written in the most superior form and position. The heading above this paragraph is a good choice for a first-degree heading.

Second-Degree Heading

If you use solid capitals centered on the page for the first-degree heading, a good choice for the second-degree headings is caps and lower case, as illustrated here. Preferably, it and any other uncapitalized head should be underscored to make it stand out, though some people say it should be only if its immediate superior is. Of course, if

you do not need the five-level breakdown here, you
could start with this form for the first-degree
head.

Third-degree heading

   To distinguish the third-degree headings from
their superiors, you may wisely choose to change
position and put them at the left margin above the
text, underscore them to make them stand out, and
write them in initial-cap form (as here) or in cap
and lower case (which would require capitalizing
the H in Heading).

   Fourth-degree heading.--For further breakdowns
into a fourth level, you may place headings at the
paragraph indention on the same line with the text
and write them as caps and lower case or as
straight lower case. They definitely need to be
underscored and separated from the first sentence,
preferably by a period and dash, as here. Some
people drop the dash.

   The fifth-degree headings can be well handled as
integral parts of the first sentence of the first
paragraph about a topic. If they are underscored

(which means italic type when printed), they will

stand out sufficiently without further distinc-

tions in form.

Nonverbal Assists to Words. Since reports so frequently present statistics (quantitative data), designs, organizational plans, and the like, they make much use of tables, charts, graphs, pictograms, drawings, and maps. But in most cases these devices only assist, not replace, words. Interpretation of graphics is not one of the three *R*'s learned by everybody. So most graphics help to explain and/or support the text only if the text helps them by telling the reader how to look at them and what they mean.

The usual procedure is a few words of interpretation, interweaving a reference to the table or the graphic presentation, then use of the best type of graph for the purpose, and then further comment on (interpretation of) the presentation.

It is important to put the table/graph and the comment close together so that the reader can see both at once; each one supplements the other; neither is complete by itself.

The graphics need to be carefully labeled as a whole and by parts, and provided with a key if necessary. Variations in colors, shadings, and kind of line (solid *versus* broken, for example) are common key devices for distinguishing the different kinds of data.

Complete discussion of the uses, advantages, and disadvantages of the various types of graphics would require more space than is appropriate here; but the following suggestions will be useful:

1. Use line graphs (perhaps marking the tops of columns in a bar chart) to represent trends according to time. Usually the perpendicular axis should represent volume and the base (or horizontal) axis should represent time. Two or more lines, usually in different colors, can show relative positions as well as the position of each at any given time.

   Unless you are using several lines or bars (but not so many as to confuse!) and are interested only in their comparative values rather than their individual changes, be sure to start at 0 as the base. If, for example, you use 40 as the base of the quantity scale and we assume that the first year represented is 50 and the second 60, the second year appears to have doubled the first, whereas it has increased only 20 per cent—as it would and should look on base 0.

   Providing grid lines will help avoid optical illusions and give the reader a quick and precise idea of just where a line is at any given time in the graph.

Remember, also, to use faired (curved) lines for continuously changing data and straight lines to connect plotted points of data that change by steps, such as enrollments in a university by semesters.

2. Use segmented bars or pie charts moving clockwise from 12:00 to represent the proportions in the breakdown of a whole. Usually the color or shading of sections distinguishes the parts (which should not be confusingly numerous), and they are labeled with both the raw figures and the percentages for precision.

3. Maps for geographical distribution of almost anything; organization charts of rectangles arranged and connected to show lines of authority and communication; flow charts, showing movement and stages in processing; blueprints, giving precise sizes and relationships; and photographs, picturing accurate size, texture, and color are all useful graphic devices in their places if they are kept simple enough for easy reading and if they concentrate on the point under discussion.

4. Use symbolic pictograms (like little men representing workers or bags of money representing profits) to add interest, especially for nontechnical readers, when you have the time and money and are preparing a report in enough copies to justify the costs. But keep all the little characters the same size (though each may represent any quantity) and vary the *number* of them to represent different total quantities. Otherwise you mislead because the volume in the pictogram involves a third dimension (depth perspective) not shown in the pictogram. Of two cylinders representing oil production, for example, one actually twice as big as the other looks only slightly bigger because of the unseen third dimension. Even in the best usage, pictograms are not precise unless you write in the exact quantities. Pictograms should be drawn to avoid prejudicial side messages, too—such as the unfavorable and irrelevant suggestion that all welfare cases are diseased, decrepit, or dumb in the drawings of a pictogram designed to represent the changing *number* of welfare cases. .

Beyond that, the writing-up of a report depends on the particular form to be used; and the form you choose should be the one best adapted to the situation, as explained along with the illustrations in Chapter XV.

[All the problems on reports are at the end of Chapter XV.]

XV. Reports: Writing Them in Appropriate Form and Style

~~~~~~

THE form in which a report is to be written should, of course, depend on the situation—mainly who its reader is, its purpose, and its length. This chapter explains in more detail and illustrates the most important forms to be learned. **The illustrations are NOT presented as perfect reports, and certainly are NOT to be followed slavishly or copied parrot-like. At best, they show acceptable content, form, and general style for their particular situations as starters to your thinking on those points for your situation.**

Though we recognize that strictly informational, periodic reports are the most numerous kind, we do not discuss them because they are mostly printed forms to be filled in with figures and perhaps a little other writing and are therefore really report-writing jobs only to the people who devise the original forms. We therefore treat the commonly used forms which do raise real report-writing problems.

WRITING THE COMPLETE ANALYTICAL REPORT

Except for extensive, formal ones, complete analytical reports usually include the nine parts explained and illustrated.

Title Page. Usually there is an outside cover with title and author's name on it. Even so, the title page is the first of the preliminary pages (counted as lower-case Roman numbers and going down to the introduction), but the *i* does not need to appear on it. Four other blocks of information do: the title itself, the name and title of the reader, the name and title of the writer, and the place and date. In many instances the name of the organization with which both writer and reader are connected is desirable information also. If the report is to be bound, remember to leave extra space on this and all other pages so that no writing will be hidden.

Like any other heading, the title should indicate precisely (not too much and not too little), concisely (without wasted words such as "A Report on . . ." or "A Survey of . . ."), and interestingly the content of the report. If you can't do that in about 20 words or less, you might consider writing a short title and supplementing it with a secondary clarifying title (usually in parentheses a couple of lines lower); but you should not use a subtitle to dodge reasonable efforts at making one title do the job well.

In looking at the accompanying illustration of the title page, note how the writer blocked her information into four parts, how she used balanced layout, and how specific she made her title. A report is information about a specific problem of a businessman or a definite group, and the title should indicate that specificness (often to the extent of naming the man or group as well as the problem). You can't answer such a general question as "Should Spot Radio Advertising Be Continued?"

Letter of Transmittal. Unless the report is an extensive and formal one, including such things as a copyright notice, letter of authorization, and letter of acceptance, page ii (counted, but not necessarily numbered) is a letter of transmittal. Written after the report is completed, in regular letter form (Chapter IV) and a style appropriate to the circumstances, it must do at least two things: transmit the report and refer to the authorization. (In the rare cases where there is no authorization, instead of the reference the writer tells enough to arouse interest in the report.) In informal situations, one sentence can do both:

WHY THE A. L. BANGS COMPANY SHOULD DISCONTINUE SPOT RADIO ADVERTISING

Prepared for

Mr. A. L. Bangs

President

by

Evelyn Lowen

Assistant Buyer

Tremont, Ohio

December 1, 195--

"Here's the report on fish poisoning you asked me to write when we were talking on May 10." Usually it needs to be a little more formal than that, but it needs no bromidic "As per your request, . . ." and rarely such formality as "In accordance with. . . ." Certainly it needs to subordinate the reference to the authorization to avoid a flat and insulting sound of seeming to tell the reader that he asked for the report, as if he were too dumb or forgetful to remember. More than likely it will say more than the minimum essential of one sentence, if for no other reason than to avoid a curt tone and to enhance the value of the report in the reader's eyes.

Some additional things it might talk about (but not all in any one letter) are

—A highlight particularly significant in affecting the findings, or a reference to special sections likely to be particularly interesting to the reader.

—A summary of conclusions and recommendations if the reader is likely to be sympathetic, provided that there is no synopsis two or three pages later. Even then, the letter can give the general decision but not supporting data.

—Side issues or facts irrelevant to the report but interesting or valuable to the reader.

—Limitations of information, time, and money—provided that they are not established in the introduction, where they naturally belong if they are true, and provided that they do not sound like lazy excuses.

The letter may appropriately end with some expression indicating the writer's attitude toward the significance of the report and/or his own appreciation for having been allowed to work on it.

The writer of the transmittal letter which appears on the next page wisely elected to incorporate her summary or synopsis in the letter, thus saving time for her reader. Had the synopsis been longer, she would have handled it separately, immediately after the Contents.

Contents.   The next part, usually page iii (with the number centered at the bottom, as always on a page with extra space at the top because of a heading), is what is commonly called "Table of Contents," or simply "Contents." It sets out the headings of the report and their beginning page numbers.

To list in it those pages that come before it looks a little odd; the reader would already have seen them. But if a separate synopsis comes after the table of contents, you list it flush left, usually as the first thing on the list. Remember that it is NOT a part of the outline and does not get an outline symbol, such as I or A, but only its name and page number (usually small Roman iv).

Then comes the real outline of the report—the headings and subheads. In most reports it's best to give all of them. They are reproduced in exactly the same wording as elsewhere but not necessarily in the same type. Preferably they should be preceded by the outline symbols —capital Romans for the major divisions (including the introduction, conclusions, and recommendations) and capital letters for their subdivisions, according to the system of outlining suggested earlier. (Remember that Romans line up on the right.) If any heading runs over to a second line, it should be cut under (indented). Each heading is then

Letterhead

December 1, 195--

Mr. A. L. Bangs, President
The A. L. Bangs Company
Tremont, Ohio

Dear Mr. Bangs:

Here is the report you requested two weeks ago concerning the advisability of
continuing the spot radio advertising which you started last May.

The cost figures gathered from Station WFRO and the Tremont News Messenger, and
analysis of your store sales figures, support the recommendation that you concentrate your advertising dollars on newspaper space.

Here are some of the significant reasons:

   --though the radio provides more extensive coverage, the newspaper
     circulation more nearly corresponds to the store's trading area

   --radio can reach more homes around Tremont because 21,368 families
     own radios but only 11,354 receive newspapers

   --radio ads cost only twice as much per family theoretically reached
     (19.9¢/1,000 vs. 10.04¢/1,000) but--because only one out of five
     families listen to commercials--27 times as much per person actually
     reached (82¢ per 1,000 vs. 3¢ per 1,000)

   --even so, people don't remember commercials as long as they do ads
     in newspapers (probably because the newspaper is available for
     reference later).

BUT THE MOST CONVINCING REASON IS THAT

   --Bangs sales of individual items spot-advertised as well as total
     sales showed little difference (1%) during the time you advertised
     by radio. The single item that showed any appreciable increase was
     maternity wear--a new department, without competition in the town.

I've enjoyed making the study. Please call on me if I can help further.

             Sincerely yours

             Evelyn Lowen
             Assistant Buyer

followed by a leader line of spaced periods leading to the page number,
as in the illustration on page 502.

Supplementary parts such as appendixes and the bibliography are
given Arabic page numbers like the body copy, but they do not get
Roman numbers to the left in the table of contents because they are
not logical parts of the discussion being outlined. The accompanying
illustration does not list a bibliography simply because the report did
not have one as a separate section. If your report does—as it probably
should unless very short—list it, flush left.

The contents may be single- or double-spaced, or single-spaced

Contents

within parts and double-spaced between, whichever makes the best appearance on the page.

Synopsis. Written after the report proper has been completed, the synopsis is a condensed version of the whole report (introduction, presentation of facts and the interpretations of them, and conclusions and recommendations—the last two either separately or together). It is the report in a nutshell. Usually it should be somewhere between a 10:1 and 20:1 reduction. In most cases the introduction should be reduced even more, and the conclusions and recommendations less because they deserve the main emphasis.

Synopsis

Savannah people are likely to buy more at a Rexwall Drug Store than Charleston
residents are, according to this market evaluation prepared for the Chairman
of the Board, Rexwall, Inc., by Factseekers, Inc.

Though metropolitan Charleston merchants serve 11,000 more customers from the
shopping area, Savannah retailers can expect some trade from almost twice as
many out-of-town buyers (340,000 versus 184,000). Savannah's 1,000 more family
units more than compensate for the fact that the Charleston family averages
3.62 people while the smaller Savannah family averages 3.4.

Savannah individuals average $85 more buying income, but the larger Charleston
families average $35 more per family for a total of half a million more annual
buying income. With less first-mortgage money to do it, 2,800 more people in
Savannah have built homes in the past four years; but 17,000 more Charlestonians
own automobiles.

The higher buying income of the individual Savannah buyer and the larger number
of customers from around Savannah explain why $2.5 million more passed through
the hands of Savannah retailers last year. Individually, Savannah residents
spent $75 more; the smaller Savannah family, however, spent only $55 more.

Though in 1948 Charleston druggists outsold those in Savannah by an average of
$3,000, last year the 61 Savannah drug-store managers and owners collected about
$5 million--$170,000 more than 62 Charleston druggists--for an average of $4,000
more per drug store in Savannah.

Overall business factors also point to Savannah as the choice. Savannah's
estimated business volume of $989 million is almost twice that of Charleston.
Since a significant part of this difference is attributable to the 10 million
more tons of cargo handled by the Savannah docks, Savannah consumers and retailers
will feel the pinch of recessions and strikes more than Charlestonians. The
extra $36 million added by Charleston manufacturing, however, is almost as un-
certain in the stability of that city as the effects of shipping are on the
economy of Savannah. Charlestonians benefit from $35 million more of the rela-
tively stable wholesale business; but $32 million more agricultural income from
farms averaging $4,000 in value helps to bolster the Savannah economy.

Certainly Savannah's business activity has been consistently better than
Charleston's in the past four years. Though the trend continues up in both
cities, construction has averaged $12 million more annually in Savannah.
Bankers in Savannah have consistently received about 10% more deposits than
their Charleston counterparts have--for $150 million more in commercial accounts
and $12 million more in savings. In both cities postmasters have collected
about 8% more each successive year, but Savannah citizens have steadily paid
for $200,000 more postage than Charlestonians have.

iv

Since the synopsis stresses results, it should not be used in a report which needs to be strongly convincing because of the reader's likely resistance; the condensed presentation of findings may not be adequate to do the necessary convincing before the reader sees the unwelcome conclusions.

But in a report which may properly follow the deductive plan because the results are probably welcome to the reader, the synopsis serves two important purposes: (1) it saves time for the busy reader who may find there all he wants; and (2) even for the reader who goes on through the whole report, the synopsis gives him a bird's-eye view which enables him to read the rest more easily and more intelligently because he can see how each fact or explanation fits into the final results which he already knows.

The letter of transmittal in the report illustrated here (p. 501) is also an example of synopsizing. For another example, read the more detailed synopsis (p. 503) of a different report long enough to make necessary a separate synopsis (the better practice in all but short reports). It specifically and concisely synopsizes a report of six major divisions (besides the introduction and the conclusions and recommendations) running to 27 pages. Desirably, it focuses on a quick presentation of results (the decisions) in the first paragraph, while also giving just enough of the introductory material for coherence and clarity. Then it summarizes the six data-filled sections in the same order and proportionate space given the topics in the full report. For readers not used to market-research data, headings like the following might have helped: Population and Buying Units, Buying Income, Retail Sales, Drug Store Sales, Over-all Business Factors and Stability, Business Activity.

Whenever possible, confine the synopsis to one page. Even though your report is double-spaced, single-space the synopsis if such spacing will help you keep to one page—for two reasons: (1) favorable reaction of your reader and (2) good training in condensation for you.

Since the synopsis is derived exclusively from the report itself—which is adequately illustrated and documented—you need neither graphics nor citations. But you do need to give the main supporting facts. Otherwise the synopsis becomes a nutshell with no meat.

Introduction.   The introduction to a complete analytical report serves primarily to answer the second of a report reader's two inevitable questions: How do you know? Rarely does it answer any part of the first question, What are the facts?

But since the introduction does begin the body of the report—which also includes the findings of fact and their interpretation, the conclusions, and the recommendations if the reader wants them—the title of the whole report appears at the top of the page, which is numbered Arabic 1 (centered at the bottom instead of at the upper right, as always on a page with extra space at the top because of a heading there).

In explaining how he knows the forthcoming facts to be reliable, the report writer states his purpose and his methods and scope, so that the reader can judge whether the research would produce information that is sound and adequate for the purpose. Unless the reader sees that the research is basically sound, he naturally discredits the whole report because he sees that the writer doesn't really know but just thinks he does.

WHY THE A. L. BANGS COMPANY SHOULD DISCONTINUE SPOT RADIO ADVERTISING

The WHY and HOW of This Report

Purpose.--After the A. L. Bangs Company of Tremont, Ohio, started using
spot radio advertising in its program, the question arose, "Is this advertising practical enough to warrant its continued use?" This study answers
that question.

Present conditions.--Since May of 19-- the Bangs Company has broadcast
spot ads on Monday, Tuesday, and Thursday at 12:35 p.m. over station WFRO AM/FM.
This time is in the Class A bracket ($4.25 for each spot if broadcast 104 times
a year), which includes the times of day when the listening audience is the
largest.

As usual, advertising continues in the Tremont News Messenger and through
stuffers sent with the monthly statements.

Scope and methods.--To determine how effective radio advertising is for
the store, I first compared trading-area coverages of the radio and the newspaper, based on an area map of the radio coverage (prepared for WFRO by a
radio-engineering firm) and subscription lists from the newspaper. To identify
the area from which the Bangs Company draws most of its business, I tabulated
the residence of each charge customer. Figures on the number of families and
of radio families in each of the principal towns came from the latest Census
of Population. Newspaper subscription lists established number of homes
reached by newspapers.

1

The introduction, then, is an important part of the conviction in the report and therefore deserves careful attention from both writer and
reader.

You can make a good start by selecting a heading for it that gives a
preview of its contents more precisely and more interestingly than the
dull, stock term "INTRODUCTION." The accompanying illustration,
you notice, does better; but you don't need to use its wording.

Besides the standard parts, an introduction may take up one or more
(rarely all) of several other possible topics. For readers who may not
know the background to the problem, it may include a little history.

2

To find out how many people were actually reached by the newspaper and the radio station, I used statistics compiled for each of them by such recognized agencies as the Audit Bureau of Circulation and the A. C. Nelson Company. Much of the information on the listening habits of Tremont people came from a survey conducted three months ago by Robert S. Conlan and Associates, Inc.

Daily sales tickets of the Bangs store showed the number of sales of each item, which I cross compared against WFRO records showing the type of merchandise spot-advertised and when.

Total Bangs sales figures for last year (from the accounting department) were adjusted to find out what sales should have been this year in the light of national sales trends as reported by the National Industrial Conference Board Publications. These adjusted sales figures are compared with actual sales to determine the overall effect of the radio advertising introduced this year.

Limitations.--Comparing number of words in a spot ad to the number of words in lines of newspaper advertising is admittedly open to question; nevertheless, it is one means of evaluating. Furthermore, the number of people listening to the radio at any one time and their concentration or inattention are impossible to verify. And the great number of factors affecting sales--weather, factory strikes, for example--make it impossible to attribute fluctuations to any one cause with absolute certainty that you are right. On the other hand, if radio spot advertising has any effect on the sales of the Bangs Company, we can reasonably assume that it would show up in some of the items specifically advertised or in the total sales over the test period.

If the background can be kept short, it is usually the first part of the introduction and leads into the statement of purpose; otherwise, to avoid delaying the statement of purpose, the writer starts with that and uses the flash-back method to follow quickly with the clarifying background to the problem. He may relegate any very long background story to the appendix and refer the needy reader to it.

Sometimes the report uses technical words or certain terms applied in a sense unfamiliar to likely readers. If so, the writer may explain them in the introduction or, preferably, in brief parenthetical statements immediately following the first use of each special term.

Any special materials, apparatus, or techniques need to be explained, to assure the reader of their soundness. Whether they are explained in the introduction, or along with the presentation of the findings, or in an appendix (where a long survey questionnaire might appear) will depend on the complexity and the detail necessary for clarity and conviction of soundness. In general, explain the whole thing in the introduction. Specific details of an experiment or specific questions on a questionnaire may, however, be best presented along with the findings. Only complex formulas or new research procedures are likely to call for a special appendix of explanation (usually for the uninitiated reader, who is referred to it). The important point is to answer the big question—How do you know?—*before* the reader asks it.

Then you are ready to present the assuredly reliable facts.

Before asking the reader to go on this mental journey, however, be sure you give him a final reminder of his route: a concise statement of plan. Such a statement should not be long or detailed in its itemization of *all* your headings. Usually one effective sentence can chart the way through to the end, like this:

> As bases for determining the more favorable market conditions, the report examines—in this order—population characteristics, buying power, retail sales and drug store sales and the attendant competition, stability of the economy, and the current business outlook.

The statement of plan is probably more useful at the end of your introductory remarks (next page), but it may be incorporated with the explanation of purpose, method, scope, or limitations.

Text. Even the lazy writer who gets by with INTRODUCTION as the heading for that part cannot get by with TEXT as a heading covering the biggest part of the report, where the writer presents his findings and analyses of them. The stock term, fitting all reports and therefore useful in talking about them, fits no one report well.

But, more important, the text section of the report is fundamentally the report; so if you try to phrase a suitable title for the section, it will be the same as the title of the whole report. Then the basic elements of your report—the factors or criteria on which the final decision is based—become third-degree headings with seemingly too little significance.

That is the first of the two major problems confronting the writer in presenting the text of his report: (1) showing the reader the organization carefully worked out as the third step in preparation and (2) phrasing well the findings of the second step and the interpretations made in the fourth step. Satisfactory solutions to both are necessary if you are to give your reader the reliable information he wants.

Your main methods for showing the over-all organization, the rela-

3

Basic plan.--To help answer the fundamental question, this report examines
both radio and newspaper coverage, cost, and retention value before analyzing
sales records.

Greater Coverage by Radio but More Selectivity through Newspaper

Both cover trading area; some waste in radio.--As you can readily see from
the three maps on the following pages /good things in the report, omitted here
for reasons of economy/, the A. L. Bangs Company's trading area is completely
covered by both the daily newspaper, the Tremont News Messenger, and radio
station WFRO AM/FM. This area includes all of Landu County and also the neigh-
boring parts of three adjoining counties.

The newspaper's coverage by carrier and mail delivery closely resembles
the Company's trading area. Mail delivery, however, is one day later than the
date of publication.

On the other hand, the radio covers the entire trading area as well as a
much larger secondary area from which the Company draws no trade.

Both the radio and the newspaper cover the trading area, but much of the
radio advertising is wasted because it goes to people who do not trade in
Tremont.

Radio covers more families.--A much better idea of the coverage comes from
comparing the number of families in the trading area reached by radio and those
reached by newspaper. According to the latest Census of Population figures
and newspaper circulation records, the number of radio families in the principal cities and towns in the retail trading area (21,368) just about doubles

tions between parts, and the relation of each part to the whole are headings and subheads, topic sentences, and summary and foreshadowing
statements. The headings and subheadings grow directly out of your
attack on the problem, where you broke it down into its elements and
further subdivided it by raising questions about each. Now that you are
presenting the facts that provide the answers, you need only phrase
those elements and questions into headings and the subheads that are
indicative, interesting, concise, and (in some cases preferably) informative to the extent of telling the most important findings about the respective parts.

4

the number of newspaper subscriptions, as shown in the following table /omitted7.
Radio families are almost 100% of the total families of the area (22,204) and
newspaper subscriptions about half that. Therefore most families in these
principal cities and towns could be exposed to radio advertising.

Although the radio ads cover some unnecessary area, they still make it
possible to reach a greater proportion of the people the Company wants to reach
than is possible through newspaper advertising.

Higher Cost of Radio Advertising

Radio costs 4:1 for same content.--To compare the costs of newspaper
advertising to those of radio advertising, I experimented with different ads
and found that on an average people read two column inches of advertising in
20 seconds, the length of the average Bangs spot ad. On the assumption that
a 20-second spot and a two-column-inch ad are comparable in content, I determined
the relative costs of $4.25 (WFRO rate chart) and $1.14 (57¢/column inch).

Those figures alone do not tell the complete story, however; for according to Paul F. Lazarsfeld and Patricia L. Kendall (Radio Listening in America,
Prentice Hall, New York, 1948, p. 373), successful spot radio advertising
depends on frequency of broadcast.

On the basis of content alone, radio spot advertising is clearly much
more expensive than newspaper advertising. The repetition necessary for success
only makes it more so.

Radio costs 2:1 for each family theoretically reached.--It is possible--
and frequently true--however, that a higher priced ad may reach so many
families that its cost per family may be lower than a less expensive one.

Just as a well-phrased heading may tell the main point about the
section over which it stands, a topic sentence can give the essence of a
paragraph and clearly foreshadow what the paragraph says. The topic
sentence puts the big point across fast, arouses the reader's interest in
seeing the supporting details that follow, and makes reading easier because of the preview. Though the resulting deductive paragraph plan is
not the only one possible, it is the most useful for most kinds of writing,
including report writing.

Reversing the plan produces a paragraph which presents a series of
facts and arguments leading to a summarizing sentence at the end.

5

To find the cost for each family theoretically reached by radio, I divided the number of homes with radios (21,368) into the cost of one spot ad ($4.25) to arrive at a cost of 19.9¢/1,000 families. The same procedure applied to a newspaper ad shows a cost of 10.04¢/1,000 subscribers ($1.14 ÷ 11,354). Since a very large part of these subscriptions go to families (only a very few to business firms), we can safely say that to reach a family by radio costs almost twice as much as by newspaper advertising.

Radio costs 27:1 for each person actually reached.--But not all radios are turned on and even if turned on some will not be tuned to WFRO.

Advertisers figure that one-third of the radio families will not be at home and another one-third will not have their radios turned on. Of the 21,368 radios in the Tremont area, then, only 7,123 are likely to be tuned to WFRO under the most optimistic circumstances.

Tremont families listen to other stations more frequently than they listen to WFRO, however. On an average 43% of the sets, 3,063, will be tuned to the local station.[1] And when a Tremont radio is on, 1.7 people are listening. Accordingly, we can reasonably assume that 5,207 people are actually exposed to the commercial and thus arrive at the cost of 81.6¢/1,000 people actually reached ($4.25 ÷ 5,207).

The News Messenger, with a circulation of 11,354 in the Bangs trading area, has a secondary readership of 3.5 persons per copy (both figures from Readership of the Tremont News Messenger, Audit Bureau of Circulation, 1954). Since the estimated number of persons exposed to a newspaper ad is 39,739

-----

[1] Study of Listening Habits--Tremont, Ohio, Robert S. Conlan and Associates, Inc., 1954, p. 5.

Both plans may be applied to larger sections as well as to paragraphs. In fact, both a paragraph's topic sentence and the first part of a larger section may reflect, summarize, or provide a transition from a preceding part, as well as give the essence and preview of what is to follow. And endings of both paragraphs and larger parts commonly summarize them, show the significance of the just-completed part to the whole problem at hand, and foreshadow what is to follow in the next section (as the ending of the illustrated introduction does). Though the summaries may indicate the advisability of a certain action, they should not go further and steal the thunder of the recommendation section by actually saying that the action should be taken.

6

(11,354 x 3.5) and the cost of the ad is \$1.14, we can for all practical purposes
assume a cost of 2.87¢/1,000. Radio, then is almost 27 times as expensive in
terms of people actually reached. [A summary table appeared here.]

Greater Retention Value of Newspaper Ads

The most significant point to establish in considering relative retention
value of advertising media, I believe, is that advertising in a small town
like Tremont to a large extent is merely keeping the store name and the merchandise before the public. People here do not respond to advertising as
quickly as they do in large cities; they wait until they had planned to go
downtown to shop before they come to the store.

Mr. J. W. Clark (President, Kirby, Clark, Inc., New York), at a recent
conference of buyers which I attended, pointed out the postponed-buying habits
of people in towns of less than 40,000 population and added that for this
reason spot radio advertising is impractical for stores located in towns the
size of Tremont. He went on to point out that a newspaper usually remains
around the home for some time and shoppers can refer back to an ad to get details
they might have forgot, whereas a radio ad once heard can never be heard or
referred to again.

Too, it is an accepted fact that almost everyone remembers things he sees
longer than those he hears. And in view of the continually confirmed fact that
only about one out of five people listen to commercials attentively, a fact
Charles Hull Wolfe re-summarized in *Modern Radio Advertising* (Funk and
Wagnalls, New York, 1953, p. 504), the greater retention value of newspaper

---

Little more need be said about how to put the findings of fact and the
interpretation into words. You have already learned to use commonly
understood words, short and direct sentences and paragraphs, itemizations, summarizing and transitional phrases and sentences, headings and
subheads, and nonverbal assists to words. You know, too, that you need
to support your statements of questionable fact with explanations, additional specific and concrete details as evidence, citations of sources, and
statistics.

But remember that graphic presentations are not complete unto
themselves, that they only help words to present facts. They cannot
interpret. The reader will consider your job only half done if you pre-

7

advertising is clearly implied--and its application to the small-town customers of the A. L. Bangs Company obvious.

We do not need to operate solely on assumption, however; company sales confirm the tentative conclusions.

Negligible Effect of Radio Ads on Sales

No significant change in sales of selected items.--Sales of seven selected items for the week before and also for the week after they were advertised on WFRO were quite irregular, as Chart 1 shows. /At this point appeared a graph with seven different-colored lines representing sales of maternity dresses, pajamas, brassieres, hose, sweaters, girdles, and coats for two successive weeks.7 The usual peak of sales on Saturday and a low on Monday is the normal pattern for the store, in no way attributable to radio advertising.

Any upward trend of sales during the second week could reasonably be attributed to the radio advertising, but sales of only one item rose signif-icantly--maternity dresses. Since this department was added to the store the week the advertising and sales were observed, the assumption that radio spot ads had anything to do with the sales is hardly justified--especially in view of the fact that this is the only maternity department in the city. /The next three pages of the report present and interpret six more small two-color line graphs--the first was for maternity dresses--showing sales for a week before and a week after spot advertising of the six other items.7

Records of sales before and after spot radio advertising of selected items do not show that spot advertising brings significant increases in sales of

sent him with a mass of undigested data and make him do the interpreting. But if you put graphics and comments about them close together so that the reader can see both at once, each supplements the other. References to the carefully chosen, most suitable graphics should be subordinated to the interpretation of the facts shown. The mere fact that the graph is there, or even the facts shown in the table or graph, are less important than the significance of those facts to the whole problem or the particular point being made at the time. So the emphasis should be on the interpretation.

those items.

No appreciable increase in total sales.--Since the number of people coming into a store may be substantially increased by advertising, total sales of the store can also be affected by the radio promotion.

But to compare last year's monthly sales to this year's would not take into consideration the fluctuations due to changes in general business activity. I therefore used National Industrial Conference Board percentages of increase and decrease of this year's sales to last year's sales (Table 2) to see what we should expect this year without radio advertising. /The statistical table of the original report is omitted here./

The difference shown in Chart 9 between what the sales actually were and what could be expected could possibly be due to the radio advertising. But the

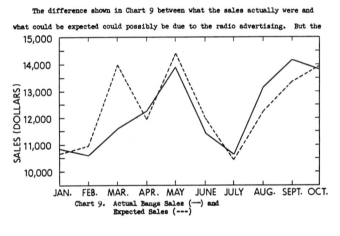

Chart 9. Actual Bangs Sales (——) and Expected Sales (- - -)

Though basically the interpretation points out trends, high and low points, and significant differences brought out by comparisons and analyses of facts and figures presented, you need not waste words by talking about "a comparison" or "analysis of" or "a study of"; if you state the significances, you imply the comparison, the analysis, or the study. And the comparisons become more significant if you put them in terms of percentages or ratios instead of, or in addition to, giving the raw figures.

To avoid monotony of both sentence pattern and length, especially in a series of similar comparisons, consider different types of sentence

9

variations between actual sales and expected sales in the months of January
through April, when radio advertising was not used in either year, suggest that
the variations from May to October cannot be definitely attributed to spot
advertising alone.

Even if we assume that the difference between what sales were and what
could have been expected was a result of the radio advertising, the extra profits
which may be attributable to it do not pay for it.

From May through October--the period observed during which the store used
spot ads--sales were $750 more (1%) than could have been expected (Table 2).
At the average net-profit margin of nearly 10%, this means radio ads increased
the store's profits by about $12.50 a month. Such an amount is not only negli-
gible when compared to the total monthly profits--it does not even pay for
one week's advertising (3 x $4.25). Clearly spot advertising has not paid its
own way at the A. L. Bangs Company.

<u>Summary of Reasons for Discontinuing Spot Advertising</u>

I recommend that the Bangs Company discontinue spot radio advertising and
concentrate on newspaper advertising because

    --spot radio ads have had apparently little effect on the sales of
      the store, either on selected items spot advertised or on total sales

    --on any basis it costs more than newspaper advertising, not only
      because of actual cost but also because of waste coverage

    --Tremont customers, like all small-town customers, are not likely
      to respond to spots, preferring to depend on their newspaper for
      reminder when they decide to shop. . .leisurely.

beginnings. Nearly always you can do better than use the expletives "It
is . . ." and "There are . . . ," which waste words, delay the idea,
and lead you to weak and awkward passive constructions.

And unless the logic of the situation clearly dictates otherwise, you'll
do best to use the present tense for both presenting and interpreting the
facts.

With the facts and analyses well organized, clearly presented, and
sharply summarized at the ends of sections, you have led the reader to
your statement of conclusions and (if he wants them) recommendations.

Conclusions and Recommendations.   When you put your conclusions and recommendations into words, they should not be surprising—and they won't be if you have done an adequate job of the preceding part. There you should have presented all the evidence and analysis necessary to support your conclusions. So no new facts or analyses should appear in the conclusions or recommendations.

Whether you separate conclusions and recommendations into two headings makes little difference. Some people prefer separation because, they say, the conclusions are strictly objective, logical results of what has been said, whereas the recommendations are the individual writer's personal suggestions of what to do about the problem. Whichever point of view and plan you use, the important thing is to be as objective as possible in stating both conclusions and recommendations.

As evidence of that objectivity in your conclusions and as a means of saving the reader the trouble of looking back into the text, you may well lift basic figures or statements from the earlier presentation and interweave them into the conclusion sentences. The writer of the synopsis illustrated on p. 503 knew that the reader of his report could not possibly retain the 200 or more facts and figures given as evidence in 27 pages of analysis. In recalling to his reader the significant evidence affecting the decision, therefore, that writer wisely attached a specific figure to every fact. Note, too, the specific wording of this ending section—as well as the selectivity and brevity.

VII.   THE PREFERRED CITY: SAVANNAH

Although a Charleston druggist enjoys the advantages of

   --a population with a half million dollars more buying
     income annually and families with $34 more to spend

   --11,000 additional potential customers

a Savannah drug store would likely sell more because of these

advantages:

   --$170,000 additional drug-store sales and $4,000 greater
     sales per drug store

   --$2.5 million more retail sales and $162 more per person
     spent in retail stores

   --1,000 more families and per-capita income $87 higher

   --four-year trend increases of 8 to 10% in construction
     ($12 million more), bank deposits ($150 million
     more), and postal receipts ($200,000 more)

   --$989 million business volume (twice as much as in
     Charleston).

Both conclusions and recommendations need to be as pointed and positive as the facts and the writer's judgment will allow. (Usually itemization will help you to make them so and help the reader to see them as such.) If you toss the problem back to the reader with indefinite conclusions or alternative suggestions, he may feel that the salary or fee he has paid you for doing the report has been wasted. Still he retains the right of final decision; so, even when he asks for your recommendations, he expects you to present them as definite suggestions but certainly not as commands. The example just cited—which is phrased specifically in terms of the objective of the report, to select the city which will likely be the more profitable scene of operations—avoids indecision on the one hand and its equally undesirable opposite, imperative command.

Appendix. Though the report reproduced here in telescoped form needed no appendix, many reports do. Frequent uses are for survey questionnaires too extensive for presentation in the introduction and not essential to the reader's understanding; for extensive formulas and statistical calculations; for extensive history, too long for the introduction; and for large maps, diagrams, or tables of figures that may be the basic data of the whole report but do not belong at any particular place in the text.

Bibliography. Most reports have a bibliography. The writer of the spot radio advertising study did not compile one because her report was short and included few published references; these few were adequately identified as she referred to them and could easily be assembled mentally by any reader in two or three minutes. In view of the circumstances under which she submitted her report, she was probably justified in omitting a formal bibliography—but that is the exception rather than the rule for any but short reports.

Most of the time when you use printed sources, the reader expects you to tell him what they are, not only to avoid the accusation of plagiarism but also to indicate reliability and perhaps provide him with places to get fuller information. Your footnotes and other citations in the text give the specific references. But at the end you list—in alphabetical order of authors' surnames, or titles if the source is unsigned—books and magazines which you have used for basic background information or for specific facts, ideas, or direct quotations.

The following bibliography (telescoped here for space economy) went with a 20-page report. (Usually the best spacing is single within items and double between them.) The items are arranged alphabetically by author (or by title if the publication had no by-line) and numbered for concise, specific citations in the text.

Publications Consulted

1. "Airlines Will Sacrifice Power to Obtain Lower Jet Noise Level," <u>Aviation Week,</u> 66:348, February 25, 1957.
2. "Boeing Sets Suppressor Flight Test," <u>Aviation Week,</u> 66:41, April 1, 1957.
3. "Portable Jet Engine Muffler Design," <u>Aviation Week,</u> 66:74–75, April 8, 1957.
4. Richards, E. G., <u>Technical Aspects of Sound</u>, Elsevier Publishing Company, New York, 1957.
5. Richards, E. J., "Research on Aerodynamic Noise from Jets and Related Problems," <u>Royal Aeronautical Society Journal,</u> 57:318–342, May, 1953.
6. "Silencing Jet Fleet Will Be Costly," <u>Aviation Week,</u> 66:47–48, May 27, 1957.

WRITING OTHER FORMS OF REPORTS

Though the report on spot radio advertising used as illustration in this chapter is not really long (many are much longer), shorter reports in different forms are more numerous. Other reports you are likely to encounter and use are letters and memos—including highly specialized forms such as justification and credit reports—and annual reports.

Letters and Memos. Regular letter form is usual for short reports going outside the organization, whereas memo (memorandum) form is more likely for intraorganizational reports.

Two common types of **letter reports** are those about job and credit applicants, already discussed on pp. 133–35 and 377–78, respectively. These two types should be informational letter reports, in that they would rely on facts and subordinate or entirely eliminate opinions— and certainly unsupported recommendations. But letter reports may be either informational or analytical.

Since the letter report is likely to be longer than the usual letter, however, and since it *is* a report, it may take on these special features of reports, while otherwise using the form explained in Chapter IV:

1. More than usually careful organization.
2. Objectivity (absence of emotional persuasion, viewing both sides of the situation, enough interweaving or implying of methods and sources to assure soundness).
3. Use of appropriate subheads and itemizations where helpful.
4. Use of graphic devices where helpful.

Depending on whether the message will likely meet with reader approval, disappointment, or resistance, the letter report should follow the Type A, Type B, or (rarely) Type C plan, as explained on pp. 28–30, 30–31, and 32–33.

Often a good letter report gives the main points of the situation and refers to one or more attachments for fuller explanation and supporting data—much as sales letters and application letters do.

Memo reports are like letter reports except in being used mostly *within* an organization and in having their own special forms. Otherwise, what has been said about letter reports will apply to memos.

Like letter reports, memos are usually short but may run to half-a-dozen or more pages.

One of the most common and effective techniques—perhaps more frequent in memos than letters—is itemization. Numbering each paragraph almost forces the writer into careful organization, precise statement, and conciseness.

The reader of memos—as of any other reports, including letter reports—will want to know what the idea is and *how you know your facts are right*. Usually you can best interweave or imply what the reader doesn't already know about your purpose, methods and sources, and scope right along with your facts and conclusions—without separate sections or even paragraphs for them.

The following illustration on the company's printed form shows a usual layout, typical direct (deductive, Type A) plan, and a typical problem:

OFFICE MEMORANDUM—Acme Insurance Company   Date 2/10/59

To   : Mr. J. G. DeWolfe, General Manager
From : R. R. Fortune, Safety & Health
Subject: HOW TO REDUCE ABSENTEEISM CAUSED BY RESPIRATORY
         DISEASES

1. Conclusion.—Our recent high rate of absenteeism seems to be a result of too low humidity. Absentees reported colds or other respiratory diseases as the cause in 73% of the cases.

2. Humidity in relation to respiratory diseases.— According to the U.S. Public Health Service, the higher the humidity in buildings the lower the rate of respiratory diseases. You can see this relationship in Figure 1 on the attached pages. The explanation is that a high humidity prevents excessive cooling from evaporation of skin moisture.

Mr. J. G. DeWolfe from R. R. Fortune, 2/10/59: ABSEN-
TEEISM, p. 2

3. <u>Desirable humidity-temperature relationships</u>.--
Although our 70 degrees is considered the best
temperature, it isn't warm enough for most
people unless the humidity is about 40. Ours is
20. As Figure 2 of the USPHS study shows, a
humidity above 50 makes most people feel clammy
and below 30 causes them to feel a dryness in
their noses and throats.

4. <u>Recommended corrective steps</u>.--To reduce absenteeism, improve the health of our personnel,
and enhance employee relations, I suggest the
following:

<u>a</u>) Raise the humidity to 40 by having a tinner
make a pan with the necessary evaporation
surface for each radiator (to be concealed
from view by the radiator covers).

<u>b</u>) Assign the janitors the job of keeping water
in the pans.

<u>c</u>) Purchase one temperature-humidity guide for
each office. Besides providing a constant
check on room conditions, these meters will
remind the employees that you have done
something about their comfort and health.

Prices range from $2 to $200. The cheapest
ones are likely to be inaccurate; but the
Wechsler at $4.50 carries the recommendation
of <u>Consumer</u> <u>Reports</u>. It looks like a small
clock with two red hands pointing to temperature and humidity scales. Hardware, department, mail-order, and specialty stores
carry it in varied colors to fit the decor
of any office.

Because of their similarities, the following **Check List for Memos**
applies to letter reports as well (except the part on form, of course).

Justification Reports.   Any analytical report could be called a justification report because it draws conclusions (and makes recommendations if wanted) and presents facts to justify them. But, as used in report writing, the justification report is a special kind.

Almost invariably it is an initiating report in which the writer makes
an original proposal, rather than a study that has been requested,
though it may well be the requested full write-up of a suggestion that
has been dropped in a suggestion box. It is deductive (Type A) presen-

CHECK LIST FOR MEMOS

1. Form:
   a) Use a neatly arranged heading, including at least the company name (usually in capitals); some wording like *Memo, Memorandum,* or *Interoffice Communication;* and a date line.
   b) Begin *To, From,* and *Subject* at the left; preferably, double-space between them; and use colons right after each *or* align all the colons with the one after *Subject.* In either case, align the beginnings of what you fill in after the colons.
   c) Use courtesy titles (Mr., Mrs., Miss) with the names of others (but not yours) if you would in talking with them; and use official titles for everybody unless all readers would know them.
   d) For emphasis, underscore or capitalize subject lines.
   e) End-of-line periods are unnecessary, even undesirable.
   f) Single-space within paragraphs and double-space between.
   g) Use itemizations, headings, tables, and charts where helpful.
   h) For pages after the first, put at least the addressee's name, the date, and the page number on the first line and triple-space below it.
   i) Use no salutation, complimentary close, or typed name of writer at the end; but you should sign nonroutine reports requiring authentication.
   j) When used, file and other references (including other people to receive carbons) may be put under a flush-right date or to the right of the To-From-Subject block. (Carbon-copy lists more commonly appear at the end instead.)
2. Organization and coverage:
   a) Bring in your main point (whether it is a request, conclusion, recommendation, or something else) in the first sentence *unless your reader might resist;* and, if he might, lead up to it with whatever facts, reasons, or explanations are necessary to convince him—especially any reader benefits you can point out.
   b) Be sure to make clear that your information is valid and pertinent by making clear what the problem is and how you got your information to solve it; but see 3b.
   c) Effective dates (for directives)—and when necessary, other time limits, places, and people concerned—are important points for coverage.
   d) Consider whether you should mention alternatives to your recommendation.
   e) Should you explain more specifically how to carry out your proposal?
   f) Be sure you have covered all points that your reader will need or want covered—especially all steps in your logic.

CHECK LIST FOR MEMOS (CONTINUED)

g) Check your sequence for coherence, logic, and psychological effect (A, B, or C plan).

3. Style:

a) Make the subject line indicate the content accurately and specifically.

b) Emphasize the important and avoid undue emphasis on the unimportant. What you found out and the likely effect are more important than how you found out or from whom; so for 2*b,* usually you should just *imply* or *interweave* in incidental phrases the necessary but unknown parts of *purpose* and *method* of the report. Usually the reader will already know the purpose; and, if not, it and your method of getting information are usually implied in stating the facts you got. "Sixty-two per cent of your employees favor . . ." indicates both what the problem is and survey method.

c) Be sure your terminology, sentence length and structure, and paragraph length and structure make for quick, clear, easy reading. Short words, sentences, and paragraphs usually help; itemizations and tabulations may help further.

d) Display really significant data, conclusions, and recommendations by such means as increasing white space, decreasing line length, itemizing, and tabulating.

e) For coherence (and often for conciseness), precede displayed items with an appropriate introducing statement.

f) Don't develop a fever (with numerous strong adjectives and adverbs, for example); keep it objective.

4. Tone:

a) Soften commands for acceptable tone; sharp imperatives rankle even in directives. "You will . . ." is too commanding for most situations. Three directives from which you can usually select an appropriate one are (in descending order of sharpness) "Please . . . ," "Will you . . . ," and "I request that you . . . ." "If you will . . ." is usually too weak.

b) Phrase recommendations for acceptable tone (depending on the reader-writer relationship and the firmness of your conviction) as "You must . . . ," "I recommend . . . ," "I suggest . . ."; "The only way . . . ," "The best solution is . . . ," and "Probably the wise decision is . . . ."

c) Accusations are always objectionable.

d) Positive is better than negative phrasing.

e) Item 2*a* is an important factor in tone.

tation that gives the recommendation immediately, followed by concise statements of the most important considerations and conclusions, before giving detailed explanations and supporting facts.

More specifically, you will provide good organization and coverage if you set up the five standard headings and do the following in this order:

a) State the purpose in one sentence. The first part, in phrase or dependent-clause structure, should mention a benefit. The second part should be the recommendation in an independent clause.

b) State the cost and saving in no more than two sentences. Don't delay the fast movement by explaining.

c) In a third part called "Procedure" or "Method of Installation," cover concisely such things as necessary space, men, training, special materials, time, and interruptions of work. Usually one to three sentences will do.

d) Itemize the conclusions, state them pointedly, and keep them to the minimum number that will cover all aspects. One of them has to be on cost and savings. One that is commonly overlooked is the good will of all people concerned. They are not always all benefits; some may point the other way.

e) In a discussion section (sometimes called "Discussion of Conclusions" or "Explanation of Advantages"), give all the details supporting the statements already made. Usually it should be itemized to match the itemized conclusions. Interweave into your explanations enough of your methods to answer the reader's question "How do you know?" That applies particularly to your method of figuring cost and savings.

The form is commonly memo, but it may be letter or some other such as that illustrated later. It may even have a title page like that of the complete analytical report. If you use memo form, of course Item 1 of the **Check List for Memos** will apply. In any form you can use the *a–e* directions above as the subheads under Item 2 of that check list and have a good **Check List for Justification Reports.**

The essential plan and techniques are illustrated by the following typical example:

How Mechanical Pencils Would Save Money for Morgan Company

Purpose.——To save the Morgan Company more than $100 in pencil expense each year, I recommend that we purchase mechanical pencils instead of wooden ones for use by employees.

Cost and Saving.——A year's supply of mechanical pencils and refills would cost only $152.40 as compared with $266.70 for wooden pencils——a yearly saving of $114.30.

Procedure.--A dependable automatic pencil manufac-
turer--Ray and Company, Rome, Georgia--would supply
the yearly need of 762 pencils with the Morgan name
on them at the quantity-discounted price of 10¢ each.
The stockroom clerk could distribute them as he does
the wooden pencils, and maintain records for control.

Conclusions.--Morgan Company would enjoy four distinct advantages by using mechanical pencils instead
of the present wooden ones.

1. We would save an estimated $114.30 a year.
2. The stockroom clerk would have fewer pencils to
   store and issue--762 as compared with 13,248.
3. Employees would be more careful about misplacing
   them.
4. Mechanical pencils stay sharp and thus provide
   uniform, neat writing without loss of time and
   patience at the pencil sharpener.

Discussion.--The following explanation of those four
advantages will show how Morgan Company would gain by
using mechanical pencils.

1. During the past three years pencils have cost us
   about 70¢ a year per employee, as shown by the
   following calculations:

	1956	1957	1958	Average
Pencil costs	$271	$227	$295	$231
Employees	450	298	395	381
Cost per employee	60¢	76¢	75¢	70¢

Converting to mechanical pencils would require,
for each employee, an estimated two pencils (@
10¢ each) and 20¢ worth of lead and eraser refills, for a total annual cost of 40¢ per employee.

Cost comparison shows a saving of $114.30 with
mechanical pencils:

Cost of wooden pencils, 381 employees @ 70¢	$266.70
Cost of mechanical pencils, 381 employees @ 40¢	152.40
Saving	$114.30

2. In the past three years, the clerk in the stockroom has had to allot space for about 1,104
   dozen, or 13,248, pencils. Also he has had to
   take the time (considerable in the aggregate) to
   distribute each one. With only 762 pencils to
   store and issue, he could use the relieved space
   and time for other things.

3. Since mechanical pencils are more valuable and
   more conspicuous (especially with the Morgan
   name on them) than wooden ones, employees would
   be more careful about carrying them home and not
   bringing them back. Also, if employees had to
   sign a receipt--which is more feasible with the
   fewer mechanical pencils--misplacements would
   occur less frequently. Those misplaced might be
   worth at least a part of their cost as advertising.

4. The mechanical pencil needs no sharpening and
   writes with the same neat uniformity throughout
   its use, instead of becoming blunt and less neat
   progressively. Moreover, mechanical pencils
   would avoid the interruptions to thinking and
   work when employees take their wooden ones to the
   pencil sharpener (which often annoys by breaking
   the lead or needing to be emptied).

Credit Reports.   The credit report illustrated as a letter report
(p. 378) is typical of those written by individual references about a
credit applicant. But various trade associations, credit bureaus, and special credit-reporting agencies have to write so many credit reports that
each develops special forms for convenience and the economy of stand-
ardization.

Because the purpose of a credit report is always the same and known
to the reader; because there is no history of the problem; and because
the methods and scope are always the same, the credit report omits the
introduction. Because the credit report is an informational rather than
analytical report, it also omits conclusions and recommendations. And
because it is a short-form report, it omits other parts of a complete report—all except the text and perhaps a synopsis. But because the credit
report must protect the writer against libel suit, it includes the necessary
legal defenses (in addition to assumed truth in the facts presented) by
specifying confidential use for the purpose of self-protection mentioned
when it was requested. Because credit decisions are always made on the

basis of the four *C*'s of credit, the report invariably covers those topics
(but not under those headings). The information includes anything
which might have a significant bearing on the credit worth of the subject (individual or firm) and omits anything else.

Different organizations still set their reports up in various forms. One
of the oldest and biggest credit-reporting agencies follows this pattern,
which covers just about everything others do in different form:

1. A subject line identifying name and address of subject, kind of business, and symbolic rating of capitalization and dependability (A-1, F-2,
   G-5, e.g.).
2. A synopsis of background, net worth, payment practice, and conditions
   and trends.
3. A history describing origin, kind of organization, shifts in organization
   or ownership, any changes of location, and growth of the business, with
   emphasis on the facts about the owners and managers (education, experience, and any significant personal details such as age, marital status,
   and health).
4. A description of operating conditions (including type and price
   ranges of stock, kind of customers, cash versus credit sales, advertising
   and other promotion, location, competition, kind and size of building,
   neighbors and other factors influencing fire hazard, insurance, and fire
   record).
5. A financial statement (signed if possible, sometimes followed by notes
   on facts that influence financial solidity).
6. Several reports from firms which have sold to the subject of the report.
   These—usually in tabulated columns—establish the highest credit extended, amount currently owed, amount past due, the terms, manner of
   payment, and length of the credit relationship.

Annual Reports. In accounting to their publics for their management of funds entrusted to them, corporations and governmental units
summarize each year's activities in their annual reports.

Back in the middle of the nineteenth century, when annual reporting
really started, stockholders were the only public considered. Since they
were usually wealthy and educated—or advised by investment specialists—early annual reports were little more than financial statements in
the formal accounting terms of the day. And the usual attitude of management was to tell as few people as possible as little as possible.

Today all that is changed. Stockholders have increased greatly (now
estimated at something above six million people, many of whom are not
acquainted with accounting terminology). Labor forces have increased
their power and have become intensely interested in the corporation's
affairs. The changed thinking of the times considers corporations essentially public institutions affecting the whole public welfare. Manage-

ment has seen that its publics include stockholders, workers, customers, government officials, and the general public. It has realized that many of these people are not educated in accounting and that many of them are interested in more than the strictly financial affairs (wages, fringe benefits to workers, products, research and development of new products, and over-all policies, for example).

Annual-report writers today, therefore, try to write so that everyone can understand, and they try to cover topics of interest to all publics. And with the realization that people are inclined to distrust and take a dim view of things they don't know about, management has shifted to the attitude of telling as many people as possible as much as possible (limited only by security regulations and information that might hurt the competitive position of the company).

Indeed, today the annual report is a major medium in the public relations programs of most corporations, a means by which they hope to tell their story to all their publics to justify their existence and their ways of doing things. They know that any business firm exists, in the long run, only with the approval and patronage of a public whose good will they have. Most corporations therefore make their reports available to anybody who asks, and some go to considerable expense to make their reports appealing and to buy newspaper advertising space or radio and television time to tell their stories to everybody. Some have gone so far in telling their stories that the reports seem more like propaganda or advertising brochures than objective reports—and have sometimes thereby lost faith and face. But the usual annual report today is highly informative about the organization it represents.

Usually today's annual reports contain a letter from the highest official as well as financial statements and the auditor's statement of opinion (sometimes called the "certificate"). Often the letter from the president or chairman of the board is only a short introduction to a review of outstanding influences, developments, and trends affecting company operations. Frequently it is both an introduction and a synopsis. And in many cases it is the entire analysis, running to 10, 12, or more pages.

Either way, most annual-report writers adapt all the devices already mentioned here—readable style, liberal use of meaningful headings, graphic illustration—to make reading easy and interesting and the reports effective public relations agents for the organizations they represent.

Annual reports deserve the study of any student of accounting. While they are not the accounting reports commonly presented by the accountant to his clients or his superiors, they are excellent studies in reporting and interpreting financial information.

You can find a tremendous volume of material about them in the library. And, as we mentioned in the chapter on application letters, you can get examples by writing to almost any company. The annual report of a company is a source of information which anybody should read before applying for a job with that company.

~~~~~

Though the following is primarily a **Check List for Complete Analytical Reports,** many of the items apply to all reports. For greatest usefulness the points appear in the order of preparation of your material, not the order of presentation when the report is assembled in its final form.

ORGANIZATION/OUTLINING (O)

1. Your title should make clear the nature and purpose of your analysis. Thus it will show the basis of classification as you phrase the major divisions of your subject, and prevent overlapping. (See Item 1, p. 483.) It may or may not reveal the outcome or reflect basic method. Answering as many of the who, what, why, where, when, and how as necessary, it should establish the boundaries of your treatment in such a manner as to imply a promise to your reader. The title "Market Factors Indicating Why a Rexwall Drug Store in Savannah Would Sell More than One in Charleston" commits you to show for each subject—Savannah and Charleston—market-factor evidence supporting your thesis.

2. In comparisons, carefully distinguish between subjects of your study and criteria (tests) which you apply to the two or more subjects from which you ultimately make a choice. In evaluating a Ford and a Chevrolet, for example, you would use both names frequently in your organization scheme, but neither would be a major heading as such. Your major headings would be the tests you decide to apply: costs (initial and operating—and possibly trade-in value), performance, comfort, and appearance. Under each head you would be obligated to analyze each subject.

3. Carefully distinguish, also, between a criterion (one of the tests you apply) and a method. A research procedure or a statistical procedure—which does need identification and probably explanation in the introductory passages—is the way you have gone about evaluating, not the basis of evaluation.

4. An outline in which the contents suggested by the title and by some other heading (usually II) are essentially the same thing shows no recognition of effective organization. Though logical, these three are all unsatisfactory:

I. Introduction	I. Introduction	I. Introduction
II. Text	II. Findings	II. Primary Considerations
III. Conclusions	III. Conclusions	III. Conclusions and Recommendations

All the basic elements of the problem are parts of the text, the section numbered II in those undesirable plans. Hence they would have to be subheads of II. Thus they would not get the emphasis they deserve, they would make II nearly all of the report (bad imbalance), and they would make the wording for the II heading almost identical with the title. They are where you present all your facts and analyses.

According to strict logic, those elements would be the only appropriate major divisions (numbered in Romans in the suggested outline form). Neither the introduction nor the conclusions and recommendations (like the synopsis and bibliography) would get major-division status. They are not logically factors, or elements, or criteria, of the topic named in the title.

Customary practice, however, DOES give major-division status (Roman numerals in the outline) to the introduction and to the conclusions and recommendations (separately or together). They deserve the emphasis, though they are not logical parts in the same breakdown of the title that gives you the text elements.

5. *Customary practice* ALSO skips a heading for the whole text and gives each major element of it a separate Roman number—for proper emphasis and better balance. So don't bury the elements or criteria in third- or fourth-order heads.

6. A heading must be phrased to cover any and all of the items listed under it. "Greater Number of Men in Milwaukee" does not cover subhead "Greater Density of Population in Buffalo"; but "More Favorable Population Characteristics in Milwaukee" could cover that as well as other points like age, color, and vocations.

7. Consider the function of your piece of information in maintaining a logical sequence without shifting viewpoint as you move from second- to third- to fourth-order heads. The relation of the part to the whole should always be clear and defensible.

8. Headings of the same class should be in the same grammatical form. Noun phrases are probably best. Complete sentences are perfectly acceptable, though often bulky.

9. When you have only one division under a heading, you have either omitted something or merely restated the governing head. True division gives at least two parts.

10. Make the heading tell something of the findings as well as establish boundaries. One-word headings only name the topic and are usually too general and all-inclusive (promising more than you cover). You cannot exclude properly with a heading like "Grocery Stores." Give your reader a tentative idea of findings with a heading like "The Increasing Importance of Grocery Stores in the Distribution of Cos-

metics." Under a second-degree heading of "CURRENT BUSINESS FACTORS FAVOR MILWAUKEE," present third-order headings such as "Milwaukee's Larger Postal Receipts," "Larger Volume of Bank Clearings in Buffalo but Greater Percentage Increase in Milwaukee," and "Milwaukee's Greater Volume of Construction."

11. Subheadings are like road markers: they keep pointing the way, providing reassurance and relief. Too many become a distraction, maybe even an irritation; too few make the going harder.

12. In phrasing headings, work for variety. Use synonyms to prevent monotony of expression. In the body of the report, with analytical passages in between, the same words used over and over again in exactly the same pattern begin to pall; but in the contents, where they are closer together, the effect is deadening.

13. Remember that the wording of any one heading must be the same, regardless of how many times it appears—or when, or where.

14. Use placement on the page, spacing, and differentiation of type of headings (with or without conventional outline numbers) to show the relative importance and relation of parts. (See p. 492.)

GRAPHICS (Gr)

1. For the convenience of your reader, place the graph, table, or any other illustrative device as close to the point discussed as you can get it.

   a) Most charts and tables you can present in small enough size to splice right into your text with additional white space on both sides, above, and below. Part of a page of graph paper will serve well for most charts.

   b) For a table or chart taking up the better part of a page, place it on the facing page to the left of the point illustrated.

   c) The laziest and least useful way is to dump all illustrations in the appendix.

2. Give all graphics or tables numbers (for economical references to them in the text), complete and accurate titles, keys if necessary, and any necessary explanations.

3. Preferably place numbers and titles of tables above, and of other graphics below.

4. Adequately label all parts of a table (the rows and columns) and of a chart if you elect to omit a key.

5. Indicate the source of your information when you use someone else's material (even when you derive your own figures from the material of another). To show the origin of your material, write *Source:* and follow up with the same information you would use in a footnote. When you assemble your own data and are thus completely and entirely responsible for it (for instance, company sales or employment figures), identify the circumstances in the "Method" section of your introduction and omit source indications under the illustration(s).

6. Give the dates that apply to your material. And be sure you have them right. Many current publications list information several years old which may or may not be applicable. And the reader should at least be

warned. You can always list the true date in parentheses immediately after the title of the table or figure.

7. Put a few lines of discussion of the specific point illustrated before placing the chart or table on the page—and preferably a few lines after—when you write up the report.

8. Call attention to the figure (preferably by number—that's why you number them) before it appears on the page. When it is on a different page from the reference to it, tell the reader where it is.

9. Charts have more interest value than tables and with accurate labels can be just as accurate.

10. When you have a number of items to present, consider the advisability of giving them in several small charts closely associated with the related text rather than in a collective (and frequently exhausting and dissociated) table.

11. In line graphs for time series, run dates along the bottom line; run quantities or percentages along the side. And be sure your starting point for quantities or percentages is 0 (unless your point is the *relative* values of two or more charted items instead of their *absolute* values, like Chart 9, p. 513).

12. Remember that bars (either simple or segmented) are read as easily as pies and often more accurately—and that pictographs may add interest but can distort information.

13. When chronology is not significant, arrange multiple bits of graphed information in an ascending or descending order of importance.

14. Number charts consecutively throughout your study; number tables consecutively in their own order. Thus you may have Chart 16 and Table 2 on page 21 of your report.

15. Use the appropriate graphic wherever one will help.

16. Avoid wasting time and space on useless graphics.

INTRODUCTION (I)

1. Focus attention on the continuing existence of the report by talking about it in the present tense. When a reader reads it, your report analyzes, presents, takes up, examines, establishes, and finally concludes. Of course, you'll have to use some past and future tenses, but in general use them for matters of historical record or things not yet done.

2. Put initial emphasis, then, on the nature and purpose of the study rather than on historical (past-tense) details of authorization, method, or history.

3. Not every report analysis needs a history section. Even if yours does, it may be more wisely handled with a subordinate reference quickly recalling the circumstances to your reader in conjunction with "Purpose" or "Method." It may be a short identification after "Purpose." It can be handled effectively and economically in the transmittal letter. And if it is extensive, consider shifting it to a preliminary section after the introduction (so that your outline would be I. Introduction II. History III. First Significant Criterion) or relegating it to the ap-

pendix, with a short statement in your introduction telling your reader where it is.

4. Definitions of terms aren't always necessary either. Even if they are, they are probably more useful as parenthetical or footnote explanations when you first employ the terms in the discussion.

5. Ordinarily you do need some explanation of procedure or method. Show in the required detail how you've gone about solving the problem with answers to the applicable when, where, how, how many, who, and why of what you did. In answering the reader's question, "How do you know?" you establish in large part the impartial, unbiased, unprejudiced nature of the report.

6. Such petty details as "Graphs have been included" are better omitted, however. Statistical exhibits are as expected in most reports as sentences are in building paragraphs.

7. Remember that references to limited amounts of time or money in the introduction may sound like excuses for poor performance. Also remember that such references—if true—may be incorporated in the transmittal letter.

8. You usually do have limitations of coverage, however, which are sometimes desirable or even necessary to show your reader why you are not covering some phase of the subject. At least, he should know that you aren't! Frequently the most coherent way to establish the scope of your analysis is in a clear explanation of the limitations of coverage, as well as the clear identification of your plan of presentation.

9. Have a clear indication of the order in which the various points confront the reader as he goes through the report. This is usually called the "Plan." Preferably end your introduction with this statement.

10. Work for combinations of these various functions to prevent overorganization and overwriting. Nature and Purpose go together naturally (and may include necessary identification of who wants the report as well as who submits it); Method, Scope, and Limitations can be combined; Scope, Limitations, and Plan might well be the label for one compact section.

11. In reports that contain a synopsis (which precedes the report itself), findings, conclusions, and recommendations are unnecessary in the introduction—even undesirable. When you have no synoptic material preceding, you may choose to place a short paragraph revealing major findings either at the beginning or the ending of your introduction.

12. Repeat the exact title of the report at the top of page 1 where you begin your introduction. But in the text paraphrase it.

STYLE (S)

1. Remember that tables and charts cannot analyze. Your words do that. Put the highlights (and low points or trends) into words and establish their significance in the light of your objective as defined in your title or the specific head. It's the message of the figure that counts, not the figure itself.

2. Refer incidentally (subordinately) to tables/charts within the sentence or at the end, not at the beginning. Don't make the figure the subject of the sentence. "Increased steel production, as shown in Chart 2, aids business in general and appliance-makers in particular" puts the emphasis where you want it. Parenthetical reference (Chart 2) does the same thing.

3. Headings are only assists; the text must read coherently without them.

4. A clear topic identification in your text as you begin a new point is vital.

5. As you move to a detailed analysis of a point involving two or more divisions, tell your reader what those divisions are and name them in the order he will meet them. This is what report writers call a "topic statement."

6. When you've finished a detailed analysis involving two or more parts, establish the significance of the over-all point in a summary statement (a short sentence or paragraph).

7. Show the relation of parts to one another and to the whole in forward-looking (and sometimes backward-looking) transitional statements. They are most useful immediately after a summary statement concluding the subject of discussion under a second-order heading. But they may coherently appear in connection with topic statements at the beginning.

As an example of 4, 5, 6, and 7, here is how one writer helped keep his reader on the track with good topic statements, summary paragraphs, and transitional ideas. For economy of space, the quoted illustration is an extraction.

II. NASHVILLE'S LARGER MARKET AREA

Since women often will travel long distances to buy clothes, the secondary area surrounding the metropolitan area is important in determining the location of a Four Cousins retail store. [Identification of principal communities and number of people in them for both Nashville and Knoxville followed.] Even though 370,000 more possible customers live within the market area of Nashville, most of the sales will come from the people within the immediate metropolitan area.

III. BETTER POPULATION FACTORS IN NASHVILLE

The total population and its rate of growth, number of women, number of employed women, and percentage of nonwhites show more clearly the potential buyers of women's clothing. [This topic statement preceded A, B, C, D headings giving the facts about and the interpretation of the topics as announced.] Even though Knoxville has a larger population, a smaller percentage of nonwhites, and about the same growth rates, Nashville has more women and a significantly larger number of employed women. Thus it furnishes the kind of customer Four Cousins sells to. [Indicates what A, B, C, and D add up to.]

Potential customers are buyers, however, only when they have sufficient buying power. [Clearly foreshadows a topic coming up and why.]

IV. MORE BUYING POWER IN NASHVILLE

Effective buying income (total and per capita), income groups, home ownership, and automobile ownership give estimates of ability to buy. [The information as promised then follows in four sections.]

[This summary statement comes at the end of the section.] The Nashville shopper has more dollars to spend, even though home- and auto-ownership figures imply more favorable financial positions of Knoxville families. Higher expenditures for homes and cars in Knoxville explain, in part, why Nashville merchants sell more.

V. GREATER RETAIL SALES AND LESS COMPETITION IN NASHVILLE

[The writer continued the use of these coherence devices throughout the report.]

8. Your topic statements should emphasize what you are taking up and the order in which you take them up; they may explain why, but only incidentally; they may even establish findings or results, but that is more the function of the textual material and summary statements.
9. To enliven your style and increase readability
   a) Choose simple, short words
   b) Make people (not things, intangibilities, or percentages) the subjects and/or objects of your sentences
   c) Use action verbs
   d) Use active voice (and thus eliminate "It is" and "There are" beginnings)
   e) Refer to quantities in simplified form (rounded off, fraction form, simplified percentages, reduced forms within the quick comprehension of any reader).

Here's a flat example which is shorter only because it forces the reader to dig in Figures 1 and 2 for the information:

The greatest majority of the students interviewed showed their preference for home buying in place of buying in the larger cities of Birming-

This rewrite is more informative, emphatic, and readable:

When University of Alabama men are ready for a new suit, they go home 78 per cent of the time. Though 4 out of 100 will buy in Tuscaloosa and 7 in Birmingham, as shown in Figure 1,

ham or Tuscaloosa. The over-all percentage for the entire body of male students represented by the sample was 78 per cent. The freshmen showed an even greater tendency for home buying by their percentage of 84.

Figure 1, below, gives a picture of the place of purchase of the entire group without regard to the nature of the group. Figure 2 divides the group according to the students' rank.

these 11 atypical cases do not warrant extensive advertising.

The Alabama man, though never weaned in the majority of cases from hometown buying, does slowly shift his clothes-buying sources from home to Birmingham to Tuscaloosa. The gain of only 13 out of every 100 purchasers over a four-year span, however (Figure 2), only confirms the suspicion that Bold Look advertising dollars in Tuscaloosa would be wasted.

10. Immediate and specific evidence (call it *support, detail,* or *substantiating facts* if you want to) is the essence of good analysis. A line doesn't sell "well"; it accounts for 19 per cent of total sales. "Many" people can be interpreted differently by each reader; "324" or "9 out of 10" can be interpreted in only one way.

11. In the analysis, point out the advisability (desirability, or profitability) of an action. But leave your recommendation(s) for the ending pages.

12. Write in present tense when you are interpreting a recognizable tendency which is likely to be continuing. (That's one of the reasons for suggesting that you incorporate dates in your charts and tables.) You have to assume that your most recent information is still applicable; hence, even though last year's sales figures are a historical record of what people *bought,* you are justified in saying, "People *buy* . . . ," meaning that they did buy, they are buying, and they will buy.

13. Treat each subject or alternative you are examining under each point (test or criterion) you take up. The surest indication of a prejudiced writer is giving information about one subject and failing to give the same kind of information for another.

14. Emotional writing, persuasive passages, and ignoring of fact are the marks of an amateur or biased writer.

15. Assumptions are necessary in any kind of analysis, but they should be plausible, and they should be clearly established as assumption rather than fact.

16. Let your unbiased, unprejudiced presentation be apparent from the careful, specific identification of your method, from the quality of your analysis, and from the objectivity of your interpretations and style. Talk about "unbiased," "impersonal," "objective" qualities brings questions to your reader's mind. If your report is all those good things, your reader will recognize it as such; if your report isn't, such disclaimers only make the situation worse.

17. Remember that many factors must be evaluated relatively as well as absolutely. The relative status (per cent, ratio, or rank—a qualitative factor) is often as important as the total (or quantitative)—and may be more important.

18. A personal style (using first- and second-person pronouns—*I, me, my, our, we, us; you, your*) is clearer, easier for both writer and reader, and more natural and interesting; yet some readers (and teachers) require an impersonal style avoiding those pronouns because they think (unjustly) that personal style loses objectivity. If you must write impersonally, you can still have highly readable copy; but you'll need to guard against an overuse of passive voice, expletive sentence beginnings (*it* and *there*), circumlocutions and other wordiness —and especially "the writer."

DOCUMENTATION (Doc)

When you use someone else's material, you are obligated to give credit to that source. The usual means of doing so are citations in the text, footnotes, source indications under graphs and tables, and a bibliography.

1. A bibliography is an alphabetical listing (either by surname of author or first significant word in the title) of all publications you have used in substantiating what you have said in the report. The usual order for a book is author's last name and given names or initials, title of publication underscored, issuing agency (publisher), place of publication, and date. Total pages may or may not be given. For an article from a periodical, the items listed are author's name, title of article in quotes, name of magazine underscored, volume number and inclusive page numbers, and date. For the specific form, see page 489. Books and periodicals may be listed under separate headings if the bibliography is extensive.

2. With a complete entry in the bibliography for each publication you use, you can economize on footnotes and parenthetical citations in the text with some simplified form which enables you to cite just enough for your reader to identify the publication in the bibliography. In footnotes you always cite the specific page or pages on which the borrowed material appears in the original.

3. Save your reader's time and confusion when you can: if you can quickly identify your reference in the text, do so. If you'll number your bibliographical entries (after arranging them alphabetically), you can use parenthetical citations like (7:215) right in the text; but you'll need to explain, the first time, that you mean page 215 in Item 7 of your bibliography. If you cite the author in the text, give no more than the publication and page reference in a footnote. The two together should be a complete reference, but duplications are useless.

4. If the reference is long and involved, relegate it to a footnote below.

5. When you cite a fact or figure which is in a table or chart, you do not need an additional footnote reference because you have the source indicated under the figure. As long as you continue to cite from the

same source, you need no further documentation. (Bibliomaniacs will insist that you do, but you won't run into them in business.) If you shift sources, however, you do need a new citation, either in a *Source:* indication, in a footnote, or in a parenthetical reference in the text.

6. *Source* indications under graphs and/or tables are just the same as footnotes: author (if there is one), name of publication, specific page or pages.

7. If you run footnotes at the bottom of the page, number them. Put a number at the end of the sentence where your borrowed material appears; put the corresponding number at the bottom of the page and give the minimum required information. Separate footnotes from text by a line, and calculate your space so that the last line of footnote material falls at your normal margin point of about $1\frac{1}{2}$ inches up from the bottom of the page.

8. If you use numbered footnotes, number them anew on each page; such a procedure is easier for you and easier for your reader than consecutive numbering throughout the entire study.

9. Information quoted from interviews, speeches, letters, and questionnaires need not be listed in a bibliography. But credit should be given at the time of quoting or paraphrasing in the text. For an interview, speech, or letter, establish the person, his title if any, the date, place, and circumstances under which the statement was made. Questionnaire information, because it is usually collective and anonymous, needs identification in the "Method" section; thereafter it need not be referred to as a source.

10. Quotations of more than two lines should be set out with additional white space all the way around (top, bottom, both sides). Further to distinguish them, they should be single-spaced. In this position, they need no quotation marks.

11. Since the synopsis and the terminal (conclusions and recommendations) are derived from the report (which is assumed to be adequately documented), these derivations commonly contain no documentation.

TERMINAL (T)

The terminal or ending section you may call by a variety of names. It may contain only significant conclusions if you have been told only to assemble facts. It may contain both conclusions and recommendation(s) if you have been asked to name the wiser or wisest course of action. You may set up two second-degree headings, one for Conclusions and another for Recommendations; or you may elect to use only one heading for the combination. You will certainly be observing good writing principles if you phrase this final section in specific wording, indicating that it is in fulfillment of the over-all objective of the report (as the two illustrations in the preceding pages of this chapter do).

1. By definition, the terminal section is a derived section—a quick recap for your reader of the most important points you have covered. Any

introduction of new material not covered in the preceding analysis is therefore an indication of haphazard planning.

2. The emphasis here should be on selectivity rather than comprehensiveness of coverage. The reasons affecting your recommendation(s), arranged in an order of importance, determine the order of presentation.

3. The more specific you can make this section, the better. Attach specific supporting figures or facts to your statements, so that your reader will not be forced back to preceding pages to find out or verify the basis for your generalization.

4. As a person of judgment (and some experience), you'll almost always have to admit that you have not built a case which is completely beyond question; you'll often do well to admit that an alternative you have not chosen does have some points in its favor. Beware of overstating your case with too strong a word like *prove*.

5. You might as well be wrong as inconclusive. Someone has paid you good money to find an answer. If you vaguely toss the problem back to the reader with alternative courses of action of equal desirability, or pass the buck in any way, you're simply not doing the job assigned you. Remember, however, that the summary, "This report does not prove a thing," is a very definite answer in the face of extensive analysis—and sometimes may be the very best conclusion.

6. The terminal must be a result of the analysis as presented in the expository passages of the report. Step by step you have analyzed and arrived at tentative conclusions in summary statements along the way. If you have analyzed and built the structure of your report well, you have kept your reader nodding his head in agreement and thus prepared him for the inevitable end result. The surprise ending is slipshod—and may be infuriating.

7. As a report writer you are rarely in the driver's seat. Someone else will make the decision. You may be expected to suggest or advise but not to command. Phrasing like the two illustrative samples presented earlier in this chapter will help you to avoid appearing peremptory or dictatorial.

8. Try itemizing your conclusions and recommendations for preciseness and conciseness; but avoid overlisting. Combine points so closely related that they should be seen together.

SYNOPSIS (Sy)

The synopsis (or epitome or précis) should NOT be attempted until the entire report has been written. It is a highly condensed summary of your entire report, written for the benefit of those readers who do not have the time or interest to read the detailed analysis and/or those who believe they can read a detailed analysis more easily if they have a summary first. It is not a preface or foreword (the functions of which are absorbed for reports in the prefatory letters). And it most certainly is not merely a rewrite of the contents table in sentence form. That would be a shell with no kernel. A good synopsis contains the most important parts of the report's kernel.

1. The synopsis which is preferable for today's busy readers contains a significant answer-to-the-problem in the first sentence. If your report ended with a recommendation, work that recommendation in as the lead; if your report merely summarized, let your lead contain the condensed significant findings.
2. Include enough of the background for coherence; but detailed explanations of method, scope, history, and plan are unnecessary here.
3. Having effectively telescoped your terminal and then your introductory functions, follow the same order of points that you have in the report itself.
4. Preferably, maintain the same proportional amount of space given to points.
5. Work in as many specific, significant statistics and other facts as you can!
6. Rely on your good order of points and short transitional words and phrases for smoothness and coherence in your synopsis. You do not have enough space here to employ the topic statements, summary statements, and transitional sentences desirable in the longer report.
7. The synopsis should stand alone (so that copies of it could be run off and circulated to many readers for coherent reading without the complete report). It should therefore neither look forward to the report itself nor backward to the preceding prefatory parts to establish a point.
8. Use of present tense is probably more desirable in the synopsis than elsewhere.
9. The synopsis concerns itself primarily with findings, not analysis (though there is more likely to be analysis in the synopsis than in the terminal section).
10. The primary difference between the synopsis and the terminal is that the terminal is highly selective; the synopsis covers the entire report.

Transmittal Letter (TL)

1. The letter of transmittal is an A-type good-news letter that should immediately and unmistakably establish the fact that the report is in the reader's hands.
2. Catch up a reference to the paraphrased topic and the time of the job assignment.
3. But tie these in naturally and conversationally. If you let the contractual aspect predominate ("Submitted herewith in accordance with your written request of April 5 . . ."), you inject an element of restraint right when you want your reader to feel most cordial toward your report.
4. If the report contains a synopsis a few pages later, you certainly do not want to dwell on findings. The only justification for including them here is to establish the value of the study (in an incidental

reference much like the sales letter writer's reference to an en-closure).

5. The introduction discusses methods and sources; rarely will you want to mention them here.

6. The emphasis of your letter should be given to showing your realization of the report's significance.

7. By implication or outright statement, express appreciation (usually your most natural way to end the letter). If you represent an agency in the business of making studies, you certainly appreciate business and always put in a bid for more. If you are a subordinate within the company structure, trying to get ahead, you certainly should appreciate the opportunity to demonstrate your ability and be eager for subsequent chances to learn more about the company and to demonstrate your good judgment and business vision.

8. The weak-kneed "I hope it will be useful" is unnecessarily disparaging. If you are that dubious about the value of your report, you'd probably better rework it.

AUTHORIZATION LETTER (Au)

As the author of the report, you will of course never write your own letter of authorization. When you do have to write one, however, keep the following points in mind.

1. Since this is akin to an order letter (it just orders services instead of tangible goods), it is an A-type letter, beginning directly with a request for information.
   a) Make it as specific as possible.
   b) Establish the report idea early—in the opening sentence or possibly in a subject line.

2. To preclude rambling, incomplete reports that will not serve your purposes, indicate
   a) The nature of the problem,
   b) The direction of the solution, and
   c) How the results are to be used.

3. Suggestions for starting points and sources of material are helpful, and they frequently save the authorizer money.

4. Be explicit in identifying
   a) When you want the completed study and
   b) How much money you are prepared to spend.

5. Eliminate brusque and unfriendly overtones by exhibiting cordiality and gratitude.

MECHANICS (M)

1. For the body of the report, margins on the sides should be at least 1 inch (10 spaces on pica type, 12 on elite), and usually no more than 1½ inches. The bottom margin is generally 1½ inches (9 spaces), top margin slightly less. If you will place your page number on the 6th or 7th line and then double-space, your top margin will be in good relationship to the others.

2. As long as you can insert a heading and two or three lines of your exposition, you need not start a new page (from the introduction through recommendations) when you go from one section to another; if you don't have that much space, start a new page. Don't, under any circumstances, isolate a caption from the beginning of the material which it headlines.

3. Spiral-bound reports are more easily prepared and handled by both reader and writer. If you use a binder on the left, allow additional margins on the left (an additional ½ inch) so that when the "bite" of the binder is taken off, your pages will still have approximately equal right and left margins.

4. Preliminary pages before the contents page need not (and probably should not) be numbered; they are figured, however, in arriving at what the number of your synopsis page or pages should be. Since the synopsis appears after the contents listing, it is assigned a number. Figure it by counting every single page after the cover (lower-case Roman numerals). Place its number 6 spaces up from the bottom of the page, centered, since this is a display page. For succeeding page numbers, place as suggested under 5.

5. The page number for page 1 (as well as all page numbers where you have a displayed heading) appears also 6 spaces up from the bottom of the page, centered. All other Arabic page numerals generally go at the top right, marking the right-hand margin. No mark of punctuation (dashes, periods, parentheses) is desirable with page numbers.

6. For typed work, remember that
   —Headings in capital letters are superior to those in capitals and lower case letters, and those in capitals and lower case superior to initial-cap heads.
   —Centered headings are superior to side headings, and side headings superior to cut-in headings.

7. Any heading not in solid capitals should be underscored to make it stand out.

8. You need at least a triple space above centered heads, a double space below.

9. Centered captions of more than one line look better double-spaced. Center the second line, too.

10. For any heading, spread the lines out; have fewer and longer lines.

11. Be consistent in whatever system you adopt for headings.

12. On the title page, display in three or four blocks
    a) The complete report title (about 2 inches or 12 spaces from the top).
    b) The person or persons receiving the report, plus title if appropriate, and name and address of the company if different from the writer's (this slightly above the center of the page).
    c) The writer, his job title, name of company, address, and date of the report (spaced so that the last line is at least 1½ inches or 9 spaces from the bottom of the page).

13. Center every line on the title page unless you have special ability to design some other good-looking layout.

14. The simple label *Contents* is adequate for the page(s) identifying your heads and page numbers.

15. By placement and type in the contents, show that the synopsis is a prefatory part. Without outline symbol, begin it at the left margin and give it its appropriate lower-case Roman page number.

16. Likewise, show by placement and type that the bibliography, appendix, and index (if you have one) are appended parts by running them (without outline symbols) at the left margin. But they are numbered in Arabic page numerals, since they follow the pages so numbered.

17. Use spaced-dot leader lines (. . . . NOT. . . . OR ....) to guide your reader's eye across the page to page-number indications. Remember to line the dots up vertically.

18. Only the page where the section begins is listed on the contents table, not inclusive page numbers.

19. Every item listed on the contents page must have a page number indicated.

20. Align all numbers to the right. If you'll put periods after outline symbols (I. A. 1.) and keep the periods lined up, you'll have no trouble.

21. For letters, observe the same conventions of placement and form as for any letter. They do not have to follow the same layout as the report (indeed, they should not).

22. Even though your report is double-spaced, if you want or need to single-space letters, parts of the contents table, or the synopsis, go ahead. You should, however, double-space between orders of headings on the contents page.

PROBLEMS

Memos and Letters

1. Prepare a memo for general distribution to all employees changing the pay-day (of a local plant where you are controller) from Thursday to Friday. Also, instead of having supervisors distribute paychecks directly to employees under their supervision, you have decided to have all employees call for paychecks at the payroll windows in the plant administration building (which is right by the parking lot). Since the plant is now running only one shift of 500 people, working from 8:00 to 4:00, regular paychecks will be distributed at the payroll windows Friday afternoons 4:00 to 5:00. The office is not open on Saturday. To accommodate those employees absent on Fridays, one payroll window will be open every afternoon from 4:00 to 5:00. The payroll period will be figured from Wednesday to Wednesday. If any employee prefers to have his check mailed to him, you'll be glad to accommodate if he will come to the employment office and sign a form authorizing the company to do so.

2. As a result of an employee survey which indicated that over 80 per cent of your employees would probably eat lunch at the plant regularly if there were a cafeteria, that nearly 50 per cent would eat the evening meal there, and that 35 per cent would eat breakfast there—your company, the Carter Manufacturing Company, Birmingham, Alabama, has decided to run such a company cafeteria. It will begin about six weeks from now in the two large supplies-storage rooms you'll refurbish in the basement of the Administration Building. It will serve food practically at cost. Mid-day meal will be served from 12:00 to 1:30; evening meal from 4:30 to 6:00; breakfast from 6:00 to 7:30. The company is now operating so that some employees work from 3:00 to 11:00, most from 7:00 to 3:00, some from 11:00 to 7:00.

The snack bar will be open from 6:00 A.M. to 12 noon. If demand for any meal does not hold up, it may have to be discontinued.

The menu, in order to keep down costs of food to the employees, will have to be kept simple, especially at first.

Miss Lucille Haven, supervisor of the L & H Cafeteria, is in charge.

As plant manager, write the memorandum.

3. The Brandon Manufacturing Company, located 10 miles outside the city limits, has 3,000 employees. During the last 2 months, several employees have submitted the suggestion that the company establish a cafeteria and serve a noon meal for employees. The vice-president of the company, John A. Guin, asked you (an independent management consultant) to investigate the advisability of following this suggestion. Would employees appreciate a cafeteria? Would the company benefit?

Questionnaires distributed to employees gave the following results:

1. What do you usually do during your lunch hour? Go home—250; bring lunch from home—1,485; eat at restaurant—1,243; do not eat lunch—22.
2. Do you believe it would be a good idea for the company to establish a cafeteria for employees here in the plant? Yes—2,622; no—188; don't know—190.
3. If there were a cafeteria here in the plant, would you probably eat lunch in it fairly regularly? Yes—2,025; no—622; don't know—353.

In a blank space left for remarks, nearly half the employees mentioned that they didn't have time during their lunch hour to go home or to go into town to a restaurant. Several of the department heads added that lateness after lunch had become so common that they usually overlooked it.

Then you interviewed the manager of a successful restaurant in town. He told you that he was quite sure that a cafeteria could sell good, low-priced meals to employees and could pay for itself if as many as 700 ate in it regularly.

When you interviewed the personnel manager of Johnson and Company, a factory in a nearby community which employs 2,000 workers, you learned that the company cafeteria established there was considered very successful. "Since we installed the cafeteria, employees have been better satisfied with their work and therefore more efficient," he said; "about 85 per cent of the personnel eat lunch there regularly. After-lunch tardiness has been almost eliminated."

P. P. Bowen, vice-president of Gensen and Company, another factory which has its own cafeteria, told you that at least 80 per cent of his employees patronize the company cafeteria. "The cafeteria has been worth any effort we put into it," he stated. "Employees get better food and more rest during the lunch hour than they did before, and they show it in their work. Morale has improved noticeably."

Write the letter report.

4. Your company, Tampa Packing Company, canners of seafood, now issues to each new woman employee five white uniforms so that she can wear a fresh one every day. (You employ women only for your sorting and stripping of crab, shrimp, *et al.*)

But you have noticed in the past couple of months a certain laxity on the part of some workers. You surmise, although you do not have any direct evidence to support you, that they either do not wear a fresh uniform each day or do not launder them after a day's wear. And you well know that an unsanitary report where the workers are concerned would lower your AAA rating.

So you set up this program: All uniforms will be turned in to the central supply room; beginning next Monday, all employees will draw from the supply room five uniforms; any employee absent on a workday will draw only four (or three, or two) uniforms the following Monday morning. Also, as an added point to stop unnecessary questions, you advise the employees that, since your supply clerk cannot personally inspect every uniform, any suit found to be unwearable (a result of laundry handling, etc.) may be turned in for another.

Point out that the company is absorbing the costs of laundering. Write a memorandum to all employees pointing out the new plan. Use the Tampa Packing Company letterhead. You are the plant manager.

5. You are the credit union officer of the Acme Corporation employee credit union, which has about $10,000 representing shares bought by employees, for lending to fellow workers. It has just recently been activated.

Prepare a memo for distribution to all employees, announcing the institution of the plan and availability of the money, provided that the loan application is approved. Employees have to pay a $1 fee for membership. Invite additional investment; you expect to pay a 3 per cent return. Employees pay 1 per cent a month interest, figured on the exact number of days the money is used. For the time being, the three-man committee that reviews all loan applications has decided on a $300 limit for any loan.

6. Rewrite the following from the assistant plant manager of Mead and Mead: "Notice to all Supervisory Personnel: On or about June 1 all supervisory personnel including assistant foremen are requested to begin making very brief weekly written reports concerning the housekeeping conditions of their respective departments. In general this report should be short and yet include all improvements or changes effected in the interim between the preceding weekly report and the present one. It is important that these reports be made regularly and promptly. Any failures so to do will be dealt with individually because of these reports importance. Your cooperation is solicited and we know it will be forthcoming and appreciated."

7. For the president of your institution prepare a directive to go to all faculty and staff members reminding them of the fact that most of the buildings on your campus are equipped with automatic sprinkler protection with an alarm bell as part of the system. In all cases the alarm bells are located on the outside walls of the buildings on the ground floor. When water begins to flow through the sprinkler system, the alarm bell rings. All persons in buildings so equipped should be aware of the fact that there is such protection and of the location of the bell. The reason for this memo is that on the 18th of last month a broken water line of the sprinkler system in the Administration Building caused approximately $1,000 damages. Several people heard the ringing of the water-flow alarm bell but did not notify the police or fire department because they were unaware of what was happening. As part of this memo you are listing all the buildings so equipped and the location of the bell. You want each employee to know the status of the building(s) where he works—and teachers to announce to their classes in buildings where applicable.

8. Using today's date, as the new general manager of Pharmaceuticals, Inc., write an interoffice memo (or a letter, as your instructor directs) to Manager R. J. Hennessy of your Pearl River Branch, indicating carbons going to C. H. Parsons, your purchasing agent, and W. J. Rumpf, your carton production manager. Your purpose is to improve efficiency and reduce operating costs. You could do so by avoiding some present unnecessary changes in setups on your automatic carton machines (that cut and fold the cardboard stock for making paper boxes). You want to use Blueprint 3914C for all its present uses and for all uses to which B/P (Blueprint) 3915C is now put. For example, Box 3123, now cut by B/P 3915C, differs from Box 3122, cut by B/P 3914C, in using heavier stock (cardboard) and in using two slightly different cuts that require 5 per cent more cardboard. The heavier stock is desirable for some of your heavier bottles, but the different cuts seem unnecessary. So Box 3123 needs to be kept as an identifying number, but Hennessy's orders for it should specify B/P 3914C. After a month's use of it by that blueprint, he is to give you a report if he finds the new cut unsatisfactory.

9. Rewrite the following memorandum for the Manager, Dormitories and Food Services Department, of your university.

TO: All Units of the Dormitories and Food Services Division
FROM: Henry Herrod, Manager
SUBJECT: Central Purchasing of Waxes, Detergents, Cleaning
              Agents and Allied Products

For some time it has been apparent that we are using too many different products for the purposes noted above in the various units of the Division. At the present time, for example, over 70 different products are in use in the Residence Halls and the Union. Many of these products are purchased in small quantities, since they may be used by only one unit, and this results in a higher cost to the University.

It was felt that by standardizing and central purchasing, advantage could be taken of quantity prices and a further saving could be obtained by taking delivery in carload or truckload lots.

To study this problem, two committees were appointed. The food area committee, headed by Louise Gardner, Union as chairman, included Dorothy Scarbrough and Carol Starkweather of the Residence Halls.

James W. Clark, served as chairman for the committee concerned with building cleaning materials. Working with James was William Huff, Residence Halls; George Schuck, Married Housing; and Alfred Fox, Union.

Results of the committee's study and recommendations does not "close the door" to all other products. The personnel agreed to continue to serve on their respective committees and their future work will involve periodic testing of new products to determine if our standardized stock should be changed.

Any salesman with a new cleaning product should be referred to Pat Murphy, Food Stores Manager. Mr. Murphy will do preliminary screening of such products for the entire Division to save each manager or maintenance man the time often consumed by salesmen.

Mr. Murphy will channel new products for testing and consideration to the respective committee chairman concerned and each unit will share in the test work.

The products listed on the attached sheet have been recommended by the committees and approved by the Administrative Staff of the Dormitories and Food Services Division for use by all departments. Most of the items will be stored at Food Stores while those marked with an asterisk (*) will be in Central Stores. [To the student: *Assume* the presence of the attached sheet listing brands and types of cleaning supplies.]

10. In charge of the Dallas plant of Vulcan Aircraft Corp., you have just finished reading an article entitled "What's Your D I I Q?" It summarizes a talk given by Professor J. W. Spiegal, of Northwestern University, to the Dallas Executives Club. D I I Q stands for Daily Idea Interruption Quotient

or the number of times daily that your associates or employees voluntarily interrupt you to offer ideas on how to improve some phase of your business. According to Spiegal, if you supervise the activities of three or more people, your D I I Q should be at least twenty. Spiegal—who has worked with General Electric, Cory, Johnson's Wax, General Shoe (*et al.*)—maintains that there is little doubt that every salesman, secretary, foreman, draftsman, and designer has many product-improvement, cost-cutting, or money-saving ideas that he or she refrains from offering to management simply because of management's attitude of "I'm the one around here who's paid to think." Spiegal has three suggestions for promoting the mental climate he feels is most productive of ideas: (1) the creative potential of every individual must be recognized, (2) any idea or suggestion is encouraged regardless of how ridiculous it may appear to the supervisor, (3) any evaluation should be limited to comments about an idea, activity, or product rather than to people. Spiegal emphasizes that the typical suggestion system, where the employee is required to sign his name, isn't the answer; best results will be accomplished only when every supervisory employee encourages subordinates to volunteer their ideas orally. Pondering all the implications of this, you decide to write a memo to all department heads raising the basic question of, "Are we stifling suggestions? Do we insist on too much conformity? Do we reward the 'Yes' man more than the man with ideas?"

11. Put the following into good memorandum form and language for staff members at a large state university:

As a further measure to facilitate and encourage the promotion of fundamental research at the University, the State Board of Trustees on 1 March last year established the Office of Research Development. One of the major functions assigned to this office is to explore the research interests of governmental agencies and national foundations and to relate such interests to corresponding research competencies here as well as to worthwhile research programs in which this institution would like to engage.

In order to respond effectively to this important and basic assignment and to support the staff in a program of research development this office asks the assistance of all staff members to supply information which will help give an overview of the research potential and primary areas of research interests at the University. It is regretted that there seems to be no way of escaping the questionnaire device to obtain the necessary information.

Each staff member is requested to execute the attached form within the next 10 days and return it via normal departmental and school channels to this office, Room 318-B, Administration Building. Where space is inadequate on the questionnaire separate sheets should be attached. The assistance of the entire staff will be sincerely appreciated in this endeavor.

To avoid a possible misunderstanding it is emphasized that the execution of this questionnaire is not the occasion for the submission of formal proposals to outside agencies for grants-in-aid, nor does the completion of the form entail a personal committment to perform research requested by an outside agency as some of these requests may not conform to the quality and variety of research appropriate for the University.

Two copies are being submitted so that a duplicate copy may be retained by staff members for reference and file.

12. Your problems with Mr. Hennessy (Problem 8, p. 544) are not yet over. A month ago you asked him to co-operate in your efficiency drive by specifying B/P 3914C for all its then-present uses and for several other boxes then calling for other blueprints. He has done so except: Recently more orders have come through for Box 3123 specifying B/P 3915C. You have asked the box shop to fill present orders as specified; but you want the change made on future orders. Write the necessary letter or memo, as directed by your instructor.

13. As advertising manager of *Seventeen* (magazine for teen-age girls) you have just had your assistant do a thorough, up-to-date, nation-wide study of the newly-wed market. You got the idea from all the questions being asked around your house about prospective purchases by your recently married eighteen-year-old daughter who lives on the other side of town. Emphasis in the report was on the ages at which girls are getting engaged and married and on the kinds of purchases newly-weds make. Pertinent findings:

   —median age for engagements, just over seventeen

   —mode of marrying ages, eighteen

   —over 500,000 teen-age girls marry annually

   —a third of the eighteen- and nineteen-year-old girls are housewives

   —besides the rings and hundreds of relatively inexpensive items which you'll see around any home, newly-weds usually buy furniture, linens, silver, appliances, draperies (or have bought for them).

   Those findings are just about what you had come to expect, from having lived through the recent marriage of your daughter. But from the standpoint of your job they mean this: Your advertising salesmen have been missing the boat in not selling advertising to the manufacturers of "goods newly-weds buy" because the salesmen have been thinking of *Seventeen* readers as unmarried high-school and college and office and store-clerking and do-nothing girls. Now you realize that many of your readers are married and many of the single ones are only a few steps from the altar—engaged, or soon to be engaged and married, and soon to be buying the "goods newly-weds buy."

   Write a memo to be distributed to your seven salesmen to start them calling on manufacturers whom they have been ignoring because of the erroneous thinking that those manufacturers' products were for homes, married people, rather than *Seventeen* readers. Cite whatever you think you need from the report findings.

14. As director of employment for Cambert Pharmaceuticals, Inc., St. Louis, prepare a directive in memo form for distribution to all employees. In it you

will want to tell them that a parking-control system is being inaugurated effective in one week's time. Parking spaces will be numbered, and each employee needing parking space will be issued a sticker corresponding to the parking space he is to occupy. Cars without stickers and cars with sticker numbers not corresponding to the number of the parking space will be towed away. They will not be released except on payment of a $5 fine. The fine will be the same amount regardless of the number of violations. Employees may pick up their stickers at the Employment Office any time between 8:30 and 5:30 during the next week; after that, the office will observe its usual hours of 9:00 to 5:00.

15. Prepare a brief memo to all employees of the Specific Electric Corporation, Schenectady, New York, reminding them of their obligation to park in assigned parking areas.

    Unless the 30,000 workers (driving to work in approximately 10,000 cars daily) park properly and economically (that is, within the designated lot and within the marked areas), general confusion results.

    All employees receive numbered permit stickers for their cars. These permits also designate the particular lot in which the car must be parked.

    Your memo must warn in tactful fashion that any car parked in any spot other than the officially designated one for that car will be towed away, and the owner will be required to pay $5 service charge to recover the car. You are plant manager.

16. As office manager, write a memo on the memo form of the Treatolite Corporation (a St. Louis chemical research and patent-leasing firm working on petroleum processing) to go to each of your seven department heads, concerning the selection of a copying machine for reproducing letters, magazine articles, drawings, and other documents. You have looked into five already, but all of them had limitations that did not make them adaptable to all-around application in Treatolite offices and laboratories. Just recently, however, Eastman Kodak has introduced a new machine that looks hopeful. You have literature on it and can see only one objection: Pages to be reproduced have to be laid flat in the machine. Magazine pages would therefore have to be torn out. Since your departments are all in one building, all your men have been able to get along pretty well with one copy of the numerous technical magazines which you subscribe to; and you would not want to mutilate them before binding them in volumes for your permanent library. You could, however, order duplicate copies wherever necessary—probably without excessive expense. Certainly you could, by using the machine, more economically and quickly reproduce the various papers that the departments have been asking your central stenographic pool to type up—to say nothing of the fact that many of the magazine articles have charts, graphs, tables, drawings, and pictures that your girls can't reproduce. You have therefore arranged with the local Eastman man to give a demonstration in your office two weeks from today. You invite the department heads to attend if they want to. Whether they come or not, you want each

to send you about five pages of material he wants reproduced (and can wait for until the demonstration date). You want to encourage them to select material that is somewhat typical but will truly test the machine's versatility. They'll have to mark the material as to source (so you can return it and the copies to the right department) and (as always) to indicate the number of copies desired. You want them to be thinking about possible ways to overcome the one known weakness of the machine so that, when they get their copied material, they can give you their suggestions on that problem, their comment on the quality of work the machine does, and their vote to buy it or not.

17. C. M. Manderson, assistant professor of English, University of Iowa, has an insurance policy with your company (Illinois Mutuals) for comprehensive coverage on his car. The policy expires the 20th of next month, and no claim has been made on it yet. Renewal is $12.

He wrote you recently, saying that he carries a policy with another company covering public liability of $5,000 a person or $10,000 for one accident and property damage of $5,000.

He is interested in combining the two policies with one company, and he is inclined to favor yours because of the dividends he has received on his policy with you in the past. Your premiums for the coverages he has with the other company are $13 for the $5-and-$10 public liability and $9 for the property damage.

Manderson has heard that recent changes in Illinois law allow suits up to $15,000 for one person or $30,000 for several persons injured in one accident. He wants your advice on whether to carry insurance to cover the maximum allowable suit. You think it advisable. The additional premium is $2.73.

Your dividends recently have been 20 per cent on all coverages except comprehensive, which has been 15 per cent. Since the old policy, No. 700416, carried a premium of $6, the dividend of $0.90 will be deducted from the renewal premium.

Write a letter report answering Manderson's questions about the various premiums and dividends. Do not use any high-pressure tactics. The only salesmanship you should use is that which grows out of the figures, your helpfulness, and your making it easy for him to give you his business.

Though this is a letter and will look like a letter, it is also a report. It should have the qualities of a report rather than those we are sometimes inclined to think characteristic of a solicited sales letter.

18. Preparatory to registration for the next session of your college, write a memo for the dean (or the director, or the head) to be distributed to all staff members connected with enrolling students. Remind them to check prerequisites for each course carefully; far too many students have had to add and drop courses after classes were under way because registration or enrollment personnel put students in classes for which they were not prepared. Emphasize

that the normal load for a student with a C average is 17 or 18 hours (or credits); that students with a B average may carry 19, and those with an A average as high as 21—but only upon written permission from the dean's (or director's, or head's) office. No student under any circumstances may carry 22 hours. Nor may any student on campus carry less than 12. Any person attempting to register for less than 12 should have written permission from the appropriate office indicating that he is either a non-degree (special) student or that he needs only a certain number less than 12 hours to complete his degree requirements. Only a student who has received a grade of F in a course may re-enroll for the second time; having received a minimum passing grade or an X or Incomplete or Deferred, he may not begin again from the beginning. Registration officials should be careful to see that students are admitted only at the times designated for them; if they are late, they have to register the last afternoon of the last day of registration; they should not be allowed to usurp the time of students who do report on time.

19. As sales engineer for the Grand Rapids branch of Warren Williams & Company, write the necessary memo to the home office in Camden concerning the wrong size of materials sent to the Lansing Heating Supply Company (see Problems 11 and 12, pp. 355, 356).

20. In the role of the industrial relations director for Republic Rolling Mill, Inc., Youngstown, Ohio, write a memo authorizing one of your assistants to submit a report evaluating various "SUB" plans now in operation in steel, auto, aluminum, rubber, and glass industries. "SUB" stands for supplemental unemployment benefits. You'd like to have as thorough a study of the various plans as is possible to obtain through available sources (magazine articles, annual reports, monographs, books) to aid your thinking and planning for an eventuality in your own company that is rapidly assuming the form of a reality. Indicate a time by which you want the report. You may want to suggest *U.S. News & World Report,* January 3, 1958, p. 73, as a starter before checking indexes for additional material.

21. As an agent of the Apex Real Estate Agency, you receive the following authorization from L. N. Rives and Company:

> Please consider this letter your authorization to find for us a suitable location for an apartment building to provide attractive accommodations for families of medium income and above.

> Our preliminary plans call for a frontage of from 100 feet to 125 feet on two streets. We expect to pay about $200,000 for the land. We feel that the location of the building must appeal to desirable tenants both because of its surroundings and because of its accessibility, in keeping with the other apartment buildings we own and operate in this city.

> We plan rental units of one to five rooms with rents ranging from $60 to $150.

You investigated several possible sites, with the following results:

A lot on the corner of Broad Street and Tenth Avenue would cost $180,-000. It is close to public transportation lines, but the L and N Railroad freight depot is only half a block away. The lot is 110 × 110. It is six blocks from the center of the downtown business area. Many businesses are located around the lot. The present old home would have to be moved or razed.

A 120 × 135 foot lot on the corner of Jackson and Lansing Streets is available at $175,000. It is in an excellent neighborhood, with fine homes nearby and a park directly across the street. Motor bus lines are ½ mile away. The closest shopping district is 2 miles away. No structure is now on the lot.

Another lot has a frontage of 120 feet on Bowie Boulevard and 140 feet on Travis Avenue. The price is $115,500. The site is one block from Larkin Boulevard, one of the principal automobile thoroughfares to the downtown district. A motor bus goes down that boulevard. It is two blocks from the streetcar line on Marsten Street. Within two blocks is a suburban shopping district, with two theaters as well as grocery, dry-goods, and variety stores. Two excellent apartment houses are in the same block, and no manufacturing is found in the neighborhood. Within a radius of about ½ mile are three churches, the Hale Memorial Library, and the Lampkin grade school. The college campus is about a mile away. This property is residential only and would have to be rezoned in order to place a business there.

Write a letter report to Mr. Rives giving your recommendation based on these facts.

22. Analyze the following tabulations and make pertinent observations and appropriate suggestions to the head of the Business Writing Department for maintaining more uniform and equitable grade distributions by the three instructors concerned. The grades for the business correspondence course were awarded over the five academic periods immediately preceding the time of this report. Set it up in the form of a memo or letter, whichever your instructor specifies. (Parenthetical figures are approximate percentages.)

Instructor M (total of 381 students)

A	B	C	D	F
18 (47)	119 (31.2)	161 (42.3)	61 (18.6)	22 (3.2)

Instructor N (total of 697 students)

A	B	C	D	F
56 (8)	151 (21.7)	379 (54.5)	68 (9.8)	43 (6)

Instructor O (total of 808 students)

A	B	C	D	F
23 (2.8)	297 (36.8)	409 (50.6)	58 (7.2)	21 (2.6)

23. In charge of the automotive finishes section of the Stabrite Paint Company, you have been asked by Apex director E. P. Hogue to find out if possible the cause of objectionable "yellowing" on the cabs of the Apex Cab Company, whose cabs have recently been repainted with your Z-202 cream enamel. You have one of the discolored panels (Cab # 104). As soon as you received it, you saw that the discoloration was due to a deposit that was re-

movable by scraping. Chemical tests revealed the presence of ferric ions. You then took a fresh door panel and painted it with your Z-202. Then you washed the panel thirty successive times (allowing ample time for complete drying) before the same yellowing surface deposit appeared as on the original door. You followed the same washing procedure used by the Apex people in their garage, using a liquid soap (Chemical 4371). Then you coated a fresh panel with Z-202, added 0.05 per cent by volume of Glodene #35 water softener, the liquid soap, and the wash water, and proceeded to wash over and over. To date the panel has been washed some 60 times with this solution, and no surface deposit has appeared; nor does there appear to be damage of any other kind to the enamel surface. Write the necessary recommendation to Mr. Hogue in the form of an interoffice memo.

24. As the sales manager for the Milton-Hamilton Hotel in St. Louis, prepare a memo for all department heads. It is to acquaint them with the hotel's official convention executive pin (which will be adopted by all Milton hotels). The pins are to be given to the convention executives when they register, to identify them as persons in charge—persons to be given VIP treatment always (and all employees are to be notified accordingly). A sample pin featuring the Milton crest will be attached to the memo. Also attached will be a sample letter which the general manager sends in advance of the convention; the letter requests the recipient to present the letter to the assistant manager when he registers so that he will receive the pin. Copy of the letter goes to the assistant manager at the time it is mailed, so that he will be familiar with the names.

25. Summary report in either memo or letter form (as your teacher directs):

Assume that you are director of the Public Opinion Research Institute, Syracuse University. You have just completed a comprehensive analysis of public survey techniques. In the morning's campus mail comes a request from the Director of Advanced Studies for a summary evaluation of personal interviews, telephone interviews, and mail questionnaires as research procedures. "Something that could be summarized in three or four typewritten pages and mimeographed for quick reading by our students," he writes.

For assistance in preparing this summary of advantages and limitations, review the discussion in your text and supplement with references/coverage that you can find in library references. Check statistics books and publications on public opinion surveying and poll-taking.

Credit

1. Rewrite the following credit information in a clear, readable credit report grouping information into clearly labeled sections of related information. Carl M. Crawford, Family Shoes, 296 Cottonwood Avenue, Phoenix. Crawford retails men's, women's, and children's shoes, most volume on credit. The price range of leather footwear once $3.95 to $6.95, then $6.95 to $9.95, is now $5.95 to $19.95. Three clerks and a bookkeeper assist. There

are two other shoe stores nearby, one selling shoes of comparable quality and price, the other shoes of lower quality and price. Shortly after going to work for his father (Marshall C. Crawford), Crawford became proprietor of the business. He graduated from the University of Southern California with a B.S. degree in business administration (1937) and then was employed by Root Bros. Construction Co. in Los Angeles. Crawford rents the store (from his father) measuring 40 × 60 feet and basement in a two-story brick building in good repair. The upper floor contains office space occupied by a publishing business and an advertising agency. He is forty-five, married, and native born. When Root Bros. closed the Los Angeles office in 1938, Crawford went to work for his father, who had started this business in 1926. New materials and changing tastes in footwear have reduced unit sales of leather footwear, but dollar volume has increased by sales emphasis on higher-priced lines and by the addition of items in gabardine, duck, canvas, straw, plastic, and silk. Sales have steadily increased; operations are continuing profitable. Crawford's wife—also native born—assists in selling and display and is carried on the payroll but does not work full-time; she is very active in club work. Inventory is heavy; capital is supplemented rather steadily by unsubordinated loans from a relative; the loans are not subordinated to claims of general creditors. In 1941 women's and children's shoes were added to the stock. The store was completely remodeled in 1946. Sales since then have shown a steady increase with the exception of 1951 and 1957, and satisfactory net profits have brought steady growth in net worth despite the rather large drawings of the owner. A stock of hosiery, purses, and costume jewelry is also carried. The store has two large show windows and aisled window display. It is located on a secondary thoroughfare in the main shopping district. In September, 1947, a small fire in the storage space in the basement caused damages estimated by Crawford and paid by the insurance company of $367. The window display is changed every week. A second fire on the ground floor (the store proper) in November, 1958, caused carpet and fixture damage of $1,569 as claimed by Crawford but settled for $1,314 by the insurance company. Crawford said, when interviewed today, that the present rather large volume of sales is partly accounted for by wide style and size assortments, which has necessitated a heavy inventory, which at December 31 was in excess of tangible net worth. This business has been in operation since 1926. On both sides of Crawford's store are one-story brick buildings also in good condition, one occupied by a jewelry store, the other by a low-to-medium-priced dress shop. In order to assist in maintaining the inventory, Crawford has obtained loans periodically from an uncle, Bryce Crawford. These loans are of amounts large enough to allow the owner to discharge obligations within purchase terms (often discounting) but have resulted in large total debt in relation to tangible net worth. Carl Crawford was on the USC varsity football and baseball teams all his eligible time in college. Bryce Crawford is an executive in an aircraft plant in Los Angeles and takes no part in the management of this business.

2. Take a local, not too large retail store (chosen by you or assigned by your teacher) and

a) Assume that you are the local Dun & Bradstreet reporter,

b) Get as much information as you can (like that in the preceding problem) by observing at the store and talking with store personnel,

c) Use calculated guesses for needed information that you can't get (like financial data), and

d) Write up a credit report on the business.

3. Using the information in Robert Wallace's "Please Remit," *Life,* December 21, 1953, pp. 42–46, 49–50, 52 (reprinted in the "Credits and Collections" section of *Writing for Business*),

a) Assume that the subject of the report in that article has just opened a small store of some kind in your community,

b) Assume that you are the local Dun & Bradstreet reporter,

c) Assume that you have been to the new store and observed carefully,

d) Use calculated guesses for needed information that is not in the article and that you can't reasonably assume you got through observation, and

e) Write a credit report covering all the kinds of information mentioned in the section on "Credit Reports" in this chapter of your book.

Justification

1. As office manager for the Lewis Department Store, Baton Rouge, Louisiana, suggest the advisability of purchasing an electric addressograph machine for billing customers each month. There are 4,000 customers, 3,000 of whom receive a statement each month. On an average, about 25 letters are returned each month because of poor typing. The addressograph plates would eliminate this; they can't make mistakes. (Completely aside from this money saving is the tangible benefit—though incalculable—of always being sure that a customer's name is correctly spelled.)

At present two of the women in the office spend four days typing addresses; their pay is $60 for a 40-hour week. The addressograph of your choice is the Audograph, which sells for $335 complete with cord and tax. It requires floor space of 4' × 6'. The Athens Supply Company gives three months' free service and, of course, guarantees the machine against mechanical defects for a full year. The estimated life is 20 years. Plates are 5¢ each. After analyzing changes in your mailing list, you estimate that you do not have more than 25 changes of address a month.

2. The stenographic work of the Colby Manufacturing Company is handled by six stenographers who are paid an average of $65 a week. Two of the girls told the office manager the first of the month that they plan to resign at the end of the month for higher pay. The manager, John Mason, has asked you, his assistant, to investigate the advisability of purchasing electric typewriters instead of hiring two new employees. He wonders if the work could be handled by four girls if they had the new machines. Would any savings be effected? What would the typists themsleves think of it? Here is the information you obtained:

Cost of new machines.......$450 for one; $425 each in groups of four or more
Present employees' typing rate.............Between 55 and 65 words a minute

Statement from Robert Whitworth, director of the Merrill Business College: "When our students who make 60 words a minute on nonelectric machines change to electric, they must practice for four or five weeks before they can get up to 60 again. However, in another three weeks most of them are making 80 or 90 words a minute without any trouble. Electric machines are so easy to operate that much of the usual strain is avoided."

One dealer offers $70 each for the six 5-year old manual typewriters now in the department. The head of the stenographic department of the Norton Company says: "Our typists have not complained of fatigue since we installed electric typewriters; the girls work more uniformly, taking fewer 'breaks' during the day."

One of the four typists in the department has had experience with electric typewriters. She says: "I'm sold on them! I can type 60 words a minute on the typewriter I am using here now, and 90 words a minute on an electric model." The other three girls have not used electric typewriters; but, because they have heard so much about the ease of operation, they are in favor of the change. Interpret these findings and incorporate them into a well-organized justification report. Assume that you would raise the pay of the four remaining stenographers to $75 a week.

Short Analytical

1. One of the junior executives of Ames, Incorporated, of San Francisco, a large manufacturer of women's clothing, suggested to the president of the company, C. D. Young, that improvement was needed in the company's correspondence. When the president brought the matter before the board of directors, there was a good deal of discussion. Some of the members felt that the suggestion was ridiculous. "Everyone in our firm knows how to write letters," one member remarked.

Enough of the members were interested, however, to pass a motion that the subject should be investigated. Accordingly, the president authorized you, one of his assistants, to determine whether correspondence improvement was needed and, if so, how it could be effected. He gave you a month.

Your first step was to read current material on letter-improvement programs. The following excerpts from current publications you considered significant:

"Conservative estimates place the cost of letters at at least $1.50 each. That means that many companies spend hundreds of thousands of dollars yearly on correspondence. To get their money's worth, they must be sure that every letter helps to improve public relations." *Source:* Article by Henry Howard in *U.S. Business,* May, page 29, entitled "Cutting Correspondence Costs."

"Bring in an instructor who has had experience in writing letters as well as in teaching. Have him conduct regular classes for several weeks.

Require all members of the firm connected with letter writing—from the president to the typist—to attend. Then watch your letters improve!" *Source:* Unsigned feature in *Printers' Week,* January, page 37, "Letter Training Program Pays Off!"

The January *Printers' Week,* on page 54, listed the names of 57 companies which had carried out letter-improvement programs. To find out what results those companies had obtained, you sent a questionnaire to the president of each. The questions and replies (55) were as follows:

I. What do you believe was the effect of your letter-improvement program on the quality of the company's letters?
1. Considerable improvement: 39
2. Slight improvement: 6
3. No noticeable difference: 10

II. What was the attitude of most of the correspondents toward the program?
1. Favorable: 42
2. Unfavorable: 4
3. Indifferent: 9

III. What do you believe was the effect of the program on your company's customer relations?
1. Considerable improvement: 38
2. Slight improvement: 11
3. No apparent change: 6

IV. Do you have a correspondence manual?
1. Yes: 28
2. No: 27

V. If yes, to IV, please answer these:
A. Do you believe it has helped to improve letter quality?
1. Yes: 24
2. No: 2
3. Don't know: 2
B. What was the approximate cost of issuing it?
Less than $200: 5
$200–$300:   4
$300–$500:   12
$500 and over: 7

VI. Do you have a correspondence supervisor or someone who assumes such duties?
1. Yes: 32
2. No: 23

VII. If yes to VI, do you believe the supervisor has helped to improve letter quality?
1. Yes: 32
2. No: 0
3. Don't know: 0

Respondents were invited to comment on each question and promised anonymity if quoted. Following are some typical comments:

> "Since completion of our training program, we have received fewer complaints than ever before and many customers have written letters of appreciation."

> "The letter improvement classes we held five years ago made correspondents conscious of their responsibilities for several months. But since there was no supervisor to encourage consistent effort to make letters effective, correspondents became lax again. Our new program provides for a supervisor who will hold regular classes for discussion of letter problems."

> "On the whole, both correspondents and typists appreciated the constructive criticism of the instructor. Nearly all were enthusiastic when they realized how important their letters were in building good will for the company."

> "The correspondence manual issued at the close of our training period served to crystallize the information presented by the instructor. It is always available for quick reference."

Meanwhile, you looked over 200 letters selected at random from the letters typed in one week by the 40 typists employed by the company. (There are about 85 dictators in the company averaging 50 letters per week.)

You found these facts:

- 15 variations in mechanical makeup
- 40 spelling errors
- 25 errors in sentence structure
- 62 participial closings
- 14 paragraphs of 15 lines or more
- 5 letters of only one sentence
- 10 letters averaging 32 words per sentence
- 54 trite expressions
- 49 instances of wordiness
- 36 expressions that would be offensive to readers
- 48 letters that were correct, complete, and original
- 33 letters that left questions unanswered
- 16 cases when the dictator individually dictated practically the same message to three or more individuals

When you interviewed Dr. R. R. Brawner of Del Monte, a professional consultant in business letters, he explained the program he has carried out in many companies. He favors classes of 2 hours each for all the correspondents and typists connected with the firm for 10 weeks. He analyzes letters dictated by each correspondent and gives individual suggestions. He stressed that, for favorable employee reaction, classes should be held during the working day in groups of no more than 20. Further, he believes that dictators and transcribers should not be taught in the same class. His fee would be $1,000 for the ten sessions.

From many sources you had heard about the letter-improvement program carried out by the Pacific Electric Company. When you interviewed Robert L. Jennings, head of the Customer Relations Department, he explained the plan as follows:

"We selected a correspondence instructor from one of the local universities to conduct a 2-hour class on Thursday afternoons. Lectures on principles of business writing, slanted toward the problems of our company, were supplemented by discussion of the carbon copies of the previous week's letters. Letters actually received from our customers were used as class problems.

"That was six years ago. By the end of the first year, the value of the course was evident. The improvement in dictation was marked. Complaints from customers were not nearly as numerous. A large file of complimentary letters from customers was accumulating.

"We are still holding those classes regularly, with one of our experienced employees in charge. The dictators know the principles, but only by regular inspection of carbon copies can it be assured that those principles are still being followed."

For some helpful information, you may want to see *American Business,* May, 1957, p. 24. Submit this analysis in formal report form with recommendations.

2. As a basis for pushing sales of his transparent wrappings and containers for a wide variety of foods, the sales manager for the Appleton (Wisconsin) Paper Company commissioned your company—The Factfinding Corp., Chicago—to run a survey of shopping habits in supermarkets. Your trained representatives in Dallas, Los Angeles, Denver, St. Paul, Cleveland, Boston, Richmond, and Jacksonville interviewed 1,754 shoppers who bought 16,378 items in 40 modern supermarkets on Tuesday through Friday two weeks ago. As the shopper entered the store, she was asked to list all food items she planned to buy; as she came to the check-out counter, this list was checked against the purchases she actually had made. Of all purchasers, the final results revealed, 25 per cent had a complete written list on entering the store, 9 per cent a partial written list, and 64 per cent only a mental "list." Of all purchases made, 33 per cent were specifically planned, 27 per cent generally planned (item but not brand), 2 per cent substituted, and 38 per cent unplanned (impulse buying). Thus 67 per cent of the buying decisions were made at the point of sale! Whereas 38 per cent of all purchases were unplanned, 58 per cent of items in transparent packaging were unplanned purchases. Though you had thousands of classifications in your original tallies (supermarkets display 2,500–3,000 items), you have narrowed your statistical tabulation down to the following representative items:

Average Profit (Per Cent)		Products Bought	Planned (Per Cent)	Generally Planned (Per Cent)	Substituted (Per Cent)	Unplanned (Per Cent)
1.	25	Breads	11	33		56
2.	26	Butter/margarine	28	45	2	25
3.	31	Candy	6	8	1	85
4.	11	Coffee	49	25	2	24
5.	23	Cookies	11	20	1	68
6.	18	Dessert mixes	17	9	1	73
7.	10	Eggs	31	48	1	20
8.	23	Fruit (canned)	21	33	3	43
9.	23	Fruit (dried)	20	30		50
10.	20	Fruit (fresh)	42	17	1	40
11.	27	Fruit (frozen)	18	48	5	29
12.	20	Fruit/veg. juices (canned)	29	29	3	39
13.	28	Gum	49			96
14.	35	Ice cream	9	32		59
15.	27	Jams/jellies/preserves	27	21	5	47
16.	19	Meat (canned)	20	18	2	60
17.	20	Meat (fresh)	41	42	2	15
18.	23	Meat (luncheon)	29	36	1	34
19.	17	Mixes, prepared	32	7	1	60
20.	28	Nuts	19	19	2	60
21.	23	Paper towels, tissues, napkins	15	19	1	65
22.	30	Pie		20		80
23.	35	Popcorn		22	11	67
24.	25	Potato chips	21	13		66
25.	17	Poultry (fresh)	67	18	2	13
26.	26	Rolls (sweet)	11	21		68
27.	11	Soap/soap flakes	49	11	1	39
28.	19	Vegetables (canned)	17	33	2	48
29.	20	Vegetables (fresh)	48	23	1	28
30.	23	Vegetables (frozen)	18	36	7	39
31.	..	Other foods	36	15	1	48

Prepare a short report with cover, title page, authorization letter, transmittal letter which contains your most significant findings, contents listings, and the analysis.

3. The Taylor Company in your community decided a month ago to purchase a vacation site where employees could spend their two-week vacations during the summer. Rooms and recreational facilities are to be furnished by the company.

The president, F. V. Taylor, asked you, the personnel manager, to find out what kind of vacation site was desired by employees. He wants you, also, to investigate available locations and to make a recommendation for the best site to purchase. The company plans to spend no more than $40,000 for the resort. It should be large enough, Mr. Taylor points out, to accommodate all the employees who would like to spend vacations there, as well as their families. It should be within 200 miles of the firm, so that employees could reach it without too much difficulty.

One of your first steps was to distribute questionnaires to the 350 employees of the company to get their reactions. All of them were in favor of the purchase; 290 said they would like to spend at least one week at the resort this year. To the question, "What kind of recreation would you like to have available?" 190 of the 350 answered fishing; 260 swimming; 93 golf; 142 boating; 96 tennis; 115 dancing. When asked whether they would prefer to stay in an individual cabin or a lodge, 280 specified a cabin, 63 mentioned a lodge, and 17 were indifferent.

You spent three weeks checking up on all possible locations. The possibilities finally narrowed down to these three:

1. A site in the Indian Mountains—small swimming pool—23 cabins—golf course—cost $25,000—tennis courts—considerable repairing needed, with costs estimated at $20,000—on U.S. Highway 290—Greyhound Bus route on highway—180 miles from firm.

2. A site on Emerald Lake—cost $32,000—25 cabins in good condition—good fishing in Serpent River, 1 mile from resort—large recreation room with fireplace—147 miles from town, 15 miles off U.S. Highway 120 on well-graded gravel road—Greyhound Bus route on highway—boathouse and small dock—golf driving range—$5,000 worth of additional equipment needed—shallow place for wading as well as swimming in lake—diving board.

3. A site on the Canook River—138 miles from firm—tennis court—lodge containing 30 double rooms and a large recreation room—good fishing—10 miles from State Highway 111—narrow, crooked dirt road from highway—very swift water, suitable only for expert swimmers—$43,000—excellent condition, with no repairs needed.

Using this information, report to Mr. Taylor ranking the three in an order of desirability in the light of employees' recreational preferences. Assemble the report with a cover and transmittal memo.

4. In an attempt to find out what leading advertisers are thinking, you as an associate editor of *Promotion,* a magazine of national circulation devoted to marketing problems, sent out questionnaires to the 400 retailers who do half the nation's over-the-counter business. From the 400 questionnaires mailed, 149 replies were returned.

On the optimistic side:

105 expect to beat last year's sales this year
 15 expect to equal them
 16 believe that this year's sales will fall below last year's level
 13 don't know
107 plan to increase their advertising*

* These 107 look at the coming year's business this way:
 68 think they'll do more business this year
 16 think they'll equal
 22 think they'll do less
  1 doesn't know

29 plan to maintain advertising at last year's level**
13 plan to curtail their advertising***

The hearty 107 can be further broken down this way: 34 food chains; 28 drug chains; 22 department stores; 14 variety chains; specialty, ready-to-wear, shoe, home furnishings, 2 each; and 1 jeweler.

The stalwart 29 like this: 11 food; 7 drug; 7 department; 1 each of jewelry, variety, ready-to-wear, and shoe.

The cowardly 13 like this: 2 department store; 2 food; 3 jewelry; 3 drug; and 3 ready-to-wear.

Write this up in short analytical report form (title page, memorandum of transmittal, and the analysis itself) for submittal to the editor, who would like to turn out the feature article himself.

5. In charge of the Placement Bureau at Haverfort University, Indianapolis, John R. Martin, director, decided to find out what personnel managers prefer in letters of application. So he asked you, director of the Research Bureau, if you would help him out. After joint consultation with the head of the Department of Business Writing, the head of the Vocational Guidance Department, and the head of Statistics, you prepared and sent the following questionnaire to 500 personnel managers in Indiana, Illinois, Ohio, Michigan, and Pennsylvania. The replies of the 324 who returned the questionnaire are tabulated on this copy. From this material prepare a short analytical report for Mr. Martin which will help him when he talks to applicants. Prepare it so that he can just hand it to an applicant with the comment, "Here, read this; it'll help you prepare your application." Copies will also be available in school libraries. Submit the report with cover, title page, letter of transmittal which is also an epitome, table of contents, and the analysis itself.

    1. *a*) Do you object to a duplicated letter of application?
           234 Yes   90 No
      b) When considering several applicants for a position, do you eliminate those who send you a duplicated letter of application?
           143 Yes   181 No
    2. *a*) Do you object to a mimeographed data sheet?
           76 Yes   248 No
      b) Do you object to a commercially printed data sheet?
           48 Yes   276 No
      c) When considering several applicants for a position, do you eliminate those who send you either of the following:

** These feel like this:
    18 expect this year's sales to be better
    6 think they'll be about the same
    4 think they'll be less
    1 doesn't know

*** These express the following guesses:
    13 think it'll equal last year's

Mimeographed data sheet   22 Yes   302 No
Commercially printed data sheet 17 Yes   307 No

3. Which of the following is more important to you in selecting an applicant?

      55 Application letter   37 Data Sheet   232 Both equal in importance

4. Which of the following do you prefer?

      123 Applicant's letter addressed to you by name, followed by your title.
      85 Applicant's letter addressed to "Personnel Manager"
      116 No preference

5. What is your reaction to the following kinds of enclosures with the application?

      Return-addressed postal card
                    29 Favorable   207 Unfavorable   88 Neutral
      Return-addressed stamped envelope
                    214 Favorable   71 Unfavorable   39 Neutral

6. *a*) What is your reaction to an applicant's sending you a follow-up letter within a month after he has mailed you his application letter and data sheet?

      252 Good   10 Annoying   62 Neutral

    b) If your answer to the above question is good, why do you favor a follow-up? (More than one reason allowed.)

      73 Shows persistence
      178 Indicates interest
      220 Lets me know he is still available.

7. In selecting inexperienced employees, which of the following backgrounds do you prefer? Please rank on a 1-2-3-4 basis (highest rank = 1).

    a) Applicant who participated in many extracurricular activities and maintained a passing grade in his sudies. (1) 37, (2) 74, (3) 114, (4) 99.

    b) Applicant who participated in several extracurricular activities and maintained above-average grades in his studies. (1) 102, (2) 124, (3) 79, (4) 19.

    c) Applicant who helped pay his own way through school and maintained above average grades in his studies. (1) 164, (2) 106, (3) 36, (4) 18.

    d) Applicant who participated in no extracurricular activities and maintained honor grades in his studies. (1) 13, (2) 13, (3) 66, (4) 232.

8. When considering several applicants for a position, do you give preference to any of the following:

35 Local applicants are given preference
107 In-state applicants are given preference over out-of-state applicants
0 Out-of-state applicants are given preference
182 Geographical location is immaterial

9. *a*) Do you want an applicant to mention beginning salary in his initial application?

   187 Yes   137 No

   b) If your answer to the above question is yes, where should he mention salary?

   97 Application letter   31 Data Sheet   96 Either

10. On many data sheets or application letters the applicant lists several specific references—usually under a caption labeled "References."

    a) When do you check these references?

    187 Before the interview   120 After the interview

    17 do not check

    b) Do you want this list of references included on the application?

    260 Yes   16 No   48 Immaterial

    c) If your answer to the above question is yes,

    1) How many references do you prefer? Please encircle your choice—

    (1) 0, (2) 16, (3) 193, (4) 72, (5) 43

    2) Where do you want these references?

    56 Application letter   137 Data Sheet   131 No preference

    3) What types of references do you prefer? (check as many as you desire)

    314 Previous employers   252 College instructors of related courses

    37 High-school teachers

    25 Dean of the college   193 (Former) supervisors

    Other (please add) Character references (banker, doctor, minister, etc.) 44

11. Many college students have worked part time while attending school. Do you want to know about these jobs, whether they are related or not?

    298 Yes   26 No

12. Many college students have worked full time during summers. Do you want to know about these jobs, whether they are related or not?

    306 Yes   18 No

13. Which of the following do you prefer from an applicant?

    9 Application letter only

    86 Application letter and data sheet

    106 Application letter with placement office credentials forwarded separately

    123 Application letter and data sheet with placement office credentials forwarded separately

6. The executive council of the American Association of Realtors met in New York early in the month. On the 10th the executive secretary, Mr. Robert Gerfen, called you (president, Research, Inc., also in New York), asking you to conduct another nation-wide survey on what kind of houses folks want to

build or buy (you did one for him five years ago). "Just urban areas," he said, "young folks earning above $6,000. We'd like to have it for distribution by the end of the month." It was easy enough for you to send to your trained representatives—in 38 cities (all over 50,000) in all sections of the country—the following questionnaire, which they used in interviewing 5,000 heads of families (about 54 per cent women, 46 per cent men) all of whom were under forty, two-thirds of whom had children, and all of whom earned over $6,000 (with an average of $6,600), and to get the replies indicated. (It was assumed that all houses would have kitchen and living room.)

1. What type of house do you prefer, single family, or row?

   Single family, detached: 4,660   Row: 40
   Two family: 240   Other or don't know: 60.

2. Do you want a one-story or two-story house?

   One-story: 4,367   Two-story: 633.

3. How many rooms do you wish your house to have (excluding bathrooms)?

   4 or less: 60   7:   1,520
   5:          570   8:   315
   6:        2,360   9 or more: 165   Don't know: 10.

4. How many bedrooms do you plan to have?

   1: 62; 2: 1,065; 3: 2,624; 4 or more: 1,245; Don't know: 4.

5. How many bathrooms:

   1: 1,844; 2: 2,572; 3: 508; 4: 76.

6. Do you plan to have your house insulated? Yes: 4,756; no: 143; don't know: 101.

7. Do you plan to have your house fire-resistant? Yes: 3,995; no: 800; don't know: 205.

8. Do you plan to have your house soundproofed? Yes: 4,231; no: 643; don't know: 126.

9. Do you plan to have your house air-conditioned? Yes: 3,726; no: 856; don't know: 418.

10. If yes to 9, do you plan to have an individual room cooler or central system? Room cooler, 215; Central system, 3,511.

11. Do you think these features are

	Necessary	Desirable but Not Necessary	Unnecessary and Not Particularly Desirable
Separate dining room..........	2,756	2,228	16
Basement....................	1,466	1,732	1,802
Family room.................	4,127	722	151
Garage (enclosed, attached).....	2,127	1,648	1,225
Carport......................	1,327	1,173	2,500
Study or library..............	576	2,552	1,872
Porch (living)................	703	1,017	3,280
Center hallway...............	1,115	2,311	1,574
Attic (with storage)..........	1,799	1,894	1,307
Utility room.................	4,556	436	8
Breakfast bar or nook.........	3,860	790	350
Laundry facilities.............	4,448	480	72
Fireplace....................	3,400	1,228	372

Submit the report to Mr. Gerfen with cover, title page, letter of transmittal which is also an epitome, contents table, and the analysis.

7. One of the projects you've inherited as director of educational research for the American Association of Collegiate Schools of Business is that of college teacher recruitment and training. Your committee of co-operating university professors of business administration (at Alabama, Indiana, Illinois, Michigan, Minnesota, Kansas, Ohio State, Pennsylvania State, Texas, and Wisconsin) administered your questionnaire to 1,260 juniors, seniors, and graduates at the eleven institutions. Prior to that, you tested your tentative questionnaire on representative students at Wade State University, and revised the "free response" questions twice in an attempt to get accurate indications of students' attitudes toward college or university teaching as a career.

Following are questions and tabulated answers which your research assistant has placed on your desk as a basis for writing a report intended for your readers—members of the AACSB, other college administrators, professional associations (accounting, marketing, management), and foundations.

1. Have you ever talked with anyone about the advantages and disadvantages of a career as a collegiate teacher of business administration?

196 answered "yes."

2. What do you consider the advantages of collegiate teaching of business administration as a career?

	Number of Times Mentioned
Prestige	441
Opportunity to help others	412
Continual learning	252
Desirable associates	128
Research opportunities	125
Consulting opportunities	124
Stimulating intellectual environment	118
Pride in doing significant work	110
Freedom of thought	40
Short hours	240
Long vacations	226
Absence of pressure	138
Pleasant duties	129
Independence in carrying out duties	62
Regularity of income	156
Increasing demand for teachers	132
Stability of job	93

3. What do you consider the disadvantages of collegiate teaching of business administration as a career?

Pay is too low	879
Industry pays more	188
Inadequate retirement benefits	122
Ability and pay not correlated	52
Monotonous, dull duties	213
Restricted expression	48
Restricted personal life	39
Promotions too slow	157

Limited room at the top............................	131
Training period too long...........................	128
Advanced-degree programs too difficult...............	118
Teachers become too theoretical/impractical..........	130
Teachers lose drive/originality......................	62
Teachers not appreciated by society..................	58

4. As a whole, would you favorably consider collegiate teaching of business administration as a career?

No   781   Don't know   303   Yes   176

5. Do you intend to teach business administration at collegiate levels?

No   1,058   Don't know   177   Yes   25

6. Do you think you have enough information about college teachers' training, duties, responsibilities, and rewards (tangible and intangible) to answer questions 4 and 5 intelligently?

No   567   Yes   569

Plan the report for final distribution with a title page, letter of transmittal, contents page, and the analysis itself (introduction, survey findings and what they establish as well as imply, and a terminal section summarizing the most significant findings together with appropriate conclusions and recommendations).

Complete Analytical

1. One of the requests coming to your desk as director of Factseekers, Inc., New York, is from the president of (name of firm supplied by your instructor). The company is a chain of retail (type of store supplied by your instructor) stores with outlets in most major cities. The chain is now contemplating opening a store in either one of two cities (names of two cities supplied by your instructor).

   You are asked to make a report evaluating the two as potential locations for this new store.

   The letter to you as director, signed by the company chairman, reads:

   Will you please submit in report form your analysis of retail-sales possibilities for (specific goods) in (specific cities)?

   Before deciding where our next branch will be, we would like the opinion of a firm of your calibre.

   Naturally, we want to know the story on population, buying power, retail sales—with special emphasis on (specific goods)—competition, and current business. But please include any other data which will be helpful to us in making our choice.

   Please do not attempt to cover taxes, wage scales, real-estate costs, or availability of sites.

   Since we plan to have the store in operation within a year's time, will you please confirm that you can submit the report no later than (specific date as assigned), subject to the same rates as on previous studies?

   This request can readily be handled without sending representatives to either city; from secondary library sources you can get all the necessary comparative data: the *Statistical Abstract of the United States, County Data Book, Market Guide of Editor and Publisher,* Rand McNally's *Commercial Atlas and Marketing Guide, Sales Management's Survey of Buying Power, Printers' Ink*'s special studies like *Sales Planning Guide* and *Major American Markets, Consumer Markets* published by the Standard Rate and Data Service. The foregoing are some of your more useful ones. But they are not intended to be an exhaustive list. You will, of course, want to consult the censuses of population, business, and manufacturers for (respectively) breakdowns of populations, influence of wholesaling and retailing on the local economy, and the value added to the economy by manufacturing. In all cases you will want the latest reliable data; recency of information is important.

Your entire analysis should be focused on the answer to the question: Which of the two towns is a better market for selling more of the specific merchandise this store sells? Population is, of course, a factor—size as well as distribution and character of. The retail market area always needs examining. Income figures are significant (a person with $4 is in a better position to buy than one with only $2). Retail sales indicate whether people are willing to spend their money (total retail sales, per capita retail sales, and retail sales figures in the particular line you're investigating—if you can find them). Sources of business strength are appropriate considerations (a manufacturing town suffers more than a distribution center during a recession; a community depending primarily upon farming for its sustenance weathers economic storms more readily than one heavily dependent upon shipbuilding, for instance). And the current business picture (as measured by construction, postal figures, employment, and bank deposits) is always examined for its diagnostic value.

The list of topics above is merely to help you start thinking about what to include; it is not intended to be inclusive, orderly, or arbitrary. For instance, no study of this kind would ever omit competitive factors.

This is assigned: Exclude any discussion of banking facilities, communications facilities (newspapers, radio stations, advertising agencies), and transportation facilities. These are adequate in both cities and so would not affect the decision. But when you set out these limitations in the introductory section of the report, indicate in a footnote the sources where the reader can quickly and easily find the information if he wants to check it or tell him frankly that such data are not available if that is the case. Furthermore, the people would have done enough reading themselves to know where the cities are—and the pertinent geographical and climate features.

Although as an intelligent approach to the analysis you will want to do some background reading about the cities (in a good encyclopedia, possibly in a Chamber of Commerce release, and perhaps in the *Saturday Evening Post,* or George Sessions Perry's *Cities of America*), *you will not use these sources as documentation (evidence) in your report.*

Once you've made the final decision of what factors to include and—just as important—the order in which to lay them out, the analysis becomes a matter of simply comparing the two cities simultaneously to show which city is the better market—more people with more money to spend, and the apparent willingness to spend it . . . especially for this kind of merchandise.

DO NOT attempt to turn out a Chamber of Commerce root-for-the-home-team piece of propaganda. Impersonally, impartially present the facts about the two cities and make your decision on the total evidence.

Devise some system of note-taking right from the start and take down complete references (author, article, publication date, volume of magazine, specific page references from which the data are taken, and total pages in the publication) every time you copy some data. Use 3×5 cards. Put separate facts on separate cards. Unless you do this job carefully and completely, you will find repeat, last-minute trips to the library necessary.

An analytical report is not just a compilation of tables and labels. Your report must depend on the quotation of facts from other sources; these are incorporated primarily in the wealth of statistical display (graphics primarily, for readability). Without these—in abundance and completely identified with publication name, date, and page(s)—your report has no base and, in the reader's mind, no authenticity. But the most significant part of the report is your own expository (analytical) comment which explains the significance of the data you have gathered.

Of course, your report will be graded on physical appearance and mechanical correctness (freedom from errors in spelling, punctuation, and grammar). It will be graded most heavily, however, on

1. Organization (the order of points for logic and emphasis)
2. Readability (stylistic factors)
3. Complete, authentic evidence and its reliability and documentation.

Submit the report with these parts in this order: cover, title page, authorization letter (you may copy the one given you and label it *COPY*), letter of transmittal, contents, synopsis, the analysis (introduction, the discussion of factors, and a terminal section), and a bibliography.

2. Write the long report authorized in Memo Problem 20, p. 550. Supplement the published data with data acquired through letters and/or interviews, as agreed upon by you and your instructor. Submit the report with cover, title page, memos of authorization and transmittal, contents, synopsis, and the analysis complete with recommendation(s).

3. Subject to approval by your instructor, choose a topic for your long report. Preferably it should be a real problem actually faced by a company or individual; if not, it should be a problem likely to be faced by someone somewhere. It should be written for one or a very limited group of specific readers; a term-theme topic or something like a textbook chapter will not do because it is not a report. It should be an analytical report: the relevant facts plus interpretation and evaluation of the advantages and disadvantages (the pros and cons) of at least two alternatives and the eventual selection of one in your final conclusions and recommendations. In other words, it must be a business problem which you help someone to solve.

It should be a topic for which you can get information in the library and through either interviews, questionnaires, or your own observation or experimentation.

The topic must be approved by your instructor. You cannot change topics after midterm for any reason.

As your instructor directs, be prepared to submit early in the course on one typed page (1) a one-sentence statement of the purpose of the report; (2) an indication of who the readers are and your relationship (actual or assumed) to them; (3) sources and/or methods of collecting data, including the titles of five items from your tentative bibliography; (4) major divisions (with subdivisions, if you like) of the coverage or body of the report.

Be prepared at any time to give your instructor a progress report in memo form, indicating what you have accomplished, what difficulties you've encountered, what remains to be done, and your plans for finishing.

At the time directed by your instructor, submit the report with appropriate cover, title page, letters of authorization and transmittal, contents listing, synopsis, body (including introduction, facts and interpretations, conclusions, recommendations), bibliography, and appendix if necessary.

Appendix A. Keyed Symbols for Significant Points about Business Writing

THIS alphabetical list of short, easy-to-remember symbols is intended as a time-saving way for a teacher to mark papers and for a student to find brief explanations of the most significant points and common errors in business writing.

The alphabetized symbols are easy for the student to find and easy for the grader to remember. They are nearly all abbreviations of already familiar grading terms. Even the few abstract, unalphabetized symbols at the end are mostly standard proofreader's marks.

Use of a symbol plus the number of the pertinent subdivision will, of course, help a student find the explanation of his particular error; but a teacher may prefer to use only the symbol and thus induce the student to review the whole topic.

Page references at the ends of some entries tell where the user can find fuller discussion and (in most cases) illustrations of those points.

Selection of the points is based on years of experience in observing the good and the unacceptable in the writing of college students. By concentrating on the most frequent trouble makers instead of giving an unnecessary systematic and complete coverage of grammar and usage, we hope to avoid wasting your time and trying your patience.

The explanations of points of grammar and usage are based solidly on the studies of linguists—the true authorities on those points.

We have used two or more symbols for some corrections because some teachers will be more accustomed to one of them and some to another.

The frequent cross-referencing is to save space and duplication; but where repetition takes little space, we feel that it is preferable to the lost time in following through on a cross-reference.

A, an   Use *a* if the following word begins with a consonant sound (including the now-pronounced *h* in *hotel* and *historical*—and combined consonant and vowel sounds, as in *European, usage, unit,* and *eulogy*); use *an* if the next word begins with a vowel sound, including words beginning with silent *h* (*hour, honor, honest*).

Ab   Abbreviation. Before abbreviating, make sure that it would be appropriate, that the reader would understand, and that you know the right form (including the capitalization, spacing, and punctuation). Ordinarily dates and states are not abbreviated. Mr., Mrs., Dr., A.M., P.M., C.O.D., F.O.B., and E.O.M. are commonly abbreviated in business writing. Chemical symbols, certain engineering terms, and certain footnote references are preferably abbreviated if you are writing to a reader who will understand. Check your dictionary if in doubt about an abbreviation.

Ac   Accuracy. Get facts, names, addresses, and statements right. Misspelling a reader's name is a strike against you. If your statement does not say what it means, or may possibly be interpreted to mean something else, restate it so that it has only one clear meaning.

Adap   Adapt better to your reader's interests, reading ability, and experience. A message that seems to be written for somebody else, or for nobody in particular, will be less effective than one which seems to fit the reader. See p. 36.

Agr   Agreement of subjects with their verbs and of pronouns with their antecedents is essential to clear, inconspicuous writing.

1. Guard particularly lest words between the subject and verb cause you to forget the number of your subject. Notice that the first sentence about agreement is an illustration: *agreement* (singular) is the subject of the verb *is;* but between them you have a prepositional phrase with four plurals. As other illustrations, consider
   —Selection of topics *is* based on the reader's knowledge and interests.
   —Government programs help make more food available to the consumer but *cost* a great deal of money.
   —Lee also tells how important the arrangement of the records offices *is*.
   Part, series, type, and other words usually followed by plural phrases are frequently pitfalls to the unwary writer:
   —The greatest part of his investments *is* in real estate.
   —A series of bank loans *has* enabled the firm to stay in business.
2. *Any, anyone, each, every, everyone, everybody, either,* and *neither* all point to singular verbs (and pronouns), except when the choice next to the verb in an either-or situation is plural:
   —Any of the men in this group *is* expected to give some of *his* time to helping the group when asked.
   —Either board members or the president *has* power to act on the point.
   —Neither the mayor nor the council members *are* allowed to use city-owned automobiles.
3. Two separate singular subjects combined by *and* require a plural verb; but when combined by *besides, together with,* or *as well as,* they take a singular:

—The honorary president and leader of this group *is* Mr. Anderson.

—Mr. Weeks and his secretary *do* the work in the central office.

—Considerable knowledge, as well as care, *is* necessary in good writing.

4. Be sure your pronouns agree in number and gender with their antecedents (words they stand for). The two biggest dangers are (1) in forgetting the number of the antecedent when many words intervene before the pronoun and (2) in deciding on the number when referring to collective nouns or pronouns.

—The benefits a student gets from studying the practical psychology, writing skills, and knowledge of business in a good course in letter writing will help *him* throughout *his* life.

—The company plans to move *its* main operations closer to *its* major source of raw materials.

—The faculty *are* allowed almost complete freedom in the conduct of *their* classes while the administration plays *its* part by providing the facilities, general policy, and record keeping.

5. Relative clauses beginning with *who, that,* or *which* require verbs agreeing with the antecedents:

—The manager is one of those persons who expect unquestioning loyalty.

6. Plural-sounding collective subjects take singular verbs when the action is that of the group but plural verbs when the action is that of various individuals:

—The board *is* having a long meeting.

—The board *have* been arguing and disagreeing on that point for months.

—Twenty-five dollars *is* a reasonable price in view of. . . .

Avoid using a collective as both singular and plural:

—The company *is* located in Chicago, but *its* (not *their*) products are sold all over the country.

7. Beware of letting the complement tempt you to make the verb agree with it:

—Our main difficulty *was* errors in billing.

—The biggest cost item *is* employees' salaries and wages.

Amb   Ambiguous—more than one possible meaning and hence not clear. Usually the temporary confusion can be cleared up by (1) correcting a faulty pronoun reference (see **Ref**) or by (2) rewording to straighten out a modifier so that it can modify only what you intend (see **Mod**).

—He took over the management of the business from his father when he was 55. (When his father reached 55, Carl took over management of the business.)

—We agreed when we signed the papers that you would pay $100. (When we signed the papers, we agreed that you would pay $100 *or* We agreed that you would pay $100 when we signed the papers.)

And   And is a strong co-ordinating conjunction—one of the most useful and most troublesome of words.

1. It should be used only to connect (in the sense of addition) things of similar quality and grammatical form. Used otherwise, it produces

faulty co-ordination between an independent and a dependent clause, misparallelism, or sentence disunity. See **Sub, Para,** and **Unit.**

—The plans call for a new four-story building, and which will cost $4,500,000. (Omit *and;* it can't connect an independent and a dependent clause.) See **Coh.**

—In this course you learn the ways of the business world, the principles of practical psychology, and to write better. (The infinitive *to write* is not parallel with the nouns *ways* and *principles.* Make them all the same form before connecting them by *and.*) See **Para.**

—We feel sure that the saw will serve you well, and we appreciate your order. (The two ideas are not closely enough related to appear in the same sentence—probably not even in the same paragraph). See **Unit.**

2. *And* is properly the most-used connective, but don't overuse it to connect a series of independent clauses into a long, stringy sentence. If the clauses deserve equal emphasis, they can be made separate sentences. If not, the weaker ones should be **Sub**ordinated.

—The consultant first talked with the executives about their letter-writing problems *and* then he took a sample of 1,000 carbon copies *and* he classified them into two groups *and* 45 per cent of them were for situations that could just as well have been handled by forms. (After talking with the executives about their letter-writing problems, the consultant classified a sample of 1,000 carbon copies from the files. He found that 45 per cent of them were for situations that could just as well. . . .)

3. *And* may be used as a sentence beginning only if you want to emphasize it.

4. *And* is not proper before *etc.;* the *et* (*et cetera*) means *and.*

5. *And* may be used with *or* (and/or), except in formal writing, to mean either one or both of two possibilities.

Ap The appearance of a letter, as of a person, should be pleasant but unobtrusive and should suggest that the writer is competent, accurate, neat, and alert. To do so, it must be on a good grade of paper, properly spaced, and typed with a reasonably fresh ribbon and clean type without messy erasures or glaring errors. Check Chapter IV.

Apos Apostrophes should be used in

1. Possessives (except *its* and the personal pronouns): before *s* in singulars (*man's*); after the *s* in plurals if the *s* was added to make the word plural (*ladies'* but *women's*);

2. Contractions: to mark the omission of a letter (*isn't, doesn't*), *it's*—meaning "it is," quite different from the possessive *its*);

3. Plurals of symbols: figures (illegible *8's*), letters of the alphabet (one *o* and two *m's*), and words written about as words (too many *and's* and *but's*).

Appr Appropriateness to the situation is an important test of good English. Is your statement too slangy, colloquial, or formal for the occasion? See **Adap,** and p. 61 for a discussion of levels of usage.

Assign   Follow the facts and directions in the assignment. Though you are expected to fill in with necessary details of your own invention, you are not to go contrary to the facts or the spirit of the problem, and you are to make only reasonable assumptions.

Au   Authorization letter. See the reports check list, p. 439.

Awk   Awkwardness in expression calls attention to itself; and it may confuse a reader. Reconstruct your sentence or change word order for a natural flow.

C   Courtesy could be improved here. See p. 15.

Cap   Capitalization is pretty well standardized except that newspapers set their own practices and hence are not guides for other writing.

1. Capitalize the names of specific things, including titles of people, but not general words. For instance you capitalize the name of any specific college, university, or department; but you write "A university education may well cost $6,000, regardless of the department in which one studies." You write "L. W. Wilson, President of the University of . . . ," or "When President Wilson came. . . ." You capitalize any specific course, room, lake, river, building, . . . , but not the general words. So you might write that you are taking Economics 215, majoring in engineering, but right now going to a history class in the Liberal Arts Building, after stopping in to see a professor in Room 115. Next summer you may fish mostly in Portage Lake and some in the Ausable River, though you prefer river to lake fishing. Of course you capitalize English, French, German—all the languages, because they derive from the names of countries.

2. In titles of books and articles, capitalize the first word and all others except articles, prepositions, and conjunctions—unless you use solid capitals.

3. Capitalize the seasons (spring, summer) only when they are personified (rare except in poetry).

4. Capitalize sections of the country (the South, the East Coast) but not directions (east, west).

5. Capitalize official titles and terms of family relationship when used in place of the name: "Yes, Son, . . . ," "The Senator then went . . . ," "After Mother had seen . . . ."

6. Capitalize the first word after a colon only if it starts a complete sentence. (In an itemized listing, you may capitalize the first word of items even though they are incomplete sentences.)

Card   Cardinal numbers (one, two, three; 6, 7, 9) are preferable to ordinals (first, second, third; 1st, 2d, 3d, 4th, or 2nd, 3rd) in dates except in very formal invitations and legal documents, or when the day is separated from the month. As a general rule, use the form that would be pronounced if read aloud. Since the simple ordinal forms may be either adjectives or adverbs, they need no -*ly* endings, ever.

    —On October 7 . . . ; sometime in November—probably about the 7th.

Case   Case is no particular problem with English nouns. One form serves for all cases except the possessive (genitive), and the only real problem there is remembering correct use of the **Apos**trophe. For pronouns:

1. Use the nominative case (*I, we, he, she, they, who*) for the subject of a verb (other than an infinitive) and for the complement of a linking verb (any form of *to be*).

2. Use the objective case (*me, us, him, her, them, whom*) as the object of a verb or preposition and as the subject of an infinitive. In informal speaking and writing, however, *who* is often used (and acceptable) as the object of a preposition unless it immediately follows the preposition: *Who* was the letter addressed to?

3. Use possessive case to show possession and to serve as the subject of a gerund (a verb form ending in *-ing* and used as a noun: "*His* accusing me of dishonesty . . . ."

CB   Comma blunders—also called comma faults—are serious errors. See **SOS**.

CF   Comma faults—also called comma blunders—are serious errors. See **SOS**.

Chop   Choppy, jerky, short sentences are slow and awkward. Usually the trouble is (1) incoherence (the sentences don't follow each other naturally—see **Coh**), (2) poor control of emphasis (all the ideas in independent clauses, though of different importance—see **Sub**), or (3) lack of variety (all the sentences of the same pattern, usually all beginning with the subject or nearly the same length—see **Var**). Try combining several of the sentences, subordinating the less important ideas, and stressing the important ones in the independent clause.

Cl   Clearness is a fundamental of good writing. Make sure your reader can get your meaning quickly and easily. Usually a statement that is not immediately clear requires fuller explanation, more exact wording, or recasting of a faulty or involved construction. See **Ac**.

Coh   Coherence—that quality of writing which shows the reader the relationships of the ideas—is essential to clear, quick, and easy reading. It comes best from a logical sequence of ideas expressed with heavy emphasis on the important ones and less on the related but less important ones, and with any necessary conjunctions to show what relationships exist. The worst kind of incoherence comes from putting apparently unrelated ideas together in the same sentence or paragraph. Be especially careful not to connect unrelated thoughts, or ideas of different importance, with *and*.

1. Plan what you want to say so that your ideas fall in a natural sequence. Sometimes a topic sentence can help hold together several otherwise seemingly unrelated ideas. For example, if you begin with "Three factors deserve special consideration," the three following sentences or paragraphs all seem related in being tied to the topic statement.

2. Be sure your ideas have the proper relative emphasis. (See **Emp** and **Sub**.) Ideas deserving emphasis should be in independent clauses (groups of words that can stand as whole sentences). If two or more of these ideas are closely related and deserve equal emphasis, they

can be put together in one sentence (compound). Ideas deserving less emphasis should be put in dependent clauses. (Since a dependent clause cannot stand alone as a sentence, it has to be attached to the independent clause most closely related in thought—making a complex sentence.)

3. Check carefully to see whether you need transitional words or phrases to help the natural sequence and sentence type show the proper relationship of your ideas. If so, see **Tr** and consider these words and others of somewhat similar meaning to select the one which fits your purpose best:

and . . . moreover, besides, in addition, also, furthermore
but . . . however, nevertheless, yet, still, although, while
either-or . . . neither-nor, else, whether
therefore . . . consequently, hence, as a result, accordingly, so, ergo
because . . . since, as, for, the reason is
then . . . after that, afterward, later, subsequently
meanwhile . . . during, simultaneously, concurrently, while
before . . . preceding, previously, prior to
if . . . provided, assuming, in case, unless

Conc   Conciseness (which is not necessarily brevity) depends on leaving out the irrelevant, leaving unsaid what you can adequately **Imply**, and cutting out deadwood. See pp. 47–50 for explanation and illustration of techniques.

Conf   Confidence in yourself, in your decisions, and in your success in obtaining the action you request will go a long way toward getting acceptance of your proposals; but you need to avoid overconfidence or presumptuousness. In an application letter, for example, the writer who is too meek or modest hurts his chances; but so does the fellow who is too cocky or aggressive. In phrasing the decision to refuse an adjustment, a writer needs to explain adequately and then assume that his decision will be acceptable. In making recommendations, usually the writer is not justified in commanding; but he needs to word them with as much confidence as the facts and the reader-writer relationship will allow. In the endings of Type-C letters, the request for action should be stated with success-consciousness (p. 41), but not with presumption. Words like *if, hope,* and *trust* indicate doubt—a lack of confidence.

—*If* you want to buy an X, just . . . . (After your sales presentation, assume that he does and tell him how: "Just fill out the handy order form and mail it today and you can have your X within . . . .")
—We *trust* this arrangement will be satisfactory. (Too much doubt. If you've explained adequately, assume acceptability of your decision.)
—When may I have an interview? (Presumptuous. The question seems to leave no alternative as to whether, the only question being when. Better: "Will you tell me a time when I may come to talk with you more fully about . . . .")

Conj   Conjunctions connect ideas to show the kind of relationship that exists.
1. Unless the relationship is already clear, put in the necessary conjunction.

2. Be sure that the one you use reflects accurately the relationship you intend. (See the list under **Coh** for groups of somewhat similar connectives with different shades of meaning.)
3. Guard particularly against using *but* when no contrast is intended, and against using either it or *and* to connect things unless they are the same grammatical structure (noun with noun, verb with verb, etc.).
4. Before using *therefore, because,* or any of the other similar words, make sure that a true cause-and-effect relationship really exists.

Conn Connotations—the overtones or related meanings of words—are often as important as the denotations, or dictionary meanings. Be sure that the words you use are appropriate in connotations as well as in denotations. Consider, for example, the connotations in the following pairs: cheap-inexpensive, secondhand-used, Complaint Department–Customer-service Department, basement store–thrift store.

Cop Copying from the assignment or from other people produces writing that doesn't sound like you. Put your ideas in your own words.

Cpr Comparisons require special attention to these points:
1. The things compared must be comparable. Usually the trouble is omission of necessary phrases like "that of," "that on," "other," or "else."
   —The mark-up on Schick shavers is higher than *that on* Remingtons. (You can't omit "that on" or you'll be comparing the height of a Remington—measured in inches—with the markup on Schicks—a percentage.)
   —Frank Mosteller sells more Fuller brushes than any *other* salesman. (Without "other," the statement is illogical if Frank is a salesman; he can't sell more than he himself sells.)
2. Incomplete comparisons mean nothing; complete them.
   —You get more miles per dollar with xxx. (More than with what?)
   —This material has a higher percentage of wool. (Higher than what?)
3. Be sure to use the correct form of comparison words. Comparisons involving two things are usually shown by adding -*er* (the comparative) to the simple form (*later, colder, slower*). Those involving more than two usually require the -*est* (or superlative) form (*latest, coldest, slowest*). For words of three syllables or more—and for many with two and some with only one—the better form is *more* plus the simple form (for the comparative) or *most* plus the simple form (for the superlative): "more frequently," "most hopeful." Some words may be used either way: oftener or more often; oftenest or most often. Attention to the sound of the expression is usually a sufficient guide to native speakers of English. When in doubt, see the dictionary.
4. Watch these idioms: Complete the "as much as" phrase and use *to* after *compare* when pointing out similarities only, *with* when pointing out any differences:
   —Price increases may be worth as much *as,* if not more than, the dividends on a common-stock purchase.
   —Comparison of x to y shows that they involve the same principles.

—Comparison of sales letters with application letters shows that they are quite similar but that they have minor differences.

5. Certain words (*unique, empty, final,* for example) are logically absolutes and hence cannot take either comparative or superlative forms.

CSP   Select a central selling point and give it the major emphasis by position and full development. Scattering your shots over too many points leaves the major ones weak. See **Emp** and **Dev.**

Date   Dates should be written in the standard form (November 2, 1961) unless you have good reason to do otherwise. Your most likely good reasons could be (1) you are in the armed services, where the form 2 November 1961 is used, or (2) you're writing a formal notice, where everything is spelled out, or (3) you're writing an informal note and may well use the form 11/2/61. Modern business writing usually does not abbreviate months and does not use the ordinal forms. See **Card.**

Dead   Deadwood phrases add nothing to the meaning but take writing and reading time because they go the long way around to say anything. For conciseness, omit them. See **Conc** and the list of frequent deadwood expressions, p. 49.

D   Diction. Use a more suitable word. The big test, of course, is whether the word conveys your thought accurately, including its connotations. Consider whether your words will be understood easily; whether they give a sharp, vivid picture by being natural and fresh instead of pompous, jargonistic, or trite; whether they give a specific, concrete meaning instead of a fuzzy or dull concept because they are general or abstract; and whether they are appropriately informal, formal, standard, technical, or nontechnical—according to the topic and reader. Watch especially the following often-confused pairs: accept-except, adapt-adopt, affect-effect, almost-most, amount-number, already-all ready, all right-"alright" (no such word), altogether-all together, are-our, beside-besides, between-among, capital-capitol, fewer-less, formerly-formally, imply-infer, it's-its, loose-lose, moral-morale, oral-verbal, personal-personnel, principal-principle, than-then, there-their, too-to-two.

Dev   Develop your point more thoroughly with more explanation, specific details, or examples to make it clearer, more interesting, more convincing, or more emphatic. See **Spec.**

Dir   Directness saves words, speeds up reading, and makes your ideas clearer. Don't waste words by beginning too far back in the background of the subject, by stating what the reader already knows, or by expressing what will be clearly implied if you begin with the key thought. Write direct, active-voice sentences beginning with the important word as the subject. The Expletives "It is . . ." and "There are . . ." are indirect, passive, and wordy.

Dng   Dangling modifier. See **Mod.**

Doc   Documentation—telling your sources—is necessary when you use the ideas of others. See pp. 488–90 for discussion and illustration. Also see the reports check list, p. 535.

Emp   Emphasis should be divided among your ideas according to their relative importance.

1. When you state important ideas, give them deserved emphasis by one or more of the following methods: putting them in the emphatic beginning or ending position of your letter or paragraph, putting them in independent clauses, developing them thoroughly, and perhaps underscoring them or writing them in solid capitals (or a different color). See p. 46 for fuller explanation.

2. When you have negative, unimportant, already known, or other ideas that don't deserve emphasis, avoid overemphasizing them. Some useful methods are putting them in unemphatic middle positions, putting them in dependent clauses or phrases, and giving them brief mention or just implying them. Particularly objectionable is overemphasis on things the reader obviously knows and on things that are (or can be) adequately implied. The first insults the reader's intelligence, and both waste words:

   —Spring is just around the corner. You'll be needing. . . . (With spring just around the corner, you'll. . . .)

   —On October 3 you asked me to write a report on. . . . I have finished it and am. . . . (Here is the report your letter of October 3 asked me to write on. . . .)

   —I have your letter of April 20 in which you ask for quotations on x. I am glad to give you our prices. Our present prices on x are. . . . (Just omit the first two sentences. They're implied in the third.)

Etc.   Etc., an abbreviation of Latin *et cetera,* meaning "and so forth," should not be used unless the reader will have a good idea of how to fill out the incomplete list (as in "Please take even-numbered seats 2, 4, 6, etc."). Otherwise it can mean only "Reader, you guess what else I mean to include," and that does not communicate. Because *etc.* is an abbreviation, it takes a period; but because it is anglicized, it need not be italicized (or underscored in typed copy). In no case should you write "and etc."; *et* means and.

Exp   Expletives (*it is, there are*) nearly always make your writing unnecessarily wordy, weak, and passive. They usually result from a misguided attempt to write an impersonal style. In general, you should avoid them, though sometimes they may help to soften a command or avoid presumptuousness in a recommendation:

   —It was thought that you would prefer. . . . (I thought you would. . . .)

   —There are four important factors involved. These are: . . . . (The four important factors are. . . .)

   —It will be necessary to have your. . . . ("You must send . . ." might be too commanding.)

Fast   Fast movement that gets to the point quickly—without cumbersome detail or explicit statement of ideas that should be implied—is desirable when your message will be accepted readily; but if you need to persuade the reader either to accept an unpleasant decision or to take a reluctant action, you have to build up your case adequately before stating the key point. Stating the bad news before adequate justifying reasons, or requesting an action before showing enough reader benefits to motivate that action, is therefore marked **Fast,** meaning "You got here too fast."

Fig Figures are better than words (except at the beginning of a sentence) for serial, telephone, page, chapter, chart, catalogue, and street numbers; for money, dimensions, and dates and time (except in formal announcements); for all quantities when several are close together (but not adjoining) in a sentence or paragraph; and for other isolated quantities above 10. (As an acceptable replacement for the Rule of 10 for isolated quantities, your teacher may authorize this: Use words if the quantity takes no more than two.)

1. If a qauntity comes at the first of a sentence, write it in words or recast the sentence.
2. When a sentence involves two different series of quantities, use figures for one and words for the other; if more than two, use a table.
   —On the qualifying exam, ten per cent of the applicants scored 90–100, thirty percent 80–89, ...
   —Please make six 2″ × 3″ black-and-white prints and three 5″ × 7″.
3. The old longhand practice of stating quantities twice—in one form followed parenthetically by the other form—is unnecessary and undesirable in type or print, though it is still sometimes used in legal documents.
4. Except in dates, street numbers, and serial numbers, use a comma between groups of three digits, counting from the right.
5. Except in tables involving some cents, periods and zeros after money quantities are wasted typing and reading.
6. Two-word quantities between 20 and 100 require the hyphen (twenty-six).
7. Cardinal numbers (1, 2, 3, 4, etc.), are preferable to ordinals (1st, 2d, 3d, 4th) in dates except when the day is separated from the month. See **Card** and **Date.**
8. Since ordinals are either adjectives or adverbs, an *-ly* ending is never necessary.

Gobb Gobbledygook is big-wordy, round-about, long-winded, or stuffed-shirt language. Characteristically it shows two or more of those traits and comes in long sentences and paragraphs. Avoid it like poison; it works against both clarity and ease of reading.

Gr Graphic devices of various kinds can often supplement words to make the information clearer, easier, or more interesting. Use them where they will help, but only if they will; make them big enough and detailed enough (but no bigger or more detailed than necessary) for your purpose; and be sure you use the most appropriate kind (line, bar, or pie chart; drawing, map, photograph, for example). See the reports check list, p. 529.

Gw Good will, the first basic requirement of a business letter, is lacking or poorly handled here. See Chapter I.

I   Introduction. See the reports check list, p. 530.

Id   Idiomatic usage—the natural, customary, accepted way of saying certain things—is correct that way simply because that is the way we say it, though it may defy grammatical analysis and rules. Idioms are so numerous and varied that they cannot be fully explained here. Usually, however, an error in idiom is use of the wrong preposition. Consider possibility *of,* possible *to,* necessity *of,* need *for,* and ability *to.* See **Prep.**

Imp   Imply rather than express the idea, to save words or avoid overemphasis. See **Emp** and pp. 48–49.

Ital   Italic print, indicated by underscoring in typewritten and handwritten copy, is used to emphasize occasional words; to mark the title of a book or journal; to mark a word, letter, or figure used as an illustration or typographical unit (instead of for its meaning); and to indicate an unanglicized foreign-language expression used in English context.
—Underscoring is *preferably not* used for titles of *parts,* such as the title of an article in a journal or a chapter in a book. Quotation marks are preferable for that purpose. (Underscoring for emphasis here.)
—Chapter III, "The Third Test of a Good Letter," in *Writing Business Letters,* stresses clear, natural style and general linguistic savoir-faire.
—*Convenience* and *questionnaire* are often misspelled.
—Use of fewer *I*'s and more *you*'s would improve many letters.

Item   Itemize complex series and lists to emphasize the points, to avoid complex punctuation problems, and to force yourself to state your points more precisely and more concisely.

Jar   Jargon is fuzzy or inappropriate writing attributable to one or more of pompousness, circumlocution, deadwood, abstractness, big words, technical terms (written to nontechnical readers), and hackneyed expressions. It is the opposite of simple, natural, clear writing. Avoid it.

Jux   Juxtapose (put side by side) facts and ideas that the reader needs to consider together. For instance, wholesale and retail prices need to be seen together (with the difference and percentage of markup figured) if they are to mean as much as they should to the retailer being asked to stock the product.

K   Awkwardness in expression calls attention to itself; and it may confuse the reader. Reconstruct your sentence or change word order for a more natural flow.

lc   Lower case needed here, instead of **Cap**ital.

Log   Logic. Avoid statements which will not stand the test of logic or for which the logic is not readily clear. Perhaps you need to write in a missing step in the logic. Maybe you need to state your idea more precisely. Or maybe you need to complete a comparison to make it logical. (If the last, see **Cpr** for fuller explanation.)

M   Mechanics. See the reports check list, p. 539.

Mod   Modifiers should be placed in the sentence where they fit most naturally and make the meaning clearest. To avoid awkwardness and write clearly, you have to make sure that each modifier relates clearly to the thing it is supposed to modify. As a general rule, the two should be as close together as natural sentence construction will allow.

1. Participles (usually phrases including a verb form ending in *-ing* or *-ed,* and usually at the beginning of a sentence) require careful attention lest you relate them to the wrong word (or nothing at all).
   —Smelling of liquor, I arrested the driver. (The officer did not intend to say that he himself had been drinking.)
   —After soaking in the prepared mixture over night, I set the specimen up to dry for two days. (The scientist didn't mean what he said.) Those errors are commonly called "misrelated modifiers" or "dangling participles." Infinitives can dangle the same way:
   —To enjoy the longest, most dependable service, the motor must be tuned up about every 100 hours of operation. (The motor cannot enjoy dependable service.)
   —In order to assist you in collecting for damages it will be necessary to fill out a company blank. (The two infinitives dangle because they are not related to any doers of the actions indicated.)

2. *Only, almost,* and *nearly* are tricky words. Watch where you put them. Consider the varied meanings from placing *only* at different spots in "I can approve payment of a $30 adjustment."

3. A so-called "split" infinitive (putting a modifier between *to* and a verb) is usually undesirable because it is usually awkward; but if it is clear and natural, you'll do better to go ahead and split the infinitive rather than write an awkward sentence trying to avoid doing so.

4. Be sure to use the correct form of modifier. Adjectives modify nouns and pronouns; adverbs modify verbs, adjectives, and other adverbs. Most adverbs end in *-ly;* but some don't. See **WF.**

Mon   Monotonous. See **Var.**

Nat   Natural writing avoids triteness, awkwardness, and pomposity. Cliches, trite and hackneyed expressions, and jargon suggest that a writer is not thinking about his subject and his reader; awkwardness suggests carelessness; and big-wordiness and pomposity suggest that the writer is trying to make an impression. He probably will—in the wrong way. Really big men think through what they want to say and put it simply, smoothly, and naturally. Though you cannot write exactly as you talk, you should try to write with the same freedom, ease, simplicity, and smoothness of your talk. See p. 54.

Neg   Negative in letter writing is defined as anything unpleasant to your reader. Since you want his good will, you should avoid the negative when you can, and subordinate it when you can't avoid it. Insofar as possible, stress the positive by telling what you have done, can do, will do, or want done instead of their negative opposites. See p. 39; and for methods of subordinating, see p. 46, **Emp,** and **Sub.**

O   Organization. See p. 482 and the reports check list, p. 527.

Obj Objectivity. Use of emotional or feverish words (especially if extensive) suggests a prejudiced rather than an objective view of the situation and therefore causes the reader to lose faith in the writer—especially a report writer. See pp. 485 and 490.

Obv Obvious statements—when they are unnecessary as bases for other statements—at least waste words; and when they are put in independent clauses, they show poor control of emphasis and may insult the reader's intelligence. When you need to state an obvious fact as the basis for something else, put it in a dependent clause and use the independent clause for the new idea. (See **Emp** and **Sub**.)

   —New York is America's biggest city. Therefore. . . . (Since New York is America's biggest city, ...)

Om Omission of a word or necessary idea. Make your statements both grammatically and logically complete. See **Tele, Log,** and **Cpr**.

   1. Conciseness is certainly a desirable quality in letters and reports, but it should not go so far as to push you into telegraphic style—omission of subjects, connective words, and articles:

       —Please send check $123 for shipment April 1.

   2. Unless the same verb form or preposition applies appropriately in a double construction, use the necessary two:

       —His interest *in* and hard work *on* accounting have. . . .

       —He should have *sold* earlier, and perhaps will now *sell,* since the market trend is clearer.

       —The product *is* new and the prospective buyers *are* numerous.

Out Outlining. See p. 482 and the reports check list topic "Organization," p. 527.

P Punctuation which follows the conventions of written English (and is therefore understood by most readers) is a helpful device for both reader and writer in communicating clearly, quickly, and easily. But when it goes contrary to the understood conventions, it does not help and may even confuse. You should not try to use even good punctuation, however, as a crutch for bad writing. Heavy punctuation cannot make a bad sentence into a good one; so the need for it suggests revising the sentence rather than trying to punctuate the involved statement. The best style is so direct and simple that it requires little punctuation except periods at the ends of sentences. Still you cannot write much without need for some internal punctuation. Here are the conventions most commonly violated:

   P1. Use a comma between two independent clauses connected by *and, but, or,* or *nor* if no other commas are in the sentence; but be sure you are connecting two clauses rather than a compound subject or verb.

       —You may buy the regular Whiz mixer at $18.75, but I think you would find the Super Whiz much more satisfactory. (Two clauses.)

       —We make two grades of Whiz mixers and sell both at prices lower than those of our competitors' products. (Compound verb; one subject.)

P2. Use a semicolon between two independent clauses unless connected by *and, but, or,* or *nor;* and, even then, use a semicolon if there are other commas in the sentence (as in this one). Typical weaker connectives requiring the semicolon between two independent clauses are *therefore, so, moreover, hence, still, accordingly, nevertheless, furthermore, consequently,* and *however.* When these words are used as simple connectors not between two independent clauses, however (as right here), they are set off by a pair of commas unless they fit so smoothly into the sentence that they require no marks.

   —Jets made airline maintenance men relearn their jobs; the jet manual is twice as thick as the old one for prop planes. (No connective.)

   —The preceding sentence could be made into two, of course; but, because the ideas are closely related, it is better as one. (Commas elsewhere require semicolon before even a strong conjunction.)

   —Good letter writing requires proper punctuation; therefore you must know how to use the semicolon. (Weak connective.)

   —The proper style for letters is simpler and less involved than most other writing, however, and therefore does not require very complex punctuation procedures. (*However* is a simple transition, *not used* between two clauses here and *not* close-knit into the phrasing the way *therefore* is; so it is set off by commas while *therefore* goes unmarked. Note, too, that the weak connective *so* requires the semicolon because it connects two clauses.)

P3. Use a comma after all dependent clauses, long phrases, or other phrases containing any form of a verb at the beginning of a sentence; but when these forms appear elsewhere in a sentence, use commas only with nonrestrictive (nonessential) ones. (Nonrestrictive statements add descriptive detail and are not necessary to the logic or grammatical completeness of the sentence; restrictive ones define, limit, or identify and are necessary to convey the intended meaning.)

   —Because the dependent clause comes at the beginning, we have to use a comma in this sentence.

   —We do not need a comma in a complex sentence if the dependent part comes at the end or in the middle and restricts the meaning the way this one does.

   —Having illustrated the two points about dependent clauses at the beginning and restrictive clauses elsewhere in the sentence, we now use this sentence to illustrate the use of a comma after a long phrase at the first of a sentence. (Because it includes a verb form, it would require a comma even if it were short, like "Having illustrated, we now leave the topic.")

   —The three points already illustrated, which are certainly important, are no more important than the point about using commas to set off nonrestrictive clauses anywhere, which this sentence illustrates. (In fact, it illustrates twice: Both the *which* clauses could be omitted; they are nonrestrictive because they merely give added information unnecessary to either the meaning or grammar of the basic sentence.)

P4. Be sure to put in both commas—or dashes or parentheses—around a parenthetical expression in the middle of a structure. Direct addresses ("Yes, Mr. Thomas, you may . . .") and appositives (restatements like this one that follow immediately to explain a term) are typical examples. But, like clauses, some appositives are restrictive or so closely related that they require no punctuation while others are nonrestrictive or so loosely related that they do.

—His starting point that good punctuation is a matter of following the conventions has not been stressed enough.

—His second point, the importance of writing letters so smoothly and naturally that they require little internal punctuation, would preclude most punctuation problems.

P5. Use commas to separate co-ordinate adjectives. As two tests for co-ordinacy, see if you can put *and* between the adjectives or invert their order without producing awkwardness. If so, they are co-ordinate and require a comma.

—Proper punctuation can help greatly in writing a clear, easy-to-read style.

—Fairly heavy white paper is best for letterheads.

P6. The comma is the usual punctuation between items in a series (preferably including one before the *and* with the last item, because it is sometimes necessary for clearness and is always correct). But if any item except the last has a comma within it, use semicolons between all the items.

—Make your writing clear, quick, and easy to read.

—Use commas between independent clauses connected by *and, but, or,* or *nor;* semicolons between independent clauses with other connectives or no connecting words; commas for dependent clauses and verbal or long phrases at the beginnings of sentences, for nonrestrictive ones elsewhere, and for simple series; and semicolons for complex series like the one in this sentence.

P7. Dashes, commas, and parentheses are all used in pairs around parenthetical expressions that interrupt the main part of the sentence. The choice depends on the desired emphasis and on the other punctuation. Two dashes (called "bridge dashes") emphasize most, commas less, and parenthesis least of all. If the parenthetical part contains internal parentheses, dashes have to be used around it; if it contains commas, dashes or parentheses have to be used around it. (Of course only a pair of parentheses can be used around a whole sentence which gives explanations, relatively unimportant additional detail, or side information not germane to the trend of the discussion, as this sentence does. In that case, the period comes inside the closing parenthesis, though it comes outside otherwise.) A single dash—made on the typewriter preferably by two hyphens without spacing before, between, or after but also by one hyphen with spacing before and after—may be used to mark an abrupt change in the trend of a sentence or to precede an added statement summarizing, contrasting, or explaining the first part. In this second function, it is commonly called the "pick-up dash."

> —Your main weaknesses in writing—misspelling, faulty punctuation, and incoherence—should be corrected before you write letters.
> —Errors in spelling, punctuation, or coherence—these all mar an otherwise good letter.
> —A letter writer must avoid the common errors in writing—misspelling, bad punctuation, and incoherence. (Of course the colon could replace the dash here; but ordinarily it should not unless the preceding statement is a formal introduction, usually indicated by the word *following,* or unless it is an introduction to an itemized list.)

P8. Hyphenate two or more words used to make a compound adjective modifying a following noun or pronoun.

> —fast-selling product, wrinkle-resistant material, long-wearing soles, never-to-be-forgotten experience.

Note that the point usually does not apply when the adjectives follow the nouns.

> —The material is highly wrinkle resistant and long wearing.

Certainly it does not apply when the adjectives modify the noun separately.

> —These slacks are made of a hard, durable material.

Nor should the compound-adjective principle be applied to various other compounds: *extracurricular, classroom,* and *textbook,* for example. For such words, unless you know for sure, the only safe guide is the dictionary. You'll find, for example, that *good will* and *week end* are both preferably two words when used as nouns but that *goodwill* and *week-end* are the preferred forms when used as adjectives.

The compound-adjective principle does apply, however, to double compounds made with one element in common, where the "suspension hyphen" follows the first: three- and five-pound cans; only light- and middle-weight boxers.

The hyphen also marks the break in a word at the end of a line. See **Syl.**

Other less-frequent uses of the hyphen include (1) spelling of fractions (*three-fourths*) and two-word quantities between 20 and 100, and (2) prefixing words or syllables to names (*post-Hitler* Germany), to other words beginning with the same vowel as the end of the prefix (*re-entry, pre-established*), or to any word that might then be confusing (*re-collect,* not *recollect; re-cover,* not *recover*).

P9. Quotation marks are used primarily for short, exact quotations of other people's words and for titles of *parts* of publications, such as magazine and newspaper stories or book chapters. (The titles of journals and books should be italicized—underlined in typed copy—or written in solid capitals. See **Ital** and **Cap.**) If a quotation is more than two or three lines long, you should indent it from each side, single-space it, and leave off quotation marks. You should not use quotation marks around a paraphrasing, but only for exact quotation. Usually you should avoid using expressions so slangy as to require quotation marks; if an expression is inappropriate without the quotes, you'd better find a different word. When closing quotation marks and other marks seem to come at the same place, the standard *American* practice is as follows: Place commas or periods *inside;* place semicolons or colons *outside;* and place question or exclamation marks inside or outside depending on whether they are part of the quotation.

P10. The colon is either an anticipating or a separating mark. As an anticipator, it is used after introductory lead-ins to explanations or quotations, especially if the lead-in includes such formalizing terms as the word *following* or if the explanation is itemized or lengthy.

—The X Company's ink was even redder: its third-quarter loss of. . . .

—Three main benefits deserve your attention: . . . . (Enumeration follows.)

—On the use of the colon, Perrin says: . . . . (Long quotation follows.)

Because the colon is also a separating mark, however—used to separate hours from minutes and volume numbers from pages, for example—it should not be used as an anticipating mark when the lead-in phrasing fits well as an integral part of a short, informal statement. Summey calls this the "obtrusive colon."

—The three main advantages are (colon would be obtrusive here) speed, economy, and convenience.

—Perrin reports that (no colon; not even a comma) *"Will* has practically replaced *shall* in. . . ."

Almost invariably words like *namely, that is, for example,* and *as follows* are wasted (and browbeating) when used with a colon. The introductory phrasing plus the colon adequately anticipate without those words.

—We had several reasons for changing: namely the. . . . (Omit *namely.*)

—We had several reasons for changing. These reasons are: . . . . (This is worse. Omit *these reasons are;* put the colon after *changing.*)

Though practice varies, usually you should capitalize the first word after a colon only if it begins a complete sentence; but if itemizations follow, you may capitalize even though each item depends on the introductory statement for completeness.

The same idea applies to the end punctuation of items following a colon. If the items make complete sentences, put a period after each; but if all are to be considered one sentence, use comma or semicolon at the end of each (except the last, of course) as in other series—or you may use no end punctuation.

P11. Underlining in typed or handwritten copy calls for italic type when printed. Its main uses are to mark titles of books and journals, to emphasize, and to indicate unanglicized words. In copy not to be printed, it should be used also for any heading not written in solid capitals. Otherwise the heading, which is really a title for the copy over which it stands, does not stand out sufficiently. (A printer would make it stand out by using big or bold-face type.)

Type underlining is preferably continuous, rather than broken by individual words, because it is easier both to type and to read that way.

P12. Besides its well-known use at the end of a question, the question mark may be used in parentheses immediately following a statement or spelling about which the writer is uncertain and unable to determine. Obviously, it should not be used as an excuse for laziness; but if you have only heard a difficult name, for example, and have to write to that person, you'd better use the mark than unconcernedly misspell the name.

A question mark should not be used after indirect questions.

—We need to know what your decision is. (Indirect question.)

Par Paragraphs in letters and reports are the same as in other writing—unified developments of topics—except that they tend to be more compressed and shorter for easier readability. (The symbol ¶ may be used to replace **Par.**)

1. Keep your paragraphs reasonably short. Long ones are discouragingly hard to read. Especially the first and last paragraphs of letters should be short (rarely more than three or four lines). Elsewhere, if a paragraph runs to more than about eight lines, you should consider breaking it up for easier readability. Usually you can find a good place. Certainly you should ignore any idea that a paragraph has to be more than one sentence. Often one sentence can say all that you need to say on a topic.

2. But develop your paragraphs adequately to clarify and support your points—by explanation, detail, facts and figures, or illustrations and examples. See **Dev.**

3. Make each paragraph coherent by taking out elements irrelevant to the topic and by showing the interrelationship of the ideas. Consider these means: (*a*) using the same key word or a synonym for it, (*b*) using a connecting word or phrase such as those listed under **Coh,** (*c*) beginning with a topic sentence or ending with a summary.

4. Show the relation of the paragraph to the preceding (by following logical sequence, carrying over key ideas, and/or using transitional

words) and to the purpose of the whole paper or section (by pointing out the significance and/or by using transitional words or sentences).

—Paragraph unity also includes. . . . (*Also* means some of the explanation has preceded.)

—Carrying over key words and using transitional words are both means of providing unity between paragraphs as well as within them. (*As well as* means we've discussed unity *in* paragraphs and now will discuss it *between* them.)

5. **Par** with **No** before it means "No new paragraph needed here because you are still on the same topic and within reasonable paragraph length."

Para Parallelism means using the same kind of grammatical structure for ideas that are used co-ordinately, as in pairs, series (including lists), comparisons, and outlines. Those structures state or imply relationships usually indicated by *and, but,* or *or* and hence should relate only full sentences to full sentences, nouns to nouns, verbs to verbs, active voice to active voice, plural to plural—indeed *any* grammatical form only to the same grammatical form in the related part. Watch for parallelism with *not only . . . but also, as well as, larger, less expensive,* and the like. (See p. 484, Item 7, for parallelism in outlines.)

—One of the duties of the airline hostess is to offer customers magazines, pillows, and hang their coats. (Two plural nouns and a verb improperly connected by the co-ordinating conjunction *and.*)

—The No-Skid knee guard is long wearing, washable, and stays in position. (Two adjectives connected by *and* to a verb.)

—John Coleman is 39, married, and a native. (Two adjectives and a noun.)

—If we fair each side of the arc, we produce a more practical airfoil section and an increase in performance is attained. (Active voice related to passive. Rewrite the last part as "increase the performance.")

—The next step is baking or catalyzation ("baking or catalyzing").

—Swimming is better exercise than to walk. (A gerund compared with an infinitive.)

Parallelism in pairs, series, and comparisons is largely a question of logic; you can add together and compare only like things. See **Log.**

Pas Passive voice (in which the subject receives rather than does the action indicated by the verb) is usually wordy, awkward, and weak. Most of your sentences should therefore use the active voice. It makes important words (usually persons or products in letters) the subjects and objects of your verbs, as they should be. Writers often use passive constructions trying to avoid *I* and *We* as the subject. If you feel that you must avoid them to prevent the monotony of sentence pattern, you should see p. 54 instead of resorting to the passive. If you feel that you must avoid them to increase objectivity, you are working under a false impression; you can be just as biased without them. (See **Obj.**) But you can avoid the first person and the passive at the same time, as explained in the first illustration below. Still you may find appropriate use for passives to meet a thesis director's or company executive's requirement that you write impersonally, to avoid a direct accusation, to put emphasis on something other than the doer of the action, or to weaken an otherwise rankling command or recommendation.

—Your Long-Flight skis were shipped this morning by our mailing department. (Can be made active and impersonal as "Two Long-Flight skis are on their way; they left the mailing department this morning.")

—The subject has been considered from the following viewpoints: . . . . (The requirement of impersonal style may justify the passive here.)

—The mower apparently has not been oiled adequately. (Avoids accusing the user.)

—The Wembley has been in great demand among the buying public for years. (The passive puts emphasis on the product rather than on the people demanding it.)

—Careful attention should be given to . . . . (Weakens a possibly rankling command.)

—It is recommended that . . . . (Weakens and avoids egotism in a recommendation.)

PD Psychological description (interpreting facts and physical features of a product in terms of reader benefits) is the real heart of selling. Unless your reader readily makes the interpretation himself, pure physical description is ineffective in selling. So when you name a physical feature of a product you're selling, show the reader what it means in terms of benefits to him. (See pp. 221–22.)

—The Bostonian Sporty shoe has Neolite soles and triple-stitched welt construction. (The Neolite soles and triple-stitched welt construction cause the Bostonian Sporty to last long and keep your feet dry.)

Per Personalized messages written for and adapted to specific readers are more effective than mass broadcasts. What seems to be for everybody has less interest to anybody. Even form letters should be worded to give each reader the feeling that the message is directed to him. Expressions such as "Those of you who . . ." and "If you are one who . . ." give just the opposite impression. (See p. 37.)

Plan Plan your letter more appropriately for the circumstances as an A, B, or C type. (See p. 28.)

Pr Follow more generally acceptable business practice.

PR Personal references (names of people or pronouns referring to them) not only help to keep the reader in the picture and produce the you-attitude (**YA**); they help to avoid the passive voice (**Pas**), to make your writing specific and concrete instead of general and abstract (**Spec**), and to make your writing easier and more interesting to read. Naming or referring to persons is an important element in readability.

Prep Prepositions indicate relationships within a sentence.

1. Be sure to use the right one for your construction. Some words require certain prepositions; others vary prepositions for different meanings:

    —ability *to;* agree *to, with,* or *in;* compare *to* (for similarities only) or *with* (for likenesses and differences); different *from.* See **Id.**

2. When you use two words that require different prepositions, use both:

    —Because of your interest *in* and aptitude *for.* . . .

3. Don't use many of the .45-caliber group prepositions (*according to, in regard to, by means of, in connection with, on the part of*) for squirrel-size ideas or your prepositions will "bulk too large," as Perrin says.

PV Insofar as possible, keep the same point of view in a sentence, paragraph, or a whole letter. Make only logically necessary shifts, and let your reader know by providing the necessary transitional words. Watch carefully for shifts in time, location, and those whose eyes you seem to be looking through. For effective you-attitude, look through the reader's eyes whenever possible. See **YA.**

R Bring your reader into the picture early and don't forget him later. He is the most important person involved with your letter. See **Per, PR, PV,** and **YA.**

Ref Reference of pronouns. Except for the few indefinite pronouns (*one, everybody, anybody,* and *it* referring to the weather), a pronoun confuses or distracts a reader unless it refers clearly to a preceding noun or pronoun and agrees with it in number and gender. *Each, every, any,* and their combinations *anybody* and *everybody,* are considered singulars requiring singular verbs and pronouns, but see **Agr** for further explanation of agreement.

1. Often the trouble with a pronoun reference is that the antecedent is just too far away. Repeat the antecedent or change the word order.

2. Guard particularly against *this, that, which, it,* and *they* making vague reference to ideas of whole preceding clauses instead of clear, one-word antecedents.

3. Of the relative pronouns, *who* usually refers only to persons, *that* to persons or things, and *which* to things, including animals and collections of persons such as boards and committees.

4. *That* usually introduces restrictive clauses (not requiring commas) and *which* usually introduces nonrestrictives ones (requiring commas).

Rep Repetition of words or ideas seems wordy and monotonous unless it serves a justifying purpose. Restatement of important ideas deserving emphasis is often desirable; but even then the restatement usually should be in somewhat different words to avoid monotony.

Res Resale material—reassuring a customer that his choice of goods and/or firm was a good one—not only shows your service attitude (**SA**); it helps keep incomplete orders and delayed shipments on the books, re-builds reader confidence when used in adjustments, and serves as a basic idea in collections. Look it up in the Index and read about it in connection with the particular type of letter involved.

S   Style. See Chapter III and the reports check list, p. 531.

SA   A service attitude—showing a genuine desire to give the reader the kinds and quality of goods and services he wants, favorable prices, and various conveniences, plus unselfish reassurance of appreciation for his business—can go a long way toward overcoming any feelings he may have that you are indifferent. Your basic techniques are to interweave into your letters some sales-promotion material (**SPM**) and resale talk (**Res**). See p. 22.

Self   Selfish interest is assumed by both reader and writer, but it does not help your cause and therefore is best not mentioned. Your reader is more interested in his own benefit and will be persuaded only if you show him what's in the situation for him. See **YA** and p. 19.

Sim   Simplify. Needlessly big words or involved sentences are hard to read.

Sin   Sincerity is essential if you are to be believed. Don't pretend or overstate your case. See p. 19.

Slow   Slow movement is desirable in a B-type letter where you must reason calmly with the reader to justify the unpleasant point you are preparing to present (see **Fast**); otherwise it is objectionable.
   1. Don't use too many words before getting to an important point. Starting too far back in the background, giving too many details, or saying things that should be implied are the most frequent faults.
   2. Don't use too many short, choppy sentences and thus slow up a message that should move fast.

SOS   Serious errors in sentence organization and structure justify the distress signal.
   1. Don't present a phrase or dependent clause as a sentence. Usually correction requires only attaching the dependent element to the preceding or following sentence (on which it depends).
        —In answer to your request concerning what the company is like, what has been accomplished, and the future prospects. Here is the information I have been able to acquire. (Replace the period with a comma.)
   2. Don't use a comma, or no punctuation at all, between two independent clauses unless a strong conjunction (*and, but, or,* or *nor*) is there. The error is not basically one of punctuation (as discussed in **P1** and **P2**) but the more serious failure to recognize what a sentence is. You need a period if the two statements are not so closely related that they ought to be in the same sentence, or a semicolon if they are.
        —The credit business is big business some people estimate that it is as much as 86% of American business. (Period needed before *some.*)
        —Running two sentences together without punctuation is about the worst error a writer can make, however it is little worse than

using a comma where a semicolon is required, as in this sentence. See **P2**.

3. Don't put words together in such unnatural, confusing relationships that the reader has to ponder to get the intended meaning. (See **K** and **Mod.**)

　　—Just because you want to sell I don't want right now to buy. (The fact that you want to sell is insufficient reason for me to buy right now.)

4. Don't put ideas together with connectives that falsely represent their relationship. See **Coh, Conj,** and **Unit.**

Sp　Spelling error. Here are some tips on spelling and a list of words frequently misspelled in business writing.

1. ie or ei: When pronounced like ee, write ie except after c or in either, neither, leisure, seize, and weird. When pronounced otherwise, write ei (as in freight, height, forfeit) except in die, lie, pie, tie, and vie.

2. Double a final single consonant preceded by a single vowel (a, e, i, o, u) in an accented syllable when you add a suffix (ing, ed, er) beginning with a vowel (plan, planning; shop, shopping). Note that if the word already ends in two consonants, or one preceded by two vowels, you do not double the last consonant (holding, helping; daubing, seeded). Note, too, that the consonant usually is not doubled unless in an accented syllable (benefit, benefited; refer, referred, references).

3. Drop a final, unpronounced e preceded by a consonant when you add a suffix beginning with a vowel (hope, hoping; change, changing; owe, owing); but you usually retain the e after c or g (noticeable, changeable).

4. Change final y to i and add es for the plural if a consonant precedes the y (ally, allies; tally, tallies); otherwise just add s (valley, valleys).

5. Add 's for the possessive of all singulars and of plurals which do not end in s; add only apostrophe for s-ending plurals (man's, men's; lady's, ladies'; Davis's, Davises').

6. Hyphenate double-word quantities between twenty and a hundred (twenty-one, thirty-two, forty-four, ninety-eight).

7. Get somebody to pronounce for you while you try to spell the following words commonly misspelled in business. Then study those you miss (along with others which give you trouble, from whatever source) until you are sure of them.

accidentally	attorneys	decision	explanation
accommodate	beginning	definitely	forty
accurate	believe	description	government
achievement	benefited	disastrous	grammar
acquaintance	category	effect (result)	guarantee
acquire	choose (chose)	embarrass	height
affect (influence)	comparative	environment	imagine
all right	conscientious	equipped	immediately
among	conscious	exaggerate	incidentally
analyze	consensus	excellence	interest
apparent	consistent	existence	interpret
argument	convenience	experience	it's (its)

laboratory	perform	procedure	stationery
led	personal	prominent	succeed
lose (loose)	personnel	psychology	surprise
moral (morale)	possession	pursue	than (then)
mortgage	practical	quantity	their (there)
necessary	precede	questionnaire	thorough
noticeable	preferred	realize	tries
occasionally	prejudiced	receive	too (to, two)
occurrence	prepare	recommend	undoubtedly
offered	principal	referring	unnecessary
omitted	principle	repetition	until
original	privilege	sense	using (useful)
paid	probably	separate	varies
passed (past)	proceed	stationary	whether (weather)
			writing (written)

Spec Specific wording, like sharpness of a photograph, helps the reader get a clear idea; general words give only a hazy view.

1. If you are inclined to use the general word for a class of things, consider the advantages of giving the specific kind in that class (machine —mower; office equipment—files, desks, chairs, and typewriters; employees—salesmen, janitors, secretaries, and others).

2. Another kind of specificness is giving supporting details, illustrations, examples, and full explanations for general statements made. If you use generalities to gain conciseness in topic and summarizing statements, be sure to follow them up with necessary supporting explanations or further details; otherwise your unsupported statements will not be accepted.

3. Still another important kind of specificness is giving the evidences of abstract qualities you may be inclined to use. If you are inclined to say that something is a bargain, outstanding offer, highest quality, revolutionary, best, ideal, or economical, give the concrete evidences for these qualities instead of the abstract words. In an application letter, if you want to convey the ideas that you are intelligent, industrious, honest, dependable, and sociable, give the evidences and let the reader draw his conclusions; you will sound too cocky if you apply those words to yourself, and your reader will not believe them anyway, unless you give the supporting concrete facts.

SPM Sales-promotional material (when appropriate and unselfish) not only shows a service attitude (see **SA**) and produces some additional sales; it helps to take the sting out of early collection letters and provides a pleasant ending for essentially bad-news letters, provided that the situation is not too seriously negative. See p. 25.

Sub Subordinate. Don't overstress negative ideas, facts known to the reader, or insignificant points. If you must say them, put them in the middle of the paragraph or letter, devote little space to them, and/or put them in dependent clauses or phrases. Since dependent clauses are particularly useful in subordinating, here are some of the main words that make clauses dependent: after, although, as, because, before, if, since, though, till, unless, until, when, where, while.

Subj Subjunctive mood is complex; but nearly all the problems with it in business writing can be solved if you remember these statements: (1)

Were is the form for present tense, regardless of person (first, second, or third); *be* is the auxiliary form (to be used with present and past participles). (2) Use the subjunctive for conditions contrary to fact (including unachieved wishes) and after commands.

—If he *were* better trained in. . . . (Present tense, third person, contrary to fact.)

—The manager directs that these topics *be discussed* thoroughly. . . . (Past participle with *be;* follows command.)

Sw   Shall-will; should-would. General usage differs so much from formal usage of *shall* and *will* that formal practice sounds unnecessarily stiff in most letters and reports. In general usage (which is usually appropriate for business writing), *will* has almost completely replaced *shall,* though formal usage still calls for *shall* with the first person and *will* with other persons to indicate the simple future, and for the reverse to indicate firm promise or determination.

More important for business writers is the distinction between the simple futures and their conditional forms, *should* and *would.* Using the simple future sometimes seems presumptuous.

—I will (or shall, if you want to be formal about it) appreciate your giving me your answer by November 20 so that. . . . (*Would,* in place of *will,* removes the presumption that the reader will answer, by using the conditional mood and saying, in effect, *"If* you will answer . . . I will appreciate it.")

Sy   Synopsis. See the reports check list, p. 537.

Syl   Divide words at the ends of lines only at syllable breaks, and then only if each part has at least two letters and is pronounceable. If in doubt about where to divide a word, check the dictionary.

T   Terminal section (of a report). See the reports check list, p. 536.

Tab   Tabulate or itemize when you have lots of figures to present or a series of distinct points to make. Itemization will make you think more sharply and state your ideas more precisely and concisely. Thus you produce clearer, quicker reading and more emphasis.

Tele   Telegraphic style (omitting subjects, connective words, and articles, as in telegrams and newspaper headlines) is not acceptable practice in letters and reports.

Ten   Watch the tense (time indicated by your verbs) for appropriateness in the individual verb and logic in the sequence of verbs. Normally you use the present, past, or future according to the time of the action you are reporting; but use the present for statements that are true regardless of time. (See the reports check list, p. 534, Item 12, for tense in reports.)

—The law of supply and demand *means.* . . .

—The 1929 edition *says.* . . .

Tone   Tone is questionable here. Watch out for a tone of indifference, undue humility, flattery, condescension, preachiness, bragging, anger, accusation, unflattering implications, sarcasm, curtness, effusiveness, and exaggeration. See p. 10.

Since salutations and complimentary closes are the first and last indications of your feelings about the formality of your relationship to your reader, be sure they represent those feelings accurately. See Chapter III.

TL   Transmittal letter. See the reports check list, p. 538.

Tr   Transitions between sentences in a paragraph and between paragraphs must show the relationship. Your best method is use of a thread of logic that will hold your thoughts together like beads on a string. When the logical thread does not make the relationship clear, however, you need to do so by repeating a key word or idea from the preceding, or by using a connecting word or phrase that shows the relationship. See **Coh** and **Unit.**

Tri   Trite expressions (a form of **Jar**gon) are usually overused and hence worn-out figures of speech that dull your writing. The remedy is to state your idea simply in natural, normal English or to use an original figure of speech.

Unit   Unity (of sentences, paragraphs, or whole pieces of writing) requires that you show how each statement fits in or belongs (is not irrelevant). Applied to a sentence or paragraph, it means that the statement seems irrelevant or that the several ideas are not closely enough related to be in the one sentence or paragraph. When applied to a whole letter or report, it means that the content seems so varied as to lack a central theme and should be put in two or more separate papers. Often, however, the writer sees relationships that justify putting things together as he has, and his fault is in not showing the reader the relationships—an error of **Coherence.**

>   —Please put your answers in ink and have your signature witnessed by two people. One of our envelopes is enclosed for your convenience. (The envelope is not a convenience in doing what is requested in the first sentence. The two unrelated ideas should not be in the same paragraph. Adding "in returning your answers" would help.)

Usa   Usage refers to the appropriateness of the language to the situation. A passage or expression marked with the symbol may be too formal and stiff, literary, flashy, or highbrow; or too slangy, familiar, crude, or lowbrow. The normal, natural English of educated people conducting their everyday affairs is neither formal nor illiterate, but informal and natural. That's what you should use for most letters and reports.

Var   Variety (of diction and of sentence pattern, type, and length) is necessary to avoid monotony, which puts readers to sleep. Achieving variety should be a part of the revision process, however, and should not distract your thoughts from saying what you want to say in writing a first draft. In your revision, see that you haven't begun too many successive sentences the same way (especially not with *I* or *we*). If you have repeated yourself, cut out the repetition unless you need it for emphasis; and then change the wording if the two statements of the same idea are close together.

The usual English sentence pattern is subject-verb-complement; in revision, vary the pattern to avoid a dull sameness. (Page 54 lists various kinds of sentence beginnings.)

Good style also requires variety in sentence type. Some of your sentences should be simple (one independent clause); some should be compound (two independent clauses stating two closely related ideas of nearly equal importance); and some should be complex (at least one independent clause and one or more dependent, all expressing related ideas but of unequal importance). Especially to be avoided are too many successive simple sentences for ideas not deserving equal emphasis or too many compound sentences connected by *and*. (See **Sub.**)

Though most of your sentences should be relatively short (averaging 12–20 words for easy readability), you will produce a monotonous choppiness if all your sentences are in that range. See **Sim** and **Chop,** and revise accordingly.

WF Word form. As you know, many words change forms slightly according to their use in the sentence. Be sure you use the right form for the purpose.

1. Verbs change according to what we call their principal parts. Here are some of the troublesome or unusual ones.

Present Tense	*Past Tense*	*Present Participle*	*Past Participle*
I begin	I began	beginning	have or had begun
blow	blew	blowing	blown
choose	chose	choosing	chosen
forget	forgot	forgetting	forgot
lay	laid	laying	laid
lead	led	leading	led
lend	lent	lending	lent
lie (recline)	lay	lying	lain
pay	paid	paying	paid
prove	proved	proving	proved
set	set	setting	set
sit	sat	sitting	sat
throw	threw	throwing	thrown
wear	wore	wearing	worn
write	wrote	writing	written

2. Adjective and adverb forms are sometimes confused. Determine whether the word modifies a noun or pronoun (for the adjective form) or a verb, adjective, or adverb (for the adverb form). Most, but not all, adverbs end in *-ly*.

3. Not only must pronouns agree with the words they refer to (see **Ref**), but they must be in the proper form (case) for their use in the sentence. Most of the troubles are cleared up in this one sentence: Use the nominative case (*I, we, he, she, they, who*) as the subject of a verb or the complement after any form of the verb *to be;* use the objective case (*me, us, him, her, them, whom*) as the object (receiving rather than doing the action) of an active-voice verb or the object of a preposition. Be especially careful to make the second of a compound object of a preposition in the objective case:

—He said that the story was a big secret, but he told it to Betty and *me*. In informal writing and speaking, you may go contrary to the general rule and use *who* at the beginning of a sentence (because that is "subject territory") even though it is really the object of a verb or preposition.

—Who would you consider the better authority on a point like this, a linguist like Fries or somebody else.

—Who did you tell? Who did you buy that for?

4. Be on guard against any of the following illiterate forms (mostly the results of bad pronunciation): "He is prejudice" (prejudiced), "He is bias" (biased), "usta" or "use to" (used to), "had of" (had), "would of" (would have), "most all" (almost all), "a savings of" (a saving of).

5. Use comparative forms (former, latter, better, more, faster, and the like) only when referring to two things; use the superlative form (best, most, fastest) only when referring to three or more. See **Cpr.**

6. Distinguish between the often-confused pairs: may be—maybe, some time—sometime, all ready—already, with regards to—in regard to, its—it's, your—you're. See **D.**

YA   You-attitude. The you-attitude is certainly one of the three most important points about letter writing. (The other two might be good will and clear style.) People do things for their own benefit, not yours. If you want to persuade them to act, then you have to show them the advantages to themselves. Both your reader and you know that you're interested in yourself. Trying to deny that fact would be insincere and disbelieved. But you need not put your selfish interests in the letter; the fact that you want something is no reason for the reader to act. The benefits he gets are. Show them to him. See **Self** and p. 33.

To show the reader what is in the situation for him, you have to visualize his way of life and show how your proposal fits in. See **Adap.**

Though using more *you's* than *I's* or *we's* may help, it is no assurance that your letter has the you-attitude.

X   Obvious error. Proofread carefully and correct such errors.

~   Invert the order or sequence of words or ideas.

◡   Close up the unnecessary space.

¶   New paragraph needed.

1. Paragraphs in letters and reports are the same as in other writing—unified developments of topics—except that they tend to be more compressed and shorter for easier readability. Especially the first and last paragraphs of letters should be short (rarely more than three or four lines). Elsewhere, if a paragraph runs to more than about eight lines, you should consider breaking it up for easier readability.

2. Develop your paragraphs adequately to support your points—by further explanation, detail, facts and figures, or illustrations and examples.

3. But avoid putting unrelated things in the same paragraphs. See pp. 56 and 58 for tips on paragraph construction.

Additional space needed here.

∂ or ℰ Delete (take out); unnecessary.

↤̣ Move in the direction pointed.

Appendix B. Letters and the Law *

BECAUSE the laws of the fifty states and the federal government vary somewhat and are continually changing, the specific details of the law as applied to letters are too voluminous to treat here—and generalizations are dangerous. Yet enough similarity exists on certain points to justify the following statements of special significance to letter writers.

RESPONSIBILITY AND RIGHTS OF POSSESSION AND PUBLICATION

The law of responsibility for a letter is fairly clear. The first name after the body of the letter is responsible. The writer's name alone at the end makes him responsible, whether on plain paper or on a company letterhead. The letterhead makes no difference. Cincinnati Lawyer Leo T. Parker says, in "Prepare to Win Lawsuits Involving Correspondence," *Industrial Marketing,* 32:37–38, 150, February, 1947: "Review of late and leading higher court decisions discloses that one requirement for an employee's relief from personal liability on letters and contracts he signs with proper authority of the employer is the employer's name precedes the agent's signature."

If the letter is about company business which the writer is authorized to handle as the company's agent, and he signs with his title, he is responsible; but he can in turn pass that responsibility on to the company under his agency agreement.

To avoid this two-step process of putting responsibility where it belongs, he can type the company name (preferably in solid capitals) a double space below the complimentary close and a quadruple space above his typed name and title, with his signature in the large space. This arrangement makes the company directly responsible for company business which a writer is authorized to handle—but, of course, not for the writer's personal business or unauthorized company business.

Because the company name defeats some of the attempts of salesmen

* Special thanks go to Mr. James J. Cavanaugh, Assistant Professor of Insurance, Law, and Real Estate Administration, Michigan State University, for a careful and helpful reading of this appendix.

to set up a feeling of personal relationship between themselves and their prospects, they often sign their letters without the company name. Conversely, putting in the company name may give the reader an additional feeling of security in dealing with an established company instead of the individual who signs the letter. The end legal effect is the same.

Regardless of who is responsible for a letter, he retains publication rights to it. The addressee who receives it has every right to keep it; but, without the consent of the responsible sender, he does not have the right to publish it in an article or book.

LEGAL ASPECTS OF BUYING AND SELLING BY MAIL

In writing sales-promotion letters, inquiries and replies about goods and services for sale, orders, and acknowledgments of orders, writers need to keep in mind what constitutes a *contract*—to be sure of forming one when desired and otherwise avoiding one.

When buyer and seller agree on a legally enforceable arrangement calling for one to act in certain ways in return for the other's acting as specified, we say they form a *contract.*

The required actions must be legal. They cannot make a contract to rob a bank or kill somebody, for example.

The phrase "in return for" means that an exchange of value—"consideration," the lawyers call it—is necessarily stated or implied. Hence many contracts which might otherwise leave a question include a phrase something like "for $1 and other valuable consideration."

And there must be agreement, or, as it is sometimes stated, "a meeting of the minds." If the terms are indefinite, unclear, or misunderstood, no contract is formed. The basic elements, then, are an *offer* and an *acceptance.*

An *offer* must be reasonably definite to provide agreement. In general, it needs to be fairly clear by explicit statement or reasonable implication in answer to Who, What, When, Where, and Why. That is, the two or more parties involved must be clear. What each agrees to do, or refrain from doing, has to be specific. In terms of goods for sale, not only the general class of goods but a fairly clear understanding of the quality, price, and number is necessary. The time the offer goes into effect and ends must be reasonably clear, by explicit statement or by implication. Where the actions are to take place is also often necessary to a valid contract. The consideration is the answer to Why.

A catalogue listing, advertisement, or sales-promotion letter is not ordinarily an offer to sell because it is usually not specific enough to answer adequately the five *W* questions. Though it may identify the prospective seller and describe the goods and give the price, it ordinarily does not indicate the number of items (another part of What), and the When and Where may not be clear enough. Simply quoting prices is not an offer.

Certainly most inquiries about products for sale do not complete contracts, both because the cataloguing or advertising of the goods was not a specific offer to sell and the inquiry is usually not an acceptance, or even an offer to buy. Hence even a specific order for goods does not usually complete a contract. More likely it has to be considered the offer, which the seller can accept or reject.

An offer by mail becomes effective when received and stands to the end of any stated time or until withdrawn, rejected, or accepted—or for a reasonable time in view of the nature of the product and the circumstances. In the absence of any statement about the duration of the offer or the amount available, an offer to sell fresh fruit at the orchard, for example, would probably last only so long as the supply lasts; but an offer to sell the orchard would last considerably longer. An offer can be withdrawn any time before acceptance, but the withdrawal has to be received to become effective.

Assuming that a valid offer has been made by mail, a letter accepting it must agree to all the terms exactly, or else it forms no contract. Thus a simple acknowledgment of receipt of an order does not complete a contract. The acknowledgment must adequately identify the order and agree to act as the offer (order) specifies. Any change in terms *required* by the receiver of an offer rejects the original offer and makes a counteroffer. The original offerer can then reject it or, to form a contract, accept it. A proposal to buy half a farm offered for sale is not an acceptance but a counteroffer. That does not mean, however, that the receiver of an offer cannot accept its terms exactly and then ask for modifications—prices, delivery schedules, quality, or the like. He forms a contract by accepting the original terms. If the original offerer agrees to the requested change, the original contract is rescinded and a new one substituted by mutual consent.

Until recently, unless the offerer had said that the contract depended on his receiving the acceptance, a properly addressed and stamped acceptance of a mailed offer became effective when posted. Thus it could not be rescinded without mutual consent, even if a message attempting to rescind arrived before the mailed acceptance. The assumption was that the letter was beyond the control of the acceptor. Postal Regulations, Sections 552 and 553, providing for the recovery of a mailed letter, now make that assumption and the law doubtful. Because of that possibility, revocation of an acceptance by other means may also be possible; but, in general, an acceptance is effective when mailed.

Warranties are closely related to contracts, in that a buyer can bring civil suit to recover for nonperformance, or to force performance, on the basis of either stated or implied warranties. Of course, any stated warranty is a part of the contract. But, in the absence of any statement to the contrary, a seller warrants by implication that he has clear title to the product sold and that it will perform the usual functions for which such products are sold. To avoid these implied warranties, a seller must be very specific; a general statement that no warranties apply if not stated does not absolve him of responsibility. For that reason, detailed denials of warranty often appear on the containers of such things as insecticides. Furthermore, if an orderer specifies the use he intends to make of a product, leaving the seller to send the appropriate thing, the seller sending the product implies warranty that the product is suitable for the specified purpose. For example, if a farmer orders a pump and says he wants it to pump water for his stock from his 100-foot well, he has a legal claim against the seller who sends a shallow-well pump; a shallow-well pump will not bring water up from that depth.

Fraud in selling by mail—intentional misrepresentation of a product to the buyer for the purpose of inducing him to buy—not only subjects the seller to civil suit by the injured buyer to recover damages sustained; it also opens the possibility of criminal prosecution by the state (and by the Post Office for use of the mails to defraud).

THE LAW OF EXCHANGING INFORMATION

Any contractual relationship in connection with the sale of goods used to be between the buyer and the seller. Therefore, information that a manufacturer distributed about his goods to consumers who bought from retailers was not a matter of contract. Thus the injured consumer had no recourse against the manufacturer in terms of contract law. Today, however, this privity of contract has been abandoned in cases about food and drugs; and it is often circumvented in other cases where most of the information about a product as inducement to purchase comes from the manufacturer directly to the consumer. The reasoning is that the dealer is the manufacturer's agent in this special sense or that the consumer is a third-party beneficiary of the manufacturer-dealer contract or that the warranty runs with the goods.

If the manufacturer intentionally misleads the consumer, however, the consumer always could and still can recover any damages in *tort* law on the basis of deceit or fraud.

Similarly, a person seeking information about other persons (credit or job applicants, for example) may sustain *tort* action for damages against an informer who intentionally or carelessly misleads him to his detriment. The informer is obligated to the inquirer to take reasonable precautions for accuracy of information and to avoid intentional deceit.

A letter writer who gives information about one person to other persons also has obligations to the state and to the person who is the subject of the report. Failure to meet the obligations subjects the informer to possible charges of *libel*—publication of defamatory statements about another person which damage that person by hurting his reputation. "Publication" in this special sense means merely giving the damaging statements to one or more other persons, or negligently allowing other persons to see them. For this reason, duns for past-due accounts and letters conveying unfavorable information about people should be sent only in sealed envelopes and addressed so that they are seen only by the debtors and other people specially privileged (as explained later).

The state assumes that the informer will be fair-minded (show good faith rather than malicious intent). Hence good faith is usually a complete defense against criminal libel charges, though truth is not if malice is present. Both good faith and truth always provide complete defense.

Civil libel suit brought by the injured person for damages to his business or profession, however, is different. The informer is obligated to tell the truth. In most legal jurisdictions truth is a complete defense against civil libel suit for damages, no matter how damaging or malicious the information may be. Where it is not, truth and absence of malicious intent are, though good faith alone is not.

Apparently for the purpose of facilitating the exchange of important business information, the law gives an informer considerable benefit of doubt and applies the principle of *privilege.* That is, a writer sending *requested* information in good faith to someone for the purpose of helping him to protect an interest (a prospective employer or creditor, for example, who could suffer considerable loss if he deals with an unworthy man) is said to be *privileged.* The information need not be absolutely true, provided that the writer has been reasonably careful to get the facts, for the privileged informer to be invulnerable to civil libel suit. One who requests information about a third party normally expects the informer to answer "to the best of your knowledge" and to include some opinion. If the informer volunteers the information, is reckless with the truth, or shows malice, however, he loses privilege as a defense.

Similarly, credit organizations that provide information about credit risks to members immediately faced with credit applications are probably protected by privilege; but if an organization distributes the information to all members, including those without immediate need or request for it, and thus forms a kind of black list, privilege probably does not apply.

A letter writer requesting personal information should show that he has an interest to protect and promise to keep the information confidential except for the particular use—to help the informer protect himself against libel suit. The informer should show that the information is requested, be reasonably careful to tell the truth and avoid any malice, and ask that the information be confidential.

In collection letters, for example, a writer disgusted with a troublesome debtor may maliciously try to get even with the debtor by making true but damaging statements about him to others who have no interest to protect. He thus provides the basis for criminal libel charges. If some of the statements are also untrue, he also throws himself open to civil libel suit for damages—without benefit of privilege because the information is going to people who have not requested it to protect an interest.

MOTIVATION BY EXTORTION

Also in collection letters—and others trying to induce a reader to act in a certain way—writers sometimes resort to threats not in due process of law to force the desired action beneficial to themselves. In so doing, they become guilty of *extortion,* a criminal offense in all state and federal jurisdictions. The due process of law for enforcing a contract (including the payment of contracted debts) is civil suit. If a writer threatens that, he is on safe legal ground, though he may lose the reader's good will; but if he threatens physical violence ("I'll beat you up") or criminal charges ("I'll report you for income tax evasion"), he is going beyond due process and is subject to criminal prosecution for extortion.

The same threatening letters—if they wilfully use abusive language to incite fear, confusion, or humiliation—also subject the senders to civil liability in tort law. The older cases usually allowed recovery only where physical harm resulted, but recent cases are supporting recovery where there is substantial mental anguish and emotional disturbance without actual physical infirmity.

Index

Practical value of letter writing, 1, 4

Praise: overdone, 10; letters of, 443

Preachiness, 12

Preliminary planning: four steps of, for letters, 57; of reports, 472

Preparation of reports, five-step process of, 472–96

Prepositions, 590

Present tense in reports, 514, 534 (12)

Prestige answers in questionnaires, 481 (6)

Presumptuousness: as overdone success consciousness, 42–43; of thanking in advance, 107

Price resistance: minimizing, 148, 233; in selling substitutes, 194, 197 (5); special letters precluding, 460

Pride appeal in collections, 415

Privilege as defense against libel, 105, 603

Procedure of collections, 404

Processed letters. *See* Forms

Product analysis, 221

Promptness: in replies, 129; in acknowledgments, 177, 188; in collections, 403

Pronouns, references of, 591 (**Ref**)

Prospecting: sales letters, 219–53; application letters, 292 ff.

Prospects, finding for sales, 222

Psychological description, 152 (4), 221–22, 234 (2), 590

Psychology: practical, learned in letter writing, 1; essential in letter writing, 5; of disappointing letters, 30, 136–43, 340

Punctuation: as element of clarity, 59; following conventions of, 59–60, 65; helps on troublesome spots of, 60, 583–88; of letter headings and inside addresses, 74, 75, 78, 79, 81

Q

Qualifications: fitting to job, 274; emphasis on in applications, 298

Quantities, writing of, 580 (**Fig**)

Questionnaires: for collecting data, 478–82; phrasing questions in, 480

Questions: as direct beginnings, 105, 110; phrasing of survey, 480

Quotation: from sources, 475; marks, use of, 587 (9)

R

Rational appeals in sales, 224

Readability: element of clearness, 56; how to improve, 56

Reader: adapting to, 36; analyzing the, 57

Reasons versus apologies in refusals, 139

Recommendations, 515, 536

Reference books, 474

References: to common experiences, for adaptation, 37; personal, for readability, 50, 57; to enclosures, 85, 153 (4d), 235 (3e); in data sheets, 285, 291 (7); to charts and tables, 532 (2); of pronouns, 591. *See also* Documentation, Footnoting, *and* Citations

Refusals: psychology and plan of, 30, 136; of requests, 136; of orders, 190; of jobs, 312; of adjustments, 340; of credit, 382

Regularity in collection series, 403

Relations of parts in reports, 532 (7)

Reminder stage of collections, 405

Remittances, methods of, 174–75

Replies: to inquiries and requests, 129–59; without sales possibilities, 130–44; with sales possibilities, 144–59

Reports: importance of, 3, 467; personnel, 133; on credit risks, 377; history, need, and functions of, 467; as tools of management, 467–70; nature and classes of, 470; characteristics of, 470; preliminary planning of, 472; collecting data for, 473–82; organization of, 482; interpretation in, 485; writing up, 488–90; types and forms of, 497–541; complete analytical, 498–517; letter and memo, 517; justification, 519; check list for memo, 520; credit, 524; annual, 525; check list for complete analytical, 527–41

Requests: special (persuasive), 106–16; justifying, 111; replies to, 129–59; for information for reports, 479

Resale: kinds, uses, and methods, 23–25, 591; in replies to inquiries, 133; in acknowledgments, 178, 182, 185, 188; in adjustments, 335; in collections, 402, 407, 414

Research: by library methods, 473; by observation, 477; by laboratory experimentation, 477; by surveys, 478

Resignations, 312

Return envelopes and cards: in requests, 115 (5d); in acknowledgments, 187 (3b); in collections, 429

Revision for tone, conciseness, coherence, and correctness, 57, 58

Reviving inactive accounts, 457

Run-on sentences, 592 (**SOS**)

S

Salary, handling in applications, 309 (6d)

Sales: letters, invited, 144–54; letters, prospecting, 219–53; strategy, 220; formulas, 227; letters, testing, 237; series, 241

This book has been set on the Linotype in 12 and 10 point Garamond No. 3, leaded 1 point. Chapter numbers and titles are in 24 point Nicolas Cochin. The size of the type page is 27 by 46½ picas.